FOOD SERVICE SCIENCE

some other AVI books

FOOD SERVICE SCIENCE

Edited by LAURA LEE W. SMITH, Ph.D. FAIC
Professor of Hotel Administration,
Emeritus Cornell University,
Ithaca, New York

and LEWIS J. MINOR, Ph.D.
Visiting Professor, School of
Business, School of Hotel,
Restaurant & Institutional
Management, Eppley Center
Michigan State University,
East Lansing, Michigan

in collaboration with specialists

WESTPORT, CONNECTICUT
THE AVI PUBLISHING COMPANY, INC
1974

Contributors

D. E. ANDERSON, Director of Technical Service, Wyandotte Chemicals Corporation, J. B. Ford Division, Wyandotte, Michigan

DEAN A. BODNER, Clinton Corn Processing Company, Clinton, Iowa

J. J. HERRINGER, Product News Editor, S. C. Johnson & Son, Racine, Wisconsin

H. W. LAWSON, Bulk Food Technical Services, Procter & Gamble Company, Miami Valley, Cincinnati, Ohio

R. V. LECHOWICH, Department of Food Science and Technology, Virginia Polytechnic Institute and State University, Blacksburg, Virginia

ROBERT W. MCINTOSH, Professor of Tourism, Department of Hotel, Restaurant and Institutional Management, Michigan State University, East Lansing, Michigan

J. RAKOSKY, JR., Central Soya Company, Chemurgy Division, Chattanooga, Tennessee

E. F. SIPOS, Central Soya Company, Chemurgy Division, Chattanooga, Tennessee

D. V. VADEHRA, Food Science and Microbiology, Cornell University, Ithaca, New York

MARK A. WOLF, Research Toxicologist, The Dow Chemical Company, Midland, Michigan

Preface

This book was written as a basic science reference textbook for students enrolled in the schools of Hotel, Restaurant and Institutional Management. The varied backgrounds including quite often a very limited training in natural and biological sciences demand a simple, useful description of those areas basic to the food service industry.

The contents of the text should aid the instructor in developing areas of interest to the student. A good basic understanding of the composition of foodstuffs and the relationships to the surrounding conditions can provide solutions to the many prob-lems that arise. A selected group of references is included in the Appendix to help both the teacher and the student. There is a continuous flow of new pertinent material available both from the industrial as well as the educational fields.

The authors are grateful to the several people of the industrial and academic disciplines for their contributions and helpful criticisms.

Laura Lee W. Smith
Lewis J. Minor

January 1973

vi

Contents

CHAPTER 1

R. McIntosh | # General Principles of Food Service

SCOPE OF THE FOOD SERVICE INDUSTRY

Eating is one of life's most pleasurable and satisfying activities. Eating "out" among the amazing variety of restaurants and other types of food services available today can and should add greatly to this pleasure and enjoyment of life. To help food purveyors make their products even more flavorful and delicious is the reason this book has been written.

Testifying to the popularity of eating out is the sheer dollar volume of food service revenues in the United States. At the time of this writing, this revenue is approaching $50 billion in some 600,000 food-serving establishments. These figures are made up of food-service industry sales, non-eating and drinking receipts, government food services, hospitals, institutions, and elementary and high school food services. The largest component by far (about 80%) is food-service industry sales, followed by government food services (11%). Food service comprises the fourth-largest industry in the United States for sales volume and is first among the service industries in the number of persons served. Total United States expenditures for food from all sources, such as grocery stores and so forth, are about $120 billion.

Future Anticipated Volume

Economic, technological, and social trends in the United States are likely to bring about a continuation of the growth of this remarkable industry. Examples of these trends are:

A. The young people's market, which is growing rapidly as the large post-WW II baby crop reaches college and young-adult age. Also, these youngsters have customarily eaten away from home since childhood and accept restaurant dining as a normal way of life.

B. The older-age group, who traditionally have constituted an excellent market for dining out, are growing in numbers to

more substantial proportions. Also, these older people now
have more income, enabling them to dine out more often.

   C. Total population growth.

   D. Higher income and growth in the economy.

   E. Increasing employment of women resulting in a larger
income for many families plus the desire to lighten household
work by dining out more often.

   F. Increase in tourism and leisure activities.

   G. Development in the restaurant industry of great ranges
in prices of meals and atmosphere, appeals to a very broad
cross-section of the market. The food-service industry now
offers "eating out" experiences to virtually everyone.

   H. Technological advances in new foods.

   I. New food presentations.

   J. New modes of customer service.

   K. More effective advertising and merchandising.

   L. Greater food-health consciousness.

Gains in total volume of business, partially due to inflation,
may increase to perhaps 25 to 50% during the '70's. But who
knows? Perhaps it will be even higher, or lower, but all the
trends appear to be favorable and toward a higher volume in
the future.

Food and Beverage

As one of America's biggest industries, foods and beverages
continue to dominate the service industries and employment.
Furthermore, social trends, such as the lowering of the drinking age to 18 in various states, is likely to increase the demand
for alcoholic beverages, and at the same time sales of restaurant meals. Soft drinks also are gaining in popularity as choices
of flavors and serving modes increase.

Wine consumption per capita in America seems to be slowly
increasing. With its connotation of the accompaniment of good
food, drinking of wine should cause a growth in restaurant sales.

Atmosphere—the total experience of dining out—is of concern to all progressive restaurateurs. This concern is mani-
fested today in a delightful array of enticing eating and drinking
establishments. Atmosphere of every conceivable variety—
from historic, to regional, geographic, to cultural themes,

themes of nature, musical or fine art—all are available and ready to serve the millions of persons who dine out every day.

It's a great business which is an essential part of our econ- omy and a true expression of the American culture.

KINDS OF FOOD SERVICE

Fast Foods

Fast foods probably are the epitome of the American contri- bution to the food-service industry. Where else in the world can a person get a complete meal for 73¢, served in about 2 minutes? The convenience and appeal of fast-food operations influence a substantial portion of the market for eating out. Fast-food restaurants particularly appeal to young people, and the food specialties prepared are the most popular. Fast foods may be eaten on the premises or taken home. A recent trend in the fast-food business seems to be provision for inside dining, to provide the convenience of all-weather dining and a chance for motorists to get out of their cars, stretch their legs, and obtain a change of atmosphere.

Many fast-food operations are franchised and have bright, highly visible exteriors. These are normally located on easily accessible sites, usually along a main highway or adjacent to an interchange of a major highway. However, there are many other types of fast-food operations in urban areas.

The quality of food served in typical fast-food operations is excellent, as a result of very careful purchasing procedures, standardization of operations, and overall management and supervision of professional caliber. Also, the vast majority of fast-food operations are of the chain or franchise variety, thus offering a uniform product wherever they may be located.

Another definite trend seems to be toward carry-out services. The convenience of eating at home can be combined with the readily available food specialties from the fast-food store.

Another trend in fast-food services is that of the exhibit-type conglomerate of food specialties from different countries. For example, counter pick-up food specialties from Italy, Spain, Greece, France, Britain, and Western U.S. may all be available side by side. The restaurant patron merely selects the type of food specialties that appeal to him for that particular meal. This technique tends to broaden the market appeal of the restaurant and makes available a delightful variety of quick-service items to satisfy the cosmopolitan appetite. Such conglomerate food services are usually found in the new mall-type shopping centers.

Fast-food operations have been the most rapidly expanding type of restaurant in the United States. In the past 5 years, this has been particularly true. Indeed, the number of these restaurants has so increased in some communities that officials are concerned that the proliferation may reach a point where none of them will be profitable. More stringent zoning and building code provisions have been enacted in some communities to more thoroughly ascertain the probability of success of a restaurant before it is constructed.

Restaurants

In restaurants, more is sold than food. Some authorities have stated that up to 60% of the satisfaction of dining out has nothing to do with the food whatsoever. The service, friendliness, atmosphere, music or other types of entertainment, napery, china, silver, glass, flowers, and other accompaniments of good dining are perhaps more important than the quality and taste of the food itself. Some of the principal elements of atmosphere are as follows:

A. Size and shape of the dining room.

B. Views obtained from windows or from various aspects of the room.

C. Type of seating—whether tables are round, square or rectangular, booths, or counters.

D. Furnishings—style, finish, period, color.

E. Layout of the seating arrangement such as elevation of portions of the room or other variations.

F. Nationality or geographic aspect of the restaurant.

G. Appearance, age, and type of uniforms of the staff.

H. Type of customers, i.e., age, social class, how they are dressed, and so forth.

I. Noise level.

J. Various colors and materials used in the decorative scheme.

K. Level of illumination.

L. Temperature or comfort level.

M. Cleanliness as evidenced by table cloths, silverware, floor, and so forth.

Some of the other considerations in restaurant types and appeals are: customer expectations; customer choice; food selected by the customer; whether the restaurant is formal or informal; the first impression of the customer as he enters the restaurant; effectiveness of the ventilation (particularly tobacco smoke and cooking odors); sound level and what that sound consists of; the anticipated value the customer will receive for his money; and the accessibility of the restaurant, such as parking facilities, ease of driving into the establishment, and similar considerations.

A significant trend today is toward larger and more elaborate restaurants; many establishments represent investments of more than $1 million. These may be located almost anywhere, but are more commonly found in large cities, shopping centers, and resort areas.

As to menu, the less elaborate menu becomes more popular year by year. This trend helps simplify restaurant operation and enhance the possibility for profits. Diet-consciousness seems to be growing in importance and the progressive restaurateur will keep this consideration in mind when preparing menus.

When possible, restaurateurs should capitalize on any views commanded by the restaurant windows, and arrange tables and elevations within the restaurant accordingly. People are more conscious of environment now, and appreciate a restaurant which has taken this factor into consideration. Where natural views are not attractive, the creation of atmosphere by the use of tapestries, oil paintings, other types of paintings or illustrations, or attractive wall patterns and fireplaces are appreciated.

The type of service will of course depend on the nature of the restaurant, but as a rule, those having more prompt service are usually the best patronized.

Services can be at all levels, from virtually self-service such as in a cafeteria to an elaborate French service in which portions of the meal are prepared at tableside. Probably the most important single element in service is the attitude, appearance, and demeanor of the waiter or waitress. In resort restaurants, for example, the guest has more hours of contact

with his waiter or waitress than any other employee at the
resort. Thus, this relationship is of major importance in
customer satisfaction. Regardless of the level of service, it
should be provided with warmth and friendliness.

School Cafeterias

Great strides have been made in improving food service in
school cafeterias. More items for selection, faster service,
use of "scramble system" cafeteria arrangements, and more
liberal provisions for "seconds" and larger quantities have
also been provided in many instances. Also incorporated in
school cafeterias have been more attractive elements of decor
and atmosphere, in order to make this portion of the school
day's activities more pleasant and enjoyable.

Increasing use of convenience foods and pre-portioned items
have increased the appeal of cafeteria meals.

One other aspect which seems to be growing is the utilization
of the school cafeteria as a practice ground for students taking
courses in food services as part of their curriculum. The
cafeteria is an ideal place for consumption of the food prepared
by students, and the customer attitudes can be surveyed and
reactions observed.

Federal school lunch programs have been expanded and this
assistance makes possible a greater value for the student for
money paid for school cafeteria meals. It also helps low-
income families with their nutritional needs via the school
cafeteria.

Hospitals

Hospital food service continues to maintain a leading position
in the amount of food served outside the home. As food is an
essential element in the recovery of the patient, it is a major
part of hospital operations and employs a substantial percentage
of the hospital staff.

Some of the innovations in hospital food service include
preparation of pre-prepared and pre-portioned food specialties.

Leasing food services to a commercial food company expanded considerably in the '60's and this is likely to continue
in the '70's. Such an arrangement relieves the hospital administrator from the responsibility of providing staff and

administrative direction to the food service of the hospital and thus transfers the responsibilities to the professional food preparation concern.

Another segment of this industry is the nursing home and retirement home food service. This particular type of organization is growing at a rapid rate as people live longer and do not find it agreeable to live with their children in advancing age. With greater income and more Federal and state-supported social programs for the elderly, this type of food service is destined to continue as one of the real growth segments of hospital food services.

Hotels

Hotels, including resort hotels and motels, have increased emphasis on food and beverage services in the past decade. In fact, most of the new motels or motor hotels being built today are larger and more elaborate than those built in the '40's and '50's. The trend is toward a more complete facility, including a dining room, bar, meeting rooms, recreational facilities and similar amenities, which make the entire establishment more broadly appealing to the traveling public.

In downtown commercial hotels, the trend has been toward the establishment of buffet services—often at noon—but also, quite common as a special evening meal at a set price. Also, the growth of the luncheon business has been outstanding, particularly in large cities and in the downtown area. However, the dinner business was for a time somewhat of a problem, but recently this has slowly improved as specialty dining rooms and increased emphasis on atmosphere make dining more of an experience.

In resorts, there has been a definite trend toward American Plan operations (includes three-meal services). Also popular is the Modified American Plan which provides two meals per day, usually breakfast—but sometimes lunch—and a rather elaborate dinner. Guests seem to prefer these plans where their time can be devoted to recreational or cultural activities rather than to purchasing food and preparing it in their own housekeeping unit. It should be noted, however, that there is also a trend toward apartment rentals in some of the largest resort areas, but these apartment dwellers customarily eat at least one meal out per day.

In motor hotels or motels the trend definitely is toward atmosphere-type dining and even a range in types of dining facilities, including a coffee shop or coffee shop section and a more elaborate dining facility. Catering for parties and banquets is another growing aspect of motor hotel food service. This service has become more important in the last decade. Breakfast and dinner continue to be the dominating demand situations for food service, but many motor hotels are developing a local luncheon market to help augment each day's volume. Beverage services have also increased in motels, and atmosphere-type bars and snack-beer areas appear to be well received by guests.

Airline Catering

The airlines have become more cost-conscious and are attempting to provide adequate customer satisfaction without increasing the cost of services. According to Marion Sadler, Chairman of the Board of Sky Chefs, an American Airline subsidiary, these are among several significant trends expected to develop within the next 5 years. He says, "The trend in air transportation has been toward more food and beverage, not less, as some have contended however there seems to be a growing need for snack services which are attractive, cleverly packaged, low in cost, and which can be served rapidly on airline flights of short duration .... The elaborate airport restaurants which have been operated profitably for many years by some caterers at large airports are going to disappear." "No longer will the caterer do any substantial amount of cooking. He will simply secure from a processer pre-prepared foods, store these foods, prepare tray set-ups for the airline and deliver the full service package to the airplane. As a service organization ... the airline caterer of the future will no longer be primarily concerned with raw food costs; its major concern will be with labor costs. This will force the caterer to a high degree of automation."

The airline catering business apparently relies more and more on prepared foods, and provides consistently high quality on all types of service according to the flight schedules in-volved.

In the jumbo or super-jet, food is prepared in its final state aboard with an increase in customer satisfaction and enjoyment.

Shopping Centers

A welcome trend in food services has been the addition of coffee shops, tea rooms, cafeterias, or lunch counters in stores and shopping centers. Particularly, this trend is seen in the enclosed mall, where a virtually atmosphere-controlled city exists. The food services are varied, interesting, and attrac-tive. Coffee-shop service, where the guest often sits at the counter or at a booth and orders from a budget-priced menu, is also a common service pattern. Finally, there is a full table service restaurant where a more elaborate menu is pre-sented, dining is more leisurely, and the expected bill higher than in any of the previously described patterns of food service. Restaurants at the present time are inclined to offer a table d'hote menu and do not list beverages or desserts in the stated price of the meal.

Diet consciousness is a definite factor; customers are in-clined to order a salad, possibly a fish or seafood entree, and often select a meal that is not as large or elaborate as was popular perhaps 10 or 15 years ago.

In 1968 there were about 12,000 shopping centers in the United States which could be classified as major retail centers, and by 1980 there may be as many as 25,000 major shopping centers, as estimated by Peter H. Plamondon, Group Vice President, Marriott Corporation. One of the most popular food services in shopping centers is the snack bar. The snack bar is characterized by having a limited yet diversified menu that will appeal to the employees of the various stores in the shopping center who may eat in the snack bar 6 days a week. Also, the typical snack bar has booths or small tables so that the foot-weary shopper can rest for a while. Cafeteria service is the usual practice.

Some snack bars have introduced the idea of allowing the customer to fix his own dish by having a super-sundae area where the customer can make his own sundaes to suit his taste.

This adds a little fun to the food selection process and helps build customer satisfaction and loyalty.

Pricing of a modest nature appeals, as the customer must be convinced that he's getting good value for his money. This is particularly true for that part of the shopping public who are value-conscious and who come to the shopping center during periods of sales or special events where they expect to get maximum values.

TRENDS IN FOOD PREPARATION, FOOD PATTERNS

The food-service industry has been growing at about 2.5 times that of the national economy; thus dynamic forces are at work to meet demands for food eaten away from home and at the same time allow the food service operator to obtain satisfactory results. With economics as the basic motivating force in the industry, the question then arises, how do we prepare food and provide patterns of food services that will result in happiness and satisfaction to the customer and financial satisfaction for the owners? The biggest problem is labor cost.

Among the trends in food preparation are the widening variety of pre-prepared items in various types of containers and forms. For example, foods previously prepared in the kitchen can now be bought ready-to-serve in cans, such as instant gravy mix, pre-prepared scalloped potatoes, ham salad, chicken and tuna salad, pre-prepared canned sauces such as sweet and sour sauce, Creole sauce or Italian sauce, au gratin potatoes, hashed brown potatoes, and many others. These and similar products are designed for maximum preparation convenience and minimum labor cost. All are ready-to-use or require the addition of water only.

Another important development or trend in food preparation has been that of better equipment, which speeds production and increases employee productivity. Just one example is a patty machine that produces meat patties as large as 1/3 lb at the rate of 1,200 per hr. A companion machine (mixer/grinder) grinds and mixes 200-lb batches of meat at the touch of a button in less than 10 min.

Food services in America's restaurants today seem to fall into three basic patterns. (1) Fast-food, quick, or limited-

menu, where the customer either eats in his car or within the
establishment with a sandwich as the main course. Usually
he has a beverage and possibly adds onion rings or French
fries to his meal. (2) Another service is the cafeteria form
wherein the customer selects any combination of principal
dishes plus beverage, but almost invariably chooses one meat
or fish entree or possibly a meat extender dish. (3) The table
service restaurant with limited or elaborate menu is the third
form, and traditional in Western culture. The greatest variety
in prices, service, and decor is found in this type of restaurant.

Equipment Development

A bewildering array of equipment is now available to the
restaurateur. In fact, it is somewhat difficult to resist being
over-equipped, as there are definitely advantages to using the
wonderfully efficient machinery and equipment that are now
available. These include microwave ovens which cook food
without heat in an unbelievably short length of time, versatile
mixers, machines that wash pots and pans, machines that will
toast 100 sandwiches an hour, and air-cooled or water-cooled
ice flake machines which produce and store from 135 to 1,875
lb of ice a day. Some other examples of this amazing array of
equipment are:

A. Disposable tableware suitable for both hot and cold food.

B. Double-deck self-cleaning convection ovens which clean
by pyrolytic process, reducing any material within the oven
to ash at 1,000°F.

C. A new high-capacity convection/recon oven, available in
both gas and electric, which can handle raw-to-done items to
be cooked with disposable aluminum trays system.

D. Cabinets which hold about 80 pieces of pressure-fried,
disjointed chicken, keeping them warm at temperatures up to
190°F, and can serve the chicken faster than a hamburger
can be fried.

E. Heavy-duty gas ranges and ovens which include 20 different
styles of cooking tops in three models.

F. A mechanical system which water-flushes, scrapes, and
prewashes chinaware, trays, etc., at a single pass, and auto-

matically flushes the waste into a disposal handling all types
of food wastes.

G. Package pubs produced and designed to the operator's
requirements.

H. Self-contained thermoelectric refrigerated cream dispensers in 3- and 6-qt capacities for perfect proportion control.

Modern technology is steadily developing new and improved
equipment for food-service operations. Keeping up with what's
available and the equipment that is suitable and necessary for
a food-service operation is a constant responsibility of a man-
aging director.

Labor Policies

The food-service industry has had relatively favorable labor
legislation and has been exempted from the Federal minimum
wage requirements and its overtime pay requirements, provided that the gross of the restaurant is less than $250,000
for the year. However, many state minimum wage laws cover
the business establishment, regardless of its volume of business; some of these laws specify a minimum number of employees or the age of the employee in determining minimum
wage requirements.

Generally, the food-service industry has had good labor re-
lations and strikes have been minimal in the past decade.
However, in a study done by the Department of Labor, Man-
power Administration, in 1969, it was concluded that the food-
service industry had a voluntary quit rate and a rate of hiring
new employees both well in excess of that of all manufacturers.
The voluntary quit rate was 7% a month and the rate of hiring
new employees was 10.4%; extended to annual rates, these
became 124% of new employees hired each year. These figures
do not include those who are involuntarily dismissed. However,
these rates tend to change with the growing levels of unemploy-
ment and slowdown in business of the nation as a whole.

To overcome this rather high turnover in personnel, the food-
service industry is challenged to develop a better image in
order to compete with the other industries. Job training and
intelligent promotion and motivational policies help to overcome
these adverse trends.

Enlightened management today does not look at its employees in an "employee-oriented" view or a "production-oriented" view. Formerly, it was assumed that a supervisor who became more employee-oriented, and thus more compassionate and interested in his workers, would find that his workers' productivity consequently declined. Conversely, if he were more production-oriented and thus more mindful of various production quotas or quality control considerations in his establishment, then the employees' morale would decline and there would be fewer satisfied workers.

University business research studies have shown that a successful supervisor can combine employee-centered and production-centered orientations, working out these concepts as a creative synergy which brings about a team viewpoint in the employee toward greater productivity and at the same time produces a satisfied and happy employee.

The best present thinking regarding labor policies is to practice good employee management. Maintenance of high standards and being present when questions arise or for decision-making is also a good policy.

Another trend which is apparently effective is profit-sharing. Many restaurants, particularly those of company-owned chain operations, have a profit-sharing and/or a retirement plan related to performance. A certain percentage of the gross or net revenues from food and beverage operations are set aside for eventual retirement.

Another effective motivator is the bonus, which is paid periodically and which is tied to the financial performance of the operation. An example of profit-sharing plans is that used by the Marriott Corporation, in which company officials state that most of their managers in individual restaurants will be millionaires by retirement and a dish washer with 20 years tenure in the company will have about $100,000 to his credit upon retirement. Handsome rewards indeed!

Better training is also one of the benefits of a more enlightened employee management policy. Large companies, particularly, have done much to prepare and put into effect training programs for their employees. A good example of such training programs is that of Burger King. This organization has a training program called Whopper College located at the company's headquarters in Miami. Whopper College utilizes a training manual accompanied by cassettes (small tape car- tridges), slides, and films. This program is offered to new franchisees and is a comprehensive course in food-service management. Another of their programs is called "training opportunities for personal success" (TOPS), an audio-visual library of 9-mm color film (with sound) cartridges. Each film shows in simple, easy steps how to perform the tasks required in a Burger King restaurant. The equipment used can be leased on a weekly fee basis by the franchisees.

Educational Advances in Training Personnel for the Industry

In spite of the somewhat negative impression which many young people have of the food-service industry as a career, there have been remarkable improvements and enlargements of educational programs for this industry. Thirteen 4-year colleges now educate young people for careers in the hotel management field, including courses in food-service manage- ment. According to *Hospitality Magazine*, 91 colleges, junior colleges, and vocational high schools and institutes currently provide food-service courses in the United States. These colleges had 1,702 students enrolled as juniors and seniors in food service, and junior colleges had 1,431 enrolled; vocational schools and institutes had an enrollment of 1,063. This makes a total of 4,216 students enrolled, at the time of their survey.

The most effective effort ever made to recruit able young people into the restaurant field was the production by the National Restaurant Association and Procter & Gamble of a 26- minute award-winning film entitled "Where Do I Go from Here?" This film won the 1970 American Personnel and Guid- ance Association Film Festival Award over 52 other entries. In addition, the NRA together with H. J. Heinz Company has pro- duced an audio-visual vocational guidance kit to acquaint America's young men and women with reasons why they should consider food service as a career.

Other outstanding educational efforts have been made by Coca Cola in cooperation with the National Restaurant Association and by the H. J. Heinz Company in cooperation with NRA.

A training manual for waitresses has been created by Sky Chefs, a subsidiary of American Airlines. Sambo's restaurants have likewise produced a brochure to interest persons in restaurant management as a career.

The Educational Institute of the American Hotel and Motel Association totals over 10,000 students in its program. EI offers special courses prepared by experts at a very modest price for anyone who may be interested. There are some 25 courses and 5 study programs, including a program leading to "certified hotel administrator" (CHA). Certification is based on a point system evaluation of the candidate. Credit is given for required courses, job performance and administrative growth, association service, such as attending meetings, being an officer, speaker, or course instructor—and examinations. The examinations are both written and oral. A research paper is also required.

The National Restaurant Association has launched a new educational program entitled the National Institute for the Foodservice Industry. Northwood Institute with campuses at Midland, Michigan, West Baden Springs, Indiana, and Cedar Hills, Texas, was chosen as the educational institution to provide direction for the program. Basically, this educational effort consists of short courses, conferences, and institutes intended to upgrade and improve management understanding and ability in the food-service field.

Project FEAST (Food Education and Service Technology), was launched in 1964 with programs at two San Francisco Bay area high schools. There are now about 17 project FEAST programs in California, and additional projects in Washington, Oregon, Nevada, Arizona, Hawaii, and Alaska. Enrollment is estimated at 1,400 students in food-service programs in the 11th and 12th grades. Of the some 2,000 students who have completed the project FEAST programs in California since 1964, about half are actively working in the food-service industry or are enrolled in higher education courses in the food-service and lodging industries. Students are taught the fundamentals of commercial food preparation and service coordinated with the other courses in their curricula.

Other high schools have done outstanding work in many parts of the country in stimulating interest in the food-service industry as a career and in making possible educational opportunities in this industry during high school. Often students who lack interest in academic subjects will show an intense interest in the vocational aspects of the industry, and these high school programs will spark a life's career in some aspect of the food-service business.

The Council on Hotel, Restaurant and Institutional Education (CHRIE) has enlarged and strengthened its key role as coordinating and stimulating motivator and guider of America's educational efforts in this field. Annual conventions of CHRIE are well attended and programs are of the highest caliber.

The Culinary Institute of America at Hyde Park, New York, is an example of an outstanding school preparing students for careers as food purveyors, particularly chefs and cooks.

In summary, some of the nation's most prominent colleges and universities, large numbers of community and junior colleges, and some of the most progressive and well-managed high schools are vigorously providing education for those wishing to develop a career in the hotel and restaurant field. Likewise, the largest and strongest associations in the public hospitality business—National Restaurant Association, American Hotel and Motel Association and The Motel Association of America—are involved in educational and certification programs to provide educational opportunities to anyone seeking better understanding and knowledge, and wishing to expand his ability as a worker in this field. So now, as never before, educational opportunities in food services are to be found in virtually all parts of the country and at any level for those who desire to grow and improve.

Tourism's Phenomenal Growth

Tourism, the business of travel, has made remarkable progress as an industry in international trade. For some countries, it is already the most important export industry and earner of foreign exchange. For other countries, tourism represents a promising new resource for economic development.

In the United States, somewhat over half of the population take at least one vacation away from home per year. This means that about 100,000 million persons take a vacation trip longer than 24 hours once a year. The amount spent for tourism in the United States is variously estimated, but about $40 billion dollars is typical of estimates made by such organizations as The Discover America Travel Organization and the American Automobile Association.

Creation of the National System of Interstate Highways has aided greatly in encouraging travel. About 85% of all recreational travel in the United States is by automobile, and thus the development of this 41,000 mile network of 4-lane divided highways is a significant achievement to encourage auto travel. Also, the nation's network of service stations, motels, and roadside food services has done much to encourage vacation experiences. As a matter of fact, fast-food operations are the most rapidly growing of all the nation's major types of food services, and are among the most popular with tourists.

America's great national parks system together with a generally excellent system of state parks and roadside parks have provided high-quality destination areas for local, instate, and interstate auto travel. The growth and popularity of recreational vehicles and camping has also increased the demand for use of public recreation areas, such as parks which provide camping facilities.

Social and economic forces have shaped the growth pattern of tourism in that most union contracts call for paid vacations and virtually all employers award some kind of vacation with pay to employees who have worked for the organization for a specified minimum time. Development of the 4-day week, which has already begun in many industries, is expected to grow in the future.

We have already seen the enactment of the ''Monday Holiday'' plan which was promoted by the Discover America Organization and is now in effect in most states. This adds 5 Mondays for holidays which formerly occurred on days during the week, and makes 3-day weekends available.

The commercial airline system of the United States is unmatched anywhere in the world. The planes provide a very high level of service and comfort and make possible rapid transportation not only to all cities that they serve in the United States but to overseas destinations and to Canada and Mexico as well.

The best air travel market of the future will grow out of that population segment of individuals having an income of $10,000 or more and also at least some college education. By the end of the '70's, economists predict that half the families of the

United States will have an income of $10,000 or more. If inflation can be kept in check, this will mean more discretionary income and thus, a growing market for air travel.

Ocean, rail, and bus travel also are expected to make modest gains during the 1970's.

As people become better educated and more aware of their fellow man, they become more curious about other parts of their country and in other countries. No longer do we have an "isolationist" attitude that America is protected by oceans on both sides. We are more interested in the cultures of other people and in getting to know them better.

In tourism we have the chance of acting as if we were in a play whose stars are ancient and modern art, old and modern culture, beautiful landscapes, archaeological and historical souvenirs, and many other touristic resources. In other words, we use as our capital not only money, but also the greatest tradition and the most remarkable achievements of mankind throughout history.

Whether people travel by car, air, bus, train, or cruise ships, they must eat, and thus food service is of great importance. In fact, many studies have shown that tourists, at least those who travel by car, spend more for food than for any other single item. Thus, as tourism grows, so does the food-service industry.

GOALS AND OPPORTUNITIES

We have seen the estimates of the growth of the food-service industry expected in the next decade, which is actually an acceleration of the remarkable growth in the past decade. What an opportunity for service to one's fellow man! Not only will there be better food-service educational opportunities, as previously noted, but also remarkable opportunities for entrance into the business at virtually any level for those properly qualified.

Every economic, technological, and social trend seems to favor the growth of the food-service industry. To accommodate the expected demand successfully, the industry must do an outstanding job and be able to satisfy its customers fully. As the industry grows and innovates, it provides increased marketing opportunities to reach even a broader segment of the population.

According to the famous management specialist, Dr. Peter Drucker, any business has only two missions—innovation and marketing. The food-service industry can be proud of its many innovations in virtually every aspect of the business, from improving taste of foods to higher productivity and more attractive decor and atmosphere. Marketing has also been vastly improved and its effectiveness is without question becoming greater each year. The volume of business that any individual food-service establishment receives is but part of its success formula. The other part is to show a profit—and a profit which is sufficient to justify the investment in management and labor devoted to the enterprise. This is the challenge of the '70's: to make a reasonable profit in return for capital investment and efforts devoted to the business. Ways must be found to make food-service operations even more efficient, to increase productivity, decrease expenses, and to sell the product at a price which the customer considers to be a good value, but which at the same time will return a sufficient profit to justify the existence of the business.

In America today, there are vast potentials of a great and growing market. We have unexcelled new educational devices and techniques as well as a large increase in the number of schools. The growing and amazing technology of American research and business enterprises produces almost daily new machinery and equipment to help make the industry more effective. New food products, new food processing, new packaging, and new methods of presentation are also evolving at a fast pace. These developments challenge the ingenuity and managerial ability of food-service industry people.

America can be proud of the tremendous diversity of its food-service industry, as well as its exciting new atmosphere, and theme specialty restaurants which are growing so rapidly. The opportunities are waiting, and so is an unequalled challenge for the career-minded of today.

Now it is necessary to discuss some of the basic scientific concepts used in this specialized area. Chapters 2 and 3 briefly cover the main subjects and later, Chapter 10 outlines those organic chemistry principles that are so needed by every knowledgeable member of this broad field of food services.

CHAPTER 2

L. L. W. Smith
L. J. Minor

Simplified Basic Concepts

Metrication and Other Units of Measurement

The use of the metric system for measurements has been in use for a long time, particularly in Europe. Weighing materials in terms of grams, kilograms, etc., walking meters and buying liquids by the liter are everyday uses. In the United States the metric system has been used only in scientific studies and taught as part of the necessary subject matter of chemistry, physics, mathematics, and other science-oriented subjects. Now the era is drawing near when these units will be used universally; 1980 has been expressed as a date for adopting the metric system. Forty countries have enacted laws which make the International System of units mandatory. These are 6 primary units; Length—meter (m), Mass—kilogram (kg), Time —second (s), Electric current—ampere (A), Temperature— degree Kelvin (K°), and Luminous intensity—candela (cd).

Measuring Standards

Measure	Unit	Definition
Length	Meter	1,650,763.73 wavelengths in vacuum of transition between energy levels $2p_{10}$ and $5d_5$ of krypton-86 atom existing at triple point of nitrogen (−210 degrees Celsius)
Mass	Kilogram	Mass of Prototype Kilogram No. 1 at International Bureau of Weights & Measures at Sèvres, France
Time	Second	9,192,631,770 cycles of frequency associated with transition between two hyperfine levels of isotope Cesium 133
Temperature	Degree Celsius (Kelvin)	1/273.16 of the thermodynamic temperature of the triple point of water (0.01 degree Celsius)

TABLE 2.1

THE 6 PRIMARY UNITS AND SOME USES

Length = meter (m) Electric current = ampere (A)
Mass = kilogram (kg) Temperature = degree Kelvin (K)[1]
Time = seconds (s) Luminous intensity = candela (cd)
Amount of substance = mole (mol)

Uses

Length (m) × width (m) = area, square meters = (m^2)
Area (m^2) × height (m) = volume = (m^3)
Distance (m) ÷ time (s) = velocity/second = m/s
Mass (kg) ÷ time (s) = rate of flow = kg/s
Volume (m^3) ÷ time (s) = rate of flow = m^3/s

In the metric system numbers are grouped into multiples of 10 represented by prefixes.

Prefix	*Symbol*	*Power*
Mega means a million times	M	10^6
Kilo means a thousand times	K	10^3
Hecto means a hundred times	h	10^2
Deca means ten times	da	10^1
Deci means a tenth part of	d	10^{-1}
Centi means a hundredth part of	c	10^{-2}
Milli means a thousandth part of	m	10^{-3}
Micro means a millionth part of	μ	10^{-6}

[1] The word degree has been eliminated from the unit of thermo-dynamic temperature (Kelvin) and the degree sign has been eliminated from its symbol (K). The word and symbol are retained in expressing Celsius or centigrade temperatures ($t = 25°C$).

Errors

In most experimental work that is done by the average technician, the results are never completely accurate. Errors are present in variable amounts. Some are attributed to human failure or skill of the experimenter and others to controlled or uncontrolled conditions. Errors are sometimes divided into systematic errors and random errors. Systematic errors are generally those which are the result of some inherent error in the method of measurement, or in the manufacture of the measuring device. Random errors are those which occur in spite of the experimenter's best efforts or skill.

TABLE 2.2

THE METRIC SYSTEM AND SOME APPROXIMATE U.S. EQUIVALENTS

1. Units of length

1 Angstrom (Å)	$= 1 \times 10^{-8}$ centimeter $= 0.00000001$ cm
10 millimeters[1] (mm)	$= 1$ centimeter $= 0.01$ meter $= 0.4$ inch
10 centimeters (cm)	$= 1$ decimeter $= 0.1$ meter $= 4$ inches
10 decimeters (dm)	$= 1$ meter about 1.1 yards or 39.39 inches
1,000 meters (m)	$= 1$ kilometer (km), about 0.62 miles
2.54 centimeters (cm)	$= 1$ inch (in.)

2. Units of Weight

10 milligrams[2] (mg)	$= 1$ centigram
10 centigrams (cg)	$= 1$ decigram
10 decigrams (dg)	$= 1$ gram
1,000 grams (gm)	$= 1$ kilogram (kg)
1 gram	$=$ about 15.43 grains (gr)
1 gram	$=$ about 0.0353 ounce (oz)
28.3 grams	$= 1$ ounce (oz)
453.59 grams	$= 1$ pound (lb)
1 kilogram	$=$ about 2.2 pounds (lbs)

3. Units of capacity

1000 milliliters (ml)	$= 1$ liter (l)
950 milliliters (ml)	$= 0.95$ l $= 1$ liquid quart (qt)
1 liter (l)	$= 1.06$ liquid quarts

---

[1] One thousandth of a millimeter (0.001 mm) is equal to 1 micron designated as μ or 10^{-3} mm. One millimicron or mμ, or 10^{-6} mm is designated as 10 Angstrom units (Å).

[2] One thousandth of a milligram or 0.000001 gm (1×10^{-6} gm) is equal to 1 microgram.

Therefore, when a number of measurements are made, the simple average may be taken as the most reliable result. Then a measure of the precision measurements may be given in terms of average deviation from the mean.

The *percentage of error* is calculated by dividing the differ-ence between the accepted value and the experimenter's mea-sured value by the accepted value, and multiplying by 100.

Energy Measurements

Temperature is a method of expressing the thermal energy of a substance. The changes which take place in water are used

TABLE 2.3

THE UNITED STATES SYSTEM,
SOME METRIC AND BRITISH EQUIVALENTS

1. Liquid Measure
   1 teaspoon (tsp)   = about 5 ml
   3 teaspooons   = 1 tablespoon (Tbsp)
   1 tablespoon (Tbsp) = about 15 ml or $\frac{1}{2}$ fluid ounce
   8 tablespoons   = 1 gill or 4 fluid ounces
   16 tablespoons   = 1 cup (c) or 8 fluid ounces
   1 cup (c)   = about 237 ml or $\frac{1}{4}$ quart
   2 cups   = 1 pint (pt)
   1 pint   = 473 ml or $\frac{1}{2}$ quart
   2 pints   = 1 quart (qt), about 0.95 l
   4 quarts   = 1 gallon (gal), about 3.79 l
   4.8 U.S. quarts   = 1 British Imperial gallon or about 4.55 liters

2. Dry Measure
   1 quart   = about 1.1 liters
   8 quarts   = 1 peck (pk) = about 8.8 liters
   4 pecks   = 1 bushel (bu) = about 35.24 liters
   4 British pecks = 1 British bushel = about 36.37 liters

3. Units of length
   1 inch (in.) = 2.54 cm
   1 foot (ft) = 0.305 m
   1 yard (yd) = 0.914 m
   1 mile (mi) = 1.609 km

4. Units of area
   1 hectare (ha) = 10,000 square meters = 2.47 acres

as the basis for the scales used in the measurement of temperature.

The *Fahrenheit scale* uses the freezing point of water or the
melting point of ice as 32°F and the boiling point of water as
212°F at standard pressure or 760 mm.

The *Celsius scale* is used in most scientific work and the
freezing point is defined as 0°C and the boiling point at 100°C
at standard pressure or 760 mm.

To convert degrees centigrade to degrees Fahrenheit the
following formula may be used.

$$1.8 \times °C = °F - 32 \text{ or degrees } F = (9/5 \times °C) + 32$$

or $°F = (1.8 \times °C) + 32$.

The third scale used in scientific work is called *Kelvin* or *Absolute*. This is based on the change of about 1/273 of its volume of gas under equal pressure as the temperature changes. The temperature on the Celsius scale can be converted to temperature on the Kelvin Scale by the addition of 273.15° to the Celsius Value: $°K = °C + 273.15°$.

A *calorie* is defined as a unit of energy. It is the amount of heat required to raise the temperature of 1 gram of water 1 degree centigrade between 14.5 and 15.5°C. The large calorie, or kilocalorie, sometimes is called the dietary Calorie (always capitalized) and is equal to 1000 small calories, or that amount of heat required to raise 1000 grams of water 1 degree centigrade. This unit is used to indicate the energy value of basic foodstuffs as follows:

1 gram protein = approximately 4 Calories
1 gram carbohydrate = approximately 4 Calories
1 gram fat = approximately 9 Calories

These figures are used in calculating the caloric values of various dietary needs.

Specific heat is defined as the calories per degree per gram. It is sometimes called the heat capacity. The specific heat of water vapor is 0.48 cal/deg/gm. The specific heat of ice is 0.45 cal/deg/gm. The specific heat of liquid water is high, 1 cal/deg/gm between 0° and 100°C. The heat of condensation of water is 540 Cal/gm at 100°C, the heat of crystallization of water at 0°C is 80 cal/gm, or the heat of fusion for the transformation from the solid state to the liquid state.

Pressure is a measure of the force per unit area exerted by a substance upon the walls of the container. The atmosphere exerts pressure and is expressed in centimeters or millimeters of mercury. By definition, 1 atmosphere is equal to 760 mm of mercury.

Standard temperature and *pressure* are defined as one atmophere pressure and zero degrees centigrade and *STP* are used to indicate these. At *STP* equal volumes of the same or different gases contain the same number of atoms or molecules, or *Avogadro's number* which is 6.023×10^{23}.

Avogadro's hypothesis and number are the basis for the concept of a *mole* of a compound. A *mole* (32 gm) of oxygen at *STP*

contains 6.023×10^{23} molecules and occupies *22.4 liters*. A *mole*
(44 gm) of carbon dioxide at STP contains 6.023×10^{23} molecules
and occupies 22.4 liters. The effect of temperature and pressure
on the volume of gases is expressed by the gas laws. The universal gas constant, R, has been omitted in the following considerations.

Boyle's law $V_1 = V_2 (p_2/p_1)$: the change in volume of a gas
at constant temperature is inversely proportional to the pressure.

Charles' law $V_1 = V_2 (T_1/T_2)$: the change in volume of a gas
at constant pressure is directly proportional to the change in
temperature.

Gay-Lussac's law is a combination of Charles' and Boyle's
laws using the same reasoning: $V_2 = V_1 \times T_2/T_1 \times p_1/p_2$.

Dalton's law states that the total pressure of a mixture of
gases at a given temperature is the sum of the partial pressure
exerted by each component. $PV = V(p_1 + p_2 + p_3$, etc.) Vapor
pressure of water must be taken into consideration when gases
are collected by water displacement. Table 2.4 presents the
vapor pressure of water at various temperatures.

The importance of temperatures, vapor pressures, and specific heats is illustrated in Table 2.5, which deals with the
storage requirements of perishable foods. Fruits such as
apples, strawberries, and bananas are dependent not only on
temperature, but on the composition of the environmental gases
such as oxygen, carbon dioxide, ammonia, ethylene, and water
vapor. The proper environment ensures that some fruits and
vegetables will be available the year-round. Metabolic processes may be hastened or retarded depending upon temperature
and environmental composition.

MATTER AND ENERGY

Our environment, our bodies, the air we breathe, the water we
drink, and the food we eat to sustain life are all chemicals. In
fact, all matter is chemical in nature. To be attuned to life, an
understanding of chemistry is essential. All about us chemical
changes occur constantly. Iron rusts, paint chalks, food spoils,
fabrics deteriorate, rubber cracks, fuel burns, and light-bulb
filaments oxidize. Plants and animals grow, iron ore yields
steel, crude oil provides a myriad of petroleum products, coal

FOOD SERVICE SCIENCE

TABLE 2.4

VAPOR PRESSURES OF WATER

Temperature, °C	Pressure, mm	Temperature, °C	Pressure, mm
0	4.58	35	42.2
5	6.54	40	55.3
10	9.21	45	71.9
15	12.79	50	92.5
20	17.54	55	118.0
21	18.65	60	149.4
22	19.83	65	187.5
23	21.1	70	234.0
24	22.4	75	289.0
25	23.8	80	355.0
26	25.2	85	434.0
27	26.7	90	526.0
28	28.3	95	634.0
29	30.0	100	760.0
30	31.8		

These figures are subtracted from the normal atmospheric readings to obtain the pressures due to the gases alone.

tar is converted to saccharin, dyes, and a multitude of other derivatives. Some of these reactions occur naturally, while others are developed through research. We live in a complex world, and our part of it—the science of food and beverage—is ever-challenging.

Matter

Matter is anything having weight or mass and occupying space. A general term that describes any specific kind of matter is *substance*. Examples are glass, protein, iron, wool, concrete, wood, and paper; these are all substances. Each has its own physical and chemical properties.

Energy

Energy may be defined as the capacity for doing work or producing changes in matter. When food is cooked, ice cream is frozen, grapes are fermented to wine, or milk fermented

TABLE 2.5[1]

STORAGE REQUIREMENTS AND PROPERTIES OF PERISHABLE FOODS[2]

Commodity	Storage Temp, °F	Relative Humidity, %	Approximate Storage Life	Water Content %	Average Freezing Point, °F	Specific Heat above Freezing[3]	Specific Heat below Freezing[3]	Latent Heat (Calculated),[4] Btu	Heat of Respiration, Btu/Ton/24 Hr
Alfalfa meal[5]	30–40	70–75	...[5]	...[5]	...	...	...	...	...
Apples	30–32	85–90	...[5]	84.1	28.2	0.87	0.45	121	1,500–12,380(70)
Apricots	31–32	85–90	1–2 wk	85.4	29.6	0.88	0.46	122	
Artichokes (globe)	31–32	90–95	1–2 wk	83.7	29.6	0.87	0.45	120	
Jerusalem	31–32	90–95	2–5 mo	79.5	27.5	0.83	0.44	114	
Asparagus	32	90–95	3–4 wk	93.0	30.4	0.94	0.48	134	
Avocados	45–55	85–90	4 wk	65.4	30.0	0.72	0.40	94	
Bananas	...[5]	85–95	...[5]	74.8	29.6	0.80	0.42	108	
Beans (green or snap)	45	85–90	8–10 days	88.9	30.2	0.91	0.47	128	6,160–52,950(70)
Lima	32–40	85–90	10–15 days	66.5	30.8	0.73	0.40	94	2,330–29,220(70)
Beer, barreled[5]	35–40	...	3–6 wk	90.2	28.0	0.92	...	...	
Beets									
Bunch	32	90–95	10–11 days	...	...	...	...	...	2,650–7,240
Topped	32	90–95	1–3 mo	87.6	29.2	0.90	0.46	126	
Blackberries	31–32	85–90	7 days	84.8	29.4	0.88	0.46	122	
Blueberries	31–32	85–90	3–6 wk	82.3	28.6	0.86	0.45	118	
Bread	0	...	Several wk	32–37	...	0.70	0.34	46–53	7,450–100,000
Broccoli, sprouting	32	90–95	7–10 days	89.9	30.3	0.92	0.47	130	
Brussels sprouts	32	90–95	3–4 wk	84.9	30.2	0.88	0.46	122	1,200–6,120(70)
Cabbage, late	32	90–95	3–4 mo	92.4	30.5	0.94	0.47	132	
Candy	0–34	40–65	...	...	...	...	...	...	
Carrots									
Bunch	32	90–95	10–14 days	...	...	...	...	...	
Prepackages	32	80–90	3–4 wk	88.2	28.8	0.90	0.46	126	2,130–8,080
Topped	32	90–95	4–5 mo	91.7	30.2	0.93	0.47	132	
Cauliflower	32	85–90	2–3 wk	88.3	30.2	0.91	0.46	126	
Celeriac	32	90–95	3–4 mo	93.7	30.9	0.95	0.48	135	1,620–14,150(70)
Celery	31–32	90–95	2–4 mo	...	...	...	...	...	1,249–13,200
Cherries	31–32	85–90	10–14 days	83.0	27.7	0.87	0.45	120	

Table 2.5 (*continued*)

Coffee (green)	35–37	80–85	2–4 mo	10–15	...	...	...	...	
Corn, sweet	31–32	85–90	4–8 days	73.9	30.8	0.79	0.42	106	6,560–61,950(80)
Cranberries	36–40	85–90	1–3 mo	87.4	30.0	0.90	0.46	124	720–1,800(50)
Cucumbers	45–50	90–95	10–14 days	96.1	30.5	0.97	0.49	137	1,690–10,460
Currants	32	80–85	10–14 days	84.7	30.2	0.88	0.45	120	
Dairy products									
Butter	32–36	80–85	2 mo	15.5–16.5	...	0.33	...	23	
Butter	−10 to −20	80–85	1 yr	15.5–16.5	...	...	0.25	23	
Cheese	35	65–70	...	37–38	28.0	0.50	0.31	54	
Cream (sweetened)	−15	...	Several mo	...	...	...	...	...	
Ice cream	−15	...	Several mo	...	22–29	0.80	0.45	96	
Skim milk									
Dried	40	...	Several mo	3.5	...	0.23	...	5	
Sweetened	35	...	Several mo	...	...	...	...	...	
Unsweetened	−15	...	Short time	...	...	...	...	...	
Dates	...[5]	...[5]	...[5]	20.0	−4.2	0.36	0.26	29	
Dewberries	31–32	85–90	7–10 days	...	29.2	...	...	...	
Dried fruits	32	50–60	9–12 mo	...	...	0.30–0.32	...	17–21	
Eggplant	45–50	85–90	10 days	92.7	30.4	0.94	0.48	132	
Eggs									
Dried spray albumen	35	Low as possible	6 mo	Up to 6.0	...	0.25	...	9	
Dried, whole	35	Low as possible	6 mo–1 yr	5.0	...	0.25	0.21	9	
Dried, yolk	35	Low as possible	6 mo–1 yr	3.0	...	0.22	0.21	4	
Fermented albumen	Rm temp	Low as possible	1 yr, plus	3–15	...	0.22–0.32	...	4–21	
Frozen	−10–0	Low as possible	1 yr, plus	73	28.0	0.74	0.42	104	
Shell	29–31[6]	85–90	8–9 mo	67.0	28.0	0.74	0.40	96	
Shell, farm cooler	40–55	75	...	67.0	28.0	0.74	0.40	96	
Endive (escarole)	32	90–95	2–3 wk	93.3	31.1	0.94	0.48	132	
Figs									
Dried	32–40	50–60	9–12 mo	24.0	...	0.39	0.27	34	
Fresh	28–32	85–90	5–7 days	78.0	27.1	0.82	0.43	112	
Fish									
Brine salted	40–50	90–95	10–12 mo	...	...	0.76	0.41	100	
Fresh	33–40	90–95	5–20 days	62–85	28.0	0.80	0.40	89–122	
Frozen	−10–0	90–95	8–10 mo	62–85	...	0.80	0.40	115	

Table 2.5 (*continued*)

Commodity									
Mild cured	28–35	75–90	4–8 mo	...	...	0.76	0.41	100	
Smoked	40–50	50–60	6–8 mo	...	...	0.70	0.39	92	
Frozen-pack fruits	−10–0	...	6–12 mo						
Frozen-pack vegetables	−10–0	...	6–12 mo						
Furs and fabrics[5]									
Garlic dry	32	70–75	6–8 mo	74.2	28.0	0.79	0.42	106	
Gooseberries	31–32	80–85	3–4 wk	88.9	30.0	0.90	0.46	126	
Grapefruit	32–50	85–90	4–8 wk	88.8	28.6	0.91	0.46	126	950–6,840(90)
Grapes									
American type	31–32	85–90	3–8 wk	81.9	29.4	0.86	0.44	116	
European type	30–31	85–90	3–6 mo	81.6	27.1	0.86	0.44	116	
Honey	...[5]	...[5]	1 yr	18.0	...	0.35	0.26	26	
Hops	29–32	50–60	Several mo	...	...	...	...	...	
Horseradish	32	90–95	10–12 mo	73.4	26.4	0.78	0.42	104	
Kale	32	90–95	3–4 wk	86.6	30.7	0.89	0.46	124	
Kohlrabi	32	90–95	2–4 wk	90.1	30.0	0.92	0.47	128	
Lard (without antioxidant)	45	90–95	4–8 mo	0	...	...	...	...	
Lard (without antioxidant)	0	90–95	12–14 mo	0	...	...	...	...	
Leeks, green	32	90–95	1–3 mo	88.2	30.4	0.90	0.46	126	
Lemons	32, 55–58	85–90	1–4 mo	89.3	29.0	0.92	0.46	127	900–5,490(80)
Lettuce	32	90–95	3–4 wk	94.8	31.2	0.96	0.48	136	
Limes	48–50	85–90	6–8 wk	86.0	28.2	0.89	0.46	122	11,320–45,890
Logan blackberries	31–32	85–90	7 days	82.9	29.5	0.86	0.45	118	
Malt syrup	...[5]	...[5]	...[5]						
Mangoes	50	85–90	2–3 wk	81.4	29.4	0.85	0.44	117	
Maple syrup	...[5]	...[5]	...[5]	36.0	...	0.49	0.31	52	
Meat									
Bacon, frozen	−10–0	90–95	4–6 mo	...	...	...	...	...	
Cured (farm style)	60–65	85	4–6 mo	13–29	...	0.30–0.43	0.24–0.29	18–41	
(packer style)	34–40	85	2–6 wk	...	...	...	...	...	
Beef, fresh	32–34	88–92	1–6 wk	62–77	28–29	0.70–0.84	0.38–0.43	89–110	
Frozen	−10–0	90–95	9–12 mo	...	...	...	...	...	
Fat backs	38–40	85–90	0–3 mo	...	...	...	...	...	
Hams and shoulders									
Fresh	32–34	85–90	7–12 days	47–54	28–29	0.58–0.63	0.34–0.36	67–77	
Cured	60–65	50–60	0–3 yr	40–45	...	0.52–0.56	0.32–0.33	57–64	

Table 2.5 (*continued*)

Frozen	−10−0	90−95	6−8 mo	...	...	...	...	...	
Lamb, fresh	32−34	85−90	5−12 days	60−70	28−29	0.68−0.76	0.38−0.51	86−100	
Frozen	−10−0	90−95	8−10 mo	...	...	...	...	...	
Livers, frozen	−10−0	90−93	3−4 mo	70.0	...	...	...	...	
Pork, fresh	32−34	85−90	3−7 days	35−42	28−29	0.48−0.54	0.30−0.32	50−60	
Frozen	−10−0	90−95	4−6 mo	...	...	...	...	...	
Sausage casings	40−45	85−90	...	...	...	...	...	...	
Smoked sausage	40−45	85−90	...	...	...	...	...	...	
Veal	32−34	90−95	5−10 days	70−80	28−29	0.76−0.84	0.42−0.51	100−114	
Melons									
Cantaloupe & Persian	45−50	85−90	1−2 wk	92.7	29.9	0.94	0.48	132	1,230−8,500
Casaba	45−50	85−90	4−6 wk	92.7	29.9	0.94	0.48	132	
Honey Dew and Honey Ball	45−50	85−90	2−4 wk	92.6	29.8	0.94	0.48	132	
Watermelons	36−40	85−90	2−3 wk	92.1	30.6	0.97	0.48	132	
Milk, powdered	32−40	Moistureproof Containers	Several wk	...	...	...	...	...	
Mushrooms[5]	32−35	85−90	3−5 days	91.1	30.0	0.93	0.47	130	6,160−58,000(70)
Mushroom spawn									
Grain spawn	32−40	75−80	2 wk	...	...	...	...	...	
Manure spawn	34	75−80	8 mo	...	...	...	...	...	
Nursery stock	32−35	85−90	3−6 mo	...	...	...	...	...	
Nuts	32−50[1]	65−75	8−12 mo	3−6	...[1]	0.22−0.25	0.21−0.22	4−8	
Oil (vegetable salad)	35	...	1 yr	0	...	...	...	...	
Okra	50	85−95	7−10 days	89.8	28.6	0.92	0.46	128	
Oleomargarine	35	60−70	1 yr	15.5	...	0.32	0.25	22	
Olives, fresh	45−50	85−90	4−6 wk	75.2	28.5	0.80	0.42	108	
Onions and onion sets	32	70−75	6−8 mo	87.5	30.1	0.90	0.46	124	1,100−4,180(70)
Oranges	32−34	85−90	8−12 wk	87.2	30.6	0.90	0.46	124	1,030−9,420(90)
Papayas	45	85−90	2−3 wk	90.8	30.1	0.82	0.47	130	
Parsnips	32	90−95	2−6 mo	78.6	29.8	0.84	0.46	112	
Peaches	31−32	85−90	2−4 wk	86.9	29.6	0.90	0.46	124	1,370−22,460(80)
Pears	29−31	85−90	...[5]	82.7	27.7	0.86	0.45	118	880−13,200
Peas, green	32	85−90	1−2 wk	74.3	30.1	0.79	0.42	106	8,360−82,920(80)
Peppers, chilli (dry)	32−40	65−75	6−9 mo	12.0	30.9	0.30	0.24	17	
Peppers, sweet	45−50	85−90	8−10 days	92.4	30.5	0.94	0.47	132	2,720−8,470
Persimmons	30	85−90	2 mo	78.2	27.5	0.84	0.43	112	

Table 2.5 (*continued*)

Commodity								
Pineapples mature green	50–60	85–90	3–4 wk	...	29.1	...	...	...	
Ripe	40–45	85–90	2–4 wk	85.3	29.7	0.88	0.45	122	
Plums, including fresh Prunes	31–32	80–85	2–4 wk[5]	85.7	28.7	0.88	0.45	123	
Pomegranates	34–35	85–90	2–4 mo	...	26.5	...	...	123	
Popcorn, unpopped	32–40	85	...[5]	13.5	...	0.31	0.24	19	
Potatoes									880–3,530(70) (Irish Potatoes)
Early crop	50–55	85–90	...[5]	...	30.0	...	...	111	
Late crop	38–50[1]	85–90	...[5]	77.8	29.8	0.82	0.43	111	
Poultry									
Fresh	32	...	1 wk	74.0	27.0	0.79	...	106	
Frozen, eviscerated	–10–0	...	9–10 mo	...	...	...	...	...	
Frozen, New York Dressed	–10–0	...	6–9 mo	...	...	...	0.37	...	
Pumpkins	50–55	70–75	2–6 mo	90.5	29.9	0.92	0.47	130	
Quinces	31–32	90–95	2–3 mo	85.3	28.1	0.88	0.45	122	
Rabbits									
Fresh	32–34	90–95	1–5 days	...	...	...	...	...	
Frozen	–10–0	90–95	0–6 mo	...	...	...	...	...	
Radishes, spring,									
Bunched, or prepackaged	32	90–95	10 days	93.6	30.1	0.95	0.48	134	
Winter	32	90–95	2–4 mo	93.6	...	0.95	0.48	134	
Raspberries									
Black	31–32	85–90	7 days	80.6	29.4	0.84	0.44	122	5,500–22,300
Frozen (red or black)	–10–0	...	1 yr	...	...	...	...	...	
Red	31–32	85–90	7 days	84.1	30.3	0.87	0.45	121	5,500–22,300
Rhubarb	32	90–95	2–3 wk	94.9	29.9	0.96	0.48	134	
Rutabagas	32	90–95	2–4 mo	89.1	29.7	0.91	0.47	127	
Salsify	32	90–95	2–4 mo	79.1	29.6	0.83	0.44	113	
Spinach	32	90–95	10–14 days	92.7	31.3	0.94	0.48	132	4,860–38,000
Squash									
Acorn	45–50	75–85	4–5 wk	...	30.0	...	...	...	
Summer	32–40	85–95	10–14 days	95.0	30.4	0.96	...	135	
Winter	50–55	70–75	4–6 mo	88.6	29.8	0.91	...	127	
Strawberries									
Fresh	31–32	85–90	7–10 days	89.9	30.2	0.92	...	129	3,800–46,400(80)

Table 2.5 (continued)

Frozen	-10-0	...	1 yr	72.0	...	...	0.42	103	
Sugar, granulated	50-100	Below 60	1-3 yr	0.5	...	0.20	0.20	72	
Sweet potatoes	55-60	90-95	4-6 mo	68.5	29.2	0.75	0.40	97	2,440-6,300
Tangerines	31-38	90-95	3-4 wk	87.3	29.5	0.90	0.46	125	
Tomatoes									
Mature green	55-70[5]	85-90[1]	2-5 wk	94.7	30.4	0.95	0.48	134	580-6,230
Ripe	32[1]	85-90[1]	7 days	94.1	30.4	0.95	0.48	134	1,020-5,640
Turnips, roots	32	90-95	4-5 mo	90.9	29.8	0.93	0.47	130	1,940-5,280
Vegetable seed	32-50	50-65	...[5]	...	...	...	...	...	
Yeast, compressed									
Baker's	31-32	...	...	70.9	...	0.77	0.41	102	

[1] From N. N. Potter, Food Science, 1968, pp. 184-189.

[2] Taken from ASRE Data Book, 1959, as modified by McCoy (1963).

[3] Calculated by Siebel's formula, see pp. 23-01 of the ASRE Data Book, 1959. For values above freezing point $S = 0.008a + 0.20$. For values below freezing point $S = 0.002a + 0.20$. (Work on the calorimetric determination of products and therefore are not included in this tabulation.)

[4] Values for latent heat (latent heat of fusion) in Btu per pound, calculated by multiplying the % of water content by the latent heat of fusion of water, 143.4 Btu. (British Thermal Unit, the quantity of heat required to raise the temperature of 1 lb of water 1°F.)

[5] See text of Chap. 23 in the ASRE Data Book, 1959, or Agr. Handbook 66. If not available for local examination, copies may be obtained from ASHRAE, New York, and from Supt. of Documents, Government Printing Office, Washington, D.C.

[6] Eggs with weak albumin freeze just below 30.

Further information can be obtained from the Agriculture Handbook No. 66, United States Department of Agriculture, Revised October, 1968.

to cheese, heat is absorbed or released. Reactions that give off heat are called *exothermic* and those that take on heat are *endothermic*.

Einstein developed a formula for the conversion of mass to energy, predicting that a small amount of mass can release a huge amount of energy. His formula is: $E = mc^2$, where E is the energy produced, m is the mass converted to energy, and c is the speed of light, amounting to 186,272 mi/sec (Table 2.6).

Laws of Conservation of Matter and Energy

When chemical changes occur, for example when wood burns, if the products of combustion are weighed, their weight is exactly equal to that of the wood and the oxygen used. This is true of all chemical changes, and has resulted in the *Law of Conservation of Matter or Mass. "In ordinary chemical changes, matter is neither created nor destroyed, but remains constant in amount."*

Energy that is stored in coal or petroleum or other substances is called *potential energy.* The Law of Conservation of Energy also applies in all chemical changes: *"In ordinary chemical reactions energy may change in form, but it is neither created nor destroyed."*

Energy, which is of such utmost importance to the world, may be needed in the future in greater amounts than can be supplied. There have been many studies projecting the energy needs for the future (year 2200) based on the population census. Energy is supplied from coal, natural gas, petroleum, hydropower, and nuclear fission. In the future energy may be obtained from wood, charcoal, wind, water wheels, geothermal sources, solar cells, radioisotopes, rocket fuels, thermonuclear reactions, and other energy sources not identified as yet.

The energy crisis behooves each student in this field to realize what he should know in every area in order to conserve both energy and the money expended for it. For instance, how hot is hot, what are the temperatures achieved by a gas flame, an electric heating coil, an acetylene torch, an alcohol lamp, an oil burner, etc.? Not only types of heating equipment need to be studied but cooling equipment as well.

Matter exists in three common forms, namely: gaseous, liquid, and solid. Gases have no definite shape unless con-

TABLE 2.6

ENERGY RELATIONSHIPS

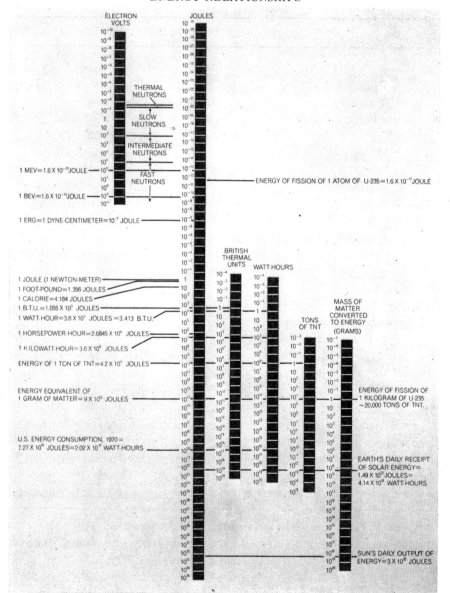

fined. Under pressure, gases can be changed to liquids and solids. For example, at constant pressure, the physical form of water depends upon the temperature. At 0° or 100°C water is a liquid; below 0°C it is a solid; above 100°C it changes to steam. These are physical changes, and not chemical changes. Thus, a substance may be changed from one physical state to another by changing the conditions of temperature and pressure under which it is maintained.

Identifying Matter

Each kind of matter has properties or characteristics by which it may be distinguished from another kind of matter. These may be classed as *physical* and *chemical* properties.

Physical properties include taste, odor, color, density, solubility, hardness, freezing point, boiling point, ductility, malleability, conductivity, melting point, viscosity, resistance to shear, texture, vapor pressure, index of refraction, surface tension, dipole moment, osmotic pressure, optical rotation, critical temperature, critical pressure, specific gravity, specific heat, specific volume, and others.

Chemical properties are based on the reactivity of the substance with oxygen, heat, water, acids, bases, enzymes, or other reactants. For example, acids or enzymes may be used to convert starch to syrup, alkali reacts with fat to produce soap and glycerol, and iron reacts with oxygen in the presence of moisture to form a type of iron oxide called rust. Each of these chemical reactions transforms matter from one form to another.

Another method of classification of matter is as *elements*, *compounds*, and *mixtures*. *Elements are grouped as metals or nonmetals. Metals* reflect light and *conduct heat or electricity.* Some are *malleable*, or workable into sheets, like gold. Others, such as copper and silver, are *ductile*, and may be drawn into fine wires.

Nonmetals are usually lighter in weight than metals, are brittle, and *will not conduct electricity. Sulfur, carbon, phosphorus*, and *chlorine* are in this class.

The elements in the lanthanide and actinide series have nearly identical properties.

This arrangement of the elements in the table is used today; however, there are other arrangements. The total number of elements that are prophesied to be made is approximately 127.

ELEMENTS AND COMPOUNDS

Elements may be defined as substances which cannot be decomposed into simpler substances by ordinary means. Examples are iron, carbon, hydrogen, and phosphorus. There is a total of 105 elements known at present; most occur naturally, but some have been made by man. The 92 elements found in nature plus the man-made have been arranged on the basis of their atomic number in a sequence termed the Periodic Table (Table 2.7).

All matter is composed of either elements alone, or of various combinations of elements. Pure substances are homogeneous, i.e., every part of the material is like every other part of the whole in every respect. A *compound* is a pure substance that can be chemically broken down into simpler pure substances, namely, *elements.*

Each element is made up of a *positively charged nucleus* surrounded by *negatively charged electrons* in varying orbits. The *atomic number* of an element is the number of *protons* or *positive charges* in the nucleus, and also represents the number of *electrons.* Each element as it exists is *electrically neutral. Neutrons* found in the nucleus do not carry a charge, and have a mass of 1.009. Electrons weigh only 0.00055 awu (atomic weight unit), or 1/1838 the mass of a proton or neutron. Table 2.8 lists the atomic weights and numbers of the elements. The number of neutrons in any nucleus is found by subtracting the number of protons (atomic number) from the atomic weight. All the atoms in most elements do not weigh the same, and different types of atoms of the same element are called isotopes.

Isotopes

Isotopes are elements having the same atomic number but different atomic weights. Their chemical properties are not significantly altered. Most elements are mixtures of isotopes. Three hydrogen isotopes have been identified: $_1H^1$, $_1H^2$, and $_1H^3$. Hydrogen having a mass of 2 was discovered by Urey in

TABLE 2.6

FISHER SCIENTIFIC / PERIODIC CHART OF THE ELEMENTS

IA	IIA	IIIB	IVB	VB	VIB	VIIB	VIII	VIII	VIII	IB	IIB	IIIA	IVA	VA	VIA	VIIA	INERT GASES
1 H 1.00797 ±0.00001																1 H 1.00797 ±0.00001	2 He 4.0026 ±0.00005
3 Li 6.939 ±0.0005	4 Be 9.0122 ±0.00005											5 B 10.811 ±0.003	6 C 12.0115 ±0.0005	7 N 14.0067 ±0.00005	8 O 15.9994 ±0.0001	9 F 18.9984 ±0.00005	10 Ne 20.183 ±0.0005
11 Na 22.9898 ±0.00005	12 Mg 24.312 ±0.005											13 Al 26.9815 ±0.00005	14 Si 28.086 ±0.001	15 P 30.9738 ±0.00005	16 S 32.064 ±0.003	17 Cl 35.453 ±0.001	18 Ar 39.948 ±0.0005
19 K 39.102 ±0.005	20 Ca 40.08 ±0.005	21 Sc 44.956 ±0.0005	22 Ti 47.90 ±0.005	23 V 50.942 ±0.0005	24 Cr 51.996 ±0.001	25 Mn 54.9380 ±0.00005	26 Fe 55.847 ±0.003	27 Co 58.9332 ±0.0005	28 Ni 58.71 ±0.005	29 Cu 63.54 ±0.005	30 Zn 65.37 ±0.005	31 Ga 69.72 ±0.005	32 Ge 72.59 ±0.005	33 As 74.9216 ±0.00005	34 Se 78.96 ±0.005	35 Br 79.909 ±0.002	36 Kr 83.80 ±0.005
37 Rb 85.47 ±0.005	38 Sr 87.62 ±0.005	39 Y 88.905 ±0.0005	40 Zr 91.22 ±0.005	41 Nb 92.906 ±0.005	42 Mo 95.94 ±0.005	43 Tc (99)	44 Ru 101.07 ±0.005	45 Rh 102.905 ±0.0005	46 Pd 106.4 ±0.05	47 Ag 107.870 ±0.003	48 Cd 112.40 ±0.005	49 In 114.82 ±0.005	50 Sn 118.69 ±0.005	51 Sb 121.75 ±0.005	52 Te 127.60 ±0.005	53 I 126.9044 ±0.00005	54 Xe 131.30 ±0.005
55 Cs 132.905 ±0.0005	56 Ba 137.34 ±0.005	57 *La 138.91 ±0.005	72 Hf 178.49 ±0.005	73 Ta 180.948 ±0.0005	74 W 183.85 ±0.005	75 Re 186.2 ±0.05	76 Os 190.2 ±0.05	77 Ir 192.2 ±0.05	78 Pt 195.09 ±0.005	79 Au 196.967 ±0.0005	80 Hg 200.59 ±0.005	81 Tl 204.37 ±0.005	82 Pb 207.19 ±0.005	83 Bi 208.980 ±0.0005	84 Po (210)	85 At (210)	86 Rn (222)
87 Fr (223)	88 Ra (226)	89 †Ac (227)															

*Lanthanum Series

58 Ce 140.12 ±0.005	59 Pr 140.907 ±0.0005	60 Nd 144.24 ±0.005	61 Pm (147)	62 Sm 150.35 ±0.005	63 Eu 151.96 ±0.005	64 Gd 157.25 ±0.005	65 Tb 158.924 ±0.0005	66 Dy 162.50 ±0.005	67 Ho 164.930 ±0.0005	68 Er 167.26 ±0.005	69 Tm 168.934 ±0.0005	70 Yb 173.04 ±0.005	71 Lu 174.97 ±0.005

†Actinium Series

90 Th 232.038 ±0.0005	91 Pa (231)	92 U 238.03 ±0.005	93 Np (237)	94 Pu (242)	95 Am (243)	96 Cm (247)	97 Bk (247)	98 Cf (249)	99 Es (254)	100 Fm (253)	101 Md (256)	102 No (253)	103 Lw (257)

() Numbers in parentheses are mass numbers of most stable or most common isotope.

Atomic Weights corrected to conform to the 1961 values of the Commission on Atomic Weights.

© 1962, by Fisher Scientific Company

TABLE 2.8

TABLE OF ELEMENTS AND ATOMIC WEIGHTS

Based on the Atomic Mass of Carbon 12.

Name	Symbol	Atomic Number	Atomic Weight
Actinium	Ac	89	. . .
Aluminum	Al	13	26.9815
Americium	Am	95	. . .
Antimony	Sb	51	121.75
Argon	Ar	18	39.948
Arsenic	As	33	74.9216
Astatine	At	85	. . .
Barium	Ba	56	137.34
Berkelium	Bk	97	. . .
Beryllium	Be	4	9.0122
Bismuth	Bi	83	208.980
Boron	B	5	10.811[a]
Bromine	Br	35	79.909[b]
Cadmium	Cd	48	112.40
Caesium	Cs	55	132.905
Calcium	Ca	20	40.08
Californium	Cf	98	. . .
Carbon	C	6	12.01115[1]
Cerium	Ce	58	140.12
Chlorine	Cl	17	35.453[b]
Chromium	Cr	24	51.996[b]
Cobalt	Co	27	58.9332
Copper	Cu	29	63.54
Curium	Cm	96	. . .
Dysprosium	Dy	66	162.50
Einsteinium	Es	99	. . .
Erbium	Er	68	167.26
Europium	Eu	63	151.96
Fermium	Fm	100	. . .
Fluorine	F	9	18.9984
Francium	Fr	87	. . .
Gadolinium	Gd	64	157.25
Gallium	Ga	31	69.72
Germanium	Ge	32	72.59
Gold	Au	79	196.967
Hafnium	Hf	72	178.49

Table 2.8 (*continued*)

Helium	He	2	4.0026
Holmium	Ho	67	164.93
Hydrogen	H	1	1.0079[1]
Indium	In	49	114.82
Iodine	I	53	126.9044
Iridium	Ir	77	192.2
Iron	Fe	26	55.74[2]
Krypton	Kr	36	83.80
Lanthanum	La	57	138.91
Lawrencium	Lw	103	...
Lead	Pb	82	207.19
Lithium	Li	3	6.939
Lutetium	Lu	71	174.97
Magnesium	Mg	12	24.312
Manganese	Mn	25	54.9380
Mendelevium	Md	101	...
Mercury	Hg	80	200.59
Molybdenum	Mo	42	95.94
Neodymium	Nd	60	144.24
Neon	Ne	10	20.183
Neptunium	Np	93	...
Nickel	Ni	28	58.41
Niobium	Nb	41	92.906
Nitrogen	N	7	14.0067
Nobelium	No	102	...
Osmium	Os	76	190.2
Oxygen	O	8	15.9994[1]
Palladium	Pd	46	106.4
Phosphorus	P	15	30.9738
Platinum	Pt	78	195.09
Plutonium	Pu	94	...
Polonium	Po	84	...
Potassium	K	19	39.102
Praseodymium	Pr	59	140.907
Promethium	Pm	61	...
Protastinium	Pa	91	...
Radium	Ra	88	...
Radon	Ru	86	...
Rhenium	Re	75	186.2
Rhodium	Rh	45	102.905
Rubidium	Rb	37	85.47
Ruthenium	Ru	44	101.07
Semarium	Sm	62	150.35
Scandium	Sc	21	44.956
Selenium	Se	34	78.96

Table 2.8 (*continued*)

Silicon	Si	14	28.086
Silver	Ag	47	107.87[2]
Sodium	Na	11	22.9898
Strontium	Sr	38	87.62
Sulfur	S	16	32.064
Tantalum	Ta	73	180.948
Technetium	Tc	43	. . .
Tellurium	Te	52	127.60
Terbium	Tb	65	158.924
Thallium	Tl	81	204.37
Thorium	Th	90	232.038
Thulium	Tm	69	168.934
Tin	Sn	50	118.69
Titanium	Ti	22	47.90
Tungsten	W	74	183.85
Uranium	U	92	238.03
Vanadium	V	23	50.942
Xenon	Xe	54	131.30
Ytterbium	Yb	70	173.04
Yttrium	Y	39	88.905
Zinc	Zn	30	65.37
Zirconium	Zr	40	91.22

[1] Atomic weights are variable because of natural variations in isotopic composition.

[2] Atomic weights are so designated because of experimental uncertainties.

1932. He named it deuterium. Hydrogen with a mass of 3 (tritium) is man-made, and is radioactive.

Heavy water consists of a two-to-one union of deuterium and oxygen atoms. When first discovered, scientists theorized that heavy water might be Ponce de Leon's long-sought "fountain of youth." Subsequent animal feeding experiments resulted in death to the animals until the same concentration was reached as naturally occurs in drinking water. At this level of heavy water the animals grew normally.

The number of outermost electrons of an element is given by the family group number in the periodic table. These outermost electrons are sometimes termed valence electrons and they do vary depending upon the electronic configuration of each element.

Elements as arranged in the periodic table tend to acquire the electronic status of a noble or inert gas. With the exception of helium, which has 2 electrons in its outer shell, the other noble gases have 8 electrons in the outermost energy level. These so-called noble gases are found in Group 0.

Symbols are used to represent the atoms (e.g., Cu represents an atom of copper). Dots are used to represent an atom's outermost electrons, the ones that are usually involved in bonding.

Bonding

Bonds are divided into 2 groups, one involving the transfer of electron(s) from 1 atom to another to produce an *ionic bond*. The other involves the sharing of electrons between two atoms to produce a *covalent bond*.

The *ionic bond* is the result of electrostatic attraction between a positive ion and a negative ion, e.g., NaCl, sodium chloride.

$$Na \cdot + \overset{\cdot\cdot}{\underset{\cdot\cdot}{Cl}} \cdot \rightarrow Na^{\oplus} + \overset{\cdot\cdot}{\underset{\cdot\cdot}{Cl}}\overset{\cdot\cdot}{:}\ ^{\ominus} \text{ or NaCl}$$

In other words, sodium chloride forms a compound due to the loss of an electron by sodium and a gain of that electron by chlorine. Sodium becomes positively charged and chlorine negatively charged; they are thus electroionically held together to form salt. In water solutions, these ions separate and the solution conducts an electric current.

When two atoms both need to acquire electrons, a sharing of electrons occurs and a *covalent bond* is formed. A simple example is the formation of a molecule of chlorine

$$(Cl_2)^{1/2} \ \overset{\cdot\cdot}{\underset{\cdot\cdot}{Cl}}\overset{\cdot\cdot}{\underset{\cdot}{Cl}}:$$

where each atom fills its need for eight electrons in its outer shell by sharing one electron with the other chlorine atom. This sharing of electrons is evident with most organic compounds (those containing carbon), such as sugar $C_{12}H_{22}O_{11}$. A water solution of sugar does not carry a current; therefore sugar is nonionic or a nonelectrolyte, all its bonds being covalent nature.

Water or H_2O, a compound, is an example of covalent bonding; oxygen with 6 electrons in its outer shell shares an electron with each of two atoms of hydrogen, thus completing its shell of eight electrons. Hydrogen shares one of oxygen's electrons to complete its outer shell of two (similar to helium).

A compound may contain both ionic and covalent bonding. Another example of bonding, namely hydrogen bonding, should be discussed here.

Oxygen has six electrons in its outer shell, and the compound water (H_2O) might be represented thus:

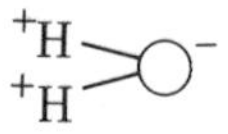

$$^+H \searrow O^-$$
$$^+H \nearrow$$

or

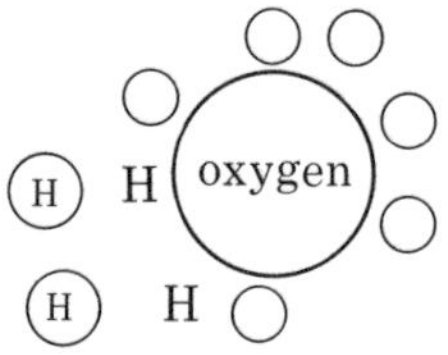

There are two sets of electrons which exert a negative polarity, thus attracting the hydrogen of another molecule of water; this results in a weak bonding termed *hydrogen bonding*, represented by dotted lines:

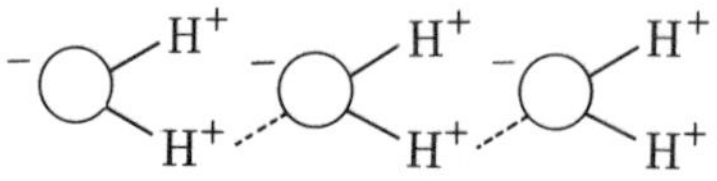

Hydrogen bonding is used as a theory for the hydration of many polysaccharides such as the starches and the hydration of proteins, such as gelatins.

Allotropes

Allotropy is a property of certain elements, such as carbon, sulfur, and phosphorus, which exist in more than one physical form. Carbon, for example, may be amorphous black, with a density of 1.8 to 2.1; graphite black, hexagonal crystals, having a density of 2.25; or diamond, colorless cubical crystals, having a density of 3.51. Both amorphous and graphite carbon sublime, that is, pass directly from solid to gas without melting, at 3652°C, whereas diamond melts at temperatures above 3500°C. All three forms boil at 4200°C. Both amorphous carbon and diamond carbon are insoluble in water, acids, and alkalies.

Graphite carbon is also insoluble in all these solvents, but unlike the other two forms it dissolves in liquid iron. This property is useful in the manufacture of iron and steel from iron ores. These three forms of carbon then are called *allotropes* or *allotropic* forms.

Free Elements

Only a few elements occur uncombined in nature, or "free." Examples are free gold in nuggets, carbon in coal, and oxygen in air. Most substances occur as compounds made up of two or more elements. Water is a compound composed of two parts hydrogen, $_1H^1$, and one part oxygen, O^{16}, having a molecular mass, MM, of 18. Oxygen has an atomic mass, am, of 16. Hydrogen has an atomic mass of 1.008. That of carbon is 12.011; but the reference standard on which the atomic weights of all other elements are based is taken as the mass of the carbon-12 isotope which is exactly 12.000. Methane is a gaseous organic compound having a molecular mass of 16; it contains one atom of carbon surrounded in a tetrahedral configuration by four atoms of hydrogen (CH_4).

Dalton's Law of Multiple Proportions states: "*When any two elements, A and B, combine to form more than one compound, the different weights of B which unite with a fixed weight of A bear a small whole number relationship to each other.*"

Formulas of Compounds

A formula reveals the exact chemical composition of a compound. The smallest particle of any compound is a molecule of that compound. Glucose has the formula $C_6H_{12}O_6$. Each glucose molecule contains six atoms of carbon, C; twelve atoms of hydrogen, H; and six atoms of oxygen, O. Sulfuric acid is H_2SO_4, indicating that two atoms of hydrogen, one of sulfur, and four of oxygen are chemically combined. This combination of symbols and subscript numbers is known as a *formula*.

Formula weights are found by looking up the atomic weights in a table of the elements, and totalling them. Sulfuric acid (H_2SO_4) contains sulfur with an atomic weight of 32, two atoms of hydrogen each having an atomic weight of 1, or a total of 2, and four atoms of oxygen each having an atomic weight of 16, or a total of 64; adding these together gives 98 as the *formula weight.* Sodium chloride is NaCl containing one atom of sodium with an atomic weight of 23, and one atom of chlorine weighing 35.4, or a molecular weight, MW, of 58.4. When the formula weight is expressed in grams it is called the *gram molecular weight, GMW,* of the compound, a convenient value for calculations.

Reactions

Equations for chemical reactions show the reactants, the *conditions* under which the reaction takes place, and the *products* formed. The reaction for photosynthesis provides a classic example.

Word Equation

$$\text{Carbon dioxide} + \text{water} \xrightarrow[\text{chlorophyll}]{\text{sunlight}} \text{glucose} + \text{oxygen}$$

Symbol Equation

$$6CO_2 + 6H_2O \xrightarrow[\text{chlorophyll}]{\text{sunlight}} C_6H_{12}O_6 + 6O_2\uparrow$$

This is a *combination reaction.* Other kinds of reactions are *decomposition reactions*:

Word equation: $\text{Sugar} \xrightarrow{\text{heat}} \text{carbon} + \text{water vapor}$

Trial equation: $C_{12}H_{22}O_{11} \xrightarrow{\text{heat}} C + H_2O$

Balanced equation: $C_{12}H_{22}O_{11} \xrightarrow{\text{heat}} 12C\downarrow + 11H_2O\uparrow$

and *displacement reactions*:

silver nitrate + sodium chloride $\longrightarrow$ silver chloride + sodium nitrate

$$AgNO_3 + NaCl \xrightarrow{\text{water}} \underset{\text{ppt} \cdot}{AgCl\downarrow} + NaNO_3$$

Density and Specific Gravity

The *density* of a substance, such as liquids or solids, is expressed in grams per milliliter (gm/ml). The density of gases is generally expressed as grams per liter. These values are

given in the Handbook of Chemistry and Physics as $D = m/v$.
The densities of elements can be readily found on complete
periodic charts. The density of some of the common gases are
of interest in air pollution.

Gas	Density (gm/ml)
ammonia	0.771
carbon dioxide	1.98
carbon monoxide	1.25
helium	0.178
hydrogen	0.09
methane	0.415^{-164}
nitric oxide	1.34
nitrous oxide	1.98
oxygen	1.43
sulfur dioxide	2.93

Specific gravity is a number which denotes the ratio of the
mass or weight of a substance in air to the mass or weight of
an equal volume of water.

$$\text{Sp gr} = \frac{\text{Weight of } V \text{ (ml) of substance}}{\text{Weight of equal } V \text{ (ml) of water}}$$

Since the volume of a given weight of a substance varies with
the temperature, the temperature at which measurements are
made must be noted, i.e., 20/4 would designate measurements
made at 20°C compared to the density of water at 4°C.

Specific gravity measurements are used in the food industry
for many purposes, such as determining the quality of potatoes
to be used for chips, French fries, baked, or boiled whole. One
pound of salt dissolved in 1 gal. of water yields a solution whose
specific gravity is 1.080. Potatoes that float in this solution
have a specific gravity less than 1.080 and are used for boiling
whole or for potato salads. Potatoes that sink in this solution
have a specific gravity greater than 1.080 and have a high solids
content. These make excellent mealy baked potatoes, French
fries, potato chips, and mashed potatoes.

Peas and onions are separated by specific gravity methods.
In the baking industry, batters are made to have a definite specific gravity to produce a desired volume. The change in the
specific gravity of milk is an indication of its dilution.

TABLE 2.9

SPECIFIC GRAVITIES AND COMPOSITION OF COMMON WINES

	Port	Sherry	Claret	Burgundy	Hock	Champagne
Specific gravity	0.995–1.050	0.995–1.015	0.990–1.015	0.990–1.020	0.990–1.008	1.040–1.055
Alcohol (g/100 ml)	13.5–20.0	13.5–20.5	7.5–12.5	7.5–12.5	7.5–12.5	10.0–14.0
% Total solids	3.3–8.4	2.0–5.0	2.0–3.5	2.0–3.5	1.5–2.5	9.5–18.0
% Free Volatile Acids (as NaC)	0.05–0.10	0.15–0.23	0.09–0.15	0.2–0.35	0.05–0.15	0.03–0.20
% Fixed acids (as H_2 Tar)	0.35–0.55	0.25–0.50	0.30–0.50	0.3–0.60	0.25–0.45	0.30–0.45
% Ash	0.25–0.35	0.35–0.55	0.2–0.3	0.2–0.40	0.10–0.25	0.25–0.45
% sugar	2.5–6.5	2.0–5.0	0.0–0.7	0.03–0.55	0.0–0.35	8.5–16.0
% phosphoric acid (P_2O_5)	0.03–0.05	0.03–0.05	0.03–0.04	0.02–0.03	0.02–0.03	0.03–0.05
% glycerin	0.3–1.3	0.4–1.0	0.3–1.0	0.3–1.0	0.25–1.3	0.3–1.0

Source: The Chemical Analysis of Food, David Pearson, 6th Ed., 1971. Academic Press, New York.

Specific gravity plays a large role in the liquor industry as shown in Table 2.9. In a pousse or cafe drink the specific gravities of the various liqueurs as shown give the main layered characteristic of the drink (Matter—Life Science Library 1963).

Liqueur	*Specific gravity*
Cognac	0.95398
Blue Curacao	1.0963
White Creme de Cacao	1.1229
Parfait Amout	1.1269
Green Creme de Menthe	1.1320
Grenadine	1.13427

A tomato juice -pineapple juice layered drink can be made by slowly pouring tomato juice down the side of a glass containing pineapple juice. The differences in specific gravity will keep the layers separated, especially if kept cool, and the mixture is very acceptable to the palate of the customer.

The specific gravities of solutions of sugars are used in the canning, syrup and confectionery industries.

CHAPTER 3

L. L. W. Smith | Solutions
L. J. Minor

TRUE SOLUTIONS

Most matter is basically electrical, and the chemical properties of materials are such that by the application of a current,
the chemical reactions that are familiar in a liquid medium
may also take place in a solid.

Water with its very high dielectric constant is able to dissociate molecules and/or ions to dissolve many materials. Ethyl
ether, petroleum solvents, and carbon tetrachloride dissolve
fats, while acetone, alcohol, and ethyl acetate are used as solvents for fingernail polish, glue, and lacquers. The fact that
all sodium, potassium, and ammonium salts are soluble in
water or that all nitrates and acetates are soluble helps one to
understand many of the reactions that take place in the food
industry. Solubilities of other inorganic materials are briefly
listed below.

Solubility in Water of Common Compounds at 20°C

1. *Nitrates and acetates*: *all soluble.*
2. *Sulfates*: soluble except those of Ba, Sr, Ca, and Pb.
3. *Chlorides*: soluble except those of Ag, Pb, and mercurous
Hg.
4. *Metallic oxides*: insoluble except Li, Na, K, Ba, Sr, and
Ca. These react with water to form hydroxides.
5. *Hydroxides*: insoluble except those of Li, Na, Ba, Ca, Sr,
K, and NH_4^+.
6. *Carbonates and phosphates*: insoluble except Na, K, and
NH_4^+.
7. *Sulfides*: insoluble except Li, Na, K, Ba, Sr, Ca, and Al.
These hydrolyze strongly.
8. *Compounds with the ammonium radical* (NH_4^+) as a cation
are soluble.

48

9. *Acid salts* are more soluble than normal salts. $Ca(HCO_3)_2$
is more soluble than $CaCO_3$.

10. All Na^+, K^+, and NH_4^+ salts are *soluble*.

Ions are electrically charged atoms or groups of atoms (the
$SO_4^=$ radical), and electrolytes are compounds that dissociate
into ions in a suitable solvent and conduct an electric current.
Solid as well as liquid electrolytes exist and the diffusion of
ions as conductors of current may take place as readily in
either medium. *Solutions are defined as uniformly dispersed
mixtures of extremely small particles of two or more substances.*

Almost any solid, liquid, or gas may act as a solvent for other
gases, liquids, and solids. Air is a gaseous solution made up
of a uniform mixture of gases. Liquid solutions result when
(1) gases such as ammonia, carbon dioxide, or oxygen, (2)
liquids such as glycerine, ethylene glycol, or acetic acid, or
(3) solids such as sodium chloride, sugar, or monosodium
glutamate are dissolved in water or, in some cases, an organic
solvent.

Solutions consist of two components: the *solute*, the dissolved
substance, and the *solvent*, the dissolving substance. Some
foods represent forms of solution; for example, milk, wine,
beer, fruit juices, other beverages, gelatin desserts, puddings,
and gravies and sauces. Before digestion, foods that are not
in solution must be broken down by enzymes present in the
digestive juices. Perspiration and urine waste products from
our bodies are solutions.

Factors which influence the solubility.of a substance are dependent upon the type of solute in relation to the kind of solvent.

Solubility is faster with finely pulverized solutes due to the
greater exposed area acted on by the solvent. Fine crystal
salt, for example, dissolves readily, whereas pretzel salt takes
longer. The rate of solution is increased by *agitation*. Stirring
sugar in coffee hastens the dissolving process.

The solubility of a solid in a liquid usually increases with a
rise in *temperature*, a physical change analogous to melting.
Energy is required to release the molecules, atoms, or ions
that are bound in the crystal. The terms *endothermic* (energy-
absorbing) and *exothermic* (energy-releasing) describe changes
which occur when some solids are dissolved in liquids.

The *solubility* of a solute *is the weight in grams required to
saturate 100 grams of solvent* at a given temperature.

Concentration of Solutions

Concentration of sugar solutions may be defined in accordance with the ratio of solute to solvent. A small amount of sugar dissolved in water is a dilute solution; a larger amount of sugar is required to prepare a *concentrated* solution. When the dissolved solute is in equilibrium with excess undissolved solute the solution is *saturated*. *Supersaturated solutions* result when a saturated solution is prepared at an elevated temperature, excess solute removed, and the solution allowed to cool undisturbed. Supersaturated solutions are metastable, that is, chemically unstable at room temperature. The excess solute will come out of solution (precipitate) as a result of stirring or adding a small crystal of solute to produce a saturated solution at that particular temperature.

Percent Solutions.—Concentration of a solution expressed in percent (parts per hundred) indicates the weight of solute compared to the weight of the solution. For example, 70% corn syrup solution contains 70 gm corn syrup and 30 gm water for every 100 gm solution. Concentration of solution may be expressed by volume; this is used in the liquor industry, e.g., 100 proof refers to 50% alcohol and 50% water.

Molar Solutions (M).—Molar solutions contain 1 gram molecular weight, GMW (molecular weight of the substance expressed as grams) made up to 1 liter of solution by adding water.

Molal Solutions (m).—A molal solution contains 1 gram molecular weight of solute dissolved in 1 liter of solvent. A 1-molal solution of sodium chloride is prepared by weighing out 58.45 gm salt and adding 1 liter of water to it.

Normal Solutions (N).—Normal solutions are solutions containing 1 gram equivalent weight of hydrogen material per liter of solution.

Normal solutions of acids that contain 1 replaceable hydrogen in the molecule (for example, HCl, HF, HNO_3) are made by dissolving 1 mole (1 gram molecular weight, GMW) of the acid in water and adjusting the volume to 1 liter. This is the same procedure as for a molar solution. However, if the acid formula contains two or more replaceable hydrogens (for example, H_2SO_4, H_3PO_4) the GMW must be divided by the number of replaceable hydrogens in order to obtain a normal solution. By definition a $1N$ solution contains 1 gm of replaceable hydrogen or its equivalent per liter.

Normal solutions of bases contain 1 replaceable hydroxyl, OH⁻,
ion in 1 liter of solution. By definition, a 1N solution of a base
contains 17 gm of OH⁻ per liter of solution.

Normal solutions of salts contain one "hydrogen equivalent"
of the salt. The GMW of the salt is divided by the hydrogen
equivalent for the salt, and this weight of salt is dissolved and
made up to 1 liter of solution. In chromic sulfate, $Cr_2(SO_4)_3$,
2 chromium atoms are equivalent to 6 hydrogen atoms, because
the sulfate radical in H_2SO_4 is equivalent to 2 hydrogen atoms
and there are 3 of these in chromic sulfate. Then the equivalent
weight is GMW/6 or 392 gm/6 = 65.3 gm of $Cr_2(SO_4)_3$ per liter
of solution, or (52 × 2) gm/6 = 104 gm/6 = 17.3 gm of chromium.

A 1N solution contains 1 gm of replaceable hydrogen per liter,
or its equivalent; for example, 17 gm of OH⁻, 23 gm of Na⁺, 20
gm of Ca⁺⁺, 17.3 gm of Cr⁺⁺, or 9 gm of Al⁺⁺⁺.

In titrations the relationship of normalities and volume is:
volume of acid used times normality of acid = volume of base
used times normality of base.

Normal solutions of oxidizing or reducing agents are based
on their equivalent weights. *The gram equivalent weight of an
oxidizing or reducing agent is found by dividing the gram formula weight by the change in oxidation number.*

$2e^- + Sn^{+4} \longrightarrow Sn^{++}$ equivalent wt. of tin solution = ½ GMW
oxidizing agent

$Fe^{++} \longrightarrow Fe^{+++} + e^-$ equivalent wt. of iron solution = GMW
reducing agent

Colligative Properties of Solutions

Colligative properties of solutions are those properties that
depend upon the number of solute particles in solution, and not
their kind. A *mole* is defined as the quantity of a substance
containing the same number of atoms as 12 gm of pure carbon
C^{12}. This is Avogadro's number that has been determined ex-
perimentally to be 6.023×10^{23}. One gram atomic weight of
any element, e.g., 55.85 gm iron, 107.87 silver, or 22.9898 gm
sodium contains 6.023×10^{23} atoms. One gram molecular
weight (1 mole) of a nonelectrolyte contains 6.023×10^{23} particles. Sugar, $C_{12}H_{22}O_{11}$, is a typical nonelectrolyte. One mole
of sugar weighs 342 gm and contains 6.023×10^{23} particles

(molecules). Electrolytes are solutes that ionize, and the number of particles in solution (ions) varies, e.g., 1 mole of sodium chloride (NaCl) contains $2 \times 6.023 \times 10^{23}$; calcium chloride ($CaCl_2$) $3 \times 6.023 \times 10^{23}$; and trisodium phosphate (Na_3PO_4) $4 \times 6.023 \times 10^{23}$ particles (ions).

Thus the effect of solutes upon the properties of the solvent varies. Raoult's Law states that: *The lowering of the vapor pressure of a solvent is directly proportional to the weight of the solute which is dissolved in a definite weight of the solvent.*

A *nonvolatile nonelectrolyte* dissolved in a liquid lowers the vapor pressure, elevates the boiling point, depresses the freezing point, and shows osmotic pressure. These four colligative properties are interrelated.

Vapor Pressure Lowering.—When sugar is added to a hot cup of coffee the vapor pressure lowering is at once apparent by noting the change in aroma. The vapor pressure is lowered because some of the volatile solvent molecules in the surface layer of the coffee are replaced by nonvolatile solute molecules.

Boiling Point Elevation.—Lowering the vapor pressure of the solvent is equivalent to raising the boiling point of the solution. According to Raoult's law, the lowering of the vapor pressure is directly proportional to the weight of solute dissolved in a definite weight of solvent. Experiments show that at standard pressure when 1 GMW of a nonvolatile *nonelectrolyte* is dissolved in 1000 gm of water, the boiling point is raised 0.52°C, whereas 1 GMW of a nonvolatile *electrolyte* in 1000 gm of water raises the boiling point 0.512°C for each ion present in the solution. Expressed as an equation then, the boiling point elevation is:

B.P. elevation = 0.52°C/GMW solute/1000 gm H_2O, for nonelectrolytes

B.P. elevation = 0.52°C/GMW solute/1000 gm H_2O/no. of ions,
for electrolytes.

With ionic substances the experimental value is slightly less than the calculated value due to energy lost in breaking the bonds.

Freezing Point Depression.—The antifreeze ethylene glycol, for the protection of car radiators, is a good example of a freezing-point depressant. Experiments show that when 1 GMW of a nonvolatile *nonelectrolyte* is dissolved in 1000 gm of water the freezing point is lowered from 0 to about −1.86°C at 760 mm pressure, whereas, 1 GMW of a nonvolatile *electrolyte* lowers the freezing point about −1.86°C for each kind of ion present in solution. A number of nonelectrolytes and electrolytes and their effects on lowering the freezing point of water are listed in Table 3.1. Deviations from the expected values will be noted, and these may be due to variations in bond energies, hydrogen bond-forming tendencies, or solubilities of the various substances. Calculated values are used in determining the amount of coolant to add when protecting a car radiator or plumbing system from freezing.

Osmotic Pressure

Osmosis is the passage of pure solvent into a solution, or from a less to a more concentrated solution, through a semipermeable membrane which is permeable to the solvent but not to to the solute. Cellophane film and parchment paper may act as semipermeable membranes. *Osmotic pressure is the excess pressure which when applied to a solution will just prevent osmosis.*

Molal solutions of different nonelectrolytes exert the same osmotic pressure, about 22.4 atmospheres, or 22.4 atm times 14.7 lb in.^{2}/atm equals 329.28 lb/in.^{2}.

When the osmotic pressure of solutions on each side of a semipermeable membrane are in equilibrium, there is an equal concentration of components, and these are called *isotonic solutions.* Consider the immersion of blood cells in a solution of sodium chloride. Since blood contains a salt concentration equivalent to 0.9% NaCl, a 0.9% NaCl solution is isotonic with respect to the blood and osmosis does not occur.

Upon immersion of the blood cells in water the cells swell and rupture, as the movement through the membrane is always from the less concentrated to the more concentrated solution. This is called a *hypotonic* solution, one of lower osmotic pressure.

Conversely, when cells are immersed in a solution of higher concentration, a *hypertonic* solution, they contract due to water removal by osmosis.

Some examples of solutions encountered daily in the food-service industry are fruit juices, soups, and beverages of all kinds. Many of these fall into various categories, from that

TABLE 3.1

HOW 1 GMW OF VARIOUS SOLUTES IN 1000 GM WATER LOWERS THE FREEZING POINT

Solute	Approximate Effect/GMW	Particles in Solution	Calculated Value Freezing Point Lowering, °C	Experimental Value Freezing Point Lowering, °C
Nonelectrolytes				
Methanol, CH_3OH	1×	6.02×10^{23}	1.86	1.85
Ethanol, C_2H_5OH	1×	6.02×10^{23}	1.86	1.83
Prestone, $C_2H_4(OH)_2$	1×	6.02×10^{23}	1.86	1.86
Glycerol, $C_3H_5(OH)_3$	1×	6.02×10^{23}	1.86	1.92
Dextrose, $C_6H_{12}O_6$	1×	6.02×10^{23}	1.86	1.92
Sucrose, $C_{12}H_{22}O_{11}$	1×	6.02×10^{23}	1.86	2.06
Electrolytes				
Sodium chloride, NaCl	2×	12.04×10^{23}	3.72	3.37
Sodium hydroxide, NaOH	2×	12.04×10^{23}	3.72	3.44
Calcium chloride, $CaCl_2$	3×	18.06×10^{23}	5.58	5.85
Hydrochloric acid, HCl	2×	12.04×10^{23}	3.72	3.94
Sulfuric acid, H_2SO_4	3×	18.06×10^{23}	5.58	4.04

TABLE 3.2

WATER SOLUTIONS, DISPERSIONS AND SUSPENSIONS

Mixture	Particle Size, mμ	Nature of Particle	Kind of Mixture	Characteristics	Examples
True solutions	0.1 to 1	Ions, atoms, molecules	Homogeneous	(1) Transparent (2) Particles do not settle (3) Pass through filter paper (4) Not visible	Air Drinking water Sugar solutions
Colloidal dispersions	1 to 1000	Large molecules large ions, small aggregates	Heterogeneous	(1) Translucent (2) Tyndall effect (3) Visible with electron microscope or ultramicroscope (4) Particles stay suspended by Brownian movement or electric charge (5) Pass through filter paper	Milk Maple syrup Jelly egg white
Suspensions	over 1000	Clumps of molecules or ions	Heterogeneous	(1) Turbid or cloudy (2) Visible in optical microscope (3) Particles settle (4) Particles do not pass through filter paper	Flour or starch in cold water Muddy water

of simple solutions through combinations, to very complex colloidal dispersions such as gravies.

Coffee and tea are generally made by the hot extraction of the basic ground coffee beans and the tea leaves. Cold-water extractions can also be made, but require 8 to 12 hr in contact with water. The latter are concentrated solutions which are then diluted to drinking strength with hot or cold water. Of course, these solutions will contain only those soluble constituents that are leached out by the cold water. The volatiles are not apparent, as in hot brewed coffee or tea.

Freeze-dried or instant coffee and tea are now accepted beverages; these solutions, too, vary from the freshly brewed product in both the amounts of extracted solutes and volatiles. Some of the work published by the Coffee Brewing Institute states that the most acceptable beverage contains 1.04 to 1.39% soluble solids with 17.5 to 21.2% extraction with 1.75 to 2.67 gal. water per pound of coffee. Another set of figures from the Midwest Research Institute indicates that for 1.25% soluble solids and 19% extraction, the formula for extraction would be 2.18 gal. water per pound. There is on the market a coffee hydrometer that measures the percentage of soluble solids at 140°F.

Chocolate and cocoa drinks represent both true solution and colloidal dispersions since they are generally made with milk. Milk itself is a complex combination of a true solution, an emulsion, and a suspension. Chocolate and cocoas vary in the percentage of fat present.

Fruit juices may be true solutions such as grape juice, or contain suspended pulp, as in orange, grapefruit, and tomato juice. In these solutions there are also soluble salts, sugars, and acids in true solution that are representative of the product.

COLLOIDAL DISPERSIONS

At one time colloids were thought to be noncrystalline and the term colloid meant glue-like or gelatinous. Experimental evidence shows that any material, even sodium chloride, under controlled conditions may exist as a colloidal dispersion. Tannin is colloidal in water but in acetic acid it is crystalloidal. Many of our foods are composed of colloidal systems.

TABLE 3.3

TYPES OF COLLOIDAL DISPERSIONS

Material	Media Dispersed in		
Dispersed	Gas	Liquid	Solid
Gases	Form true solutions (non-colloidal)	*Foams* Ice cream soda Whipped cream Beaten egg whites	*Solid foams* Plaster Pumice stone Floating soaps Bread
Liquids	*Fogs* Mists Clouds Sprays	*Emulsions* Mayonnaise milk blood	Butter cheese hydrogenated shortening
Solids	*Smokes* Dust Fumes	*Sols* Gelatin (warm) cooked starch in water	Colored glass Porcelain Paper Some alloys gelatin gels fruit jellies

The colloidal state is defined by the size of dispersed parti-cles, and if the particle size is between 1 and 500 millimicrons (mμ or mm) the dispersion is called colloidal. Actually, the range is not definite, and the upper and lower limits are arbi-trary; it lies just below the resolving limit of the optical microscope. Colloidal particles are from 10 angstroms to 1 micron in diameter. A micron or micrometer (μ or μm) is 1 millionth of a meter (10^{-6} m); an angstrom is one hundred millionth of a centimeter (10^{-8} cm) or one ten-thousandth of a micron ($10^{-4}\mu$). Then, the dimensional limits of colloidal parti-cles are 1 millimicron (1 mμ) to 1 micron (1 μ) in diameter. Colloidal particles have a large ratio of surface area to volume and possess the characteristic of adsorption. Their dimensions do not permit them to diffuse through most membranes, but they do pass through filters. Colloids may be either large mole-cules or aggregates of smaller molecules. Proteins (gelatin, egg yolk, and casein) and carbohydrates such as pectin, algin, starch, and cellulose are examples of high molecular weight colloidal substances.

TABLE 3.4

A BRIEF COMPARISON OF COLLOIDAL SYSTEMS
VS. TRUE SOLUTIONS

Property	Solution	Colloidal Dispersion	Suspension
Diam. of particle (Solid, liquid or gas)	$0.5-2.5A^1$	10–1000A	1000A
Effect of gravity	Kinetic motion no effect of gravity	Brownian movement. no effect of gravity	Separates due to pull of gravity
Light	Transparent	Translucent to opaque resulting in Tyndall effect	Translucent to opaque (Tyndall effect may be apparent)
Filterability	Non	Non	Filterable
Homogeneity	Homogeneous	Homogeneous ↓ Borderline ↓ Heterogeneous	Heterogeneous
No. of phases	One	At least 2	At least 2
Examples	Sugar and water Alcohol and water Salt and water	Raw egg white Raw egg yolk Gelatin gel Mayonnaise	Clay and water, Starch and water, etc.

[1] A = angstrom = 10^{-8} cm. Other terms that are used in discussing colloidal phenomena are:

Micelle or micellar colloids which represent aggregates of many small molecular or groups of atoms which are held together by secondary valences such as cohesive or van der Waals forces. A micelle is usually less stable than a macromolecule. An example of a macromolecule would be rubber $(C_5H_8)_{2000}$ or glycogen $[C_6H_7O_2-(OH)_3]_{5000}$. Micellar colloids are usually much more complex than

Table 3.4 (*continued*)
molecular colloids. Micellar colloids such as an emulsion always
contain a stabilizing layer around each droplet.

Colloids

Molecular	Micellar
Macromolecules in solution. Do not exist in units smaller than macromolecules. Examples are: starch, albumin, polystyrene, silicones.	The dispersed substance can exist in units smaller than colloidal particles such as sulfur, gold, iron hydroxide, soaps, emulsions.

Tyndall Effect

In a movie theater dust particles appear as spots of reflected
light when one looks through the projection beam from either
side. Tyndall noted this effect in colloidal systems, but not in
true solutions, and thus it is called the *Tyndall Effect*. An ultramicroscope utilizes the Tyndall Effect by passing an intense
beam of light at right angles through a droplet of a colloidal
dispersion mounted on a dark background; pinpoints of light
reflected by the particles can be seen through the eyepiece,
though the particles themselves cannot be resolved.

Brownian Movement

Colloidal particles show Brownian movement. Examination
of a colloidal dispersion with an ultramicroscope reveals colloidal particles as bright specks moving in random zigzag paths.
A particle's pathway changes as a result of bombardment by
the molecules of the solvent. These collisions cause the particles to move in many directions simultaneously and keeps them
in suspension; this phenomenon is called *Brownian Movement*.
The particles do not coagulate, since they all bear like charges
and repel one another.

Colloidal systems are intermediate between true solutions and
suspensions, and may exist in all combinations of the three
states of matter excepting gas in gas. Gases mix in air to give
true solutions. Thus, the systems possible include solid-in-
solid, solid-in-liquid, solid-in-gas, liquid-in-solid, liquid-in-
liquid, liquid-in-gas, gas-in-solid, and gas-in-liquid. These

are summarized in tables 3.2, 3.3 and 3.4. Foams, emulsions, gels, and sols are among the important systems in foods.

Methods of Preparation

Colloids are intermediate in size between dissolved molecules in solution and coarse matter in suspensions. Coarse matter may be broken down to colloidal size, or molecular size particles can be agglomerated or built up.

The term *lyophobic* refers to material which exists in the colloidal state without having any significant affinity for the medium. *Lyophilic* refers to material which readily goes into colloidal suspension or has an affinity for the medium; if water, the term *hydrophilic* is used. When the medium is fat the term used is *lipophilic*.

A summary of classifications, although complicated and does not cover all cases, might be:

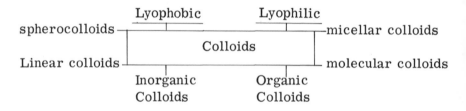

Colloids containing particles of very different sizes are called *polydispersed sols*. The opposite of polydispersed would be *monodispersed*, implying that all particles are of the same size. There are few of this type known.

The term *emulsoid* generally refers to lyophilic colloidal systems; *suspensoid* frequently refers to lyophobic sols. These are sometimes misleading and indicate some of the confusion that exists in this field.

Mechanical dispersion occurs in nature as water cuts through soil and rocks. Mustard seed and spices may be ground to a colloidal dispersion in a *colloid mill*. Milk, salad dressing, and other foods may be stabilized by pumping them through a tiny orifice under high pressure in a machine called an *homogenizer*. Fat globules in milk may be dispersed by agitation, but they will soon coalesce. Homogenization breaks the globules into colloidal particles that remain emulsified.

Peptization

Digestion of food occurs by mechanical and chemical action. After breaking the food down with the teeth, gastric juices and enzymes (organic catalysts) reduce or peptize the food particles to colloidal size. Chemicals that cause peptization are called peptizing agents.

SOLS, GELS, AND EMULSIONS

Sols are liquid colloidal suspensoids or dispersions that appear to be homogeneous but are not.

Gels are semi-rigid colloidal dispersions of a solid in a liquid or gas, such as jelly, glue, and gelatin gels. Viscosity may vary widely in gels. Some are thixotropic, that is, they are semi-solid gels until stirring or heating causes a loss of viscosity. A starch suspension may be a sol at high temperatures and a gel at room temperature.

Emulsions are intimate mixtures of immiscible liquids in which one liquid is dispersed as droplets throughout the other. French dressing is an *emulsion* of vinegar (a water solution of acetic acid) and oil. When mixed intimately by high-speed agitation the oil droplets remain in suspension, but when agitation stops, coalescence of the droplets takes place rapidly. To prevent this separation, as in mayonnaise an emulsifying agent must be added. Egg yolk contains lecithin that coats the oil droplets and stabilizes the emulsion. Lecithin serves as a *protective colloid* and keeps the dispersed particles apart as it possesses both hydrophobic and hydrophilic properties.

Agitation of foods incorporates air, and a *foam* forms as a result of low surface tension. In beer and soft drinks, foam is desirable, and it is essential in whipped cream and egg whites. Foam stability is increased by the addition of acids or their salts. Egg whites have a larger volume when whipped at room temperature than at refrigerator temperature.

Milk froth forms when milk is agitated at 30° to 60°C. Whipped cream forms best when the cream is chilled to 10°C (50°F) or lower. Aging the cream up to 48 hr improves its whipping properties. Pasteurization and homogenization of the cream reduces foam volume and shortens stability. Care must be taken to avoid over-whipping cream as butter may then be formed.

OTHER PROPERTIES OF COLLOIDS

Some of the other important properties of colloids include adsorption, dialysis, electrophoresis, ultracentrifugation, coagulation, imbibition, syneresis, hysteresis, and hydration.

Adsorption

Gas masks contain finely divided activated charcoal that adsorbs many harmful gases. Adhesion of one substance to the surface of another is called adsorption. The adsorption capacity of a substance is a function of the exposed surface area, and the properties of the materials involved. An increase in pressure will increase the rate of adsorption of a gas on activated charcoal, whereas an increase in temperature reduces it.

Dialysis

Electrolytes may shorten the life of colloidal suspensions. Accordingly, their removal from the solution is desirable. Colloidal particles are impeded by membranes such as parchment, collodion, animal bladders, or cellophane, whereas the ions or molecules of a solute pass through their pores. Experiment: When a mixture of starch gel, salt, and water is placed in a dialyzing bag and immersed in a beaker of distilled water, the sodium and chloride ions move through the bag and into the distilled water. Addition of silver nitrate solution to the distilled water at the start gives no reaction, but then as the sodium and chloride ions pass through, a white opalescent precipitate of silver chloride forms. Upon addition of potassium iodide solution to the gel in the bag a blue color forms, indicating the presence of starch.

Electrophoresis

Complex proteins such as casein from milk and myoglobin from meat consist of various fractions, each with its own electrical migration tendencies. A technique called starch gel electrophoresis may be used to separate them. When a colloidal dispersion is placed between two electrodes, the migration is in one direction but the rate varies, making it possible to separate and purify the fractions. This migration of colloidal particles under the influence of an electrical potential is called *electrophoresis.* A colloidal solution does not conduct a current as readily as an electrolyte, since the number of colloid particles in solution is extremely small compared to the number of ions in a solution of electrolyte.

Ultracentrifugation

An ordinary centrifuge will not cause colloidal particles to settle, as electrostatic charges and other forces keep them in suspension. An ultracentrifuge spinning at a speed that produces a force equivalent to 400,000 times the force of gravity can settle the colloidal particles. This process is called *ultracentrifugation.*

Coagulation

When the electrical charges on colloidal particles are removed or neutralized the colloid coagulates and precipitates. This may occur as a result of adding an acid, base, or salt. Clay particles in the Mississippi river coagulate and form a delta at the river's mouth due to neutralization of their negative charges by the positive sodium ions in the salt water of the Gulf.

Addition of another colloid having an opposite charge may also cause precipitation to occur.

Cottrell precipitators are used for industrial smoke abatement. Colloidal particles in smoke and flue dust are electrically charged. When passed between plates carrying opposite charges the colloidal particles migrate to the plate having the charge opposite to their own. The dust coagulates and falls from the plates, and is collected. In some systems two endless belts are used to carry the charges. These belts pass over scrapers and through an oil bath which process cleans them.

Imbibition or Absorption

Colloids may imbibe or absorb liquid. Egg white has a strong affinity for water, and starch will swell even against a pressure of 250 atmospheres when heated in the presence of water. Imbibition by proteins is affected by pH. At the isoelectric point, the pH at which the charge on the molecule is zero, imbibition is at a minimum. There is a marked increase in water-holding capacity (imbibition) on either the acid or alkaline side with a maximum at pH 2.5 and pH 10.5. (Carbohydrate gels show a maximum imbibition tendency at or near their isoelectric points.)

Syneresis

Syneresis is the separation of a liquid phase from some solid or semi-solid food stuffs. This is not necessarily water, but a dilute solution. Examples are the liquid that collects around gelatin gels, puddings, or on gravy left in a refrigerator; "leaky" butter; and the juice that exudes from cooked meat.

Hysteresis

This is an aging phenomenon in which older tissues lose their imbibing capacity. Skins form on puddings and gravies as the dehydrated micelles (electrically charged particles) aggregate. Aging of a gel is characterized by a weakening of the forces that hold the liquid. Collagen in old animals is less dispersible than that in young animals.

Hydration

Proteins and carbohydrates are hydrophilic colloids that have a strong affinity for water. This is a function of both adsorption and absorption. Bound water is the water of hydration in bio-colloids. Control of hydration is important in improving the storage quality of foods.

COLLOIDS IN CONFECTIONS

Colloids are used in confections to prevent crystallization and serve as protective emulsifiers of any fat present.

Pectin is obtained from apple pomace and citrus peel. High methoxyl pectin of 150 grade will produce jelly of described strength from 150 lb of sugar under standardized conditions. The setting time for gelled candies is regulated by adjusting the pH with citric acid and the alkaline buffer salt, sodium citrate. Browning during cooking is avoided by holding the pH below 5.2, and it is still high enough, above pH 4, to retard the rate of production of invert sugar.

Gelatin is rated on the basis of bloom (gel strength) which varies from 50 to 300 Bloom. These numbers express firmness of the gel product. A relatively small percentage of gelatin softens the texture in a high-sugar formula. This gives a soft, smooth-textured marshmallow, cream, or nougat.

Protein whipping agents are used to provide lightness of texture and low density in confections. Egg albumin, soy protein, and milk protein are the principal agents used, and for most applications egg albumin is superior. Natural gums, such as arabic and tragacanth, have been replaced by starch, pectin, gelatin, and dextrin in gumdrop and lozenge manufacture. *Lecithin* derived from the soya bean is used in chocolate to reduce the amount of cocoa butter required and to lower the viscosity. Enrobing is improved with lecithinated chocolate. Lecithin keeps the butter fat and water emulsified in butter brittles. It is also beneficial in toffees and caramels.

These are examples of *protective colloids*, a phenomenon that occurs in many food products. In a cream tomato soup, the colloidally dispersed casein of the milk is protected by the presence of the cooked starch of the cream sauce from the action of the acid in the tomato juice. Casein is a negatively charged colloid which is precipitated by addition of hydrogen ion to produce a curdled effect. This is illustrated when acid or vinegar is added to milk to form a curd, as in the manufacture of cottage cheese.

CHAPTER 4

L. L. W. Smith
L. J. Minor

Gas Components

Without oxygen man cannot survive longer than a few minutes. He can live without water for a few days, and without food for a few weeks. The atmosphere provides man with oxygen and plants with carbon dioxide. It is the source of rain, the shield that absorbs excessive ultraviolet radiation from the sun, and the barrier that disperses most of the high-energy cosmic rays from outer space. It is a protective shield burning out the meteors that would otherwise scar the earth's surface with craters, and constantly destroy life. It also scatters the sun's electromagnetic radiation, thus providing us with light.

Furthermore, this atmospheric ocean equilibrates the temperature and climate of the earth. Otherwise the equator temperature would be as high as 180°F during the day and as low as –220°F at night. Radio communication, sound propagation, and flight are all possible because of the atmosphere.

The atmosphere, for better or worse, is the air we breathe and feel. Together with sound, light, and visual sensations it is a major environmental factor. When man leaves this planet to explore outer space, the moon, or other planets, he must take oxygen with him. In normal air travel, cabins must be pressurized, and oxygen masks are provided as stand-by emergency equipment. It is important for a food-service manager to understand the science of the air, so that he may provide maximum comfort and safety for both guests and employees. External air pollution may cause an area to be excluded when other factors indicate that the location would be ideal for an inn. Internal air pollution can also cause an otherwise excellent facility, discerning customers to avoid using.

PROPERTIES OF THE ATMOSPHERE

The earth is surrounded by a layer of gases, vapors, atoms, ions, and rays 6,000 miles thick that comprises less than 1/1,000,000th part of the planet by mass. This atmosphere of

TABLE 4.1

AVERAGE COMPOSITION OF THE AIR AT THE EARTH'S SURFACE

Gas	Percent By Volume	Density Gm per Liter
Nitrogen	78.03	1.25
Oxygen	20.99	1.43
Carbon dioxide	0.03	1.98
Water vapor	Varies	
Argon	0.93	1.78
Neon	0.0018	0.90
Helium	0.0005	0.18
Krypton	0.0001	3.71
Xenon	0.000009	5.85

The composition of 1 million cubic feet of dry air in cubic feet is as follows:

Nitrogen	780,840	krypton	1.14
Oxygen	209,460	xenon	0.086
Argon	9,340	hydrocarbons	1
Carbon dioxide	300	hydrogen	0.5
Neon	18.18	acetylene	0.02
Helium	5.24		

Carbon dioxide, hydrocarbon, hydrogen, and acetylene content vary with location

the earth is highly oxidized, and fortunately contains almost no explosive hydrogen.

We live in the troposphere or lowest region of the atmosphere, which extends to an average height of 11 km. The *troposphere* is where all important weather processes occur. This then is the layer of the atmosphere with which man is primarily concerned. By controlling the reactions that occur in this region it may be possible some day to manufacture seasons to our liking and be able to prevent flood and wind damage. An average composition of the air at the earth's surface is given in Table 4.1.

The *stratosphere* is a region extending from 7 to 19 miles above the earth. Vertical mixing of nuclear bomb debris is slow in this layer of the atmosphere, indicating a uniform tem-

perature. Since the water-vapor content is low, only a few percent in the stratosphere, the transfer of latent heat of vaporization and condensation is negligible. Ozone is generated in
the upper portion of the stratosphere; apart from ozone and
water vapor, gaseous proportions are the same in the troposphere and stratosphere.

The oxygen we breathe is molecular oxygen consisting of two
atoms of oxygen, having the formula O_2. When three atoms of
oxygen combine, O_3, it is called ozone and it is highly reactive
and poisonous gas. It is formed, at least partially by electrical
discharges (lightning) or by ultraviolet radiation. Ozone absorbs ultraviolet light having wavelengths of less than 4000 Å,
thus making biological processes on earth possible. As super-
sonic jets will be flying through this poisonous layer of ozone
gas, planes must be designed to keep ozone out of the cabin,
and a new ozone-proof plastic will have to be developed for this
purpose.

The *mesosphere* extends from 19 to 50 miles above the earth.
Ozone is generated in this layer and there is some ionization of
gases. At times clouds are seen at a 50-mile height from the
light of the rising or setting sun. The composition is fairly
constant: 78% nitrogen and 21% oxygen at this level.

The *ionosphere* reaches from 50 to 400 miles above earth.
At 60 miles up, ions and atoms form, lighter nitrogen diffuses
away, causing the ratio of oxygen to nitrogen to change. At
80 miles there are more oxygen than nitrogen atoms. Above
90 miles most oxygen is atomic or ionic and nitrogen changes
from molecular to atomic. Air-glow emissions, including the
aurora, occur in the ionosphere.

The *exosphere* goes beyond 400 miles; here helium and hydrogen predominate. Randomly moving molecules in this region suffer no collisions unless they return to the lower atmosphere.

ATMOSPHERIC EVAPORATION

Evaporation occurs as molecules of terrestrial water change
from the liquid to the vapor state. When molecules of water in
snow or glaciers move directly from the solid to the vapor
phase, the process is called *sublimation*. Clouds, fog, dew,
rain, snow, hail, sleet, and frost originate from the water
vapor in the atmosphere. Water evaporates from the oceans,

TABLE 4.2
BOILING TEMPERATURES OF WATER AT VARIOUS ALTITUDES[1]

Altitude, ft	Boiling Point of Water °F	°C
Sea level	212.0	100.0
2,000	208.4	98.4
5,000	203.0	95.0
7,500	198.4	92.4
10,000	194.0	90.0
15,000	185.0	85.0
30,000	158.0	70.0

[1] About 2°F or 1°C should be added to the thermometer reading for each additional 1,000 feet in altitude when frying foods in deep fat.

lakes, rivers, ponds, ice and snow fields, the soil, and from leaves of plants or trees.

ATMOSPHERIC PRESSURE

The atmosphere at standard temperature (0°C) and pressure (760 mm mercury, Hg) weighs 1.29 gm/l. *A column of air 1 inch square exerts a pressure of 14.7 lb/in^2*. To measure atmospheric pressure an instrument called a *barometer* is used. In simplest form, this consists of a sealed glass tube filled with mercury. The open end is inverted and submerged in a mercury pool. Any variation in pressure causes a change in the tube's mercury level. *At sea level the height of the mercury column reaches 760 mm*, about 80 in. Weather reports often express barometric pressure as inches of mercury. *Standard conditions of temperature and pressure (STP) for physical constants are 0°C and 760 mm Hg pressure.*

Changes Due to Altitude

Atmospheric pressures change appreciably as altitudes vary. This affects the boiling temperatures of water, the pressures of steam, and the formulation of cake recipes as shown in Tables 4.2, 4.3, and 4.4.

Temperature in the troposphere decreases with height at the rate of about 6.5°C per kilometer. There is a corresponding change in the density of the atmosphere from 1220 to 425

TABLE 4.3

STEAM PRESSURES AT VARIOUS ALTITUDES[1]

| Temperature | | Steam Pressure (lb) at | | | |
°F	°C	Sea Level	4,000 ft	6,000 ft	7,500 ft
228	109	5	7	8	9
240	115	10	12	13	14
150	121	15	17	18	19
159	126	20	22	23	24

[1] When cooking foods at higher altitudes $\frac{1}{2}$ lb should be added to the gauge pressure for each additional 1,000 ft in altitude.

TABLE 4.4

CAKE RECIPE ADJUSTMENTS FOR HIGH ALTITUDES[1]

Adjustment	3,000 ft	5,000 ft	7,000 ft
Baking powder reduction per tsp in recipe use	1/8 tsp less	1/8 to 1/4 tsp less	1/4 tsp less
Sugar reduction per cup in recipe use	0 to 1 tbsp less	0 to 2 tbsp less	1 to 3 tbsp less
Liquid increase per cup in recipe use	1 to 2 tbsp more	2 to 4 tbsp more	3 to 4 tbsp more

[1] At altitudes above 5,000 feet starch gelatinization in a double boiler is impractical. Direct heat and adequate stirring must be used.

gm per cubic meter. Velocity of sound in the media changes from 345 meters per second at sea level to 310 meters per second at 10 kilometers.

PROPERTIES OF AIR

Air is heavy, even though the weight of 1 liter is only 1.29 gm at STP. The air in a kitchen having dimensions of 50 × 40 × 15 ft weighs about 2600 lb. Ventilation at a rate of one air change per hour means that blowers must put in and take out more than 10 tons of air every 8 hr.

Each day an average man consumes 4.5 lb water, 2.8 lb food, and 30 lb air. Think of how this quantity of air compares with the weight of food produced, and an idea of the logistical implications in air movement can be gained. As the lungs take in the atmosphere, the effects vary with the quality of what is breathed in and out. A clean atmosphere is beneficial to those who are immersed in it, but an atmosphere fouled with tobacco smoke can have bad effects on health, especially after frequent and prolonged inhalation.

Air is a mixture of gases. Ordinary air contains about four-fifths nitrogen and one-fifth oxygen. Thorough mixing keeps the chemical composition of the troposphere uniform in normal dry, uncontaminated air. Nitrogen and oxygen constitute 99.03%; these two gases plus argon and carbon dioxide comprise 99.997% by volume of clean, dry air. Other atmospheric gases in descending order of concentration are: neon, helium, krypton, xenon, hydrogen, methane, nitrous oxide, ozone, sulfur dioxide, nitrogen dioxide, ammonia, carbon monoxide, and iodine. Taken together, these minor constituents represent only 0.003% of the total percentage by volume of dry, clean air. Water vapor content varies over a wide range from 20 gm or more per kilogram of tropical air to 0.5 gm per kilogram of air in the dry polar regions. When cooled and compressed air changes to a liquid. When liquid air boils, helium distils off first at –269°C, then neon at –249°C, nitrogen at –196°C, argon at –186°C, oxygen at –183°C, krypton at –153°C, and xenon at –107°C. Carbon dioxide sublimes.

Water vapor and carbon dioxide are important though minor constituents of the atmosphere. One scientist explains, "The water vapor and carbon dioxide in the air not only absorb infrared radiation from the earth but reradiate it back to the earth. Thus, they tend to hold in the heat of the earth's lower atmosphere—rather like the glass of a greenhouse."

Alveolar Air

As rapidly as blood traverses the alveoli or air cells of the lungs, the hemoglobin is nearly saturated with oxygen. At the oxygen tension in the tissues nearly half the oxygen is released, and this is replaced by an equal amount of carbon dioxide to be expired (see Table 4.5). Glucose is oxidized to CO_2 and H_2O by all tissues except the red blood cells and vigorously exercising muscles. The latter convert glucose to lactic acid, releasing part of the energy it contains. Proteins are also oxidized and provide energy.

TABLE 4.5

GAS COMPOSITION OF INSPIRED, EXPIRED, AND ALVEOLAR AIR

	Nitrogen	Oxygen	Carbon Dioxide	Water Vapor
Inspired air	78.5	20.8	0.04	0.66
Expired air	74.8	15.3	3.80	6.10
Alveolar air	75.1	13.5	5.30	6.10

Emphysema is a crippling disease that develops in the lungs of smokers. Fibrosis of the lung walls is caused by inhalation of sulfur dioxide, nitrogen oxides, and tars. Expansion and contraction of the lungs is lost, and the lung capacity is reduced.

There is some fear that the carbon dioxide content of the troposphere, which has increased from about 0.0290% in 1890 to 0.0314% in 1966, a gain of about 8%, has caused an increase in the temperature of the troposphere. The earth's climate does seem to be rising slowly, and in both polar regions, glaciers are receding. Not all the carbon dioxide that moves into the atmosphere remains there. Plant life and the oceans absorb or utilize about one-half of the total input.

CARBON DIOXIDE

Carbon Dioxide and the Carbon Cycle

Compared to nitrogen and oxygen, the amount of carbon dioxide in the atmosphere is small, 0.03%. However, this gas controls both temperature and infrared radiation with the help of water vapor. Furthermore, this minute concentration of carbon dioxide in the air maintains plant life by way of photosynthesis. Removal of carbon from the atmosphere takes place in two ways: first, by photosynthesis, which occurs in the presence of sunlight and water vapor together with the essential green pigment of plants, chlorophyll, as carbon dioxide is taken in and oxygen is liberated; second, by the weathering of rocks as the carbonates find their way into soil and ground water. Decay processes, animal respiration, and combustion of fuels, can more **than** compensate for this removal of carbon from the atmosphere.

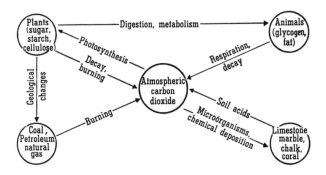

FIG. 4.1. THE CARBON-DIOXIDE CYCLE

Decomposition of organic matter from plants and animals *by bacterial action* liberates carbon and hydrogen, the end products are mainly carbon dioxide, methane, and water. Rich soil has a high carbon-nitrogen ratio; a low ratio suggests poor soil. Many soil microorganisms are capable of decomposing simple carbohydrates and proteins, but relatively few can act on cellulose and nucleoproteins. Cellulose may be digested by bacteria of the genera Cellulomonas, Cellvibrio, Clostridium, Pseudomonas, Actinomyces, and some molds. Both *aerobic* bacteria (grow best in free oxygen) and *anaerobic* bacteria (can grow without either air or free oxygen) are involved in the carbon cycle.

Carbon atoms can be traced by means of radioactive tag compounds through a cycle from carbon dioxide in air, to plant tissue, to animal tissue, and back to air again. This cycle is known as the carbon dioxide or carbon cycle as shown in Fig. 4.1.

Carbon dioxide is a colorless, odorless, and tasteless gas. It weighs 1.96 gm per liter and is moderately soluble in water (0.145 gm per 100 gm water at 25°C). It is easily liquefied and solidified. When the liquid is allowed to escape from a pressure tank of carbon dioxide, the heat of evaporation is sufficient to cool part of the gas until it solidifies into carbon dioxide snow, known as "Dry Ice."

Carbon dioxide reacts slowly with water to form carbonic acid. Commercial uses for CO_2 are as a preservative in foods to prevent oxidation (canned coffee), and as a propellant in aerosols, pellet guns, etc.

Air containing 15% carbon dioxide will not support combustion; hence, common portable fire extinguishers contain separate solutions of acid and bicarbonate solutions which when combined by shaking form a fire-quenching mixture. Other uses of carbon dioxide include the manufacture of sodium bicarbonate by the Solvay process. In the production of soda water and soft drinks, carbon dioxide is a source of bubbles in both alcoholic and non-alcoholic beverages. As a refrigerant, it melts at −57°C, or when mixed with ether or acetone will produce a temperature of −80°C.

Carbon dioxide is a leavening agent in the baking industry. The sources of carbon dioxide are (1) the reaction of sodium bicarbonate ($NaHCO_3$) and an acid ingredient, and (2) the action of heat on ammonium carbonate, both primary and secondary.

The history of the growth and use of baking powders is a fascinating one. The first formula for baking powder was developed in the United States in 1850 as a cream of tartar baking powder. In 1853, V. C. Price of Troy, N. Y., compounded a baking powder using cream of tartar, baking soda, and starch or flour as a stabilizing ingredient. In 1856, E. N. Horsford at Harvard University proposed a compound using monocalcium phosphate as the acid ingredient. Later, in 1892, alum or sodium aluminum sulfate was introduced, labeled as S.A.S. baking powder, and termed a "double-acting" baking powder.

A baking powder consists of baking soda ($NaHCO_3$) and an acid ingredient together with a filler of starch or other inert ingredients, which may be calcium sulfate or small percentages of dried egg white. The composition of baking powder is such that it will produce 14% by weight of CO_2, the law requiring a minimum of 12%. Of course, some baking powders can be so constructed as to produce more, actually as high as 17%. Baking powders are now produced to release carbon dioxide at various intervals, some slowly at room temperature and some more rapidly at baking temperatures. Table 4.6 gives not only a brief history of leavening but an idea of the relative rates of the release of carbon dioxide.

Other acid ingredients are used and these have been selected mainly because they leave no off-flavored or toxic residue. Glucono-delta-lactone was selected for use in making a bread mix for Army Field Kitchens, which required only addition of water and a short time to proof; when baked, it resembled a

TABLE 4.6

*MAJOR STEPS IN THE HISTORY OF LEAVENING

Leavening Agent Type or Brand First Use Chemical Description	% Leavening Gas Released			Applications	Comments	
	2 Min After Mixing	10 – 15 Min Bench Action	During Baking		Advantages	Disadvantages
Yeasts (from early times)	None	Unpredictable	Destroyed	All bread or dough mixtures	Yeasty flavors, tender crust	Action very slow
Sour milk or buttermilk $CH_3CHOHCOOH$ (lactic acid)	Almost all	None	Very little	All bread or dough mixtures	Flavor	Inconsistent re-
Eggs (whites or whole fresh)	None	None	Very little	Cake doughs	Excellent emulsifier improves texture and flavor	Cost is high
Varying alcohols from wines, etc.	None	None	Very little	Cake doughs	Suitable for flavor of festive cakes	Expensive little leavening action
$KHC_4H_4O_6$ Cream of tartar (1835)	About 70%	Very little	About 30%	All mixtures	Flavor pH adjustment	Expensive gas release too rapid Poor shelf life

Table 4.6 (*continued*)

Leavening Agent Type or Brand First Use Chemical Description	% Leavening Gas Released			Applications	Comments	
	2 Min After Mixing	10 – 15 Min Bench Action	During Baking		Advantages	Disadvantages
$(CH(OH)COOH)_2$ Tartaric acid with cream of tartar (1845–1850)	70–80%	Slow	10–20%	General	Flavor; lower cost	Unstable
Crude monocalcium phosphate, monohydrate, used in baking powders	60–70%	None	30–40%	General	No aftertaste. Low in cost.	Works too rapidly. Used with slower acting phosphates
$Al_2(SO_4) \cdot Na_2SO_4 \cdot 24H_2O$ Sodium aluminum sulfate (1885)	None	None	All	General	Low Cost	Acts slowly Accelerates rancidity of flour. Can't be used alone
CH_3COOH (acetic acid), vinegar (early 1900's)	100%			General	Adjusts pH	Results variable
$Na_2H_2P_2O_7 \cdot 6H_2O$ (SAPP) (early 1900's)				General	Very good leavening action	Bitter after-flavor in baked goods

				Use	Action
$CH_3CHOHCOOH$ (lactic acid) dried buttermilk or powdered cultured skimmed milk (1916)	100%			All mixture in which a buttermilk flavor is desired	Buttermilk flavor. Very little leavening action which is lost in mixing
$Na_2H_2P_2O_7$ "Perfection" (SAPP) high-purity	40%	8%	52%	To speed reaction of slower acting SAPP's	Fastest acting SAPP
$Na_2H_2P_2O_7$ "Donut Pyro"	36%	8%	56%	Prepared doughnut mixes for automatic machines	Designed for machine type doughnuts
$Na_2H_2P_2O_7$ "Victor Cream" (SAPP)	32%	8%	60%	Prepared mixes	Universal SAPP for all types of prepared mixes
$Na_2H_2P_2O_7$ "B.P.Pyro"	28%	8%	64%	Refrigerated biscuit dough	Minimum bench action with fast leavening following application of heat
$Na_2H_2P_2O_7$ (SAPP #4)	22%	11%	67%	Canned biscuits	Slowest acting SAPP with maximum tolerance for baking temperatures
Monocalcium phosphate monohydrate	60%	None	40%	Mixes	Increased batter aeration, greater

Table 4.6 (*continued*)

Leavening Agent Type or Brand First Use Chemical Description	% Leavening Gas Released			Applications	Comments	
	2 Min After Mixing	10–15 Min Bench Action	During Baking		Advantages	Disadvantages
$CaH_4(PO_4)_2 \cdot H_2O$ "Regent 12XX" (1937)					volume and texture; adjusts pH	
Anhydrous coated monocalcium phosphate $CaH_4(PO_4)_2$ "V-90" (1939)	15%	35%	50%	Mixes	A slowly soluble phosphate coating on every crystal retards release of CO_2	
$CaHPO_4 \cdot 2H_2O$ Dicalcium phosphate dihydrate, N.F.	0%	0%	100%	Usually formulated with MCP or Levair to adjust pH	Releases acid only during baking cycle	
$NaH_{14}Al_3(PO_4)_8 \cdot 4H_2O$ "Levair" (sodium aluminum phosphate) (1951)	22%	9%	69%	Mixes	Slow reaction. Improves tenderness and moisture of baked products	
"actif-8" Combination of sodium aluminum phosphate and V-90 (above)	27%	20%	53%	Self-rising flour	Stable for extended shelf-life. Flexible in manufacturing and baking. No after-flavor	

typical yeast-produced loaf of bread. The flavor and aroma were obtained by adding yeast by-products. The substitution of buttermilk and baking soda in biscuits, quick breads and cakes involves lactic acid as the acid ingredient.

Carbon Dioxide as a Leavening Agent

Baking Powders.—All baking powders contain the following: a source of hydrogen ion, sodium bicarbonate as the source of carbon dioxide, and cornstarch or other inert ingredients as fillers.

The amount of carbon dioxide released from baking powder is 12 to 14% by weight. The following factors affect the rate at which carbon dioxide is evolved: (1) solubility of the baking powder ingredients, (2) temperature, and (3) indirectly, the viscosity of the batter. In general, one teaspoon of baking powder (4 gm) is used to leaven 1 cup of flour.

Types of baking powders (trade names in parentheses)
   (1) Tartrate baking powder (Royal)
   (2) Phosphate baking powder (V-90, Happy Family, Rumford)
   (3) Pyrophosphate-phosphate baking powder (Fleischman's)
   (4) Alum-phosphate baking powder (Calumet, Davis)
   (5) Sodium aluminum phosphate (S.A.P.)
Reaction of baking powders
   (1) Tartrate baking powder (Acid ingred.: cream of tartar, tartaric acid. Residues: potassium sodium tartrate, secondary sodium tartrate.)
      (a) $KHC_4H_4O_6 + NaHCO_3 \rightarrow KNaC_4H_4O_6 + H_2O + CO_2\uparrow$
      (b) $H_2C_4H_4O_6 + 2NaHCO_3 \rightarrow Na_2C_4H_4O_6 + 2H_2O + 2CO_2\uparrow$
   (2) Phosphate baking powder – also called ortho phosphate b.p. or mono calcium phosphate b.p. (Acid ingred.: primary calcium phosphate. Residues: secondary calcium phosphate, secondary sodium phosphate.)
      (a) $Ca(H_2PO_4)_2 + 2NaHCO_3 \rightarrow CaHPO_4 + Na_2HPO_4 + 2H_2O + 2CO_2\uparrow$
   (3) Pyrophosphate-phosphate b.p. (Acid ingred.: primary calcium phosphate, secondary sodium pyrophosphate. Residues: secondary calcium phosphate, secondary sodium phosphate, normal sodium pyrophosphate.)
      (a) $Ca(H_2PO_4)_2 + 2NaHCO_3 \rightarrow CaHPO_4 + Na_2HPO_4 + 2H_2O + 2CO_2\uparrow$

(b) $Na_2H_2P_2O_7 + 2NaHCO_3 \rightarrow Na_4P_2O_7 + 2H_2O + 2CO_2\uparrow$

(4) Alum-phosphate b.p.—also called S.A.S. or "double acting" b.p. (Acid ingred.: primary calcium phosphate, aluminum sulfate. Residues: secondary calcium phosphate, secondary sodium phosphate, aluminum hydroxide, sodium sulfate.)

    (a) $Ca(H_2PO_4)_2 + 2NaHCO_3 \rightarrow CaHPO_4 + Na_2HPO_4 +$
$$2H_2O + 2CO_2\uparrow$$

    (b) $Al_2(SO_4)_3 + 6H_2O \rightarrow 2Al(OH)_3 + 3H_2SO_4$

    (c) $3H_2SO_4 + 6NaHCO_3 \rightarrow 3Na_2SO_4 + 6H_2O + 6CO_2\uparrow$

(5) Sodium aluminum phosphate (S.A.P.) — delayed action leavener (Acid ingred.: sodium aluminum hydrogen phosphate. Residues: disodium hydrogen phosphate which is inert). ("Active-8")

    (a) $2NaAl_3H_{14}(PO_4)_8 . 4H_2O + 23NaHCO_3 \rightarrow$
$Na_5Al_6(PO_4)_6(OH)_5 . 12H_2O + 10Na_2HPO_4 + 23CO_2\uparrow +$
$$14H_2O$$

Some other sources of leavening and their reactions

(1) Glucono delta lactone (Acid ingred.: gluconic acid. Residue: sodium gluconate).

$C_6H_{10}O_6 + H_2O \rightarrow HC_6H_{11}O_7$

$HC_6H_{11}O_7 + NaHCO_3 \rightarrow NaC_6H_{11}O_7 + H_2O + CO_2\uparrow$

(2) Ammonium bicarbonate

$NH_4HCO_3 + H_2O \rightarrow 2H_2O + NH_3\uparrow + CO_2\uparrow$ (no residue)

Some other acid ingredients and their reactions with NaHCO₃

(1) Acetic acid (vinegar): $HC_2H_3O_2$

$HC_2H_3O_2 + NaHCO_3 \rightarrow NaC_2H_3O_2 + H_2O + CO_2\uparrow$

(2) Lactic acid (sour milk or buttermilk): $HC_3H_5O_3$

$HC_3H_5O_3 + NaHCO_3 \rightarrow NaC_3H_5O_3 + H_2O + CO_2\uparrow$

(3) Aconitic acid (molasses): $H_3C_6H_3O_6$

$H_3C_6H_3O_6 + 3NaHCO_3 \rightarrow Na_3C_6H_3O_6 + 3H_2O + 3CO_2\uparrow$

(4) Citric acid (citrus juices): $H_3C_6H_5O_7$

$H_3C_6H_5O_7 + 3NaHCO_3 \rightarrow Na_3C_6H_5O_7 + 3H_2O + 3CO_2\uparrow$

Yeast Fermentation in Bread Making

Yeasts are defined as true fungi whose usual and dominant growth form is unicellular. The yeast strain used in bread making is *Saccharomyces cerevisiae*, one of about 3,000 species of yeast plants. Yeast has an average composition of 70% water, 15% protein, 10% glycogen, 0.5% fat, 2.0% cellulose, and 2.5% minerals. It is rich in the B complex vitamins and many enzymes necessary for growth and reproduction, such as diastase,invertase,maltase,zymase,and proteases.

Yeast is added on the basis of about 2 lb per 100 lb flour, plus water, salt, sometimes yeast food, sugar, malt, nonfat milk solids, and fats. During fermentation of the dough the following basic reactions take place.

$$\text{Starch + water} \xrightarrow[\text{yeast}]{\text{diastase}} \text{maltose} \tag{1}$$

$$(C_6H_{10}O_5)_x + \frac{x}{2} H_2O \longrightarrow \frac{x}{2} C_{12}H_{22}O_{11}$$

$$\text{Maltose + water} \xrightarrow[\text{yeast}]{\text{maltase}} \text{2 molecules glucose} \tag{2}$$

$$C_{12}H_{22}O_{11} + H_2O \longrightarrow 2 C_6H_{12}O_6$$

$$\text{Glucose} \xrightarrow[\text{yeast}]{\text{zymase}} \text{2 molecules ethyl alcohol +}$$

$$\text{2 molecules } CO_2 + 50{,}000 \text{ Cal} \tag{3}$$

$$C_6H_{12}O_6 \longrightarrow 2C_2H_5OH + 2CO_2\uparrow + 50{,}000 \text{ Cal}$$

The carbon dioxide produced is redistributed throughout the batter during rising, kneading, proofing, and baking.

In the fermentation of alcoholic beverages the action of yeast on the glucose and/or sucrose present takes place under controlled conditions to yield the type of beverage wanted. In nonalcoholic beverages, carbon dioxide is introduced and maintained under pressure in the container.

NITROGEN AND THE NITROGEN CYCLE

Nitrogen constitutes 78% or nearly four-fifths of the atmosphere. Free atmospheric nitrogen is semiactive and does not combine readily. It occurs as diatomic molecules in which the 2 nitrogen atoms share a triple covalent bond consisting of 3 pairs of electrons, :N:::N: Since the bond is strong, and the electrons are tightly held, the molecule is not assimilated by plants and animals, as is the case with carbon dioxide. Fortunately for man, certain bacteria convert or "fix" nitrogen from the air in nodules on the roots of soybeans and other legumes to a form of nitrogen compounds that the roots can absorb. Still other microbes cause the decay of dead plants and animals, and thus release nitrogen compounds for use by plants.

Nitrogen Cycle

Oxides of nitrogen are formed whenever lightning flashes convert atmospheric oxygen to ozone, which reacts with nitrogen to produce them. Rain water combines with these oxides, forming nitrite and nitrate compounds that penetrate well-cultivated soil and reach the roots of plants. Plants supply proteins to animals, which in turn convert less desirable plant proteins to more desirable animal proteins for human consumption. This nitrogen conversion process is known as the nitrogen cycle (Fig 4.2).

Ozone

An allotrope of oxygen forms when ultraviolet rays from the sun act on oxygen high in the atmosphere.

$$3O_2 \xrightarrow[\text{light}]{\text{ultraviolet}} 2O_3$$

Its color is light blue. A high-voltage electric charge acts on oxygen the same way.

Nitrogen dioxide from car exhausts reacts with oxygen in the presence of ultraviolet light to produce ozone and nitric oxide, a daytime reaction that dangerously pollutes air. It is a reversible reaction.

$$NO_2 + O_2 \underset{\text{ultraviolet light}}{\overset{\longrightarrow}{\longleftarrow}} O_3 + NO$$

The odor of ozone is unique and is often noticeable near X-ray machines and around TV tubes, or after a nearby lightning flash.

Ozone at $-115°C$ and 1 atm is a dark-blue liquid. At $-249.6°C$ ozone solidifies to a dark-violet crystalline mass. It is more soluble in water, and is more active chemically than oxygen, and is readily soluble in carbon tetrachloride.

A strong and rapid oxidizing agent, it is used in France to purify municipal water supplies, as a germicide, to remove odors from air by subsequent charcoal absorption, and to artificially age tobacco, wine, and meats. Other uses have included purifying oysters, and increasing storage time of eggs, fruits, and vegetables.

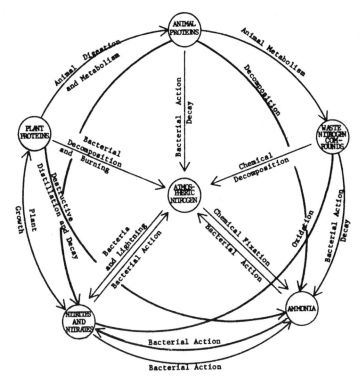

FIG. 4.2. NITROGEN CYCLE IN NATURE
Reprinted by permission of the publisher, from W. H. Nebergall, F. C.
Schmidt, and H. F. Holtzclaw, College Chemistry, D.C. Heath and
Company, 1968.

A powerful poison, ozone at 500 ppm in air will kill man
instantly. As a constituent of smog, lower concentrations
cause edema, bronchopneumonia, and death in 2 to 10 days.
The American Conference of Governmental Industrial Hygienists has set a toxic threshold limit of 0.1 ppm in air.

Ozone attacks rubber severely, causing cracking. Fats form
peroxides readily with ozone; off-flavors and rancidity, or
both, may develop rapidly in foods exposed to its action.

Carbon Monoxide

Carbon monoxide, CO, is an odorless, colorless, and poisonous gas formed when fossil fuels such as gasoline, natural

gas, coal, or wood burn without adequate air or oxygen.

$$2CH_4 + 3O_2 \longrightarrow 2CO + 4H_2O$$

Carbon monoxide reacts with hemoglobin 210 times faster than with oxygen. Then the blood can no longer take on oxygen. In a dilution of 1 part carbon monoxide in 200 parts air, death occurs in 2 min. In a ratio of 1 to 500, asphyxiation requires less than 1 hr.

Aerosols

Aerosols in the troposphere include dust, fog, smoke, bacteria, pollen, sea spray, organic materials, and volcanic ash. They are instrumental in cloud and fog formation, rainfall, atmospheric electrification, and the heat balance of the atmosphere. They act as nuclei for water droplets and ice crystals, and thus profoundly influence the weather. Aerosol particles are extremely small, having radii of less than 0.1 micron. Research on atmospheric freezing processes is complicated by the minute size of aerosol particles as each nuclei weighs only about 10^{-15} gm.

Controlling the weather is one of the more recent goals of meteorology. Cloudseeding with dry ice began in November 1946 over Mt. Greylock in western Massachusetts, when Dr. Vincent J. Schaefer dropped 2.7 kg of crushed dry ice from a small plane into a supercooled cloud, and water was converted into ice crystals, which fell earthward as snow.

Later that same year, Dr. Bernard Vonnegut, demonstrated that silver iodide, a compound having a crystalline structure resembling that of ice, could also be used for cloud seeding. Silver iodide is easier to handle than dry ice, and is now the most widely used substance for precipitating rain from supercooled clouds. Cloudseeding research indicates that rainfall in the eastern U.S. can be increased an average of 10 to 20%.

Liquid Air, Liquid Oxygen, and Liquid Nitrogen

Liquid air resembles water in appearance, and boils at −190°C. Dewar flasks or Thermos-type double-walled containers, having the space between the walls evacuated, are used in storing liquid air. When plants, or polymers such as plastic and rubber are immersed in liquid air they freeze solid. As they are dropped to a hard surface they shatter like glass. Nitrogen, oxygen, and other atmospheric gases are obtained from liquid air.

Uses of Air.—Carbon dioxide and nitrogen gases are obtained from air for use as refrigerants and inert-atmosphere storage or packaging. Air is used as a foaming agent in confections, icings, souffles, whipped cream, and mousses. In dough batters, air and water are leaveners. Leavening means increasing the surface area of a dough by including many gas bubbles: 1 vol. $H_2O = 1,600$ vols. steam. Overrun in ice cream is a function of the trapped air content. Although air is the heating medium in ovens and the cooling agent in blast freezers, its low *specific heat* or capacity to hold and give up heat is only 0.25 as compared to 0.5 for steam and 1.0 for water. Aeration of water containing iron and hydrogen sulfide combined with settling, filtering, and softening greatly improves the quality of some well waters. *Aeration* is necessary to improve the drinking quality of boiled water. Classification and transport of flour, spices and seeds, spray drying, lint removal, and jar cleaning are some other useful applications of air.

OXYGEN AND OXIDATION

Oxygen is the most abundant element on earth, constituting 50% of the solid crust of the earth, 89% of the water, and 20% of the atmosphere. Oxidation of food occurs in the respiration process, giving energy to the body and cells; it is accompanied by release of carbon dioxide and water. (see Table 4.7).

Physical Properties of Oxygen

Oxygen is a colorless, odorless, and tasteless gas. It is diatomic and occurs as O_2. It cannot be liquefied until cooled to –118.84°C, its critical temperature, at a pressure of 49.71 atm, its critical pressure. Under a pressure of 1 atm, oxygen liquefies at a temperature of –182.97°C, its boiling point. At STP oxygen has a density of 1.42 gm/l. Molecular oxygen has two unpaired electrons, since magnetic studies reveal that the molecule is strongly attracted by a magnetic field. Although oxygen is only slightly soluble in water, fish use the dissolved oxygen.

Chemical Properties of Oxygen

Oxidation reactions include metabolism, combustion of gasoline, coal, natural gas, wood, and other fuels, and the oxidation of metals. They may be slow as in rusting of iron, or explosive as in the burning of hydrogen at 600°C.

Oxygen combined in rocks and minerals together with oxygen in water and the atmosphere amounts to 49.2% of the earth's matter. This makes oxygen first in abundance on earth, but third in the universe, where hydrogen is first, and helium second. All the elements except the rare gases (helium, argon, neon, and krypton) react with oxygen to form compounds.

Oxygen is used in the manufacture of steel, and in acetylene torches that cut steel while operating at flame temperatures of over 4,000°C.

Acetylene + oxygen $\longrightarrow$ carbon dioxide + water + heat

Hospitals use oxygen for treatment of pneumonia and heart diseases and with anesthetics during surgery. Emergency squads carry oxygen to revive gas or smoke victims or for artificial respiration in treatment of electric shock, drowning, or heart attack. High-pressure oxygen is used to resuscitate persons poisoned with carbon monoxide.

Oxygen is provided in modern aircraft that fly at altitudes of several miles above the earth. However, it is only used when the pressurizing system for the cabin fails. Mountain climbers who conquer peaks like Mt. Everest use oxygen tanks at the highest levels. The astronauts who walked on the moon took oxygen with them; and liquid oxygen was used for liftoff of the spaceship.

Photosynthesis provides oxygen. Chlorophyllaceous plants in the presence of sunlight manufacture more oxygen than they require. The excess oxygen is released to the atmosphere for use by animals. Chlorophyll activated by ultraviolet light catalyzes, or speeds up, the conversion of carbon dioxide and water by plants to simple sugar and oxygen.

$$\text{Carbon dioxide + water} \xrightarrow[\text{sunlight}]{\text{chlorophyll}} \text{glucose + oxygen}$$
$$6CO_2 + 6H_2O \longrightarrow C_6H_{12}O_6 + 6O_2$$

Oxidation of food uses oxygen. At night plants oxidize the sugar formed by photosynthesis. Both plants and animals convert food to energy needed for life.

glucose + oxygen $\longrightarrow$ carbon dioxide + water + energy
$$C_6H_{12}O_6 \longrightarrow 6CO_2 + 6H_2O + \text{calories}$$

This reaction is the reverse of photosynthesis.

Waste destruction requires oxygen. Dead animal and plant
materials require oxygen as well as bacteria and sunlight for
the process of decay. These processes restore nitrate, nitrite, sulfate, and phosphate to the soil, and carbon dioxide
and water to the atmosphere. Streams and lakes require oxygen
to satisfy the biochemical oxygen demand (BOD). As the organic
waste load increases, more oxygen is needed to inactivate
pathogenic bacteria. Some cities aerate their water supplies
by spraying the water in air or pumping air into the river to
provide an aerobic medium. Molds, oxidative scum yeasts,
wine yeasts, and aerobic bacteria require free or uncombined
oxygen.

Oxygen and Fire

Controlling combustion is achieved by governing the rate
of reaction. Flour in mass does not burn, but when atomized
in fine particles, and exposed to a spark an explosion may
occur.

Three conditions are required for combustion, namely: fuel,
heat, and sufficient oxygen.

*The kindling temperature of a solid, or flash point of a
liquid* is that temperature at which light and flame occur as a
result of rapid oxidation.

Small pieces of fuel kindle readily by the heat of a match.
Larger pieces of wood or coal must reach the kindling temperature before burning. The more air supplied, the more
rapidly the fuel is oxidized.

Complete *combustion* is accomplished when oxygen is supplied in sufficient quantity to make a gas flame burn with a
bright blue hue. A yellow flame indicates incomplete combustion due to carbon that has not been burned. This yellow flame
blackens cooking utensils or kerosene lamps, and represents a
waste of fuel.

methane + oxygen $\xrightarrow{\text{heat}}$ carbon dioxide + water + heat

$$CH_4 + 2O_2 \longrightarrow CO_2 + 2H_2O + 212 \text{ kilocalories}$$

The principal products of any combustion are carbon dioxide
and water. Carbon monoxide and carbon are liberated when
combustion is incomplete due to lack of oxygen.

The main products of combustion from coal are the same.
However, impurities in coal result in sulfur dioxide and sulfur

trioxide as by-products. Gasoline yields other atmospheric
pollutants including: hydrocarbons that have not burned, aldehydes, organic acids, carbon monoxide, nitric and nitrous
oxides, ozone, and lead, boron, or other organometallic additives.

Proper ventilation and venting of all gas-fired equipment is
essential to safety. A wise manager will check all possible
sources that may lead to asphyxiation from carbon monoxide
or other chemical fumes such as chlorinated solvents.

Spontaneous combustion may result from careless disposition of oily or solvent-laden paint rags. Heat may accumulate,
causing the temperature to rise to the kindling point. This
process is known as spontaneous combustion. Pollution is so
great in the Cuyahoga River in Cleveland's Flats that fires break
out on the water's surface weekly as chemicals pour into the
saturated water. Bowling alleys often burn down as a result of
spontaneous combustion by pin-cleaning materials. The best
procedure is to burn solvent-soaked rags in an incinerator. Do
not keep them around.

Fire control is dependent upon controlling at least one of the
three factors responsible for combustion, namely, *fuel, heat,*
and *oxygen*. Recognize the importance of *exposed surface*. A
lump of coal won't burn when subjected to a lighted match. On
the other hand, a coal dust explosion may be set off with a
lighted match. Paint seals wood or metal away from air, preventing decay or rusting and retarding flammability. Store
combustible materials away from heat sources.

Fire extinguishers function by smothering or cooling the
fire. Carbon dioxide stored under high pressure is used for
extinguishing fat fires that the use of water might spread.
Carbon dioxide extinguishers are especially helpful in kitchens.
Extinguishers filled with plain water may be provided for
dining areas.

The soda-acid extinguisher contains sulfuric acid in a loosely
stoppered bottle that mixes with sodium bicarbonate solution
when the tank is turned upside down. Carbon dioxide gas and
the water expelled with it are the active agents.

$$2NaHCO_3 + H_2SO_4 \longrightarrow 2CO_2 + 2H_2O + Na_2SO_4$$

Another extinguisher of this type liberates a foaming substance that blankets the fire. The carbon dioxide combines
with the foam to exclude oxygen. Obviously either of these

latter types would make food unusable.

Often all that is needed to put a cooking fire out is a metal cover with a handle in the center that will smother the flames, by cutting off the oxygen supply.

Flame Retardants[1]

(1) *Flame-resistant treatment* is *not fireproofing. Asbestos* and *glass* are the only materials which will not char or be destroyed when exposed to fire; treated fabrics can be destroyed.

(2) Treated fabrics will *char* and possibly *glow;* however they do not burst into flame and thus spread the fire.

(3) *Glow* remains or occurs when the charred area is red hot after the igniting flame is gone. *Glow is dangerous.* Some flame retardants *shorten* the *duration* of the *glow time* and keep it from spreading.

(4) Most flame-retardant solutions are used for materials kept under *cover;* they are *not weather-proof.*

(5) Flame-retardant solutions given here are not effective on synthetic materials unless so specified.

(6) These solutions are applied (a) by dipping, (b) by spraying and (c) by sprinkling.

(7) Resin-treated fabrics, etc., which resist wetting may be treated by adding 1 tsp of a wetting agent (any synthetic detergent) to each gallon of solution.

(8) Materials must be *dry* before being treated. Completely wet them with solution.

(9) Do not apply solutions to materials that water would injure.

(10) Solutions of borax ($Na_2B_4O_7$) and boric acid (H_3BO_3) or diammonium phosphate $(NH_4)_2HPO_4$ are cheap and easily prepared.

(11) Organopolyphosphorus compounds are used as flame retardants for rayon, paper, wood products, and synthetic fibers; they are also used as a lubricating oil and as gasoline additives.

(12) *Solution A.*   Glow lasts about 30 seconds.

Borax.........7 oz
Boric acid......3 oz

[1]References: (1) USDA Leaflet No. 454, 1959. (2) Michigan Chemical Corporation. (3) *C. &En.*, p. 102, Sept. 1960.

Water (hot)..... 2 qt
Dissolve boric acid by making a paste with small quantity
of water. Add this and the borax to the remaining hot
water. Stir until solution is clear.

(13) In the laboratory use:

Borax..........10.3 gm
Boric acid...... 4.4 gm
Water (hot).....100 ml
Dip piece of *litmus paper* or *cloth—dry* and *test reaction*.

AIR POLLUTION

Urbanization, technical advances, and a population concentration from 106 million people in cities in 1920 to 170 million in 1960 (projected to 280 million by the year 2000) have been the factors responsible for the pollution dilemma. Just as bacterial cells die off when waste products poison their substrate, men can't survive if immersed in filth. Air pollution attacks the lungs, the digestive tract, and the eyes and ears. Air pollutants damage crops, corrode metal and stone, destroy fabrics and paints, besides endangering the health of many people. Gases, vapors, solids, and noise are polluting the atmosphere. The total emission of atmospheric pollutants in 1966 was estimated as 125 million tons per year by the National Academy of Sciences. About 60% come from transportation, 19% from manufacturing, 13% from power generators, 6% from heating units, and 3% from refuse disposal.

Management must be cognizant of these environmental hazards when choosing locations for hotels, motels, restaurants, and inns. Formerly, emphasis was placed on potable water, adequate sewage facilities, power, transportation, and the market potential in selecting a suitable building site. Pollution problems have caused the Federal Government to name 57 air quality control regions. The Air Quality Control Act of 1967 requires that states set and enforce pollution standards on a regional basis.

Sulfur Dioxide

Many air pollution experts believe sulfur dioxide is most

damaging. The result of oxidation of sulfur dioxide to sulfur trioxide, which reacts readily with atmospheric moisture, forms sulfuric acid aerosols. These chemicals severely attack the respiratory systems of persons inhaling them.

New technology includes oxidation processes for removing sulfur oxides from stack gases. Recent tests using natural gas instead of gasoline to propel automobiles have resulted in a claimed reduction of 90% in pollutants. However, the automobile remains the number one cause of serious air pollution.

Ozone (O_3)

One hour of sunlight brings the ozone concentration to a peak on a crowded highway. Olefins (unsaturated hydrocarbons) are emitted from the car exhaust. These olefins bond ozone that forms as a product of the reaction between nitrogen dioxide and oxygen in the presence of ultraviolet light. The reaction is reversible.

$$NO_2 + O_2 \xrightleftharpoons[\text{UV light}]{} O_3 + NO$$

At a level of 6 parts per million (ppm) in air ozone kills laboratory animals within 4 hr. Lung edema and hemorrhage are the cause of death. Russian studies indicate that 3 ppm results in the lung disease emphysema.

The great French scientist Carnot showed mathematically that the internal combustion engine has a maximum efficiency total of 26%. Thus 74% or more of the fuel is wasted, and after being exhausted, pollutes the atmosphere.

Tobacco Smoke

According to Carr, who is a smoker himself, "smoking is air pollution on a minor-league scale." Engineers design an air supply system on the basis of the quality of outside air available for ventilation, together with the smoke and body emanations from people. However, designs are usually planned to minimize cooling and heating losses. This means that the make-up of fresh air is minimal.

Society today consists of 60% nonsmokers and 40% smokers. Susceptibility to smoke from cigarettes, pipes, and cigars varies from one person to another. Age is a prime factor, as babies and older people are affected the most. Allergens from tobacco volatiles have a pronounced effect, causing nausea, headache, insomnia, and loss of appetite in many persons.

Emphysema can occur in nonsmokers who play poker or billiards in smoke-filled rooms. Travellers on trains, buses, planes, or in cars may be subjected to extremely high concentrations of these gaseous toxicants. Meeting rooms are frequently fouled and so are study areas. Permissiveness with regard to smokers has perhaps had further deleterious effects on society than simply loss of health and life.

Clothing, hair, skin, upholstery, rugs, linens, telephone mouthpieces, in fact, all surfaces contacted by tobacco smoke are fouled. A nonsmoker, upon entering an empty room saturated with tobacco smoke volatiles from its previous occupant(s), often has a sensation of nausea. A wise manager should realize the predicament of the nonsmoker, and try to look after his needs as well as he does the smoker's. Certainly, a person should have a choice. Rooms, furnishings, and surfaces should be cleaned and freshened immediately when vacated. Smoke-free dining and meeting rooms or areas should be provided.

Cigarettes.—The average smoker takes 2-sec 35-ml puffs once a minute to a butt length of 23 mm. About 1/3 of the smoke is mainstream or inhaled and blown out. The gaseous phase is absorbed in the oral cavity and lungs, and 16% of the particulate matter stays in the mouth. The other 2/3 of the cigarette smoke is side-stream, and passes directly into the atmosphere. The side-stream contains 1000 ppm of carbon monoxide as compared to an average concentration of 70 ppm in the Holland tunnel.

Particulate matter is "tar"; of this, 70 mg per cigarette is emitted together with 60 mg of dry smoke containing 4 to 5 mg nicotine in the side-stream and 20 to 25 mg with 1 to 1.5 mg nicotine in the main-stream.

Gas phase constituents in the main-stream average 77 mg CO_2, 23 mg CO, and 0.6 mg H_2 per 9 puffs. Other gases include oxygen and nitrogen, which are innocuous. Side-stream concentrations are probably three times as high.

Carbon monoxide (*CO*) gas is colorless and odorless, but has a slight garlic odor at levels above the toxic threshold. The organs of carbon monoxide-poisoned victims have a garlic-like aroma. Hemoglobin's affinity for CO is about 210 times as strong as for oxygen, yielding carboxyhemoglobin (COHb). Victims skins redden with the COHb complex instead of oxy-hemoglobin, and the brain becomes oxygen starved. Revival is

TABLE 4.7
EFFECT OF CIGARETTE FILTERS ON THE YIELD OF SOME
OF THE VAPORIZED COMPONENTS. 85 MM BLENDED
CIGARETTES, COMPONENTS IN ORDER OF INCREASING
BOILING POINT FOR EACH CLASS

Material	Yield in micrograms per 40 ml puff		
	No Filter	Acetate Filter	Combined Acetate Adsorbent Filter
Hydrocarbons			
methane	97.0	117.0	108.0
ethylene	22.0	21.0	20.0
ethane	51.0	67.0	61.0
propene	25.0	27.0	24.0
propane	23.0	26.0	22.0
2-methylpropene	6.6	7.7	4.4
1,3-butadiene	4.3	5.4	2.8
butane	7.0	8.4	4.5
cis -2-butene	4.1	4.4	2.8
isoprene (2-methyl-1,3-butadiene)	47.0	47.0	18.0
2-methyl-2-butene	6.8	8.5	3.2
benzene	6.1	5.9	1.9
toluene	9.7	8.7	2.9
Alcohols			
methanol	13.0	10.0	1.8
Aldehydes			
formaldehyde	4.1	3.6	3.5
acetaldehyde	81.0	82.0	48.0
propionaldehyde	6.9	6.7	2.4
acrolein	8.2	7.9	2.9
isobutyralsehyde	3.6	3.3	1.0
Ketones			
acetone	42.0	39.0	13.0
2-butanone	10.0	9.4	2.3
butenone	3.7	3.5	0.9
2,3-butanedione	15.0	15.0	3.9
Esters			
methyl formate	3.6	3.5	1.2
Cyclic Ethers			
furan	4.6	4.3	1.7
2-methylfuran	5.8	5.4	1.5
2,5-dimethylfuran	4.9	4.5	1.0
Nitriles			
hydrogen cyanide	32.0	29.0	11.0
acetonitrile	18.0	15.0	5.8

Table 4.7 (*continued*)

| Material | Yield in micrograms per 40 ml puff | | |
	No Filter	Acetate Filter	Combined Acetate Adsorbent Filter
Miscellaneous			
nitric oxide	30.0	35.0	41.0
methyl chloride	19.0	24.0	22.0
hydrogen sulfide	3.4	3.1	1.3
ammonia[1]	12.0	13.0	7.6

[1] Total of ammoniacal compounds determinable by the Nessler procedure, expressed as the equivalent micrograms of ammonia.
Source: From Tobacco Science, 1965, Vol. 9.

possible by promptly placing the patient in a high-pressure oxygen chamber.

Airplane crashes and auto accidents have been traced to CO effects on the brain, causing faulty vision and judgment. Cigarette smoking coupled with high temperature in the range of 85 to 100°F makes brain impairment at lower concentrations of CO possible.

Heating equipment, stoves, water heaters, and charcoal broilers must be adequately vented and provided with a fresh air supply that insures complete combustion of fuel. Insufficient oxygen or faulty and dirty equipment may cause formation of carbon monoxide instead of carbon dioxide and water.

TABLE 4.8
BODY EMANATIONS

Gas	Concentration, Mg
Ammonium	297
CO	278 (nonsmokers)
CO	417 (smokers)
Hydrocarbons	504
Aldehydes	0.6
Ketones	232
Mercaptans and H_2S	5
Fatty acids	89

American hygienists recently set 50 ppm of CO in the atmosphere as a maximum for safety. The Russians set 1 ppm as a
maximum, California has set 30 ppm in smog, and in 1965
Chicago's air averaged 17 ppm.

The air pollutants listed in Table 4.7, when added to smog,
may cause asphyxiation. People who breathe through their
noses are partly protected from particulates, but like filters
on cigarettes, the hairs of the nose do not affect the concentration of gases. Cigar and pipe smoke may be even more
dangerous.

Cigars and Pipes.—Studies indicate that concentrations of
nitrogen dioxide in cigar and pipe smoke greatly exceed the
levels of toxicity for humans. These concentrations are 3 to 4
times NO_2 content of cigarette smoke. The origin of nitrogen
oxides in tobacco smoke is probably burned organic nitrogen
from nicotine and tobacco protein. Long-term exposure to less
than 3 ppm of NO_2 will result in emphysema.

Body Emanations

Sweat, bad breath, intestinal gas discharges, flakes of psoria-
sis, dandruff, lint from clothing, and perfume from people are
other pollutants. The amounts of gases given off by the adult
male in 24 hr are shown in Table 4.8. Women and children
would release less.

EFFECTS OF AIR ON FOODS

Light, oxygen, and water vapor are the only chemically active
agents in air, but next to microbes they have the most destructive effect on food.

$$O_2 + \text{fruit and vegetables} \xrightarrow{\text{respiration}} CO_2 + H_2O$$

$$\text{Low } O_2 + \text{fruits and vegetables} \xrightarrow[\text{microorganisms}]{\text{fermentative}} \text{off-flavors}$$

Both nutritive value and flavor loss accompany oxidation of fats
and oils, destruction of some vitamins, and deterioration of
the biological value of proteins. Milk powder stored in air loses
the amino acids arginine, histidine, lysine, and methionine.
Vitamins A, B, B_6, C, E, K, and biotin are susceptible to oxidation.

TABLE 4.9

OXYGEN CONSUMPTION OF MAN COMPARED WITH MACHINES

	Oxygen consumption, Moles/Hr
Man (resting)	0.8
average daily activity	3.0
extreme physical activity	16.0
Automobile	
30 mph, 15 mpg	47.0
60 mph, 15 mpg	94.0
Oil-fired furnace (winter)	137.0
Jet airplane (4 jets	
Mach 0.9 at 35,000 ft)	450,000.0
Open-hearth blast furnace	
(6400 tons pig iron daily)	9,700,000.0
Steam turbine-driven	
electric generator (500 megawatts)	10,800,000.0

Light plus oxygen will bring about color changes in many foodstuffs. *Oxygen promotes* oxidative rancidity, and foods of low lipid content are as susceptible as fatty foods. Accelerating catalysts, or *enzymes*, in the complex food matrix are responsible for these changes. Nonenzymatic accelerators are metals, metal salts, and organic compounds of metals. Oxidative enzymes such as lipoxidases or peroxidases, other enzymes and biological catalysts such as hemoglobin and hematins, and light-sensitive photochemical pigments and carbonyl compounds in heated fats may act as pro-oxidants.

Light-induced oxidation of milk fat gives a different organoleptic, or taste-odor, reaction than spontaneously oxidized milk. Irradiated fat also has a characteristic odor. Each reaction product differs depending upon the circumstances. Furthermore, irradiated meat odor differs from irradiated butterfat odor; this may be due to the presence of higher concentrations of sulfur compounds in meat.

Orange juice undergoes oxidative changes associated with rancidity, whereas volatile oils from the skins give a "terpeney" off-flavor.

Fresh pork sausage, even though refrigerated, often spoils by oxidative rancidity. Frozen hamburger oxidizes in a few weeks even at 0°F. Turkey fat turns rancid within a few days

TABLE 4.10

ESTIMATED VEGETATION REQUIRED TO SUPPLY
THE DAILY OXYGEN REQUIREMENTS OF AN ADULT[1]

Vegetation	Area, Sq m
Corn	17
Oak-Pine forest	22
Wheat	36
Lawn turf	350
Ocean	400

[1]Heichel, G. H., "Plants, Oxygen and People," Frontiers of Plant Science, November, 1971, page 6, Connecticut Agricultural Experiment Station, Storis, Conn.

after freezing. So do oils in pre-cooked chicken and fish sticks during frozen storage. Ice creams may develop an oxidized flavor resembling cardboard or tallow.

Oxidized fats and oils develop tallowy, painty, burned, fish, metallic, grassy, and other off-flavors that characterize rancidity. *Flavor reversion* of soybean oil occurs with a light oxidation, or one percent of that required for rancidity, and results in "fishy," "beany," and "painty" odors.

Raw frozen vegetables develop a "hay" flavor which could be partly due to the action of oxidative enzymes on the ascorbic acid (vitamin C). Dehydrated potatoes contain only 0.5% fat, yet oxidation of this small amount of fat can result in off-flavors and odors.

Oxidative changes in the fermentation of tea are responsible for building up a concentration of 10% by weight of polyphenolic end-products in the finished tea.

Strawberries discolor because of oxygen in cold storage and turn purple or fade. Cherries oxidize and darken, and blackberries discolor badly, turning brown and souring. The use of carbon dioxide in cold storage retards these processes.

Photochemical oxidation occurs with some jar-packed products, since there is a pronounced tendency for pigments to lighten due to photochemical effects of light, heat, and oxygen catalysis. Wines are especially susceptible to photochemical oxidation reactions, and must be kept away from light and heat to retain their best flavor. Flexible packaging in laminated aluminum foil, though costlier and lacking in the sales advantage that transparency offers, provides protection from both light and oxygen. Permeability of films such as polyethylene, polypropylene, vinylidine chloride, cellulose acetate, and other transparent polymer packaging materials to oxygen may make them advantageous for use with some foods and not with others.

Preventing Oxidation

Complete removal of air and peroxides should make fat keep indefinitely. Unfortunately, this is not practical to achieve and antioxidants are added. Deodorization is the removal of peroxides to stabilize fats against oxidation.

Tomato juice and chopped cabbage require a "hot-break" to inactivate oxidative enzymes, or 50% of the ascorbic acid in these products is lost. De-aeration of juice is necessary to preserve fresh flavor. This reduces oxygen and oil content. The steam-distilled oil is returned to the juice to add flavor.

Vegetables are blanched in boiling water to inactivate enzymes, preclude browning, and remove oxygen so that ascorbic acid may be retained. Steam blanching for 2 to 3 min gives a higher percentage of retention of ascorbic acid than water blanching at 160° to 204°F.

Odors such as paint, smoke, fish, and solvents are absorbed by fats, butter, or fat-containing foods, including coffee, chocolate, milk, cheese, and many others. These off-flavors are highly objectionable and should be avoided at all times.

Mold spores, often present in the atmosphere, are picked up in the manufacture of bread, syrups, chocolate, fruits, vegetables, sausage, bacon, cheese, and spices. Molds require oxygen for growth. Incorporation of mycostats that inhibit mold growth, such as sorbates, acetates, and propionates, is sometimes necessary. These additives are used in specific products with government approval.

Drying or hardening and skinning-over often occur in cooked sauces, puddings, gelatins, glazes, and other preparations. A thin oil coating may be used over sauces and glazes that must be held under refrigeration. A modified form of waxy-maize starch may be used to retard *syneresis*, or moisture separation. Puddings and gelatins should be covered with aluminum foil or suitable plastic film to avoid moisture change at the surface. This hardening and skinning increases with age and may be caused by hydrogen bonding that forms molec- ular aggregates that become difficult to break up or reincor- porate.

Headspace oxygen is encountered in canned foods, carbonated beverages, and wines. The amount of air retained in a sealed can or bottle varies with the filling method. Mechanical vacuum may be applied to the filled container. Nitrogen, carbon dioxide, or steam purging of the headspace can help to eliminate oxygen.

AIR AS A COOKING MEDIUM

Air as a conductor of heat is not as efficient as water or some other cooking media, but most of the equipment is based on the use of air.

Convection Cooking and Thawing

The movement of air in an oven with a blower results in more uniform and faster cooking. Ovens designed and built on this principle are called convection ovens, and they are becoming increasingly popular for both cooking and thawing. Rapid move- ment of warmed air in large amounts compensates somewhat for air's low specific heat. Humidification of the oven chamber is recommended to speed cooking by raising the specific heat of the air by moisture addition. A blast type of convection oven was first introduced by the Germans. It is used princi- pally for thawing frozen foods. In many respects it is pre- ferred to the microwave oven.

Microwave Cooking, Thawing, and Drying

Microwave heating utilizes an alternating current that re- verses itself 915 to 2450 million times per second. As food molecules, such as water, are polar and have positive charges on one end and negative charges on the other, they are turned around millions or billions of times every second. This fric- tion creates the heat necessary in the food to do the actual cooking. Moisture is the carrier for microwaves and when the final drop of water is driven off, heating automatically stops. (Metal pans or dishes cannot be used in microwave ovens, since the waves are reflected and tend to burn out the generator.)

This means that ceramic or other porous materials which have low electrical losses must be used to hold the food during cooking or thawing. Research to find other suitable materials continues.

Microwave steam cooking of poultry for pre-cooked, breaded, brown-and-serve parts was commercialized in 1966. Live steam cooks the outer 1/4 in. of chicken meat in 6 to 8 min, while the microwave finishes cooking to the bone in an additional 6 min. Quality and yield are improved by combining the two media as a result of greater retention of natural juices.

Micro-aire cooking is a combination of the microwave and convection cooking units.

Microwave drying is one of the successful applications of microwaves; it effects finish-drying of potato chips fried to color from 6 to 2% moisture. This can be accomplished without darkening the chips in the manner customarily encountered by finishing them completely in the deep-fat fryer.

Air and Foods

Air is used in food processing besides leavening and drying. Air is incorporated into food products such as whipped cream, ice cream, or whipped butter. It can be undesirable due to oxidative products formed.

Batters and doughs incorporate air as a result of egg-white, fat and sugar, and flour aeration. During baking the entrapped gases expand 1/273 of their volume per degree centigrade rise in temperature at standard pressure. Air inclusion makes leavening more effective since it expands with the steam. Since 1 volume of water forms 1600 volumes of steam, about 2/3 to 3/4 of the total expansion is attributable to the presence of water. Nevertheless, in the absence of air cells, water vapor escapes and there is no volume increase. Thus air is essential in air-steam leavening.

Ice cream is made from a mix and during freezing, air is incorporated. The increase in volume resulting from aeration is called overrun. Federal ice cream standards require a minimum milk fat content of 10%. Thus, if 5-gal. of mix weighing 9 lb/gal. containing 4.5 lb/gal. of 20% cream is aerated to a volume of 9.5 gal. and frozen, the overrun is 90% and the ice cream has a butterfat content of 10%.

$$\% \text{ overrun} = \frac{\text{volume of ice cream} - \text{volume of mix}}{\text{volume of mix}} =$$

$$\frac{9.5 \text{ gal.} - 5 \text{ gal.}}{5 \text{ gal.}} \times 100 = 90\%$$

$$\% \text{ butterfat} = \frac{\text{weight of butterfat}}{\text{weight of ice cream}} \times 100 =$$

$$\frac{4.5 \text{ lb/gal.} \times 5 \text{ gal.} \times 20\%}{45 \text{ lb}} \times 100 = 10\%$$

$$\text{Weight/gal. of ice cream} = \frac{\text{wt of mix}}{\text{volume of ice cream}} =$$

$$\frac{9 \text{ lb/gal.} \times 5 \text{ gal.}}{9.5 \text{ gal.}} = 4.726 \text{ lb/gal.}$$

CHAPTER 5

L. L. W. Smith

L. J. Minor

Water: Properties and Role in Foods

Water is a transparent, odorless, tasteless liquid, a compound of hydrogen and oxygen, H_2O, freezing at 32°F or 0°C, and boiling at 212°F or 100°C, which in a more or less impure state constitutes rain, snow, glaciers, ice, oceans, lakes, rivers, and wells; it contains 11.188% hydrogen and 88.812% oxygen by weight.

Water is abundant on earth, though scarce in many regions. Man's environment is inadequate without a sufficient supply of safe, or potable, water for drinking, cooking, and sanitation needs (see Figs. 5.1 and 5.2). The distribution of natural water is summarized in Tables 5.1 and 5.2.

Water Sources

Presently, the only practical source of water to supply man's needs is fresh water from lakes, rivers, and wells. The Great Lakes contain one-third of all available fresh water. Glacier ice is a potentially rich source of pure, natural water, resulting from the firnication (pressure packing) of snow. Recent studies indicate that towing glaciers from Polar regions and pumping the water inland may prove more economical and practical than distillation of seawater. Arizona's underground water level has dropped 2000 ft since 1930.

Distillation of seawater is costly both in fuel and equipment. Furthermore, for every 100 gal. of distilled water obtained there is a 300-lb salt residue to dispose of. It has been suggested that this by-product be used to manufacture plastic-salt bricks or walls for structural purposes.

CHEMISTRY AND PHYSICS OF WATER

Pure water is made up of H_2O^{16} except for 0.3% which consists of 18 different isotopes and 15 different ions, or a total of 33 different substances. Hydrogen, H^1, deuterium, H^2, tritium, H^3, O^{16}, O^{17}, and O^{18} are responsible for these variants.

102

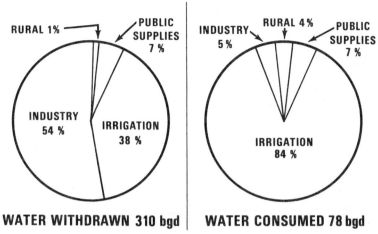

WATER WITHDRAWN 310 bgd | **WATER CONSUMED 78 bgd**

FIG. 5.1. WATER USE IN UNITED STATES
Source: Estimated Use of Water in the United States 1965 C. Richard
Murray, Geological Survey Circular 556 (1968).

TABLE 5.1

DISTRIBUTION OF NATURAL WATERS

Source	% of Total
Seawater	98.33
Continental ice	1.64
Fresh water	0.1
Water vapor	0.003

Density of Water

The unit of mass in the metric system is based on 1 ml of
water at 4°C having a mass of 1.0000 gm. The density, D, of
a substance is its mass, or weight, per unit of volume, $D =$
gm/ml. Water's density of 1.00 makes it a reference standard.

Specific Gravity

The term specific gravity (sp. gr.) means the ratio of the
mass of a substance to the mass of an equal volume of a reference substance. Water is normally used as a reference substance for liquids and solids, whereas air and hydrogen are
used for gases. Hydrometers are sealed cylinders with a
weighted bulb used to measure the specific gravity of liquids.

Withdrawal Use _____ **310 bgd**

Self-supplied Industry ___ **167 bgd**

Irrigation _____ **118 bgd**

Public Supplies _____ **22 bgd**

Self-supplied Rural _____ **3 bgd**

Consumptive Use _____ **78 bgd**

Irrigation _____**65.5 bgd**

Public Supplies_____ **5.5 bgd**

Self-supplied Industry ___ **3.9 bgd**

Self-supplied Rural _____ **3.1 bgd**

FIG. 5.2. TABLE OF
WATER USE IN THE
UNITED STATES
Source: Estimated Use of
Water in the United States
1965 C. Richard Murray,
Geological Survey Circular
556 (1968).

Water has a specific gravity of 1.00; substances that sink in water have specific gravities greater than 1, and those that float on water have specific gravities less than 1.

Temperature Reference

Standard reference temperatures are the freezing point of water at 0°C or 32°F and the boiling point at 100°C or 212°F at standard pressure. On the thermometer scales 180 Fahrenheit degrees equals 100 centigrade degrees, or vice versa as shown in the following equations:

$$\frac{°F - 32}{180} = \frac{°C}{100}; \ °C = \frac{5}{9}(°F - 32); \ °F = \frac{9}{5}°C + 32; \ °K = °C + 273$$

Calorie

A calorie is defined as the heat required to raise the temperature of 1 gm of water from 14.5° to 15.5°C. This is called the small calorie (cal or c.). The large calorie (Cal or C.) is equal to 1,000 small calories and is called a kilocalorie. In nutrition, calories are counted as large calories (Cal) or kilocalories.

Another unit of heat measurement is the British thermal unit, Btu; it is the amount of heat required to raise one pound of water 1°F (70° to 71°F).

TABLE 5.2
WORLD WATER BUDGET

Water Item	Volume, Cubic Miles	Volume, Cubic Kilometers	% of Total Water
Supply			
Water in land areas			
Fresh-water lakes	30,000	125,000	0.009
Saline lakes and inland seas	25,000	104,000	0.008
Rivers (average instantane-			
ous volume)	300	1,250	0.0001
Soil moisture	16,000	67,000	0.005
Ground water to depth of $2\frac{1}{2}$			
miles (4,000 m)	2,000,000	8,350,000	0.61
Icecaps and glaciers	7,000,000	29,200,000	2.14
Total in land area	9,700,000	37,800,000	2.8
Atmosphere	3,100	13,000	0.001
World ocean	317,000,000	1,320,000,000	97.3
Total, all items	326,000,000	1,360,000,000	100
Budget			
Annual Evaporation[1]			
From world ocean	84,000	350,000	0.026
From land areas	17,000	70,000	0.005
Total	101,000	420,000	0.031
Annual precipitation			
On world ocean	77,000	320,000	0.024
On land areas	24,000	100,000	0.007
Total	101,000	420,000	0.031
Annual runoff to oceans from			
rivers and icecaps	9,100	38,000	0.003
Ground-water outflow to oceans[2]	400	1,600	0.0001
Total	9,500	39,600	0.0031

[1] Evaporation 84,000 cubic miles (420,000 km^3) is a measure of total water participating annually in the hydrological cycle.
[2] Arbitrarily set equal to about 5% of surface runoff.
  Note: Values in the table are approximations based on data com-
      piled from many sources. They should not be construed to
      mean that any of the values is precise.
  Source: Modified after Raymond L. Nace, U.S. Geological Survey.

Specific Heat

The specific heat of a substance is the heat required to raise
1 gm of the substance 1°C. Water has a specific heat of 1,

sand 0.2, air 0.25, steam 0.5, and iron 0.1. Water's high specific heat, or capacity for absorbing or releasing heat, makes it an ideal coolant for engines and heating medium for buildings. Canners cool their products in water to below 90°F; otherwise stack burn occurs when heat-processed products are stored without adequate cooling.

Heat of Fusion and Heat of Vaporization

One gram of ice must absorb 80 calories (the heat of fusion) of heat before it melts at 0°C; conversely, 1 gm of water must release 80 calories of heat (heat of crystallization) before freezing at 0°C. Similarly, the conversion of 1 gm of water at 100°C to 1 gm of steam at 100°C requires 540 calories. Therefore, the *heat of vaporization* of water is 540 cal.

To convert 1 gm of ice to 1 gm of steam the heat required is 80 cal plus 100 cal, the heat required to raise the temperature of 1 gm of water at 0° to 100°C, plus *540* calories, the heat of vaporization of water. Therefore a total of 720 calories is needed to convert 1 gm of ice to 1 gm of steam.

The same number of calories would have to be removed (720 cal) to convert 1 gm of steam to 1 gm of ice.

Hydrogen Bonding

Water being a polar molecule tends to form temporary bridges that are called *hydrogen bonds*. The energy of forming and breaking these bonds has been measured, and amounts to about 3 kilocalories per mile of H_2O. This residual energy explains the high boiling point, freezing point, specific heat, density, and other unique properties of water.

When water freezes it assumes a hexagonal structure, the water molecules retain their individuality. Water locks itself into a crystalline structure and expands by about 10% when it freezes.

Hydrogen-ion Concentration (pH)

In food and other biochemical materials the concentrations of acid and base are low, and changes in acid or base concentrations are prevented by the presence of substances called *buffers*. Hydrogen-ion concentration, $[H^+]$, is used to measure acidity and hydroxyl-ion concentration, $[OH^-]$, to measure basicity in biological systems. Though it is highly associated, water does dissociate slightly into hydrogen and hydroxyl ions, the concentrations being very small but equal.

Precise measurements of the conductivity of pure water show that the hydrogen-ion concentration of water is 1/10,000,-000th or 10^{-7} mole per liter. The logarithm of the reciprocal of this value to the base 10 is 7, which is called the pH of water. This is the neutral point at which the hydrogen and hydroxyl-ion concentrations are equal; since each is 10^{-7}, their product is 10^{-14}. The definition of pH is the log of the reciprocal of the hydrogen-ion concentration, and the pH of pure water is 7, the neutral point.

$$pH = \log \frac{1}{[H^+]} \qquad pH_{H_2O} = \log \frac{1}{[10^{-7}]} = 7$$

All substances having values of pH lower than 7 are more acidic, and those higher than 7 more basic than pure water. Some common pH values are given in **Table 5.3**.

Reactions Involving Water

Hydrolysis is the reaction in which water plays a role as well as the medium. Hydrolysis will assume greater importance as the study of the composition and treatment of food stuffs is developed. The major constituent of most food products is water. Vegetables and fruits average 60 to 90% water, raw lean hamburger has 68% moisture and about 60% after cooking. Even crackers, a so-called dry product, contain 4.3% water. Water is necessary for bacterial action, and thus plays a role in sanitation, and is very important in all cleaning reactions.

To understand some of these basic reactions it will be necessary to cover some of the inorganic chemistry involved.

Water reacts with oxides of nonmetals to form acids. Phosphorus pentoxide combines with water to form phosphoric acid, and carbon dioxide combines with water to form carbonic acid.

$$P_2O_5 + 3H_2O \longrightarrow 2H_3PO_4$$
$$CO_2 + H_2O \longrightarrow H_2CO_3$$

Water reacts with oxides of metals to form bases. Quicklime or calcium oxide (CaO) combines with water to form slaked lime or calcium hydroxide, $Ca(OH)_2$, by the reaction $CaO + H_2O \rightarrow Ca(OH)_2$. Sodium oxide, Na_2O reacts so readily with water to form sodium that heat is given off. It is an *exothermic* reaction.

Acidimetry

In the food-science industry, where biological reactions occur in aqueous solutions, the concentration of the hydrogen

TABLE 5.3

APPROXIMATE pH OF SOME COMMON SUBSTANCES

Apples	*2.9–3.3*	Grapefruit	3.0–3.8
Apricots, dried stewed	3.3–3.5	Grapes	2.8–3.8
Apricot nectar, canned	3.8	Hominy, lye	6.9–7.9
Asparagus, fresh, cooked	6.0–6.2	Honey	3.7–3.9
Asparagus, canned	5.2–5.3	Jams, fruit	3.5–4.0
Bananas	5.0–5.3	Jellies, fruit	3.0–3.5
Beans, home-baked	5.0–6.0	Lemon juice	*2.2–2.4*
Beans, Kidney, cooked	5.9–6.1	Lobster or shrimp,	
		cooked	7.1–7.3
Beans, green lima, cooked	6.2–6.4	Magnesia, milk of	10.5
Beans, green, cooked	5.7–6.2	Meat, freshly killed	7.2–7.4
Beers	4.0–5.0	Meat, ripened	5.6–5.8
Beet greens, cooked	6.0–7.0	Meat, cooked	5.6–7.0
Beets, cooked	5.2–5.9	Milk, cows	*6.3–6.8*
Blackberries	3.9–4.5	Milk, cows, sour	4.7–5.7
Blood, human	7.4	Milk, human	6.6–7.6
Blueberries	3.1–3.2	Molasses	*4.7–5.7*
Bread, white	5.3–5.7	Olives, ripe, canned	6.0
Bread, whole wheat	5.3–5.7	Oranges	*3.6–4.3*
Buttermilk	*4.4–4.8*	Peaches, raw	3.3–4.1
Cabbage, green, cooked	6.4–6.8	Pears, raw	3.5–4.1
Cabbage, green, raw	5.8–6.3	Peas, cooked	6.2–6.9
Carrots, cooked	5.6–5.9	Pickles, dill	3.2–3.5
Carrots, raw	5.9–6.0	Pickles, sour	3.0–3.5
Cheese, Cheddar, Amer.		Plums, fresh	2.8–5.0
& Eng.	4.9–5.0	Potatoes, Irish, cooked	5.2–6.2
Cherries	3.2–4.5	Potatoes, sweet, cooked	5.3–6.0
Chocolate	*5.2–6.0*	Pumpkin	4.8–5.2
Cider	*2.9–3.3*	Raspberries, raw	3.5–4.0
Cocoa	6.5	Rhubarb, stewed	3.1–3.3
Cocoa, breakfast	5.2–6.0	Saliva, human	*6.0–7.6*
Cocoa, Dutch Process	6.0–8.8	Sauerkraut, cooked	3.5
Coffee, infusion, clear	4.7–5.0	Spinach, cooked	5.5–7.2
Corn, cooked	6.3–7.0	Squash, Hubbard,	
Corn syrups	4.9–5.1	cooked	6.0–6.2
Cracker dough, optimum	7.1	Strawberries, fresh	3.1–3.5
Crackers, soda	5.7–8.5	Tea, infusion, clear	5.8
Dates	4.6–4.8	Tomatoes, raw or	
Eggs, new-laid,		cooked	*4.0–4.5*
Whole	*6.6*	Turnips, yellow,	
White	8.0	cooked	5.2–5.8

Table 5.3 (*continued*)

Yolk	6.1	Urine, human	*4.8–8.4*
Eggs, cold storage		Vinegar, Cider	2.4–3.4
Whole	7.5–8.2	Water, mineral	6.2–9.4
White	8.6–9.0	Water, sea	8.0–8.4
Yolk	6.4–6.9	Water, distilled	
Fish, cooked	6.0–6.9	(equilibrium with air)	*5.8*
Flour, wheat	6.0–6.5	Water, distilled	*6.8–7.0*
Gastric contents, human	*1.0–3.0*	(CO_2 free)	
Gingerale	2.0–4.0	Water, drinking	*6.0–8.2*
Gooseberries	2.8–3.1	Wines	2.8–3.8

ion (H^+) or hydronium ion (H_3O^+) is very important. The concentration of hydrogen ion is expressed by definition as:

$$pH = \text{negative log } [H^+] \text{ or } pH = -\log [H^+]$$

The concentration of hydrogen ion $[H^+]$ is expressed as moles per liter. A very convenient way of showing this relationship is:

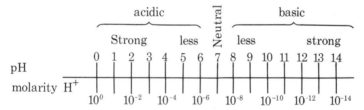

The log of a number between 1 and 10 can be found in a table of logarithms or from the following relationship:

The pH or H^+ concentration of some of the common solutions and mixtures can very accurately be determined by use of the Beckman pH meter. Colored test papers can be used to obtain approximate pH readings. Such papers as "Accutint," Hydrion, Oxyphen, etc., are used; the latter will give values within 0.2 to 0.3 pH value.

Some fruits change color over a pH range. Joslyn gives the following color changes of the water-soluble pigments; beets remain red throughout the acid range, red apples, blackberries, blueberries, black cherries, cranberries, and grapes

TABLE 5.4

ACID CONCENTRATION OF CARBONATED BEVERAGES
AND FRUIT JUICES

Flavor	Carbonated Beverages			Fruit Juices		
	Acid,%	pH	Acid Used for Calculations	Acid,%	pH	Acid Used for Calculations
Apple	0.10	3.5	Malic, citric	0.5	3.3	Malic
Blackberry	0.12	3.0	Citric	1.4	3.0	Malic
Cherry	0.10	3.0	Citric, malic	1.2	3.2	Malic
Grape	0.10	3.0	Tartaric	1.2	3.0	Tartaric
Pineapple	0.12	3.3	Citric	0.8	3.2	Citric
Raspberry	0.10	3.0	Citric	1.3	3.6	Malic
Strawberry	0.10	3.0	Citric	1.1	3.3	Malic
Grapefruit	0.18	3.0	Citric	1.5	3.2	Citric
Lemon	0.13	2.7	Citric	6.0	2.2	Citric
Lime	0.14	2.6	Citric	7.0	2.0	Citric
Orange	0.08	3.5	Citric	1.2	3.3	Citric
Celery	0.02	5.7	Malic, citric			
Cream soda	0.02	5.5	Citric			
Ginger Ale						
Golden	0.12	2.8	Citric			
Pale Dry	0.24	2.8	Citric			
Kola	0.05	2.3	Phosphoric			
Root Beer	0.01	5.0	Phosphoric			
Sarsaparilla	0.01	4.5	Phosphoric			
Tom Collins	0.30	3.2	Citric			

Source: Carbonated Beverages by Morris C. Jacobs. Chemical
Publishing Co., 1959.

change from red in the acid to black in the alkaline range.
Loganberries, black and red raspberries, and strawberries
change from bright red in acid solution to blue or bluish green
in alkaline solution. Red cabbage remains a brighter red in
acid and changes to a bluish green in alkaline media.

Tables 5.3, 5.4, and 5.5 give the approximate pH of some
common food substances; and the approximate pH of the water
in the states is given on the map which illustrates the degree of
hardness of water (see Fig. 5.3).

Inorganic salts resulting from the reaction of strong acids
such as HCl and strong bases such as NaOH do not undergo
hydrolysis. This means that sodium chloride ions do not react

TABLE 5.5

pH OF SOME PREPARED DISHES

pH 4 = 4.9	pH 5 = 5.9	pH = 6 or higher
Soups		
Consomme Madrilene	Crabmeat Jumbo	Corn Chowder
Stockless Vegetable	Cream of Tomato Soup	Cream Soups except
Tomato Bouillon	French Onion Soup	Tomato
	Minestrone	New England Clam
	Mulligatawny	Chowder
	Navy Bean Soup	Oyster Stew
	Split Pea Soup	Potato Chowder
	Philadelphia Clam	
	Chowder	
Main dishes		
Baked Beans	American Chop Suey	Beef Stew
Chili Con Carne	Austrian Ravioli	Scalloped Eggs and
Creole Franks	Hungarian Goulash	Vegetables
Creole Spaghetti	Chicken or Turkey	Ham or Meat Loaf
Potato Salad	Salad	Tuna or Chicken Pie
Spanish Rice	White Bread Stuffing	Chicken or Turkey
Vegetable Chop Suey		a la King
		Corn Bread Stuffing

with water to produce changes in the normal concentration of
hydrogen and hydroxyl ions from the water.

Salts of a strong base and weak acid, or of a strong acid
and a weak base, do undergo hydrolysis, the degree of hydrolysis being called the *hydrolysis constant*. Obviously, it is
the weak acid and weak base that are affected.

Fats, carbohydrates, and proteins are subject to both chemical and enzymatic hydrolysis reactions that split compounds
as they take up hydrogen and hydroxyl groups from water.

Bound water

Part of the water in carbohydrate and protein foods is *bound*
by hydrogen bonding to free electron pairs within the molecule;
this is called *bound water*. Some of its characteristics are
that its solvent action is lost; its vapor pressure is small;
it cannot be frozen or pressed out of tissue; and it is very
dense. About 5 to 10% of the total water in a tissue is bound.
Water that contains soluble substances, for example, salts,

Degree of Hardness of Water and pH

(Water hardness expressed as ppm of $CaCO_3$.)

$CaCO_3$	Soft	Moderately Soft	Moderately Hard	Hard
ppm	up to 50	51-100	101-200	211-500
grains/gal. *	up to 3	3^+-6	6^+-12	12^+-30

* Divide ppm/17.1 = grains per gallon

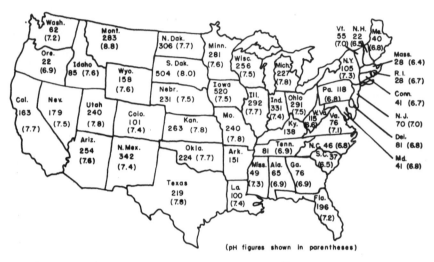

(pH figures shown in parentheses)

Cornell University water = raw water = pH 7.8, alkalinity = 78 ppm.
     = processed water = pH 6.6, alkalinity = 50 ppm.
Ithaca water averages 95-113 ppm.

FIG. 5.3. DEGREE OF HARDNESS OF WATER AND pH

amino acids, proteins, and sugars, is called *free water*, that can be pressed or frozen out of the tissue.

Bound water protects living tissue from freezing in the winter, and dehydrating in the summer. One gram of dry gelatin contains about 0.5 gm of bound water. At least a portion of bound water may become free, or vice versa.

Metabolic Water

About 60% of the carbohydrate, 2% of the protein, and 100% of the fat eaten by animals are oxidized in metabolic processes to furnish energy; water and carbon dioxide are also produced:

carbohydrates: $C_6H_{12}O_6 + 6O_2 \longrightarrow 6CO_2 + 6H_2O + 4$ Cal/gm

fats: $C_{57}H_{104}O_6 + 80 O_2 \longrightarrow 57 CO_2 + 52 H_2O + 9$ Cal/gm

A normal mixed diet, by oxidation, supplies the body with

about 1 liter of water a day. Another 1.5 liters of drinking water are needed to replace daily losses from perspiration, respiration, and excretion. Since fat yields more metabolic water, stored fats are used by hibernating animals in winter. Camels' humps may contain 100 lb of fat, which can supply 400,000 calories and 50 quarts of water.

Sublimation and Freeze-drying

On a cold, sunny, wintry day the laundry is hung on the porch of a Swiss Chalet high in the mountains. How does it dry? The sun's rays warm the surface layer of ice and the wind removes it as vapor. In time the clothes are free of ice and completely dry. This change of a solid directly into a gas is known as sublimation.

Freeze-drying of foods utilizes this principle, but speeds it up with vacuum. First the food is frozen, then placed on a warm surface, and subjected to a high vacuum. The ice sublimes to water vapor.

Absorption, Adsorption, Capillarity, and Coalescence

Water is *absorbed* by a sponge, paper, or cloth towel meaning that the water is bound by hydrogen bonding to the material by which it is absorbed.

When the bottom portion of a towel is immersed in water the water moves upward until the entire towel is wet; this is called capillary action. This principle is applied in paper chromatography, which is a method of separating mixtures of soluble organic compounds.

Rain water and melted snow that seeps into the ground providing moisture for plant life and man's needs is called ground water; it is absorbed through capillary action by the plants. After passing through soil and porous rocks it finally reaches the water table or the level of the water beneath the surface. Where the soil is moist, capillary action is effective, but when the earth is dry the water runs off as it will from a very dry surface.

Flour, starch, dextrose, gelatin, egg white, and gums are a few finely divided food ingredients that absorb water.

Adsorption and coalescence occur when the tiny water droplets in clouds coalesce or come together until large drops form and precipitate. Air pollutants such as oxides of nitrogen and sulfur attract water vapor and are *adsorbed*, that is, concentrated on the surfaces of the water molecules.

Meat-smoking studies revealed that smoke deposition is an adsorption rather than a settling process, and the rate of deposition of phenols from the burning of damp hardwood sawdust is 20 times as high for wet compared to dry surfaces. Continuous electrostatic smoking of meats is accomplished by ionizing the smoke particles with 50,000 volts of electricity about 8 in. from the grounded meat; the ionized smoke is then rapidly adsorbed, a surface phenomenon.

Surface Tension

Hydrogen bonding accounts for the high surface tension of water. Intermolecular attractive forces are balanced in the body of the liquid, while at the surface the only molecules above are those few in the vapor phase. Accordingly, molecules in the surface layer are drawn inward, and the liquid assumes a shape having a minimum surface area, namely, a sphere. This phenomenon is called surface tension.

The high surface tension of water causes capillarity in glass tubes, spherical droplets, solvent power, and a surface skin that will support a needle laid carefully upon it, or water bugs that race across it without sinking.

Hydrates and Water of Hydration

Many substances when crystallized from a water solution unite chemically with a definite proportion of water to form the crystal; this is called water of *hydration*. Formulas of some hydrates are shown in Table 5.6. Water may be mechanically enclosed in crystals, but this is not water of crystallization. Upon heating such crystals decrepitation—miniature explosions from the escape of steam—often occurs. Hydrates lose their water noiselessly when heated. Monosodium glutamate monohydrate is the commerical form in which this flavor enhancer is marketed. The use of moisture barriers prevents any variation in weight of packaged food ingredients stored in damp atmospheres.

When purchasing and using cleaning compounds, water of hydration should be taken into consideration. Soda ash, $Na_2CO_3 \cdot 10H_2O$, loses its water of hydration by gentle heating, and the resulting salt is called anhydrous sodium carbonate, Na_2CO_3. A comparison of molecular weight shows that the

TABLE 5.6

HYDRATE FORMULAS

Compound	Formula	Name
Sodium carbonate, soda ash	$Na_2CO_3 \cdot 10H_2O$	Sodium carbonate decahydrate
Aluminum sulfate, filter alum	$Al_2(SO_4)_3 \cdot 18H_2O$	Aluminum sulfate octadecahydrate
Alpha-d-Glucose	$C_6H_{12}O_6 \cdot H_2O$	Alpha-D-glucose-monohydrate
Monosodium Glutamate	$COOH(CH_2)CHNH_2(COONa \cdot H_2O)$	Monosodium glutamate monohydrate
Potassium alum	$KAL(SO_4)_2 \cdot 12H_2O$	Potassium aluminum sulfate, dodecahydrate
Copper sulfate, blue vitriol	$CuSO_4 \cdot 5H_2O$	Cupric sulfate pentahydrate
Calcium chloride	$CaCl_2 \cdot H_2O$	Calcium chloride monohydrate
Sodium aluminum sulfate	$Na_2SO_4 \cdot Al_2(SO_4)_3 \cdot 24H_2O$	Sodium aluminum sulfate tetracosanehydrate
Sodium hydrogen phosphate	$NaH_2PO_4 \cdot H_2O$	Primary sodium phosphate monohydrate

hydrate weight is 286 gm/mole and contains about 63% water, whereas the anhydrous product weighs 106 gm/mole. Since the cleaning effectiveness of the dry product is nearly three times that of the hydrate, the anhydrous product is more economical.

Efflorescence and Deliquescence

Many substances such as sodium carbonate, $Na_2CO_3 \cdot 10H_2O$, lose their water of crystallization when exposed to air and crumble to anhydrous powder. Loss of water by crystals when exposed to air is called *efflorescence*.

Salt and sugar contain traces of magnesium chloride and molasses, respectively, and in humid weather they become sticky as a result of adsorbing moisture from the air; these and similar solids possess *deliquescent* or *hygroscopic* properties. Starch, trisodium phosphate, magnesium stearate, or sodium carbonate are sometimes added at low concentrations to coat the salt or sugar impurities. This tends to keep the products free-flowing. Packaging materials with moisture-proof barriers are now used for hygroscopic materials such as dextrose, chocolate, gelatin, dry milk powder, malted milk, instant coffee powders, etc.

Dehydrated onion powder is so hygroscopic that processors pack it in tin containers with a small bag of silica gel, a *dehydrating agent*, to keep it dry.

Calcium chloride is used to dry the atmosphere in basements as a dehydrating agent, and is applied to dirt roads for its *deliquescence*.

Humectancy

Humectants are substances having an affinity for water, and are used to stabilize the moisture content of a product. Glycerol and sorbitol are used as humectants; both are rich in hydroxy groups that effectively hold water by hydrogen bonding within their molecules.

RELATIVE HUMIDITY

Two factors affect the moisture content of the air, namely, air temperature and relative proximity to earth sources of water. Plants and especially trees continually remove water from the ground and add water vapor to the air. A single full-grown tree may add as much as 5000 gal. of water as vapor to the air during a single summer.

Absolute humidity is the number of grams of water vapor per cubic meter of air. It may also be expressed in terms of the actual pressure of the water vapor present. Air-conditioning engineers measure humidity in units of grains of moisture; a grain is 1/7000 of a pound of water, per cubic foot of air. The total amount of water vapor that air can hold is dependent upon its pressure and temperature. At a pressure of 30 in. Hg, air at 0°F will hold about 0.5 grain of water vapor per cubic foot; at 32°F, about 2 grains; at 70°F, about 8 grains; and at 100°F about 20 grains. When more water vapor is forced into the atmosphere than it will hold, moisture will be deposited on objects and surfaces that are at the same or lower temperature than the air. Beyond the point of saturation, a molecule of water vapor will be deposited from the air for every molecule of water vapor evaporated into the air.

Any matter containing water will evaporate its content proportionately. Air in homes and other buildings gets its moisture content from everything containing water, such as food preparation, hot water, and filled bath tubs, all of which evaporate water into the air.

Dew point temperature is that temperature at which air becomes saturated with water vapor. The dropping of temperature below the dew point results in condensation of some of the water vapor present. Dew point temperature always gives a true indication of the water vapor present in a given sample of air, for the relative humidity is dependent upon saturation. The dew point is usually determined from tables in textbooks or manuals. Knowledge of the dew point temperature is useful in predicting the drop in dry-bulb temperature that will cause air at a prevailing relative humidity to lose its moisture.

Relative humidity is the amount of water vapor in a unit volume of air compared to the total amount that could be contained in the same volume of air under the same conditions of atmospheric pressure and temperature. For example, at normal pressure, a cubic foot of air can hold 8 grains of moisture. Accordingly, air with 3.2 grains contains only 0.4 of its capacity, that is, the relative humidity is 40%.

Relative humidities reported by weather bureaus are correct for the outdoor relative humidity at the location where the readings were taken. However, that of any specific locality may be different, depending on its distance from the weather station and other factors. Indoor relative humidity has little relationship to the outdoor figure, especially during the colder months, when the house is heated. *Hygrometers* are instruments that measure the water-vapor content of the atmosphere, and there are several types. For accurate data the well-known wet-and-dry-bulb psychrometer is commonly used (Table 5.7).

From the table it can be seen that if the dry-bulb reading is 70°F and the wet-bulb reading 60°F, the relative humidity is 55%. Assuming that the dry-bulb reading is 68°F and the wet-bulb reading is 54°F the relative humidity would be 38%.

FOOD SERVICE SCIENCE

TABLE 5.7

RELATIVE HUMIDITY

Dry-bulb Reading, °F	Difference Between Dry-bulb and Wet-bulb Readings																	
	1°	2°	3°	4°	5°	6°	7°	8°	9°	10°	11°	12°	13°	14°	15°	16°	17°	18°
50	93	87	80	74	67	61	55	50	44	38	33	27	22	16	11	6	1	0
52	94	87	81	75	69	63	57	51	46	40	35	30	24	20	15	10	5	0
54	94	88	82	76	70	64	59	53	48	43	38	32	28	23	18	13	8	4
56	94	88	82	77	71	65	60	55	50	44	40	35	30	25	21	16	12	8
58	94	89	83	78	72	67	61	56	51	46	42	37	33	28	24	19	15	11
60	94	89	84	78	73	68	63	58	53	48	44	39	34	30	26	22	18	14
62	95	89	84	79	74	69	64	59	54	50	45	41	37	32	28	24	20	16
64	95	90	85	79	74	70	65	60	56	51	47	43	38	34	30	27	23	19
66	95	90	85	80	75	71	66	61	57	53	49	45	40	36	32	29	25	22
68	95	90	85	81	76	71	67	63	58	54	50	46	42	38	34	31	27	24
70	95	90	86	81	77	72	68	64	60	55	52	48	44	40	36	33	29	26
72	95	91	86	82	77	73	69	65	61	57	53	49	45	42	38	35	31	28
74	95	91	86	82	78	74	70	66	62	58	54	50	47	43	40	36	33	30
76	95	91	87	82	78	74	70	66	63	59	55	52	48	45	41	38	35	31
78	96	91	87	83	79	75	71	67	63	60	56	53	49	46	43	39	36	33
80	96	92	87	83	79	75	72	68	64	61	57	54	51	47	44	41	38	35

Effects of Humidity on Foods

Humid air may cause microbiological contamination and spoilage of foods. Refrigerators where vegetables are stored may have mold-laden atmospheres. Fresh fruits and vegetables with bruised skins—for example, apples, peaches, pears, and celery—may spoil during refrigeration. Warm foods placed in cold rooms will draw in the cool air unless tightly covered. Proper sanitation of cold-storage rooms is essential to maintaining a clean atmosphere.

Another troublesome problem in cold-storage areas is foul odors caused by the growth of *Pseudomonas* organisms on poultry skins or meats. This organism thrives on moist fatty protein media. An unclean cold-storage plant may give off a strong *Pseudomonas* odor that can be smelled a block away.

Controlling the relative humidity of a food storage atmosphere is an important method of preventing incipient spoilage on food surfaces. Microorganisms require sufficient moisture at the substrate-cell interface for growth to occur. Each type of organism, yeast, mold, or bacteria, has a general range

of water activity. Water activity, a/w, is a ratio of the vapor
pressure of a solution to the vapor pressure of pure water at
the same temperature. Most microbes require a water activity
ranging from 0.75 to 1.00 as shown in Table 5.8.

Storage of fresh, frozen, and dried foods will always detract
from food flavor and quality, the degree of deterioration being
proportional to the storage time and temperature. At lower
temperatures and humidities there is less bacterial or enzyme
action. All should understand that freezing does not inactivate
all organisms present in the food at the time it is frozen. Dehydration does not preclude the presence of microbial species,
but rather may preserve them. The shrinkage in meat, vegetables, or fruits, is appreciable at humidities of 75% as compared to 95%. Quick turnover, and a first-in first-out method
of using stored food inventories is mandatory (Table 5.9).

Dry Products

Leaveners, salt, sweeteners, cereals, flour, pastas, rice,
starches, dry condiments, seasonings, gelatin (plain and
flavored), dried fruits, dried beans, peas, lentils, dehydrated
vegetables and cracker meal, cocoa, instant coffee, ground
coffee, tea, and instant fruit drinks can be stored safely in
moisture-proof containers at room temperature (60°F) for
approximately 6 mo to 1 yr. Potato chips and other snack
items of this caliber may be stored at room temperature in
moisture-proof packages that also retard the penetration of
certain light waves. Flavoring extracts must also be stored
in the dark. Shelled nuts in moisture proof packages may be
kept for 1 yr in the frozen state and need not be thawed
prior to use. When stored products are opened to remove
portions, the packages must be thoroughly resealed before
restoring.

Humidity Affects Foods that Are Hygroscopic

Dried foods are hygroscopic, and must be kept hermetically
sealed. These include dextrose, spray-dried hydrolyzed
proteins, onion powder, chocolate, gelatin, dry milk powder,
malted milk, instant coffee powders and granules, foam-dried
fruit, pulled sugar decorations, and many others. Desiccants
such as silica gel in moisture permeable bags are sometimes

TABLE 5.8

LOWEST A/W AND RH VALUES PERMITTING GROWTH OF SPOILAGE ORGANISMS

Microorganisms	Minimum a/w	Equilibrium RH* %	Storage RH %	Susceptible Foods
Normal bacteria	0.91	91	below 90	meat, fish, poultry, eggs, milk
Normal yeasts	0.88	88	below 87	syrups, puddings
Normal molds	0.80	80	below 79	fruits, vegetables, meats, cereals, bread
Halophilic bacteria	0.75	75	below 74	cured meats
Xerophilic fungi	0.65	65	below 64	dried meats
Osmophilic yeasts	0.60	60	below 59	jams, jellies, syrups, honey

Source: Frazier (1958)

An a/w of 0.70 inhibits spoilage at room temperature. This is approximated in dry milk at 8% moisture, dried whole egg at 10 to 11%, flour at 13 to 15%, nonfat dry milk at 15%, dehydrated fat-free meat at 15%, seeds of leguminous crops at 15%, dehydrated vegetables at 14 to 20%, dehydrated fruits at 18 to 25% and starch at 18%.

*RH is relative humidity.

packed in with moisture susceptible foods, and these pref-
erentially absorb atmospheric moisture. Dry storage rooms
or process rooms are often equipped with dehumidifiers that
maintain relative humidities of less than 30%.

Storage of Canned Foods.—Canned food containers may deteriorate when stored in damp, corrosive atmospheres. Whenever exterior rust occurs the vacuum in the can should be
checked and verified. Loss of vacuum indicates that air leakage
has occurred and that the *product is unsafe*. Occasionally
vacuum loss may be attributable to hydrogen formation at the
product-container interface. This is called a hydrogen swell,
and the contents should be discarded though not necessarily
spoiled.

Spices, Coffee, Onion Powder.—Spices are stored in a
dark room at 60° to 70°F using air-tight metal containers.
Oxidation occurs readily in spice oils and oleoresins. Coffee
beans contain 15 to 17% oil after roasting; they are readily
susceptible to oxidation and should be stored at temperatures
below 40°F. Ground coffee beans start to oxidize immediately,
and hence should be brewed promptly to capture their full
flavor. Instant coffees are hygroscopic and must be kept
tightly sealed to preclude absorption of atmospheric moisture.
Onion powder is extremely hygroscopic and is often packed
in sealed metal cans together with a desiccant in a semipermeable pouch.

Storage of Wine.—A wine cellar should be maintained at a
uniform temperature of 60°F and a humidity of 50%. When
stored, each bottle of wine must be laid in a horizontal position
so that the wine keeps the cork moistened. The room should
be darkened, free from drafts, and mechanical or sound vibrations.

Frozen food storage at 0°F has been proposed by the Association of Food and Drug Officials of the United States. Many
foods would be better stored at − 20°F. Presently, this is impractical except for large installations. Variations in temperature above and below zero damages most frozen foods.
All parts of freezer storage should be checked daily by means
of recording thermometer charts. A summary of conditions
that have proven satisfactory for general food storage is
given in Table 5.9. A good rule is to test regularly. Freshness
and goodness can only be maintained by constant care.

TABLE 5.9
STORAGE TEMPERATURE AND RELATIVE HUMIDITIES

Product	Temperature,°F		RH,%
Meat	32–34		88–92
Mild-cured hams	60–65		50–60
Poultry	32		85
Fish	33–40		90–95
Scallops, shucked clams, oysters, lobster meat, crab meat, shrimp	0	4–6 mo	---
Eggs			
Fresh eggs	29–31		80–85
Frozen whole eggs, yolks, whites	32	1 yr	Low as possible
Eggs dehydrated	35	6 mo	Moisture proof container
Dairy products			
Butter	32–36	2 mo	
	–10 to –20	1 yr	80–85
Cheese (hard)	35		65–70
Milk, dry non-fat	40	6 mo	Moisture proof container
Milk, dry whole	32–40		Moisture proof container
Milk, evaporated	35	1 yr	60
Fats and oils			
Margarine	32–36	2 mo	50
Salad dressings	35	1 mo	---
Vegetable oils	35	1 yr	---
Vegetable shortenings	50		---
Animal fats, lard	32–35	1 mo	---
Chicken fat	32–35	1 mo	---
Turkey fat	32–35	2 wk	---
Fruits and Vegetables			
Fruits	32–50		80–90
Corn (fresh)	31–32	4–8 da	90–95
Mushrooms	32–35	Use at Once	80–90
Prepeeled Potatoes	32–35	5 da	85–90
New potatoes	50–55		85–90
Mature potatoes	38–50		85–90
Ripe tomatoes	32	7 da	85–90
Unripe tomatoes	55–70	2–5 wk	85–90
Avocados	40–55	4 wk	85–90

Table 5.9 (*continued*)

Dry Products

Leaveners, salt, sweeteners, cereals, flour, pastas, rice, starches, dry condiments, seasonings, gelatin (plain and flavored), dried fruits, dried beans, peas, lentils, dehydrated vegetables and cracker meal, cocoa, instant coffee, ground coffee, tea, and instant fruit drinks can be stored safely in moisture-proof containers at room temperature (60°F) for approximately 6 mo to 1 yr. Potato chips and other snack items of this caliber may be stored at room temperature in moisture-proof packages that also retard the penetration of certain light waves. Flavoring extracts must also be stored in the dark. Shelled nuts in moisture proof packages may be kept for one yr in the frozen state and need not be thawed prior to use. When stored products are opened to remove portions, the packages must be thoroughly resealed before restoring.

Freezing, Thawing, and Cooking

The various methods of heating food are by means of convections and conduction (cooking and frying), direct contact with heat source (roasting), or radiation (grilling). These methods depend upon conduction of heat from the outside inward. Food is a poor conductor of heat.

The *specific heat* is the heat required to raise 1 gm of a substance 1°C. Air has a specific heat of about 0.25, steam 0.50, and water 1.0. At the same temperature, water will heat or cool 4 times as fast as air, and 2 times as fast as steam. Since air has a very low specific heat, a large amount of air must be passed over bunker coils in air-blast freezing. For example, at 2100 ft^3/min (cfm) and a temperature of $-20°F$, 5.2 hr are required for a 15-lb block of fish fillets having dimensions of $2\frac{1}{4} \times 13 \times 17$ in. to reach 0°F.

Human Comfort as Related to Relative Humidity

A relative humidity of 50% has a lethal effect on nearly all infectious bacteria and viruses. At this moisture level germs from sneezing and coughing settle to the floor and die. In dry air mucus and saliva cells dry up and may be suspended in the atmosphere for several weeks. Dust, pollen, and other allergens in the environment may affect sensitized nasal membranes during the fall and winter months.

As the human body gives off heat there is a cooling effect on the surface of the body due to moisture evaporation (an endothermic reaction). Research indicates that there is no direct relationship between temperature and relative humidity at temperatures between 73° and 77°F and relative humidities of 30 to 80%. Dry sunny days with temperatures in the 80's or even higher may permit a high rate of activity and still be comfortable. However, cloudy days that are cooler are often sticky due to the higher relative humidity. Then perspiration rates are slowed and discomfort sets in. Personal reactions vary greatly among individuals, and with physical condition. An index, known as the Temperature-Humidity Index, or "T-HI" has been developed as a numerical index to comfort. Nearly everyone is comfortable at a T-HI of 71.

Humidifiers may be installed to regulate humidity in cold weather. *Dehumidifiers containing* $(CaCl_2)$ *or air conditioners* will remove excess moisture from the building during the summer, spring, and fall months. Ideal conditions require a high level of relative humidity, about 50%, with a dry-bulb temperature of 73° to 77°F for best human performance. However, with modern construction methods this high level of moisture would lead to condensation problems during the heating season. Damage to paint, insulation, and sheathing would result. A compromise between the recommended 50% level and that relative humidity at which there is no excessive condensation on the interior window panes is advisable. Authorities agree on the following values:

Outdoor Temperature,°F	Indoor Relative Humidity, %
20	35
10	30
0	25
−10	20
−20	15

Human Health and Relative Humidity

During cold weather much of our time is spent in surroundings that are excessively heated, inadequately ventilated, and deficient in humidity. This hot, dry environment is a threat to health. Head colds and respiratory infections set-in when heat dries the membranes of the nose, throat, and bronchial tubes. A humidity of 40 to 50% is required, as one of the primary functions of the nose is to supply moisture to the inhaled air for a humidity of 85% when it reaches the lungs.

WATER IMPURITIES

The earth's water cycle illustrates how water becomes impure and is, in turn, purified by nature. Rain, nearly pure as it starts to fall, quickly gathers dust, smoke, living organisms, and gases. It even dissolves minerals transported by the winds. After only a short fall through the atmosphere, rain water thus picks up a number of suspended and dissolved impurities.

In comparison to atmospheric water, surface water in streams, rivers, and lakes may be exposed to its environment for weeks or months before it reaches the sea or evaporates. Thus, it has greater opportunity to pick up impurities. Water can take on color and many organic impurities as it flows through swampy areas, and may also acquire objectionable tastes and odors from decaying plants and animal life.

Water which flows over the earth's surface often becomes turbid, or cloudy, as it gathers solid impurities, such as silt, sand, mud, and clay that build up river deltas. Millions of tons of suspended solids may be carried each year by a single river. For example, the Mississippi River carries about 600 million tons of earth into the Gulf of Mexico each year. In nine months, this river carries as much soil as was dug from the Panama Canal in ten years. The Indians named a river "Missouri," meaning "big muddy," long before the white man appeared in North America. The Colorado River has been described as a little too thick to drink, and a little too thin to plow.

Groundwater is in contact with its environment even longer than surface water. By using tritium, a radioactive form of hydrogen as a tracer, scientists have been able to estimate the age of certain waters from deep wells. Based on the known concentration of tritium in rain, its known rate of decomposition, and measurements of the remaining concentration, the ages of deep-well water in several locations in Nebraska were calculated at 14 to 61 years, and in Illinois, at 50 to more than 100 years.

When surface water seeps into the ground, the earth acts as a fine sieve, removing living organisms and turbidity. Thus, well water is usually clear, but contains greater concentrations of dissolved minerals.

While water impurities vary widely in kind and amount, they may be classified generally as (a) living organisms, (b) suspended substances, (c) dissolved gases, (d) dissolved solids (Table 5.10).

Measuring Water Impurities

Very small amounts of impurities can cause water problems. The water chemist measures and expresses these small quantities by using the terms "grains per gallon" (gpg) and "parts per million" (ppm). The grain weight was originally derived from the average weight of a dry grain of wheat. One grain is 1/7,000 of a pound; 1 grain per gallon is 1/7,000 of a pound of an impurity in a gallon of water; 1 part per million is 1 milligram per liter, or 1/1,000 gm of impurity in 1,000 gm (about 1,000 cubic centimeters; exactly 1,000 milliliters; or 1 liter) of water. One grain per gallon equals 17.1 ppm (in Canada, 14.2 ppm).

To convert grains per U.S. gallon into parts per million, multiply by 17.1. To convert grains per Imperial gallon (Canada) into parts per million, multiply by 14.2. To convert parts per million into grains per U.S. gallon, multiply by 0.058. To convert parts per million into grains per Imperial gallon (Canada), multiply by 0.07.

Water impurities are usually reported as ions, or as ions expressed as the equivalent concentration of calcium carbonate. While these are small units of measure, the volume of water used in the home, as well as in commercial and industrial establishments, is large. Thus, even small amounts of impurities can cause severe problems.

Water Hardness

Caused chiefly by dissolved calcium and magnesium from the earth's crust, water hardness occurs in significant amounts in more than 85% of the United States and Canada.

Carbon dioxide, picked up from the air and from decaying vegetation, unites with water to form carbonic acid:

$$CO_2 + H_2O \rightarrow H_2CO_3$$

carbon dioxide   water   carbonic acid

This weak acid increases the ability of water to dissolve rock. Thus, common limestone (calcium carbonate and magnesium

TABLE 5.10

SUBSTANCES OCCURRING IN NATURAL WATERS

Origin	Suspended	Colloidal	Gases	Non-ionized Solids and Dipoles	Positive Ions	Negative Ions
Mineral soils and rocks	Clay, sand, inorganic soils	Clay SiO_2 Fe_2O_3 Al_2O_3 MnO_2	CO_2		Ca^{++} Fe^{++} Mg^{++} Mn^{++} Na^+ Zn^{++} K^+	HCO_3^{--} $HSiO_3^-$ Cl^- $H_2BO_3^-$ SO_4^{--} $HPO_4^=$ NO_3^- $H_2PO_4^-$ CO_3^{--} OH^- F^-
Atmosphere			N_2, O_2 CO_2, SO_2		H^+	HCO_3^- SO_4^{--}
Organic decomposition	Organic soil, organic wastes	Vegetable coloring matter, organic wastes	CO_2, H_2S NH_3, CH_4 O_2, H_2 N_2 Odori-vectors	Vegetable coloring matter, organic wastes	Na^+ NH_4^+ H^+	Cl^- NO_3^- HCO_3^- OH^- NO_2^- HS^- Organic radicals
Living organisms	Fish, algae, diatoms, minute animals	Viruses, bacteria, algae, and diatoms				

carbonate), since the primary salts are sparingly soluble in pure water, is the principal source of water hardness.

$$\underset{\text{carbonic acid}}{H_2CO_3} + \underset{\substack{\text{dolomitic}\\\text{limestone}}}{\begin{array}{c}(Ca)\\(Mg)\end{array}} \quad CO_3 \rightarrow \underset{\substack{\text{calcium and mag-}\\\text{nesium bicarbonates}}}{\begin{array}{c}(Ca)\\(Mg)\end{array}} (HCO_3)_2$$

Other sources of hardness are gypsum (calcium sulfate), epsomite or epsom salts (magnesium sulfate), and calcium and magnesium chloride.

Natural water supplies usually contain sufficient hardness to make them objectionable and inefficient to use. Hardness can range from less than 1 grain to several hundred grains per gallon, as calcium carbonate. Most water supplies are in the 3.0 to 30.0 grains per gallon range. The U.S. Geological Survey reports the average hardness of 1315 larger cities in the United States as 7.0 grains per gallon. Of course, these are principally surface water supplies (Fig. 5.3). Well-water supplies are normally higher in hardness than surface-water supplies, and most of the hardness enters rivers and lakes from underground water sources.

Hardness of surface water supplies can vary seasonally, depending on the amount of rainfall and, in northern climates, on freezing. Lack of rainfall and freezing shuts off surface water, causing hardness to increase. For example, the Mississippi River at Moline, Ill., doubles its hardness (from 8 to 16 grains per gallon) in winter. The hardness of large bodies of water, such as the Great Lakes, remains quite constant; Lake Michigan has a hardness of 7.5 grains per gallon, as compared to 4 grains per gallon for Lake Superior.

Snow has been found to contain over 1 grain per gallon of hardness, hail as much as 3 grains per gallon, and rain water as much as 3 grains per gallon, even after hours of continuous rain. Cistern water often contains 5 to 10 grains of hardness. By comparison, an ion-exchange water softener produces water that has less than 1 grain per gallon of hardness.

Hard Water Problems.—Water hardness would cause few problems if it remained dissolved and invisible, but it doesn't. When hard water is heated, a portion of the hardness turns back into insoluble limestone (scale). This scale deposits in hot water pipes, coffee urns, valves, and dishwasher jets as solid rock, where it chokes off water flow. It also accumulates in water heaters, where it acts as an insulator, decreasing heating efficiency and increasing fuel bills.

Calcium and magnesium bicarbonates partially decompose on heating to form a carbonate scale, as illustrated by the following equation:

$$Ca\,(HCO_3)_2 \quad + \quad \rightarrow \quad CaCO_3 \quad\quad CO_2 \quad + \quad H_2O$$

Calcium bicarbonate Heat   Calcium carbonate   Carbon   water
(soluble in water) applied   Limestone   dioxide
                            (insoluble in water)
                            "Lime" scale which
                            forms in water
                            heaters and boilers

Calcium sulfate increases in solubility with heating to about 104°F, but becomes less soluble upon further increase in temperature to boiling. Thus calcium sulfate can also precipitate at elevated temperatures to form a hard, adherent scale.

Sludge.—Loose deposits are commonly referred to as sludge. Whether scale is soft or hard, or whether the impurities are present as a sludge or as adherent scale, both are insulators and reduce heating efficiency.

Scale Removal.—The only available methods for rapid removal of hard water scale, once it has formed, are acid treatment or mechanical removal. However, periodic removal is costly. The best solution is to prevent the formation of scale by removing hardness from the water. Water softening not only eliminates the problem, but soft water also will gradually remove previously formed scale deposits, bringing water heaters back to their original efficiency and restoring most of the original carrying capacity of hot-water pipes.

Iron and Manganese

Iron occurs quite frequently in groundwater supplies. Manganese is more rarely found. Considering the low percentages of these substances present, however, they affect the usability of a water supply to a surprising degree and can be very troublesome.

As little as 0.3 of 1 part per million of iron in water (about) $2\frac{1}{2}$ lb per million gallons) has been known to cause staining of porcelain, but concentrations of up to 5.0 parts per million, or more, are not uncommon in well-water supplies.

Well water which contains iron is usually clear and color-less as it is drawn from the faucet, but when it is allowed to stand in a container, or is used for cooking, the invisible dissolved ferrous iron combines with oxygen from the air to form a reddish-brown precipitate (ferric hydroxide).

$$2Fe^{++} + 4HCO_3^- + H_2O + 1/2O_2 \rightarrow 2Fe(OH)_3 + 4CO_2$$

ferrous ion	bicar-bonate	water	oxygen	ferric hydroxide	carbon dioxide

Manganese oxidizes more slowly, but in a similar manner, forming a black precipitate.

$$2Mn^{++} + 4HCO_3^- + H_2O + 1/2O_2 \longrightarrow 2Mn(OH)_3 + 4CO_2$$

manga-nous ion	bicar-bonate	water	oxygen	manganic hydroxide (black rust)	carbon dioxide

These impurities impart a disagreeable metallic taste to water and can destroy the flavor and appearance of coffee, tea, and other beverages. Iron and manganese produce rusty or black stains on plumbing fixtures, dishes, and utensils. Iron and manganese deposits can build up in pressure tanks, water heaters, and pipes, breaking loose periodically to cause rusty water at the faucet.

In their soluble, ionized forms, small to moderate amounts of iron, manganese, and other metallic impurities are re-moved by a water softener. Larger amounts of iron and man-ganese can be removed by oxidation and filtration.

Hydrogen Sulfide Problems

Hydrogen sulfide is an offensive, gaseous impurity found in many well water supplies. Its "rotten egg" odor can be recognized at concentrations below 1 ppm. It corrodes iron pipe and produces "slugs" of black water. It forms black streaks on fabrics and porcelain. It readily tarnishes copper and silverware. The preferred method for removal is by oxidation and filtration.

Corrosion Problems

Corrosive water in groundwater supplies can usually be attributed to the presence of carbonic acid, though mineral acids may be present in some areas. The problem is usually characterized by rusty water and stains from iron pipe, and blue-green stains from copper pipe, along with premature failure of the pipes. Corrosion due to acid water may be corrected by neutralization.

Corrosion due to dissolved oxygen may occur in surface water supplies or ground water in arid regions. Corrosion may be accelerated by high mineralization, which increases the electrical conductivity of water. These problems can best be corrected by feeding film-forming materials, such as polyphosphates and silicates in the water system.

Turbidity

While not characteristic of well-water supplies, turbidity, or cloudiness in water, can be caused by rust particles or other suspended matter, or by dirt, silt, and sand in surface-water supplies. Such water is not palatable or acceptable. Turbidity can cause sedimentation and rumbling in water heaters and erosion of pipes and valves in water-using appliances. It is best corrected by filtration.

Color

A yellow to brown color due to dissolved organic substances, such as tannin and humic materials from vegetation, may be found in some surface water supplies, and less frequently in ground water. Such water is not palatable and can cause staining. Preferred methods of correction are adsorption on activated carbon, coagulation, filtration, and oxidation.

Taste and Odor

Iron can impart an objectionable metallic taste to well-water supplies and hydrogen sulfide a "rotten egg" odor. Highly mineralized water may also have a disagreeable taste. In surface-water supplies, taste and odor may occur as a result of decomposition of aquatic life, such as algae, man-made contaminants, and even chlorine. Preferred methods of treatment include adsorption on activated carbon, distillation or demineralization, oxidation, and filtration.

High Mineralization

Contrary to popular belief, the oceans are not the only areas where salty and highly mineralized water is found. Such water occurs in many inland localities. Water which contains large amounts of dissolved minerals, but is less salty than sea water, is termed brackish, or saline water.

CHARACTERISTICS OF MINERALIZED WATERS

Description of Water	Concentration of Dissolved Solids, ppm
Brackish	1,000–3,000
Saline	3,000–10,000
Sea water	10,000–36,000
Brine[1]	36,000+

[1] As found in the Dead Sea, Salt Lake, and brine wells.

The Drinking Water Standards of the U.S. Public Health Service recommend that water containing more than 250 ppm of chlorides or sulfates, or 500 ppm of dissolved solids, should not be used if other less mineralized supplies are available.

Many communities in saline or brackish water areas, as well as commercial establishments, are isolated and have no other source of supply. Heretofore, importation of water has been the only feasible solution. Today, several new methods of water treatment hold promise. These involve substantial removal of dissolved minerals from the water by newer demineralization techniques, by electrodialysis, and by reverse osmosis.

Iron and manganese present serious problems in the preparation of beverages, particularly coffee, tea, and whiskey, since the tannins in these beverages react with the metals in water producing a black coloration which destroys appearance and flavor. Complete removal of iron and manganese is therefore essential for virtually all beverage preparation.

Alkalinity in water reacts with and neutralizes carefully balanced acidic beverage flavors. It also prevents proper carbonation of fountain-prepared soft drinks, making them flat and lifeless. This is why most bottling plants treat their water to reduce the alkalinity to less than 50 ppm. Highly alkaline water also produces excessively dark coffee and tea, with a harsh taste which masks the true beverage flavor. Hard waters make cloudy and unappetizing tea. This effect is particularly noticeable when the tea is iced. The processes of reverse osmosis or partial demineralization are the most suitable for removing dissolved minerals and taste-and odor-producing substances in the water which can adversely affect the beverages.

Ice Making

All the esthetically offensive materials found in water, including iron, manganese, color, taste, odor, and turbidity, create obvious problems in ice served in beverages or with foods. Thus removal of these materials is a major requirement for good ice.

Not so obvious are problems caused by dissolved minerals in water. High concentration of minerals can reduce the production capacity of an ice machine, produce a brittle ice of poor quality, and can cause serious scale problems in the ice machine. Softening the water by ion exchange will usually improve the situation, but since it does not reduce the total mineral concentration, softening will not eliminate all these problems, and other equipment must be applied. The best approach is to reduce the concentration of minerals in the water with reverse osmosis or partial demineralization.

WATER-CONDITIONING METHODS

A number of water-conditioning methods are available to improve water quality in restaurants and institutions. These processes are basic, economical, and effective. Operation of equipment is usually automatic. In most cases, the water is treated for a specific purpose at or near the point of use, and the treatment applied is commensurate with the purpose for which the water is to be used, such as food and beverage preparation, dishwashing, or general cleaning.

Filtration is the most basic of water-treatment methods, and may be used to remove solid particles such as dirt, sand, precipitated iron and other suspended matter from water. The filtering media may be sand or similar granular material, which is backwashed for cleaning, or may be an essentially rigid element which is discarded after a single use. A number of replaceable cartridges of paper, cloth, or wound yard are used for this purpose.

Activated carbon is a special type of filter medium, and is applied where removal of chlorine, hydrogen sulfide, and taste and odor is desired. Granular activated carbon in large tanks is often used as both an adsorbent and a mechanical filter medium. Powdered, or very fine, activated carbon is also incorporated into many of the cartridge filters because of its adsorbent action.

The granular media filters are usually relatively large, and are normally installed to treat the total water supply where large volumes of water of high flow rates are required. Cartridge filters are smaller in size, and are commonly installed near the point of use for small water volumes or special use requirements.

Water for drinking, cooking, and beverage use may be treated by reverse osmosis to produce a high-quality water which is crystal-clear and very palatable.

Since many water impurities exist as ions, water-conditioning methods frequently employed involve ion exchange or deionization.

When sodium chloride (table salt) is dissolved in water, each molecule ionized produces two ions, a sodium ion with a single positive charge and a chloride ion with a single negative charge.

$$NaCl \longrightarrow Na^+ + Cl^-$$
sodium chloride molecule   sodium ion   chloride ion

Ions exist independently in solution and possess specific properties, which may differ greatly from those of their atoms or molecules. For example, metallic sodium reacts violently with water, producing hydrogen gas and caustic soda, but sodium ions exist calmly in solution. Chlorine gas is poisonous, but chloride ions are not. In fact, both sodium and chloride ions are essential to life.

Many water impurities exist as ions in solution. The most common of these are:

Cations		Anions	
Calcium	Ca^{++}	Bicarbonate	HCO_3^-
Magnesium	Mg^{++}	Chloride	Cl^-
Sodium	Na^+	Sulfate	SO_4^{--}
Iron	Fe^{++}	Nitrate	NO_3^-
Manganese	Mn^{++}	Carbonate	CO_3^{--}

These electrically charged dissolved particles make ordinary natural water a good conductor of electricity. Conversely, pure water has a high electrical resistance, and resistance is frequently used as a measure of its purity.

Ion Exchange.—The most widely applied process of ion separation in use today is ion exchange. This method is used in water softeners to remove the hardness ions, calcium, and magnesium. It is estimated that there are over $5\frac{1}{2}$ million water softeners in homes, and many hundreds of thousands more in commercial and industrial applications today.

Ion exchange may be defined as the interchange of ions in a solution with ions present in a solid, insoluble material. In practical application, it involves trading of more desirable ions for less desirable ions.

Cation Exchange.—In water softening, a cation exchange process, small beads of ion-exchange resin are contained in a tank, and are initially charged with replaceable sodium ions.

As the hard water passes down through the bed of resin particles, the calcium and magnesium ions come in intimate contact with the beads. Since the calcium and magnesium ions have a greater affinity for the ion-exchange resin than do the sodium ions, the hardness ions are held by the beads, and a chemically equivalent number of sodium ions are released into the water.

$$Ca^{++} \quad + \quad Na_2R \longrightarrow 2Na^+ \quad + \quad CaR$$
$$Mg^{++} \quad + \quad Na_2R \longrightarrow 2Na^+ \quad + \quad MgR$$

Hardness ions in water	Ion exchange resin in softener	Sodium ions in water	Exhausted resin in softener

Although only calcium and magnesium are shown in the above equations, iron, manganese, and other metallic ions can be removed in the same manner.

This process continues automatically until the supply of sodium ions in the exchange resin is almost depleted. When this occurs, increasing numbers of the hardness ions pass through the bed, unremoved, and the softener is termed exhausted. To restore the bed of ion-exchange resin to its original condition, a strong solution of common salt is passed through it. Because of the high concentration of sodium ions in the salt solution, the affinity of the hardness ions for the resin is overcome, and the calcium and magnesium ions are forced out of the resin and rinsed to waste. Sodium ions from the salt brine are held by the resin, and after rinsing, the resin is ready for another softening cycle.

Today's water softeners use automatic valves which perform the complete "regeneration" or "recharging" with little need for attention. Heretofore, the recharging of automatic water softeners has been initiated by a timer on a predetermined time sequence — a system which cannot follow variations in water use or water hardness. Some commercial and industrial water softeners were recharged on a gallonage basis, using a water meter, but even this costly and cumbersome system cannot accommodate itself to variations in water hardness.

One of the very recent developments is an electronic sensing device which initiates recharging just before the softener is exhausted and the water becomes hard. This device keeps pace with varying water demands and varying water hardness. When water usage, or hardness, increases, the softener recharges more frequently; when water usage is very low, for example on the day a restaurant is closed, the softener doesn't recharge. Thus the water softener recharges only as needed.

In the new electronically automated water softener, two pairs of electrodes are located near the bottom of the bed of ion-exchange resin. A form of Wheatstone bridge continuously measures the resistances between each pair of electrodes. As long as the ion-exchange resin is in the recharged state, the resistances are equal and the system is in balance. However, when the resin nears the limit of its capacity to produce soft water, the resistance changes between one pair of electrodes. This change is detected and a small electric signal is passed to a solid-state amplifier. The amplified current then activates the recharge controller, when and only when recharging is required.

Anion Exchange.—Ion-exchange resins which have the ability to exchange anions have been developed in recent years. One of the uses for these resins is the exchange of bicarbonates, sulfates, and even nitrates in water, for chlorides from the resins. This process may be used for reducing the alkalinity of water, for removing laxative sulfate concentrations and even nitrates from drinking water. Note, however, that substantially all the anions in the water would be converted to chlorides, which may impart a salty taste if the water is high in dissolved minerals. Further overexhausting the resin may result in a "throw" of high concentrations of some of the previously removed ions into the treated water. Thus nitrate removal with this process should be carried on only under careful supervision. Again, common salt is used as a source of chloride ions for regeneration in this process.

$$(AR) - Cl_x + \begin{matrix} (HCO_3^-) \\ (SO_4^{--}) \\ (NO_3^-) \\ (CO_3^{--}) \end{matrix} \longrightarrow (AR) - \begin{matrix} (HCO_3) \\ (SO_4) \\ (NO_3) \\ (CO_3) \end{matrix} + X\ Cl^-$$

Chloride form anion resin in tank	Anions in water		Exhausted anion resin in tank	Chloride ions in water

As with water softening, anion exchange in the chloride cycle does not reduce the concentration of minerals, but simply converts anions in the water to chlorides.

Demineralization

Dissolved ionized solids can be removed from water almost completely by a combination cation and anion exchange process. In fact, the process is superior to distillation for the removal of dissolved minerals.

Two types of ion-exchange resins are used in this "demineralization" or "deionization" process. The first is the same ion-exchange resin used in water softening, except that it is initially charged with hydrogen ions, rather than sodium.

As water passes through the bed of resin, the hydrogen ions are released into the water and the positively charged mineral ions (calcium, magnesium, sodium, iron, etc.) from the water are held by the resin. At this point the water is strongly acid, for it contains only the hydrogen ions and the various negatively charged ions.

$$(CR)-H_x + \begin{matrix} (Ca^{++}) \\ (Mg^{++}) \\ (Na^+) \\ (Fe^{++}) \end{matrix} + \begin{matrix} (HCO_3^-) \\ (Cl^-) \\ (SO_4^{--}) \\ (NO_3^-) \\ (CO_3^{--}) \end{matrix} \longrightarrow (CR) - \begin{matrix} (Ca) \\ (Mg) \\ (Na) \\ (Fe) \end{matrix} + X\,H^+ + \begin{matrix} (HCO_3^-) \\ (Cl^-) \\ (SO_4^{--}) \\ (NO_3^-) \\ (CO_3^{--}) \end{matrix}$$

Hydrogen form cation resin in tank	Cations in water	Anions in water	Exhausted cation resin in tank	Hydrogen ions in water	Anions in water

The water is then immediately passed through a bed of anion resin, which has been initially charged with hydroxyl (OH⁻) ions.

In a manner similar to the ion-exchange reactions described above, these hydroxyl ions are released into the water and negative ions, such as bicarbonates, chlorides, sulfates, and nitrates from the water, are held by the resin. Thus, dissolved minerals are removed from the raw water in exchange for hydrogen and hydroxyl ions which form additional pure water.

$$(AR)-(OH)_x + H_x^+ + \begin{pmatrix} (HCO_3^-) \\ (Cl^-) \\ (SO_4^{--}) \\ (NO_3^-) \\ (CO_3^{--}) \end{pmatrix} \longrightarrow (AR) - \begin{pmatrix} (HCO_3) \\ (Cl) \\ (SO_4) \\ (NO_3) \\ (CO_3) \end{pmatrix} + H_x^+ + (OH^-)_x$$

Hydroxide form anion resin in tank	Hydrogen ions in water	Anions in water	Exhausted anion resin in tank	Hydrogen & Hydroxide ions in water

$$= HOH \text{ or } H_2O$$
Pure water

As in water softening, the two resins used in the process ulti- mately become exhausted, and are then regenerated. A solution of strong acid, such as sulfuric or hydrochloric, is used to re- generate the cation resin, and a solution of strong alkali (caus- tic soda, sodium hydroxide) is used to regenerate the anion resin. Strong solutions of these regenerants overcome the affinity of the ions removed from the water and the resins are recharged with their original hydrogen and hydroxyl ions. The waste products are then rinsed from the beds for disposal.

Two beds of the ion-exchange resin may not completely remove dissolved minerals, because of opposing reactions. Therefore, a second pair of action and anion exchange resin beds is frequently used to produce a higher-quality water.

The ultimate in water quality can be produced by mixing the beds of cation and anion resins in a single tank, producing the equivalent of an almost infinite number of pairs of beds in series. This mixed-bed demineralization process routinely produces water of amazing chemical purity, far superior to even multiple distillations under the best of conditions. The resins in the mixed beds are separated for regeneration by their differences in density.

Demineralization is relatively expensive, as compared to simple softening, because of the cost of the acids and caustic used for regeneration, the need for acid- and alkali-resistant materials of construction, and the cost of the neutralization of regeneration wastes for disposal. The method is most advan- tageous for waters of low to moderate mineral concentrations

since regeneration costs increase with higher mineral concentrations. Yet its simplicity in the production of high-quality
water has many advantages. Demineralization units can be
operated intermittently, and under varied flow requirements,
with no need for water storage and are frequently used in
laboratories and commercial and industrial establishments.

Distillation

Distillation is one of the oldest methods known of separating
fresh water from a solution of minerals, ions, organic matter,
and other soluble and suspended materials. In the simplest
form of distillation, water is boiled to convert it into steam,
and the steam is then cooled to condense it into fresh water.
The minerals and other foreign materials are left behind in
the process. Thus distillation involves adding heat to vaporize
the water, and then removing heat from the vapor to condense
it into fresh water.

While it takes 1 Btu to raise the temperature of 1 lb of water
1°F, it takes approximately 980 Btu to convert that same pound
of water to steam, even after the water has been heated to
boiling temperature. Thus, if the steps of heat addition and
cooling are accomplished independently, distillation is a very
costly and inefficient process. Therefore, a number of designs
have been developed to recover much of the heat released by
the condensing steam. Modern systems are limited, not so
much by the development of heat-recovery systems, but by
problems with scale formation and corrosion. In any case,
such complex systems are extremely costly and must be operated under close technical control. They are suited to only
large installations such as government-operated desalination
plants, or to huge industrial or power generation plants. They
are not practical for use in small installations.

Small simple stills are sometimes used in laboratories where
convenience outweighs economy and operating efficiency. Also
small household counter-top stills are available to provide
drinking water in areas where only poor quality water is available. Distilled water, however, is not necessarily "pure" or
even of very high quality. Commercial bottled distilled water
commonly contains 10 to 20 ppm of minerals due to carry-over
with the steam, and poorly operated stills can produce very poor
water indeed. Where high-quality water must be produced by

distillation, repeated distillation of the same water in special apparatus is necessary.

Two new processes show considerable promise for reducing the mineral concentrations of sea, saline, and brackish water to levels suitable for commercial, industrial, and household applications. These processes are electrodialysis and reverse osmosis.

Electrodialysis

In the electrodialysis process, the water to be treated is passed between pairs of semipermeable membranes, which are similar in their composition to the ion exchange used in de-mineralization. Each of the membranes will allow only one type of ion, either cations or anions, to pass through. To move ions through these membranes, a direct current is applied to the water from electrodes in compartments outside the membranes. Positive ions are attracted to the negative electrode, and pass through the cation-permeable membrane into the concentrated stream compartment. These streams of high mineral concentration are directed to waste, and the purified stream from the center compartment is directed to storage for use. In simple three-compartment cells such as directed above, the efficiency is relatively poor, because of the quantities of water wasted, and current-consuming reactions at the electrodes. To improve this efficiency, multiple units are used containing parallel cells with alternating membranes, but still only two electrodes.

The electrodialysis process works best if operated continuously; thus storage must be available for intermittent demands. Prefiltration of the water is frequently desirable because of possible fouling of the membranes with organic matter or certain inorganic precipitates.

As minerals are removed, power requirements increase, because of an increase in the electrical resistance of the water. Multiple units in series are required to produce the purest water, but the water will not be as good as that produced by demineralization. However, the cost can be much less, and the unit does not require regeneration.

Osmosis

Osmosis (Fig. 5.4) is the familiar process whereby trees and other plants acquire water and nutrients from the ground, and

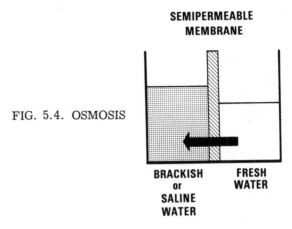

FIG. 5.4. OSMOSIS

lift these solutions throughout their structures. When two aqueous solutions of different concentrations are separated by a semipermeable membrane, such as a root hair, water passes through the membrane from the less concentrated to the more concentrated solution. The osmotic pressure developed by this solvent movement can raise the more concentrated solution a considerable distance.

Reverse osmosis (Fig. 5.5), is the opposite of the action just described. In water technology, pressure is applied to the more concentrated fluid (saline or brackish water) to force water through the special membrane. The membrane is permeable to the water but less permeable to water impurities. This process results in a separation of water from its impurities, both soluble and suspended.

Reverse osmosis holds great promise as an effective and economical process for large-scale treatment of water contain excessive amounts of dissolved minerals. Today, reverse osmosis can furnish high-quality water at a reasonable cost.

Reverse osmosis membranes remove living organisms, such as bacteria and viruses. They also remove colloidal and other nondissolved solid materials, and reject practically all the dissolved minerals in water. With sufficient pressure, only pure water passes through the membrane by a process of diffusing into and through its structure. Therefore, reverse osmosis really involves only three things: water to be treated, the reverse osmosis membrane, and water pressure.

Reverse osmosis is a versatile process. It removes suspended solids as well as ionized and un-ionized dissolved

SEMIPERMEABLE
MEMBRANE

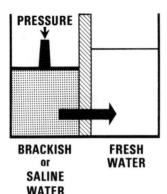

FIG. 5.5. REVERSE OSMOSIS

BRACKISH   FRESH
or   WATER
SALINE
WATER

solids. Thus it removes minerals, synthetic detergents, and other organic contaminants, taste- and color-producing sub-stances, and odor. It even has potential application in the re-moval of bacteria and viruses.

As with electrodialysis, prefiltration is sometimes necessary to reduce fouling of the membrane. Since it is a continuous process, storage capacity is necessary for treated water. However, the only energy required is that for the production of pressure, and this unit operates on available water pressure.

Analytical reports of water samples taken before and after household reverse osmosis units, at actual installations, dem-onstrate the effectiveness of this device. On a brackish water, such as that of Fort Morgan, Colorado, the unit reduced the total dissolved solids from 1420 to 84 mg per liter. On a similar water in Lumberton, New Mexico, the reduction was from 1150 to 71 mg per liter. A report from an installation in Tawas City, Michigan, shows a large reduction from 1440 to 228 mg per liter.

Even better water quality is produced by reverse osmosis when used on water supplies of lower total dissolved solids content. For example, Kansas City, Missouri, water is reduced from 635 to 38 mg per liter, and Las Vegas, Nevada, water is reduced from 336 to 23 mg per liter. This latter product water is in the same range as many commercial distilled waters. Even better quality water is produced by reverse osmosis if higher operating pressure is available.

The potential for reverse osmosis is enormous, since it is basically a simple process, with no moving parts, no regeneration, and requires a minimum of energy. Related possibilities are for selective membranes, which would permit the passage of specific ions, while preventing the passage of others. However, even in the present state of development, reverse osmosis makes brackish or saline water fresh for people or animals, and improves normal water to virtually demineralized water quality.

A number of ion separation processes and equipment have been considered. Each has its own particular features and range of applications. Ion exchange water softening removes all but traces of calcium, magnesium, and other heavy-metal ions in exchange for sodium, but does not reduce total mineral concentration. Yet it is an economical method of water treatment for the elimination of hard water scale, and it increases the effectiveness of virtually every washing and cleaning process, improves sanitation, and provides a substantial reduction in the quantities of cleaning materials required.

Small-scale distillation is relatively costly and inconvenient, but it can be used to reduce the mineral concentrations of small quantities of water where other methods may not be available or practical.

Electrodialysis is used to reduce the mineral concentrations of sea, saline, and brackish waters for general use, at costs between that of simple softening and complete mineral removal. Generally, the process is applied in fairly large installations where an effluent quality of 500 ppm or above is acceptable, because of increased power requirements as mineral concentrations in the water are reduced.

Because of its inherent simplicity and lower power requirements, reverse osmosis, the most recent development, is finding application in the treatment of normal, saline, and brackish water supplies. While the quality of water from a single unit varies with the quality of the water treated, and the pressure applied, reverse osmosis can produce water containing only a few parts per million of dissolved minerals.

All these methods are adaptations and extensions of processes which occur in nature. Ion exchange occurs in soils, which hold nutrients against the leaching effects of rainfall, but then release them to support plant life. Distillation occurs in nature as the evaporation and condensation steps of the water cycle. Electrodialysis is based on a reversal of natural galvanic cells developed between dissimilar metals, combined with a form of ion exchange. Reverse osmosis clearly parallels natural cell membrane functions.

Thus many natural processes involving ions have been duplicated and adapted and this knowledge used in the treatment of water for the benefit of man. Although costs vary over a considerable range, the apparatus and knowledge to produce water of virtually any quality which might be required is at hand.

PHOSPHATES

One of the elements singled out in the anti-pollution program is phosphorus. In its oxidized form it is a member of a large group of "phosphate" compounds. Phosphorus in one form 'or another is necessary for both vegetable and animal growth. It is an ingredient of all complete fertilizers, whether animal or mineral. It is present in all living creatures as a part of the skeletal structure; in a 70-kg man there is about 700 gm of phosphorus, 80% in teeth and bones, 35 to 45 mg in each 100 ml of blood where it is concentrated in the red blood cells; the remainder is in the tissue, particularly the nervous tissue. Part of the buffer system of the blood and urine is due to the presence of $H_2PO_4^-$ and $HPO_4^=$ ions. In one or more of the following forms it has been and is used in detergents as sodium triphosphate, Na_3PO_4, as sodium polyphosphate, $Na_5P_3O_{10}$, and as tetrasodium pyrophosphate, $Na_4P_2O_7$.

Phosphates and polyphosphates are also used in food processing because of their effects on the various properties of food products. They may be added to aid in controlling the acidic and buffering properties necessary. The acid ingredient in baking powders may be one or more of the following: $CaHPO_4$, $Ca(H_2PO_4)_2$, $NaAl_3H_{14}(PO_4)_8 \cdot 4H_2O$ and $Na_2H_2P_2O_7$. As buffers in food products NaH_2PO_4 and its mono and dihydrate, $Ca(H_2PO_4)_2$ and $Na_2H_2P_2O_7$, are used; orthophosphoric acid itself is an acidifying agent in various food products such as cola drinks.

The polyphosphates, including sodium hexametaphosphate $[Na_6(PO_3)_6]$, are employed as sequestering agents to remove metal ions such as calcium or ferrous ions. These polyphosphates also form insoluble salts with multiple-charged metal ions; they can be used as precipitating agents such as Mg-$(NH_4)PO_4 \cdot 6H_2O$ struvite crystals found in canned tuna, which are often mistaken for broken glass by consumers.

Polyphosphates have the ability to be adsorbed on the surface of colloidal particles, usually increasing the negative charge. As a result these particles may be held in dispersion or deflocculated in an aqueous medium. Polyphosphates also are able to interact as anions with the cationic functions of large molecules such as proteins, etc.

All of the above properties interreact in various foodstuffs to produce an acceptable end product. Table 5.11 shows many food applications of the phosphates. At the present time the use of phosphates is replacing the use of nitrates and nitrites in the curing of meats.

The excess phosphates present in water are to be curtailed by reducing and in most cases, eliminating those compounds present in all detergents. Perhaps it should be inserted here that it is through proper treatment and control of sewage wastes and water that recycled water will be fit for human consumption.

WATER FOR RESTAURANTS AND INSTITUTIONS[1]

Bacteriological Quality

The primary requirement for water used in restaurants and institutions for drinking, the preparation of food, and even for dishwashing and many cleaning operations, is its bacteriological safety. Such water must be free of pathogens—organisms capable of causing disease. In the United States, statistical evidence of freedom from coliform organisms (organisms which are normally present in human and animal wastes) is accepted as an indication of freedom from pathogens.

Municipal water supplies are normally free of both pathogens and coliform organisms, either naturally, or as a result of treatment, and such water may be used without concern. Private water supplies, however, should be checked periodically to assure sanitary quality. Chlorination and other disinfection processes are often used as an added safety factor, but should not be depended upon to make a water from a questionable or polluted source safe for drinking and other purposes.

[1]George Klumb, Culligan, Inc. prepared this chapter section

TABLE 5.11

MAJOR APPLICATIONS OF THE PHOSPHATES IN FOODS[1]

Industry and Products	Phosphate[2] Employed	Prime Function of Phosphate
Baking Industry		
Phosphated flour	MCP	Solid acid (1)[3]
Self-rising flours	SALP, AMCP, SAPP	Solid acid (1)
Baking powders	MCP, SAPP	Solid acid (1)
Dough conditioners	MCP, DCP, TCP	pH control (1) and bacteriocide (5)
Flour enrichment	DCP, TCP, DSP, IP	Nutrient (6)
Prepared mixes	SALP, SAPP, AMCP, MCP, DCP, IP	Solid acid (1)
Cake doughnuts	SAPP, AMCP, SALP	Solid acid (1)
Angel-food cake mixes and me-ringue mixes	Glasses, AMCP, MCP SAPP	Protein reaction (5) and pH control (1)
Refrigerated and frozen biscuits	SAPP, SALP	Solid acid (1)
Cereal Products		
Macaroni products	DSP, IP	pH control (1) and nutrient (6)
Cooked cereals	DSP, IP	pH control (1) and nutrient (6)
Instant puddings	TSPP, DSP	Dispersion (4) and protein reaction (5)
Modified starches	MSP, DSP, POCl$_3$, STP	Phosphate esterifi-cation (1)
Dairy Industry		
Process cheeses	MSP, PA, DSP, TSP, SALP, and TSPP, STP, Glasses	Protein reaction (5) dispersion (4) and complexing (2)
Evaporated milk	DSP	Protein reaction (5) and dispersion (4)
Malted-milk powders	TSPP	Dispersion (4)
Synthetic whipped creams	Glasses, TSPP	Protein reaction (5)
Ice cream and ice milks	TSPP	Protein reaction (5) and dispersion (4)
Buttermilk	STP	Dispersion (4)
Meat Products		
Cured hams	STP, DSP, TSPP	Dispersion (4), pH control (1) and pro-tein reaction (5)

Table 5.11 (*continued*)

Industry and Products	Phosphate[2] Employed	Prime Function of Phosphate
Sausage meats	Glasses, TSPP, KK, etc.	Protein reaction (5)
Frankfurters	Glasses, TSPP, KK, etc.	Protein reaction (5) and dispersion (4)
Soft-drink Industry		
Carbonated beverages	PA	pH control (1)
Beverage dry base	MCP	Solid acid (1)
Fruit and Vegetable Processing		
Potatoes	SAPP	Complexing (2)
Legumes	Glasses, STP	Complexing (2)
Jams and jellies	STP, glasses, PA	Complexing (2)
Fats and Oil Industry		
Vegetable shortenings	PA	pH control (1) and complexing (2)
Lard	TCP, TSP	Adsorption (4) and pH control (1)
Salad dressing	PA	pH control (4)
Fermentation Industry		
Yeasts and other fermentation products	PA, MAP, DAP, MKP	Nutrient (6)
Wines	Glasses	Complexing (2)

[1] Symposium: Phosphates in Food Processing, 1970. J. M. DeMann and P. Melnychyn. p. 16.

[2] MCP = monocalcium phosphate monohydrate; DAP = diammonium phosphate; DCP = dicalcium phosphate; DSP = disodium phosphate; Glasses = vitreous sodium phosphates including the "tetraphosphate," the so-called "hexametaphosphate," and Calgon®; IP = iron phosphates; MAP = monoammonium phosphate; AMCP = anhydrous coated monocalcium phosphate; MKP = monopotassium phosphate; SAPP = sodium acid pyrophosphate, $Na_2H_2P_2O_7$; STP = sodium tripolyphosphate; TCP = precipitated hydroxylapatite, the so-called "tricalcium phosphate"; TSP = trisodium phosphate; TSPP = tetrasodium pyrophosphate; PA = orthophosphoric acid; SALP = sodium aluminum phosphate; KK = cross-linked Kurrol's salt, $(KPO_3)_n$; MSP = monosodium phosphate.

[3] The number in parentheses refers to the respective phosphate property listed in the text.

Washing and Cleaning Problems

The demand for higher standards of health and cleanliness increases more and more the awareness of the problems that hard water causes in washing and cleaning. The efficiency and effectiveness of soaps, detergents, and washing compounds are greatly reduced when they must overcome water hardness.

It takes many times as much soap to produce skimpy suds in hard water as it does to produce luxurious suds in soft water. Soap combines with calcium and magnesium in hard water to form a gummy, insoluble precipitate called soap scum, or soap curd. Thus water hardness consumes soap. Conversely, soap softens water by precipitating hardness, but water softening with soap is expensive, and the gummy product of such softening remains in the wash water to cause further trouble.

Iron, manganese, and color present major washing and cleaning problems because of the severe stains caused by these materials. Once formed, iron and manganese stains are set by the common bleaches, alkaline cleansers, and washing compounds, and often can be removed only by treatment with acids. The use of abrasive cleansers on light surfaces may remove some stains, but it also roughens the surfaces and makes later stains even more difficult to remove. Stains due to organic materials may sometimes be removed with hypochlorite bleaches, provided the stained surface are not adversely affected.

Dishwashing Problems

Problems in mechanical dishwashing appear as inadequate removal of food soil, spotting, streaking, and heavy white deposits, fading of pattern, etching, and rust stains. Deposits formed in dishwashing are of real concern. From an aesthetic standpoint they can hold food particles and dirt. From a sanitary standpoint, they can hold and protect bacteria.

Inadequate Soil Removal.—This problem is usually caused by inadequate washing and rinsing, due to the use of too little dishwashing compound or improper stacking of dishes, which prevents uniform washing and rinsing. It is important that wash and rinse water reach each dish. Blocking of water flow pattern will give poor results.

Spotting and Streaking.—Many commercial TV skits illustrate this problem which can appear in a variety of forms, from cloudy spots or film to heavy white encrustations. These are normally caused by water hardness. They may also result from the use of excessive amounts of dishwashing compound and inadequate rinsing.

The necessity for removing adherent food substances containing protein and fat requires powerful hydraulic action, which limits the choice of a cleansing agent in mechanical dishwashers. The best method for removing food greases and fats in dishwashing is by emulsification, which is the process by which soap cleans. Therefore, it would be expected that soap would be the best choice as a cleansing agent for machine dishwashing. Unfortunately, because of their ability to form suds, neither soaps nor sudsing synthetic detergents can be used as cleansing agents in dishwashers. Foaming or sudsing seriously interferes with water action. Even though their ability to emulsify greasy and fatty soil is poorer than that of soaps or synthetic detergents, alkali compounds, which are similar to soap and synthetic detergent builders, must be used almost exclusively in dishwashing compounds because they do not produce suds. It is essential, of course, to maintain sufficient alkalinity in the washing solution to remove greasy food deposits.

Sodium carbonate, trisodium phosphate, sodium metasilicate, and other silicates make up the largest portion of household dishwashing compounds. Other ingredients may be small amounts of non-sudsing synthetic detergents or wetting agents, emulsifiers, such as carboxy methyl cellulose or similar compounds, and chelating or sequestering agents, such as the tetrasodium salt of ethylenediaminetetraacetic acid (EDTA, Versene) or sodium hexametaphosphate (Calgon), which are non-precipitating water softeners. The chelating or sequestering agents are added to counteract water hardness, but excessive amounts can be corrosive. Due to potential corrosion problems, economic considerations, and wide variation in water hardness, not enough of these agents are normally added to soften water completely. When softened water is used for dishwashing, the quantities of chelating or sequestering agents can be reduced to a minimum in the dishwashing compound. With softened water, the chelating or sequestering agents counteract the calcium in food soil, such as milk. They also serve as an aid to detergency by helping in the emulsification and saponification of greases and in the solubilizing of proteins. Silicates have a good dispersing action on food deposits and a protective action on glassware and on metals such as aluminum.

Disinfectants, such as chlorine or quaternary ammonium compounds, are added to commercial dishwashing compounds. Chlorine compounds also help remove coffee staining, but they have the disadvantage of odor and harshness on plasticware and on overglaze patterns when used in household dishwashing compounds. The perborates are used to remove stains from plasticwares. In commercial dishwashing, health departments frequently require a very hot water or steam rinse or a disinfectant dip.

Softened water has several advantages in mechanical dishwashing.

(1) Softened water eliminates limestone scale, formed by precipitation from calcium bicarbonate in hard water by heat. Hard water scale can form on dishwashing equipment and on the articles being washed.

(2) Softened water eliminates deposits or scum formed by the reaction of alkalies in dishwashing compounds with water hardness. Sodium carbonate, trisodium phosphate, and sodium silicate react with calcium and magnesium bicarbonate, sulfate, and chloride in hard water to form insoluble precipitates of calcium and magnesium carbonate (limestone), tricalcium phosphate, and calcium silicate.

(3) While soap is not employed directly in mechanical dishwashing, small amounts of it can be formed indirectly when alkali substances in the dishwashing compounds react with fats from food. Soap formed in this manner then combines with water hardness to form soap curd, which prevents proper cleaning.

Cooking Problems

If vegetables that contain protein and carbohydrates, such as beans and peas, are cooked in water containing calcium and magnesium compounds (hardness), these elements are chelated by the protein and pectins, and the vegetables become tough, and rubbery. This effect will also be produced when vegetables of this type are canned in hard water. The reaction which takes place indicates that peas and beans are, in a sense, "water softeners." During the process of softening the water, these vegetables take up hardness. Generally, the degree of hardening has been found to be directly proportional to the amount of calcium and magnesium present in the water. Calcium compounds have a greater hardening effect than magnesium compounds. This is important because calcium compounds are usually present in hard water in greater quantity than are magnesium compounds.

Softened water should be used for canning vegetables of this type. In addition, it is important that any salt brine which is used in the canning process be made from a salt which contains as little calcium and magnesium as possible, as calcium and magnesium from the salt also contribute to the hardening effect.

The use of hard water in canning beets results in a white coating on the surface of the beets. This makes them less attractive and reduces their commercial value, and is due to the fact that beets contain a soluble oxalate (sodium oxalate) which is changed to insoluble calcium and magnesium oxalate. The beets canned in hard water are very firm.

The following vegetables should be cooked or canned in soft water for best results: Navy beans, California pink beans, Jap pinto beans, soy beans, red kidney beans, ripe lima beans, California black eye beans, beets, and peas.

Excessive hardness can retard the fermentation of yeasts used in bread, although according to one report, too little calcium softens the gluten to produce a soggy bread. However, for cake and some cracker baking, completely softened water appears to give the best results.

Highly mineralized waters can produce a variety of problems, due to adverse tastes as well as undesirable reactions with the foods. Many of the sugars used in candy making can be decomposed by even the weak alkalies found in some waters, producing discoloration, a change in flavor, a bitter taste, and a strong, pungent, acrid aftertaste as decomposition becomes greater. Completely or partially demineralized water should be used to avoid such problems.

Iron, manganese, and color in water can produce unappetizing discolorations in almost any food preparation or processing.

CHAPTER 6

D. E. Anderson | # Chemical Specialties in Institutional Sanitation

All businesses are concerned with maintenance of environment, not only as a matter of pride, but of economic advantage the manufacturer gets better production from employees under attractive working conditions, the hospital cures better under aseptic conditions, and all organizations which serve the public are constantly being judged on appearance and cleanliness.

Chemical specialties, which may be described as custom combinations of chemical compounds, are specifically designed to accomplish numerous tasks in the easiest way, to help maintain clean, attractive surroundings.

The development, production, and sales of such chemical specialties has become a large industry which is highly technical. It is an industry characterized by a great deal of customer service, since best results are obtained when these highly specialized products are used correctly.

DETERGENTS

Detergents are the most widely used chemical specialties, and those which would be most quickly recognized as such. If soil is defined as "matter in the wrong place," then detergents may be defined as agents which can remove matter from the wrong place.

Although it is not often regarded as a detergent, water can be considered the most common "chemical" used for cleaning. The simple acts of rinsing one's hands or a soiled dish under a faucet are detergent processes. Although other solvents are sometimes used in detergent systems, such as those used in dry cleaning and spot removal, water is by far the most common cleaning agent.

Man has known for many centuries that water could be improved upon when it was being used for cleaning. Soap as well as niter is mentioned in Old Testament history for washing (Jer. 11:22).

Until the twentieth century the additives used in aqueous systems were relatively unsophisticated: soap, alkalies (soda ash), modified carbonates (sal soda), and finely divided clays and abrasive materials (bentonite and pumice).

Although these materials certainly improved the performance of water for cleaning, natural waters carry impurities and properties which have undesirable side effects. Calcium and magnesium salts dissolved in water (commonly known as water hardness) react with soap to form gummy precipitates, leaving difficult-to-remove deposits on hard surfaces. Iron and manganese ions in water caused discoloration on objects to be cleaned.

The rapidly expanding chemical industry has provided innumerable new agents for the improvement of aqueous detergent systems.

Mechanisms of Detergency

Studies in detergency have greatly expanded knowledge of the mechanisms whereby these agents accomplish their task. Rather simply stated, it is necessary that a detergent:

(1) *Separate the soil from the surface.* Most systems employ agents that reduce surface tension of water to aid in penetration.

(2) *Disperse the soil.* In general the soil must become separated into small enough particles to be lifted into the detergent system.

(3) *Suspend the soil.* Once dispersed, the small particles must not be allowed to rejoin, or agglomerate, which would cause them to tend to fall back on the surface to be cleaned prior to being flushed or rinsed away.

Other factors besides the chemicals used affect the detergent system:

(1) Time: The length of exposure of a soil to the detergent solution is, of course, a factor in the end result.

(2) Temperature: In general, the mechanisms which cause detergency are more effective at higher temperatures. As detergent systems are improved, of course, satisfactory results are made possible at somewhat lower temperatures, with reductions in heating costs. However, today's detergents require quite high temperatures for removal of most heavy soils.

(3) Concentration: There is usually an economic optimum concentration for each detergent. Under-use of a detergent can be a complete waste of money, as the desired result may not

be attained. On the other hand, over-use, besides being un-necessary expense, may cause damage to the surface or material being cleaned, or require extra effort in subsequent operations such as rinsing.

(4) Physical Action: Most cleaning operations today are assisted by mechanical action, such as brushes, sprays, or circulation systems. Proper maintenance of the mechanisms, and operation that assures proper action are very important.

Detergent Raw Materials

The raw materials available to the manufacturer of specialty detergents are now almost limitless. A review of some of the more commonly used will illustrate how they can be combined to the benefit of the user. It is beyond the intent of this text to try to be all-inclusive, and indeed new chemicals are being added so rapidly to the list of those useful in these systems that even the expert is hard-pressed to stay current in this field.

Alkaline Materials.—Most of the powdered or granular products contain one or more of the raw materials discussed here.

Caustic soda, or sodium hydroxide, commonly known as lye, is used in very heavy-duty cleaners. It will react with fatty and protein soils. It is used in drain cleaners, oven cleaners, laundering alkalies, and sometimes in heavy-duty cement floor cleaners. It forms very highly alkaline solutions in water, is corrosive to the skin and eyes, and is most safely used in closed cleaning systems.

Sodium carbonates, anhydrous or hydrated, provide alkalinity in detergent systems without the degree of hazard of the hy-droxide. For many years the dairy industry used modified sodium carbonates for cleaning, to avoid using soap which might cause off-flavors in the milk.

A whole family of phosphates is employed in the detergent industry. The first to be commonly used was trisodium ortho-phosphate. Like most of the earlier cleaning alkalies, when added to hard water, it precipitated the hardness, leaving softened water in which the excess phosphate salt was dissolved; this provided not only alkalinity but rather effective dispersing properties. Other phosphates will be discussed under water-conditioning ingredients.

Similarly, a large family of silicate salts is used in detergents. These are formed of combinations of alkalies of sodium or potassium with silicon dioxide, and can be found commercially in a great number of ratios, providing low to high alkalinity and varying properties. They are good soil "suspenders."

Surface-tension Depressants.—To obtain penetration and lifting of soil, chemicals are used to reduce the surface tension of water. These are often referred to as wetting agents. Soap was the original wetting agent; but since the 1930's, synthetic detergents have grown in popularity until today in the United States they are more widely used than soap.

Soaps should not be discounted, however, as there is still a wide variety in use. They are formed by the reaction between an alkaline material and natural fatty acids, either animal or vegetable. Soaps made from sodium hydroxide are usually "hard," and are typified by bar or chip soaps. Soaps made from potassium hydroxide are "soft," and are found in many liquid preparations such as shampoos.

Hard soaps, or "tallow soaps," are made from animal fats, they have higher melting points and are slow to dissolve, but have good soil-removing properties. Soft soaps, such as those made from coconut oil and potassium hydroxide, dissolve easily at lower temperatures and are useful where temperature limitations are encountered, but are be quite as good detergents as hard soaps.

All surface-tension depressants cause water to foam or "suds." Soap also reacts with the calcium and magnesium salts in natural water to form insoluble precipitates which do not aid in the reduction of surface tension. Therefore, in hard waters part of the soap used in the water is ineffective, and only when an excess has been achieved does sudsing occur and the process of detergency begin. Traditionally, the effectiveness of a washing solution has been judged by the visible suds, and copious suds were always considered essential. When soap alone was used, this was indeed true, and if the solution went "flat," a gray wash was sure to result. This same effect can be noticed in using bar soap in hard water when washing the hands. A considerable amount of soap has to be dissolved from the bar onto the hands before a lather is developed that is effective in removing soil.

Synthetic detergents (Syndets) with properties similar to soap in wetting and loosening soil, have the added advantage of not forming precipitates with the dissolved calcium and magnesium in natural waters.

Although sulfated and sulfonated organic synthetic detergents were known as long ago as 1900, commercial practicability did not occur until the late 1930's and early 1940's because of the shortage of soap during World War II, and because competitively priced sodium alkyl aryl sulfonate became available.

Synthetic detergents are classified by industry as anionic, nonionic, and cationic. An anionic synthetic detergent is one which in solution has an active anion (carrying a negative charge). Soap is anionic, as is the sodium alkyl aryl sulfonate mentioned above. In this class is found a whole series of organic sulfates and sulfonates, each with its particular properties which may make it the preferred choice for a particular task.

In detergent applications, the nonionics are growing rapidly. These do not ionize in aqueous systems. The most commonly used nonionic detergents are condensation products of ethylene oxide with fatty acids, alkyl phenols, polypropylene glycols, and alcohols. It has been found that these types of detergents can be tailor-made for different detergent systems by varying the molecular structure of the hydrophilic (water-loving) and the lipophilic (oil-loving) ends of the compound. Some of these nonionic detergents are lower-foaming than the anionics, and are used to control foam where this is desirable in an aqueous system. A good example is in machine dishwashing, where lowering of surface tension is desirable, but where sprays and agitation would create undesirable amounts of foam.

Cationic detergents are those which in water solution provide cations (ions with a positive charge), which are hydrophilic. For the most part these are not very effective detergents, but uses are found in fabric softeners, and the alkyl benzyl ammonium chlorides are useful because of their bactericidal properties. They are employed in a number of detergent germicides used in maintenance cleaning, and have been used in dishwashing sanitizing operations.

A word about biodegradability is in order. This terms refers to the decomposition of a material by natural biochemical and environmental influences. Soap, as it passes into sewage disposal systems or into natural streams, is rapidly decomposed or degraded. Synthetic detergents require varying times to degraded and become inactive. During the early 1960's, in the interest of pollution control, the detergent industry voluntarily changed its production of alkyl benzene sulfonates to the straight-chain alkyl type, referred to as linear alkylate sulfonate, or LAS, which greatly increased its biodegradability. All types of detergents now in use are carefully classified and controlled for biodegradability.

Acid Cleaning Agents.—Some soils are more susceptible to removal by acids than by alkalies. For example, removal of hard water scale, rust, and cement stains is best accomplished with acids. Bowl cleaners in liquid form contain hydrochloric acid or phosphoric acid, and sodium acid sulfate in powdered form. Acid fluoride salts are used in laundering for rust stain removal from fabrics as well as for proper pH control on finished fabrics (souring). Citric, gluconic, sulfamic, and other acids are used for scale removal.

Sequestrants or Chelating Agents.—These terms apply to chemicals which when placed in water solution will complex with metallic ions, such as calcium, magnesium, and iron ions, removing them from interference with the detergent system. The complex phosphates are very widely used for this purpose, the most common being sodium tripolyphosphate; others are tetrasodium pyrophosphate and sodium hexametaphosphate. The detergency of even the synthetic detergents in hard water is improved by the addition of these agents.

Several new organic chelating agents are being used. Sodium gluconate is effective in alkaline cleaning systems. Ethylenediamine tetraacetic acid and its salts are used, particularly in liquid cleaners. Nitrilotriacetate salts are also effective.

Additives.—A number of chemicals are used to assist in making proprietary detergents more effective or attractive.

Sodium carboxymethylcellulose imparts a soil-suspending property to laundering detergents. Indeed, until this was introduced in the mid-1940's, detergents using the alkyl aryl sulfonate type of wetting agent did not perform as well as soap-based materials.

Certain *amines* and fatty amides used in detergent products tend to stabilize the foam or suds, and although they may lend minor detergent boosting, the primary purpose is to satisfy the user that the product is active because of the long-lasting visible suds.

Bleaches are used in many detergent processes. Bleaching is most commonly associated with laundering, but oxidizing agents are also frequently used in detergents in machine dishwashing and in food-processing sanitation. Bleaches are generally placed in one of three classes: oxidizing, reducing, and "optical." Oxidizing bleaches include sodium and calcium hypochlorites, chlorinated trisodium phosphate, chlorinated organic compounds such as chlorinated hydantoins and derivatives of cyanuric acid, perborate, and peroxygen compounds. Reducing agents such as oxalic acid, sodium sulfite and sodium thiosulfate, also are effective as stain removers. Optical brighteners are used, primarily in laundry detergents, to cause fabrics to fluoresce, giving a pleasing, intensified whitening effect to the eye. These are, in fact, dyes rather than bleaches in the technical sense of the word.

Inhibitors are necessary ingredients in many chemical specialties to protect the surfaces being cleaned from chemical attack. Alkaline detergents may be harmful to aluminum, and a careful balance of alkalinity and silicate content will prevent such attack. Acid detergents used in scale removal can attack steel or aluminum. Complex organic inhibitors, such as amines and thiols, are used to prevent this. Detergents used for spray washing of tin-coated baking pans have for a number of years contained chromates to protect the tin from attack.

Dyes and *perfumes* are used to add to the appeal of proprietary detergents. If they encourage the use of detergents to create more sanitary conditions, they undoubtedly serve a useful purpose.

Enzymes, or organic catalysts, are finding special uses in digesting stubborn soils, and are included in some laundering detergents for the purpose of attacking specific stains.

It can be seen that the choice of materials from which a complex detergent can be manufactured is extremely diverse. A modern chemical specialties manufacturer will need to inventory several hundred raw materials to provide a complete line of institutional products.

In addition, a continuous search goes on for new chemicals

and new methods to accomplish special institutional cleaning and sanitizing problems.

While detergents constitute the major part of the chemical specialties used by institutions, there are a number of other necessary specialties, such as polishes, sanitizers and germicides, fabric softeners, starches, insecticides, and dust-laying oils. Some of these will now be discussed.

BUILDING MAINTENANCE CLEANING

Walls and Painted Surfaces

Mild alkaline cleaners and synthetic detergents are used for this purpose. The strength of the detergent is, of course, limited by its possible effects on the painted surface and by the fact that most of this type of washing exposes the user's hands to the washing solution.

Windows and Glass Panels

Light-duty synthetic detergents, solvents, and ammonia are common ingredients in cleaning solutions for glass. In most cases, cleaning is fairly frequent and soil accumulation is light. In such applications it is important that the detergent leave a minimum of residue and be volatile, to prevent unnecessary effort in removing detergent after the soil has been loosened.

Porcelain, Tile, and Porcelain Fixtures

These materials are most commonly found in bathrooms and rest-room facilities, where management should be most particular to keep fastidiously clean. Ceramic surfaces have traditionally been cleaned with abrasive cleaners. Care should be taken to be sure that the abrasive is of good quality to prevent damage to the glazed surfaces. Most abrasive cleaners contain synthetic detergents to aid in penetration and rinsing. Many also contain a source of available chlorine (bleach) to aid in stain removal, disinfecting and deodorizing.

Detergent-disinfectants, based on cleaning ingredients and phenolic or quaternary ammonium bactericidal agents, are also useful in these areas.

Special attention must be given to toilets and urinals; and, as mentioned earlier, special acid cleaners are used to pre-

vent and remove scale accumulations in these fixtures. Acid
cleaners should be confined to cleaning true porcelain, as
they may damage enamelled or painted surfaces.

Floors

Maintenance of floors is the most time-consuming task in
building cleaning, and it deserves analysis and supervision on
a continuing basis.

Floors are classified three ways: carpeted, resilient (asphalt,
vinyl, linoleum, cork, and wood), and hard (marble, terrazzo,
quarry tile, etc.).

Carpeting has had a resurgence in institutional and industrial
use since the advent of synthetic fibers. Nylon and polyester
yarns are proving quite stain-resistant, and it has been found
that regular maintenance with synthetic detergents can pick up
the surface soil, if performed on a frequent basis. Periodic
cleaning in depth is used to pull penetrating soil from carpets.
Wool is best cleaned with neutral or even slightly acid detergents. Synthetic fibers allow the use of more highly alkaline
detergents.

Light daily surface cleaning may be accomplished with
moistened sponge mops. More heavily soiled carpets are
now being cleaned with special machines which apply and remove foaming-type detergents. A compromise is achieved
between depth of cleaning and the period of time the carpet
is out of service while drying.

Resilient floors have varying resistance to maintenance
procedures. In general, the manufacturers prefer that solvents, strong alkalies, and acids be avoided in the cleaning
detergents. Traditionally, these floors were cleaned with
"soft" liquid soaps. However, synthetic detergents, in combination with other ingredients, have now largely taken over
this duty. It is necessary that the detergent have no adverse
effects on the tile being cleaned, that it loosen soil without
requiring undue physical action, that it rinse easily with the
soil still in suspension, and that the suds level be low enough
to permit easy rinsing with a mop. With machine cleaning,
excess suds interfere with cleaning action and vacuum pickup.

Most resilient floor maintenance procedures today include
a floor-polish application. These are water emulsions of
either natural or synthetic waxes and/or synthetic polymers

(polyethylene, polystyrene, etc.). Solvent-based polishes are not recommended because of their effect on this type of flooring.

By varying the properties of these emulsions, polishes can be manufactured which dry to varying degrees of (1) gloss, (2) resistance to marking or scuffing, (3) buffability, and (4) resistance to water or detergent solutions. There is no one polish that meets the requirements for all situations. An open corridor, such as a school or hospital corridor, may be most easily maintained by damp mopping and buffing every night because of the heavy traffic. An office area, with many desk, files, and other pieces of furniture, may not easily lend itself to maintenance with a buffing machine, and a non-buffable polish applied frequently with light coats may prove most desirable.

In an area where water spillage is frequent, a water and detergent resistant polish may be desired. On the other hand, an area where much ground-in soil is carried in from out of doors may be protected best by frequent removal and reapplication of the polish.

In general, stripping and re-establishing of the polish protective film should not be necessary more than two or three times a year. The program of maintenance between stripping should be regular damp-mopping or dry-mopping, with spray-buffing or light applications of polish where needed.

Wood flooring requires a different type of maintenance. Water-based cleaners and polishes are used only where sealers have been applied which make the floor impervious to water. Solvent-based seals and varnishes are used, and frequently the total maintenance program is built around solvent-based waxes and cleaners.

Hard floors, such as terrazzo and marble, were for years maintained with abrasive cleaners. However, the labor required to remove the abrasive material in the rinsing operation became too costly. Soaps were not entirely satisfactory because they tended to form films which dulled the appearance of the floor. These films were the result of reaction between the calcium in the floor and the soap. Synthetic detergents, as mentioned earlier, avoid this reaction, and they are widely used today on this type of flooring. Where films have formed on this type of floor, a water-softening chemical may be used to safely remove them. Acids should never be used on hard floors, except baked tile floors which are installed with acid-resistant grouting.

FOOD SERVICE AREAS

Another area in institutional sanitation where chemical specialties have played a major role is the kitchen. Special products have been manufactured for cleaning and sanitizing food contact surfaces, ovens and ventilating hoods, garbage disposal areas, and deep-fat frying equipment. Care should be taken to use the products which have been developed for these tasks, as there are problems associated with each of these operations which are avoided with proper products. As examples, many deep-fat fryers are made of aluminum, which should not be cleaned with strong alkalies; some oven finishes also are not resistant to alkalies.

In institutions using re-usable food service ware, dishwashing is a major operation. Smaller operations and remote service locations may still use hand-dishwashing procedures; but most larger institutions now use dishwashing machines, except for bulky irregular-shaped pans and utensils.

The accepted cycle for dishwashing, whether by hand or machine, is to (1) wash, (2) rinse, and (3) sanitize. The objective is to obtain ware which is visually clean, with no residual detergent or water deposits, and bacteriologically acceptable public health standards. Except in hospitals where highly contagious and dangerous diseases are treated (such as tuberculosis), dishes are not "sterilized," but are "sanitized." This means a reduction to a count of 100 bacteria per square inch of surface.

In hand dishwashing, dishes are usually prescraped by hand to remove gross food, flushed to remove much of the remaining food particles, washed in a soap or synthetic detergent, rinsed in an overflowing sink compartment, then sanitized by immersing in a chemical solution. For many years, immersion in hot water was used (180°F for 1 min); but in most areas, chemical sanitizing has replaced hot water, because it can be performed at lower temperature and thus is more comfortable for the operator. The sanitizer can be a solution containing available chlorine, iodine, quaternary ammonium compound or other safe chemicals which will provide the equivalent bactericidal power of 100 ppm of available chlorine in a specified time.

In machine dishwashing, prescraping may be accomplished by hand in smaller operations with semi-automatic flushing into garbage disposal units, or in larger operations by completely automatic spray-washer compartments called pre-scrapers. Washing, rinsing, and sanitizing are accomplished either by cycling the operations in a single-compartment machine, or by conveying the dishes or utensils through a series of compartments to accomplish a wash-recirculating rinse, and a high-temperature final fresh-water rinse.

The standards for the performance of such machines, as agreed upon by representatives of manufacturers, users, and public health officials, have been published by the National Sanitation Foundation in Ann Arbor, Michigan. These standards are the result of research which has determined the minimum pressures, flow rates, temperatures, and time of exposure to each operation to obtain satisfactory results.

The majority of the work of cleaning dishes and utensils in a dishwashing machine is certainly performed by the action of the water and the physical action of the machine, but the addition of detergents and other chemical specialties is absolutely necessary for maximum results.

A pre-soak for silverware has proved beneficial in volume operations. When soiled silver is returned to the dishwashing area, it is immediately dropped into a detergent solution which softens dried-on soils and makes the action in the dishwashing machine much more effective. These solutions normally include a synthetic detergent and sometimes also inorganic electrolytes which remove sulfide tarnish when the silver is placed in contact with aluminum. Detarnishing of this type is not effective with stainless-steel flatware.

In dishwashing operations, the manufacturers of chemical specialties have performed a high degree of service. In addition to providing detergents which are effective and safe for each intended purpose, they make available accessories to the dishwashing machines which automatically control and feed detergents to the wash-and-rinse sections of the machine, and representatives of these firms instruct personnel on the operation of the equipment, inspect the dishwashing machine operation, and make necessary minor corrections to assure best results. Since experience has shown that unless the total mechanical operation is in order, the chemicals cannot be expected to perform as intended, so these services become extremely important.

LAUNDERING

Chemical specialties play a major role in institutional laundering. Again, water is the medium in which the process is conducted. In most institutions of any size, the water is softened for laundering purposes, as it has been found through experience that the detergency process may be conducted with the greatest economy without having to soften the water during the laundering procedure.

Except for special treatment for certain soils and stains, the traditional cotton fabric used in institutions has been subjected to a standard cycle of laundering such as the following:

(1) *Flush*. A hot water rinse to remove gross soils.

(2) *Break*. An alkaline detergent step to loosen soils.

(3) *Suds*. A soap or synthetic addition to further loosen soil and to suspend it in the solution.

(4) *Rinse*. Sufficient rinses to remove the majority of soil and to reduce alkalinity to a level that will allow efficient bleaching.

(5) *Bleach*. The addition of an oxidizing agent to improve whiteness and to remove stubborn stains. This has traditionally been a product which provides available chlorine. Some of the modern chemical specialties based on organic chlorine-releasing compounds have provided much improved fabric safety.

(6) *Rinse*. Sufficient number of rinses to eliminate traces of chlorine to make subsequent operations safe and to remove vestiges of remaining soil.

(7) *Sour and Other Final Washwheel Operations*. These may be combined or separate steps, but they include "souring," or treatment of the fabric with a carefully controlled acid bath. This produces a fabric with a specified pH, being sure that there is no residual alkalinity, and making the fabric much

more manageable in the finishing operations, such as pressing and folding. In these final operations in the washwheel, chemical specialties play a large part. Certainly everyone recognizes the role that *starches* have played in the final finishing of laundered fabrics. Starches are becoming much more complex and useful; they are readily soluble, do not need the "cooking" operation of the older types, and are tailored to the various fabric compositions now available.

Fabric softeners based on cationic compounds impart a good "hand" or "feel" to fabrics.

Optical brighteners, mentioned earlier, may be used to highlight colors and intensify whiteness.

Bacteriostatic agents or fungicidal agents may be added to improve sanitary conditions or to prevent mildew from forming on soiled linens.

Oil treatments may be given to mop heads and wiping cloths to impart the ability to pick up dust and to hold it so that it is not redistributed.

Again, in laundering, the principles of time, temperature, concentration, and physical action must be followed closely to obtain proper results.

It is obvious that the shorter the time cycles in laundering, the greater the efficiency—more production in less time with less labor. In all cases, however, a minimum cycle is necessary for satisfactory results.

Proper control of temperature is a vital factor in each laundering operation. Without an adequate supply of hot water, quality is sacrificed; but economy will be cast to the winds if lower temperatures are not used in those operations where they are permissible. Control of the use of chemical specialties in washroom operations is also important. Underuse usually results in poor quality. Overuse is not only wasteful, but in some cases may actually damage the fabric involved.

The use of synthetic fibers in institutional fabrics is growing rapidly. These can require adjustments in the washing techniques and changes in the chemical specialties used for the most effective and economical results. Textile manufacturers are originating and competing with many kinds of special finishes, soil-release agents, permanent-press features, and other innovations which require knowledge of changing laundering techniques.

Again the manufacturer of chemical specialties provides a service in staying current with these changes by translating them into products and procedures which the institution can use safely and economically.

OTHER CHEMICAL SPECIALTIES

This chapter reviews some of the principles in use and properties of chemical specialties in the institutional field. It should be noted that there are practically no operations in institutions where chemical specialties are not used. Not covered are insecticides, furniture and metal polishes, specific stain removers, boiler-water treatments, the role of aerosols in cleaning, and a host of other items which might be considered chemical specialties.

It is true, however, that this is a very competitive and fast-changing field. Most chemical specialties have a commercial life of less than ten years, at which time it is necessary to have a new product or method of accomplishing the result intended. The institutional manager must recognize these changes and continue to be open-minded to new products and methods.

CHAPTER 7

L. L. W. Smith
L. J. Minor

Metals

Food-processing equipment, packaging machinery, piping, work tables, handling equipment, storage bins and racks, dollies, conveyors, sanitizing machines, tableware and utensils are generally fabricated from metals. Many food products, including milk, eggs, meats, sauerkraut, tomatoes, pickles, mustard, Worchestershire and Soya sauces, and fruit juices react with metals, causing pitting or other forms of corrosion. Humid air, atmospheric pollutants, heat, and electrolytes or other pollutants in water accelerate the breakdown of metals by chemical and electrochemical reactions.

Corrosion is the deterioration of a substance (usually a metal) due to reaction with its environment, as distinguished from erosion by mechanical action. Oxidation is the most common cause, though corrosion is fundamentally an electro-chemical phenomenon. Dry air or oxygen-free water will not rust iron. Thus both air and water together promote corrosion. Electrolytes such as salt, acids, and bases accelerate the process. Heating and placing strains on metal will accelerate corrosion. Iron in contact with a more active metal such as zinc has less tendency to oxidize, whereas with less-active metals such as tin, lead, or copper, corrosion tendencies seem to increase.

Corrosion occurs rapidly when iron, copper, tin, lead, or aluminum are exposed to food chemicals including lactic acid, vinegar solutions, ammonia, carbon dioxide, hydrogen sulfide, and sulfur dioxide encountered in cooking foods. In the presence of moisture, corrosive acids form with carbon dioxide, hydrogen sulfide, and sulfur dioxide. Occasionally, as in the case of sulfuric acid, dilute solutions are more corrosive then 100% concentrated acid. The most important food additive, salt, is corrosive in kitchen atmospheres and cooking liquids. Corrosion resistance is affected by the nature and concentration of the chemical and by the temperature and time of exposure.

Corrosion resistance in metals has led to the development of metal alloys or surface coatings for metals in the food industry. *Porcelain or vitreous enamel* coatings have been used on low-cost kitchen utensils for many years. More useful and successful applications for these materials have been for the protection of metals used in food-storage rooms, freezers, refrigerators, stoves and cabinets. Porcelain enamel is defined by the American Society for Testing and Materials as "a substantially vitreous or glassy, inorganic coating bonded to metal by fusion at a temperature of 800°F." Glazes included in vitreous coatings may contain poisonous heavy metals that tend to migrate from the utensil to the food. Porosity is a problem with enameled surfaces, as it is with plastics. After certain foods are cooked or served in them the interiors stain. The main failure of porcelain surfaces is chipping as a result of brittleness that leads to exposure and rusting of the base metal.

Tin coatings have been used inside copper utensils for many years, and in France chefs still use and prefer this class of kitchen ware. The metal is applied by "hot-dipping" or covering the clean copper surface with molten tin. Abrasion and cleaning together with the corrosive action of certain foods soon removes the tin coating, and then the copper must be re-coated. Chefs in large hotels often have their own facilities for "hot-dipping." The excellent heat-transfer characteristics of copper make these pots and pans ideal for the preparation of heat-sensitive consomme, sauces, roux, and souffles.

Tests made on food cooked in tinned steel frying pans contained up to 80 ppm of lead. Tin formulas may contain varying amounts of lead and other poisonous heavy metals.

Tin coatings for cans may be applied by either "hot-dipping" or coating the base steel plate electrolytically. A unit called the "base box" is used by can manufacturers. Hot-dipped tinplate averages 1.25 lb of tin per base box of steel plate. During World War II when tin imports, were limited, electrolytic plates varying from 0.1 to 0.75 lb of tin per base box were tested as containers for fruits and vegetables. These cans were made up plain and with various coatings. Side seams were stripped to re-coat burned areas next to them after soldering. Low-tin solders were also tested, and efforts were made to produce an enamel-coated blackplate can. The Germans succeeded in doing this by stitch-welding the side seams.

Electrolytic tin coating of cans has progressed since World War II, and this process, followed by enameling of the inner can surface, is used extensively in can manufacture today. Development of the aluminum can is another technological advance for the container industry.

Pin-holing in the enamel coatings on cans, together with cracking due to brittleness, are problems that shorten can life. Plain tin cans are corroded by nearly all foods, but extensive tests with monkeys proved that the metal pickup by the food is non-toxic. A reduction in content of such elements as sulfur and phosphorus increases the corrosion resistance of cans for low-pH products such as bean sprouts packed in citric acid.

Corn is packed in enameled cans using coatings that contain zinc oxide. Formerly, the sulfur in corn reacted with iron to form black iron sulfide that made the product unsightly. By including zinc oxide in the C-enamel formulation the sulfur reacts with the more active zinc and forms white zinc sulfide. Sour cherries are packed in cans coated with a special enamel that safeguards the wholesomeness and appearance of the product.

Cans that fail to protect the product usually have faulty top-seams or side-seams. Can bodies are formed by the container manufacturer; side seams are hooked together and soldered ends are flanged, and the can bottom is sealed on at the factory. Covers and bottoms are flanged and a sealing compound containing latex is used to ensure air and water tightness after the cover and bottom hooks are formed and rolled tight on the sealing machines.

When covers are applied after filling the cans, care must be taken to prevent any of the product from lodging in the seam. The operator must also adhere closely to the manufacturer's "specs" for body and cover hook length, which is checked at frequent intervals with a micrometer. When tolerances are not met the operator, who has been trained by the container manufacturer, carefully adjusts the sealing machine. Since the rate of filling and sealing often exceeds 100 cans per min, the importance of this operation is apparent.

Side-seam failure is caused by enamel burning when these seams are soldered. Just as cover hook failure must be controlled by the canner, side-seam control is the responsibility of the manufacturer. When spoilage occurs trained microbiologists can usually determine the cause and who is responsible.

Aluminum cookware is used extensively in kitchens throughout the United States, but despite technological advances in the metallurgy of aluminum alloys the metal has serious drawbacks. Abrasion resistance has been improved by anodizing high-voltage electrolytic treatment, in which the metal serves as the anode in a bath containing sulfuric, chromic, or oxalic acid, resulting in an oxide coating.

Aluminum is attacked by water, ammonia, sulfur dioxide, and hydrogen sulfide from cooked foods, by vinegar, lactic acid, sodium chloride and ammonium chloride in soups, sauces, seasonings, sauerkraut, and the like. Pitting is most likely to occur in the presence of chloride ions and oxygen, and the damage increases with temperature rise. Alkali attacks the metal when cleaning with detergents.

Aluminum oxide is easily formed on the surface of aluminum utensils. It is removed by the action of acids or bases, the former by the acids in foods such as applesauce, rhubarb, and tomatoes. The action by bases or alkalies is in the detergents or scouring powders used.

This oxide coating on utensils can be removed when using a metal whip in an aluminum vessel when making white sauces or mashing potatoes, and the result is a gray or off-colored product. This type of reaction is prevented by the following treatments of aluminum cooking utensils.

Anodized aluminum used in light-weight cooking utensils consisting of aluminum or aluminum alloys is sealed and coated with oils, fats, waxes, or resins by absorption. Aluminum and its alloys are protected from lactic acid by using a nickel coating 0.03 mm thick. Fluorinated hydrocarbon resin coatings including Teflon are electroplated or flame-sprayed on aluminum nonstick cooking utensils.

Aluminum and its alloys are used in the dairy, brewing, vegetable oil-refining, and sugar industries for fabricated equipment ranging from small sieves to large storage tanks.

Copper is widely used in the confectionery, food, and fermen-

tation industries despite its corrosion tendencies. Poor resistance to sulfur compounds, ammonia, and organic acids
in the presence of oxygen and heat in solution are characteristic
of copper. In the pH range 4 to 6 copper is attacked by organic
acids, such as amino acids and their salts, yielding copper
compounds called chelates that do not precipitate from solution. For this reason, soya sauce and other hydrolyzed protein
derivatives should not be held in containers of copper, stainless steel containing small amounts of copper, or Monel
metal.

Copper is ductile and malleable and is an ideal metal for
fabricating tubing, kettles, stills or other equipment. Heat
transfer and electrical conductivity are excellent. Uniform
heating results when stainless steel cooking utensil bottoms
are copper-clad.

Copper tubing is extensively used for plumbing, as the joints
and fittings may be soldered rapidly with silver solder. Managers should be sure that copper and galvanized iron piping
are not joined together for expediency, as this causes corrosion
resulting from a galvanic cell at the interface of the dissimilar
metals.

Another food spoilage problem caused by copper even in trace
amounts is oxidative rancidity. Copper is a powerful prooxidant
that rapidly ruins the taste of fatty foods, including dairy
products.

Hailey in his novel "Hotel" tells of rancid French-fried
potatoes. When the manager and the chef checked the equipment they found hairline scratches in the plating on the bottoms
of the baskets used for immersion of the product in the hot
fat. Thus the brass underneath (containing copper) was exposed. The problem was eliminated by having the baskets
electroplated.

An interesting case of rancidity in foods was caused by
trace copper in salt that had been passed through Monel metal
screening. When the different grades were used in potato
chips, cheese, butter, and other salted products oxidative
rancidity developed rapidly. Trace copper acted as a catalytic
prooxidant. Replacement of the Monel screening with copper-
free stainless steel solved the problem.

Care should be taken to eliminate brass fittings from pumps
and filters used in deep-fat frying systems. Copper contact

with food should always be avoided. Iron also acts as a milder prooxidant, but fortunately hot fat seals or is adsorbed on iron surfaces, minimizing the effect.

Monel metal is produced when a blend of nickel, copper, and iron sulfide are roasted and subsequently reduced with carbon. An alloy (containing nickel, iron, and copper) results and has high corrosion resistance. Hot-water heaters with long-life capabilities are lined with Monel rather than the cheaper vitreous-enameled steel.

Corrosion and abrasion resistance of Monel is better than aluminum, but does not equal that of stainless steel. Furthermore, the copper content of Monel may cause undesirable contamination of food and pitting of the metal.

Utensils made from Monel may be drawn by spinning a sheet while pressing it over a spindle. This kitchenware is highly polished and attractive, and buyers often purchase it as stainless steel. Unfortunately, this unwariness is due to a lack of knowledge concerning the metal's corrosive tendency. Exposure of the metal to salty solutions in the pH range 4 to 6 leads to rapid corrosion and contamination of the product, besides ruining the utensil.

Galvanized iron is iron that has been zinc-coated by hot-dipping steel plate in a vat of molten zinc and rolling the sheet, or electro-galvanizing it in a plating bath. By either method an alloy of the two metals results at the iron interface with a layer of zinc on the surface. An advantage of electro-galvanizing is that the zinc layer thickness may be controlled and altered as desired.

Sherardizing is a process for zinc-coating small iron objects, such as nuts, bolts, pulleys and the like, by placing them in zinc dust inside a revolving drum and applying heat to melt the zinc dust into the surface. A corrosion-resistant coating results.

Metallizing is a process by which molten zinc is sprayed with force against iron.

Uses of galvanized iron in food plants includes meat hooks, pipe legs for stainless-steel table tops, storage racks, dollies, and other noncontact applications. The zinc coating retards rusting, but in salt-laden or other polluted atmospheres, including cooking vapors, the protection is short-lived. (Zinc coating reacts with acids present in foodstuffs, producing toxic compounds.) A surprising amount of galvanized iron is found in meat-cutting plants. The abrasion resistance of galvanized iron is poor.

Polymers such as Teflon, epoxy-chlorohydrin, and epoxy-amino resins are being used in limited applications as surface coatings for wood and metal contacting food. Teflon is a tetrafluoroethylene ($CF_2 = CF_2$) polymer used on nonstick pot, frying pans, and griddle surfaces. Unfortunately, the coating is an unsightly black, and does not withstand abrasion. Even hairline scratches in the material result in food sticking to the metal beneath. Modified epoxy resins have been used successfully for lining sugar tanks.

Steel is an alloy of iron with small percentages of carbon and other elements combined in definite proportions to produce strength, toughness, and hardness. *Mild steels* contain up to 0.2%, *medium steels* 0.2 to 0.6%, and *high-carbon steels* 0.6 to 1.5% carbon. The latter are used in springs, cutlery, razor blades, and surgical instruments. Heating steel to redness and then cooling slowly is called *annealing*. *Tempered* steel is made by quenching the hot metal rapidly in water or oil, followed by controlled reheating. *Case-hardened* steel is obtained when low-carbon steel parts immersed in carbon inside a closed container are heated, then removed, and quenched in oil.

Besides iron and carbon, sulfur, silicon, manganese, molybdenum, chromium, vanadium, phosphorus, and other elements are present in alloy steels. Sulfur imparts machinability, and phosphorus strengthens steel alloys. Steels having low sulfur and phosphorus content are used in acid-resistant steel plate.

Stainless steels are alloys containing chromium and nickel, which greatly increase corrosion resistance to food chemicals, including acidic hydrogen sulfide and sulfur dioxide gases in solution. Manganese may be added to increase hardness.

Stainless steels, as the name implies, are steel alloys that resists staining. However, they are not entirely stain-free, but develop spots as a result of staining with fruit juices, hard water, and the like; thus they are not 100% stain-proof. Yet, these alloys represent the finest metal surfaces available for use in food plant doors and hardware, processing equipment, cookware and tableware. A list of steels and alloy steels, their compositions, properties, and uses are given in Table 7.1.

Stainless steel formula 18-8, containing 18% chromium and 8% nickel has proved to be a successful alloy for dairy and food-processing equipment. In a 4% sodium chloride solution in the pH range 4 to 8 this 18-8 alloy pits, and in the pH range 2 to 3 hydrogen is evolved at the metal-solution interface. Pitting of stainless steel is likely to occur in the presence of chloride ions and oxygen.

Other formulations containing 5 to 7% manganese, 17 to 19% chromium, and 3.5 to 4.5% nickel are about equal to 18-8 in all branches of the food industry tested.

The porous crystalline nature of nickel helps to bond chromium and other metals to steel. Copper is plated on first, followed by nickel and chromium. The dense crystals of chromium form a hard and continuous lubricating surface, which aids in heat transfer when starch, protein, or fat are heated in agitated steam-jacketed kettles. Any buildups of these food materials on metal surfaces decreases the rate of heat transfer.

Sterling silver contains 7.5% copper to increase its strength; it is used for British "sterling silver" coins. Coin silver in the United States contains 10 and jewelry 20% copper.

A major use of sterling silver in the United States is in tableware. Hydrogen sulfide from air polluted with coal smoke or cooked foods reacts readily with silver alloys to form black silver sulfide. To protect silverware from tarnishing, protective coatings may be applied. However, washing and abrasion remove this protective layer in time. Contact with sulfur-rich food materials such as mustard, onion, garlic, leeks, meats, and eggs blackens silver.

Stainless steel of high luster is replacing sterling silver in table service ware. Maintenance and replacement costs are lower, and the appearance of quality stainless alloys has improved.

Pewter is an alloy of tin with 5 to 15% antimony, 0 to 3% copper and 0 to 15% lead. White metal and Britannia metal are also of this general composition. In Colonial days pewterware of ornate design was used extensively at the table. Today its usage is limited to salt and pepper dispensers, and beer mugs.

TABLE 7.1
STEEL AND ALLOY STEELS

Steel	Composition	Properties	Uses
Low-carbon	0.05–0.25% C	Malleable, weldable	Boiler plates, sheet and structural steel, wire
Medium-carbon	0.25–0.75% C	Durable, castable	Axles, piston rods, rails, projectiles
High-carbon	0.75–1.2% C	Hard, strong	Springs, drills, axes, lathe tools, knives
Alloy Steels Chrome	Less than 3% Cr	Strong, resistant to strains	Files, gears, axles, projectiles
Chrome-tungsten	0.25–1.0% C 4–25% W 2–10% Cr	Retain temper at high temperatures	High speed cutting tools
Manganese	10–18% Mn	Hard, tough, resistant to wear	Rails, armor plate, safes
Nickel-chromium	1–4% Ni 0.5–2% Cr	Hard, resistant to strains	Tools, axles, gears, auto parts, drive shafts
Chrome-vanadium	1–10% Cr 0.15% V	Strong, strain-resistant	Axles
Permalloy	78% Ni	High magnetic susceptibility	Ocean cables
Silicon	Less than 5% Si 16% Si	Corrosion-resistant Acid-resistant	Dynamos Chemical ware and plumbing
Stainless	13% Cr	Corrosion resistant	Cutlery
	13–20%	Corrosion resistant	Food and chemical processing equipment

Lead is a soft metal, heavy, but lacking in tensile strength. When freshly cut it has a metallic luster, but acquires a dull gray color in moist air. Water reacts with the metal in the presence of oxygen to form lead hydroxide.

Pewterware is dark and unattractive. Like sterling it must be polished regularly or coated with a polymeric protective material to maintain its best appearance.

The average daily intake of lead from food is 0.3 mg. Formerly, when lead pipe plumbing was used in soft-water systems, and pewterware was popular, the ingestion of lead was considerable from these sources. Insecticide residues that contaminate our food, together with migrant lead compounds from pottery used in food service, may contribute considerable amounts of lead in the diet. Accordingly, managers should seek to eliminate sources of lead contamination from their food service by careful washing of fresh fruits and vegetables and avoidance of lead-containing ware.

METHODS OF CLEANING METALS

Aluminum vessels that are dull can be brightened by cooking acid foods, such as tomatoes, apples, rhubarb, or by heating a solution of vinegar or cream of tartar. Lime scale can be removed by heating vinegar solution and burnt particles by a solution of sodium bicarbonate. An abrasive can be used. Some commercial pan cleaners have a very low pH, 2 to 3, and pans soaked in these become clean and lose some of their metal.

Brass and *bronze* are generally cleaned by using a mild abrasive of salt or rottenstone in an acid (vinegar) medium. Commercial cleaners are available on the market.

Copper must be kept clean and shiny. Copper salts are poisonous and are removed by salt or a mild abrasive plus acid (vinegar). Generally, copper items are lacquered to keep their luster.

Iron utensils are thoroughly scrubbed, then seasoned with fat for 2 to 3 hours at 250–300°F, wiped or washed, and dried thoroughly.

Pewter vessels are washed with detergent and polished with a mild abrasive.

Dull or stained silverware is treated as follows: Removal of sulfide or dark stains is quickly and cheaply accomplished by the electrolytic method. This is a simple procedure that involves (a) covering the silver with hot water in which are dissolved 1 tbsp salt and 1 tbsp baking soda per quart; (b) the presence of aluminum, either as the pan or as aluminum foil, lining the pan or in the water, and (c) keeping the silver in contact with the aluminum. This method requires but a few seconds to clean; then the silver is removed, rinsed, and wiped dry. This electrolytic procedure cannot be used with silver decorated with oxidized silver, since it removes the oxidized silver along with the stain. The advantages of this method are (a) it is inexpensive, (b) quick, and (c) redeposits the silver on the article cleaned, no silver being lost. This equation summarizes the reactions which take place.

$$6NaHCO_3 + 2Al + 3Ag_2S \xrightarrow[NaCl]{heat} 2Na_3AlO_3 +$$
$$6Ag\downarrow + 3H_2S\uparrow + 6CO_2\uparrow$$

Commercial abrasive cleaners can be used, but they remove silver permanently and require more labor. Commercial dips are effective, but must be handled carefully and the manufacturers' directions must be followed explicitly. These are based on organic chelating agents to remove surface material and leave the surface like one polished mechanically.

Stainless Steel is washed with soaps or detergents, and abrasives can be used to remove discoloration. Commercial dressings are on the market for countertops that remove stains, etc.

Tin is washed with detergents and mild abrasives can be used to remove rust, etc. Keep dry to prevent rusting.

Polishing

The polishing phenomenon seems to be a smoothing of the surface on a molecular scale. It could be of a molecular fluidity akin to melting with the result that the surface acquires a smooth coat.

A powder's polishing ability depends on the relative hardness of the materials at the temperature produced at the rubbed surface. This implies that polishing mechanism is abrasion.

After polishing, underlying scratches reappear after the film formed on the surface by polishing is removed. This property has enabled coin collectors to use an etchant to recover the worn-off date on a coin, the metal where the date was stamped having been deformed. Polishing removes these scratches but the application of an etchant rediscloses the location of the original groves.

Experiments have shown that polishing smooths the surface not by redistribution but by removing material from the surface.

Polishing is not abrasive, is not smearing, and is not based on melting. What then is it?

Burnishing is polishing without the use of abrasives; it is accomplished by rubbing the surface with another hard solid or a cloth. Burnishing is generally carried out at low pressure and often against a resilient surface. The temperature rise is minimal. It is suggested that burnishing removes molecules of the substance at the surface or redistributes these surface molecules.

Polishing with a cloth and a very fine abrasive or burnishing with a very fine mesh gives a very high degree of polish. Polishing with a cloth containing very fine diamond grains (one micron in diameter) gives a pressure per contact point much smaller than burnishing; a standard copper specimen was polished in minutes compared to burnishing, which required hours.

Polishing, like burnishing, is governed by a critical pressure; below this critical pressure the process entails the removal of material by the molecule.

The electrolytic method of polishing involves the immersion of the surface in the solution, the protuberances on the surface being dissolved away as the current is passed through the solution. A surface polished this way looks exactly like one polished mechanically. Robinowiez (1967) gives a more detailed discussion.

Burnishing machines on the market are principled by rubbing one surface with another, namely steel balls against the silver surface. Some are so built to include the electrolytic method of removing stain.

CHAPTER 8

J. J. Herringer

Floor and Building Maintenance

The commercial building manager today has more responsibility than ever before. New and up-dated buildings represent larger investments to protect, and modern facilities require more specialized care. Increased employee and customer traffic requires more rigid safety and health precautions. With the public's increasing demands for good appearance, buildings and floors must be maintained constantly at the highest possible level.

This maintenance, as most building managers are painfully aware, is expensive. It is estimated that American businesses spend as much as $25 billion annually on housekeeping.

Floor maintenance operations alone account for 40% of this figure, the remaining 60% going for other housekeeping operations such as washroom maintenance, cleaning of furniture, fixtures, equipment, and insect control.

The fundamental housekeeping goals for any building include: (1) cleanliness and sanitation; (2) health, safety, and comfort; (3) protection of valuable property and surfaces; (4) good appearance.

Considering the estimated $25 billion annual outlay for the achievement of these goals, cutting down expenses while maintaining the highest possible level of floor care and general building appearance becomes the name of the game.

But a building manager faces some severe problems in cutting costs. One of the more important to be considered is the increasing price of labor.

It has been estimated that the removal of a single pound of dirt from a building costs as much as $600. Of that cost, equipment and supplies take only about 5%, or $30. The remaining $570 goes for labor.

This, from the very beginning, points out the importance of such measures as value analysis in purchasing to avoid the pitfalls of ordering inferior products, only to find that in the long run the labor costs they add eat up your maintenance budget.

180

The most effective approach to housekeeping involves application of a technique called the "systems approach"— more specifically, the use of several systems incorporated into an effective program designed to meet the particular needs of the building.

It is wise in the beginning, in fact necessary, to evaluate the building with emphasis on housekeeping *needs, desires,* and *problems.*

Following a complete survey of a given building, and objective evaluation of observations, the most effective and economical housekeeping program for that building can be developed. The total program breaks down into a series of systems. In a typical school, for example, the program might consist of these separate but interdependent systems:

(1) *Preventive Maintenance System*: Control of dust and dirt at all outside and inside sources. Some of the more basic preventive measures include adequate cleaning schedules in outside entrance areas, the use of floor mats at doorway and elevator entrances, sweeping of dirt and shoveling of snow from sidewalks, and other common-sense measures.

(2) *Floor Maintenance System*: Locations, types of flooring, and specific problem areas determine recommendations for nonbuffable, buffable floor maintenance systems, or carpet-care systems.

(3) *General Cleaning System*: For all areas and surfaces other than floors—furniture, walls, glass, etc.

(4) *Washroom Sanitation System.*

(5) *Insect Control System.*

(6) *Gymnasium Floor Maintenance System.*

Properly thought out, developed and modified for the particular needs of your building, these basic systems make up the total housekeeping program.

FLOOR MAINTENANCE

Since floor maintenance takes the largest single share of the housekeeping budget, it will be examined first, beginning with its development from the earliest coating of wooden parquet floors with beeswax to the point where floor maintenance products and procedures now stand.

To gain a historical perspective of the business of maintaining floors, let us consider that manufacturers have reached a highly advanced stage of development in floor-care systems. They now think in terms of high gloss, water and detergent resistance, black heel mark resistance, resistance to spills and chemicals, and floor finishes that can be recoated or removed selectively and under tight control.

Such characteristics are far removed from beeswax, which was first recorded in the 13th century as being used on mosaic tile floors that were beginning to gain popularity in Italy. But even beeswax so improved the appearance of the tile that its use was expanded to include the polishing of marble, stone, and terrazzo floors. It was in the following century, however, when wooden parquetry flooring was introduced in France, that the use of floor wax as we commonly know it became widespread. The beeswax used in those early days was melted onto the floor with hot irons, then polished by serfs and servants skating around on the waxed surface with their feet bound in rags. If these maintenance procedures were primitive, their intention was the same as ours today. They were designed to make the floor shiny, give it a good appearance, make it easy to keep clean, and protect the wood, tile, or marble.

The next step in the long line of developmental changes that is still going on was the use of turpentine in which the beeswax could be dispersed. This thinning of the wax with a solvent meant that the wax could be spread on the floor rather than melted on, and was the forerunner of modern paste and liquid waxes.

The methods of using polished waxes also progressed. Skating around on the floor gave way to hands-and-knees buffing with rags and brushes. But for nearly five centuries there was little change in the raw material composition of floor waxes.

Beeswax continued to hold the spotlight until the late 18th century, when carnauba wax was discovered on the leaves of the carnauba palm trees of eastern Brazil. Explorers in the area noted that the wax enabled the trees to hold enough moisture to survive the hot, dry winds that withered nearly all other vegetation.

The natives had been harvesting and using carnauba for domestic purposes for years, but it was not until the latter part of the 19th century that it became an important commodity in commerce. By then, wax manufacturers had found that carnauba wax could be used in a floor-wax formulation that would give a much longer-lasting finish and produce a much higher gloss than was possible with beeswax alone. Carnauba was indeed a vast improvement, but its lack of transparency, relatively dark color and difficulty of application made it much less than a perfect finish. Since floors were rarely washed and never stripped of their old wax coatings (the feeling was, the more wax on the floor, the better) the floors developed a dark, mellow glow which looked much better than nothing and was considerably more slippery. The slippery quality, however, was considered proof of shine, and if the layers on layers of wax scuffed easily, they buffed back to a shine just as easily.

The chain of events which brought floor finishing up to the point at which it now stands began over 80 years ago, when prepared floor wax was first introduced for sale to the general public. It was basically the same carnauba wax, but was dissolved in a naphtha (a more economical solvent) rather than turpentine. With naphthas the drying rate could be controlled. It was put on by hand and polished by hand, using a stone wrapped in lamb's wool or flannel. Although the prepared wax still offered much in the way of hard work, it did serve to introduce floor polish into the average home.

About 40 years ago, the "better way" that housewives had been looking for since they started waxing their floors was introduced. It was called "self-polishing wax," and was considered quite an achievement. Since it could simply be spread on the floor and allowed to dry to a shine, it proved to be a big seller. The increased sales meant new demands for carnauba wax, which could only be obtained in Brazil; and as waxmakers and carbon paper manufacturers, the only other users, increased their demands for the commodity, the Brazilian government increased its prices.

When the price of raw carnauba wax had reached $1.00 a pound, a search for a new supply or substitute was launched. It was soon discovered that carnauba palms would grow straight and tall in the southern U.S., but that they would not produce wax. After screening of some 1,500 possible substitutes, it was discovered that sugar cane produced a wax which was a good substitute in carbon paper, but not floor polish. By this time the price of Brazilian carnauba had reached $1.40 a pound.

The breakthrough on carbon paper manufacture, however, convinced the Brazilian government that, inevitably, another substitute would be found for use in floor polish. They dropped their price back to $0.70 a pound, and the wax manufacturers, accepting this, continued to work with carnauba-formulated self-polishing waxes for nearly 20 years.

Even though the price of carnauba wax had come down, the problems of its dark color, its lack of water resistance, the fact that it was readily affected by cleaning solutions and scuffed easily still remained.

Then, around 1950, came another breakthrough: the formulation of emulsion floor polishes made from synthetic resins. The timing was right, since modifications and improvements in natural materials had about reached their limit.

The floor finishes, made up of interlaced polymer molecules which formed a thin, nearly transparent film over the floor, solved many of the problems, though at first they created new ones. For instance, where wax emulsion floor polishes had insufficient resistance to water, the experimental polymers were very resistant. This was clearly not suitable, because once the finish had been put on the floor it was very difficult to remove when the floor needed refinishing.

The finishes that resulted from trying to overcome the new problems were often compromises. They had enough resistance to withstand light cleaning solutions and water, but not enough to withstand strong cleaning solutions.

The introduction of metal-complexed sealers and finishes only a few years ago solved these problems and introduced several noteworthy performance characteristics. First of all, these finishes have a high degree of detergent and water resistance and can be washed repeatedly, or even machine-scrubbed, without materially affecting their original gloss. They also resist spotting or dulling from spilled or tracked-in liquids. Their gloss increases with additional coatings, and most of them can be removed without difficulty with chemically compatible strippers sold as part of the floor care system. The better-quality metal-complexed finishes also retain the most desirable properties of conventional polymer finishes, especially resistance to black heel marking, dirt pick-up, and clarity of multiple coats.

Combining detergent resistance and easy removability in the same product had, up until this point, been an unattainable goal. Any formulation which increased water and detergent resistance also made removal more difficult, sometimes impossible. On the other hand, easy removability almost meant poor water and detergent resistance.

To understand how these metal-complexed sealers and finishes solved the problems, let us look at what happens to a floor finish or sealer after it has been applied to a floor. As water evaporates from the emulsion, the molecules coalesce into a continuous film. The film, however, would be as difficult to remove as a varnish or lacquer, except that chemists build in what they call "break points." These "break points" are sensitive to detergents and strippers, so that the polymer film can be broken up and removed when desired.

This is the place where conventional polymer finishes stopped. Because the "break points" are affected by water, some of the finish was removed and the gloss dulled whenever the floor was washed. The "break points" were also vulnerable to attack by spilled and tracked-in liquids, and spotting resulted.

By incorporating certain metallic ions, called "interlocks," into the polymer chain, chemists were able to protect the "break points" from attack by water and other liquids, detergents and conventional strippers. After application, the drying film acutally undergoes a chemical reaction as water evaporates. The metallic ions cross-link the molecules, and an entirely new water-resistant polymer chain is formed on the floor. Removal, when desired, is simpler and easier for a metal-complexed finish. A specially selected reagent dissolves the "interlocks" and leaves the "break points" again vulnerable to attack.

To the building maintenance manager, metal-complexed systems mean significant savings in time and labor. The floor can be subjected to repeated detergent scrubbing without dulling the gloss. The interval between refinishings is greatly extended, and the sealer will last through repeated removals of the top finish. Because of the resistance of the finish to black marking and dirt pick-up, day-to-day maintenance involves little more than sweeping or damp mopping.

Manufacturers who are able to formulate their own resins and metal-complexed polymers have the advantage here, since they can develop chemically matched products—a sealer, finish, maintainer and stripper—to be used together as a complete floor care system.

The widespread acceptance of these products indicates that metal-complexing may prove to be the most important development in floor maintenance since self-polishing waxes were introduced nearly 40 years ago.

FLOORING TYPES

In planning a basic maintenance program for a building, the types of flooring to be taken into consideration will usually include combinations of the following:

(1) Resilient: vinyl, vinyl asbestos, asphalt and rubber tile, linoleum. (2) Non-resilient: concrete, terrazzo, mosaic, and quarry tile. (3) Wooden: nowadays mainly gymnasium floors. (4) Carpeting.

Resilient

Of the four varieties mentioned above, resilient flooring is by far the most widely used in the commercial field, representing as much as 70% of the total. Resilient floors fall into six basic categories: asphalt tile; vinyl asbestos tile; vinyl tile; vinyl sheet; linoleum and rubber tile.

Asphalt tile was the most popular floor covering for many years. Since the introduction of vinyl asbestos, however, it has steadily lost ground for commercial and industrial use.

Vinyl is also gaining in popularity, but is still relatively limited in commercial use. Linoleum and vinyl sheet flooring are widely used in homes, but to a lesser degree in commercial buildings. Rubber tile, once quite widely used, is now rapidly disappearing.

Both vinyl asbestos and asphalt tiles are composed essentially of resin, asbestos and inert mineral fillers. Asphalt tile differs from vinyl asbestos primarily in the resins used. Originally asphalt tile contained asphaltic resin. For this reason, it was always dark in color—black, brown, and maroon were common. It was also highly sensitive to grease and solvents.

Later, to achieve lighter colors, other, more expensive resins were brought into use. Although these were not asphaltic resins, the tile was and still is called "asphalt tile." It was

sold at a premium price, and since it exhibits some tolerance
for grease, it was offered as "grease-resistant."

With the introduction of vinyl resins, complete grease resistance was achieved and a broad selection of colors was
made available. These tiles are identified as vinyl asbestos
and are sold as grease-proof.

In either category, whether asphalt or vinyl asbestos, the
cheaper grades contain a high percentage of mineral filler.
From the standpoint of maintenance, the cheapest grade is the
most difficult to maintain. The better, more expensive grades,
with a high percentage of resin, are the easiest to maintain,
last longer, and look better on a floor. Tile with a high inorganic filler content suffers particularly from continuous
cleaning, which destroys the resin bond and leaves a faded,
rough surface.

One of the major determining factors to be considered in
setting up a maintenance system for floors is simply whether
the flooring is new or whether it has been on the floor for a
length of time and has been previously maintained with finishes
and cleaners.

New Floors.—When a newly laid floor is to go into service
for the first time, the job of setting up a maintenance program
commonly includes overcoming three problems with the floor.
They are: (1) mill finish, (2) construction dirt; (3) plasticizer
migration.

Mill Finish.—The successful use of any floor finish depends
on preparation of the floor than on any other factor. The most
common cause of massive failure of floor finish, accounting
for more than half of all complaints received by manufacturers,
is poor adhesion resulting from improper preparation.

Mill finish found on new floor tile complicates the preparation
considerably. The broad category of agents commonly called
mill finishes are usually organic release agents applied at the
time the tile is manufactured. Although these agents are applied
to allow the tile to pass through the rollers and prevent sticking, they are subjected to such high levels of heat and pressure
that they actually become part of the tile surface.

As a side effect, they also act to improve the appearance of
the newly manufactured tile and give it a reasonable shine.
But mill finish is not floor finish, and it is not a good base for
floor finish. For maximum floor polish performance mill

finish must be removed completely before applying sealer or finish. This thorough stripping can be accomplished with some of the new stripping products now being marketed by major floor-finish manufacturers.

It is to be remembered that careful and complete stripping at this time can save many headaches and the retracing of steps later on.

Construction Dirt.—In all construction—new buildings, building additions, remodeling—construction dirt and dust in the form of cement, plaster, sand, paper and insulation fibers, acoustical material, etc., will present housekeeping problems for some time. This air-borne and tracked-in dirt will collect on all horizontal surfaces, particularly on floors, and will cause problems until it has been completely removed.

Plasticizer Migration.—The manufacture of vinyl-bonded floors requires the use of plasticizers for flexibility and re-silience. The tougher the resin, the more difficult it is to plasticize. Some of the plasticizers used in vinyl-bonded floors are also compatible with or have an affinity for certain floor-polish ingredients and will migrate into the floor-polish film. The problems this causes vary with the amount of plasti-cizer that has migrated into the film. In mild cases, the polish will become slightly tacky or sticky, and will pick up increased amounts of dirt. In severe cases, furniture sticks to the tile and the tile is marred, or a piece of the tile pulled out when the furniture is moved.

Although this problem can be severe, there are available on the market sealers whose formulation includes the ability to control plasticizer migration. Once the sealer gives evidence that it will not fail under these conditions, the finishing is simple.

Floors in Use.—When setting up a new maintenance system for a floor already in use, proper preparation is again the first and most important task. The three steps in the proper preparation of the floor are: (1) complete stripping of the existing finish; (2) thorough rinsing with clean water; (3) complete and proper sealing.

Again the absolute necessity of carefully completing these steps must be stressed. If they are done properly, floor maintenance becomes easy. If they are done poorly or not at all, good floor maintenance becomes virtually impossible.

Another of the main sources of floor maintenance trouble is weather, and winter is the season in which the majority of this trouble occurs. Winter is the season of snow, rain, ice, and artificial heat. Each of these cause trouble directly or indirectly. Rain and snow make mud of ordinary street dirt. In this form it sticks to shoes and is tracked into buildings. The accumulation of dirt in a building on a rainy or snowy day may be 50 or 100 times as great as on a normal dry day.

Remembering the estimates of dirt removal costing nearly $600 a pound, one can readily see the importance of stopping as much of this dirt at the door as is possible. This can be done fairly simple by the use of well-placed foot mats, hall runners, and the placement of rubber mats near doors and elevators to catch dripping boots and umbrellas.

With winter comes ice, and with ice comes sand and salt, used by the millions of tons annually as antislip and melting agents on roads and sidewalks. Either sand or salt, each in its own way, is a notorious destroyer of floor finishes and of the floors themselves. Salt, after being tracked in as salt water, dries and becomes crystalline and abrasive. It can severely scratch both floors and finishes. Sand, in even moderate quantities, is highly abrasive and will destroy virtually any floor finish and eventually the floor itself. As stated earlier, the place to stop these problems is at the door.

Although the destructive character of sand and salt is easy to understand, artificial heat is not as readily identified as a troublemaker. It does, however, cause its share of problems. By removing most of the humidity from the air, artificial heat makes many substances light enough to become air-borne. Included are such things as paper, textile and wood fibers, chalk dust, and so on. It is basically the same accumulation that is called "dust" when found on furniture, but is called "powder" when on the floor. In many cases the accumulation of this "powder" is believed to be caused by the actual powdering of the floor finish. This, however, occurs very rarely.

Non-resilient floors

There are many types of non-resilient flooring, such as slate, marble, granite and stone. But only three are found in large enough quantities to warrant attention here: terrazzo,

quarry tile, and concrete. Each of these flooring materials has
its own characteristics and problems.

Terrazzo, which is made by floating marble chips in a bed or
matrix of concrete, can be profoundly affected by the quality
and quantity of the chips used and the care and skill employed
in laying the floor. Characteristically, a good terrazzo floor is
hard and smooth and, being seamless, should be easy to
maintain. The surface is ground and polished to a smooth
finish after the concrete has cured, and usually gives a fine
appearance. Specific problems arise, however, from the
fact that marble chips are sensitive to acids, even mild acids.
The grout, or concrete between the chips, on the other hand, is
porous and sensitive to free alkali, present in many detergents.
Casual exposure of the marble chips to mild acids, such as
rinsing with vinegar or using an acid hardener, can erode and
roughen the surface of the marble. Even more troublesome is
the tendency of the porous grout to absorb oil, grease, and
soap. When this has happened the use of common floor maintenance systems becomes very difficult. To minimize the chances
of running into trouble with a terrazzo floor, a coat or two of a
good-quality sealer, followed by maintenance with a high-
quality finish is important. Effective sealing is really the
important element.

Quarry tile is characteristically very dense and hard. It
takes finish very well, however, and is usually easy to prepare.
The best procedure is to strip the floor properly and thoroughly,
then apply a good sealer and a quality finish.

Concrete, as used for flooring, is a mixture of cement, sand,
crushed stone or other aggregate, and water. It differs from
mortar in that concrete must retain nearly all the water in the
mix in order to cure properly. The water in a concrete mix is
needed to combine chemically and permanently with essential
ingredients in Portland cement in the process of hydration.
This process hardens the cement matrix and binds the aggregate into a solid mass. Because of various chemical agents
used as coating films to hold the water in the concrete as it
hardens, a good application of a high-quality sealer coat will
be necessary to make possible easy maintenance of the floor.
Besides preventing any further chemical activity of these
chemical hardening agents which might prove harmful or
disastrous to floor finishes, application of a good sealer coat

will provide benefits in the form of elimination of concrete dusting, improved gloss and appearance, protection against spilled liquids and stains, and easier maintenance.

Wooden Floors

To today's manufacturers of floor finishes, wooden floors usually mean gymnasium floors. Maintaining a gymnasium floor which is in good condition is a simple matter of keeping it free of dirt and dust. A gymnasium floor which is in bad or deteriorating condition, however, will eventually require stripping, sealing, and refinishing.

Booklets outlining the procedures for stripping and refinishing a gymnasium floor are available from most major finish manufacturers on request, and will provide detailed instructions for the process.

Care of wooden floors other than gymnasium floors can be summarized in one statement. Never use water. Water will raise the grain in wood and leave a rough and damaged surface. Solvent waxes should be used for cleaning and waxing. They must, of course, be buffed to maintain a gloss.

Carpeting

Of all the materials available for carpeting, only wool and certain kinds of synthetics are considered satisfactory for commercial use. Wool, dating back to the hand-woven Oriental rugs of Persia, is still considered best in terms of resilience and resistance to soiling, and is most easily cleaned and maintained. On the other hand, it does not wear as long as nylon. Nylon offers the most in terms of wear and is less expensive than wool. It does not have wool's resilience and soils more readily, but it is also easily cleaned. And it is naturally moth and mildew-proof, as are all the synthetics.

New synthetic fibers now on the market are acrylic, polyester, and olefin. Acrylic carpeting has most of the features of nylon but is not quite as resistant to wear. Olefin, one of the latest man-made fibers to be offered for carpet use, is made of polypropylene and offers three advantages: (1) absence of static electricity build-up; (2) high wearability; (3) excellent stain resistance.

Cotton and rayon and other synthetics are also available and can be considered for installation where cost and light service are prime factors. Both cotton and rayon have poor resilience, soil quickly, and are difficult to clean.

The color dyes used in today's carpeting present little or no problem to the user, except that he should be aware that those used in wool are usually fixed by acid solution and are generally endangered by the use of strong alkaline cleaning agents.

The tweeds, or "salt and pepper" color combination usually show the least amount of dirt and are easiest to keep looking clean and presentable.

Although the carpet buyer must largely rely on the reputation of the manufacturer as to the quality of the backing, many precise specifications have been developed as to the surface.

The most important of these, after basic construction and fiber type, is pile weight, or the actual amount of pile yarn in the carpet itself. Anything under 20 oz per sq yd is generally considered of poor quality; medium quality runs from 20 to 40 oz per sq yd, and carpeting of over 40 oz is considered excellent. A carpet's total weight per square yard is not important, since extra sizing on the back does not add to wearability.

Cleaning of Carpets.—One reason for the rapidly growing popularity of carpeting in commercial installations is the growing recognition of the fact that carpet maintenance is no longer either difficult or costly. The development of ever more efficient equipment designed specifically for carpet care is helping convert what was once thought of as a "cleaning problem" into another part of a simple maintenance program.

One of the basic elements of this program should be regular vacuum cleanings. A considerable amount of granular soil works its way past the surface of the carpet, into the pile and down into the backing. It is this soil, cutting into the carpet fibers by the grinding action of passing feet, which does the real damage to carpeting. It must be eliminated through a regular cleaning program with machines and cleaners specifically designed for that purpose.

Eventually all carpeting picks up oil-based or greasy dirt and reaches a point where vacuuming is no longer effective. At this point the cleaning process requires the use of solvents or detergents as well as agitation. So-called "mop-on" cleaners supply the solvent with little agitation. These are easy to apply

and effective for touch-up of high traffic areas such as eleva-
ors. A different type of measure is "dry-cleaning," which
supplements the action of the solvent with more active agitation.
These preparations usually consist of a solvent-saturated
powder, often based on sawdust or ground corncobs. It is
sprinkled on the carpet and worked into the pile with a stiff
brush. When dry it is simply vacuumed up. One major disadvantage of this type of cleaning, however, is that only very
vigorous vacuuming can lift all the sawdust or powder back out
of the carpet pile. If any is permitted to remain, it can cause
abrasion and wear.

Far more popular is wet shampooing, even though it requires
more drying time. The use of liquid detergents and a good deal
of agitation is the only way to emulsify oily soils and at the
same time disperse and suspend soil to a point where it can
easily be picked up. Wet shampooing can be done with a standard rotary floor machine equipped with a carpet brush. In
the better models, the detergent solution is fed through the
brush itself from a tank on the handle. The brush works the
detergent into a foam as it goes and the foam can be picked up
with a wet/dry vacuum cleaner, bringing the dirt with it. The
dirty foam should be picked up almost immediately if short
drying times are to be achieved. Experts recommend the job
be done with a two-man crew, one running the floor machine
and another following with the wet/dry vacuum. After the rug
has been shampooed and allowed to dry, a stiff brush or up-
right vacuum can be used to set the pile. Properly done, a
shampooed carpet will dry overnight.

One of the newest developments in carpet cleaning is an
adaptation of the rotary floor-care brush in which a foam-
generating tank is mounted on a conventional unit. In this
process, the detergent solution is whipped into a foam before it
is delivered to the brush edge. The dry foam has the same
cleaning power as the wet detergents, but with as little as 5% of
the moisture. There are also now on the market reel-type
machines to do dry-foam carpet cleaning. Some experts feel
that the reel types are better for cut-pile carpeting since they
clean the carpet in the direction of the pile, with no twisting of
the fibers. The most efficient of these machines is a combination vacuum cleaner, foam generator, and wet/dry vacuum,
accomplishing the entire carpet cleaning cycle in one pass.

General Housekeeping

Having now covered the basic types of flooring to be found in today's commercial buildings, we can look back and see that some basic rules for housekeeping seem to have emerged. The first of these is selection of the proper maintenance systems in the beginning. We must consider in this selection the needs of the user, traffic volume and conditions, the type of floor maintenance desired by the user and the condition and type of flooring.

A brief look at user preferences in floor finish shows that the non-buffables, the polymer and metal-complexed polymer finishes are the most widely used, and that they can be used virtually wherever the building supervisor and custodial staff is willing to take the time to prepare the floor and apply the system properly.

The polymers and metal-complexed polymers are the most desirable type of floor finish wherever black heel marking is a problem, such as in building lobbies and schools, and wherever frequent scrubbing is necessary, as in hospitals. They are also desirable in areas where spills are common, such as in restaurants and cafeterias.

The oldest of the self-polishing finishes, the buffable self-polishing waxes, still hold a major share of the floor finish market. Their significant advantage is their buffability; their gloss can be restored easily.

These finishes require more daily maintenance than the non-buffables, but are useful in areas where extremely fine appearance is desired, such as in executive offices, and where the extra work of buffing is considered to be worthwhile. These systems can be used wherever buffability is desired by the user and scrubbability is of little importance; where the user wants to brighten the floor frequently by buffing and where he will scrub infrequently.

It should be noted here that a technique called "spray buffing" can be used to brighten the finishes which are commonly referred to as non-buffable. "Spray buffing," however, is not a maintenance system in itself. It is a good shortcut toward eliminating scuffs and black heel marks from a floor between refinishings.

INSECT CONTROL

Another area of building maintenance which a beginner will rapidly learn not to neglect is that of insect control. Estimates are that damage to foodstuffs and clothing, not to mention building appearance, run into millions of dollars annually.

One of the fallacies of insect hunting is that killing bugs in the commercial and institutional field is quite different from the everyday household and backyard problem. The areas are larger, such as in warehouses, beer depots, bakeries, canneries and packing plants, so there are more bugs. But bugs are bugs, cockroaches, or flies, and can be effectively handled by the new heavy-duty liquid and aerosol products offered by leading insecticide product manufacturers, in many cases without the harmful after-effects of DDT and other damaging insecticides now, or soon to be, illegal.

Of the 600 species of flying and crawling insects, rodents and bugs which are considered damaging, the most important is the German cockroach. Next come rats and mice, termites and all other insects, moths, bedbugs, wasps, and beetles. These creatures account for some 90% of pest damage in commercial installations.

When the supervisor of a building or business discovers he has cockroaches or other pests to get rid of, he has the choice of calling in a professional pest control operator or of doing the job himself. In actuality, however, insect control is a constant problem no matter how diligently a maintenance or pest control program is followed in any building. Good housekeeping, especially in areas where food is prepared, served, or stored, is the single most important factor in preventing infestations.

WASHROOM MAINTENANCE

The last, but one of the most important areas to be considered in this chapter, is that of washroom maintenance. The purposes and use of commercial washrooms call for more cleaning and more specialized cleaning procedures than any other public facility—probably as much as 1 hr of cleaning for each 100 times the room is used.

There is no other location in any building where regular, systematic maintenance is so important and necessary as in the washrooms. Here an untidy appearance, offensive odors, and uncontrolled disease-producing germs will not only present an unfavorable impression, but can actually pose a threat to the health of employees and customers. A daily maintenance program, carefully planned and followed through, is the only way to assure a sanitary, clean, and presentable washroom at all times. Cleaning should be divided up into a general program for walls and floors, a regular cleaning schedule for toilets and urinals, glass mirrors, and towel holders, and liberal use of disinfectant sprays and air fresheners. In most cases the products necessary will be available from the same manufacturer who supplies floor-finishing products and maintenance needs.

CHAPTER 9

R. V. Lechowich

Relationships of Microorganisms in Foods and in Food-Service Systems

The presence of bacteria is an important factor in any food-handling or preparation system. These plant forms are characterized by their very small size, possession of rigid cell walls, lack of chlorophyll or other photosynthetic pigments, have no demonstrable nucleus, generally lack a means of sexual reproduction, and multiply extremely rapidly by simple transverse fission. The very small size of a common bacterium can be illustrated by the fact that one trillion (1,000,000,000,000 or 1×10^{12}) *Escherichia coli* bacteria, the common intestinal bacterium, can be placed in the volume of one cubic centimeter.

The composition of the bacterial cell is much like that of the human body in that both systems contain about 85% water. The remaining 15% of dry material is composed of 50% carbon, about 8% hydrogen, 10 to 12% nitrogen, 25 to 30% oxygen, and about 5 to 10% minerals.

Bacterial cells can be regarded as complex sacs of chemicals and enzymes. A bacterium such as *Escherichia coli* contains all the necessary enzymes to be able to grow well in a simple solution containing only the sugar glucose, ammonium chloride as a nitrogen source, and minerals.

The lactic acid bacterium *Streptococcus lactis* is used in the production of fermented dairy products, such as cottage cheese and yogurt. This microorganism does not have the ability to produce certain enzymes needed to synthesize necessary growth compounds. Therefore, pre-manufactured materials such as 16 to 17 amino acids, peptides, vitamins, sugars, sodium citrate, and fatty acids must be supplied to this microorganism if it is to grow.

SOURCES OF MICROBIAL CONTAMINATION

The multiplicity of energy-obtaining schemes possessed by the thousands of different bacterial species has enabled them to adapt to almost every conceivable ecological scheme in nature.

Thus, bacteria are extremely widespread and are found in soil, water, and the air. Soil contains by far both the greatest quantity and variety of types of microorganisms. Microorganisms are also encountered in the air, which serves as the transport mechanism for microorganisms found on dust particles or on water droplets. The third important microbial distribution system is water, which is another way of transporting microorganisms under natural conditions, as well as under commercial food-processing or food-preparation conditions.

In food-service systems, other important sources of microbial contamination can be utensils, counter-top surfaces, the clothing and hands of kitchen workers. The utensils may be contaminated with bacteria from the soil and water originating from fresh vegetables. Lack of proper cleaning techniques for table tops and cutting boards can introduce bacteria into relatively uncontaminated food sources. An example is the cutting or dicing of cooked meat items on uncleaned and unsanitized cutting boards previously used to cut up raw meats or poultry.

The air supply in a food preparation area in which there is much physical activity may contain many bacteria per cubic foot of air. Besides the dust particles in air that contain bacteria, water droplets may be introduced into the air by kitchen workers who sneeze or cough and thus add bacterial contamination to the air, which can then be transferred to food items or to work surfaces.

Colds also serve to transmit microorganisms to workers' hands when the affected worker covers his mouth when sneezing or coughing or after use of a handkerchief. Workers' hands may also transmit microorganisms from fecal sources if proper handwashing is not followed after using toilet facilities. In addition, infected cuts or infections on the hands are the best sources of contaminating a food material with the food-poisoning bacterium *Staphylococcus aureus*. This microorganism will be discussed in the section of this chapter on food-poisoning microorganisms.

Proper sanitation of exposed work surfaces may not be sufficient to minimize bacterial contamination if poor housekeeping habits are practiced. Thus, open doors and windows must be screened to prevent entrance of flies that can efficiently transfer large numbers of bacteria from decomposing garbage to work surfaces and utensils.

Bacteria present in the soil and food residues on the floors and in crevices on table tops or between work surfaces and walls can be spread to otherwise clean areas by flies and cockroaches. An effective insect-control program is necessary to prevent or minimize bacterial transmission from walls and floors to work surfaces by insects.

Microbial transmission by mice and rats can be a serious problem if an adequate rodent-control program is not used. The attraction of the food supply necessitates the proper disposal of kitchen waste and proper masonry construction of food preparation areas to minimize the entry of rodent pests. Traps or Warfarin-containing bait stations should be used if the presence of rodents is detected, and their means of entry located and sealed. The importance of sanitation in overall quality control of food preparation will be covered in the last section of this chapter.

TESTING FOR THE PRESENCE OF MICROORGANISMS

Given the facts that bacteria are generally widely distributed in soil, water, air, on workers' hands, in their nasal passages, and on utensils and equipment surfaces, let us examine the significance of the presence of these microorganisms. The numbers of bacteria in these environments can be readily established by performing standard quantitative bacterial plate counts. Quantitative plating of microorganisms is a very common technique that is used in microbiology to give some idea of the numbers of microorganisms that actually may be present in a given environment. However, the technique has some definite limitations.

Under most conditions, only those numbers of bacteria that are alive and that can grow in the presence of air will be detected. To accomplish this, the microorganisms from a piece of equipment or working surface are removed, or if from a food sample, they can be weighed and diluted with either sterile water or some common diluent such as a phosphate buffer or saline. Dilution of the bacteria is continued until the point is reached where a certain easily countable number, hopefully between 30 to 300 microorganisms, will be added to sterile Petri dishes. A good bacteriological growth medium plus the solidifying agent, agar, is added to the plates and the agar is allowed to solidify. The plates are placed in an incubator and after a certain length of time, the bacteria grow to form visible colonies and their number are counted and multiplied by the dilution factor. One must keep in mind that this procedure counts only live bacteria which are capable of growth in air. As microorganisms that are inhibited by air (anaerobes), are not detected with this technique, a true total microbial picture may not be obtained; but this procedure produces a reasonably good index of the microorganisms present in a food or on a surface.

A high total plate count does not necessarily indicate an improper preparation or poor raw materials, but it does indicate poor cleaning and sanitation. The bacteriological nature of each sample also has to be considered. For example, a high bacteriological plate count of an unpasteurized cottage cheese, or fermented sausage, or ground beef should not be surprising because these bacteria are either used in their manufacture or are normally present.

What then do bacteriological counts mean, since an absolute number of microorganisms present may not be obtained? Very often the relative numbers obtained from bacteriological counts can be used as indicators of the sanitary quality of equipment, foodstuffs, or any other material. For example, if equipment surfaces or utensils are to be examined and bacteriological counts of a given surface are obtained, this indicates how effective the clean-up is. It may indicate how conditions vary from day to day or after clean-up, for example. Count data may be very helpful and are excellent aids in microbiology.

What are some of the common microbiological counting techniques that can be used for equipment surfaces? One of the most widely used is the swab technique. This utilizes a swab, such as a cotton or sodium alginate wool-tipped wooden stick, to wipe off a certain area of a working surface; then the tip of the swab is broken off in a sterile tube of diluent such as peptone water or buffer. The diluent is plated out, using the previously described bacteriological technique to determine the number of microorganisms removed from the area.

However, a simpler method called the "agar-sausage" technique can be used. In this instance, a sterile agar is added to a sterile cellulose casing, such as a sausage casing, the casing tied, and allowed to solidify. The sterile "agar sausage" can be taken to a food preparation area and the end sliced off with a sterile knife. The sausage is partially squeezed out of the casing and touched to an equipment surface. A disc of this material is then cut off with the sterile knife, placed in a Pétri dish, and allowed to incubate. Depending upon the contamination present on the surface, the number of microorganisms present can be counted, or an estimate made as to light, moderate or heavy contamination on any given area. A third method is to purchase sterile media in small flexible vinyl Petri dishes such as the "Rodac" contact plate. The top of the plate is removed, the agar surface pressed against the surface to be tested, the top replaced, and the plate allowed to incubate. These are rapid techniques to be used where exact quantitation is not required. Follow-up tests should be run to determine the effectiveness of clean-up and sanitation.

Similar techniques can be performed on kitchen workers to determine the presence of fecal contaminants or food-poisoning microorganisms on their hands. The performance and inter-pretation of this type of testing can be performed by the local Board of Health officials or a commercial laboratory.

PRINCIPAL MICROORGANISMS THAT MAY CONTAMINATE FOODS

Bacteria are always present in foods and in food-preparation areas as a result of the wide distribution of bacteria, the pres-ence of food that permits bacteria to grow, and other suitable conditions such as oxygen, acidity, and so on. Bacteria behave according to one of the most basic of natural laws—preserva-tion of the species. They attempt to grow, divide and reproduce to the best degree possible, considering their environment. Thus, food handlers must recognize the presence of bacteria and their mode of growth, in order to control bacterial growth and maintain the quality that initially was present in the food-stuffs.

There are three basic types of microorganisms: the bacteria, the yeasts, and the molds. Each is important to food handlers because of their unique adaptations to environmental conditions.

In his excellent book entitled "Modern Food Microbiology," Professor J. M. Jay states that 25 different genera of bacteria, 16 different molds, and 9 different yeasts comprise the most

common and important microbial genera involved in food spoilage and food poisoning. Of these 25 bacteria, the most important genera in food operations would be: *Achromobacter,*
Alcaligenes, Bacillus, Clostridium, Corynebacterium, Entero-
bacter, Erwinia, Escherichia, Flavobacterium, Lactobacillus,
Leuconostoc, Micrococcus, Pseudomonas, Salmonella, Sarcina,
Shigella, Staphylococcus, and *Streptococcus.*

These bacteria are important because of their different abili-
ties to grow at different temperatures. Bacteria can be divided
into four major groups with respect to their growth temperature
classification.

Mesophiles

Mesophilic bacteria are those that can grow in the temperature
range of 15° to 40°C (59° to 104°F), and that have their maximum
rate of growth at 30° to 32°C (86° to 90°F). Thus if kitchen
temperatures are about 90°F, one would expect bacteria to grow
at a very rapid rate on counter tops or working surfaces that
are coated with thin layers of food.

Bacterial growth rates can be quite dramatic. The presence
of only 100 bacteria per sq in. of working surface can lead to
more than 6,500,000 bacteria per sq in. within only 2 hr! This
situation would result from a mesophilic bacteria that could
divide every 0.5 hr, growing without interference. Some bacterial growth and off-flavor development may take place if
Bacillus, Clostridia, Enterobacter, Escherichia or the lactic
acid bacteria such as *Lactobacillus, Leuconostoc,* or *Strepto-*
coccus are present.

Besides bacteria, yeasts and molds include many mesophilic
genera that have temperature optima that exceed 25°C (77°F).
Thus, the multicellular fungi or the molds included in the genera
Alternaria, Aspergillus, Botrytis, Cephalosporium, Clado-
sporium, Fusarium, Geotrichum, Gleosporium, Helminosporium,
Mucor, Penicillium, Rhizopus, Sporotrichum, and *Thamnidium*
are important in food spoilage. Yeasts, or single-celled fungi,
also includes many mesophilic species in the various genera of
Saccharomyces, Schizosaccharomyces, Torulopsis, and others.
These yeasts and molds are chiefly a problem in acid fruits,
where they grow more quickly than bacteria in the presence
of substantial amounts of sugar.

Facultative Thermophiles

Some food-poisoning bacteria may grow at mesophilic temperatures, but definitely grow better at 37° to 45°C (98° to 113°F). *Clostridium botulinum* types A and B, *Clostridium perfringens*, *Salmonella* species, and *Staphylococcus aureus* can be considered facultative thermophiles, that is they grow best at higher temperatures, but do not necessarily require these for growth. The fairly rare occurrence of *Clostridium botulinum* makes only the *C. perfringens*, *Salmonella* and *S. aureus* microorganisms a real hazard in food-preparation areas.

Obligate Thermophiles

This term denotes all the microorganisms that have a strict requirement for high temperatures for growth. The optimum temperature for growth of this group is 55°C (131°F).

Psychrophiles

Psychrophilic microorganisms can be defined as those microorganisms that are capable of growth at 0°C (32°F) or less, but their optimal growth temperature is about 25°C (77°F). There are also some microorganisms, including some of the bacteria that are termed psychrotrophic or cold-loving, that can grow at refrigerator temperatures. However, the optimum temperature for the psychrotrophs is above 25°C (77°F).

Psychrophilic bacteria that are a major problem in foods and food-handling systems include the genera *Achromobacter*, *Corynebacterium*, *Erwinia*, *Flavobacterium*, *Microbacterium*, and *Pseudomonas*. Also, the yeasts and molds are capable of slow growth at refrigerator temperatures.

FACTORS THAT AFFECT MICROBIAL GROWTH

Time-Temperature Effects

There are many environmental factors that affect microbial growth. Temperature was stated to have a marked effect upon microbial growth, but the time bacteria are maintained at a given temperature is also important.

Examination of the growth of a mesophilic bacterium growing at different temperatures will illustrate this time-temperature effect. Growth data for the microorganisms indicate that the

doubling or generation time at the optimum growth temperature
of 37°C (98°F) is about 30 min and that the lag or adaptation
period is only about 2.5 hr at this temperature. About 100 million or 1×10^8 bacteria per ml are produced after only 12 hr
of growth at 37°C. At 45°C (113°F) the rate of division and the
maximum population of one million (1×10^6) bacteria per ml are
considerably less than those produced at the optimum temperature. Reduction in growth temperature to 20°C (68°F) increased
the lag period to about 8 hr and also decreased the rate of
growth. If a food contained about 100 bacteria per gm and was
kept at 37°C for 8 hr, more than one million bacteria would be
present.

Effects of Moisture

There is a universal need for water in the life processes of
living organisms. The water content of the human body and
that of microorganisms is remarkably similar. Water is used
as the solvent to transport sugars and waste products in living
cells. The water contents of fresh foods are basically the same
as the plant or animal they were obtained from, while processed
foods generally have had some water removed during preparation.

pH

The optimum pH for growth of most bacteria is near neutrality (pH 7.0) with a minimum value of about 5.0 and a maximum
value of 8.0. There are some bacteria, however, that can grow
below pH 3.0 and up to pH 11.0. The pH of most food products
is slightly below 7.0; this includes the highly perishable meat,
poultry and fish items, vegetables, milk, and dairy products.
Proper temperature control must be used with these products,
since acidic vegetables such as tomatoes (pH 4.5), pimentoes
(pH 4.7), potatoes (pH 5.1), or other acidic products such as
fruits or fruit juices (pH 3.0 to 4.0), cranberry sauce (pH 2.3),
or pickle products (pH 3.0 to 3.7), are usually fairly safe.

Gaseous Environment

Most of the kitchen environment will encourage the growth
of air-loving microorganisms, or aerobic microbes. However,

the inner portion of a large roast of meat or a large covered
deep container containing a gravy or cream soup may have
little if any dissolved oxygen present. Heating drives off the
dissolved oxygen that was originally present, and can lead to
anaerobic environments in these viscous products. These systems, essentially lacking in air, may permit the growth of
obligate (strict) anaerobic or facultative anaerobic spore
formers. The facultative anaerobes are capable of growth in
both air-containing and air-lacking systems. Examples of
facultative anaerobic nonspore-forming microorganisms are
Staphylococcus and *Lactobacillus*.

MICROORGANISM-SUBSTRATE RELATIONSHIPS

Microorganisms are extremely rapid in growth and are capable of growth on a wide variety of food sources or substrates.
When this growth is used in the preparation of cottage cheese
or fermented sausages, it is a method of food manufacturing.
However, the appearance of an unwanted microorganism such
as a *Penicillium* mold on the cottage cheese or sausage would
be considered spoilage.

Carbohydrate Foods

About 20% of all harvested fruits and vegetables are lost be-.
cause of microbial spoilage by one or more of 250 different
diseases that may attack them. These diseases are for the
most part caused by molds and bacteria.

These molds and bacteria are particularly well suited to grow
in vegetables that contain about 88% water, 8.5% carbohydrates,
1.9% protein, 0.3% fat, and 0.85% minerals. The presence of
large amounts of water and available sugars and starches,
favorable pH range, and generally aerobic conditions favor the
growth of bacteria. Thus, soft rots produced by the *Erwina*
bacteria or gray mold rots caused by the genus *Botyritis* are
the most common causes of microbial spoilage.

Proteinaceous Foods

Meats, poultry, and fish contain all the nutrients required for
the growth of microorganisms and because of this, they constitute the most perishable class of foods. This high-protein

class of foods contain about 76% water, 18% protein, 3.0% fat,
1.6% nonprotein nitrogenous substances, 1.2% carbohydrate,
and about 0.6% minerals. The presence of high moisture, high
B vitamin content, low glucose content, aerobic nature of fresh
meat, and use of refrigerated storage generally cause an increase in the number of pseudomonad group of bacteria present
on meat and fish. Molds can also grow well on meats at refrigerator temperatures, but do not grow as quickly as some
bacteria. Most of the changes produced by bacterial growth in
meat products are off-flavors and odors which cause marked
quality losses in these products.

Fatty Foods

Foods high in fat or lipid, such as butter, margarine, salad
dressings, or nuts, do not generally spoil from microbial causes
because of their relatively low water content. Although certain
lipolytic or fat-splitting microorganisms such as certain species
of *Pseudomonas* can hydrolyze the fat and cause rancidity, the
principal cause of change in high-fat foods is oxidative rancidity
produced by chemical combination of oxygen in the air with the
fat.

PRECAUTIONS TO BE TAKEN WITH VARIOUS CLASSES OF FOOD

It has been pointed out that bacteria are present everywhere
within the kitchen environment on food materials, work surfaces,
utensils, and emanating from the workers.

Communicable diseases can readily be passed from workers
to persons consuming prepared food. Persons who are ill with
respiratory diseases or colds should not work with food. Periodic medical check-ups of employees is ideal but not always
practical, though many apparently healthy persons can be
carriers of both salmonella and *C. perfringens* bacteria. Food
poisoning and spoilage bacteria may also be introduced into
foods by insects or rodents, or may already be present on
meats, poultry, shellfish, and the kitchen environment.

Carbohydrate Foods

Foods high in carbohydrates but low in protein include fresh,
frozen, and canned fruits, dried fruits, honey syrups, potatoes,

sweet potatoes, and starch-thickened gravies, sauces, stews, and puddings, These items, because of their carbohydrate content, low protein and amino acid content and generally higher acidity (low pH) do not spoil as readily as other foods, such as meat or vegetables. However, proper care and sanitation should be used in their preparation from the initial washing of the product until it is served. Again, maintenance of quality should be the prime concern of the food-service operator.

Many vegetables, such as corn, lima beans, squash, broccoli, carrots, Brussels sprouts, and peas, contain large to moderate percentages of carbohydrates, and also contain varying amounts of protein. String beans and corn are two examples of this type of product. Because these items contain more necessary growth factors for bacteria, bacteria can readily grow in them to produce undesirable changes. Thus maintenance of proper temperature control to keep products out of the range of 40° to 140°F is very important with vegetables of this class.

Protein Foods

The high-protein foods are meat, poultry, fish, milk, dairy products, and eggs; these contain all the necessary growth factors for excellent growth of most bacteria. They are thus the most perishable class of foods. They also may contain to a highly variable extent certain of the food-poisoning bacteria. Thus salmonella microorganisms may be found in about 15% of all pork products and about 40% of all poultry products, while *C. perfringens* microorganisms occurs in 26% of beef products. Both of these microorganisms may be found in all meat-type items, while sea food and fishery products are known to be contaminated with type E *C. botulinum* microorganisms.

Salmonella and *C. botulinum* type E microorganisms are readily killed by proper heating to temperatures of 180°F. Recontamination of the cooked product from the work surfaces or utensils used for raw product preparation should not occur.

C. perfringens bacteria are not killed by normal heating procedures, so strict temperature control to keep high-protein products out of the range of 40° to 140°F is most essential. Rapid cooling of left-over materials is also necessary. Shallow pans should be used to cool foods in the refrigerator or cooler as soon as they are taken from steam tables, food warmers, or from preparation areas.

Fatty Foods

This class of food does not pose a microbiological problem, but proper usage and storage of butter, margarine, cooking oils, mayonnaise, and nuts will keep them from losing quality. Oxidative changes leading to rancidity will cause flavor changes of these products, so cold storage in covered containers and use of oldest products first is strongly recommended.

KITCHEN CONTROLS FOR DIFFERENT FOOD PRODUCTS

The varying composition of various classes of food has been described in relation to the ability of each class of food to support microbial growth and the types of microorganisms that may be present. Each foodstuff may be then subjected to various types of processing treatments that also affect the microorganisms present and their subsequent ability to grow.

Canned Food

There are two basic classes of food within the category of canned goods: (1) those that are commercially sterile and thus shelf-stable at normal room temperatures, and (2) nonsterile canned foods, which include canned hams greater in size than 3 lb that are only pasteurized to retain maximum texture and flavor of the ham.

Shelf-stable canned products that literally include every product from apples to zucchini should be stored in a cool, dry storeroom. Again, proper inventory control to use the oldest product first is important, since some quality loss and container damage can occur if canned products are stored for more than 6 months to a year.

Pasteurized canned meats and poultry, that may include hams, luncheon meats, and chicken or turkey products, must be stored in a refrigerator operated at 36° to 38°F with sufficient cooling capacity to cool warmer products when first placed under refrigeration. The canned poultry products are almost always received frozen, and they should be stored in a freezer and transferred to a refrigerator only for thawing prior to preparation.

Dents and bulges appearing in canned goods generally indicate a possibility of bacterial spoilage and should be discarded.

Frozen Foods

Almost every food item from appetizers, entrees, and desserts may be frozen. The food item may be a single component, such as a fruit or meat product, or main meal items that have been previously prepared and portion-controlled and packaged. Frozen items have been frozen when the food was at peak quality; frozen storage at −10°F will maintain this quality better than when higher storage temperatures are used, such as 0°F or −5°F. Proper freezer operation to prevent or minimize temperature cycling between 0 to −10°F is also important, since substantial quality loss through large ice crystal formation can occur.

The "first-in, first-out" rule of food storage also applies to frozen foods, if the foods are to be served at their best quality.

Frozen foods should be allowed to thaw in the sealed package under running cold water or in the refrigerator prior to use. They should be served immediately after thawing. If the packaged and unpackaged frozen food never exceeds refrigerator temperatures, no microbiological hazard will occur, but refreezing will bring about quality loss by slow-freezing methods.

Dehydrated Foods

Dried vegetables, fruits, bouillion, and cereals should also be stored in a cool dry storeroom. Temperature fluctuation should be prevented, since moisture condensation in the room and on packages could occur. Low humidity conditions are essential to maintain optimum product quality and to prevent mold formation on the product surfaces.

PROCESS CONTROLS

Each step in food preparation should be carefully controlled so that the quality of the food item as originally purchased and received is maintained throughout preparation and handling to the point where the food is consumed. Proper food preparation and handling will ensure minimal microbiological growth problems.

Heating

Prompt and thorough cooking of food items to temperatures of 160° to 180°F should rid them of harmful microorganisms. Certain items such as Hollandaise sauces cannot be heated excessively, but many items that undergo considerable handling in their preparation should be sufficiently cooked. These include deep-fat and pan-fried items, creamed foods, meat and poultry pies, casseroles, and left-overs.

Cooling

Prompt and efficient cooling to keep cooked food in the bacterial growth range of 40° to 140°F for the shortest possible time is essential. High-protein foods should be spread in shallow layers in shallow pans to cool. Cream-style soups and gravies prepared in large steam-jacketed kettles should be cooled in the kettle by circulating refrigerated water through the jacket and stirring the product continually while cooling. Once the product is cooled to at least 50°F, it may be covered to prevent drying or discoloration while in the refrigerator.

Freezing

Prompt cooling must take place prior to freezing, as discussed in the previous section. The product to be frozen may be put in covered shallow pans and placed in a freezer in a rack or tray that permits maximum air movement all around it. The freezer should be equipped with an air blower to provide forced convection currents to achieve good heat transfer between the air and the product. Frozen products should be stored at −10°F or less.

Storage

The rationale for proper storage of refrigerated, frozen, and dried foods has been discussed. Two basic principles that must be considered in storage procedures are that some quality loss will occur in storage, and that therefore storage times should be minimal, sufficient only for proper and most efficient operation. The first-in, first-out rule should be always used to prevent undue storage of products.

Handling

Every handling step involves labor and money. Efficient kitchen layouts and proper instruction of personnel should be used to keep handling to a minimum. Also, the more handling a product receives, the greater the chance for bacterial contamination and subsequent quality loss.

CHAPTER 10

L. L. W. Smith
L. J. Minor

Organic Chemistry

Biochemists approach food chemistry by studying the living cell, whereas *organic chemists* use the carbon atom as a starting point. Since the living cell's complexity requires a fundamental knowledge of both organic chemistry and microbiology to develop and comprehend its role in foods, the function of the carbon atom in compounds becomes the basis of food chemistry.

CARBON

Carbon is in Group IV A in the central portion of the Periodic Table. Accordingly carbon is neither strongly electronegative (electron-attracting) nor electropositive (electron-repelling). It has an atomic number of 6 with a total of 6 orbital electrons. Two electrons are in the first (K) shell, and four electrons are in the valence (L) shell. Carbon atoms tend to share electrons with other carbon atoms to form long chains (*aliphatic compounds*), or six membered carbon rings having alternating double and single pairs of electron bonds between the carbon atoms (aromatic compounds). Carbon with a valence of four tends to form covalent bonds not only with other carbon atoms but with hydrogen, oxygen, nitrogen or other specific elements. A million or more organic compounds are known and the number is ever increasing.

The conformation or space arrangement of the carbon atom is a regular tetrahedron with bonds extending from it to the corners of the tetrahedron.

Chains of carbon atoms, either straight or branched, as well as *rings*, occupy three dimensions. However, the hydrocarbon C_8H_{18}(octane) for convenience in printing is shown as:

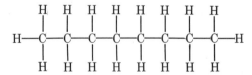

Hydrocarbons are compounds made up of carbon and hydrogen.

ALIPHATIC HYDROCARBONS

Formulas such as C_8H_8, showing the elements and number of atoms of each element present in a compound, are *molecular formulas* that reveal nothing concerning the structure of a compound. In order to indicate the *arrangement of atoms within molecule, structural formulas* are used.

Compounds having the same *molecular formulas* but different *structural formulas* are called *isomers*. For example the molecular formula C_4H_{10} may represent either normal butane (*n*-butane), a straight-chain compound, or 2-methyl propane (isobutane), a branched-chain compound.

n-butane—m.p. $-135°C$ 2-methyl propane
b.p. $-0.5°C$ or isobutane

m.p. $-145°C$
b.p. $-10°C$

Condensed formulas are used and are a short-hand molecular formula, but do show the position of the functional groups.

C_2H_5OH (ethanol)   vs CH_3OCH_3 (methoxymethane)
$(CH_3)_3CCHCH_2$ vs $(CH_2)_6$
3,3-dimethylbutene-1   cyclohexane

Skeletal formulas are another expression of configuration in which the hydrogens attached to the carbons are not shown.

Homologous Series

Hydrocarbons are divided into 3 homologous series called alkanes or paraffins (general formula C_nH_{2n+2}); alkenes or olefins (general formula C_nH_{2n}); and alkynes or acetylenes (C_nH_{2n-2}). Members of a homologous series are separated from each other by a constant factor such as —CH_2— (methylene group). The *alkene* series has a double covalent bond between two adjacent carbon atoms, while the *alkyne* series has a triple covalent bond between two adjacent carbon atoms; these two series are called *unsaturated compounds* with reactive sites. The reactivity of alkynes is greater than that of alkenes, which in turn are more reactive than the *saturated alkanes*. Alkynes and alkenes form *addition compounds* and alkanes form *sub - stitution compounds*.

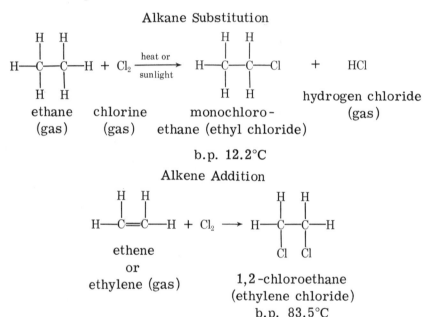

Alkane Substitution

ethane (gas)   chlorine (gas)   monochloro-ethane (ethyl chloride)   hydrogen chloride (gas)

b.p. 12.2°C

Alkene Addition

ethene or ethylene (gas)

1,2-chloroethane (ethylene chloride)
b.p. 83.5°C

The 1,2-means that on the first and second carbon in the chain, there is a chlorine atom bonded.

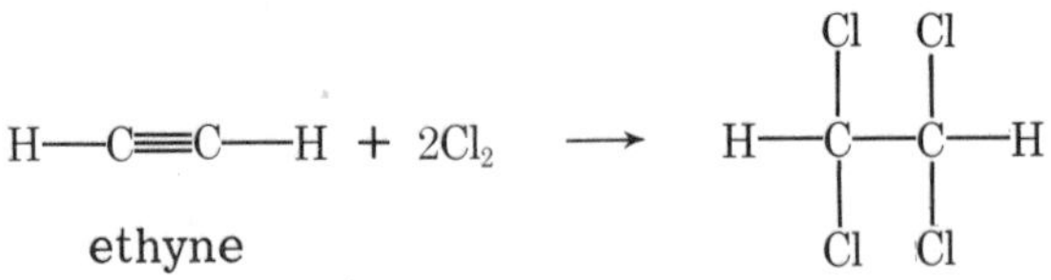

ethyne (acetylene gas)

1,1,2,2-tetrachloroethane

Alkene Addition

Reactions produce a mixture of products that must be separated by distillation, crystallization, sublimation, or other means. The examples given are for purpose of illustration.

Aliphatic compounds are so-called because the term orig-inally referred to fats. The modern meaning is substances re-lated to methane; either saturated or unsaturated open-chain or cyclic compounds not containing a benzene ring.

Nomenclature

A system for naming carbon compounds has been developed by the International Union of Pure and Applied Chemistry, I.U.P.A.C. The rules are:

(1) The general name for paraffin or saturated hydrocarbons is *alkane*; that for olefins or hydrocarbons with double bonds between adjacent carbon atoms is *alkene*, and for acetylenes or hydrocarbons with triple bonds between adjacent carbon atoms is *alkyne*.

(2) In naming branched hydrocarbons, use the longest con-tinuous chain of carbon atoms in the molecule as the basis for naming the compound. An examination of the compound

$$CH_3-CH_2-\underset{3}{\overset{\overset{\displaystyle CH_3}{|}}{CH}}-CH_2-CH_2-CH_3$$
$$\underset{1}{}\underset{2}{}\underset{3}{}\underset{4}{}\underset{5}{}\underset{6}{}$$

reveals that the longest continuous chain has 6 carbon atoms, and is thus a hexane compound.

(3) Numbering of the carbon atoms begins at the end nearest the branch, as shown.

(4) The substituent has one carbon atom and the name is derived from the paraffin hydrocarbon methane, CH_4, by chang-ing the *-ane* ending to *-yl*, making it a methyl group. Since the methyl group is attached to the 3-carbon of the longest chain the name of the compound is 3-methylhexane.

(5) When numbering the longest chain the substituents must have the lowest possible numbers. Had the chain been numbered from right to left the name would be 4-methylhexane. That would be incorrect. Other examples are:

2,2-dimethylpentane   2,2-dibromopropane

TABLE 10.1

A HOMOLOGOUS SERIES OF ALKANES, ALKENES, AND ALKYNES

Alkanes C_nH_{2n+2}	b.p., °C	Alkenes C_nH_{2n}	b.p., °C	Alkynes C_nH_{2n-2}	b.p., °C
CH_4, methane	−162				
C_2H_6, ethane	− 88	C_2H_4, ethylene	−104	C_2H_2, acetylene	−84
C_3H_8, propane	− 42	C_3H_6, propene	− 47	C_3H_4, propyne	−23
C_4H_{10}, butane	− 0.5	C_4H_8, 1-butene	− 5	C_4H_6, 1-butyne	9
isobutane	− 10.2	2-butene	2.5	2-butyne	27
C_5H_{12}, pentane	36	C_5H_{10}, 1-pentene	30	C_5H_8, 1-pentyne	40
Isopentane	28	2-pentene	36	2-pentyne	56
Neopentane	9.5				
C_6H_{14}, hexane	69	C_6H_{12}, 1-hexene	63	C_6H_{10}, 1-hexyne	72
2-methyl-pentane	60	2-hexene	68	2-hexyne	84
3-methyl-pentane	64	3-hexene	68	3-hexyne	
C_7H_{16}, heptane	98	C_7H_{14}, 1-heptene	96	C_7H_{12}, 1-heptyne	100
2-methyl-hexane	90	2-heptene	98	2-heptyne	112
3-methyl-hexane	92	3-heptene	92	3-heptyne	107
C_8H_{18}, octane	125	C_8H_{16}, octylene	123	C_8H_{14}, 1-octyne	126
2-methyl-heptane	117			2-octyne	137
3-methyl-heptane	119			3-octyne	133
C_9H_{20}, nonane	151	C_9H_{18}, 1-nonylene	147	C_9H_{16}, 1-nonyne	160
$C_{10}H_{22}$, decane	174	$C_{10}H_{20}$, 1-decene	171	$C_{10}H_{18}$, 1-decyne	

A homologous series of alkanes, alkenes, and alkynes is given in Table 10.1. Note that the boiling point rises as the carbon chain lengthens. Unsaturated compound boiling points are higher when unsaturation is at the second carbon than at either the first or third positions. Boiling point differences between saturated and unsaturated compounds are remarkably small. Branched compounds have lower boiling points at the C_2 as compared to the C_3 position, and branching lowers the boiling points of compounds having the same number of carbon atoms in a straight chain.

Boiling point and melting point are the physical constants
most often used to identify unknown compounds. Separations
by distillation or crystallization are also made on the basis
of differences in boiling point or melting point.

All hydrocarbons float in water and are almost completely
insoluble in water. The viscosity increases as the chain length
increases.

Major sources of hydrocarbons are the fossil fuels, whose
products of incomplete combustion poison the atmospheres of
congested highways and cities. These include coal, petroleum
and natural gas. Other sources are plant waxes C_{25} to C_{37},
pine turpentine (heptane), and marsh gas (CH_4).

COAL, PETROLEUM, AND NATURAL GAS

Coal

Coal is a black or dark brown combustible mineral substance
consisting of carbonized vegetable matter. Originally as cellulose $(C_6H_{10}O_5)_x$, in which x represents variable multiples of
units from photosynthesis in a primeval forest 300 million years
ago, coal was formed by high pressure and some heating in the
presence of water and absence of air. Methane (CH_4), carbon
dioxide (CO_2), and ammonia (NH_3) gases were released as car-
bonization progressed. This reduction in hydrogen, oxygen,
and nitrogen content enriched the carbon concentration in stages
from peat (11%), to lignite (22%), to bituminous (60%), and
finally to anthracite (80%).

Coke is the solid by-product resulting from the destructive
distillation of coal in an oven or closed chamber or by imperfect
combustion; it is chiefly carbon. A ton of coal yields about 3/4
ton of coke. Besides being used as a smokeless fuel, coke is an
effective reducing agent for converting metal oxides to metals.
Pig iron is made from molten iron oxide by adding coke to form
carbon monoxide and cast iron containing 3 to 4% carbon together with sulfur, phosphorus, silicon, and manganese.

Steel is made from iron by burning out the impurities with
oxygen at very high temperatures.

Useful by-products per ton of coal other than coke include
10 to 12 thousand cu ft of fuel gas; 6 to 9 gal. coal tar, from
which synthetic dyes and medicines are derived; 5 to 6 lb ammonia used for fertilizers; and 2 to 3 gal. light oil, from which

benzene, toluene, naphtha, benzaldehyde, and phenol are distilled. Naphthalene, cresol, cyanogen, and ferricyanide are also
obtained, together with hundreds of by-products including:
benzoic acid, and sodium benzoate food preservatives; sac-
charine, a food sweetener; food colors, disinfectants, refrigerants, antiseptics, paper sizings, paints, varnishes, plastics,
explosives, lampblack pigment, and hundreds of related products.

Petroleum

Petroleum means rock oil resulting from the decomposition of
plants and animals living in the strata when rocks were formed,
and consists mainly of a complex mixture of hydrocarbons. Re-
fineries produce petroleum ether solvent, gasoline, kerosene,
fuel oil, lubricating oils, paraffin wax, and asphalt from crude
oil by fractional distillation.

Natural Gas

Natural gas is found with petroleum deposits. It is composed
mainly of methane (CH_4), and ethane (C_2H_6), together with
smaller amounts of propane (C_3H_8) and butane (C_4H_{10}), and
traces of pentane (C_5H_{12}) and hexane (C_6H_{14}). Some hydrocarbons
from petroleum and natural gas, and their uses are given in
Table 10.2.

TYPES OF ORGANIC REACTIONS

Changing hydrocarbon structures is important, since straight-
chain hydrocarbons as shown in Table 10.2 have high knock
tendencies in motor fuel. Isooctane (2,2,4-trimethylpentane) has
the formula $CH_3C(CH_3)_2CH_2CH(CH_3)_2$ and is rated as 100-octane
gasoline. Heptane with the formula $CH_3(CH_2)_5CH_3$ has an octane
rating of zero.

A motor fuel having an octane rating of less than 100 would
perform like a blend of isooctane and heptane. The addition of
tetraethyl lead

$$C_2H_5 \atop | \atop C_2H_5\!-\!\!-Pb\!-\!\!-C_2H_5 \atop | \atop C_2H_5$$

TABLE 10.2

PARAFFIN (SATURATED) HYDROCARBONS FROM PETROLEUM AND NATURAL GAS

Hydrocarbon	Formula	b.p., °C	Use
Methane	CH_4	-162	Natural gas
Ethane	C_2H_6	-88	Natural gas
Propane	C_3H_8	-42	Bottled gas
Butane	C_4H_{10}	-0.5	Bottled gas
Pentane	C_5H_{12}	36	Hi-knock motor fuel
Hexane	C_6H_{14}	69	Hi-knock motor fuel
Heptane	C_7H_{16}	98	Hi-knock motor fuel
Octane	C_8H_{18}	123	Hi-knock motor fuel
Iso-octane	$CH_3-C(CH_3)_2-CH_2-CH(CH_3)-CH_3$	99	No-knock motor fuel
Nonane	C_9H_{20}	151	Kerosene
Decane	$C_{10}H_{22}$	174	Kerosene
Hendecane	$C_{11}H_{24}$	196	Kerosene
Dodecane	$C_{12}H_{26}$	215	Kerosene
Hexadecane	$C_{16}H_{34}$	288	Fuel oil
Heptadecane	$C_{17}H_{36}$	303	Fuel oil
Octadecane	$C_{18}H_{38}$	317	Fuel oil
	$C_{19}H_{38}-C_{20}H_{42}$		Lubricating oil
	$C_{20}H_{42}-C_{22}H_{48}$		Grease
	$C_{20}H_{42}-C_{24}H_{50}$		Paraffin wax

to isooctane increases the octane rating to above 100. Some modern gasolines have octane ratings higher than 200 for use in specific engines.

Isomerization or conversion of straight chain to branched hydrocarbons is essential to the production of high-octane motor fuel. This may be accomplished by means of heating hydrocarbon gases under pressure in the presence of a catalyst as in the conversion of butane to isobutane.

$$CH_3-CH_2-CH_2-CH_3 \xrightarrow[70-100°C]{AlCl_3} CH_3-\overset{\overset{\displaystyle CH_3}{|}}{CH}-CH_3$$

n-butane   isobutane
(bp -0.5°C)   (bp -10°C)

Actually, in the refining of crude oil, distillation is used to separate propane and butane, heavy gasoline and naphthas, kerosene and diesel fuel, fuel oil, petrolatum, and paraffin in crude cuts.

Butane is converted to motor or aviation gasoline by isomerization and alkylation. Fuel oil is subjected to catalytic cracking and thermal cracking to produce motor gasoline. Both of these unit processes, together with hydroforming, are important.

Alkylation is the process of combining a saturated with an unsaturated hydrocarbon. Isooctane is formed when isobutene and isobutane react in the presence of sulfuric acid (catalyst).

$$CH_3-C=CH_2 \;+\; H-\overset{\displaystyle CH_3}{\underset{\displaystyle CH_3}{C}}-CH_3 \xrightarrow{H_2SO_4} CH_3-CH-CH_2-\overset{\displaystyle CH_3}{\underset{\displaystyle CH_3}{C}}-CH_3$$

isobutene	isobutane	2,2,4-trimethylpentane
2-methyl propene	2-methyl propane	

$$CH_3(CH_2)_{10}CH_3 \xrightarrow[\text{catalyst}]{\text{heat pressure}}$$
$$CH_2=CH(CH_2)_3CH_3 \;+\; CH_3(CH_2)_4CH_3$$

1-hexene	n-hexane

$$CH_3(CH_2)_4CH_3 \xrightarrow[\text{catalyst}]{\text{heat pressure}} CH_2=CHCH_3 \;+\; CH_3CH_2CH_3$$

propene	propane

Catalytic cracking is used to produce ethylene, propylene, and butylene used for the manufacture of ethylene glycol (permanent antifreeze), polyethylene and polypropylene packaging films, synthetic rubber, and high-octane fuels.

Polymerization is a process by which many small molecules unite to produce a giant molecule called a *polymer*. Starch, proteins, pectin and natural rubber are polymers. Polymerized molecules are the source of nylon and other manufactured fibers, plastics, and synthetic rubber.

Hydroforming is a process for converting straight-chain hydrocarbons into cyclic and aromatic hydrocarbons by the use of heat, pressure, and catalysts in the presence of hydrogen.

$$CH_3(CH_2)_4CH_3 \xrightarrow[\text{heat}]{\text{platinum catalyst}}$$

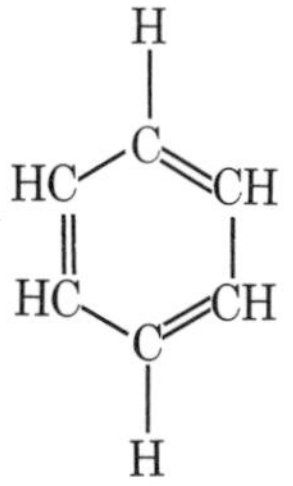

n-hexane

benzene

$+\ 4H_2$

Aromatization is another name for hydroforming. Its main use is to convert low-grade products such as straight-run gasolines or naphtha into high-octane motor fuels. Another application is to produce benzene, toluene, and xylene from petroleum by the conversion of hexane, heptane, or octane to the corresponding aromatic hydrocarbon. This involves hydrogen release and cyclizing the respective molecules.

Hydrogenation is the process of adding hydrogen to an unsaturated molecule in the presence of a catalyst. Vegetable oils are converted to shortening by this method. An example of hydrocarbon saturation with hydrogen is the conversion of the olefin, 1-butene, to butane.

$$CH_2{=}CHCH_2CH_3 + H_2 \xrightarrow[\substack{\text{pressure,}\\ \text{heat}}]{\text{platinum}} CH_3CH_2CH_2CH_3$$

n-butene   n-butane

Dehydrogenation is the removal of hydrogen from a saturated hydrocarbon in the presence of a catalyst.

$$CH_3CH_2CH_2CH_3 \xrightarrow{\text{catalyst}} CH_2{=}CH{-}CH_2{-}CH_3$$

butane   1-butene

$$CH_2{=}CH{-}CH_2{-}CH_3 \xrightarrow{\text{catalyst}} CH_2{=}CH{-}CH{=}CH_2$$

1-butene   1,3-butadiene

Butadiene is polymerized to make an important form of synthetic rubber.

The various unit processes described exemplify how the petroleum industry has developed methods of tailoring organic molecules for use in a myriad of products. Obviously, these methods and modifications of them are useful in other chemical industries.

Organic compounds burn in air with a yellow flame (a result of incomplete combustion), and release of energy as heat.

This phenomenon is important in the use of gas fuel or the combustion of methane, natural gas, or the bottled gases, propane and butane. The regulation or control of the burner valves to obtain the maximum amount of heat is an economical must. The combustion of these gases, if complete, yields carbon dioxide, water and heat.

$$C_nH_{2n+2} + \frac{3n + 1}{2} O_2 \longrightarrow nCO_2 + n + 1\ H_2O + \Delta$$

The number of calories released per mole is called the *heat of combustion* and for methane is 211 kcal/mole.

Heats of combustion have a nearly constant increase per —CH_2— unit of 156 kcal/mole between homologues.

HYDROCARBON DERIVATIVES

Alcohols and phenols may be regarded as the aliphatic (R—OH) and aromatic (Ar—OH) analogs of water (H—OH), in which R usually represents an *alkyl* group (C_nH_{2n+1}) and Ar represents the phenyl group (C_6H_5). Replacement of a hydrogen atom in a saturated or unsaturated hydrocarbon by a hydroxyl group (—OH) yields the corresponding alcohol. Phenol is formed when a hydrogen atom in the benzene ring is replaced by a hydroxyl group. The properties of alcohols and phenols are derived from the *functional group* —OH.

Hydrogen bonding is a characteristic of alcohols and phenols. Ethyl alcohol, the product of fruit and grain fermentations, is infinitely soluble in water, and is used as a preservative in fruit extracts and flavors. Phenol is less soluble due to the presence of the ring, which hinders solubility. In fact naphthol, with two rings, is only very slightly soluble. Solubility of the aliphatic alcohols decreases as the chain length increases. Octanol ($C_8H_{17}OH$) is soluble, but nonanol ($C_9H_{19}OH$) is insoluble. Branched-chain alcohols are less soluble than their straight-chain isomers.

Alcohols

Methanol [(CH$_3$OH) Methyl Alcohol, Wood Alcohol].—So-called because it was formerly manufactured by the distillation of wood. Now it is synthesized from carbon monoxide by hydrogenation.

$$CO + 2H_2 \xrightarrow[\substack{150 \text{ atm} \\ \text{catalyst}}]{400°C} CH_3OH$$

Although the odor and taste somewhat resemble that of ethyl alcohol, it is extremely poisonous when inhaled or imbibed: blindness and death may result. Its uses include manufacture of formaldehyde (H—CHO); antifreeze; solvent for shellac, guns, and resins; paint removers; inks; rocket fuel; and dehydration of natural gas.

Ethanol [(C$_2$H$_5$OH), Ethyl Alcohol, Grain Alcohol, or Simply Alcohol].—May be prepared from starch, cellulose, and sugars of certain plants by alcoholic fermentation, but most is synthesized from ethylene. It is the principal industrial alcohol. Three commercial methods are used to produce ethanol; methods (1) and (2) are fermentations:

(1) $C_{12}H_{22}O_{11} + H_2O \xrightarrow[\text{zymase}]{\text{yeast}} 4CH_3CH_2OH + 4CO_2$

cane sugar in   ethyl alcohol
blackstrap
molasses

(2) starch $\xrightarrow{\text{enzymes}}$ glucose $(C_6H_{12}O_6)$

$C_6H_{12}O_6 \xrightarrow[\text{zymase}]{\text{yeast}} 2C_2H_5OH + 2CO_2$

glucose
(simple sugar)

(3) $CH_2{=}CH_2 \xrightarrow{98\% \ H_2SO_4} CH_3CH_2OSO_3H \xrightarrow{H_2O, \ heat}$

ethylene   ethyl hydrogen
(ethene)   sulfate

$$CH_3CH_2OH + H_2SO_4$$

ethanol

95% of all commercial alcohol in the United States is produced by method (3).

Uses of ethyl alcohol include: solvent in making tinctures, *essences*, *extracts*, and varnishes; *vinegar*; medicinals, dyes, and perfumes; antifreeze; explosives; and *beverages*.

Handling precautions are necessary as ethanol is highly *flammable*.

Commercial alcohol is a constant-boiling mixture of 95% alcohol and 5% water that cannot be further purified by distillation. To make *absolute alcohol* quicklime (CaO) is added that reacts with the water, but does not affect the alcohol.

Proof is a term used for alcoholic beverages, and is twice the percent of alcohol present.

Percentages of Alcohol in Beverages: Beer, 2 to 5%, ale 6%, wine 7 to 12%, fortified wine 17 to 20%, whiskey, brandy, gin, rum, etc. 40 to 75%.

The body oxidizes about one-half gram of alcohol per kilogram of body weight in 24 hr.

Ethylene Glycol. —[$C_2H_4(OH)_2$] contains two —OH groups, and is termed a dihydric alcohol. It is the permanent antifreeze used in car radiators because of its high boiling point, 197°C. It will burn, but is not considered flammable.

Glycerol [CH_2OH $CHOH$ CH_2OH, 1,2,3-propanetriol (glycerine)] is a trihydric alcohol produced when fats or oils are digested with sodium or potassium hydroxide or is obtained from propylene ($CH_3CH{=}CH_2$) synthetically. It is a syrupy, viscous, colorless, high-boiling liquid that is soluble in water and alcohol, and has a pronounced sweet taste. Hydrogen bonding tendencies are pronounced as a result of the three (—OH) groups in the glycerol molecule; as a moistening agent (humectant) it conditions tobacco. *Uses of glycerol* include alkyd resins and ester gums; explosives, tobacco, cellophane, cosmetics and dentifrices; paper coatings and finishes; explosives; drugs; corks and gaskets; liqueurs; perfumery; lubricant and softener; bacteriostat; penetrant; solvent; humectant. Glycerol is combustible but not highly flammable.

AROMATIC HYDROCARBONS

Aromatic compounds were originally referred to as natural products having characteristic aromatic odors. Today, chemists classify aromatic compounds as substances having structures related to benzene. *Heterocyclic compounds* are the third large class of organic substances; they are cyclic compounds having at least one element other than carbon as a member of the ring, such as oxygen, nitrogen, sulfur, or some other element.

Benzene has six carbon atoms in its ring with one hydrogen atom attached to each carbon atom. Research indicates that the hydrogen and carbon atoms lie in the same plane with a covalent bond joining each carbon-hydrogen (C:H) pair. There are three single and three double pairs of electrons distributed in the ring with the double bonds forming layers of negative charge above and below the plane of carbon atoms. It is believed that benzene is a *stable resonance hybrid structure* composed of all possible classical structures.

These symbols

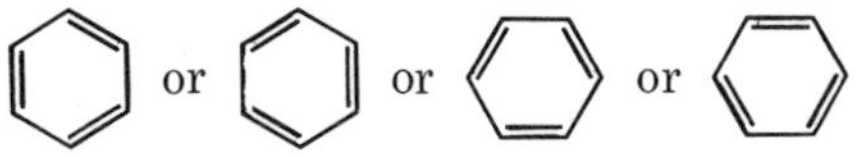

show that the electron pairs are constantly moving in the ring. At each point of the hexagonal ring there is a C:H group. The abbreviation for the benzene structure is:

in which the circle is made up of three pairs of electrons constantly moving, whereas, the hexagonal ring contains six C:H groups.

Aromatic hydrocarbons that are both aromatic and aliphatic are:

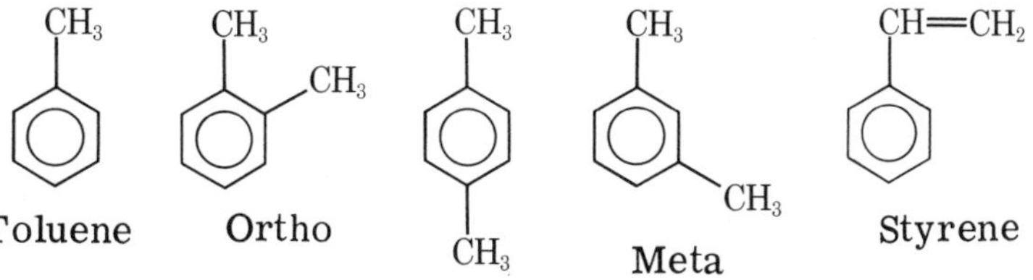

Toluene   Ortho

Para
Xylene, a mixture of isomers

Styrene

Note that commercial xylene is a mixture of the ortho (two

adjacent ring substituents or radicals), para (two opposite), and meta (with a third carbon atom between the two substitu- ents).

Multiple aromatic ring compounds include

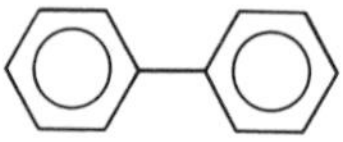

diphenyl
$C_{12}H_{10}$
or "condensed" rings

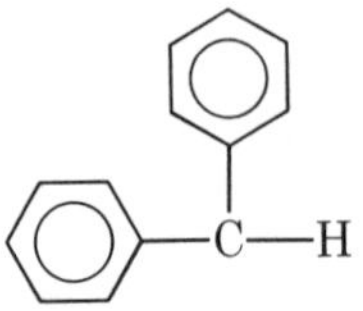

diphenylmethane
$C_{13}H_{14}$

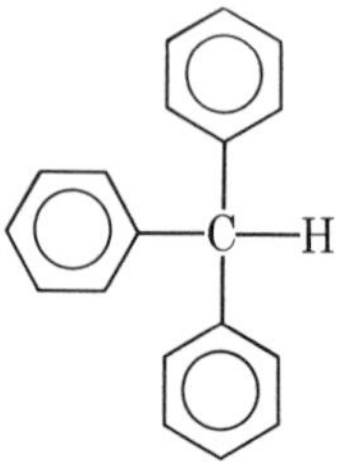

triphenylmethane
$C_{19}H_{16}$

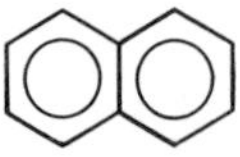

naphthalene
$C_{10}H_8$

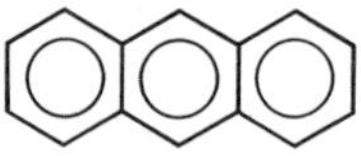

anthracene
$C_{14}H_{10}$

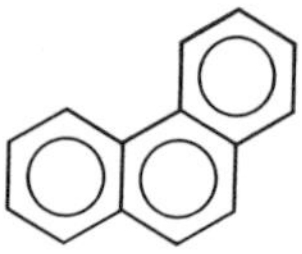

phenanthrene
$C_{14}H_{10}$

Aromatic nomenclature has been developed for the general class of compounds called *arenes*. A typical *aryl* group is the *phenyl* group consisting

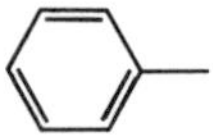

or C_6H_5

of a benzene ring with one hydrogen removed.

A numbering system is used when more than one hydrogen in the ring is substituted:

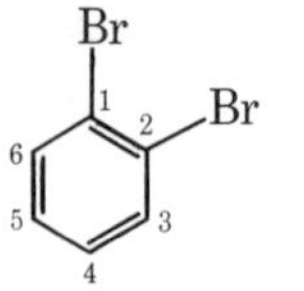

ortho-dibromobenzene
(1,2-dibromobenzene)

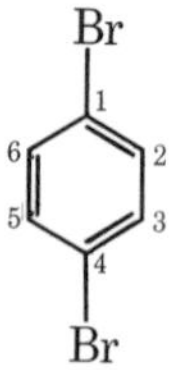

para-dibromobenzene
(1,4-dibromobenzene)

meta-dibromobenzene
(1,3-dibromobenzene)

When three or more substituents are in the ring a numbering system is used.

Phenols

Phenols are derivatives of benzene which have one or more hydroxyl (—OH) groups attached directly to carbon atoms in the benzene ring. Phenol itself, C_6H_5OH, is known as carbolic acid, with an ionization constant, K_a, of 1×10^{-10}. An important constituent of coal tar, phenol is produced synthetically from chlorobenzene by hydrolyzing with alkali.

Treatment with carbon dioxide liberates the phenol from its sodium salt.

Uses of phenol include phenolic resins; epoxy resins; nylon-6; 2,4-D weed killers; selective solvent for refining lubricating oils; salicylic acid; pentachlorophenol; germicidal paints; pharmaceuticals.

Handling precautions are necessary with phenol. It has a corrosive action on tissues, blisters skin, irritates mucous membranes, and may paralyze the central nervous system, causing death. Many persons are allergic to medicines containing phenol or its derivatives.

Ethers

Ethers have the general formulas R—O—R and Ar—O—R, the functional group being $\geq$C—O—C$\leq$. Structurally it is related to water, H—OH, both hydrogens being replaced by alkyl, R, groups, Generally, ethers are isomers of alcohols with the same number of carbon atoms.

CH_3—CH_2—OH   and CH_3—O—CH_3

ethyl alcohol   dimethyl ether

Ethers are prepared by the condensation (elimination of water) of alcohols. Concentrated sulfuric acid may be added as a dehydrating agent.

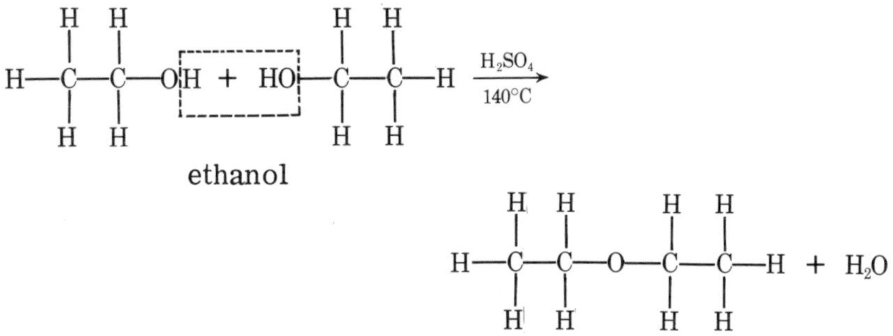

ethanol

diethyl ether (ethyl ether)
bp 35°C

Diethyl ether is used as an anaesthetic and solvent for fats, gums and waxes. *Caution: it is extremely flammable.*

Other important ethers are dimethyl ether, used as a refrigerant, and diphenyl ether, b.p. 259°C, used as a heat-transfer medium.

Some important aromatic compounds containing the ether, —C—O—C—, functional group are: eugenol (oil of cloves)

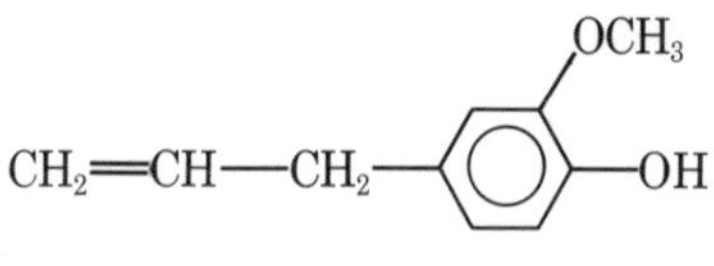

and anethole (oil of anise)

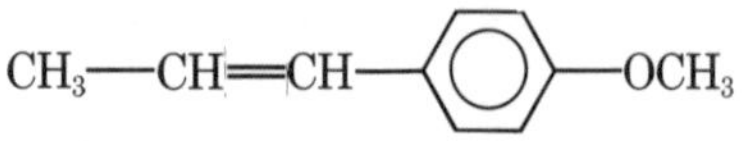

Aldehydes and Ketones

Oxidation of hydrocarbons gives alcohols first, and with further oxidation aldehydes are produced having the functional group —CHO. Methanol is oxidized to formaldehyde more

$$2H—\overset{\displaystyle H}{\underset{\displaystyle H}{\overset{|}{\underset{|}{C}}}}—OH + O_2 \longrightarrow 2H—\overset{\displaystyle H}{\overset{|}{C}}=O + 2H_2O$$

easily than methane is oxidized to methanol. Oxidation takes place at the carbon atom that is already oxidized to an alcohol. Oxidation of *primary alcohols* gives aldehydes,

$$R—\overset{\displaystyle H}{\underset{\displaystyle H}{\overset{|}{\underset{|}{C}}}}—OH \xrightarrow{[OH]} \left[R—\overset{\displaystyle OH}{\underset{\displaystyle H}{\overset{|}{\underset{|}{C}}}}—OH \right] \xrightarrow{-H_2O} R—\overset{\displaystyle H}{\overset{|}{C}}=O$$

primary   intermediate   aldehyde
alcohol

and oxidation of secondary alcohols produces ketones.

$$R—\overset{\displaystyle H}{\underset{\displaystyle R^1}{\overset{|}{\underset{|}{C}}}}—OH \xrightarrow{[OH]} \left[R—\overset{\displaystyle OH}{\underset{\displaystyle R^1}{\overset{|}{\underset{|}{C}}}}—OH \right] \longrightarrow R—\overset{\displaystyle }{\underset{\displaystyle R^1}{\overset{|}{\underset{|}{C}}}}=O$$

secondary   intermediate   ketone
alcohol

Formaldehyde, or methanal, HCHO, is a gas with a pungent, irritating odor, and is marketed in an aqueous solution containing 37–37.5% by weight of formaldehyde, known as *formalin*. Methyl alcohol is added to inhibit polymerization. Bakelite resin is a reaction product of phenol and formaldehyde; it was the first commercially successful plastic. Proteins coagulate in the presence of formaldehyde, making it useful in the preservation of anatomical specimens and in embalming fluids. Other uses are as a disinfectant and as a reducing agent in the production of silver mirrors.

Acetaldehyde [ethanal, CH_3CHO] is a colorless, water-soluble liquid, b.p. 20.2°C, with an odor resembling freshly cut green apples. It occurs in many foods, and volatilizes during cooking. Its uses include: acetic acid, acetic anhydride and *n*-butyl alcohol production; phenol and urea condensation products; and as an intermediate for drugs, perfumes, and photographic agents. Over a hundred chemicals including DDT and butadiene may be made from acetaldehyde. Environmental pollution of plants, birds, fish, animals and humans has caused many governments to ban the use of DDT, para, para'-dichlorodiphenyl trichloroethane. Storage of DDT by the body occurs in the fatty tissues, where it remains and builds up.

Acetone [dimethylketone, or propanone, CH_3COCH_3] is the simplest and most important ketone, a colorless liquid, b.p. 56.5°C, with a characteristic pungent odor and sweet taste. Like acetaldehyde, acetone is ubiquitous in foods. Its uses include: synthesis of acetic anhydride; solvent for cellulose acetate; solvent in paints, lacquers, and adhesives; absorbent for acetylene gas; general solvent uses; epoxy resins; fibers; pharmaceuticals; rubber antioxidants; an electronic parts cleanser and drying agent.

Aldehydes and ketones generally are referred to as carbonyl compounds as they contain the carbonyl ($>C{=}O$) group. Many natural substances are aldehydes and ketones, for example, flavors from almonds, cinnamon, and vanilla, perfumes, camphor, riboflavin (vitamin B_2), ascorbic acid (vitamin C), vitamin K, and the hormones estrone, progesterone, and testosterone.

CARBOXYLIC ACIDS

Organic acids may be thought of as the further oxidation products of aldehydes. Plants and animals synthesize many products, including organic acids from carbon, hydrogen, oxygen, and nitrogen by enzymatic action. Substances containing the carboxyl group, a name derived from carbonyl and hydroxyl

$$-C\diagup_{\diagdown OH}^{O}$$

as a functional group are known as *carboxylic* acids.

Aliphatic acids have the general formula R—COOH and aromatic acids Ar—COOH.

Fatty acids are found in fats and belong to the aliphatic alkane series; and some of the important ones are given in Table 10.3. Acids have names ending in "*ic*," for example, formic or methanoic acid, HCOOH; acetic or ethanoic acid, CH_3COOH; propionic or propanoic acid, CH_3CH_2COOH; and butyric or butanoic acid, $CH_3CH_2CH_2COOH$. It is important to be able to recognize both the common and the I.U.P.A.C. name for each of the acids.

Butterfat contains the broadest spectrum of fatty acids found in any natural fat or oil including: butyric, caprylic, capric, lauric, myristic, stearic, oleic, linoleic, palmitoleic, myris-toleic, and several others..

Low molecular weight fatty acids generally have pungent, penetrating, disagreeable odors characteristically present in limburger cheese, perspiration, unclean locker rooms and other sources of decomposed fat. Formic acid has a pungent penetrating odor; acetic, very pungent; propionic, strong and persistent; butyric, rancid; caproic, limburger cheese; caprylic, a barny or animal odor. The C_1 to C_{10} acids are liquids, and those above C_{10} are waxy solids.

Formic acid [methanoic acid, HCOOH] was originally obtained by distilling red ants, and is an irritant in ant bites and bee stings. In nature it occurs in plant lipids, and animal blood; it is not a true fatty acid.

Acetic acid [ethanoic acid, CH_3COOH] is important as a precursor of body cholesterol, as the active ingredient in vinegar for pickles, and a component of cellulose acetate. It is a mild acid with an ionization constant, Ka, of 1.8×10^{-5}. Chain length has little effect on the ionization constants of the higher molecular weight fatty acids. When hydrogen atoms on the alpha-carbon atom are replaced by chlorine, the acidity increases markedly due to the strong electron-attracting capacity of chlorine. The alpha-carbon is the one adjacent to the functional, or —COOH group; the beta-carbon is second, the gamma third, the delta fourth, the epsilson fifth, etc.

acetic acid $\quad$ monochloroacetic acid $\quad$ trichloroacetic acid
Ka 1.8×10^{-5} $\qquad$ Ka 1.5×10^{-3} $\qquad$ Ka 2.0×10^{-1}

TABLE 10.3

CARBOXYLIC ACIDS

Formula	Common Name	I.U.P.A.C. Name	Source	Food Uses[1]
HCOOH	Formic	Methanoic	Synthesis	Fermentation aid, preservative
CH_3COOH	Acetic	Ethanoic	Vinegar	Pickles, preservative
CH_3CH_2COOH	Propionic	Propanoic	Synthesis	Fruit flavors, bread mold inhibitors
$CH_3(CH_2)_2COOH$	n-butyric	Butanoic	Milk fat	Flavors
$CH_3(CH_2)_4COOH$	n-caproic	Hexanoic	Milk fat	Flavors
$CH_3(CH_2)_5COOH$	Enanthic	Heptanoic	Oxidation of heptaldehyde	Flavors
$CH_3(CH_2)_6COOH$	Caprylic	Octanoic	Coconut oil	Flavors
$CH_3(CH_2)_{10}COOH$	Lauric	Dodecanoic	Coconut oil	Flavors
$CH_3(CH_2)_{12}COOH$	Myristic	Tetradecanoic	Coconut oil	Flavors
$CH_3(CH_2)_{14}COOH$	Palmitic	Hexadecanoic	Whale fat (spermacetic) lard, cocoa, butter	Interesterification in fat synthesis
$CH_3(CH_2)_{16}COOH$	Stearic	Octadecanoic	Beef fat (tallow)	Packaging
$CH_3(CH_2)_7CH:CH(CH_2)_7COOH$	Oleic	Cis-9-octadecanoic	Pork fat (lard)	Lubricant

Structural Formula	Name	Chemical Name	Source	Use
$CH_3(CH_2)_4CH:CHCH_2CH:CH(CH_2)_7COOH$	Linoleic	9,11- or 9,12-octadecadienoic	Safflower oil, Vegetable oils	Essential in diet; Emulsifying agent
$CH_3CH_2(CH)_2CH_2(CH)_2CH_2(CH)_2(CH)_7COOH$	Linolenic	9,12,15-octadecatrienoic	Linseed oil, vegetable oils	Essential in diet
$CH_3CH(OH)COOH$	Lactic	Alpha-hydroxy-propionic	Sour milk, sauerkraut	Acidulant, flavoring
$COOHCH_2COHCOOH:CH_2COOH$	Citric	2-hydroxy-1,2,3-propane-tricarboxylic acid	Citrus fruits	Confections, flavors beverages
$COOHCH_2CHOHCOOH$	Malic	Hydroxy succinic	Green apples, gooseberries	Acidulant, aging of wine
$COOH—COOH$	Oxalic	Ethanedioic	Rhubarb, spinach	Purification of baking powder
$CH_3CH=CHCH=CHCOOH$	Sorbic	2,4-hexadienoic	Synthesis	Food preservative
$COOHCH_2CH_2COOH$	Succinic	Butadioic	Broccoli, rhubarb, fresh meat extracts	Non-hydroscopic acidulant
$COOHCHOHCHOHCOOH$	Tartaric	2,3-dihydroxy butadioic	Grape, currant, raspberry, etc.	Acidulant to augment fruit flavors

[1]Handbook of Food Additives, 1968, The Chemical Rubber Company.

Formic acid has a Ka of 2.1×10^{-4} and for the aromatic acid
benzoic, C_6H_5COOH, $Ka = 6.6 \times 10^{-5}$.

Lactic acid [alphahydroxy propanoic acid, $CH_3CHOHCOOH$]
is produced in milk by the fermentative action of lactobacillus
on lactose, milk sugar. Buttermilk and sour milk derive their
taste from lactic acid. During muscle contraction lactic acid
forms as the animal starch, glycogen, is fermented by enzymes.

Fermented sausages such as cervelat, thuringer, Lebanon
bologna, and dry summer sausages are preserved by the lactic
acid produced intentionally by fermenting the added sugar.
Stability is obtained by lowering the pH of the meat with lactic
acid, adding salt, and partially drying. A similar process is
used in cheese making.

Citric acid [β-hydroxy-β-carboxypentadioic acid), COOH
$CH_2COHCOOH$ CH_2 COOH] has four functional groups; three
are carboxyls and one a hydroxyl. It is a white crystalline
polyfunctional compound having a strong acidic taste, and is
used in flavorings, confections and beverages. Citric acid is
added to fruits in combination with ascorbic acid before freezing to inhibit enzyme action that destroys the natural fruit
color and flavor.

Sorbic acid [2,4-hexadienoic acid), $CH_3CH:CHCH:CHCOOH$]
is used in cheese, pickles, fruits, salads, baked goods, syrups,
candies and margarine to inhibit the growth of molds, yeast,
and aerobes. Commercially, sorbic acid is produced synthetically.

Vegetable and animal fats contain the important saturated
fatty acids lauric (C_{12}), myristic (C_{14}), palmitic (C_{16}), and
stearic (C_{18}), together with the monounsaturated oleic (C_{18}),
the diunsaturated linoleic (C_{18}), and the triunsaturated linolenic
(C_{18}). The latter two (linoleic and linolenic) are essential fatty
acids, necessary in the diet as the body does not synthesize
them.

Physical properties of fatty acids that are important, besides
the unusual odors described for members up to C_{10}, include boiling points, which range from 101°C for formic (C_1) to 383°C for
stearic (C_{18}), and solubility in water, which decreases with
chain length. The C_1 to C_4 fatty acids are miscible, C_5 to C_8
slightly soluble, and C_9 and higher are virtually insoluble.

Organic salts, RCOONa and ArCOONa, are obtained by neutralizing an acid with sodium or potassium hydroxide usually,

and removing the water by evaporation.

These organic salts are usually water-soluble, resulting in slightly alkaline solutions by hydrolysis to a weak acid and a strong base. Sodium acetate, CH_3COONa, when in water solution hydrolyzes to sodium ions, Na^+, and acetate ions, CH_3COO^-. Water is only slightly ionized, but the hydrogen ions, H^+, present will react with some of the acetate ions to form acetic acid, CH_3COOH, and an equal number of hydroxyl ions, OH^-, will unite with sodium ions to form sodium hydroxide, $NaOH$. Since acetic acid is a weak acid and sodium hydroxide is a strong base the resulting solution will be alkaline.

Soaps are salts of long-chain fatty acids. Addition of sodium hydroxide to a long-chain fatty acid produces a harder and less soluble soap than that resulting from the use of potassium hydroxide.

$$CH_3CH_2CH_2CH_2CH_2CH_2CH_2CH_2CH{=}CHCH_2CH_2CH_2CH_2CH_2CH_2CH_2C{\diagup}{\overset{O}{\underset{ONa}{}}}$$

sodium oleate
(hard soap)

$$CH_3CH_2CH_2CH_2CH_2CH_2CH_2CH_2CH{=}CHCH_2CH_2CH_2CH_2CH_2CH_2CH_2C{\diagup}{\overset{O}{\underset{OK}{}}}$$

potassium oleate
(soft soap)

Hard water contains calcium, Ca^{++}, magnesium, Mg^{++}, and iron, Fe^{++}, ions. Soaps are precipitated as insoluble salts by these metal ions; thus the softening of water becomes imperative.

Sodium benzoate, (benzene ring)$-C{\diagup}{\overset{O}{\underset{ONa}{}}}$

is widely used as a food preservative especially in fruits and fruit drinks at a maximum level of 0.1%. It is obtained by neutralizing benzoic acid with bicarbonate of soda. Sodium benzoate is a white, odorless powder, having a sweetish astringent taste, and is soluble in water or alcohol.

ESTERS

Esters, RCOOR and ArCOOR, are organic compounds derived from the reaction of an acid with an alcohol by heating the mix-

ture in the presence of a mineral acid catalyst. Esters are
named as derivatives of the alkyl radical furnished by the alcohol, and the ending "-ic" of the acid changes to "ate."

$$CH_3C\overset{\displaystyle O}{\diagup}\!\!-OH \quad + \quad CH_3CH_2OH \quad \xrightarrow[(H_2SO_4)]{H^+} \quad CH_3C\overset{\displaystyle O}{\diagup}\!\!-OC_2H_5$$

(ethanoic acid)   ethanol   (ethyl ethanoate)
(acetic acid)   (ethyl alcohol)   (ethyl acetate)

Fragrant synthetic flavors are synthesized from mixtures of
alcohols, acids, aldehydes, ketones, ethers, and esters. Some
of these products have been matched more closely to true
natural flavors within the past few years as a result of gas
chromatography research. Natural aromas are analyzed by
this method of separating the numerous flavor components.
Then a synthetic product is made up from pure chemicals in
an attempt to match the natural flavor.

Some typical characteristic ester aromas are artificial rum,
ethyl formate; bananas, *n*-amyl acetate; oranges, octyl acetate;
pineapples, ethyl butyrate, and apricots, amyl butyrate. Strawberry, raspberry, cherry, blackberry, apple, and other fruit
flavors are largely blends of various esters, and are stable
toward oxidation. Citrus flavors, on the other hand, are extracted from the fruits, and are highly susceptible to oxidative
changes that spoil their flavors.

Wines owe to the formation of esters some of their delightful
aromatic properties that develop as a result of aging. This
is a slow process, but red wines from a great vintage year
may be stored for decades in order to achieve their full flavor
potential.

AMINES AND AMIDES

Amines, RNH_2 and $ArNH_2$, are organic compounds of nitrogen
that may be thought of as derivatives of ammonia, NH_3, with
the hydrogen atoms replaced by alkyl or aryl groups, such as
CH_3NH_2 (methylamine) and $C_6H_5NH_2$ (aniline). All amines are
basic, and will react readily with hydrochloric or other strong
acids to form salts. Meat, poultry, fish, and vegetable volatiles
that are released in cooking contain amines. One method of
rating the freshness of fish is by assaying the trimethylamine
content.

Primary, secondary, and tertiary amines are possible by replacing one, two, or three of the hydrogen atoms of ammonia with organic radicals. Mixed or straight amines containing both aliphatic and aromatic groups are possible. Amines are names from the alkyl or aryl groups attached to the nitrogen.

$$H-\overset{\overset{\displaystyle H}{|}}{N}-H \qquad CH_3-\overset{\overset{\displaystyle H}{|}}{N}-H \qquad CH_3-\overset{\overset{\displaystyle CH_3}{|}}{N}-H \qquad CH_3-\overset{\overset{\displaystyle CH_3}{|}}{N}-CH_3$$

ammonia	methylamine	dimethylamine	trimethylamine
	primary	secondary	tertiary
	aliphatic	aliphatic	aliphatic

aniline	diphenylamine	N,N-Dimethylaniline
primary aromatic	secondary aromatic	tertiary mixed

Lower molecular weight amines are readily soluble in water, giving basic solutions. Amine odors are fishlike.

Indole (benzopyrrole) and skatole (β-methylindole) are found in decomposed meat together with the two diamines, putrescine and cadaverine; they have foul odors, and are putrefied food substances known as ptomaines. All ptomaines are not poisonous, but no one generally eats food so putrid.

Amides are organic compounds having the functional group —$CONH_2$. Examples are acetamide, CH_3CONH_2, a lacquer solvent, and urea, $CO(NH_2)_2$ used as a fertilizer, animal feed, and in urea resins.

THIOLS, SULFIDES AND DISULFIDES

Organic sulfur compounds that may be thought of as derivatives of hydrogen sulfide (H_2S) are called *thiols* or *mercaptans*, R—SH; *sulfides*, R—S—R; and disulfides, R—SS—R; they are also known as analogs of alcohols, R—OH, and ethers, R—O—R. Cooked meat and poultry odors are due largely to sulfur compounds, including hydrogen sulfide, ammonium sulfide, mercaptans, and organic sulfides and disulfides. Thiols have strong disagreeable odors; hydrogen sulfide odor has been identified with rotten eggs; sulfides and disulfides also have powerful, penetrating, disagreeable odors. Yet at low concentrations a tolerance and acceptance of strong, unpleasant smells is not uncommon, as shown by the appetizing vapors of meat and poultry.

Sulfur compounds in vegetables tend to bleach the chlorophyll during cooking; thus green vegetables should be cooked in uncovered pans to purge them of hydrogen sulfide, dimethyl sulfide, and other volatile sulfur compounds. Mustard, onions, garlic, and similar vegetables owe their characteristic flavors to sulfur compounds and a complex compound called sinigrin, $KC_{10}H_{16}NO_9S_2 \cdot H_2O$ indigenous to cauliflower and other members of the genus *Brassica* family. Diallyl sulfide $(CH_2\!\!=\!\!CHCH_2)_2S$, is the active ingredient in oil of garlic, and also occurs in onions or the genus *Allium* family of plants.

Natural and manufactured fuel gases are odorless, and to warn householders of gas leaks a few parts per million of thiols are sometimes used to give the gas a potent disagreeable odor that can easily be detected by the nose.

POLYMERS

Polymers are high molecular weight compounds built up by uniting a large number of small molecules in a natural or synthetic process called *polymerization*. Examples of polymers found in nature are rubber, pectin, starch, cellulose, proteins, and gums.

Cellulose and silk are natural linear polymers that may have molecular weights greater than 1,000,000. Van der Waals forces are strong enough to prevent molecules from slipping past each other at high temperatures; hence they do not soften or decompose at temperatures high enough to break covalent bonds. Van der Waals forces are the attractive forces between molecules. Polymers of lower molecular weights, from 10,000 to 300,000, soften when heated. Here the Van der Waals forces are such that the molecules slip past each other upon heating. These polymers are said to be thermoplastic and can be molded and extruded to form fibers, etc.

The basic unit of a polymer is termed a monomer; two monomers are called a dimer; three monomers, a trimer; beyond this, the term polymer is generally used. Polymerization is accomplished by addition or by condensation reactions; in the biological field the condensation involves the loss of water molecules. For a polymeric molecule to result, the monomers must be polyfunctional. The resulting polymer may be linear, branched or crosslinked, depending upon the number of functional groups present in the monomer.

Natural rubber consists of long chains of isoprene [(2-methyl-1-3-butadiene) CH_2=$CHCH_3CH$=CH_2]. The molecules are united by 1,4-addition.

$$CH_2=\underset{\underset{\displaystyle CH_3}{|}}{C}-CH=CH_2 \xrightarrow{\text{catalyst}} -(CH_2-\underset{\underset{\displaystyle CH_3}{|}}{C}=CHCH_2)_n-$$

isoprene unit

Natural rubber from the sap (latex) of the rubber tree is made up of molecules containing about 2000 isoprene units, and has a molecular weight of approximately 136,000.

Synthetic rubber of many types has been developed through research. *Neoprene* is made from acetylene and hydrochloric acid.

$$2CH\equiv CH \xrightarrow[\substack{\text{ammonium} \\ \text{chloride}}]{\substack{\text{cuprous} \\ \text{chloride}}} CH_2=CH-CH\equiv CH \xrightarrow{HCl} CH_2C-\underset{\underset{\displaystyle Cl}{|}}{C}=CH_2$$

vinylacetylene   chloroprene

$$nCH_2=CH-\underset{\underset{\displaystyle Cl}{|}}{C}=CH_2 \xrightarrow{\text{catalyst}} -(CH_2-CH=\underset{\underset{\displaystyle Cl}{|}}{C}-CH_2)_n-$$

neoprene

Note that neoprene, like isoprene, polymerizes by 1,4-addition. Neoprene is used in oil-, solvent-, heat-, and weather-resistant resilient products, adhesive cements, paints and putties, crepe soles for shoes, and as a binder for rocket fuels.

Dacron is a polyester fiber made from the reaction between terephthalic acid and ethylene glycol. (See formula, page 240.) Suits, made from Dacron and wool and shirts or blouses made from Dacron and cotton are crease-resistant. Other uses of dacron include curtains, rope, belts, and fire hose. *Mylar* packaging film is a variant of Dacron polyester.

$$n \left[\text{HO}-\overset{\text{O}}{\underset{|}{\text{C}}}-\langle \bigcirc \rangle-\overset{\text{O}}{\underset{\|}{\text{C}}}\text{--OH} + \text{HO}-\text{CH}_2\text{CH}_2\text{OH} + \right.$$

terephthalic acid   glycol

$$\left. \text{HO--}\overset{\text{O}}{\underset{\|}{\text{C}}}-\langle \bigcirc \rangle-\overset{\text{O}}{\underset{\|}{\text{C}}}\text{--OH} + \text{HOCH}_2\text{CH}_2\text{OH} \right] \longrightarrow$$

$$\text{HOCH}_2\text{CH}_2\text{O--}\left[-\overset{\text{O}}{\underset{\|}{\text{C}}}-\langle \bigcirc \rangle-\overset{\text{O}}{\underset{\|}{\text{C}}}-\text{OCH}_2\text{CH}_2\text{O--} \right]_n\text{--H}$$

Dacron

Alkyd resins for surface coating paints, varnishes and print-ing inks are polyesters of *phthalic anhydride, glycerol*, and *fatty acids*.

Nylon is a polyamide that has proved superior to silk in many ways.

Many other kinds of synthetic fibers have been developed through research.

Other polymers include *Delrin* an $-(\text{OCH}_2-)_n$ resin derived from formaldehyde used for molding; *polyethylene* used in making packaging film and containers; *Lucite* a methacrylate polymer that is transparent (known also as Plexiglas); *Orlon*, an acrylonitrile, $-\text{CH}_2\!\!=\!\!\text{CH--CN}$, polymer used for textiles; Acrilan used in carpets; and many others.

Some *food polymers* that are rather exciting in their new forms and uses are the starches, pectins, alginates and car-boxymethylcellulose. The gelatins have not been changed to a great extent. The above have been covered in the sections on carbohydrates. However, as polymers, Table 10.4 gives a relationship as to monomers and linkage.

HALOGEN COMPOUNDS

Compounds containing carbon, C, hydrogen, H, and a halogen, X, are made synthetically and used extensively for organic

TABLE 10.4
SOME FOOD POLYMERS, MONOMERS, LINKAGE AND USES

	Principal Monomer	Linkage	Repeating Unit	Uses
Starch	α-D-glucose	—C—O—C—	(ring structure)	Thickening, etc.
Pectins	α-D-galacturonic acid	—C—O—C—	(ring structure, COOH)	Gel formation, etc.
Algins	β-D-mannuronic acid	—C—O—C—	(ring structure, COOH)	Emulsifier stabilizer, etc.
Carboxymethycellulose	β-D-glucose	—C—O—C—	(ring structure)	Stabilizer, etc.
Gelatin	α-amino acids	—CONH—	$R—CH(NH_2)COOH$	Protein

synthesis. The general formula for aliphatic halogen compounds is RX and for aromatics ArX. *Halogens* are the chemically related elements of Group VII A; in descending order
of activity they are fluorine, chlorine, bromine and iodine.
Uses of organic halogen compounds include insecticides, fire
extinguishing, refrigerants, disinfectants, and dry-cleaning
solvents.

Alkyl and Aryl halides, RX and ArX, react with magnesium
to form the Grignard reagent. *Silicones* are produced by reacting the Grignard reagent with silicon tetrachloride, $SiCl_4$ and
hydrolyzing the silane, $RSiCl_2$.

$$CH_3I \quad + \; Mg \quad \xrightarrow{\text{ether}} \quad CH_3MgI$$

methyl-iodide   methyl magnesium iodide

bromobenzene   phenyl magnesium bromide

$$2R\overset{-\;+}{M}gX + SiCl_4 \longrightarrow R_2SiCl_2 + 2Mg^{++}X^-Cl^-$$

dichloroalkyl silane

$$R_2SiCl_2 + H_2O \longrightarrow \left(\!\!\begin{array}{c} R \\ | \\ -Si-O-Si-O- \\ | \\ R \end{array}\!\!\begin{array}{c} R \\ | \\ \\ | \\ R \end{array}\!\!\right)_n + 2HCl$$

Silicones are heat-stable, serviceable over a wide temperature span, oxygen- and weather-resistant, and water-repellent.
Uses include greases, rubbers, surface-coatings, and foamable
powders.

Alkyl halides, RX, condense with aromatic hydrocarbons in
the presence of aluminum chloride, a catalyst to replace one or
more of the ring hydrogens with an alkyl group. This is known
as the Friedel-Crafts synthesis.

benzene   ethylbenzene

$$\bigcirc \ + \ 3CH_3CH_2Br \xrightarrow[\text{24 hrs}]{AlCl_3} \quad \text{(1,3,5-triethylbenzene)} \ + \ 3HBr$$

ethyl bromide

1,3,5-triethylbenzene

Synthetic organic chemistry is based on reactions of this type. *"Styrofoam"* is made by polymerizing styrene,

$$\bigcirc \ + \ CH_2{=}CH_2 \xrightarrow[\text{80°C}]{AlCl_3} \bigcirc{-}CH_2CH_3 \xrightarrow[\text{$-H_2$}]{\text{catalyst}} \bigcirc{-}CH{=}CH_2$$

benzene   ethylene   ethylbenzene   styrene

$$\bigcirc{-}CH{=}CH_2 \xrightarrow{\text{catalyst}} \left[\bigcirc{-}CH{-}CH_2{-} \right]_n$$

polystyrene

and is widely used as insulating wallboard.

"*Freons*" are mixed alkyl halides. Freon-11 (trichloromonofluoromethane, CCl_3F) is used as a refrigerant and in high-pressure aerosols for insecticides. Freon-12 (dichlorodifluoromethane, CCl_2F_2) is used as a refrigerant and aerosol propellant. Freon-13 (monochlorotrifluoromethane, $CClF_3$) is used as a refrigerant and metal hardener. Freon-13B (monobromotrifluoromethane, $CBrF_3$) is used as a refrigerant, metal hardener, and fire extinguisher. Freon-22 (monochlorodifluoromethane, $CHClF_2$) is used as a contact freezing medium for foods. Freon-C-318 (octafluorocyclobutane, $C_4H_2F_8$) is used as a food-grade propellant together with nitrous oxide, N_2O, as a propellant for flavoring extracts, spices, dessert topping, salad dressing, frosting, and other pressurized food products.

FUNCTIONAL GROUPS

Organic compounds derive their characteristic properties from their functional groups. These groups are the reactive parts that are responsible for classes of compounds, and make it possible to classify over a million organic compounds into a small number of groups, as shown in Table 10.5.

Three factors determine the properties and chemistry of carbon compounds, namely:

TABLE 10.5

CLASSIFICATION OF ALIPHATIC COMPOUNDS

Functional Group	Type of Compound	Ending	Example	Name	
				I.U.P.C.A.	Common
—C—C— alkane	Saturated hydrocarbon C_nH_{2n+2}	ane	C_2H_6	Ethane	Ethane
R (1 less hydrogen)	Radical— C_nH_{2n+1}	yl	C_2H_5	Ethyl	Ethyl
—C=C— alkene	Olefin— C_nH_{2n}	ene	C_2H_4	Ethene	Ethylene
—C≡C— alkyne	Acetylene— C_nH_{2n-2}	yne	C_2H_2	Ethyne	Acetylene
—C=C—C=C—	Polyolefin C_nH_{2n-2}	diene	C_4H_6	1–3 butadiene	Butadiene
—C—O—H	Alcohol primary, secondary, and tertiary	ol	CH_3CH_2OH	Ethanol	Ethyl alcohol
H —C=O	Aldehyde	al	CH_3CHO	Ethanal	Acetaldehyde

Structure	Name	Suffix	Formula	IUPAC name	Common name
$\diagup{C}{=}O$	Ketone	one	CH_3COCH_3	Propanone	Acetone
$-C(=O)-O-H$	Acid	o-ic acid	CH_3COOH	Ethanoic acid	Acetic acid
$-C(=O)-O-R$	Ester	o-ate	CH_3COOCH_3	Methyl ethanoate	Methyl-acetate
$R-O-R(\equiv C-O-C\equiv)$	Ether	---	$C_2H_5OC_2H_5$	Ethoxy ethane	Ethyl ether
$R-\underset{H}{N}-H$	Amine—primary, secondary & tertiary	---	CH_3NH_2	Mono amino methane	Methyl-amine
$R-X$	Alkyl halide	---	CH_3Cl	Mono chloro methane	Methyl-chloride
$R-C(=O)-NH_2$	Amides	---	$CH_3-\underset{NH_2}{C}=O$	Ethanamide	Acetamide
$R-\underset{NH_2}{CHC}-O-H$	α-amino acid	α amino o-ic acid	$\underset{NH_2}{CH_2}-COOH$	α amino ethanoic acid	Glycine

R = alkyl radical, X = halogen.

(1) Length of the chain and/or the number of carbon atoms in the molecule.

(2) Type of bonds—single, double, triple or aromatic.

(3) Functional groups present in the molecule.

OPTICAL ROTATION

Optically active compounds have a definite arrangement of atoms and groups in their molecules. When dissolved in water and subjected to a beam of plane polarized light, these molecules due to their unique structures rotate the plane of polarized light to the left or right. A characteristic of substances having optical activity is that one or more carbon atoms in the molecule is attached to four different atoms or groups. Lactic acid for example:

$$
\begin{array}{c}
H \\
| \\
CH_3C^*\!\!-\!\!COOH \\
| \\
OH
\end{array}
$$

has the carbon atom marked* attached to an —H, an —OH, a —CH$_3$ and a —COOH. The C* is an asymmetric carbon atom.

Three forms of lactic acid are known. One turns the plane of polarized light to the right, and is called *dextro* (+) lactic acid; the other turns it to the left and is called *levo* (−) lactic acid; the third is inactive, and is made up of equal parts of the dextro and levo forms.

The *dextro* and *levo* forms of lactic acid are mirror images of each other, or opposite forms, known as *enantiomorphs*.

$$
\begin{array}{cc}
\begin{array}{c}
CH_3 \\
| \\
H\!-\!C\!-\!OH \\
| \\
COOH
\end{array}
&
\begin{array}{c}
CH_3 \\
| \\
HO\!-\!C\!-\!H \\
| \\
COOH
\end{array}
\\
\text{d+ lactic acid} & \text{l− lactic acid}
\end{array}
$$

Plane-polarized light is light in which the vibrations lie in one plane, as distinguished from ordinary light which vibrates in all directions. When light is passed through a Nicol prism, consisting of two crystals of calcite cemented together with Canada Balsam, the light emerging vibrates in a single plane. *Polarimeters* are instruments incorporating a light source emitting unpolarized light, a polarizing prism, sample tube with the dissolved optically active substance in it, and an analyzer prism calibrated to measure the angle of rotation in degrees.

Temperature, wavelength of light used, concentration of the sample, and length of the sample tube must be standardized in order to compare the optical activity of different substances and their relative purity.

Levorotatory substances have the angle of rotation expressed as a *negative* value (−), and *dextrorotatory* values are *positive* (+).

Optically active food chemicals include proteins, amino acids, sugars, lactic and tartaric acids, and numerous others.

Resolution of racemic mixtures into their (+) and (−) components may be accomplished by the mechanical separation of crystals using a magnifying lens and tweezers; biochemical resolution by feeding one isomer to a microorganism that leaves the other; and conversion to *diastereoisomers*, or isomers that are not mirror images, by adding a base and converting the racemic mixture of acids to diastereoisomeric salts that may be separated by recrystallization. Each individual salt is then reconverted to the original acid.

When compounds containing an asymmetric carbon atom are synthesized, a combination 50-50 dextro-levo molecules designated as inactive, and known as a *"racemic"* mixture is obtained. Separation of racemic mixtures is costly and difficult.

Sour milk contains the "racemic" variety. Dextro-lactic acid occurs in meat, meat extracts, blood and urine. When muscle contracts *glycogen* (animal starch) is converted to lactic acid, and studies show that animals rested ante-mortem give more tender meat post-mortem, other factors being equal. *Levo*-lactic acid is obtained from sugar fermented with *bacillus acidi levolactici*; this is the commercial method of producing lactic acid from corn sugar.

Levo-glutamic acid is found in cereal, fish, poultry and meat proteins: Levo-monosodium glutamate, MSG, is manufactured biosynthetically, and is widely used as a protein flavor accentuator.

$$\overset{\text{H}}{\underset{\text{NH}_2}{\text{COOHCO}_2\text{CH}_2{-}\overset{|}{\underset{|}{\text{C}}}{-}\text{COOH}}} \qquad \overset{\text{H}}{\underset{\text{NH}_2}{\text{COOHCH}_2\text{CH}_2\overset{|}{\underset{|}{\text{C}}}{-}\text{COONa.H}_2\text{O}}}$$

Levo-glutamic acid   Levo-monosodium glutamate
monohydrate

The natural or L-form of glutamic acid, when neutralized carefully with sodium hydroxide to pH 7, enhances and accentuates protein flavors in vegetables, grains, fish, poultry, and meat. When the L-form is racemized by excessive heating it loses its flavor-amplifying activity. A synthetic DL mixture has only one-half the flavor-potentiating properties of the L-form. Since glutamate activity is based upon palate sensitization to protein flavors, it may be concluded that the taste receptors are attuned only to the L-form.

CHAPTER 11

L. L. W. Smith
L. J. Minor
Food Flavor

In closing the world's protein gap, flavor control is a vital factor. Food primarily must be nutritious to sustain life, but unless the flavor is acceptable to the human palate, it may not be eaten. Today, new ways are being found to upgrade natural foods lacking flavor and to add flavor to new man-made meat substitutes having a high nutritive content.

Flavor chemistry is the newest branch of food chemistry in the United States. Gas chromatography, whereby food flavor volatiles can be separated into their manifold chemical components, is being perfected. Other physicochemical techniques are also being used with the help of the human nose and brain, which are more sensitive than mechanical devices to identify these chemicals.

New and improved synthetic fruit flavors have already been developed, as there are not enough natural fruits grown to meet the demand for these flavors in foods. Similarly, beef extract is being replaced with flavor potentiators: MSG (monosodium glutamate); HVP (hydrolyzed plant proteins); and the flavor nucleotides: 5'-IMP (inosine-5'-monophosphate) that occurs in meat and fish muscle, and 5'-GMP (guanosine-5'-monophosphate), produced biochemically from yeast and yeast derivatives. Progress has been made with meat substitutes. Natural flavorings derived from beef, chicken, and ham have been combined with soy, yeast, or algae protein to make simulated meats.

The Importance of Flavor

Food may be nutritious and possess maximum eye appeal, but when flavor is lacking it is neither acceptable nor marketable. Nature itself provides many interesting examples. Apples having a beautiful, lustrous red color may be discarded after

249

one bite if they are dry and pithy. It is a rare treat to taste a really good melon. Green fruits shipped to market and then ripened are seldom tasty. Some tough meat can look tempting when purchased, but no matter how it is cooked, the toughness remains. Chicken breast meat or lobster meat with eye appeal may be tasteless, dry, and tough after preparation for the table.

Research and quality control have been helpful in combating both the quirks of nature and a combination of handling, storage, and cooking variables. Yet, within limits, products still vary. Generally, nature provides the best and most nutritive product when the fruit, vegetable, meat, poultry, or fish has attained its ripest, tenderest, and most succulent stage. Accordingly, tenderometers are applied to representative samples of fruits and vegetables prior to harvest in order to check their maturity. Meats and poultry are tested with shear meters. Many other physical and chemical methods are employed in upgrading and safeguarding the yield, nutrition, and flavor of food.

Ecologically speaking the simple relationship between food and man is better appreciated than the interrelationship of food nutrition, food flavor, and man. Perhaps one of the most memorable instances of this neglect of flavor occurred during World War II with respect to the Army's canned C-rations (meat and vegetable stew, meat and vegetable hash, meat and beans, etc.). These rations were found unpalatable by the soldiers because of a combination of factors, including effects of canning and storage and lack of added flavoring or enhancers.

Proof of this flavor inadequacy was obtained by fortuitous circumstance. Hungry soldiers wouldn't eat their rations: indeed Caul reported that soldiers stationed in the Arctic region preferred hunger to unpleasant-tasting though nutritive foods. Then the soldiers found by experimentation that the bouillon powder contained in their K-rations could be used to flavor the C-rations and thus improve palatability.

Another valuable lesson was learned at a later date in connection with the Marshall Plan program of feeding Europe after the war. Grain, vegetable oil, and milk powder combinations were formulated both with and without added monosodium glutamate, hydrolyzed plant proteins, and spices for flavoring. Since the flavor additives increased the cost about 5%, the procurement officers decided that flavoring was unnecessary, maintaining that the primary object was to provide calories and protein, not flavor. When General Lucius D. Clay attempted to feed these ersatz products without seasoning to the hungry masses of Europe, they were rejected. Eventually he was forced to order millions of pounds of this unpalatable food to be dumped into the ocean.

Daily thousands of kitchens in the United States prepare food items that are either partly or entirely rejected at the table. Garbage cans and disposals are frequently filled with discarded or uneaten foods. This wanton waste could be eliminated by intelligent leadership in the food-service industries, for example, by giving proper recognition to the importance of flavor in food preparation. Chef-less food preparation in a quantity kitchen for a captive pensioner audience should be as acceptable as chef-prepared-to-order food for a millionaire.

The renowned American food scientist I. J. Hutchings stated: "Food must be made not only nutritious but more appealing to the consumer. Food scientists have been negligent in the area of developing or creating food flavors." In a similar vein, the eminent nutritionist and late president of Wisconsin University C. A. Elvehjem predicted: "Just as individual nutrients such as vitamins were identified, isolated, synthesized, and then used for enriching foods, so a similar attack will be made on flavors and aromas present in foods and food products. By 1980 foods combined to meet specific nutritional requirements may be enriched with these flavors just as we now enrich with vitamins."

Sounds and sights may be recorded or photographed, but flavors are transient, complex, and indefinable chemicals that register mental impressions. Odor and the sense of smell are of paramount importance in flavor, and taste plays a lesser role.

What is Flavor?

Flavor may be described as consisting of three fundamental parts: (1) *taste* of the nonvolatile constituents including sweetness, saltiness, sourness, bitterness, and monosodium or nucleotide-enhancing effects (which emphasize taste bud sensitizing and mouth feel in protein foods); (2) *odor*, consisting of the volatile constituents of fruits and spices and of cooked meat, poultry, fish, vegetables, eggs, etc; and (3) *kinesthetic flavors*, such as texture and other physical qualities, that may affect the senses of sight, touch, or hearing.

In 1969 the Society of Flavor Chemists gave the following definition for the physiological sensations. "Flavor is the sensation caused by and those properties of, any substance taken in the mouth, which stimulates one or both of the senses of taste and smell and/or also the general pain, tactile and temperature receptors in the mouth."

A *flavor* is a substance which may be a single chemical entity or a blend of chemicals of natural or synthetic origin, whose primary purpose is to provide all or part of the particular effect to any food or other product taken in the mouth.

Numerous definitions of flavor could be given, but the one chosen is that of Kazeniac, who used four designations as proposed by Sjöström and Cairncross. The first was taste, consisting of saltiness, sweetness, sourness, and bitterness, to which Moncrieff has recently added metallic. The second was aroma, which described odor sensations. The third was body, which referred to the texture or sensation caused by chewing, but having nothing to do with taste or aroma. The fourth was mouth satisfaction, which implied salivary stimulation, blending, and pleasantness. Thus defined, flavor is an interaction of these four basic sensations.

Taste, smell, and feel are our chemical senses. By realizing that all matter is electrical in nature and that temperature affects reaction rates, we may conclude that our chemical senses are affected by both electrochemical and thermochemical phenomena. Salivary enzymes (protein catalysts) often cause chemical changes to occur within the food even while it is being chewed. Furthermore, texture must be considered in any overall concept of taste. Tactile sensations (which affect the sense of touch) as well as the responses resulting from seeing or hearing (as in the case of water-chestnuts or popcorn when they are being chewed) the food are important in evaluating its physical characteristics. Hence, both kinds of taste effects—chemical and kinesthetic or physical—are involved.

Since the two chief parts of flavor are taste and odor, separate discussions of each follow. Taste will be considered first.

TASTE

Taste is a relatively simple physical sensation which originates in the taste buds in the mouth. The taste buds are stimulated by the food's chemical make-up, its temperature, pH
(relative acidity), and the interplay of other senses: smell,
touch (biting, chewing, tongue feel, swallowing), eye-appeal,
and so on. Taste and odor work together, reaching the taste
buds with or without other sensory side effects, such as sight
and hearing. The brain combines these sensory reactions
into the complex response called flavor.

Taste Physiology

Taste is one of the simpler senses. There are only five
principal dimensions in taste as compared to countless varieties
of odors. Yet the innervation of taste is more complex than that
of smell.

Taste receptors are called taste buds. They are located on
moist body surfaces, i.e., in the mouth cavity of human
beings, on the gills of fish, and on the feet of butterflies. The
taste buds are embedded in the covering of papillae, which are
minute projections located mostly on the tongue but also on
the inside surface of the cheek and on the epiglottis. There
are about 245 taste buds in each papilla and approximately
9,000 taste buds in all.

Taste buds consist of sensory cells in the mouth surface
tissue (epithelium) that are motivated by nerve endings. Taste
occurs when a chemical compound dissolved in the saliva
seeps into the taste bud and stimulates the nerve ending, which
transmits an electrical impulse to the brain. Tasting doesn't
always require ingestion of the compound directly into the
mouth. For instance, when an antibiotic is injected into the
arm or thigh of a medical patient, the patient may experience a
bitter taste almost instantly via the bloodstream as the taste
buds absorb it from the blood.

The tongue is the principal instrument of taste and can dif-
ferentiate between two separate stimuli occurring simultaneously only 0.05 in. apart. Tasting is a rapid reaction. Experimental results show that the papillae of the rat will respond
to the taste of a sodium chloride solution within 0.05 sec.

According to Kazeniac, sweetness is detected mainly at the

tip of the tongue, saltiness at the frontal edges, sourness at the sides, and bitterness at the back of the tongue. Taste perception zones as shown by Crocker deviate appreciably from those ascribed to the tongue by Kazeniac. However, as will be clarified in the next section, this appraisal of taste bud functions with respect to location may be passé. Taste buds have been known to migrate with age. Sweet-sensitive buds located in the cheeks of infants and small children disappear as the children grow older.

Dysautonomic patients (persons with malfunctioning autonomic nervous systems) are unable to perceive taste or discriminate between tastes. But in most people tasting ability is taken for granted, although it can be dulled or sharpened. Smokers and heavy coffee or liquor drinkers experience a fatiguing effect on their taste buds. One distinguished epicurean club called Quando Manducamus ("When Do We Eat?") has placed a taboo on smoking until after dining is completed and coffee has been served. A glass of sherry and a cup of consommé preceding the meat attune the diner's taste mechanism by stimulating the flow of gastric juices. Tobacco chewers, as distinguished from smokers, are often proficient tasters. So one might assume that constant mastication stimulates the salivary gland and cleanses the taste buds.

A series of classic experiments concerned with the salt, sour, sweet, and bitter tastes were reported by Moncrieff. Later, this same worker showed that bitterness in chemical compounds increases in direct proportion to the molecular weight.

Taste Theories

Recently, Von Békésy proposed a "duplexity theory" of taste. First he studied the relationships between warm and cold stimuli and the four basic taste stimuli—sweet, salty, sour, and bitter. Then he separated the tongue sensations into two general groupings: (1) bitter, warm, and sweet and (2) sour, cold, and salty. He also concluded that sour and salty tastes merge together at the center of the tongue, whereas sweet and sour tastes do not.

The newest concept of taste-bud action is based on studies of electron micrographs of taste buds. Two cell types exist, one light and the other dark. The light-colored cells are

compared to bricks in a building, and the darker cells are
likened to the mortar, as they bind the lighter cells together.
Dark cells absorb the element osmium, but light cells do not.
Both kinds of cells, together with a hair-like nerve cell that
transmits taste responses to the brain, are present in taste
buds. Taste buds vary in shape, and their position in the
epithelium (mouth's surface tissue) may undergo change.
Accordingly, experimental evidence indicates that the nature
of the taste bud may be that of a migratory lymph cell.

Taste Psychology

Historically, taste classification is based ón phenomenologi-
cal evidence. The Swedish botanist Carolus Linnaeus (1707-
1778) enumerated eleven tastes: sweet, sour, salty, fatty,
bitter, aqueous, viscous, astringent, nauseous, sharp, and
insipid. Wilhelm Wundt (1832–1920), founder of the first experimental psychology laboratory, reduced the number of
tastes to six: sweet, sour, salty, bitter, alkaline, and metallic.
Later, Wundt held to the basic four consisting of sweet, sour,
salty, and bitter, as proposed by Crocker. General acceptance
of this four-dimensional characterization of the taste phenomenon led Henning to develop the taste tetrahedron concept. Now,
Moncrieff holds that it is necessary to add metallic to the
four primaries of Crocker.

A psychophysical scale that measures gustatory values of
different foods has been devised by Beebe-Center and Waddell.
Since taste is synonymous with the term "gustation," a unit
of taste called the "gust" was devised. The "gust" is based
on the taste of a 1% sugar solution. On the scale, undiluted
lime, lemon, or pickle juice has a rating of over 100 gusts.
Acceptable foods rarely exceed 50 gusts. Therefore, foodstuffs
are usually served that occupy positions near the middle of the
scale.

Off-tastes can profoundly influence likes or dislikes for
food. Tomato juice or other fruit or vegetable juices from a
can may have a fishy or metallic taste due to the reaction
between the acid in the juice and the metals of the container.
Packing in glass or in drawn metal cans having acid-resisting
enamelled surfaces corrects this problem. Orange juice
served warm and coffee served cold have objectionable tastes.
Foods that should be sweet but taste salty, or vice versa, are

highly unacceptable. Too much monosodium glutamate (MSG) is not good either.

In food service a common fault is leaving onion soup or consomme on the steam table too long before tasting it to see if evaporation has caused too high a salt concentration. Adding the correct amount of water is a simple antidote, but this is often overlooked. Food should always be tasted prior to serving and checked at frequent intervals whenever it is held hot. A good cook, according to Escoffier, uses the freshest and finest ingredients, exercises utmost care in meal preparation, and uses his nose and his tongue to test the food.

Sometimes the sense of taste can warn that the food being consumed may be harmful to health. For example, medical researchers find that burned fat volatiles deposited on charcoal-broiled steaks contain benzopyrene, the cancer-causing chemical found in cigarette smoke. Spent fat from the potato-chip industry, when added to chicken rations, caused breast cancer in the chickens. For meats other than pork, cooking time and temperature should be held to a minimum whenever possible.

Taste blending is important. Salt in small percentages enhances sweetness and masks sourness. Monosodium glutamate (MSG) in small proportions reduces earthiness and/or bitterness in potatoes, onions, and bean sprouts. Nucleotides and monosodium glutamate act synergistically to reduce bitterness and disguise other bizarre notes in vegetable products such as onions. In short, these so-called flavor potentiators can make a vegetable dish tolerable to a meat eater by improving the flavor profile, providing they are used as directed.

Often two similar products can be combined to form a single superior product. Tomato juice from the West Coast is added to tomato juice from the Midwest to reduce the acidity and improve the color of the midwestern product. Likewise Niagara and Concord grape wines of the East and Midwest are blended with California wines, because the fruits from California are sweeter and less acid than those from the eastern United States and yield wines of higher alcohol content.

Food patterns and tastes are in a constant state of flux. For example, pickles are milder, ham is less salty, and wieners are seasoned with MSG, as are soups and stews. Within the past 25 years food scientists have learned to make these and many other changes in order to increase consumer acceptance.

Taste Control

Taste may be controlled, within the limits of natural variance, by taste-testing together with careful grading, weighing, processing, and handling of foods. Taste-testing may be done directly by the organoleptic methods of feeling, smelling, and tasting, or indirectly by chemical and instrumental testing. Taste-testing in the manufacturing of foods requires stringent control of the seasoning profile and careful consideration of the kinesthetic and chemical factors in taste. The influence of processing (chlorination, washing, heating-cooling, freezing-thawing, etc.) on sensory properties of food must likewise be controlled to ensure taste acceptance.

Quality.—Consumer preference, detection of difference, difference-preference, selection of the best sample or process, and determination of grade or quality level may be studied by taste panels. The attributes of quality included under taste are texture, temperature, appearance, sweetness, bitterness, and metallicness. Glutamate and nucleotide effects should also be considered whenever these potentiators are added to protein foods. Fiber, moisture, fat, protein, carbohydrate, and ash are determined by chemical procedures. Minerals such as sodium, potassium, arsenic, and lead are assayed by spectrographic, polarographic, and X-ray diffraction or chemical techniques.

Texture.—Characteristics of texture as related to touch and taste are measured directly by sight and by mouth or finger feel. Texture can further be determined by instrument testing: firmness and juiciness are tested by compression, chewiness by shear-pressure, fibrousness by comminution (cutting fine), and stickiness by tensile strength. Grittiness is measured by comminution, sedimentation, and elution (separation of material by washing). Mealiness is measured by starch or gum analysis. Color measurements have also proved useful in the realm of kinesthetic factors. Temperature is tested directly by feel and indirectly by either a thermometer or a potentiometer.

Taste Chemicals.—The chemical tastes may be easy or difficult to measure depending on their nature. Sugar, salt, pH, monosodium glutamate, and the 5' nucleotides usually occur in natural or prepared foods at concentrations that permit either chemical or biochemical and physicochemical measurements. The Glutamate Manufacturers Technical Committee has published methods for determining the monosodium glutamate content of foods, and Pabst Laboratories has perfected techniques for the 5' nucleotides. Components of food that impart bitter notes are difficult to assay due to their complex chemical nature.

Taste Stimuli.—According to Sharon, taste stimuli may cause both direct and indirect reactions. When food is put into the mouth, there is a direct response to it. Salivary and gastric stimulation may also result from the sight of food. This indirect response to taste stimuli can measurably increase pancreatic secretion when the food is being digested in the intestine later on.

There are other responses to eating besides stimulation of the taste buds and the stomach. When lumps of meat are chewed, the soft palate tissue, tooth membranes, muscles, and joints are stimulated. Thus more gastric juices result from eating stew than from eating hash.

Continuing research is essential in the taste area of food science. Currently, however, the emphasis is being placed on food odor analysis. The problems involved in first analyzing and then synthesizing or biochemically producing food odors is a timely challenge that food scientists have accepted.

ODOR

Odor has been termed the most important sensory component of flavor by Moncrieff. Evidence of the importance of olfaction can be obtained readily by holding the nose and tasting first an apple and then a potato. If you hold your nose when you are blindfolded, you cannot tell the difference between the apple and the potato. Moncrieff says, "gustation is to taste as olfaction is to smell."

Odor is a complex physiological response occurring at specific chemical receptor loci known as the hairs of the olfactory cell, and due to electrochemical, thermochemical, and kinesthetic reactions at those specific sites. Whenever smell, with or without superimposed feeling, contacts the receptor site concomitantly, the brain computes the overall effect of the complex response known as odor.

Odor Physiology

By comparing the chemical senses of taste and smell, Moncrieff found that the brain is capable of recognizing more than 200,000 different odors, and that while the palate and tongue have thousands of taste receptors, the nasal cleft has millions of olfactory receptors. These are embedded in the small patch of mucous membrane situated on each wall of the nasal cleft, which is a narrow space in the uppermost compartment of the nose.

According to Von Frisch, rabbits, dogs, and eels possess many more olfactory receptors than man. The olfactory bulb of the rabbit contains 100,000,000 receptor cells with 6 to 12 hairs per cell. Man's total is 50,000,000 glomeruli receptors served by 45,000 secondary neurons connected to the olfactory brain. The rabbit has only 25,000 of the secondary neurons leading to the cortex of the brain.

In a series of classic experiments, Gesteland and Lettvin measured the electrical responses of individual olfactory nerve cells in the olfactory organ of the frog. (Frogs are the species most frequently chosen for olfaction experiments because their neural anatomy resembles that of man). These workers connected microelectrodes to the individual cells, and their experiments demonstrated that specific cells react selectively with specific odors. Eight kinds of odor receptors were identified in the frog, and 5 of these receptor-types reacted with the 7 primary odors which Amoore described. Thus, Gesteland and Lettvin's experiments give support to the stereochemical theory of odor (see next section), proposed by Amoore, Johnston, and Rubin. They have been successful in establishing the fact that the sense of smell is governed by an electrical process that originates in the olfactory nerve whenever a whiff of odor hits the lining of the nose.

The human nose is an instrument of remarkable sensitivity and precision. Even though the sensitivity to odors varies between individuals, most people can detect vanillin at a concentration of 1 part in 10^6. Odor thresholds also vary according to the chemical compound that is being smelled. For example, ethyl mercaptan—the active ingredient in skunk odor—can be detected in as low a concentration as 0.000000000000071 ounce (7×10^{-14} ounce). Yet this is equivalent to more than 19 billion (19×10^9) molecules of ethyl mercaptan. As odor sensitivity is about 10,000 times that of taste sensitivity, ordinary chemical methods are often impractical in the study of food odors.

Odor Theories

More than 2,000 years ago the Roman poet Lucretius postulated that the palate contains small pores of various sizes and shapes. Odor perception was attributed by Lucretius to the specific shapes of the odorous molecules together with their capabilities of fitting particular pores in the palate.

In 1949, Moncrieff proposed a so-called new theory of odor remarkably similar to the ancient one of Lucretius, but based on modern scientific evidence. According to Moncrieff's deductions, the odorant must be volatile and must possess a molecular configuration complementary to that of a specific site on the olfactory receptor. He stated that olfaction occurs in six stages: (1) odorant molecules pervade the air; (2) odor-containing air is inspired by the subject, and sniffed into the nasal cleft; (3) molecules lodge themselves on sites of suitable receptors; (4) lodgement may cause an energy change, such as a reduction in surface tension; (5) the energy shift in the receptors sends discrete electrical messages up the olfactory nerve to the brain; and (6) the brain processes and computes the smell.

About 15 years later, after more than a decade of experimentation with hundreds of organic odor compounds, Amoore and co-workers proposed the stereochemical theory of odor. While there are 3 primary colors of sight, these workers chose 7 primary odors: camphoraceous, musky, floral, pepperminty, ethereal, pungent, and putrid. The first 5 of these 7 primary odors are complementary to the 7 receptor sites, which resemble cavities and slots. According to Amoore, each of these 5 primary odors can be identified by the size and shape of its molecules, and particular odors fit into specific openings. Pungent and putrid odors are distinguished by electrical charge rather than by shape. Thus, these workers proposed a complex odor spectrum for smell that resembles the simpler color spectrum for sight.

Experimental evidence substantiates the stereochemical theory of odor. The first direct support of the Amoore theory is Gesteland and Lettvin's experimental discovery of differ-

entiated receptor sites in the olfactory organ of the frog.
Obviously, Amoore's theory is of great value, although it may
prove to be an oversimplified explanation of the complex
phenomenon of odor. Further studies will place the stereochemical theory of odor in proper perspective.

Instrumentation

So far man has devised no instrument to equal the performance of the human nose and brain. Work is being done to
develop better instruments for detecting odors. In making
such efforts, scientists are learning more about the way
the human nose functions.

According to Moncrieff, the smell stimulus is a physiochemical adsorptive process, and the molecules responsible for
a particular flavor lend themselves to instrumentation. His
mechanical nose is made up of a thermostat coated with a
peanut protein film and a glass-enclosed thermistor having
a resistance capacity of 2000 ohms, with a drop in resistance
of 60 ohms per °C rise in temperature. When an odorant vapor
in air is passed over the coated thermostat at a controlled
rate of one liter of air per minute, a temperature rise occurs
which unbalances the Wheatstone bridge resistance circuit.
This device, while more sensitive to acetone than the human
nose, is inferior to the nose in detecting vanilla or musk
odors.

Quite recently, investigations of the sense of smell were
begun at Honeywell Research Center, Hopkins, Minnesota.
The ultimate goal of this research effort is to develop electronic
sensors capable of detecting and identifying odors.

Odor Psychology

Both good and bad odors exert remarkable psychological
influence on our lives. Food appetites and personal performance can be whetted or dulled by the odors in the air. Emo-
tional effects of odors can also profoundly affect food sales.

A pleasant feeling and salivary stimulation can result from
inhaling food aromas. Consider for example: the fragrant
essence of freshly picked tree-ripened oranges, apples, peaches, pears, or bananas; the yeasty aroma of homemade bread

baking; the smell of beef roasting, corn popping, coffee perco-
lating, cheese curing, hops brewing, or fudge cooling on a
marble slab. These fragrances can cause us to recollect childhood smelling experiences and to reminisce. In contrast, the
lachrymatory effect of peeled onions cause tears to flow; the
sickening gassy smell of sour milk, spoiled meat or fermented
fruits and vegetables turns the stomach.

Hazardous odors serve as a warning mechanism with the aid
of our chemical senses. Gas leaks are identified by means of
the mercaptan stench that is purposely added to natural-gas
supplies. Yet, recently a patent was granted for the use of
methyl mercaptan as a coffee flavor booster. The application
of excessive heat to fat when frying foods causes the release
of some polynuclear hydrocarbons that the nose may detect.
Hence, our chemical warning system protects us today as it
did primitive man many thousands of years ago.

Odor transfer problems have plagued engineers for many
years. Design engineering is needed to minimize problems of
odor transfer in apartment buildings, refrigerators, and food
packages. Tests prove that tarry or oily materials are espec-
cially receptive to certain odors. Butter or chocolate can be
ruined by exposure to paint and varnish fumes. Butter should
not be cut with a knife that hasn't been cleaned after being
used on fish, onions, or garlic; butter should not be exposed
to raw fish, smoked ham, onion, garlic, sauerkraut, or limburger cheese volatiles. Chefs, on the other hand, sometimes
use odor transfer advantageously. For example, a lobster
butter is produced by incorporating cooked lobster essence
into creamery butter.

Sight Psychology.—Taste panels were used by Borsenik to
study the effect of 11 different light sources on 8 foods. Food
illuminated with incandescent and white fluorescent lamps was
preferred to those with soft white, warm white, cool white, gold,
daylight, pink, blue, green, and red fluorescent lighting.

Odor Analysis

Odor has been called the principal part of flavor. Consequently, the problem of odor analysis is being attacked with ever-
increasing vigor by food scientists in all parts of the world.
Taste analysis is comparatively much less complicated—the

taste, or nonvolatile portions of flavor, are fewer in number
and occur naturally in foods at high enough concentrations to
permit either direct chemical or microbiological analysis.
Odor analysis is much more difficult. The odor or volatile
parts of flavor are low in concentration to start with. And
as the many individual components are separated for subsequent analysis, further reduction in sample size occurs.
Accordingly sophisticated chemical and/or instrumental methods of analysis are being developed to cope with the situation.
Some of these will be described later.

There is a growing awareness that the determination of what
chemicals constitute an odor may be the simplest part of solving
an odor problem. For, beyond this, it is essential to determine
the relative concentrations of all the chemicals constituting the
odor. Since it is not uncommon for a food odor to contain more
than 200 different chemicals at varying concentrations, the
tasks of analyzing a particular food odor and then matching it
by synthesis are extremely difficult both chemically and mathematically speaking.

Even this concept of food odor analysis is oversimplified,
however, for food is living matter that is in a constant state of
flux. Fruit enzymes, for instance, are constantly forming
esters from acids and alcohols present in the fruit. Meanwhile other enzymes are hydrolyzing esters to form alcohols
and acids. Many other chemical changes are concomitantly
occurring. These changes happen even while an apple, orange,
or banana is being eaten. Analysis showed that crushed fresh
strawberries contain 1 part in 2 million of the alcohol hexane-
2-ol, whereas none of this particular alcohol was present in
the whole fresh fruit. Mere crushing, a physical effect, thus
changes the chemical nature of strawberries and alters their
flavor.

In applying modern research instruments to the study of
flavor, scientists are continually discovering more complexity
in the natural flavors of all foods, although there are a few
common-denominator type factors. Many of the same chemical
compounds have been found in different foods at varying levels
of concentration. Thus it has been established that there may
be some qualitative chemical similarities accompanied by both
qualitative and quantitative chemical differences between foods.

Functional groups have profound effects on characteristic

flavors; for example, a phenyl group and a side chain of at least four carbons gives the so-called "bite" of black pepper's active ingredient peperine. Pungent compounds indigenous to red pepper spice are derivatives of ortho-methoxy-phenol. Sweetness, menthol coolness, and glutamate effect are all influenced by isomerism. Sweet and bitter taste-producing compounds are complex, while salty or acid tastes are more uniform. Nevertheless, despite the complexity of flavor, functional-group analysis together with gas chromatography are providing some answers.

Exact predictions of what compounds will be sweet or bitter is impossible, but Moncrieff has provided the following guidelines. Polyhydroxy and polyhalogenated aliphatic compounds and alpha-amino acids are usually sweet. One nitro group in a molecule imparts sweetness, but 2 or 3 nitro groups result in bitterness. Some aldehydes are sweet; ketones are never sweet; alkaloids are bitter. Phenyl group substitution in a sweet compound such as glycerol causes a bitter taste. Symmetrical ureas are not sweet, but 1,1-dimethylurea is very sweet.

Natives in West Africa chew the pulp of miracle fruit, a small red berry, to make their stale and acidulated maize bread more palatable, and to give sweetness to sour palm wine and beer. A glycoprotein in the fruit modifies the tongue's receptors, making sour substances taste sweet. Gymnenic acid converts the taste of table sugar to grittiness. After 1 or 2 hours the effect wears off.

Gas chromatographic methods for separating flavor volatiles are complex and expensive. It is safe to estimate that the rate of improvement in gas chromatographs during the past five years has been at least five times as great as the rate of change in automobile models during the same period. Constant development and refinement of gas chromatographs is still going on.

For example, the results of a gas chromatographic study of cooked chicken volatiles by Minor *et al.* was published in 1965. A total of less than 30 peaks representing at least that many chemical entities was obtained on each of the chromatograms for breast and leg muscle, using a packed column and temperature programming. During the two-year interim from the start of the study to the publication of the results, gas chromatographs equipped with electron-capture detectors and capillary column fractionators resulted in the separation of about 200 peaks, indicative of that number of individual compounds in cooked chicken aroma. However, separation has proved to be much easier than subsequent identification of the peaks, each of which may represent either one discrete entity or several chemical entities combined. In other words, the more peaks one separates by gas chromatography the more involved their identification may become.

Separating the volatiles is only the first step in analyzing a particular food odor. Samples of odorous materials injected into a gas chromatograph average about 1 or 2 milliliters of concentrated flavor volatiles. Fractionation ideally involves separation of this small amount of flavor compounds into 100 or more discrete and minute component fractions. Subsequent identification of these fractions requires sensitive instruments. For example, a combination of the human nose, mass spectrometry, nuclear magnetic resonance, and infrared and ultraviolet spectrophotometry is being used by Day in studies on the analysis of cheese volatiles. Progress is being made in the analysis of food odors by applying organoleptic tests, chemical tests, instrumentation, and other physiochemical methods, together with physiological studies. Using a variety of instrumental techniques based mainly on tandem hookups of the gas chromatograph and time-in-flight mass spectrometer, trace amounts of volatile chemical constituents of food are being detected at everincreasing rates.

Food flavor research is progressing on bread, wine, red meats, poultry, fish, milk, cultured dairy products, cheese, potato, onion, hops, peaches, pears, and other fruits, coffee, and flavor potentiators such as monosodium glutamate and the sodium salts of the 5' nucleotides. For example, a total of 200 compounds were reported in coffee volatiles in 1967. This number was raised to 363 compounds in coffee by mid 1969. The final number of components predicted for coffee is 600. This same pattern holds for other food-flavor volatiles.

PRACTICAL USE OF FLAVOR RESEARCH DEVELOPMENTS

For centuries salt, sugar, spices, and wood smoke have been added to supplement the natural flavors that occur in foods. These additives lend savory richness to certain dishes.

Soya sauce as a flavoring and monosodium glutamate as a seasoning and flavor potentiator were developed in the Orient to make vegetable protein foods tolerable to a meat eater.

Soya sauce with vinegar and spices is the base for Worcestershire sauce. Prime quality soya sauce is made from wheat and soy beans by a slow fermentation process. MSG occurs naturally in wheat, meat, poultry, and other foods, and since the early 1900's it has been manufactured by several methods. Today it is being produced by microbiological or enzyme action from low-cost sources.

Vanilla bean extract is another flavoring of antique origin. Other extracts such as oil of wintergreen, spice oils, oleoresinous extracts from spices, and natural fruit extracts have also been used as food flavorings for decades. Hydrolyzed plant proteins from grain and yeast sources, and the sodium salts of the 5' nucleotides from Japan represent more recent developments that are being applied to complement or replace beef extract which is expensive and in short supply.

A list totalling 1,023 flavoring ingredients was compiled recently. We may wonder why so many flavoring materials, both synthetic and natural, are needed. Let us consider one small facet of the total fruit flavor picture—strawberry flavor. Based on the annual consumption of strawberry flavoring (imitation) and the average annual production of strawberries in the United States, it has been calculated that the entire strawberry crop, if used only to provide a natural flavor extract, would yield only enough to satisfy the annual needs of a city the size of Pittsburgh, leaving none for the rest of the country. Thus synthetic flavorings are useful and necessary supplements to natural fruit flavor supplies.

Fruit flavors have been worked on for several decades by organic chemists. Synthetic strawberry, raspberry, and cherry flavors have been used in candies and gelatin desserts for three decades or longer. One key advantage of these synthetics is their stability toward oxygen in the air.

Duplicating even the simplest of the true natural flavors has not been successful. Qualitative and quantitative factors combine to magnify the problem to and perhaps beyond computer proportions. Thus flavor chemistry may offer the food scientist a never-ending challenge, as the relationship between chemical structure and flavor is essentially unknown. Of more than

TABLE 11.1

FRUIT AROMAS

Source	Compounds Found to Date[1]	No. of GRAS List
Pineapple	38	19
Banana	37	22
Passion fruit	4	4
Black currant	89	45
Apple	84	58
Pear	69	39
Peach	33	25
Raspberry	61	33
Strawberry	137	66
Grapefruit	31	16
Lemon	61	39
Lime	46	23
Orange	124	73
Grape	83	48

[1]Adapted from Nursten, H. E., and A. A. Williams, March, 1967. Chem. Ind., pp. 486–497.

1,100 flavor substances now on the GRAS (generally regarded as safe by the FDA) list the majority occur naturally in foods and the others are closely related to them in chemical structure (Table 11.1).

It is easiest to synthesize imitations of fruit flavors. Vegetable flavors are harder, and butter and cheese flavors harder still to imitate, although biochemists are producing useful cheese essences. Most difficult of all flavors to simulate are those of meat, fish, and poultry. Research on meat flavor began nearly two centuries ago when chemistry was in its infancy in Europe. At that time scientists had begun studying the chemical composition of meat extract.

Beef extract, hydrolyzed vegetable proteins, casein digests, and yeast autolyzate extracts are flavorings that have characteristic amino acid, peptide, protein, nucleotide, and "browning reaction" flavors. Each hydrolyzed plant protein is different from the other; the protein source and the manufacturing process chosen are responsible for flavor differences. Yet these products are compatible or synergistic with one another and/or with certain meats or meat and vegetable mixtures. In short, these are meat and vegetable flavor synergists that work with meat flavor to enrich or supplement it. Occurring as by-products of glutamate manufactured from plant protein hydrolyzates, they are related to monosodium glutamate as molasses is to sugar. In other words, they are the compounds present in the mother liquor from which MSG is isolated by chemically controlled crystallization.

Pure chemical compounds that are likewise synergistic with the flavorings described above, with meat, and with each other are MSG, DSG, and DSI. Their primary function is to provide flavor enrichment by blending flavors synergistically and additively. The secret of flavor development according to Sjöström and Cairncross is "blended flavor." Of all the condiments, however, meat extract provides the truest resemblance to the mouth satisfaction indigenous to freshly prepared meat stock. In fact, there is no flavor substitute that matches real meat taste and aroma.

Meat Substitutes

Liebig's classic meat extract preparation and analysis was prompted by meat shortages in Europe resulting from the Napoleonic wars. Today there are about 3.2 billion people in the world, 550 million of whom consume over 90% of the meat supply.

In the search for ways to close the ever-widening protein versus population gap, the Japanese have turned to fishing. A Frenchman, Champagnat, has succeeded in producing protein from crude petroleum by developing strains of yeast that can subsist on petroleum hydrocarbons. A soy-protein matrix perfected by Boyer is flavored with beef-like, ham-like, bacon-like, and chicken-like flavors. A Purdue research team has recently announced development of a lysine-rich mutant strain of corn in their efforts to alleviate Kwashiorkor (protein deficiency disease) among infants in underfed countries. Furthermore, lysine and most of the other essential amino acids are now produced by synthesis or microbiologically. But in their present stage, none of these developments or any combination of them can go far toward alleviating protein shortages.

Man improves the biological efficiency of grain proteins by feeding them to ruminants, thus converting them to animal protein of relatively high biological value. However, it takes 7 calories of plant carbohydrate to produce 1 calorie of beef protein and $3\frac{1}{2}$ calories of plant carbohydrate to produce 1 calorie of chicken protein. Meanwhile, the natural resource holding the most serious threat to our food supply and living standard is water. About 330 gal. of water are required to provide enough wheat for one person to subsist on for one day; and 4200 gal. are needed to produce only 1 lb of beef.

One must look to the Orient for guidance in making practical substitutions of vegetables for meat and in flavoring these substitute foods. Bean sprouts produced from either soy or mung beans sprouts are highly nutritious and flavorful. Furthermore, the Chinese have discovered that a combination of green soybeans with Chinese cabbage provides a complete and balanced spectrum of the essential amino acids in adequate amounts to support growth and maintenance of the human body.

Flavor satisfaction is achieved by adding soya sauce, monosodium glutamate, and the sodium salts of the 5' nucleotides to the bland vegetables and rice that make up their main diet. For centuries the Japanese have used sea tangle for its glutamate effect and dried bonito for its nucleotide effect in seasoning their meals.

It was reported by Ikeda that the principal flavor component of sea tangle extract is monosodium glutamate (MSG). Today most of the MSG is produced by direct fermentation processes. The world's supply, which was recently reported to be 150 million lb per year valued at about $80 million, comes mainly from Japan. Production in the United States is less than one-fourth of the total amount produced. When one considers that monosodium glutamate usage is at a level of one-tenth the concentration of salt used in food, and that its use is restricted to protein foods, one begins to appreciate the impact of this Oriental seasoning on American food habits. About 30 billion lb of protein foods are seasoned annually (about 150 lb per person per year) with MSG, and the use is increasing.

Monosodium glutamate and the sodium salts of the 5' nucleotides are natural seasonings that act at the receptor surface of the taste buds. Food flavor is affected by nucleotide binding of metal ions that sensitizes tasting sites that are otherwise not active in enhancement of flavors. These effects have been reported by Beidler.

The 5' nucleotides may also be used to flavor meat substitutes. Inosinic acid, an important 5' nucleotide, was first isolated from beef muscle in 1847 by Liebig, who named it after the Greek word meaning muscle. This nucleic acid, upon neutralizing with mild alkali, yields the flavor nucleotide disodium inosinate (DSI). It is interesting to note that this flavor nucleotide is a constituent of ribonucleic acid, which is present in the muscle and brain of mammals and fish.

Ribonucleic acid (RNA) is present in every living cell. There are several types of RNA, one of which transmits information within a cell. When RNA from the brains of trained rats was injected into the brains of untrained rats the latter responded immediately at the learning level of the trained rats. The precursor of RNA, desoxyribonucleic acid (DNA), is the key compound in genetic modification. Some day RNA may be used to determine human behavioral characteristics.

Apparently there are key relationships between flavor and life. It is interesting to note that compounds which contribute to life processes occurring in nature may also be isolated, purified, and neutralized to serve as food-flavor potentiators.

First of all there is MSG, the monosodium salt of glutamic acid, which is a building block of protein and is the most widely occurring amino acid found in natural proteins. Next, there is the nucleotide disodium inosinate (DSI), which occurs in the RNA of muscle and may be derived directly from RNA by acid hydrolysis, followed by neutralization with sodium hydroxide, or by enzyme action. DSI contributes an amazing synergistic action to the flavor-accentuating powers of MSG and the hydrolyzed plant proteins. Disodium guanylate (DSG), another nucleotide, is derived from yeast cells and is about 20 times as effective as DSI, but in a little different manner.

The nucleotides are effective in seasoning protein foods at concentrations in the range of one-twentieth of the level of MSG or less. A blend of nucleotides consisting of 50% DSI and 50% DSG, derived from yeast, is being marketed in the United States. This product is imported from Japan and sells for $25 a pound, though the price is dropping. At present its main use is to partially replace beef extract. By modifying and improving hydrolyzed plant protein flavors, the nucleotides

achieve a meatier connotation of flavor than is possible with
MSG alone. Scientists have proved that inosinic acid, the
precursor of the flavor nucleotide, is one of the major active
ingredients in natural beef, chicken, and fish muscle, present
in the nonvolatile flavor fraction of cooked meat.

Scientific research may one day close the protein gap by
applying biochemical principles to the conversion of air, water,
carbohydrates, or carbon to protein. This kind of protein,
when available, will have to be modified in texture, appearance, taste, and aroma. For unless the synthetic product is
acceptable in both nutrition and flavor, it will not be eaten.

FLAVORING MATERIALS

Various flavoring materials used in food and beverage manufacture are derived from plants. These include fruits, flowers,
roots, barks, seeds, and leaves that yield herbs and spices
together with their derivatives, namely; fruit juices, essential
oils, and oleoresins and extracts.

Essential Oils

Essential oils are aromatic volatile oils derived from plants
that usually carry the flavor of the plant. Terpenes and many
other classes of chemical compounds may be present, including acids, esters, alcohols, aldehydes, ketones, sulfides,
mercaptans (thiols), lactones, and others. They are distinguished from fixed oils, such as vegetable oils, that are glycerides of fatty acids and hence saponifiable. Essential oils
(except those containing esters) are nonsaponifiable. Some
essential oils, such as oil of wintergreen (methyl salicylate),
are nearly pure single compounds. Others, for example oil
of bitter almond (benzaldehyde, hydrocyanic acid), are mixtures. From the flavoring viewpoint they are strong and convenient sources of desirable aroma.

The essential oils may be concentrated in special cells within the plant or its parts. For example, citrus oils occur in the
cells of the skin, whereas oil of celery may be derived either
from the seed or leaf. Yields of oils from lemon, lime, or
orange skins vary to a maximum of 1%. Peppercorns yield
about 10%, caraway seeds 7%, and rose petals 0.02%.

Methods of extraction include: (a) steam distillation; (b) pressing (fruit rinds); (c) percolation with solvent (vanilla); extraction with volatile solvents which are afterwards distilled off; (e) maceration in fixed oil or fat extraction with solvent, and isolation or distilling; and (f) enfleurage, exposing odorless fats to aromatics contained in flower petals until strongly scented, and then extracting with solvent.

Terpeneless oils are obtained by removal of 90% or more of the terpenes from citrus or other oils by fractional vacuum distillation. Thus the nonterpene components are concentrated five-or tenfold. Their increased stability toward oxidation is important. However, they lose some of the original flavor potency of the fruits or leaves.

Storage and handling techniques must be designed to safeguard essential oils from exposure to light, air, heat, or cold. Photochemical effects induced by exposure to light catalyze their deterioration. Oxidation of terpenes resulting from exposure to air causes objectionable "turpentine odor" and sticky polymeric compounds to develop. Heat accelerates resin formation. Cold shock causes the oil to separate. Accordingly, essential oils are protected by packaging them in dark-glass or tin containers, and storing in the dark at room temperature (60 to 70°F).

Uses of essential oils are mainly for flavoring foods and beverages. Some important volatile oils used in flavoring foods are shown in Table 11.2.

Oleoresins

Oleoresins are semisolid mixtures of the resin and essential oil of the plant from which they exude. They have pungent tastes and characteristic odors sometimes termed balsamic.

Solvent extraction by percolation followed by removal of the solvent by distillation are the processes used to separate oleoresins from spices and herbs. Ethylene dichloride is the preferred solvent for oleoresin of pepper, but must be carefully removed from the finished product as it is toxic in food products except in trace amounts.

Ground pepper powder often contains undesirable filth including microbial, insect, and rodent contamination. Oleoresins overcome these problems, and provide a convenient

TABLE 11.2.
CHARACTERISTICS OF ESSENTIAL OILS

Oil	Description of Odor	Taste	Important Components
Garlic	Pungent, sulfury	Biting	Diallyl disulfide and other sulfur compounds
Leek	Pungent, sulfury	Biting	Vinyl sulfide, thiols, aldehyde
Onion	Pungent, lachrymatory	Biting	Sulfur compounds, and allyl aldehyde
Ginger	Pungent, spicy, fragrant	Burning	Zingerone, citral
Cardamon	Fragrant, camphoric, spicy	Burning	Cinede, camphor borneol, terpineol
Pepper	Pungent, piney	Burning	Terpenes, camphor
Nutmeg	Spicy, turpentinic, lemony	Bitter	Terpenes, terpene alcohols, eugenol, esters, aldehydes
Cinnamon (bark)	Cinnamon	Sweet	85% cinnamic aldehyde
Cassia (bark)	Cinnamon	Sweet	70–85% cinnamic aldehyde
Bitter almond	Peach kernels	---	Benzaldehyde, prussic acid
Apple (skin)	Fragrance of apples	---	Acetaldehyde, amyl esters
Peach (skin)	Fragrance of peaches	---	Acetaldehyde, methyl esters, linalool, aldehyde
Lime (skin)	Lemony	---	Citrol and 4 other aldehydes, dipentene
Lemon	Lemony	---	4–5% citrol (90% cipentene)
Orange (sweet)	Orangey	---	Linalyl esters, terpineol, u-decyl aldehyde (95% dipentene)
Cloves	Fragrant, spicy, pungent	Numbing	About 85% eugenol
Coriander	Lavenderlike	---	Linalool
Celery (seed)	Celery	---	Sedanonic lactone, dipentene
Caraway	Distinctive caraway	---	50% carvone, dipentene
Dill	Like caraway	---	Carvone, dipentene, dill apiole
Sage	Spicy, herbaceous	---	Camphor, cineole, terpenes
Marjoram	Lavenderlike	---	Terpineol, esters, terpenes
Thyme	Spicy, phenolic, herbaceous	---	50–70% carvacrol

Source: Crocker (1945).

means of standardizing flavor quality and strength. They provide good stability in storage. When freshly made, oleoresin black pepper is a dark green viscous liquid with a pungent aroma. On standing, peperine crystallizes out. Hence it is necessary to warm and stir the product before using in order to assure homogeneity and uniformity.

Propylene glycol may be added in amounts up to 20% by weight of the oleoresin. This solvent solubilizes the piperine. The resultant ''liquid pepper'' may be blended into either a salt or dextrose carrier at a concentration of 7 lb ''liquid pepper'' per 100 lb carrying media. Uniform distribution may be achieved by heating the ''liquid pepper'' and stirring to bring the oleoresin into solutions. Addition to 10 lb aliquots of the carrier accompanied by thorough blending distributes the ''liquid pepper'' uniformly over each particle of carrier. The ''soluble pepper'' thus produced may be used pound for pound to replace ground pepper in a given formula.

''Soluble pepper'' on a salt carrier or similar preparations made from other herb or spice oleoresins provide convenient sanitary, standardized flavorings for meats, salad dressings, prepared entrees, soups and other foods. ''Soluble ginger,'' ''soluble mace,'' ''soluble cinnamon,'' ''soluble nutmeg,'' etc., on a dextrose carrier are ideal for bakery products and beverages.

Important oleoresins include: oleoresin pepper, oleoresin capsicum, oleoresin paprika, oleoresin celery, oleoresin vanilla, and oleoresin ginger.

Other Flavorings

Juices are important flavoring raw materials. However, they are usually fortified with their essential oils or synthetic chemicals.

Research on essential oil and fruit flavors has resulted in the identification of compounds that are active flavoring ingredients. These include: vanillin (vanilla), benzaldehyde (almonds), cinnamaldehyde (cinnamon), ethyl formate (artificial rum flavor), n-amyl acetate (bananas), octyl acetate (oranges), ethyl butyrate (pineapples), amyl butyrate (apricots), and hundreds of others. Accordingly, synthetic flavors are of major importance in the food industry.

TABLE 11.3.
ORANGE FLAVOR INGREDIENTS

Quality Sought	Formulation	
"Character Impact" or "Characterizing Flavor Notes"	Orange oils	5.0 lb
	5 Fold orange oil	2.0 lb
	Terpeneless orange oil	0.125 lb
"Contributor Notes" (not essential)	Citrus Oils	1–2 lb
"Contributor Notes" essential for juice character	Orange juice fortified,[1] imitation (mixture of aroma chemicals properly blended)	0.5 lb

[1] The imitation orange juice fortifier is prepared as follows:

Quality Sought	Formulation	
"Neutral Base" present in most synthetic fruit flavors	Isoamyl Acetate	
	Ethyl Acetate	
	Ethyl Butyrate (Optional)	
	Isoamyl Butyrate	
	Benzyl Alcohol	49.0 parts
"Primer"—character impact note	Decyl aldehyde	10.0 parts
"Naturalizer" rounds out the composition	Orange Oil (s)	20.5 parts
"Toner" imparts secondary notes	Ethyl Anthranalate	
	Acetal	
	Ethyl Formate	
	Octyl Aldehyde	20.0 parts
"Lifts" or accentuates the flavor	Organic Acid	0.50 parts
		100.0 parts

Source: Melillo (1968)

Of more than 1,100 substances now used in flavors most have been found to occur naturally or are closely related chemically to those already analytically identified in foods. Vanillin flavor is used three times more than natural vanilla, synthetic strawberry flavor two times more than natural strawberry, and synthetic Concord grape five times its equivalent in Concord-type grapes grown for all purposes.

Flavors are of two general classes: natural or true, and synthetic or imitation. Natural flavors include those already discussed. Imitation flavor materials include mixtures of aromatic chemicals, either alone or blended with natural flavors. These serve as the flavorist's structural materials for building flavor. Table 11.3 shows the ingredients of an orange flavor.

Flavor ingredients may be stabilized with sodium benzoate to avoid microbiological spoilage. Chemical deterioration is most often due to their reaction with oxygen of the air. To preclude this type of spoilage, suitable antioxidants are added to the oils prior to or during processing.

Conclusion

Essential oils, oleoresins, extracts, and fruit juices are important food and beverage flavorings. Today, blander food components and greater use of synthetic flavors may be needed for economic reasons. Since the requirement of safety in food additives includes flavorings, more stringent regulation by FDA may stifle flavor industry advancement. Analogy with existing materials whose safety is known may be a significant criterion for approval. See appendix for chart on the uses of spices and herbs in various foodstuffs.

CHAPTER 12

L. L. W. Smith
L. J. Minor

Vegetables

Vegetables may be classified as to parts of a plant, such as *root*, for example, carrots, beets, and sweet potatoes. Potatoes and asparagus represent the *stem*; celery, spinach, kale, and rhubarb represent the *leaves*, while the onion represents leaf scales. The *flowers* of the plants are broccoli and cauliflower; the *fruits* are tomatoes, squash, cucumbers, peppers, snap beans, and snow peas, while the *seeds* are corn, beans, and peas.

Vegetables may be classified as to color as green, yellow, orange, red, white and all shades in between.

Vegetables may be classified as to flavor as strong, e.g., the members of the cabbage or brassica family and the onion or allium family. The mild-flavored vegetables are potatoes and corn.

There are other classifications such as high and low sugar, high and low fat, high and low protein, high and low sodium or calcium, and high or low pH value, etc.

The average composition of fresh vegetables is in general water 97 to 66%, carbohydrates 28 to 5%, protein about 3%, and fat 1% or less. The minerals present are sodium, potassium, calcium, magnesium, iron and salts of trace elements. The vitamins vary as to the percentages of fat-soluble (A, D, E and K) and water-soluble (B complex and vitamin C).

The quality of fruits and vegetables depends upon varietal differences, maturity at harvest, storage and marketing procedures. The intended use of a vegetable, such as cooked vs. serving raw, also determines the kind and quality. Experience is the best teacher in learning how to purchase fruits and vegetables properly; but alas, time does not always allow for experience. There are available for the inexperienced excellent sources of material from the land grant colleges in each state, the United States Department of Agriculture, Superintendent of Documents in Washington, D.C., the United Fresh Fruit and

Vegetable Association, and the Western Growers Association, etc.

The cooking of fruits and vegetables is a method of preserving certain qualities of the product, such as the color, flavor, and aroma, and to produce a pleasing texture while maintaining as much nutritive value as possible. The texture is modified; cellulose fiber or roughage is softened; protopectins are changed to more soluble pectin products; starch grains tend to swell and disperse; proteins are denatured; and some organic acids, salts and simple sugars are released into the surround- ing media. Aroma and flavor are developed and some released; some loss of ascorbic acid and thiamine is inevitable, but losses of vitamin A, riboflavin and niacin are not so great. The color may or may not change since it depends upon the pigments present, the pH of the product and media and the time and final temperature of heating.

Color

The green color of plants is a nonwater-soluble pigment called chlorophyll. Chlorophyll exists in two forms, the α or $C_{32}H_{30}$-

$$ON_4Mg \Big\langle \begin{array}{l} COOCH_3 \\ COOC_{20}H_{39} \end{array} \quad \text{and the } \beta \text{ or } C_{32}H_{28}O_2N_4Mg \Big\langle \begin{array}{l} COOCH_3 \\ COOC_{20}H_{39} \end{array} \quad \text{forms.}$$

The chlorophylls are always accompanied by the *fat-soluble* or *nonwater-soluble yellow* to *red pigments* known as the *ca-rotenoids*, such as the carotenes ($C_{40}H_{56}$) and xanthophylls ($C_{40}H_{56}O_2$). Some water-soluble flavones (white to yellow color) may also be present.

The basic group of the chlorophyll molecule is the pyrrole group,

$$\begin{array}{c} -C \!\!-\!\! C- \\ \| \quad | \\ -C \!\!\diagdown\!\! {}_N\!\!\diagup\!\! C- \end{array}$$

four of these are joined by a methylene group —HC= and the nitrogen of each pyrrole group is oriented to the magnesium. Chlorophyll β differs from α by having an aldehyde group in carbon atom no. 3. These are called methyl phytyl chlorophyll-ides and are bound to lipoproteins in the plastid portion of the cell.

phytol ester   methyl ester

For purposes of simplification the formula for chlorophyll, whether α or β, will be written as $\times \text{Mg} \begin{smallmatrix} \text{COOCH}_3 \\ \text{COOC}_{20}\text{H}_{39} \end{smallmatrix}$.

Chlorophylls are easily acted upon by weak acids, bases, heat, copper salts and enzymes. The reaction with acid or in acid media is represented as follows:

(a) $\text{XMg} \begin{smallmatrix} \text{COOCH}_3 \\ \text{COOC}_{20}\text{H}_{39} \end{smallmatrix} + 2\text{CH}_3\text{COOH} \longrightarrow \text{XH}_2 \begin{smallmatrix} \text{COOCH}_3 \\ \text{COOC}_{20}\text{H}_{39} \end{smallmatrix} + \text{Mg(CH}_3\text{COO)}_2$

$$\text{XH}_2 \begin{smallmatrix} \text{COOCH}_3 \\ \text{COOC}_{20}\text{H}_{39} \end{smallmatrix}$$

is called phaeophytin, and is a dull or olive green color. Canned green beans are typical of the change from a bright green to a dull green color. The reaction which occurs in alkaline media by the addition of NaHCO_3, is represented as follows:

(b) $\text{XMg} \begin{smallmatrix} \text{COOCH}_3 \\ \text{COOC}_{20}\text{H}_{39} \end{smallmatrix} + 2\text{NaOH} \longrightarrow \text{XMg(COONa)}_2 + \text{CH}_3\text{OH} + \text{C}_{20}\text{H}_{39}\text{OH}$

X Mg(COONa)_2 is called chlorophyllin and is a bright green color. The alcohols methanol (CH_3OH) and phytol ($\text{C}_{20}\text{H}_{39}\text{OH}$) are released.

The difficulty with adding baking soda to the cooking water is not knowing the amount to add, since softening of the texture is definitely a by-product of cooking in alkaline media as well as producing off-flavors.

The *carotenes or carotenoids* range from yellow to deep red. $C_{40}H_{56}$ is a polyene based on the isoprene monomer which is of

$$-C=\underset{\underset{C}{|}}{C}- \quad C=C-$$

the *trans* configuration in nature. Carotene has cyclic ends and lycopene has open ends. Carotene is the primary coloring agent in carrots and lycopene is the chief pigment in tomatoes, along with other carotenes and xanthophylls.

Carotene is the precursor of vitamin A which represents one half of the β-carotene molecule:

Xanthophylls ($C_{40}H_{50}O$ and $C_{40}H_{56}O_2$) are the chief yellow pigments in corn, squash and sweet potatoes.

Lutein ($C_{40}H_{56}O_2$) is present in egg yolks. There are many carotenoids; at one time it was estimated that about 80 different forms exist. These pigments are fairly stable to most cooking procedures. They will oxidize and change from the *trans* to *cis* form under *excessive* cooking methods.

The *water-soluble* pigments are the *anthocyanins*, the *flavones* and the *tannins*. These are polyphenols giving an astringency stimulus to the mouth and tongue and can even be detected by the lips.

The *anthocyanins* cover the red to blue to purple range and are glucosides, such as cyanidin. They are red in acid media, blue in alkaline media.

The *flavones* are colorless or white to pale yellow, and similar in structure to the anthocyanins. Some have —OH groups and some have —OCH$_3$ or methoxy groups; they are white in acid media and yellow in alkaline media.

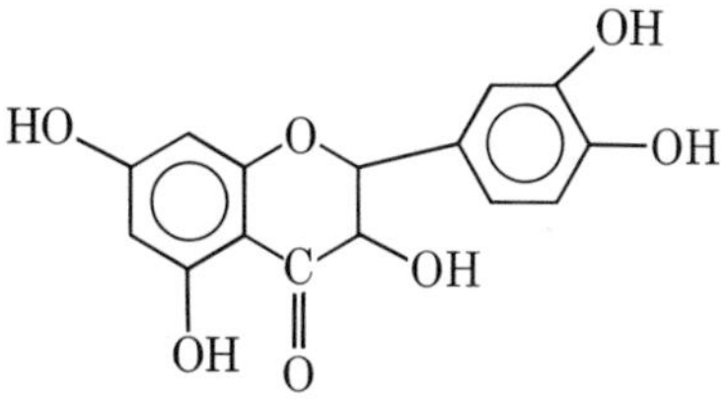

quercetin

The *tannins* vary from brown to red coloring, and tend to affect both color and flavor of the product.

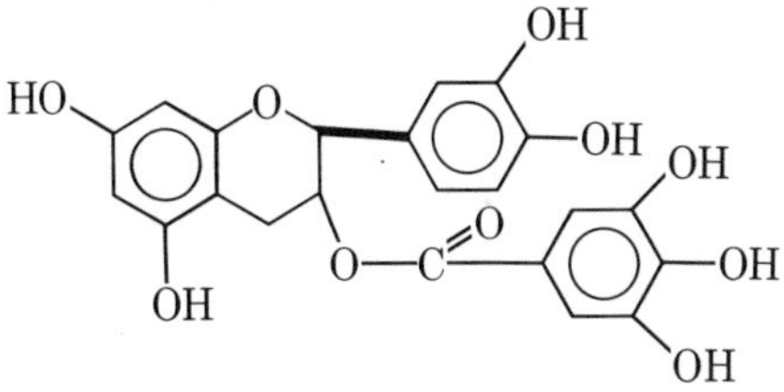

gallocatechingallate

Tannins are present in teas, chocolate, apples, bananas, hops, coffee, persimmons, pears and dates, and produce an astringency, especially in the immature product. Tannins darken during the fermentation process; green tea becomes black tea. Tannins react with polyphenoloxidases to contribute to enzymatic browning of fruits and vegetables such as the browning of sliced raw peaches, apples or potatoes. This enzymatic browning reaction is the result of the action of oxygen and polyphenoloxidase on polyphenols to produce a melanin, which varies from a pink to brown to black discoloration. This is controlled by cooking, which denatures the enzyme, or by dipping the raw product for a minute in a solution of sodium bisulfite ($NaHSO_3$) in a concentration of 2 oz of the salt per gallon of water. Commercial products generally contain sodium bisulfite, or citric or tartaric acid products to be made into solutions. These acid-reacting solutions keep oxygen from the cut product and the low pH tends to inhibit enzymatic action and thus prevent discoloration. Tannins react to heavy metals such as lead, mercury and iron, and are more soluble in hot water than cold water. Cold extracts of tea and coffee contain less tannins.

Other color changes in fruits and vegetables may be due not to the pigments or compounds discussed but to other chemical

TABLE 12.1
PLANT ACIDS

Common Name	Formula and I.U.P.A.C. Name	Where Found or Used
	Volatile monocarboxylic acids	
Formic acid	HCOOH Methanoic acid	Asparagus, cauliflower, cabbage, peas, etc.
Acetic acid	CH_3COOH Ethanoic acid	
Propionic acid	C_2H_5COOH Propanoic acid	
Butyric acid	C_3H_7COOH Butanoic acid	
Valeric acid	C_4H_9COOH Pentanoic acid	
Caproic acid	$C_5H_{11}COOH$ Hexanoic acid	
	Nonvolatile acids, dicarboxylic	
Oxalic acid	COOHCOOH Ethandioic acid	Sorrel, rhubarb, spinach, grapes, tomatoes
Malonic acid	$COOHCH_2COOH$ Propandioic acid	Ester in many products
Succinic acid	$COOH(CH_2)_2COOH$ butadioic acid	Blackberries, broccoli, beer, rice
Glutamic acid	$COOH(CH_2)_3COOH$ pentadioic acid	Sugar beets, etc.
Adipic acid	$COOH(CH_2)_4COOH$ hexadioic acid	Beet juice, acid ingredient in baking powder
Oxalacetic acid	$COOHCOCH_2COOH$ α-ketobutadioic acid	Very common but only found in traces

Fumaric acid	$COOH(CH)_2COOH$ *trans*-butendioic acid	Low hydroscopic and used in powdered beverages and pudding, found in all plant and animal tissues
Maleic acid	$COOH(CH)_2COOH$ *cis*-butendioic acid	Used chiefly in the manufacture of maleic acid hydrozide, a sprout inhibitor

Hydroxydicarboxylic acids are the α forms

Malic acid	$COOHCHOHCH_2COOH$ α-hydroxybutadioic acid	Apples, rhubarb, grapes, etc. and as calcium salt in maple syrup and referred to as "sugar sand"
Tartaric acid	$COOH(CHOH)_2COOH$ α,β-dihydroxy butadioic acid	Grapes, used as an ingredient in flavoring foods or as an acid ingredient in baking powders

Aminodicarboxylic acids

Aspartic acid	$COOHCHNH_2CH_2COOH$ α-aminobutadioic acid	Sugar cane, sugar beets
Glutamic acid	$COOHCHNH_2(CH_2)_2COOH$ α-aminopentadioic acid	Used to improve taste of beer and as the monosodium salt, a flavor enhancer

Tricarboxylic acids

Citric acid	$COOHCH_2C(OH)(COOH)CH_2COOH$ 2-hydroxy-1,2,3-propanetricarboxylic acid	Found chiefly in citrus fruits

Table 12.1 (continued)

Common Name	Formula and I.U.P.A.C. Name	Where Found or Used
Aconitic acid	COOHCH$_2$C(COOH)CHCOOH Cis-1, 2, 3-prop-2-ene tricarboxylic acid	Found in molasses
	Aromatic plant acids [1]	
Benzoic acid	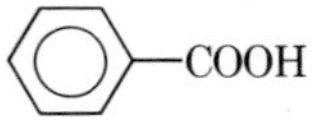 ⬡—COOH Benzoic acid	Cranberries, plums and as the sodium salt used as a preservative
Salicylic acid	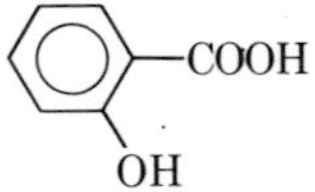 ⬡—COOH (OH) o-hydroxybenzoic acid	Cherry back, anise, tea, raspberries
Methyl salicylate	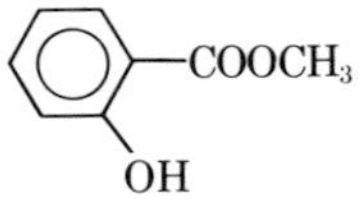 ⬡—COOCH$_3$ (OH) Methyl-o-hydroxybenzoate	Oil of wintergreen
Acetyl salicylate	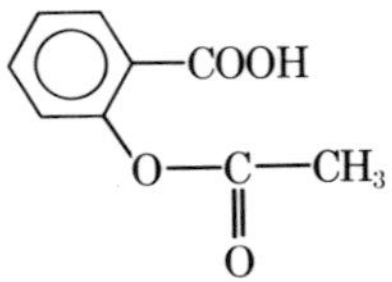 ⬡—COOH, O—C—CH$_3$ ‖ O o-acetylbenzoic acid	Aspirin
Cinnamic acid	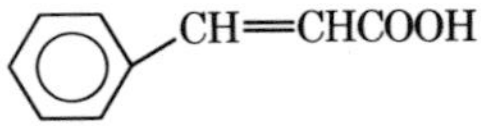 ⬡—CH=CHCOOH 3-phenylpropenoic acid	Flavoring agent

Vanillic acid	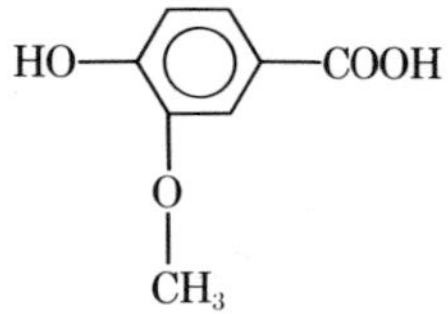 COOH	3-methoxy-4-hydroxy-benzoic acid	Vanilla bean, flavoring
Caffeic acid	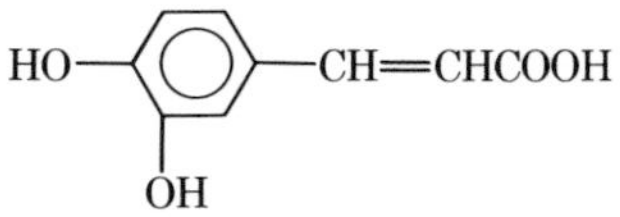 CH=CHCOOH	3,4-dihydroxy cinnamic acid	Found in plants in conjugated form. Green and roasted coffee
Oil of almonds	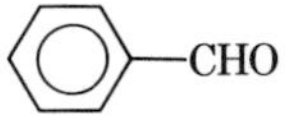 CHO	Benzaldehyde	Almonds, cherry pits casses back, used in baked goods and hand lotions
Benzyl alcohol	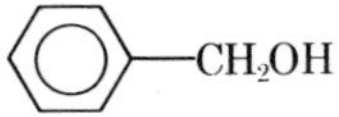 CH₂OH		Raspberries and tea used in synthetic flavorings.
Eugenol	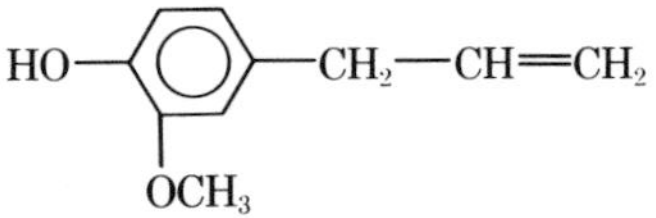 CH₂—CH=CH₂	3(3-methoxy-4-hydroxyphenyl) propene-1	Oil of cloves
Ethyl acetate Ethyl butyrate	CH₃COOC₂H₅ C₃H₇COOC₂H₅	Ethyl ethanoate Ethyl butanoate	Apples, bananas, pineapples, etc. Apples, strawberries, in alcoholic solution known as pineapple oil
Diacetyl Acetoin	CH₃COCOCH₃ CH₃CHOHCOCH₃	Butadione 3-hydroxy-2-butanone	Butter Butter
Allyl isothiocyanate	CH₂CHCH₂NCS	3 isothiocyanopropene-1	Oil of mustard, horseradish, onion

Table 12.1 (*continued*)

Common Name	Formula and I.U.P.A.C. Name		Where Found or Used
Asparagine	$H_2NCOCH_2CH(NH_2)COOH$	α-aminosuccinamic acid	Found in young plants
Sinigrin	$CH_2CHCHNC \begin{smallmatrix} OSO_3K \\ SC_6H_{11}O_5 \end{smallmatrix}$	potassium myronate (a β-glucopyranoside	In Crucifers and some members of the allium family
Diallyl sulfide	$(CH_2CHCH_2)_2S$	di(2 propenyl) sulfide	Garlic, onions
Allyl propyl disulfide	$(CH_2CHCH_2)\!-\!S$ $CH_3CH_2CH_2\!-\!S$	2-propenylpropyl disulfide	Leek, garlic, onion
Allyl mercaptan	CH_2CHCH_2SH	2-propene-1-thiol	Garlic
Methyl cysteine sulfoxide	$CH_3\!-\!S\!-\!CH_2CH(NH_2)COOH$ $\overset{\|}{\underset{O}{}}$	Methyl cysteine sulfoxide	Onion, garlic
Allinin	$CH_2\!=\!CHCH_2SCH_2CH(NH_2)COOH$ $\overset{\|}{\underset{O}{}}$	2-propenyl cysteine sulfoxide	Onion, garlic
Allyl amine[2]	$CH_2CHCH_2NH_2$	2-propenylamine	Strong odor of old fish
Putrecine	$NH_2(CH_2)_4NH_2$	1,4-diaminobutane	Spoiled meat products
Cadaverine	$NH_2(CH_2)_5NH_2$	1,5-diaminopentane	Spoiled meat products

[1]Occur as salts, esters, and are sometimes linked with sugar.
[2]The amines contribute to the "fishy" odor and the strong odors of spoiled protein materials in particular.

phenomena, such as the after-cooking darkening of cooked potatoes, which appears to result from the action of ferric iron and orthodihydric phenols, probably chlorgenic acid. This phenomenon appears first under the skin at the stem end of the potato and decreases in intensity toward the apical end. Treatment with secondary sodium acid pyrophosphate completely prevents discoloration in dehydrated potato products, in mashed potatoes prepared from fresh produce, in boiled whole peeled potatoes, in French fries, in prepared potato salad and peeled small whole or sliced frozen potatoes. A 1 to $1\frac{1}{2}\%$ dip of $Na_2H_2P_2O_7$ is effective. It can be used in potato products which have already developed after-cooking darkening; here the dark color is considerably lightened. This latter procedure may be used with steamed whole peeled potatoes, dipped in the S. A. P. P. solution from a half to several minutes until the dark color is lightened or disappears. (See Smith, Potatoes: Production, Storing, Processing.)

The flavor of plant products is a result of the acids, salts, esters, aldehydes, ketones, alcohols, amines, aromatic compounds and sulfur compounds present or produced. These contribute to either the taste or odor of both the raw and cooked product.

Plant acids serve several purposes, such as controlling the acidity, which varies with maturity; they are part of the buffering systems, and function as preservatives and sometimes act as synergists to the natural antioxidant (Vitamin E or tocophenol) present (Table 12.1.).

Recently, work done in England on the volatile flavors of some vegetables, both raw and cooked, itemized approximately 33 identified chemical compounds classified as flavor volatiles. Much has been done on the variation of preparation and cooking methods on the flavor volatiles and vitamin C content of cabbage, both fresh and dehydrated.

CHAPTER 13

L. L. W. Smith

L. J. Minor

Amino Acids, Food
Proteins, and Enzymes

AMINO ACIDS

Alpha-amino acids

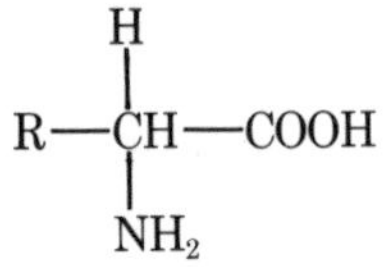

$$\begin{array}{c} H \\ | \\ R\!-\!CH\!-\!COOH \\ | \\ NH_2 \end{array}$$

have the amino group on the alpha carbon atom next to the carboxyl group. *They are the building blocks of proteins,* and
when protein solutions are hydrolyzed with acid the hydrolyzate
contains a mixture of about 22 levorotatory alpha-amino acids.
Individual amino acids may be separated from protein hydrolyzates and their concentrations determined mechanically by
column chromatography.

Determining the *sequence of amino acids in a protein molecule* is a difficult and tedious task requiring special training
and experience in biochemical research. Yet the sequential
order of amino acids has been elucidated for several proteins
including the enzyme ribonuclease, cytochrome-C, tobacco
mosaic virus, and hemoglobin.

Classification of amino acids is possible in various ways;
three classes are chosen based upon amino acids having (1)
an equal number of basic or amino (—NH₂) and acid or carboxyl
(—COOH) groups, (2) more amino than carboxyl groups, and
(3) more carboxyl than amino groups. The ten essential amino
acids necessary in an adequate human and rat diet are: lysine,
tryptophan, histidine, phenylalanine, leucine, isoleucine,
threonine, valine, arginine, and methionine. Each is identified
in Table 13.1 by an asterisk.

Essential and nonessential amino acids are shown in Table
13.1. Arginine and histidine are borderline, arginine being
essential for maximum growth in children, and histidine being
required in the diet of some adults. By definition, essential

288

amino acids are those that cannot be synthesized in adequate amounts in the body, and are thus necessary in the diet.

Cystine can replace about one-sixth of the methionine require-ment and tyrosine about one-half of the phenylalanine require-ment, but they are nonfunctional in the absence of methionine or phenylalanine, respectively. Either glutamic acid or proline can substitute effectively for arginine in the diet.

Non-essential amino acids also serve as a source of energy in the diet.

The properties of amino acids that constitute a protein are to a large extent responsible for the chemical and physical characteristics of that protein. The amino acids in Table 13.1 are white, crystalline solids with melting points above 200°C. Many are readily soluble in water, but relatively in-soluble in the organic solvents alcohol, ether, and benzene.

Amino acids are optically active, since the alpha protein's carbon adjacent to the carboxyl group is asymmetric. Proteins also exhibit optical activity.

Dissociation of amino acids in water solutions results in the formation of a dipolar ion, sometimes called a "zwitterion," that becomes both positively and negatively charged. Com-pounds that react as both acids and bases in the formation of salts are called *amphoteric,* and since amino acids have both an acidic or carboxyl (–COOH) group, and a basic or amino (–NH$_2$) group they have this property.

$$\left[H_2N-\underset{\underset{R}{|}}{CH}-COO- \right] \underset{H_2O}{\overset{[OH^-]}{\rightleftarrows}}$$

Basic salt form, as
in the sodium salt
of the amino acid

$$\left[H_3\overset{+}{N}-\underset{\underset{R}{|}}{CH}-COO- \right] \overset{[H^+]}{\rightleftarrows} \left[H_3\overset{+}{N}-\underset{\underset{R}{|}}{CH}-COOH \right]$$

Normal salt form,   Acidic salt form,
as in the free   as in the amino
amino acid   acid hydrochloride

Amino acids are buffers that are charged positively in acid so-lutions and negatively in basic solutions. At the *isoelectric point, pI,* the pH at which migration to either the positive

TABLE 13.1

TWENTY NATURALLY OCCURRING AMINO ACIDS

Name	Formula	Abbreviation
A. *Acidic Amino Acids*		
1. Aspartic acid	$HOOC-CH_2-\underset{\underset{NH_2}{\vert}}{CH}-COOH$	Asp
2. Glutamic acid	$HOOC-CH_2-CH_2-\underset{\underset{NH_2}{\vert}}{CH}-COOH$	Glu
B. *Basic Amino Acids*		
3. Arginine*[1]	$HN{=}\underset{\underset{H}{\vert}}{C}-N-CH_2CH_2CH_2-\underset{\underset{NH_2}{\vert}}{\overset{\overset{NH_2}{\vert}}{}}{CH}-COOH$	Arg
4. Lysine*	$\underset{\underset{NH_2}{\vert}}{CH_2}-CH_2-CH_2-CH_2-\underset{\underset{NH_2}{\vert}}{CH}-COOH$	Lys
5. Histidine*	$\underset{N \quad NH}{\underset{\diagdown\,\diagup}{\underset{CH}{}}}\,\, CH{=}CH-CH_2-\underset{\underset{NH_2}{\vert}}{CH}-COOH$	His
C. *Equal in Acidic and Basic Groups*		
6. Glycine	$\underset{\underset{NH_2}{\vert}}{CH_2}-COOH$	Gly
7. Alanine	$CH_3-\underset{\underset{NH_2}{\vert}}{CH}-COOH$	Ala
8. Phenylalanine*	⬡$-CH_2CH-COOH$ $\quad\quad\quad\;\underset{NH_2}{\vert}$	Phe
9. Tyrosine	$HO-$⬡$-CH_2CH-COOH$ $\quad\quad\quad\quad\quad\;\underset{NH_2}{\vert}$	Tyr
10. Tryptophan*	$CH_2CH-COOH$ $\underset{NH_2}{\vert}$	Trp

Table 13.1 (*continued*)

Name	Formula	Abbreviation
11. Thyroxine	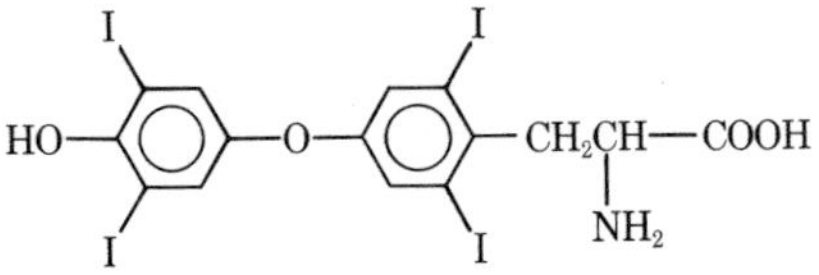 $HO-\langle\rangle-O-\langle\rangle-CH_2CH-COOH$ (with I substituents on rings; NH_2 on the CH)	Thy
12. Serine	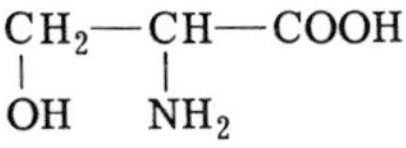 $CH_2-CH-COOH$, with OH and NH_2	Ser
13. Threonine*	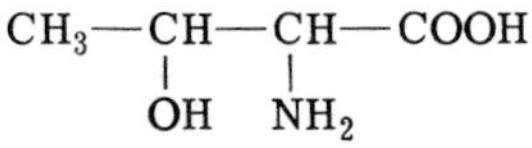 $CH_3-CH-CH-COOH$, with OH and NH_2	Thr
14. Valine*	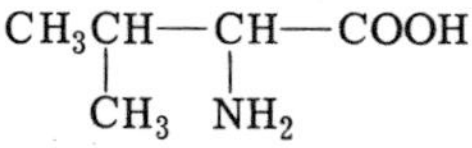 $CH_3CH-CH-COOH$, with CH_3 and NH_2	Val
15. Leucine*	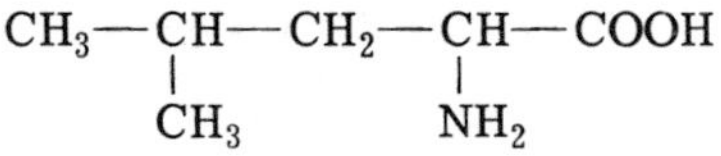 $CH_3-CH-CH_2-CH-COOH$, with CH_3 and NH_2	Leu
16. Isoleucine*	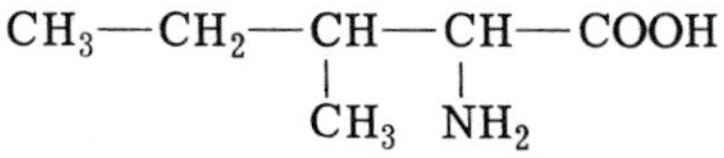 $CH_3-CH_2-CH-CH-COOH$, with CH_3 and NH_2	Ileu
17. Proline	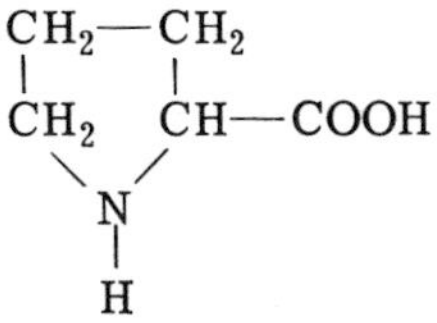 ring: CH_2-CH_2 / CH_2 $CH-COOH$ joined through $N-H$	Pro
18. Hydroxyproline	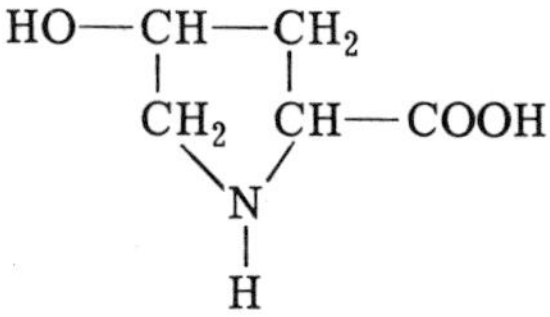 $HO-CH-CH_2$ / CH_2 $CH-COOH$ joined through $N-H$	Hyp
19. Methionine*	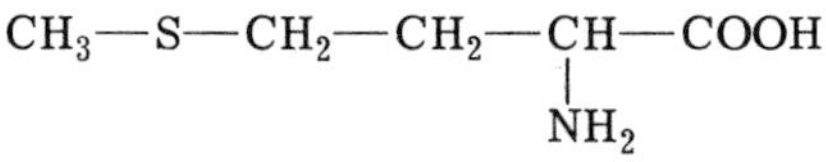 $CH_3-S-CH_2-CH_2-CH-COOH$, with NH_2	Met
20. Cystine[2]	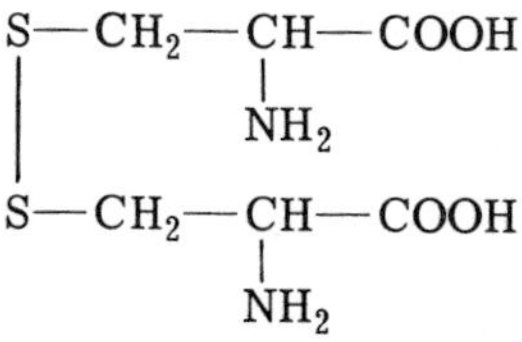 $S-CH_2-CH-COOH$ (NH_2) and $S-CH_2-CH-COOH$ (NH_2)	CyS-S-S-CyS

TABLE 13.1 (*continued*)

Name	Formula 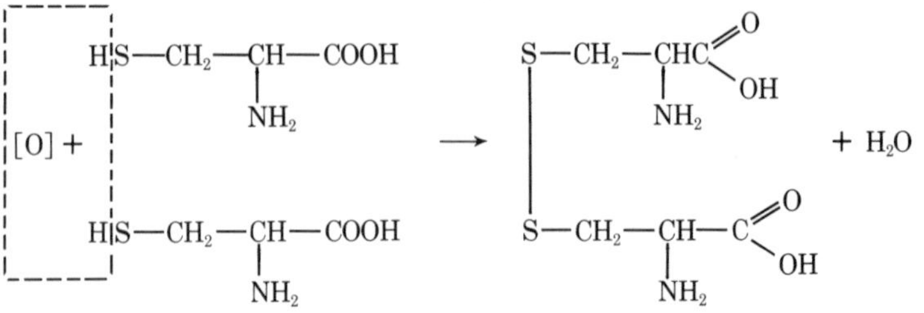	Abbreviation

$$[O] + \left\{ \begin{array}{l} HS-CH_2-CH-COOH \\ \hspace{2.2cm} NH_2 \\[1em] HS-CH_2-CH-COOH \\ \hspace{2.2cm} NH_2 \end{array} \right. \longrightarrow \left. \begin{array}{l} S-CH_2-CHC{\nwarrow}^{O}_{OH} \\ \hspace{1.8cm} NH_2 \\[1em] S-CH_2-CH-C{\nwarrow}^{O}_{OH} \\ \hspace{1.8cm} NH_2 \end{array} \right\} + H_2O$$

[1]Asterisk denotes the essential amino acids.
[2]Cystine is obtained by the oxidation of two molecules of
   cysteine. (CyS).

(anode) or negative (cathode) **pole** in an electrolyzed solution
ceases, the dipolar form of the amino acid exists with a net
charge of zero. Amino acids precipitate out of the solution at
their isoelectric point pH values. Some of these values are
given in Table 13.2.

Chemical properties of the essential amino acids may be
categorized by considering the R-group of each amino acid,

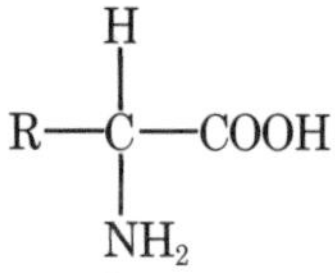

$$R-\underset{\underset{NH_2}{|}}{\overset{\overset{H}{|}}{C}}-COOH$$

The categories would then be *hydrocarbon* for valine, leucine
and isoleucine where R is, respectively: $(CH_3)_2CH^-$; $(CH_3)_2$.
$CHCH_2^-$ and $CH_3CH_2CH(CH_3)^-$. The R value for threonine contains the hydroxy group; $CH_3CH(OH)^-$; the sulfur group in
methionine, $CH_3SCH_2CH_2^-$. Lysine with 2 amino groups is basic
$NH_2(CH_2)_4CH(NH_2)^-$, as is arginine, $NH_2C(NH)NH(CH_2)_3CH(NH_2)^-$,
and histidine, which is heterocyclic,

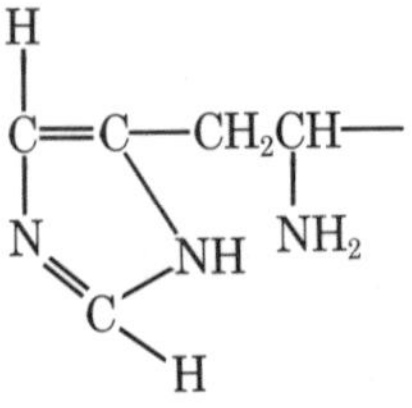

$$\underset{\underset{\underset{\underset{H}{\diagdown}}{C}}{N\diagdown \hspace{0.3cm} \diagup NH}}{\overset{\overset{H}{|}}{C}}=C-CH_2CH- \quad \text{and}$$

TABLE 13.2

APPARENT pI VALUES FOR AMINO ACIDS AT 25°C[1]

Amino Acid	pI
Alanine	6.00
Arginine	10.76
Aspartic acid	2.77
Cysteine (30°)	5.07
Cystine (30°)	4.60
Glutamic acid	3.22
Glycine	5.97
Histidine	7.59
Hydroxyproline	5.83
Isoleucine	6.02
Leucine	5.98
Lysine	9.74
Phenylalanine	5.48
Proline	6.30
Serine	5.68
Tryptophan	5.89
Tyrosine	5.66
Valine	5.96

[1]pI value indicates the pH values at the isoelectric point.

basic for lysine,

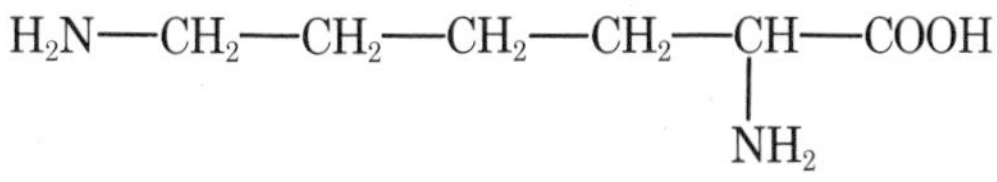

$$H_2N-CH_2-CH_2-CH_2-CH_2-CH-COOH$$
$$|$$
$$NH_2$$

and arginine;

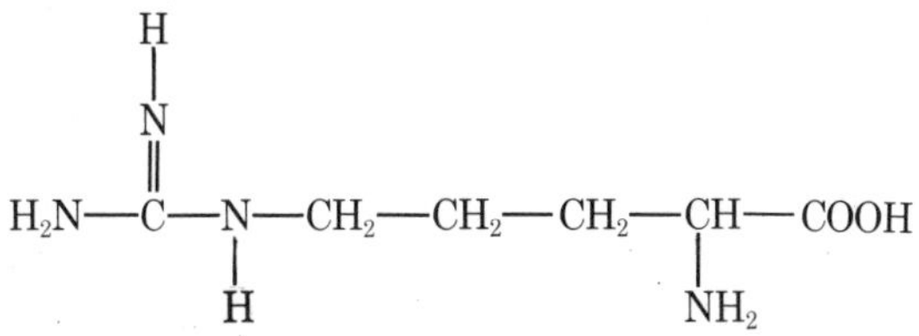

$$\begin{array}{c} H \\ | \\ N \\ \| \end{array}$$
$$H_2N-C-N-CH_2-CH_2-CH_2-CH-COOH$$
$$\qquad\quad | \qquad\qquad\qquad\qquad\quad |$$
$$\qquad\quad H \qquad\qquad\qquad\qquad\quad NH_2$$

aromatic for phenylalanine,

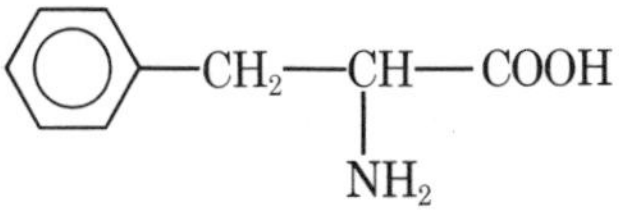

$$\langle O \rangle -CH_2-CH-COOH$$
$$|$$
$$NH_2$$

and heterocyclic for tryptophan,

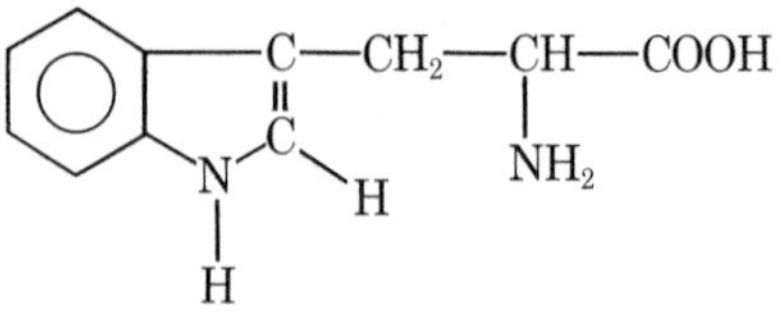

(may also be classed as aromatic)

and histidine

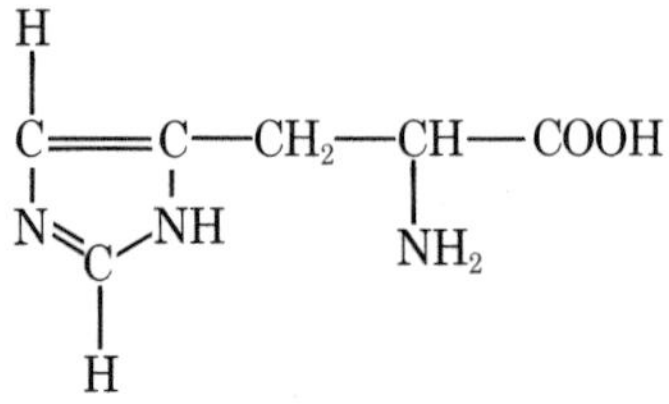

(may also be classed as basic).

Protein digestion or hydrolysis by enzymes from mammals: (trypsin, chymotrypsin) or less specific plant and animal enzymes (papain, pepsin, elastase), or bacterial enzymes (pronase, subtilin) splits peptide bonds indiscriminately. Chemical cleavage requires strong acid or base and elevated temperature.

Vegetable protein hydrolyzates are solutions of amino acids, salt, ammonium chloride, and colored reaction products resulting from interactions between amino acids and reducing sugars (sugars having a free carbonyl $C=O$ group).

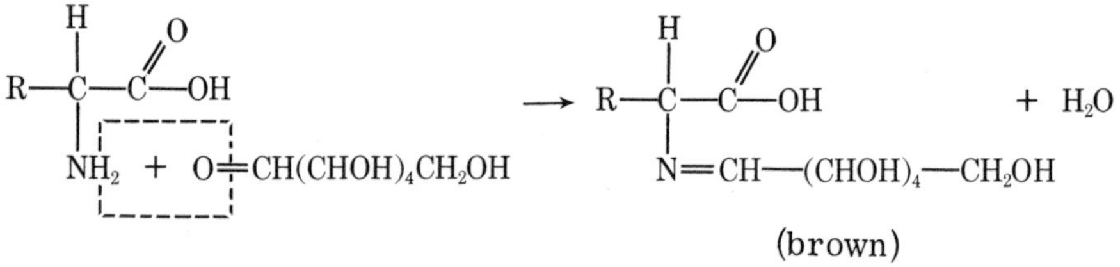

(brown)

Alpha-amino acid-reducing sugar condensation products result from the Maillard or *"browning" reaction* which may take place at a wide range of temperatures. Roast beef color and flavor is characterized by the presence of these compounds.

Each protein, when hydrolyzed, gives a product having a characteristic flavor. This is due to differences in the amino-acid spectra of wheat gluten, corn gluten, soy protein, casein and yeast protein. Hydrochloric acid is used to digest these and other proteins, and when hydrolysis is complete, as shown by analytical tests, the solution is neutralized with pure sodium hydroxide to a pH of about 5.5. This neutralization results in the formation of common salt and ammonium chloride. Sometimes the ammonium chloride is removed from the hydrolyzate to give a milder-tasting product, as ammonium chloride has a harsh, brackish taste.

Soya sauce is a typical hydrolyzed plant protein. Although the original product from the Orient was fermented by adding molds such as Aspergillus flavus or Aspergillus oryzae to a mixture of cooked soybeans, and cracked wheat, the modern version is the result of hydrolyzing a blend of soy protein and wheat gluten with constant-boiling hydrochloric acid. After hydrolysis the pH is adjusted to 5.4 and a mixture of caramel and corn syrup is added. The caramel imparts a dark color, whereas the glucose adds sweetness and stabilizes the amino acid suspension, preventing precipitation of leucine. Soya sauce is the flavor base in Worcestershire sauce. A discussion of protein hydrolyzate flavors and seasonings is given in the chapter on Flavor.

Yeast autolyzates are flavor potentiators resulting from the digestion of debittered or primary brewers yeast by the enzymes that are indigenous to those protein sources. Yeast proteins are rich sources of amino and nucleic acids that enrich broths and gravies.

PROTEINS

Proteins are complex organic substances that are polymers of amino acids joined by amide or peptide linkages,

$$-\overset{\overset{\textstyle O}{\|}}{C}-NH-$$

Their molecular weights are high, ranging from 20,000 to 20,000,000, and their structures vary from *fibrillar* to *globular* and *conjugated* classes. Protein molecules are large polypeptides, the terminal functional groups being the amino group on one end and the carboxyl group on the other.

Peptides are chains of amino acids joined together. *Dipeptides* consist of two amino acids united by a peptide bond (amide linkage).

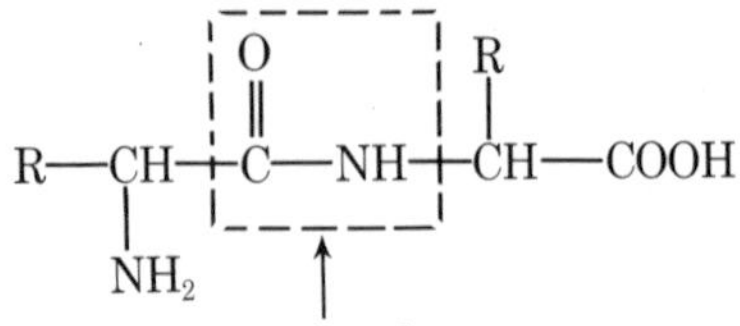

$$R—CH—C—NH—CH—COOH$$

with structure showing O (double bond to C), R, NH_2, and "peptide bond"

Glutathione (glutamyl-cysteinyl-glycine) is a tripeptide found in nearly all living cells. A unique property of its structure is that the amide linkage between the glutamic and cysteine molecules is obtained from the gamma rather than the alpha carboxyl group of glutamic acid.

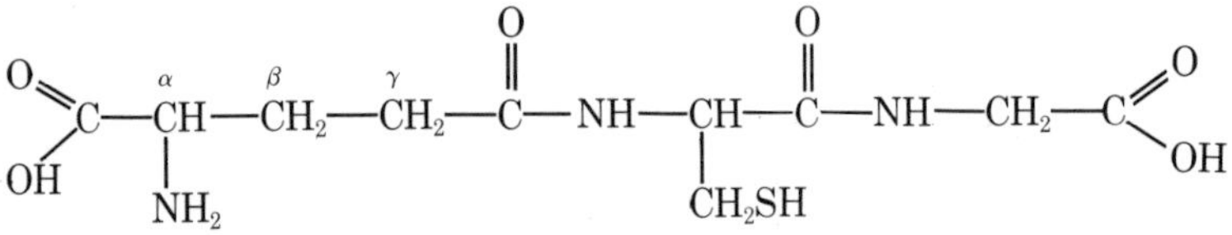

$$\underset{OH}{\overset{O}{C}}—\underset{NH_2}{\overset{\alpha}{CH}}—\overset{\beta}{CH_2}—\overset{\gamma}{CH_2}—\overset{O}{C}—NH—\underset{CH_2SH}{CH}—\overset{O}{C}—NH—CH_2—\overset{O}{C}{\overset{\diagup O}{\diagdown OH}}$$

Oxytocin, a cyclic octapeptide,

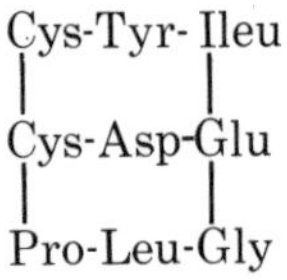

Cys-Tyr-Ileu
| |
Cys-Asp-Glu
| |
Pro-Leu-Gly

is a hormone that was studied by V. du Vigneaud at Cornell University. In 1955 he determined its amino acid sequence and structure and synthesized the molecule. He was awarded the Nobel prize for this basic work. This hormone functions in uterine contractions and lactation.

Insulin contains 16 different kinds of amino acid residues. Frederick Sanger, an Englishman, received the Nobel prize in 1958 for elucidating the structure of insulin, a task that required about ten years of research.

Automated instruments are now available for determining the sequence of amino acids in proteins in three steps. First the N-terminal amino acid is reacted to form a phenylthiocarbamyl derivative, then this is treated with an anhydrous acid, and the reaction products formed are identified by thin-layer or gas chromatography.

Protein structure studies by Linus Pauling were rewarded by his acceptance of the Nobel Prize in 1954. His research showed that some proteins form helical structures that fold to accommodate large numbers of amino acid residues. The levels of structure are termed primary, secondary, tertiary, and quaternary.

Primary structure is the result of amino acid sequence, peptide bond formation, and includes —S—S— bonds.

Secondary structure occurs as a result of hydrogen bond formation between adjacent or nearby amino acid units that produces coiling or twisting of the polypeptide chain into an alpha helix. Then R-groups are bent out from all sides of the alpha helix, causing great reactivity between adjacent molecules. As the helical formation takes place, hydrogen bonding occurs between

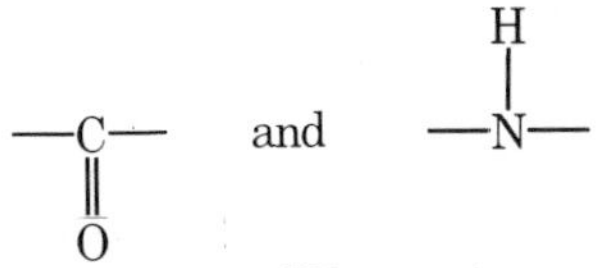

$$-\underset{\underset{O}{\parallel}}{C}- \qquad and \qquad -\underset{}{\overset{H}{\underset{|}{N}}}-$$

groups. These bonds are about 3 to 4 peptide units apart. Only part of the polypeptide chain is coiled in the alpha-helix configuration.

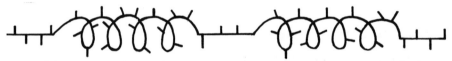

Tertiary structure involves bonding between rather distant amino acid residues to produce a folding of the molecules. Disulfide bonds, hydrogen bonds between R-groups, hydrophobic bonds between R-groups of the hydrocarbon amino acid units, and ionic bonds between positively and negatively charged R-groups or ends of the polypeptide chain are postulated in tertiary structural formation.

Region of
tertiary
bonds

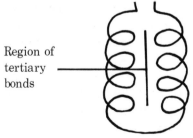

Tertiary Structure

Characteristically, tertiary bonds are relatively far apart.

Quaternary structure involves the same types of bonds as tertiary structure, but involves bonding between subunits in large protein molecules.

Disulfide bonds are formed between two cysteine units that are oxidized to cystine.

Hydrophobic bonding in the tertiary structure may result from the R-groups of alanine, valine, leucine, isoleucine, phenylalanine, trypotophan, and proline.

Protein three-dimensional structures result from a spontaneous folding due to interaction between amino acid sequences. A one-dimensional string of peptide-linked amino acids is transformed into an active enzyme protein by the action of messenger ribonucleic acid, m-RNA.

Ionic bonds may originate from the charge on each of seven sources. Positive charges may come from four sources, namely, terminal ($-NH_2$), lysine ($-NH_2$), arginine ($-NH_2$), and histidine ($-NH_2$). Negative charges may be due to terminal $-COOH$, aspartic acid ($-COOH$), or glutamic acid ($-COOH$). Bonding then occurs between the positively and the negatively charged areas of the protein molecule.

Classification of Proteins

Proteins may be classed as *simple proteins* (polypeptides) or *conjugated proteins* (peptide units joined to a nonprotein group).

Fibrillar proteins have a fibrous helical structure resembling that of rope, and are not soluble in water. These include *collagen* present in the muscle and hides of animals that breaks down partially or completely into gelatin, glue, or bone stock. When cooked in water or steam, elastin in muscle is not affected, and is rubbery, tough, and chewy. Reticulin is closely related to collagen; keratin in the horn, hoofs, hair and wool of animals, and fibroin from silk are other examples of fibrillar proteins.

Gelatin is a low nutritive value protein made up of about 27% glycine and an equal total percentage of proline and hydroxyproline, with small percentages of other amino acids but no tryptophan. Keratin contains small percentages of the 20 important amino acids, and is rich in the sulfur-containing amino acid cystine. However, like collagen and gelatin, keratin is nutritionally inadequate.

Globular proteins are structurally more complex than fibrous proteins. Besides having a rope-like helix, the helices are folded and compacted into a kind of ball. The most nutritious proteins, including milk, eggs, meat, soy, and wheat protein, are globular proteins. Solubility and dispersibility in water are more pronounced, and they are far more sensitive to heat, pH, and salt than fibrous proteins.

Subclasses of the globular proteins are based upon their solubility in various solvents and include albumins, globulins, glutelins, prolamines, histones, and protamines.

Wheat gluten proteins contain 35% glutamic acid, and 14% proline. Gliadin's alpha helix content is twice that of glutenin. Since alpha helices are stabilized by hydrophobic amino acids, the higher hydrophobicity (water repellency) is understandable. Hydrogen bonds are involved in stabilizing dough structure, and protein quality may be a function of the ratio of disulfide to sulfhydryl groups.

Conjugated proteins consist of a polypeptide joined with a nonprotein group. Hemoglobin, consisting of 96% globin protein and 4% heme-containing iron, is a typical conjugated protein. As a transport medium, blood hemoglobin moves oxygen from the lungs to the tissues of the body. Enzymes, phosphoproteins (caseins) in milk, and nucleoproteins in the living cell are other examples of conjugated proteins.

Derived proteins or protein hydrolyzates are the result of the action of enzymes on proteins. These reactions are those of hydrolysis, the resulting product depends on the degree of the reaction. The stepwise breakdown is sometimes designated as protein to meta-protein, to proteases, to peptones, to polypeptides to dipeptides, and finally to amino acids.

These protein hydrolyzates have produced the protein analogs currently on the market.

Enzymes belong to two general classes, hydrolytic and oxidative-reductive. Usually, hydrolytic enzymes are simple proteins, whereas nonprotein *prosthetic* groups characterize enzymes responsible for oxidation-reduction reactions. *Adenosine triphosphate* (ATP) and *adenosine diphosphate* (ADP) are important examples of compounds having prosthetic groups such as high-energy pyrophosphate linkages important in the conservation of cell energy during oxidative reactions.

Nucleoproteins contain a nitrogenous base, a sugar, and

phosphoric acid as their prosthetic groups; they are typified
by *ribonucleic acid* (RNA) and *deoxyribonucleic acid* (DNA)
in the living cell. Viruses are giant molecules. Wendell Stanley,
an American biochemist, received the Nobel Prize in 1946 for
his work on tobacco mosaic virus, a nucleoprotein with a
molecular weight of about 40 million.

Molecular weights of proteins are unusually high; their determination can be made by measuring *sedimentation velocity* and
sedimentation equilibrium in a Svedberg ultracentrifuge.
Light-scattering may be used to determine the molecular
weight and the shape of protein molecules.

Optical rotation of proteins in the natural state averages
from $-30°$ to $-60°$ (levorotation); after cooking, the structures
are altered to values of $-80°$ to $-120°$. Doty reported that an
optical rotation reading of $-10°$ represents a 100% helical
coil, whereas one of $-90°$ is indicative of a 100% random coil;
these readings may be used to measure the extent of protein
denaturation.

Denaturation of protein is exemplified by the difference
between a raw and cooked egg. During cooking, hydrogen
bonds are disrupted causing a breakdown of the tertiary structure. Denaturating agents other than heat include organic
solvents, acids, bases, severe vibration, UV light, and other
harsh treatments. Denatured proteins are less soluble than
native proteins, and the enzymatic activity of biologically
active substances is lost. Denaturation changes are generally
irreversible. Other effects of denaturation by cooking are
liberation of ammonia and hydrogen sulfide from the unfolded
structure, increase in levorotation, increase in susceptibility
to enzyme hydrolysis, and loss of crystallizability.

Browning or Maillard reactions occur when the amino groups,
$-NH_2$, of proteins, amino acids, or amines react with the
carbonyl groups, $>C=O$, of reducing sugars to produce
brown-colored reaction products called glycosylamines.

$$R_1-NH_2 \ + \ O=CH(R_2) \ \longrightarrow \ R_1-N=CH(R_2) + H_2O$$
proteins or   reducing   glycosylamines
amino acids   sugars

This is the general type of reaction that occurs in nonenzymatic browning of foods. Optimal conditions for the Maillard
reaction are low water content, pH 7 to 10, and dehydration

temperatures. Many mechanisms, not just the one shown, are involved in browning, which is affected by traces of metals, light, and a wide range of pH. Flavor and color in bread crust, potato chips, ready-to-eat cereal flakes, maple syrup, roasted meat, coffee, and cacao beans may be excellent or poor depending upon the control of baking, roasting, or the heat used.

In some cases the browning reaction improves food odors, colors, and flavors; an example is the brown color in the crust of baked products. The effect can be undesirable, as in the darkening of dehydrated eggs caused by the reaction of proteins and free amino acids in eggs with the glucose of egg white.

Fish muscle darkening may be due to browning reactions which probably result from the interaction of the 5-carbon sugar, ribose, with the lysine residue in fish protein. Browning in beef and pork is masked by oxyhemoglobin, but when these meats are heated or dehydrated the free ribose combines with amino acids.

Color in soya sauce is due to the browning reaction that contributes to the sauce's complex flavor.

Dark-colored potato chips result when varieties of potatoes having high reducing sugar content are used for chipping. Tubers may be reconditioned to convert some of the accumulated reducing sugars to starch when stored for a period of time at 70°F, resulting in chips of better or lighter color. Although enzymatic browning is caused by the enzyme polyphenoloxidase reacting with oxygen, other enzymes that break down starch to sugars, or proteins to amino acids, unless controlled may indirectly be the cause of browning in potato chips.

Browning in dairy products occurs when the lactose content increases as a result of water removal. Evaporated milk turns brown unless high-temperature-short-time sterilization is used. When corn sugar, glucose, is added, browning increases in condensed milk, whereas the addition of the non-reducing sugar sucrose has very little or no deleterious effect on color. Ultraviolet irradiation of milk increases browning, and off-odors are produced by splitting amino acids from the casein. A malty flavor comes from acetaldehyde with alanine as the precursor. Cooked flavors in milk are due to the production of methyl sulfide from methionine. A boiled cabbage or burnt-protein flavor in homogenized milk arise from the formation of beta-mercaptopropionaldehyde, which is caused by the ultraviolet-catalyzed breakdown of methionine in the presence of riboflavin.

Nonenzymatic browning control in foods is dependent largely on controlling pH, temperature, time of heating, and moisture content. Dehydrated products containing intermediate amounts of moisture are especially susceptible to browning during storage, and low holding temperatures retard browning.

Liquid eggs are fermented before drying, or are treated with yeast, bacteria, or the enzyme, glucose oxidase, to remove the reducing sugar and prevent browning. Sulfhydryl groups in cystine prevented browning in mixtures of monosodium glutamate and dextrose. Other additives including sucrose, when added before dehydration, tend to retard the Maillard reaction.

Tests for Amino Acids, Peptides, and Proteins

Several methods are used for isolating and determining proteins and amino acids besides the column chromatography method, namely, ninhydrin for amino acids and ultracentrifugation for proteins. Chemical, physicochemical methods and combinations have been incorporated into instruments that improve precision and save time.

Zone electrophoresis involves the movement of proteins, amino acids, or peptides through a starch-film medium. High voltages are required and migration rates vary according to the charge on the molecule. Mixtures of compounds may be separated by electrophoretic movement.

Paper chromatography is a proven method for separating and identifying amino acids by capillary movement on filter paper immersed in a water-organic solvent solution. A few microliters of protein hydrolyzate are spotted on the paper together with a control solution of pure amino acids. Each amino acid has its own migration rate, and is identified with a ninhydrin spray after the solvent front has moved a sufficient distance. After drying the paper in a low-temperature oven, the spots show clearly and the distance migrated by each is used to identify the amino acids comprising the hydrolyzate solution.

Biuret reactions occur when protein is mixed with a concentrated solution of sodium hydroxide and a drop or two of dilute copper sulfate solution. A violet to pink color is obtained; the more pinkish the color the simpler the protein. Nearly all substances containing two groups attached to each other through the same nitrogen atom give the reaction.

Xanthoproteic reactions occur when a protein solution is heated with concentrated nitric acid to produce a yellow color; the color is due to formation of a nitro compound, and turns to orange on addition of excess of ammonium hydroxide.

Ion-exchange resins are used in separating proteins or amino acids by column chromatography.

Molecular sieves made of dextrans from cane sugar have been used to fractionate mixtures of proteins.

Millon's reaction involves the phenolic derivative tyrosine that gives a brick-red color on addition of a solution of mercury in nitric acid.

Hopkins-Cole: Mix protein with glyoxylic acid and concentrated sulfuric acid, and a violet ring is obtained due to the presence of tryptophan in the protein molecule.

Molisch: Upon addition of alpha-naphthol and concentrated sulfuric acid to a protein solution a violet ring forms due to the presence of glucosamine in the protein molecule.

Any substance that gives two or more color reactions may be a protein. Proteins are precipitated by the salts of heavy metals, such as lead acetate, mercuric chloride, or copper sulfate. The "alkaloidal reagents" phosphotungstic, phosphomolybdic, tannic, and picric acids precipitate proteins. Many proteins, including the albumins and globulins, coagulate on heating.

FOOD PROTEINS

Our protein supply depends upon the photosynthesis of plants that utilize the sun's energy, water, carbon dioxide, and chlorophyll to provide the food energy needed by all forms of animal life. Food proteins of animal origin are of prime importance in the diet of the human race, including proteins from meat, milk, and eggs.

Meat protein is derived mainly from the muscle of the animal body, and consists largely of the protein *myosin*.

TABLE 13.3

AMINO ACID COMPOSITION OF FRESH BEEF, PORK,
LAMB, AND CURED AND PROCESSED MEATS[1]

Amino Acid	Beef, %	Pork, %	Lamb, %	Cured and Processed Meats
Essential				
Arginine	6.6	5.4	6.9	6.6
Histidine	2.9	3.2	2.7	2.8
Isoleucine	5.1	4.9	4.8	4.9
Leucine	8.4	7.5	7.4	7.4
Lysine	8.4	7.8	7.6	7.4
Methionine	2.3	2.5	2.3	2.2
Phenylalanine	4.0	4.1	3.9	4.0
Threonine	4.0	5.1	4.9	3.9
Tryptophan	1.1	1.4	1.3	1.0
Valine	5.7	5.0	5.0	5.2
Nonessential				
Alanine	6.4	6.3	6.3	6.4
Aspartic acid	8.8	8.9	8.5	9.1
Cystine	1.4	1.3	1.3	1.5
Glutamic acid	14.4	14.5	14.4	12.9
Glycine	7.1	6.1	6.7	8.0
Proline	5.4	4.6	4.8	5.2
Serine	3.8	4.0	3.9	4.2
Tyrosine	3.2	3.0	3.2	2.9

[1]All values are expressed as percentage in the crude protein
(N × 6.25).

Source: Schweigert and Payne, 1956

Gelatin is derived from collagen found in muscle tissues.
Blood proteins are also present in meat. Vitamins and minerals in the form of conjugated proteins are plentiful in the
liver and other soft glandular tissues.

The isoelectric point of myosin is at pH 5.4. It is soluble
at pH 4.2, and nearly insoluble from pH 4.3 to 7.5. At pH's
above 8.0, myosin forms a *thixotropic gel* (liquefies when
agitated and re-solidifies at rest). The approximate amino
acid content of some meat proteins is given in Table 13.3.
A comparison of the water and protein contents of raw and
cooked meats is shown in Table 13.4.

Milk proteins include casein, phosphoprotein, lactalbumin, and lactoglobulin. Casein constitutes 80% of the total. In milk, casein averages 2.6%, lactalbumin 0.5%, and lactoglobulin 0.15%. Whey proteins total between 0.60 to 0.80% and include β-lactoglobulin, α-lactalbumin, serum albumin, immune globulins, and proteose-peptones. These undenatured proteins resemble egg white in their functional properties. They may be modified to produce excellent substitutes for eggs in a wide variety of baked goods.

Casein is not precipitated by heat, but coagulates in the presence of small amounts of acid, and is dispersed by excess acid. In cheese making it is precipitated by the proteolytic enzyme, rennin, obtained from calves' stomachs. Freshly precipitated casein has an isoelectric point of 4.6.

The amino acid content of milk proteins is shown in Table 13.5. Compared to egg proteins as a standard, cows' milk is low in cystine-methionine content.

Egg proteins constitute about 13% of hens eggs, the balance being water. Egg yolk contains less than 50% water and the protein content is 16%, as shown in Table 13.4, but the fat content is 32%, compared to 0.0 to 0.05% in the white. Egg-white proteins include ovalbumin, conalbumin, ovomucin, ovomucoid and ovoglobulin. The egg yolk proteins are vitellin and livetin. The amino acid contents of whole egg albumin are shown in Table 13.6.

Cereal proteins are predominantly *globulins* in the seeds of many plants, but are present in small amounts in the cereal endosperm. Quantitatively, glutelins, prolamins, albumins, globulins, proteoses, amino acids, and acido amides occur in that order in cereals.

Protein contents vary in any given protein, whereas the amino acid spectra of different proteins impart characteristic flavors to the hydrolyzates of corn, barley, rice, oat, wheat, soybean, cottonseed, and peanut proteins. The amino acid content of the cereals and soybean is given in Table 13.7.

Wheat-gluten proteins are low in lysine. Its protein content is below that of rice, oats, and rye in nutritional value, and is on a par with that of corn and barley. Modern cereals utilize blends of corn, wheat, rice, and soybean flakes to boost their nutritional value. A new variety of corn having a high lysine content has been developed. Addition of small per-

TABLE 13.4

AVERAGE PROTEIN, FAT, AND WATER
CONTENT OF MEAT, POULTRY AND SEAFOOD

Name	Water %	Protein %	Fat %
Beef			
Round, raw	71	20	8
Round, cooked	59	27	13
Hamburger, raw	59	15	25
Hamburger, cooked	47	22	30
Lamb			
Leg roast, raw	64	18	17
Leg roast, cooked	56	24	19
Pork			
Ham, fresh, raw	53	15	31
Ham, cured, cooked	39	23	33
Veal			
Cutlet, raw	68	19	12
Cutlet, cooked	60	28	11
Fish			
Halibut, raw	75	19	5
Halibut, cooked	64	26	8
Salmon, raw	63	17	17
Salmon, canned	65	20	13
Chicken			
Roasters, raw	66	20	13
Chicken, canned	62	30	8
Turkey			
Turkey, raw	58	20	20
Duck and goose			
Duck, raw	54	16	30
Goose, raw	50	16	34
Eggs, raw			
White	88	11	0
Yolk	50	16	32
Whole	74	13	12
Eggs, dried			
White	3	86	0
Yolk	3	31	61
Whole	5	47	42

Table 13.4 (*continued*)

Name	Water %	Protein %	Fat %
Milk, cow			
Fluid, whole	87	4	4
Fluid, nonfat	91	3.5	0.1
Evaporated, canned	74	7	8
Nonfat, dry	3.5	36	1
Cheese			
Cheddar	37	25	34
Cheddar, processed	40	23	30
Cottage	77	20	0.5
Cream	51	9	37
Fats, oils, and shortenings			
Butter, margarine	16	0.6	61
Cooking fats, oils	0	0	100
Mayonnaise	16	1.5	78
French dressing	40	0.6	36
Cereals			
Wheat (grain)	13	14.0	2.2
Gluten flour[1]	8.5	41.4	1.9
Bread (white)[2]	35.8	8.7	3.2
Bread (whole wheat)	36.4	10.5	3.0
Corn (sweet)	72.7	3.5	1.0
Oatmeat (dry form)	8.3	14.2	7.4
Soybean flour			
Full fat	8.0	36.7	20.3
Low fat	8.0	43.4	6.7
Soybean protein	8.2	74.9	0.1
Soybean proteinate	5.5	80.6	0.1
Yeast (dry)	5.0	36.9	1.6

[1]Gluten flour (45% gluten, 55% patent flour).
[2]See appendix for Cornell bread formula.

centages of lysine to cereals doubles their nutritive value.

Soybean proteins when cooked and heated have high digestibility. Methionine and cystine levels are inadequate in soy protein to support maximum growth in animals. When methionine is added to supplement the raw protein after cooking, the nutritive value of soybean is about equal to that of some meat products.

Lysine is susceptible to decomposition by heat. Wheat is low in lysine, and when bread is toasted the lysine content

TABLE 13.5

APPROXIMATE AMINO ACID CONTENT (IN GRAMS) OF COW MILK PROTEINS[1]

Amino Acid	Protein	Casein	Lactalbumin	Beta Lactoglobulin
Essential				
Arginine	4.3	4.2	3.9	3.0
Histidine	2.6	3.0	2.1	1.5
Isoleucine	8.5	6.5	6.4	7.0
Leucine	11.3	9.9	10.4	15.3
Lysine	7.5	7.9	9.6	11.4
Methionine	3.4	3.5	2.7	3.6
Phenylalanine	5.7	5.6	5.4	5.2
Threonine	4.5	4.1	5.4	6.0
Tryptophan	1.6	1.2	2.5	2.0
Valine	8.4	6.7	6.4	7.0
Nonessential				
Cystine	1.0	0.3	4.1	3.5
Glycine	2.3	2.1	—	—
Tyrosine	5.3	6.9	4.4	4.3

[1]All values are expressed as percentage in the crude protein (N × 6.25).

Source: Svedberg and Eriksson—Quensel, 1936.

is lowered still further, so that untoasted bread is more nutritious than toasted. Flavor is improved by toasting cereals, but some nutritive value is lost.

Mung beans (*Phaseolus aureus*) are in truth legumes. They are used to produce bean sprouts which have a bland flavor. Larger sprouts with stronger flavor result when soybeans are sprouted by hydroponic culture. Bean sprouts contain 7.5% protein and about 90% water. Actually, the protein is broken down to peptides and amino acids during sprouting, thus making bean sprouts more readily digestible.

Yeast proteins may be obtained by the growing yeast on waste products, thus producing food that is rich in protein, minerals, and vitamins and that resembles the casein of cows' milk. Nutritionally, yeast protein ranks higher than that of other vegetable proteins, but is low in palatability. Recently, the petroleum industry has developed yeast protein

TABLE 13. 6

APPROXIMATE AMINO ACID CONTENT (IN GRAMS) OF
WHOLE EGG AND EGG ALBUMIN[1]

Amino Acid	Whole Egg	Egg Albumin
Essential		
Arginine	6.4	5.7
Histidine	2.1	2.4
Isoleucine	8.2	7.1
Leucine	9.2	9.4
Lysine	7.2	5.0
Methionine	4.1	5.5
Phenylalanine	6.3	6.4
Threonine	4.9	3.8
Tryptophan	1.5	1.4
Valine	7.3	7.3
Nonessential		
Cystine	2.4	2.9
Glycine	2.2	2.3
Tyrosine	4.5	4.2

[1]All values are expressed as percentages in the crude protein
$(N \times 6.25)$
Source: Block and Mitchell, 1946–47.

from crude oil, using the substrate afterward to produce
gasoline and other petroleum by-products.

Monosodium glutamate is unique as a flavor potentiator for
protein foods. Only the levorotatory form, derived from
naturally occurring glutamic acid, has an effect on the taste
buds called the "glutamate effect."

Pure monosodium glutamate, MSG, has no flavor itself,
but tastes salty, sweet, sour, bitter, and metallic. Gluta-
ate's intensifying effect on *protein flavor* may be due to the
sensitization of the taste mechanism to the total flavor of
proteinaceous foods.

When an excess of MSG is added, a glutamate taste is superimposed on the natural flavor of the food. Uusally, in pork
and poultry products a concentration of 1 part MSG per 1000
parts of food by weight suffices. Beef requires $2\frac{1}{2}$ parts of
MSG per 1000 parts of beef products.

TABLE 13.7

AMINO ACID CONTENT OF THE CEREALS AND SOYBEAN[1]

Amino Acid	Whole Wheat	Wheat Gluten	Wheat Germ	Whole Maize	Maize Gluten	Maize Germ	White Rice	Whole Rye	Rolled Oats	Soybean
Essential										
Arginine	4.2	3.9	6.0	4.8	3.1	8.1	7.2	4.3	6.0	7.1
Histidine	2.1	2.2	2.5	2.2	1.6	2.9	1.5	1.4	2.2	2.3
Isoleucine	3.6	3.7	—	4.0	6.0	4.0	5.3	4.0	5.6	6.6
Leucine	6.8	7.5	6.7	22.0	24.0	13.0	9.0	6.2	8.3	5.0
Lysine	2.7	2.0	5.5	2.0	0.8	5.8	3.2	4.2	3.3	5.0
Methionine	2.5	1.0	—	3.1	2.5	1.6	3.4	1.3	2.4	2.0
Phenylalanine	5.7	5.5	4.2	5.0	6.4	5.5	6.7	5.6	6.6	5.7
Threonine	3.3	2.7	3.8	3.7	4.1	4.7	4.1	3.0	3.5	4.0
Tryptophan	1.2	1.0	1.0	0.8	0.7	1.3	1.3	1.3	1.2	1.2
Valine	4.5	4.2	—	5.0	5.0	6.0	6.3	5.0	6.3	4.2
Nonessential										
Cystine	1.8	1.9	0.8	1.5	1.1	1.8	1.4	—	1.8	1.9
Glycine	—	7.3	—	—	4.3	—	10.3	—	—	high
Tyrosine	4.4	3.8	3.8	5.5	6.7	6.7	5.6	—	4.6	4.1

[1]All values are expressed as percentages in the crude protein (N × 6.25)

Source: Block and Mitchell, 1946–47.

Since MSG is derived from glutamic acid, the most abundant protein building block in nature, those who are allergic or sensitive to proteins may also be sensitive to MSG. A "Chinese restaurant syndrome" characterized by headaches has been reported; it is due to the use of excessive amounts of MSG in the food. However, generally only those who are sensitive to wheat and other proteins are affected, and they represent only 0.1% of the population.

Bad flavors are intensified by the addition of MSG. For example, when stag meat is used in sausage at concentrations as low as 1 or 2% addition of MSG brings out a strong urine taste and odor, especially upon heating. In other words, MSG not only cannot improve a bad product, but makes it taste worse. In meat products made from old and tainted meats MSG is eliminated from their formulas, and peppery concotions substituted that smell like pizza. These strongly flavored preparations anesthetize the taste buds, and mask the spoiled meat flavor.

Protein hydrolyzates from wheat gluten, corn gluten, casein, and soy protein have characteristic flavors that complement meat flavor. Worcestershire sauce is flavored with soya sauce garnished with spices, and is preserved with vinegar as a flavor base.

Hydrolyzed vegetable proteins are used to flavor meats, fish, poultry, vegetables, and bouillon cubes. *Soya sauce* is made in the United States by hydrolyzing mixtures of wheat gluten and soy protein with constant-boiling hydrochloric acid. Acid hydrolysis has replaced the fermentation method of soy sauce production, but research may yet reverse this trend.

Nucleotide seasonings derived from yeast or other microbiological sources are replacing part of the MSG used for flavor potentiation. Disodium inosinate and disodium guanylate added to MSG at a concentration of 5 parts nucleotide per 100 parts MSG substantially reduces the proportion of seasoning required to potentiate protein flavors. Yeast autolyzate seasoned with disodium inosinate and disodium guanylate is being used as a substitute for beef extract.

Beef extract is obtained by extracting lean beef with water by prolonged heating. Concentration of the extract to a solids content of more than 80% results in extensive browning. A foul, disagreeable odor characterizes the product, but addition of 1 part to 100 parts of vegetable soup suffices to remove off-flavor notes, and imparts a mouth-satisfying quality to the soup.

Enzymes

Enzymes are colloidal, protein biological catalysts produced by living organisms. Enzymes are important factors in the production of cheese, production and clarification of beer, wine, and fruit juices, and the conversion of starch to syrup. Phosphatase in milk and catalase in vegetables are useful enzyme-indicators of pasteurization of dairy products and blanching of vegetable products, respectively. Their presence is evidence that processing is inadequate, whereas their absence indicates that processing is adequate. Food spoilage due to enzymes is responsible for changes in texture, flavor, and color that make the product aesthetically objectionable though not necessarily toxic.

Enzymes are usually simple or conjugated proteins of two types: those controlling hydrolytic changes are mostly simple proteins, and those influencing oxidation-reduction reactions are conjugated proteins. Enzymes have names ending in- -*ase* or -*in*. At least 1000 individual enzymes are involved in the body's biochemistry, controlling energy needed for breathing, heart pumping, nerve transmission, and digestion. Synthetic ribonuclease has been produced by a series of 369 chemical reactions in 11,931 steps by an automatic enzyme synthesizer working 24 hr a day for three weeks to link 124 amino-acid molecules together in proper sequence. When placed in solution it folds itself into its natural three-dimensional configuration.

Classification of enzymes according to the recommendation of the Commission of Enzymes of the International Union of Biochemistry was published in 1961. There are six major classes, as follows:

(1) Oxidoreductases: catalyze oxidation-reduction reactions.

(2) Transferases: catalyze group transfer reaction.

(3) Hydrolases: catalyze hydrolytic reactions.

(4) Lyases: catalyze reactions involving the removal of a group leaving a double bond, or the addition of a group to a double bond.

(5) Isomerases: catalyze isomerization reactions.

(6) Ligases or synthetases: catalyze reactions involving the joining together of two molecules, coupled with the breakdown of a pyrophosphate bond in ATP, or similar triphosphate.

Each specific enzyme is each given a code number of four digits:

1.1.1.1 Alcohol dehydrogenase
2.1.1.1 Nicotinamide methyltransferase
3.1.1.1 Carboxyesterase
4.1.1.1 Pyruvate decarboxylase
5.1.1.1 Alanine racemase
6.1.1.1 Tyrosyl - S - RNA synthetase

Enzyme specificity is the most characteristic feature of enzyme activity, both with respect to the kind of reaction catalyzed and the substrate acted upon. Peptidases exemplify substrate specificity.

Pepsin hydrolysis is favored when a phenylalanine or tyrosine residue occupies either side of the peptide bond. Ester bonds are not affected by pepsin.

Trypsin splits bonds of the carboxyl groups of the basic amino acids lysine and arginine. Amides split more easily than peptides and esters hydrolyze most readily.

Chymotrypsin splits the peptide linkages of aromatic amino acid residues, especially tyrosine, and hydrolyzes esters.

Peroxisomes are tiny enzyme packages that may control plant and animal growth. Slow-growing plants, including spinach, wheat and tobacco, are rich in peroxisomes, while fast-growing crops have few. Peroxisomes apparently break down glycolic acid molecules that affect growth.

Proenzymes are inactive precursors of enzymes called *zymogens*, and are concerned with proteolytic activity. *Pepsinogen* in the gastric mucosa is converted to pepsin by hydrochloric acid by removal of one-fifth of the peptide chain. *Trypsinogen* in the pancreas is changed to trypsin by reaction with the enzyme enterokinase. *Chymotrypsinogen* in the pancreas is converted to chymotrypsin by the peptide-fragmenting activity of trypsin. *Cytochrome-C*, a small respiratory enzyme, is a prehistoric photosynthetic bacterial protein present in all living things. Biochemists are studying cytochrome-C, and its relationship to the beginnings of evolution.

Enzyme action tremendously increases the rate of a chemical reaction. Enzymes are very specific because of their specific primary amino-acid sequences. The present theory of enzyme action includes close proximity of the active site of the enzyme to the substrate and the formation of definite compounds when the enzyme and substrate react. Enzymes undergo changes in their active sites after reaction with a substrate molecule to form an activated complex. This last concept envisions a reaction between the enzyme and the substrate to produce an "induced fit." The new product breaks away, leaving the enzyme intact.

Research on the enzyme ribonuclease has resulted recently in identifying the active sites in its chemical structure. Ribonuclease catalyzes the breakdown of RNA in a two-step reaction involving just three of the enzyme's 124 amino acid molecules.

Inhibitors of enzyme action may be specific and nonspecific, reversible and nonreversible, or competitive and noncompetitive in their action. The last classification has increased knowledge of the mode of action of enzymes and of identification of amino-acid residues making up the active site.

Enzyme spoilage is chemical action that doubles in rate for every 10°C rise in temperature. Pasteurization of milk and cheese, blanching of fruits and vegetables, freezing of foods, and control of pH are some methods used to prevent or retard enzyme action. Chemical inhibitors such as ascorbic acid (vitamin C) have been used to retard color darkening in fruits due to polyphenol oxidase enzyme activity, and the brown color in meat caused by oxidation of myoglobin to metmyoglobin. Fat-splitting enzymes are the principal causes of off-flavors in freeze-dried fruits, vegetables, and meats as well as in frozen products. Antioxidant additives may inhibit oxidation due to enzymes, but may contribute off-flavors of their own.

Enzyme spoilage is responsible for flavor, texture and color changes that frequently make refrigerated and food products undesirable or unacceptable when stored at an unsuitable temperature or for too long a period of time. Some important enzymes and their uses are given in Table 13.8.

Enzymes are more efficient than ordinary inorganic catalysts. Reactions are promoted under very mild conditions of temperature. Each enzyme has an optimum operating temperature above and below which activity declines.

Reactions are generally accelerated by the addition of heat, but too much heat deactivates enzymes, since they are proteins and are denatured by heat. The blanching of foods to be frozen is done to inactivate the enzymes, which can initiate reactions that produce off-flavors in the frozen product.

The speed of an enzyme-catalyzed reaction depends somewhat on the concentration of the enzyme present. Very small amounts of invertase are needed to bring about the inversion of sucrose.

Enzyme manufacturing is a specialty activity involved mainly with the food industry. Table 13.8 lists some commercial enzymes.

Fungal amylases are used instead of malt in distilleries or to augment malt activity in beer making. Diastases, a name given to enzymes that act upon starches, are used for making corn syrup as well as in the pharmaceutical field and in many fermentation industries.

The action of enzymes on cabbage is used in the production of sauerkraut under very controlled conditions. In the baking industry the action of enzymes on the starches and sugars present is necessary for the formation of carbon dioxide. Under special conditions the action of diastases produces soluble starch adhesives used in the textile and paper industries.

Proteolytic enzymes—those which act upon proteins—are used in the tanning and baking industries. Meat tenderizers such as papain, bromelin, ficin, rhozyme, and trypsin are. used. Proteases are also used in brewing, dry cleaning, and for the production of protein hydrolyzates especially from soya protein. Pectinases or pectinolytic enzymes are employed in making and clarifying fruit juices and concentrates and in the wine industry.

One of industry's newest uses of specific enzymes has been to produce those which will react at the pH of detergent solutions and at reasonably high temperatures.

The functioning of many enzymes is dependent upon the presence of a metallic ion such as $Ni(II)$, iron, molybdenum, cobalt, etc. Some enzymes contain metal ions at their active sites, such as Zn^{++} in carboxypeptidase, and carbonic anhydrase, Mn^{++} in malic enzyme, and Mg^{++} in a variety of kinases.

TABLE 13.8

SOME COMMERCIAL ENZYMES

Class	Enzymes	Source	Uses
Proteases	Acid fungal protease	Mold	Hydrolysis of proteins at low pH replaces pepsin for chill-proofing in beer; cereal treatment, rennet extender
	Bromelin	Pineapple plant	Meat tenderizer; baking, to produce texture (waffles, pancakes, etc.)
	Fungal protease	Aspergillus oryzae	Bread baking (texture, loaf volume, color improved), meat tenderizing (used with plant proteolytic enzymes)
	Ficin	Latex of the fig tree	Tenderizer for meat and sausage casings, brewings (prevents haze formation in beer)
	Papain	Latex of fruit of Carici Papaya	Meat tenderizer, used in on-the-hoof
	Pepsin	Stomach mucosa	Production of "instant" cereals
	HT proteolytic	Bacteria	Baking (shortening baking time and improves flavor of crackers and cookies)
	Rennin	Abomasum	Clotting of casein (cheese curds)
Pectinases	Takamine pectinases	Molds	(a) jellies: destroys pectin in fruit juices so that a standard pectin may be added (b) apple juice: clarifies the juice (c) purées: from peaches, currants, rasp-

Oxidases	Glucose oxidase	Fungi	berries, apricots, strawberries, and other fruits (aids in processing) (d) grape juice and wines: filters, aid by digesting pectin that blocks filters. (a) Eggs: desugars whites, yolks or whole eggs (b) Beverages: removes oxygen thus increasing shelf-life (c) Oxygen sensitive foods; removes oxygen
Catalases	Catalase B	Microbial	Decomposes hydrogen peroxide to water and oxygen
	Catalase L	Beef livers	Destroys residual peroxide used in Swiss-style cheese manufacture
Cellulose	Cellulase	Fungal	(a) Citrus: clarifies juices by removing cellulose cloud (b) Beer: increases body (c) Pomace: catalyzes hydrolysis to sugars
Hemicellulose	Hemicellulase	Bacterial	Splits hemicelluloses and gums (a) Coffee: breakdown gums (b) Gums: splits locust bean gum, carboxymethyne, cellulose, and other gums
Pancreatize lipase	Pancreatic lipase	Hog pancreas	Splits fats Hydrolyzes triglycerides to glycerine and fatty acids with di- and monoglycerides as intermediate products
Amylase	Fungal	Fungal	Bread baking: gives better color, retards staling

Other enzymes require the presence of an ion such as Na^+, K^+ or NH_4^+ for stabilization of a particular conformation responsible for maximum catalytic activity.

Metal ions that all living organisms require are sodium, potassium, magnesium, calcium, manganese, iron, cobalt, copper, and zinc. In addition, there are small quantities of vanadium, chromium, molybdenum, niobium, and cadmium found in particular living organisms. Recently selenium, a nonmetal, has been added to the list of necessary trace elements.

CHAPTER 14

L. L. W. Smith
L. J. Minor

Meat

Meat is easily the most important single item in the diet, primarily because of its palatability and high nutritive value for man; only milk, milk products, and eggs rank higher than meat, poultry, and fish. Meat is appealing to the eye and to the palate; its aroma, flavor, color, and texture add interest to meals; it lends variety to the diet; its lasting value is satisfying; it is highly digestible. Meat most closely resembles the composition of the tissues it is to replace, being very high in essential food nutrients, namely, protein, the energy-producing elements phosphorus, iron, and copper, and certain vitamins.

The digestibility of meat and meat products is very high, approximately 97% of the protein, 95% of the fat, and 98% of the carbohydrate being utilized by the body. Fat meats require longer periods of time for complete digestion; however, this increased length of time does not interfere with completeness of digestibility. Meat is readily absorbed after digestion, leaving little residue in the intestines.

PHYSICAL AND CHEMICAL COMPOSITION OF MEAT

The composition, both physical and chemical, of meat, poultry, and fish is of extreme importance. Certain components are inherent in the product, while others can be influenced to a greater or lesser extent by man and by environment.

Composition has been determined by actual experimental investigation and by estimation from existing data. The most accurate method is an analysis of the entire body, devoid of the digestive tract and urinary contents. An analysis of the dressed carcass would probably be the next best method. Since both of these are time-consuming and costly, research workers have endeavored to discover and develop simple estimating methods, and some success has been achieved.

Schoenheimer and others have suggested that all components of living matter, whether functional or structural, of simple or of complex nature, are in a steady state of rapid flux, and that all regenerative reactions are enzymatic in nature.

Physical composition is largely concerned with lean, fat, and bone and their relative proportions. Studies with beef, lamb, and mutton carcasses have indicated a very close relationship between the separable muscle or lean, separable fat, and separable bone in the rib cut and comparable constituents of the entire carcass; hence an analysis of this cut has been employed to estimate the gross physical composition of the carcass.

In general, studies of the approximate average physical composition of the primal or wholesale cuts of steer carcasses have indicated that the higher the grade, the greater the percentage of edible meat (separable lean plus separable fat) and fat, and the lower the percentage of lean and bone and gristle.

Chemical Composition and Nutritive Value

Chemically, meat components can be classified in a number of ways. The grouping may be organic or inorganic. The discussion that follows divides meat into its principal components, biochemically. The chief components of meat are water, protein, fat, minerals, and certain of the vitamins. Meat is composed of approximately 75% water, 18% protein, 3.5% soluble nonprotein substances, and 3% fat.

All meats contain water. The moisture content varies somewhat with age, younger animals having a relatively greater proportion of water. Approximately 70 to 75% of muscle is water; about 40 to 70% of the ordinary cuts of meat is water.

Proteins represent the most important component of the edible portion of animal tissues; muscle proteins are the principal solids of meat. Protein content is calculated as total nitrogen multiplied by the factor 6.25 (protein contains 16% nitrogen, thus the ratio of protein to nitrogen is 100:16 or 6.25). The protein content of the edible portion of meat, on a fresh basis, varies from 15 to 20%, the higher values being more typical of beef, veal, and lab, and the lower values usually of pork. The amount of protein varies in a specific cut, to a large extent, with its fat content. As the fat content increases, the percentage of protein decreases, that is, there is an inverse relationship between fat and protein content. Protein content is also affected by age or stage of growth, and is higher in young animals.

The proteins of meat may be divided into the soluble and the insoluble forms. Heat alone will coagulate the soluble proteins, which include the globulins, albumins, myoalbumin, and myosin. The insoluble proteins are collagen, elastin, and keratin (characteristic of hair, horns, hoofs, and nails). Otherwise, the proteins in meat may be divided into the albuminoids or myosin, contained in muscle and lean meat, these being the most valuable because of a similarity in composition to the heterogeneous compounds of the body and most prevalent; the gelatinoids, which comprise collagen (contained in tendons and in connective tissue); and ossein (the principal protein of the organic matrix of bone in which mineral salts are deposited).

Actomyosin, the globulin complex which is the most abundant muscle protein—the component involved in the contraction of muscle—consists of two proteins: actin and myosin. Edible muscle tissue also contains collagen, elastin, and reticulin (structural elements related to skeletal attachment), respiratory pigments (mostly myoglobin, the muscle pigment), nucleoproteins (concerned with heritability characteristics), enzymes (catalysts for cellular metabolic changes), and other protein components involved in a variety of miscellaneous functions.

Protein is also found in considerable amounts in the inedible portion of meat, i.e., collagen (the principal component of skin, tendons, bone). *Collagen* is the most abundant protein in the animal kingdom; it is the major fibrous component of the skin, tendon, ligaments, cartilage, and bone. In the tendon it has a tensile strength equal to that of a light steel wire; in the cornea it is as transparent as water. It accounts for the toughness of leather, the tenacity of glue, and the viscosity of gelatin. It underlies the crippling deformities associated with rheumatic disease, etc.

Collagen is basically a molecule composed of three polypeptide chains, each composed of about 1000 amino acids. Hydroxyproline (4-hydroxy-2-pyrolidine carboxylic acid) and hydroxylysine (α,e, -diamino-Δ-hydroxyhexanoic acid) make up about 25% of the links in the collagen molecule. The greater the percentage of these two amino acids, the higher the resistance of the molecule to heat or chemical denaturation. Another distinctive feature in the long chain is that every fourth position seems to be occupied by glycine, followed by proline or hydroxy-proline. This makes about 30% of the chain glycine. The basic molecular chain is twisted into a left-handed helix, and three such helixes are wrapped around each other to form a right-handed superhelix. These are held together by hydrogen bonding to the oxygen at the peptide linkage and to the nitrogen at the peptide bond.

Collagen has an isoelectric point of pH 7 to 8. It is distinguished from elastin by hydrolyzing to gelatin in water at 80°C. Collagen in the aging process becomes more and more unaffected and requires stronger acids and heat for hydrolysis.

Collagen is the principal constituent of the connective skin of attaching muscle fibers and of the tendons which attach muscles to bones. *Elastin* is more important as a ligament, as it connects bones to bones and/or cartilage. Elastin fibers stretch and return to their original form, whereas collagen fibers are flexible, but offer great resistance to pulling force. Elastin fibers when damaged are not replaced, as are collagen fibers, and this accounts for the lack of elasticity in scar tissue.

The collagen content of meat cuts varies with the lower amount present in large muscle of the ribs, 9, 10, and 11, and the tenderloin. Round, porterhouse, sirloin, chuck steaks rank second as to the lower amount of collagen. Short ribs have more elastin than collagen, while foreshanks are highest in collagen, as well as muscles from low-grade animals, the young and the undernourished.

Another class of functional proteins comprises those of the *blood plasma, lymph,* and *similar body fluids.* Body fluids represent a 0.9% solution and the blood represents 1/11th to 1/12th of the body weight, or about 6 liters in volume.

In blood there are about 70 gm of dissolved albumins and globulins per liter, of which about 4 gm are fibrinogen. This body fluid aids in the maintenance of a constant osmotic pressure within the body. It contains the buffering agents $CO_3^=$, HCO_3^-, $H_2PO_4^-$, $HPO_4^=$, and the amino acids. It acts as a carrier for the amino acids, enzymes, ions, glucose, lipids, etc., to provide nutrients for the body mechanisms.

The clotting of the blood is a property of the blood plasma. When blood clots, the soluble protein fibrinogen is converted to insoluble fibrin, whose fibers form a mat-like clot. The average clotting time is 5 to 8 min. A brief description of the clotting mechanism is as follows:

Prothrombin (protein) + Ca^{++} and thromboplastin from the tissues yield thrombin, an enzyme. Thrombin plus fibrinogen then produces fibrin. The blood clot represents a gel of about 99% water and the cellular elements enmeshed in a network of the fibrous strands of fibrin. Vitamin K is necessary for the production and function of fibrinogen.

Another group of important proteins are the *respiratory proteins*, those which transport oxygen from the respiratory organs to the consuming tissues such as hemoglobin. The oxygen is then held in the tissues by other respiratory proteins such as myoglobin. *Hemoglobin* has a molecular weight of about 68,000, contains 4 iron atoms; its 10,000 atoms are assembled into 4 chains with 4 pigment groups. *Myoglobin*, on the other hand, represents a molecular weight of about 17,000, has 1 iron atom, represents about 96% globin and 4% heme. It is responsible for the color of meat. It is similar to the configuration of the chlorophyll molecule, containing porphyrin groups bound together with ferrous iron; the colored body is attached to the globin portion.

The degree of red color is important to the consumer, sometimes more so than the quality. There are many examples of buying by the eye as to color rather than quality. *Myoglobin* in cut meat is a purplish red; when exposed to the oxygen of the air it turns bright red. It is then called *oxymyoglobin* and is said to have been *oxygenated*. When cooked or exposed to heat the ferrous iron becomes ferric iron and the color a dark brown, and the term *metmyoglobin* is used. During the curing of ham the sodium or potassium nitrites used produce a *nitrosomyoglobin*, which has a pinkish hue. Here again, when the ham or cured pork is heated, the product turns brownish and the protein is *nitroso-metmyoglobin*. In both the metmyoglobins, the protein has been denatured by cooking.

The packaging of meat requires material which allows the presence of oxygen so the meat remains bright red.

Other protein materials present in animal flesh are *enzymes*, *hormones*, and the *chromosomes* or *genes* found in every cell. The *mucoproteins*, those proteins conjugated with carbohydrate material, are the highly viscous body fluids. The saliva, gastrointestinal fluids, and the fluids of the joints are mucoidal in character.

Quantitative analyses for the amino-acid content of meat indicate that meat contains all the essential or indispensable amino acids in liberal percentages, and that meat proteins are biologically complete. The lean tissues of different cuts from the same carcass and of the various kinds of meat are very similar in amino-acid composition. The muscle tissues of mammals, birds, fish, and shellfish, are quite similar in amino-acid pattern.

Fat is the most variable component of the animal body. All fats are combinations of glycerol or glycerin and fatty acids; hence the common name glycerides. Each species contains a combination of fatty acids peculiar to or typical of that species, and differing from the combinations in any other species. Fats are carriers of the so-called fat-soluble vitamins A, D, E, and K, and are sources of certain fatty acids necessary for the proper functioning of the body that can be obtained in no other way, particularly the so-called essential fatty acids, linoleic, linolenic, and arachidonic. The fat content of most cuts of meat varies from 5 to 30%.

Meat furnishes significant amounts of phosphorus, iron, copper, manganese, zinc, cobalt, magnesium, and iodine; it cannot be considered a good source of calcium.

In vitamin value, the chief strength of meat is in the B-complex vitamins. Meat has been found to be a significant source of all the B-complex vitamins. Vitamins A, D, and C occur in significant concentration only in organ meats.

Nitrogenous and nonnitrogenous extractives are found in meat; the former is believed to contribute heavily to the distinctive flavor of meat. Myoglobin is the pigment which is the principal color characteristic of meat. Its quantity may vary from muscle to muscle, giving a graduation in color, rather than the homogeneity (alikeness) common to some muscles and kinds of meat, e.g., veal.

Meat is cooked to increase palatability and to destroy any harmful organisms present. Therefore, the eating quality of meat is dependent upon the method of cooking, the temperature and time. Tender cuts of meat become less tender on cooking. Meat cooked to rare degree of doneness results in tender muscle fibers and tough connective tissue, and the residue flavor is one of saltiness. Those cuts with large amounts of connective tissue require both temperature and time for softening. Temperature is important for muscle protein toughening. Therefore, less-tender cuts require a long time at low temperatures in moist heat for a satisfactory result. Tender cuts are cooked in dry heat for a short time.

Various cuts of meat do not respond in the same way to any one set of cooking conditions. A loin steak may be tender when broiled rare, while bottom round will be tough when broiled similarly. If both cuts are braised, then the bottom round is tender and the loin is tough. Moist heat results in rapid heat penetration, while dry heat achieves a low rate of heat penetration.

SOME BASIC CHANGES IN PROTEIN, FATS AND CARBOHYDRATES OF MEAT DURING AGING AND COOKING

The fundamental changes which take place during the aging of meat are (1) formation of actomyosin, (2) decrease in pH from about 7.4 to pH 5.5 due to the formation of lactic acid, and (3) decrease in tenderness during rigor mortis followed by gradual increase 7 to 10 days after slaughter due mainly to the action of proteolytic enzymes. "Proten" beef is beef from cattle slaughtered after the administration of proteolytic enzymes intravenously. This meat, though tender, has not become too popular, as it often has a texture similar to that of cooked liver.

Cooking

The changes which take place during cooking vary greatly depending upon cut of meat, method of preparation, and the desired product.

(a) Changes in color

(1) The change in myoglobin (red) to hematin (grayish-brown) or metmyoglobin, a denaturing process due to heat, results in the breaking of bonds and the exposure of groups, thus enlarging the molecule. This change also results in loss of some moisture and salts.

(2) The *Maillard* or *browning reaction* is due to the reaction of the amino acid groups and the reducing sugars present. This produces both flavor and color changes especially on the outer portion of the piece of meat.

(3) Charring, of course, is reducing or oxidizing organic compounds down to carbon.

(b) Loss in weight and change in volume

(1) Some of these changes can be related to denaturation of the protein present with accompanying loss of moisture and salts.

(2) The collagen present is hydrolyzed to gelatin. Mammalian collagen generally shrinks to less than one third its original length; the shrink point temperatures have been determined for the collagen present in halibut, shark, pike, carp and lung fish. These shrinkage temperatures are much lower than that of mammalian collagen. When meat is not heated to the shrink point of the collagen, tenderness is forfeited. Fat is melted and exuded into the drippings. Volatile materials are lost, such as moisture and odor compounds.

(c) The changes in the fatty tissue are loss of fat due to melting, loss of fatty acids due to hydrolysis of fats, and shrinkage of adipose tissue which is protein in nature.

(d) The intracellular proteins and those of the muscle fibers are hydrolyzed by the enzymes present into various constituents until heat destroys these enzymes. Glucose is broken from the conjugated protein, etc. The heat-denatured proteins are more susceptible to the action of digestive enzymes.

(e) There is a loss in thiamine (about 25 to 50%), but about 70% of niacin, riboflavin, and pantothenic acid is retained.

(f) Most minerals are retained, and some can even be made more soluble such as the Ca^{++} in calcium acetate when meat is cooked in an acid (vinegar) medium.

(g) Microorganisms are destroyed, particularly *trichinella spiralis* which is present in pork; though it is destroyed at 137°F, it is recommended that pork be cooked to 165°F for safety. These organisms are also destroyed if the product is held at freezing temperatures of −15°C for ten days prior to cooking.

(h) Meat is cooked to produce flavor; raw meat, while very tender, has little flavor, and quite often the after-taste is one of salt.

Flavor production is due to enzymatic hydrolysis up to the inhibition of this reaction by heat, and then to heat hydrolysis, depending upon temperature and time. There are the products resulting from the Maillard reaction, due to the release of

fluids and salts and to the release or melting of fat, and some
fat hydrolysis and the hydrolysis of protein material. These
products are represented by volatile and nonvolatile constituents
such as acids, alcohols, aldehydes, mercaptans, sulfides, and
amines. The drippings generally contain salts, amines, acids,
gelatin, and the purine bodies besides water. These all add up
to gravy flavor.

Tenderness, juiciness, and flavor are the main factors in
palatability. Tenderness may be related to marbling, to the
effects or conditions of slaughtering and aging. Juiciness varies
inversely with the cooking losses or degree of doneness; rare
meat is juicier than well-done meat. Flavor is developed by
the various methods of cooking and/or preparation for consumption.

Methods of cooking may be either with or without moisture.
Roasting is described as uncovered dry-heat cooking of meat.
The question of searing is one of improving external appearance. Roasting at low oven temperatures tends to give a more
tender product, more juice, more flavor, more uniform doneness, less cooking time, and less loss in weight, volume and
drippings. Higher-grade beef, i.e., that with more marbling,
will have more dripping losses from fat but less from evaporation. The longer cooking time at lower temperature has shown
lower cost in fuel per serving.

Meat cooked to an internal temperature of 55° to 60°C is considered rare, 60° to 70°C, medium and 75° to 80°C well-done.
The temperature of meat continues to rise after removal from
the oven and this must be considered, especially when preparing large cuts of meat. The degree of rise depends upon
oven temperature, internal temperature, and size of roast.

Boning does not cause important changes in the quality of
the cooked product, but the removal of the bone aids in slicing
or in locker space if it is to be frozen.

The final report of a study of different handling methods for
frozen roasts in institutional food service completed in 1969
states the following from the data collected: Roasts cooked
from the frozen state yield as much meat as roasts partially
or completely thawed prior to cooking. Dripping losses were
greater when cooked from the frozen state, and of course these
required a longer cooking time. Evaporation loss during the
cooking process was only slightly less than drip loss. This

report does not discuss the relative palatability of the cooked products.

Braising is slow-cooking in a moist atmosphere, whether the meat is in a covered container or wrapped in aluminum foil; steam and pressure cooking are more rapid methods. Here again a more flavorful and tender product can be obtained at low temperatures. Less-tender cuts are used for braising and are cooked until well-done. Tender cuts prepared in this manner would tend to be stringy and dryer. Here denaturation of the protein material is more complete; much of its water-holding capacity is lost and a dry strawlike product results. However, the muscle fibers are easily separated, since most of the collagen material has been hydrolyzed.

Broiling is a dry-heat method which can be done over an open flame, whether gas, charcoal or electric. It can also be accomplished by pan-frying and by deep-fat frying. Here the skill of the operator proves a valuable asset.

Meat can be roasted more quickly with the use of skewers, metal or gas-filled (Freon and carbon dioxide). These conduct the heat into the product, shorten the cooking time and are used generally in the preparation of large turkeys, etc.

Microwave cooking with high-frequency electromagnetic waves shortens cooking time. The waves only penetrate about 2 in. and the electric field created oscillates the polar molecules in the food, converting this molecular motion to heat, thus cooking the food. The cooking losses are very great. The size of the food product must be regulated or the outside of the meat tends to become so dehydrated that it resembles leather.

Although meat cooks from the outside inward, Decareau states that if a 7-lb rib roast is removed from an electronic oven when the internal temperature is about 27°C or 80°F, and allowed to stand 45 min at room temperature, the meat will eventually have a temperature range of 135° to 145°F throughout. The average 10-lb beef roast cooked in the microwave ovens here at Cornell School of Hotel Administration for the past 15 years have shown a very small rise in internal temperature after removal from the oven.

Generally, microwave cooking is used for reconstituting procedures or delayed cooking. The latter involves partially cooking, chilling or freezing quickly, and later thawing and/or completing the cooking procedure.

Tenderizing

Methods used to tenderize meat are (a) mechanical, such as cutting, grinding, scoring, and pounding and (b) chemical, the use of proteolytic enzymes (injection prior to slaughter and rubbed on the meat itself). These enzymes are papain from papaya, bromelin from pineapple, ficin from figs, Rhozyme from fungus, and trypsin from animal stomachs. They act on the surface protein, for the penetration is only from 0.5 to 2 mm, to produce the various protein hydrolyzates. They are active at room temperature and low-cooking temperatures and are soon inactivated as the cooking proceeds.

Marinating

There seems to be a rather misguided myth that marinating is a tenderizing procedure. Here again it is a surface activity of acid hydrolysis of collagen and denaturing of surface protein material. It preserves the meat, as the microorganisms find it difficult to grow in the pH of the marinating sauces. The size of the piece, the age, and the kind of meat determine any action that would result from soaking a piece of meat for several days. If cooked in the sauce, then the flavor is imparted to the final product, as in sauerbraten.

Proteins and Other Meat Values

Salt (NaCl) added to ground meat tends to increase the water-holding capacity of the protein. Sodium polyphosphate ($Na_5P_3O_7$) and sodium acid pyrophosphate ($Na_2H_2P_2O_7$) have also been used for the same purpose in ground meat products and sausages. When the water-holding capacity is increased the products are more tender upon cooking, if not overcooked.

There is little or no nutritional quality change in the protein by standard cooking or processing methods, as indicated by the availability of tryptophan, methionine, and lysine. Little if any of the essential amino acids are destroyed. Lysine, after severe heat treatment, is not fully digested; therefore the protein quality under these conditions would be decreased. The B vitamins present are generally not affected, except thiamine. The protein present in meat furnishes 4 cal/gm, the fat 9 Cal/gm, and the carbohydrate 4 Cal/gm.

Fish protein reacts similarly to the protein of animal flesh, the major difference being that it occurs in thinner layers and less fat is present. It requires a shorter cooking time at lower temperatures. Overcooked fish flesh has the texture of straw, and practically no flavor. The flavoring compounds formed are lost to the cooking media, as in chowders, etc.

Most crustaceans are heated to boiling, then simmered for a very short time in order to obtain a tender, flavorful product.

The changing eating habits of the public have resulted in the use of more processed meats (comminuted, e.g., sausages), prefabricated, and portion cuts. The constant improvements in preservation techniques, particularly freezing and the trans- porting and holding of these products, have resulted in an in- creased use and acceptability of meat so handled. Precooked meats are marketed for institutional uses such as rare, medium, and well-done roasts, precooked and frozen hamburger patties, corn beef, pork roasts, pre-seared steaks, and chops, etc. The development of molded or formed steaks, combinations of cuts, encased or bound with natural meat salts or binders will tend to increase. Roasts made from pieces of meat have been developed and accepted.

Meat is especially valuable for growth, reproduction, and lactation. From the nutritional standpoint, its high content of protein, iron, phosphorus, thiamine, riboflavin, niacin, and calories contributes to these physiological functions. An ade- quate intake of meat furnishes high-quality protein for growth, iron and copper for the formation of hemoglobin and rich red blood cells, phosphorus for skeletal growth and tooth develop- ment, vitamins for the promotion of growth and the protection of health, and calories for energy. As food for adults, meat satisfies many of the nutritional needs for maintenance. Meat is recommended for weight gaining, reducing, and maintenance. The fatter meats are used in weight-gaining diets. For weight- reducing, all the necessary food elements must be carefully supplied to the body. A considerable proportion of these daily needs are furnished by meat. Lean meat, with its low caloric content, is an ideal weight-reducing food. In addition to its nutri- tive value, meat's satiety or lasting value gives it "staying power," and thus avoids the hungry feeling so often experienced when reducing.

MEAT INSPECTION

Meat inspection is the examination of meat (all parts suitable for human consumption) and meat products, relative to their proper origin and wholesomeness as food for man. This examination is complete when it extends not only to all parts of the slaughtered animal, but also to the live animal from which this food is obtained. It therefore includes an antemortem, as well as a postmortem examination.

In the United States, at least three forms of meat inspection are officially practiced: Federal or United States inspection, a function of the Meat Inspection Division, Consumer and Marketing Service, United States Department of Agriculture; state inspection, a function of the Department of Agriculture of specific states in the United States; and local inspection, a function of various counties and municipalities throughout the United States. The most highly developed of these programs is that sponsored by the Federal government.

U.S. Government or Federal Inspection is under the jurisdiction of the Consumer Protection Programs Division, Consumer and Marketing Service, U.S. Department of Agriculture. State Inspection is under the jurisdiction of the respective State Departments of Agriculture. More than 35 states have some form of state meat inspection, most relating more to the processing plant than to meat *per se*. Municipal or local inspection is usually under county or local departments of health.

Federal inspection takes precedence and is the usual pattern for the other forms of inspection. The inspection notation, "Inspected and Passed," (Fig. 14.1) at any level, means that at the time the meat or meat product was examined it was wholesome; however, this is no guarantee that when the product reaches the hotel or restaurant such a situation still exists. Thus it is essential that all meat and meat products be checked carefully for "condition" on receipt and before acceptance.

The Meat Inspection Act of 1890 authorized the inspection of salted pork and bacon ... and live animals intended for export (including the authorized inspection and quarantine of imported animals).

On June 20, 1906, Congress passed the Meat Inspection Act, which is in effect at the present time. A number of amendments to this Act have been passed: particularly the addition of horses

FIG. 14.1. FEDERAL INSPECTION INDICIA FOR POULTRY (TOP) AND MEAT (BOTTOM)

to the list of animals slaughtered (1919); the Poultry Products Inspection Act, establishing Federal Inspection of all poultry in interstate and foreign commerce (1957); the National Humane Slaughter Act, setting standards for methods of equipment used in slaughtering livestock and poultry (1958); the Wholesome Meat Act, providing for the establishment of a uniform standard for State and Federally inspected meats (1967); and the Wholesome Poultry Products Act (1968), providing the same provisions for poultry inspection as the Wholesome Meat Act (1967) provided for meat inspection.

The main purposes of the present system of Federal Meat Inspection are:

(a) To supervise the sanitation of plants, particularly with respect to approval for the plant's construction and equipment.

(b) To examine food animals, including cattle, calves, sheep, swine, goats, and horses, prior to slaughter, to eliminate diseased animals (antemortem examination).

(c) To conduct a thorough postmortem examination of each animal at the time of slaughter to discover and eliminate dis-eased and otherwise unfit meat.

(d) To assure proper postmortem diagnosis and disposition of carcasses in unusual cases, as well as to destroy for food purposes diseased, unsound, and otherwise unfit meat.

(e) To see that meat and meat food products are kept clean and wholesome during all stages of preparation and processing into articles of food.

(f) To guard against the use of harmful preservatives, chemicals, dyes, or other deleterious ingredients.

(g) To cause sound and wholesome meat and meat food products to be marked, stamped, tagged, or labeled appropriately as "Inspected and Passed," and to cause unsound, unhealthful, and unwholesome meat and meat food products to be marked, stamped, tagged, or labeled "Inspected and condemned," the number on the stamp being that of the establishment.

(h) To require informative labeling which is accurate, and at the same time to prevent the use of false and deceptive labeling on meat and meat food products.

(i) To certify meat and meat food products for export.

(j) To inspect meat and meat food products offered for importation into the United States.

(k) To examine meat and meat food products for compliance with specification requirements of governmental purchasing agents.

(l) To maintain laboratories to obtain chemical and biological (microbiological, pathological, parasitological, and seriological) information, for the purpose of conducting those investigations necessary to ensure the accuracy and effectiveness of inspection procedures.

(m) To supervise the manufacture and labeling of processed or renovated butter.

(n) To set standards for methods of equipment used in slaughtering livestock and poultry in a humane manner.

(o) To see to it that meat and poultry which does not cross state lines is inspected according to programs "at least equal to Federal Inspection."

The Federal examination of meat and meat food products (and poultry and poultry food products) is mandatory if any of the following conditions exist:

(a) Livestock and poultry are slaughtered for transportation in interstate (from one state to another) or foreign (imported or exported) commerce; even if only one product in a plant falls in this category, the entire plant must be under Federal Inspection; there is no such thing as partial Federal Inspection in an establishment.

(b) Meat and meat food products and poultry and poultry food products, purchased by various government agencies, such as the armed forces, hospitals, and other institutions.

Federal meat and poultry inspection is administered by the Consumer and Marketing Service of the United States Department of Agriculture.

It is absolutely essential that for food-service industry usage, all meat be inspected at some level before it is accepted. In addition, on receipt, meat should be examined carefully to establish an absence of discoloration, off-odors, sliminess, etc., all earmarks of spoilage.

MEAT GRADING

Grading is the examination, identification, and certification of products according to definite standards or specifications. Grades indicate the ultimate worth of the product to the consumer, and therefore determine product value. The grade names are commonly accepted designations of relative desirability. Grading is based on certain definite preference-determining factors. These factors have been: (1) conformation (form, shape, ratio of meat to bone, contour, outline, muscling, meatiness, etc.), (2) finish (fatness), and (3) quality (character of lean—color, texture, firmness; fat—distribution and marbling; and bone—maturity). In the last several years, these factors have lost their individual identity.

Conformation, as determined in the carcass, side, or cut, in the final analysis, indicates the proportion of more desirable to less desirable cuts. As objectively ascertained in determining yield grades, it is a major consideration.

Finish, occasionally referred to as condition (particularly in the live animal), and the amount, color (if applicable), character, and distribution of fat, externally, internally, or intramuscularly (marbling), are being related closely to maturity factors, according to present grading practice.

Quality, the more nebulous consideration, is at the same time probably the most important factor. It is largely a characteristic of flesh (color, texture, firmness); fat (evenness of distribution, marbling, i.e., fine particles of fat interspersed in lean being preferable to "seams" of fat); and bone (size, color, consistency, or hardness). Bone is the principal indicator of maturity (chronological age). Boneless cuts of meat cannot be Federally graded. Youthful bone is bloody, porous, moist, and shows evi-

dence of cartilage, a form of connective tissue which will
eventually become solid bone; it is soft and white when immature,
e.g., the so-called "buttons" at the ends of the chine bones,
principally related to ribs of beef.

U.S. Government grades for meat have undergone a number
of changes since the present system of grading went into effect
(beef was the first kind of meat Federally graded according to
the modern system, in 1939). Yield grades have been in effect
in connection with beef grading since 1965; for lamb, since 1969.
Separate identification is given to "quality" and to cuttability.
The evaluation of conformation provides that carcasses can
meet this requirement for a grade either through a specified
development of muscling or a specified development of muscling
and fat combined.

For beef, the system also included a requirement that all
carcasses be ribbed (partially separated into a hindquarter
and forequarter, on one side, to expose the ribeye muscle between the 12th and 13th ribs) prior to grading. Standards were
developed for cuttability grades of carcasses and certain wholesale cuts of all classes of beef. A subdivision was made on the
basis of the sex condition of the animal from which the carcass
was obtained (steer, heifer, cow, stag, and bull).

The grade of a beef carcass, under the present system, is
based on separate evaluations of two considerations: (1) palatability, indicating characteristics of the lean, and conformation,
now referred to as "quality;" and (2) the percentage of trimmed,
boneless, major retail cuts derived from the carcass, referred
to as "cuttability." The grade of beef carcass given by the
Federal meat grader may, however, consist of an evaluation for
the quality designation, the cuttability designation, or a combination of both. Previous grade standards for beef used the
term "quality" only for the palatability-indicating characteristics of the lean without reference to conformation (present
usage does not imply that variations in conformation are either
directly or indirectly related to differences in palatability).

Quality and cuttability standards are now written separately,
with a further separation into three sections of applicability:
(1) steers, heifers, and cows, without reference to or identification with respect to sex; (2) bulls; and (3) stags. There are five
cuttability groups applicable to all classes, denoted by Nos. 1
through 5, group 1 representing the highest degree of cuttability,

USDA PRIME   USDA CHOICE   USDA GOOD   USDA COMRCL   USDA UTILITY

FIG. 14.2. STAMPS SHOWING AVAILABLE USDA MEAT GRADES

i.e., greatest yield. Eight quality designations (Prime, Choice, Good, Standard, Commercial, Utility, Cutter, and Canner) are applicable to steer, heifer, and cow carcasses, except that cow carcasses are ineligible for Prime. Quality designations for bull and stag carcasses are Choice, Good, Commercial, Utility, Cutter, and Canner.

The final quality grade of a carcass or primal cut is based on a composite evaluation of conformation and quality. Among the major considerations is the relationship between marbling (interspersion of fat particles in the lean), maturity (as expressed by relative ossification of bone), and quality (that part of the final grade that represents the palatability of the lean, color, texture, firmness, marbling), shown in Table 14.1.

The cuttability group of a beef carcass is determined by 4 factors: (1) the amount of external fat (fat thickness over the ribeye muscle); (2) the amount of kidney, pelvic, and heart fat (according to a factor established by the quality grade); (3) the area of the ribeye muscle; and (4) the carcass weight. The actual cuttability group is determined on the basis of the following equation: cuttability group + 2.50 + 2.50× adjusted fat thickness (in.) + (0.0038× hot carcass weight in lb) − 0.32× ribeye area in sq in.).

The assigned grade appears in the form of a "ribbon" roll, which is applied in harmless purple vegetable ink on the entire carcass (Fig. 14.2). The initials appearing in the ribbon roll are a code for the individual grade. The cuttability grade appears in the form of a shield on each of the wholesale or primal cuts.

The Federal grades of beef (quality), veal, lamb, and mutton (quality), and pork are listed in Table 14.1.

Lamb yield grades became available for industry use in 1969.[1] The yield grades are 1, 2, 3, 4, and 5 (yield grade No. 1 carcasses have the highest yield of retail cuts; yield grade No. 5 the lowest). These grades represent a uniform method of identifying carcasses for differences in "cuttability," specifi-

---

[1] USDA Yield Grades for Lamb. USDA Marketing Bulletin No. 52, 1970.

TABLE 14.1

FEDERAL GRADES OF BEEF, VEAL AND CALF, LAMB AND MUTTON, AND PORK

Beef[1]		Veal and Calf[1]	Lamb and Mutton[1]	Pork[2]
Steers, Heifers, and Cows	Bulls and Stags			
Prime	Choice	Prime	Prime	U.S. No. 1
Choice	Good	Choice	Choice	U.S. No. 2
Good	Commercial	Good	Good	U.S. No. 3
Standard	Utility	Standard	Utility	U.S. No. 4
Commercial	Cutter	Utility	Cull	U.S. Utility
Utility	Canner	Cull		
Cutter				
Canner				

[1] Service and Regulatory Announcements 99 (1965), 114 (1956), 123 (1960), C&MS, USDA.
[2] USDA Grades for Pork Carcasses, USDA Marketing Bulletin No. 49, 1970.

cally the yields of closely trimmed, boneless, retail cuts from the leg, loin, hotel rack, and shoulder. The three factors on which lamb yield grades are based are: (1) amount of external fat as measured by the thickness of external fat over the center of the ribeye muscle between the 12th and 13th ribs (measured by probing); (2) the amount of kidney and pelvic fat, measured subjectively and expressed as a percentage of carcass weight; and (3) conformation grade of the legs, as described in the quality grade standards. Yield grade descriptions primarily apply to carcasses. These standards are also applicable to sides, foresaddles, hindsaddles, forequarters, hindquarters, hotel racks, loins, and combinations of regular or trimmed wholesale cuts, which include either the hotel rack or loin.

Standards for grades of pork carcasses are based on those attributes that determine value and utility: the quality of the lean and the yield of the four principal lean cuts (hams, loins, picnics, and Boston butts). Quality of lean is acceptable (U.S. No. 1, 2, 3, or 4) or unacceptable (U.S. Utility). Of the 5 classes (based on the sex condition of the animal at the time of slaughter), namely, barrows, gilts, sows, stags, and boars, only bar-

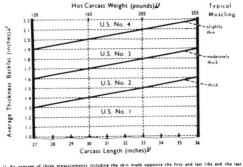

FIG. 14.3. RELATIONSHIP BETWEEN AVERAGE THICKNESS OF
BACKFAT, CARCASS LENGTH OR WEIGHT, AND GRADE FOR CAR-
CASSES WITH MUSCLING TYPICAL OF THEIR DEGREE OF FATNESS.
USDA Marketing Bulletin No. 49, 1970.

rows and gilts are graded. Grading is on the basis of: (1)
quality-indicating characteristics of the lean, including firmness
of fat and lean, amount of feathering between the ribs, the color
of lean (ideally a pinkish grey), unless a cut surface is visible;
and (2) expected combined yields of the 4 lean cuts. With a
1/4-in. fat trim, these expected yields, based on chilled carcass
weight, by grade, are[2]:

Grade	Yield (%)
U.S. No. 1	53 and over
U.S. No. 2	50 to 52.9
U.S. No. 3	47 to 49.9
U.S. No. 4	Less than 47

[2] USDA Grades for Pork Carcasses. USDA Marketing Bulletin No. 49,
1970.

CHAPTER 15

D. V. Vadehra | Poultry Meat

The almost universal acceptance of poultry meat (with the exception of vegetarians) and the rapid generation time and fast growth rates of broilers have revolutionized the poultry industry during the last two decades. Blaxter (1961) said that "the United States poultry industry is one of the most amazing pieces of integrated work that has ever been done." At one time, poultry was raised in the backyard and was considered a "fancy" item. However, times have changed and new marketing trends have made the broiler a prime item in the supermarket. Chicken and turkey production increased by 143% during the 1940–1960 period. This has happened because of the phenomenal progress and success achieved by poultry "husbandry" scientists, who have made great strides in the areas of nutrition, genetics, and disease control. As an illustration, it took 14 weeks and 4 to $4\frac{1}{2}$ lb of feed in the mid-30's and 8 weeks and 2 to $2\frac{1}{2}$ lb of feed in the mid-60's for each pound of gain under commercial conditions; current estimates are 1.8 to 1.9 lb of feed per lb of body weight. The basic sciences of nutrition with respect to essential vitamins and amino acids have played a significant role in the increased production. This chapter will discuss the inspection, grading, chemical composition, and utilization of poultry and poultry products.

CLASSES OF POULTRY

With the development of grading of market poultry in the United States it has become necessary to divide each species of poultry into classes according to their physical characteristics. The following classes and specifications are quite generally used in the different markets of this country (Tables 15.1 and 15.2).

339

TABLE 15.1

INDICATIONS OF AGE IN POULTRY

	Young Birds	Mature Birds
Comb chickens	Pliable, resilient, not wrinkled, points sharp	Wrinkled, coarser, thicker points, rounded
Bill, ducks	Pliable, not completely hardened	Hardened
Plumage	Fresh, glossy appearance	Faded, worn except in birds which have recently molted
Fat	Smooth layers with brighter color. Not lumpy over feather tracts	Generally darker in color, inclined to lumpiness over heavy feather tracts
Breastbone	Cartilage, if present, pliable and soft	End of keel; hardened cartilage, bony
Pinbone	Pliable	Not pliable
Shanks	Scales on shanks, smooth, small	Scales, larger, rough, and slightly raised
Oil sac	Small, soft	Enlarged, often hardened
Spurs (male) chickens, turkeys occasionally adult females	Small, underdeveloped corn-like	Spurs gradually increase in length with age, becoming somewhat curved and sharper. Hens often have fine, sharp spurs after first year
Windpipe, ducks, geese	Easily dented	Hardened, almost bony-like to the touch
Flesh	Tender meated, translucent appearance, fine texture	Coarser texture, darker, hardened muscle fibers
Drumsticks	Lacking in development, muscles easily dented	Generally rounded, full, firm

Chicken

Fryer or broiler: young chicken (usually under 12 weeks of age, more often 8 to 9 weeks) of either sex that is tender-

TABLE 15.2

INDICATION OF SEX IN POULTRY

	Males	Females
Head	Usually larger with larger and longer attachments, such as comb and wattles; coarser than that of females in appearance	Smaller, rather fine and delicate in appearance compared with males. Hen turkeys have hair on center line of head
Plumage	Feathers usually long and pointed at the ends. Tail feathers in chickens long and curved. Parti-colored varieties, have more brilliant colors than have the females. Most male ducks have a curl in the tail feathers	Feathers inclined to be shorter and more blunt than those of the male. Tail feathers short and straight in comparison with the male. Modest colors in parti-colored varieties
Body	Larger and generally more angular than the female. Depth from keel to back greater on same weight birds. Bones, including shanks, longer, larger, and coarser	Finer boned, body more rounded
Skin	Slightly coarser, particularly in old birds. Feather follicles larger. Less fat under skin between heavy feather tracts and over back	Smoother, generally a better distribution of fat between feather tracts. Feather tracts narrower but carrying more fat
Keel	Longer with fleshing tending to taper at the base	Shorter with more rounded appearance over the breast
Legs	Drumstick and thigh relatively long with flesh tending to show less full until mature	Drumstick and thigh relatively shorter with drumstick more inclined to roundness, increasingly so with age

meated with soft, pliable, smooth-textured skin, and flexible breastbone cartilage.

Roaster: young chicken (usually under 4 months of age), of either sex, that is tender-meated with soft, pliable, smooth-textured skin, and breastbone cartilage somewhat less flexible than that of a broiler or fryer.

Capon: an unsexed male chicken (usually under 6 months of age) that is tender-meated with soft, pliable, smooth-textured skin.

Hen or stewing chicken or fowl: a mature female chicken (usually more than 10 months of age) with meat less tender than that of a roaster and nonflexible breastbone.

Cock or old rooster: a mature male chicken with coarse skin, toughened and darkened meat, and hardened breastbone.

Turkeys

Fryers or roasters: a young turkey (usually under 16 weeks of age) of either sex, that is tender-meated with soft, pliable, smooth-textured skin, and flexible breastbone cartilage.

Young hen turkey: a young female (usually under 7 months of age) that is tender-meated with soft, pliable, smooth-textured skin, and breastbone cartilage somewhat less flexible than that in a turkey fryer.

Young tom turkey: a young male (usually under 7 months of age) that is tender-meated with soft, pliable, smooth-textured skin, and breastbone cartilage somewhat less flexible than that in a turkey fryer.

Hen turkey: a mature or old hen turkey (usually over 10 months of age) with toughened flesh and hardened breastbone. It may have coarse or dry skin and patchy areas of surface fat.

Tom turkey: a mature male turkey or old male turkey (usually over 10 months of age) with coarse skin, toughened flesh, and hardened breastbone.

Ducks

Broiler or fryer duckling: a young duck (usually under 8 weeks of age) of either sex, that is tender-meated and has a soft bill and soft windpipe.

Roaster duckling: a young duck (usually under 14 weeks of age) of either sex, that is tender-meated and has a bill that is not completely hardened and a windpipe that is easily dented.

Mature or old duck: a duck (usually over 6 months of age) of either sex, with toughened flesh, hardened bill, and hardened windpipe.

Geese

Young goose: a goose of either sex, tender-meated, with a windpipe that is easily dented.

Mature or old goose: a goose of either sex with toughened flesh and hardened windpipe.

Guineas

Young guinea: may be of either sex and is tender-meated.

Mature or old guinea: may be of either sex and has toughened flesh.

Pigeons

Squab: a young pigeon of either sex which is extra tender-meated.

Pigeons: a mature bird of either sex, with coarse skin and toughened flesh.

STANDARDS AND GRADES

The standards of quality list various factors, such as fat covering, fleshing, exposed flesh, discolorations, etc., which when evaluated collectively determine the grade of the bird (Table 15.3). The grades used at the retail level are referred to as U.S. Consumer grades, and these are: U.S. Grade A, U.S. Grade B, and U.S. Grade C. The U.S. procurement grades are designed primarily for institutional trade and these include U.S. procurement grade I and U.S. procurement grade II. These grades place more emphasis on yield than on appearance.

POULTRY PROCESSING

The broilers are generally caught at night for loading. This results in an easier catch, less struggle, and the bird settles down in the coops much faster. Also, in summer, the temperature is an important factor.

Weighing.—The weight of the empty crates and the truck is generally taken at a public scale followed by loading and re-weighing at the public scale close to the processing plant.

TABLE 15.3

SUMMARY OF STANDARDS OF QUALITY FOR LIVE POULTRY ON AN INDIVIDUAL BIRD BASIS

	A or No. 1 Quality	B or No. 2 Quality	C or No. 3 Quality
Health and Vigor	Alert, bright eyes, healthy vigorous	Good health and vigor	Lacking in vigor
Feathering	Well covered with feathers	Fairly well covered with feathers	Complete lack of plumage feathers on back
	Slight scattering of pin feathers	Moderate number of feathers	Large number of pin feathers
Conformation			
Breast bone	Normal Slight curve, $\frac{1}{8}$ in. dent (chick.) $\frac{1}{4}$ in. dent (turk.)	Practically normal Slightly crooked	Abnormal Crooked
Back	Normal (except slight curve)	Moderately crooked	Crooked or hunch back
Legs and Wings	Normal	Slightly misshapen	Misshapen
Fleshing	Well covered, some fat under long breast	Fairly well fleshed	Poorly developed, narrow breast, thin covering of flesh

	Grade A	Grade B	Grade C
Fat Covering	Well covered, some fat under skin over entire carcass	Enough fat on breast and legs to prevent a distinct appearance of flesh through skin	Lacking in fat covering on back and thighs, small amount in feather tracts
	Chicken fryers and turkey fryers and young toms only moderate covering	Hens or fowl may have excessive abdominal fat	
Defects			
Tears and broken bones	Slight	Moderate	Serious
	Free	Free	Free
Bruises, scratches, and callouses	Slight skin bruises, scratches and callouses	Moderate (except only slight flesh bruises)	Unlimited to extent no part unfit for food
Shanks	Slightly scaly	Moderately scaly	Seriously scaly

Shrinkage.—The term refers to the weight loss during the hauling process. Contract hauling, the most commonly used procedure, allows for a shrinkage of 3 to 4%, depending on the area. Other modifications of the hauling processes are used in different areas.

Slaughtering.—After the birds have been delivered to the processing plants, they are killed as soon as possible. Stunning prior to slaughter may or may not be utilized. In turkeys electric shock is generally used, while in broilers the jugular vein is cut directly. There are several ways of cutting poultry for bleeding, the most common being the "Modified Kosher," in which the jugular vein is severed just below the jowls so that the windpipe and esophagus remain uncut.

Scalding.—Various times and temperatures are recommended for the several types of poultry in different regions of the country. Poultry immersed in water heated to 160° to 180°F for 30 to 60 sec is considered as hard scald; the temperatures for subscald and soft scalding are 138° to 140°F for 30 to 75 sec and 123° to 130°F for 90 to 120 sec, respectively. The decision on the temperature is generally based on the ease of removing feathers as well as damage and discoloration to the skin and epidermis.

Picking.—The feathers are now removed almost exclusively by automatic rubber-fingered feather pickers. Wax picking, however, is still being used for water-fowl carcass.

Singeing.—This is an essential process for the removal of the hair-like appendages called filoplumes.

These procedures are followed by washing, scrubbing, and the removal of the shanks and oil glands.

Dressing.—Dressing of the carcass is followed by evisceration, which is generally done on a separate line. The process includes positioning of the carcass, followed by opening of the body cavity to remove the viscera. At this point, the carcass is generally inspected for wholesomeness, followed by removal of lungs (generally by vacuum) as well as of the head, crop, windpipe, and neck. The carcasses are then automatically sorted according to weight, and dropped into chill tanks.

Chilling.—According to the U.S.D.A. Standards, the carcass must be chilled to a final temperature of 40°F. Several types of equipment have been designed for this purpose, including the "drag" chiller, oscillating vat chillers, parallel-flow

TABLE 15.3a.

NUMBER OF MICROORGANISMS ON POULTRY
AND IN PROCESSING WATER

Points of Sampling	Usual Range of Numbers[1]
Skin of live bird	600–8,100
Scald water (137°–140°F)	5,900–17,000
Fresh chill water	50,000–210,000
Aerated chill water	34,000–240,000
Skin after rough pick	8,100–45,000
Skin after neck pick	3,300–32,000
Skin after singe	13,000–210,000
Skin after evisceration	11,000–93,000
Cavity after evisceration	1,400–12,000
In chill tank	50,000–600,000
Final product	4,000–33,000

[1]Counts per square centimeter or per milliliters. Walker and Ayers, 1956.

tumble chillers, and counter-flow tumble chillers, all of which use a mixture of crushed ice and water.

After chilling, the poultry is ice-packed in wire-bound wooden boxes which generally contain 25 to 30 birds and approximately 30 to 35 lb of ice per box.

During the ice-chilling process, the birds generally pick up a certain amount of water. This is regulated by the U.S.D.A. according to the size of the bird. The general guidelines are given below:

Ready to cook weight	Pickup allowed(%)
Turkey, 20 lb or over	4.5
Turkey, 10 to 20 lb	6.0
Turkey under 10 lb	8.0
Chicken, 5 lb and under	8.0
All other kinds and weights of poultry	6.0

It has been well documented that chilling poultry in ice water is far from an ideal procedure from the microbiological and shelf-life standpoint. The data on Table 15.3 illustrate the

typical microbiological count at various processing points
and illustrate the drawbacks of the water-chilling process.

The above data clearly indicate that chill water is an important source of microorganisms, and is in large measure
responsible for the relatively short shelf-life of fresh poultry.
Several recent advances in chilling have been reported by
several commercial concerns, including chill pack, air-chill-
ing, and carbon dioxide snow. All these processes are aimed
at increasing the shelf-life and quality of fresh broilers.

CHEMICAL COMPOSITION

Table 15.4 gives the gross chemical composition of various
cut-up parts of broilers and other poultry. The composition
of cooked poultry meat depends on the method of cooking and
can also be found in Tables 15.4 and 15.7.

Proteins

The meat proteins in general are made up of three classes
depending on their solubility in various solvents. The sarco-
plasmic proteins, soluble in weak salt solution, are the proteins of the cytoplasm and contain the meat pigment and enzymes. The myofibrillar proteins, which are soluble in high
salt solution, consist of actin and myosin, tropomyosin and
several minor components. These are often referred to as
contractile proteins because they are responsible for the
contraction and relaxation of the muscle. The so-called "insoluble" proteins are the connective tissue proteins, collagen.
elastin, and reticulin. From a functional standpoint, the
myofibrillar proteins are responsible for emulsification, and
the connective tissue proteins at least in part are responsible
for the toughness of the meat.

Poultry meat contains all the essential amino acids in good
proportions. The distribution of amino acids in turkey and
chicken is very similar.

Lipids

The lipid content varies considerably with the age, sex, and
species of poultry. In poultry, most of the fat is located under-

neath the skin, while the distribution in the tissues is rather low. Poultry meat in general contains higher percentages of unsaturated fatty acids and lower percentages of cholesterol than do red meats. Saturated fatty acids are 28 to 31%, while unsaturated fatty acids constitute about 70% of the total lipid.

Other nutrients, such as minerals and vitamins, are also well supplied by poultry meat. Like other meat, it is almost devoid of carbohydrates.

PRESERVATION OF POULTRY

The preservation of any food product is based on extending its shelf-life. This is achieved either by retarding microbial growth and chemical reaction by refrigeration, or by destroying the bacteria partially or completely by pasteurization or sterilization. The extent of heat used for these processes also inactivates most of the enzymes.

Unfrozen Poultry

Poultry meat poses some special preservation problems, with broilers in particular. In this country, nearly all broilers are sold fresh, which limits their shelf-life. The housewife is not yet ready to purchase frozen broilers. Ironically, she will, however, purchase fresh broilers, which are often used as "loss leaders" in the supermarkets, and freeze them herself. Since her packaging material and freezing temperatures are not as close to optimum as would be found in a commercial establishment, the end product is often not as good as a commercially frozen broiler would be. The shelf-life of ice-packed chicken stored at 40°F (4.4°C) is approximately 6 days, while at 32°F (0°C) it is 14 days. The advocates of air chilling, chill pack, and carbon dioxide snow pack claim shelf-lives as high as 20 to 30 days.

Freezing

Broilers are frozen for longer storage. Fairly rapid freezing results in less drip (weep) on thawing and the product does not dry out as much during cooking. Most poultry is sharp-frozen at –20°F (–30°C) and stored at this temperature.

TABLE 15.4
COMPOSITION OF FOODS (100 GRAMS) EDIBLE PORTION

Food and Description	Water, %	Food Energy, Calories	Protein, Grams	Fat, Grams	Carbohydrate Total, Grams	Fiber, Grams	Ash, Grams
Chicken (all classes)							
Light meat without skin							
Raw	73.7	117	23.4	1.9	0	0	1.0
Cooked, roasted	63.8	166	31.6	3.4	0	0	1.2
Dark meat without skin							
Raw	73.7	130	20.6	4.7	0	0	1.0
Cooked, roasted	64.4	176	28.0	6.3	0	0	1.2
Broilers, flesh only, cooked, broiled	71.0	136	23.8	3.8	0		1.1
Fryers (weight, ready to cook, with giblets, more than 1¾ lbs)							
Flesh, skin, and giblets							
Raw	75.7	124	18.6	4.9	0	0	0.8
Cooked, fried	53.3	249	30.7	11.8	2.9	—	1.3
Flesh and skin							
Raw	75.4	126	18.8	5.1	0	0	0.7
Cooked, fried	53.5	250	30.6	11.9	2.8	0	1.2
Flesh only							
Raw	77.2	107	19.3	2.7	0	0	0.8
Cooked, fried	58.6	209	31.2	7.8	1.2	—	1.2
Skin only							
Raw	66.3	223	16.1	17.1	0	0	0.5
Cooked, fried	32.5	419	28.3	28.9	9.1	—	1.2
Giblets							
Raw	78.4	103	17.5	3.1	0.1	0	0.9
Cooked, fried	51.7	252	30.8	11.2	4.7	0	1.6

Light meat with skin						
Raw	77.2	101	20.5	1.5	0	0	0.8
Cooked, fried	55.0	234	31.5	9.9	2.4	–	1.2
Dark meat with skin						
Raw	75.3	132	17.7	6.3	0	0	0.7
Cooked, fried	52.1	263	29.9	13.6	3.1	–	1.3
Light meat without skin						
Raw	77.2	101	20.5	1.5	0	0	0.8
Cooked, fried	59.5	197	32.1	6.1	1.1	0	1.2
Dark meat without skin						
Raw	77.3	112	18.1	3.8	0	0	0.8
Cooked, fried	57.5	220	30.4	9.3	1.5	–	1.3
Cut-up parts						
Backs						
Raw	73.3	157	16.5	9.6	0	0	0.6
Cooked, fried	40.5	347	30.0	21.2	6.8	0	1.5
Drumstick						
Raw	76.5	115	18.8	3.9	0	0	0.8
Cooked, fried	55.0	235	32.6	10.2	1.0	–	1.2
Neck						
Raw	74.5	151	15.5	9.4	0	0	0.6
Cooked, fried	50.2	289	26.7	17.4	4.5	–	1.2
Rib						
Raw	76.2	124	17.7	5.4	0	0	0.7
Cooked, fried	45.7	298	31.5	15.4	5.9	–	1.5
Thigh						
Raw	75.5	128	18.1	5.6	0	0	0.8
Cooked, fried	55.8	237	29.1	11.4	2.5	–	1.2
Wing						
Raw	73.5	146	18.5	7.4	0	0	0.6
Cooked, fried	52.6	268	29.0	14.8	2.7	–	0.9

Source: U.S.D.A. Handbook No. 8.

In no case should storage temperature be higher than 0°F (–18°C). The humidity during storage is also important from the standpoint of drying of the carcass.

In contrast to the "fresh" unfrozen marketing of broilers, turkeys, ducks, and geese are invariably sold in the frozen form. This is primarily because of the seasonal nature of turkey and the regional nature of rearing ducks and geese.

Canning

The percentage of poultry used for canning varies between 5 and 7% for chicken and 10 and 15% for turkeys. A number of products are available in the canned form, including whole fowl, broiler and disjointed chicken packed in broth or gravy, boned poultry meat, turkey breasts, chicken liver products, chicken and noodles, chicken à la king, chicken stew, and several more. A large percentage of poultry meat, mainly fowl, is also used in various soups. The time and temperature for sterilization during the canning process will depend on type of product, size of the can, and previous treatment.

Dehydration

This preservation method is used mainly for dehydrated soup mixtures and chicken sandwiches. Recent advances in freeze-drying have been applied to poultry meat, and although some of these products are being manufactured today, high production costs are still a major factor in their availability.

Radiation

The use of cathode or gamma rays for the preservation of poultry has been the subject of much research and has a great potential because flavor and color changes are minimal. However, the FDA has not approved its use as of this date.

MERCHANDIZING OF POULTRY

Merchandizing of poultry has progressed from the selling of live birds, to New York dressed, to ready-to-cook poultry, the form in which it is sold at present. The availability of cut-up parts for portion and part control is the result of improved merchandizing techniques. In order to purchase cut-up poultry intelligently, it is necessary to know the proportions of the various parts of poultry. Tables 15.5 and 15.6 show the percentage distribution of cut-up parts of broilers, turkeys, ducks, and geese.

COOKING OF POULTRY

There are four basic procedures used for cooking poultry.

(1) **Broiling.**—Usually, the smallest broiler-fryers are selected for this method. The highest part of the chicken should be about 4 to 5 in. from the heat source. The chickens are generally brushed with seasoned butter or oil and the total cooking time is approximately 35 to 45 min.

(2) **Frying.**—Chicken of any weight can be used, and the carcass is usually cut into parts before cooking. Several variations, such as pan-frying, deep fat-frying or oven-frying can be used. Cooking times and temperatures vary with the method employed.

(3) **Roasting.**—Chickens, turkeys, ducks, and geese can be roasted, and may be cooked stuffed or unstuffed. The bird is generally oiled before cooking; no water is added to the pan and the bird is not covered. Covering the pan or wrapping in foil stews the bird rather than roasts it, and produces a steamed flavor, with unsatisfactory browning. Drying of the skin can be prevented by basting with the pan drippings. Recommended oven temperature is usually 325°F. In larger birds, a thermometer should be used as an indication of doneness. End points recommended are 185°F in the center of the breast, 190°F in the thigh muscle, and 165°F in the center of the stuffing. Temperatures as low as 200° to 250°F have been recommended for a juicier product, but it should be remembered that at this temperature the food remains a dangerously long time in a temperature range favorable to bacterial growth. Stuffing should be cooked separately.

(3a) **Roasting in Bag.**—This innovation has come into practice recently; it provides the convenience of no oven cleanups, and the manufacturers claim a juicier and more flavorful product.

(4) **Moist Heat.**—Older poultry such as fowl are generally cooked with moist heat. The poultry can be fricasseed (equivalent to braising), steamed, or simmered. Two to 3 hr are

required for fowl weighing 3 to 4 lb. Chicken cooked in this manner are the basis for a wide variety of other dishes such as salads, casseroles, creamed chicken, and sandwiches.

Table 15.7 shows the percentage yield of poultry cooked by different methods.

Commercial Cooking Procedures

During the last decade the broiler industry has experienced phenomenal growth, contributed to in large measure by the success of "take-out" restaurants such as Kentucky Fried Chicken, etc.

Although slightly different cooking procedures are used, the basic principle involves frying under pressure. K.F.C. uses 250°F for 15 min at 15-lb pressure; Henny Penny employs 325°F for 12 min at 9-lb pressure for cut-up broiler parts, while Broaster uses a much higher pressure, 30 lb. These processes are patented by the companies that developed them.

A second innovation has been the merchandizing of fully cooked prebrowned chicken. The processing involved in this method varies, but generally the major portion of the cooking is performed by steaming, deep fat-frying being used only for browning. This product is sold mainly in the frozen form, but merchandizing from the refrigerated meat cases would add greater convenience and could increase sales.

The third innovation involves the use of microwave cookery. This is being used by several commercial companies. Several researchers have shown the economic advantage of this method. The fast rate of cooking is the primary benefit, though there are conflicting reports on the improvement of juiciness.

A FEW TECHNOLOGICAL PROBLEMS

Although the problems in the processing and cooking of poultry are minimal, the following two are rather important and need discussion:

(1) *Darkening of the Bones.*—This is a discoloration that is often observed in cooked broilers which have been frozen when raw. Uncooked broilers will also show the darkening, but heating accentuates the color. It is due to the leakage of the internal contents of the long bones during freezing and

TABLE 15.5

PERCENTAGE DISTRIBUTION OF CUT-UP PARTS IN DIFFERENT SPECIES OF READY-TO-COOK POULTRY

Kinds	Number of Birds	Average Age, Weeks	Average Live Weight, Lb	Legs and Thighs, %	Breasts, %	Back and Ribs,[1] %	Wings, Neck, %	Gizzard, Liver, %	Heart, %
Broilers									
Male	10	10	3.9	34.1	25.4	17.0	13.3	3.5	2.6	0.6
Female	10	10	3.0	32.4	25.7	16.6	13.6	4.1	2.8	0.7
Turkeys Small									
Male	10	16	10.0	29.3	28.3	19.9	13.0	3.3	2.3	1.0
Female	10	16	7.0	29.0	29.9	20.0	12.0	3.7	2.1	0.4
Large									
Male	10	28	22.0	24.1	41.3	18.4	9.5	3.4	1.1	0.4
Female	10	28	14.0	25.5	35.5	20.6	11.3	2.4	1.6	0.3
Ducks									
Male	10	7.5	7.1	23.4	29.7	23.0	10.6	5.4	2.7	0.9
Female	10	7.5	6.3	23.5	30.1	23.6	10.8	4.7	2.5	0.9
Geese	20	10-12	10.8	21.9	23.8	21.3	16.0	6.3	3.5	0.9

[1]Ribs separated from breast and attached to back. Pelvic meat attached to thighs.
Source: Winter and Clements (1957).

TABLE 15.6

WEIGHTS OF THE SEVERAL PARTS OF VARIOUS KINDS OF POULTRY PROCESSED AT ONTARIO[3]

COMMERCIAL PROCESSING PLANTS

Kinds	Sex	Age Weeks	No. of Birds	Live	Hot-Dressed	Heads	Legs	Carcass and Neck	Hearts	Liver	Gizzard	Total	Total[1] Ready-to-Cook	Chilled[2] Carcass and Neck	Water Uptake in Cooling
										Giblets					
Chicken Broilers	M	8.5	105	3.8	3.5	0.1	0.2	2.7	0.02	0.08	0.07	0.17	2.9	2.7	0.02
	F	8.5	105	3.0	2.8	0.1	0.1	2.1	0.02	0.07	0.07	0.15	2.3	2.2	0.04
	M	10.6	100	5.4	5.1	0.1	0.2	4.0	0.02	0.10	0.08	0.21	4.2	4.1	0.13
	F	10.6	100	4.1	3.8	0.1	0.2	3.0	0.01	0.08	0.09	0.19	3.2	3.1	0.03
Capons		18.7	104	8.7	7.8	0.2	0.3	6.2	0.03	0.14	0.17	0.35	6.5	6.3	0.10
Turkeys,	M	26.0	100	27.0	25.0	0.5	0.4	20.8	0.11	0.51	0.34	0.96	21.7	21.6	0.80
B.B.W.	F	23.0	100	16.2	14.9	0.3	0.4	12.3	0.06	0.27	0.25	0.59	12.9	12.8	0.50
Broilers	M	16.4	100	12.0	10.8	0.4	0.4	9.1	0.05	0.15	0.17	0.38	9.5	9.6	0.50
B.B.W.	F	16.4	100	8.0	7.4	0.2	0.2	6.1	0.13[4]		0.12	0.25	6.4	6.4	0.30
Ducks	M	7.6	100	5.8	5.0	0.2	0.1	3.8	0.04	0.19	0.10	0.33	4.1	4.0	0.20
Pekin	F	7.6	100	5.5	4.7	0.2	0.1	3.6	0.04	0.17	0.10	0.31	3.9	3.7	0.10
Pheasants	M	21.0	79	3.1	2.8	0.1	0.1	2.3	0.01	0.05	0.05	0.13	2.5	2.4	0.10
	F	21.0	75	2.4	2.1	0.1	0.05	1.8	0.01	0.04	0.05	0.10	1.9	1.9	0.10

Average Weight, Lb

[1]Ready-to-Cook = carcass + neck + giblets
[2]Cooled by procedure prevailing in each plant.
[3]Under supervision of authors.
[4]Hearts and Livers.
Source: Snyder and Orr (1964), Ontario Agriculture College.

TABLE 15.7

PERCENTAGE YIELDS OF POULTRY COOKED
BY DIFFERENT METHODS[1]

Cooking Method	Average	Range
Chicken		
Broiled	74	82–62
Fricassee	82	82–81
Fried	79	83–74
Roasted	72	83–61
Stewed or braised	68	77–51
Turkey		
Roasted		
under 5 lb	79	82–73 without giblets
over 5 lb	72	82–56 without giblets
Boiled or stewed	71	74–68 without giblets
Steamed	69	75–65 without giblets
Pressure cooked	72	74–70 with giblets
Duck, not reported	82	85–74
Gosling, roasted	66	72–61

[1]Computed from ready-to-cook weights, U.S.D.A. Handbook No. 102.

thawing. The bones of the young birds at the time of slaughter
are generally quite porous, due to the lack of insufficient
deposition of calcium at this stage of development. When
the thawed frozen broilers are cooked the bone marrow material (hemoglobin) which has leaked out changes color, becoming dark. Although objectionable to some people, the eating
quality and nutritional value of the meat are unaffected. It
has been reported that this discoloration can be prevented
by microwave thawing of the frozen birds.

(2) *Shelf-life*.—Cooked poultry generally has a shorter shelf-
life than red meats and terms like "warmed up" flavor, and
"feathery" flavor have often been used to describe these
flavor changes. Two possible factors may contribute to this
off-flavor: (a) the presence of skin, which is edible in poultry
but is removed from red meat carcasses, and (b) the high
degree of unsaturated fatty acids in poultry fat which undergo
autooxidation more readily.

CHAPTER 16

D. V. Vadehra | Eggs

The use of eggs in human diet for their nutritional and functional properties was a diversification from the primary biological function of eggs for propagation of species. Because
of the latter role, the egg contents are well protected both
from within and outside. The exteriors (the cuticle, shell, and
its membrane) are often referred to as the first natural packaging material.

In this chapter, the formation, structure, chemical composition, grading, preservation, and functions of the egg will be
discussed. The term egg will be used to refer to the eggs of
domestic fowl (*Gallus gallus*). It may be worthwhile to point
out that the business of producing eggs is getting closer to an
industrial concept than farming. It is not unusual to find big
complexes producing a million eggs a day. Not too many other
industries can match production figures of 200,000,000 units
(eggs) per day!

FORMATION OF THE EGG

The reproductive system of the hen consists of the ovary and
an oviduct. The formation of an egg takes 25 to 27 hr; during
this period the ovary provides yolk, while the oviduct secretes
albumen, shell membranes, shell, and the cuticle (Fig. 16.1).

The ovary is a cluster of developing yolk much like a bunch
of grapes. The left ovary (right ovary is nonfunctional) is
fully formed when the chick is hatched and contains approximately 3600 to 4000 minute ova, each with its own sac or follicle. The formation of yolk takes place in three stages; the first
stage is completed before the chick hatches; the second is
completed within 8 to 10 days before sexual maturity; the
third involves accelerated growth of the yolk. As much as
2.8 gm of yolk is added per day during the maximal growth
period. The yolk is completely mature approximately 2 days
before ovulation. Ovulation is the process of release of mature

358

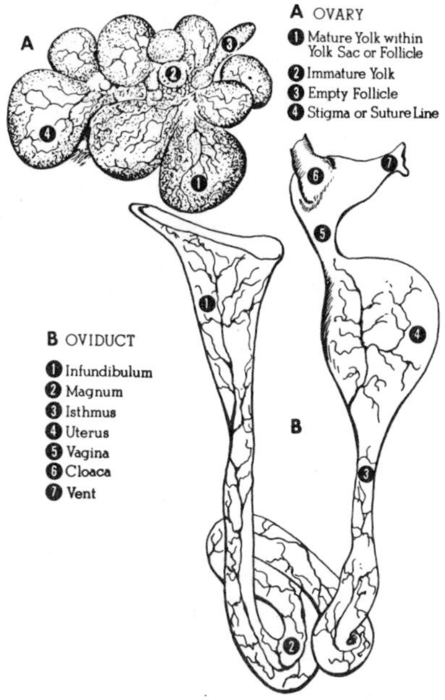

A OVARY
❶ Mature Yolk within Yolk Sac or Follicle
❷ Immature Yolk
❸ Empty Follicle
❹ Stigma or Suture Line

B OVIDUCT
❶ Infundibulum
❷ Magnum
❸ Isthmus
❹ Uterus
❺ Vagina
❻ Cloaca
❼ Vent

FIG. 16.1. ENLARGED DRAW-INGS OF A, OVARY, B, OVI-DUCT

yolk (ovum) by the ovary. The yolk sac is well supplied with blood vessels, but there is an area called stigma or suture line which is devoid of blood vessels. It is in this area that the ovulation takes place. In a good-laying hen ovulation takes place 30 min after the fully developed egg is laid.

The formation of other egg structures takes place in the oviduct, a long (25 to 27-in.) tube-like organ lying along the backbone. The oviduct may be divided into 5 parts according to their functions.

The first part is the *infundibulum*, about 3 to 4 in. long and often called funnel because of its shape. The infundibulum opens into the body cavity; when ovulation occurs, it engulfs the yolk and triggers the mechanism for the formation of the egg. The infundibulum also serves as a reservoir of male spermatozoa which fertilizes the germ. The yolk moves on to the next part in about 15 min by means of peristaltic action.

The second part, the *magnum*, is about 15 in. long. The thick white which comprises 55% of the total egg white is secreted in this portion of the oviduct. This process requires about 3 hr. The quality of albumen is largely determined by the amount of ovomucin secreted in this part of the oviduct.

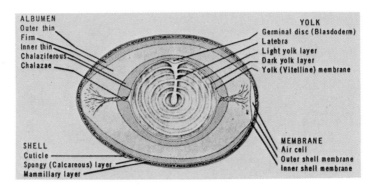

FIG. 16.2.   THE PARTS OF AN EGG

The third part is the *isthmus*, which is a constricted area about 4 in. long. The two shell membranes, together with some water and minerals, are secreted in this part. The developing egg passes through this part in $1\frac{1}{4}$ hr.

The fourth part is the *uterus*. This is the thickest part of the oviduct and is approximately 4 in. long. The final complement of the egg white and the minerals pass through the membranes by osmotic pressure; the shell, the shell pigments and the cuticle are secreted in this part. It takes about 19 to 21 hr for the completion of these activities in the uterus.

Finally, the egg moves through the vagina (2 in.), cloaca, and the vent from which it is laid. Within 1 hr another ovulation takes place and the whole process is started over again.

STRUCTURE OF THE EGG

The formation of the various components of the egg has been discussed above. This section will deal with their chemical nature and properties (Fig. 16.2).

The outermost layer of the egg is the *cuticle* ("bloom") which is believed to be a mucoprotein (a conjugated protein with a carbohydrate moiety). The cuticle plays an important role in preventing the microbial spoilage of eggs. Cuticle is also believed to retard the escape of carbon dioxide and thus preserve the internal quality of eggs. There is considerable controversy in regard to the role of cuticle in washed eggs and as to whether or not commercial egg-washing procedures remove this important structure.

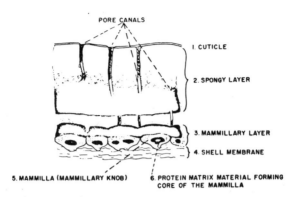

FIG. 16.3.   MAGNIFIED RADIAL SECTION THROUGH THE SHELL

The *shell* is the next structure and is made up of two layers:
(1) the mamillary layer, and (2) the spongy layer. The mamillary layer, so-called because of its shape, consists of calcite
crystals which are set perpendicular to the surface of the
shell. The spongy layer is also made up of calcite, but the
crystals are much smaller and are less oriented for the most
part except at the surface. The shell is 300 to 340 μ thick
$(1 \ \mu = 10^{-6}$ meter), and is *very* porous (7,000 to 8,000 pores
per egg). These pores are generally funnel-shaped and allow
the exchange of gases (Fig. 16.3).

The *membranes*, which are tough and fibrous, lie beneath
the shell, and are made up of proteins, lipids and carbohydrates. The membrane proteins are insoluble in most solvents
and have been thought to be very similar to the hair proteins
(keratins). However, their exact nature is not yet known. The
two membranes, often referred to as the outer and inner shell
membranes, adhere to each other except at the blunt end of
the egg, where they separate to form the air cell. The air cell
is produced only on storage and is not present in eggs at the
time of laying. The outer shell membrane thickness is approximately 5 times that of the inner shell membrane. Nutritionally, these membranes are not an important factor,
but from the ecological standpoint, disposal of the shells from
commercial egg-breaking plants is becoming a problem.

Egg white, constituting about 58% of the weight of the egg,
is made up of 4 well recognized layers. The *outer thin layer*
lies next to the membranes except at the two ends of the egg,

and constitutes about 21% of the albumen. The *thick or firm layer* is attached to the shell membrane at each end of the egg. It holds the inner thin white and the yolk. This layer is the most important factor in egg quality for it gives the albumen its gel or firm structure. The thick white makes up approximately 55% of the albumen. The *inner thin layer* surrounds the fourth layer and represents 21% of the total albumen. The *chalaziferous layer* surrounds the egg yolk and is continuous with the chalazae cords. This is a very firm but thin layer and comprises only 3% of the albumen.

The *chalazae* are continuous with the chalaziferous layer of albumen; to the visual eye these look like ropy cords. They are produced from the ovomucin during the spiral movement of the egg through the oviduct.

The *vitelline membrane,* also referred to as the yolk membrane, gives shape and integrity to the yolk. It also supports the germ cell (blasdoderm) and the chalaza cord. The permeability of this membrane may be affected during storage which allows inward movement of the moisture and contents of the albumen.

The yolk consists of a *latebra, germinal disc*—concentric rings of yolk material surrounded by the yolk membranes. Yolk is rich in fatty substances and constitutes 31% of the egg.

EGG ABNORMALITIES

The formation of the egg is a complex phenomenon involving several physiological activities in the bird. In nature, there are always some slips, which result in the formation of abnormal eggs. Some of the abnormalities and their causes are discussed below:

Blood Spots.—As the name suggests, small accumulation of red blood cells in the albumen are produced when the egg does not break at the stigma and one or more of the blood vessels is ruptured.

Meat Spots.—These are reddish-brown, brown, or tan spots resulting from either (a) sloughed tissue from the reproductive organs, or (b) chemical oxidation of the blood spots.

Double-yolked Eggs.—These occur as the result of release of two yolks at one time; it can also be due to pick-up of the "lost" yolk from the previous ovulation day.

TABLE 16.1
GROSS CHEMICAL COMPOSITION OF THE
MAJOR COMPONENTS OF THE EGG

Component	% of Total	Water	Protein	Fat	Ash
Whole egg	100	65.5	11.8	11.0	11.7
White	58	88.0	11.0	0.2	0.8
Yolk	31	48.0	17.5	32.5	2.0
		$CaCO_3$	$MgCO_3$	$Ca_3(PO_4)_2$	Organic matter
Shell (including cuticle)	11	94.0%	1.0%	1.0%	4.0%

TABLE 16.2
SOME STANDARD DIMENSIONS OF THE AVERAGE EGG

Weight	58.0 gm
Volume	53.0 cc
Specific gravity	1.09
Long axis	5.7 cm
Short axis	4.2 cm
Long circumference	15.7 cm
Short circumference	13.5 cm
Surface area	68.0 cm^2

Yolk-less Eggs.—The release of the ovum is under hormonal control, while the secretion of the other egg parts are both hormonal and stimulating. Sometimes the sloughed material from the ovary or oviduct stimulates these secretions, and this results in the production of an egg without any yolk.

Shell-less Eggs.—This is due to some stress (disease) which prevents the eggs from staying in the uterus for a long enough period to complete the secretions and deposition of shell material.

Other abnormalities like thin-shell eggs, off-color, and off-flavor eggs are mostly due to disease or feed.

CHEMICAL COMPOSITION

From the human consumption standpoint, egg white and egg yolk are the only important components and these will be discussed in detail (Tables 16.1 and 16.2).

TABLE 16.3

DISTRIBUTION OF VARIOUS INDIVIDUAL
PROTEINS IN EGG WHITE

Constituent	% of Dry Weight, Albumen
Ovalbumin	54
Conalbumin	13
Ovomucoid	11
Lysozyme	3.5
Ovomucin	1.5
Uncharacterized proteins	8.0
Flavoproteins	0.8
Ovoinhibitor	0.1
Avidin	0.05
Nonprotein material	8.0

Egg White

Egg white is an important biological and nutritional part
of the egg and is made up almost entirely of water, proteins,
vitamins, and traces of lipids. The carbohydrates are generally
bound to the proteins. The albumen has 5 major protein constituents and 7 to 9 minor constituents, each of which has an
interesting biological activity. Except for the amount of ovomucin, the 4 layers of egg white are very similar in composition and contain all the component proteins. Table 16.3 gives
an approximate distribution of various proteins in egg white.

Ovalbumin.—Ovalbumin is the major component; it plays an
important role in the foaming, coagulation, and characteristic
texture and color of egg white. It contains sulfhydryl groups
which upon heating produce hydrogen sulfide and other sulfur-
containing compounds which give the characteristic "egg"
flavor.

Conalbumin.—Conalbumin is the second most abundant protein
of egg white; it is characterized by its ability to bind metal
ions. One molecule of conalbumin will bind two atoms of Fe^{+++},
Cu^{++} or Zn^{++} to form rust-red, greenish-yellow and colorless
complexes. This property is important because the metal-
protein complex is more resistant to heat and enzymatic denaturation. This metal-binding ability also gives conalbumin

antibacterial property, particularly against the organisms that require these metal ions for growth.

Ovomucoid.—This protein, which makes up 10 to 11% of albumen, can be distinguished from others by its high carbohydrate content (20 to 22%), its high heat stability (75° to 100°C does not cause coagulation), and its resistance to precipitation by acids. Ovomucoid possesses an important antitryptic biological activity which was of concern to nutritionists until it was observed that chicken ovomucoid is not specific for human trypsin.

Lysozyme (Muramidase).—This is probably the best-characterized protein of egg white, as its primary, secondary, and tertiary structure is now known. It can be identified by its basic isoelectric point (pH 10.7) and antibacterial properties. Lysozyme attacks N-acetylglycosamine linkages in the cell wall of gram-positive organisms, thus causing lysis of the bacteria. It has been shown that most gram-positive bacteria contain large amounts of this substrate and therefore are more susceptible to lysis by lysozyme. This explains why the spoilage of eggs is due to gram-negative bacteria. Since lysozyme is a basic protein, it has a tendency to complex with other proteins of the albumen, particularly, ovomucin. Such a complex with ovomucin has been used to describe the gel structure of thick egg white.

Ovomucin.—This is a glycoprotein, characterized by its precipitation by dilution of egg white with several volumes of water. It can also be precipitated by lowering the pH to 4.0 or below. Ovomucin is generally believed to be an important part of the gel structure of egg white and is also the major component of the chalazae cords. Recently, it has been shown that this protein has antihemagglutination properties against viruses, which are probably due to the high percentage of sialic acid in this protein.

Minor Protein Constituents.—*Avidin.* This protein binds biotin (one of the B vitamins), giving avidin antibacterial properties.

Ovoinhibitor. This protein can be distinguished on the basis of its action against trypsin and other bacterial and fungal proteases.

Flavoprotein. This protein binds riboflavin and gives the characteristic greenish color to egg white.

Globulins and other minor constituents have not been fully characterized in terms of their functional properties.

Egg Yolk

Egg yolk contains proteins, lipids and water in approximately a 1:2:3 ratio, all of which is in the form of macromolecules (large molecules). Yolk is the primary source of nutrients for the developing embryo during incubation and several hours after hatching. Most of the lipids and proteins in the yolk occur as conjugated moieties called lipoproteins. The lipoproteins of egg yolk are generally divided into low-density (containing large amounts of lipids) and high-density. Some important lipoproteins are lipovitellin and lipovitellenin. These lipoproteins contain lecithin as an important lipid fraction and contribute significantly to its emulsifying properties. The lipid-free proteins include livetin and phosvitin. In addition, egg yolk contains significant percentages of cholesterol, which is also important in the functional properties of yolk and perhaps in health. The yellow color of the yolk is due to the pigment xanthophyll.

NUTRITIONAL PROPERTIES OF EGG

An average chicken egg weighs 57 to 58 gm (2 oz). It is a very good source of high-quality proteins, minerals, and vitamins. The proteins of egg contains all the essential amino acids in well-balanced proportions. The albumen also contain water-soluble vitamins, particularly riboflavin, which is responsible for the greenish color of the albumen.

Egg yolk is rich in lipids, which are a source of energy. The yolk contains most all vitamins except C. Egg yolk is also rich in minerals, particularly iron, phosphorus, sulfur, and copper, as well as potassium, sodium, magnesium, calcium, and manganese.

There are some common misgivings in regard to the nutritional and functional qualities of brown and white eggs. As far as it can be ascertained from the literature, there are no differences in the overall properties of the two, except that brown eggs have a greater amount of the pigment ovoporphyrin in the shell. The differences in their preference

are due to the background of consumer rather than to actual
nutritional differences. Also, it may be worth while to mention the differences between fertile and unfertile eggs. Once
again, there are no major differences; however, it is possible
that there may be slight differences due to the type of feed
used for the breeding hen.

GRADING OF EGGS

Grading in general may be defined as the sorting of products
according to quality, size, weight, and other factors that determine their relative monetary value. Eggs are no exception,
and shell eggs are graded into different classes according to
established government standards. The U.S. standards are
based on the following factors: (1) Exterior factors, (a) cleanliness, (b) soundness of the shell; (2) Interior factors, (a) condition of the albumen, (b) condition of the yolk, (c) size and
condition of air cell.

Eggs are also classified according to weight; even though
they are generally sold by the dozen, they still have to meet
fairly narrow weight requirements (Table 16.4).

Color of eggs is not a consideration in classification; however, it is an important marketing factor. Eggs are packaged
and sold separately by color rather than in mixed colors.

An important fact to keep in mind is the difference between
class of eggs based on weight and grade of eggs based on
quality. Medium eggs weighing less could still be A or AA
grade. Another point to remember is that there are no great
differences in the qualitative nutritional value of different
grades; however, the functional quality changes considerably.
Grade B eggs can be easily used in cookery, where appearance
of the egg *per se* is not a factor, while higher grades are
generally used for poached, fried, and boiled eggs.

Exterior Quality Factors

The shape of the egg has to conform to more or less the
ideal shape; eggs which do not do so are down-graded. Some
of the common unusual shapes of eggs include eggs with ridges,
rough areas, and thin spots. These abnormalities usually result from disease (physical condition) or malnutrition. The

TABLE 16.4

U.S. WEIGHT CLASSES FOR CONSUMER
GRADES FOR SHELL EGGS

Size or Weight Class	Minimum Net Weight per Dozen, oz	Minimum Net Weight per 30 Dozen, lb	Minimum Weight for Individual Eggs at Rate per dozen, oz
Jumbo	30	56	29
Extra large	27	50-1/2	26
Large	24	45	23
Medium	21	39-1/2	20
Small	18	34	17
Peewee	15	28	

term "body check" is often used to refer to eggs which have a rough surface. This is generally due to an *in vivo* (in the body) crack which has repaired itself by recalcification. The three terms often used in grading include: practically normal (Quality AA and A), slightly abnormal (Quality B), and abnormal (Quality C). The terms check and leaker are used to describe the condition of the membranes and shell. A check has a cracked shell but the membranes are intact, while in a leaker both the membrane and shells are broken; these are regarded as condemned. Another factor is shell cleanliness. The terms clean (Quality AA and A), slightly stained (Quality B), moderate stain (Quality C), and dirty are used for this classification.

Classification of Internal Quality

This quality is judged on the basis of: (a) candling; (b) Haugh units; (c) less commonly used indicators: (1) albumen index; (2) yolk index.

Candling.—This is done automatically, semiautomatically, and by hand. Basically, in candling one holds the egg with the large end up and rotates it in front of a high-intensity lamp in a dark room. Shadow and mobility of the yolk, size of air cell, and presence of blood or meat spots can be seen

by an experienced candler. Some of these will be discussed
briefly.

Air Cell.—The air cell is a measure of quality; the table
below illustrates some of the specifications.

Quality	Depth	Movement
AA	1/8 in.	2/8 in.
A	3/16 in.	2/8 in.
B	3/8 in.	May be free or bubbly
C	No limit	No limit

Descriptive terms used are: Practically regular (AA, A),
free air cell (B), bubbly air cell (C).

Yolk and White.—Appearance of the yolk when the egg is
twirled during candling is considered as one of the best indicators of internal quality. The appearance of the yolk is
dependent mostly on the condition of the albumen, particularly
its thickness; however, the following factors are also important (Tables 16.5 and 16.6): (1) Distinctness of yolk shadow
outline; (2) Size and shape of yolk; (3) Defects and germ development.

Internal quality based on the breakout method. Two important
procedures are used: (1) U.S.D.A. breakout standards; (2)
Haugh units.

U.S.D.A. breakfast grades can be best shown by a diagram
(Fig. 16.4). The primary considerations are the height and
the spreading of the albumen.

Haugh Units.—This is probably the best objective measure of
egg quality. It has been well accepted both in research and
industry as an important procedure. It includes the weighing
of eggs, followed by breaking with the sharp edge of a knife
and determining the height of albumen. These data are used
to calculate Haugh units based on the following equation:

$$\text{H.U.} = 100 \log \left[\frac{H - \sqrt{g}\,(30W^{0.37} - 100)}{100} + 1.9 \right]$$

which can be simplified to give H.U. $= 100 \log (H + 7.57 -
1.7W^{0.37})$. H = height of thick albumen in millimeters; W =
weight of egg in gm, g is the gravitational constant.

Haugh units have been found to have a good correlation
with U.S.D.A. grades; however, sometimes the relation-

TABLE 16.5

SUMMARY OF UNITED STATES STANDARDS FOR QUALITY OF INDIVIDUAL SHELL EGGS

Specifications for Each Quality Factor

Quality Factor	AA Quality	A Quality	B Quality	C Quality
Shell	Clean unbroken, practically normal	Clean unbroken, practically normal	Clean; to very slightly stained, unbroken, may be slightly abnormal	Clean, to moderately stained, unbroken, may be abnormal
Air Cell	1/8 in. or less in depth Practically regular	3/16 in. or less in depth Practically regular	3/8 in. or less in depth May be free or bubbly	May be over 3/8 in. in depth May be free or bubbly
White	Clear, Firm (72 Haugh units or higher)	Clear, may be reasonably firm (60 to 72 Haugh units)	Clear, may be slightly weak (31 to 60 Haugh units)	May be weak and watery, small blood clots or spots may be present[1] (less than 31 Haugh units)
Yolk	Outline slightly defined, practically free from defects	Outline may be fairly well defined, practically free from defects	Outline may be well defined May be slightly enlarged and flattened, may show definite but not serious defects	Outline may be plainly visible, may be enlarged and flattened, may show clearly visible germ development but no blood, may show other serious defects

[1]If they are small (aggregating not more than 1/8 in. in diameter).

TABLE 16.6

SUMMARY OF U.S. CONSUMER GRADES FOR SHELL EGGS

	Quality Required	Tolerance Permitted	
		%	Quality
U.S. Consumer Grade (origin)			
Grade AA or Fresh Fancy Quality	85% AA	Up to 15	A
		Not over 5	B, C, or check
Grade A	85% A or better	Up to 15	B
		Not over 5	C or check
Grade B	85% B or better	Not over 10	Checks
U.S. Consumer grade (destination)			
Grade AA or Fresh Fancy Quality	80% AA	Up to 20	A
		Not over 5	B, C, or check
		Not over 0.5	Leakers or dirties
Grade A	80% A or better	Up to 20	B
		Not over 5	C or check
		Not over 0.5	Leakers or dirties
Grade B	80% B or better	Up to 20	C
		Not over 10	Checks
		Not over 0.5	Leakers or dirties

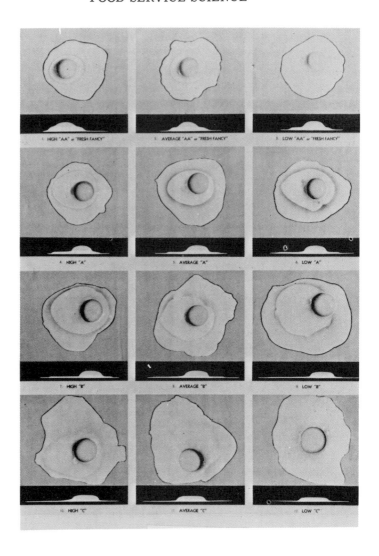

FIG. 16.4. INTERIOR QUALITY OF EGGS

The pictures on this chart show the interior quality of eggs that meet the specifications of the United States Standards for Quality of Individual Shell Eggs with respect to albumen and yolk quality. Quality factors dealing with the shell, air cell, and defects are not included. Scores 1, 2, and 3 represent the appearance of broken-out eggs of high, average, and low AA Quality or Fresh Fancy Quality; 4, 5, and 6 represent high, average, and low A Quality; 7, 8, and 9, high, average, and low B Quality, and 10, 11, and 12, high, average, and low C Quality.

TABLE 16.7

NUMBER OF WHOLE EGG, WHITES AND YOLKS PER CUP

	Number per Cup		
Size	Whole Egg	Whites	Yolks
Extra large	4	6	12
Large	5	7	14
Medium	6	8	16
Small	7	10	18

ships found with candling are not straight-line in nature. Also, the temperature of the eggs should be kept as close to a selec- ted narrow range as possible (7° to 15°C). Generally one does not use the above equations for calculations because charts and slide rules are available for this purpose (Table 16.7).

STORAGE AND PRESERVATION OF EGGS

The quality of egg decreases almost linearily with storage. However, the degree, extent and the rate of decrease in quality depends on temperature, humidity, and other atmo- spheric conditions. The apparent results of storage are de- crease in egg weight, increase in the size of air cell, de- crease in the albumen quality as evidenced by breakdown of the gel structures, and decrease in Haugh units. There is also an increase in the pH of the albumen.

Changes in the Air Cell.—The increase in the size of the air cell is due to evaporation of moisture, which induces changes in the height, diameter, and volume of the cell. At constant temperature and humidity these changes are a function of time.

Changes in the Albumen.—The first visual change in the albumen is loss of gel structure, such that the broken-out egg will spread over a large area. This thinning is a chemical phenomenon involving interactions of the albumen proteins (mucin, lysozyme). These changes affect the functional quality of the eggs considerably. It has been reported that thinning of the albumen also affects the flavor of the egg.

Changes in Yolk.—The yolk is covered by the vitellin membrane, and the changes in size, shape, and color of the yolk are governed considerably by changes in this membrane. As the egg ages, the permeability of the vitellin membrane increases; this allows passage of water, minerals, and certain protein components from the albumen into the yolk. The yolk index (yolk height/yolk width) shows a decrease. The changes are time- and temperature-dependent. In very old eggs, the yolk membrane may even break.

Changes in pH.—The pH of the albumen of the egg as it is laid is 7.6. On storage, the albumen of the egg white becomes more alkaline; within a week (depending on storage conditions) it may become as high as 9.7, and generally remains constant at that value. This increase in pH of the albumen is due to loss of carbon dioxide from the egg. Besides containing free dissolved carbon dioxide, the albumen has dissolved bicarbonate of sodium and potassium, which also act as sources of carbon dioxide. There are also changes in the pH of the yolk, but these are less drastic and are generally attributed to albumen. The pH of the yolk changes from 6.0 to 6.8 on storage.

PRESERVATION OF EGGS

The main objective of preserving eggs is to delay chemical and microbiological changes during storage. This is important from both a marketing and public health safety point of view. The preservation methods rely chiefly on temperature and humidity controls. The lower the temperature of storage, the longer the shelf-life. A relative humidity between 80 and 85% is considered ideal. Higher humidity values favor the growth of molds and lower humidity increase the loss of moisture.

The sealing of eggs with oil and other inert material has been extensively studied, and is a recommended procedure for increasing shelf-life. The eggs are either dipped or sprayed with an oil that must be colorless, odorless, and tasteless. Mineral oil is generally used because it meets these criteria. The oil retards the escape of carbon dioxide. The work done in our laboratory indicates that the quality of eggs can be preserved even at room temperature if the eggs are covered with an impermeable film which creates a microenvironment of carbon dioxide around the egg.

Thermostabilization of Eggs. This procedure is almost a
century old and is based on the principle of stabilizing the
interior quality of the egg by application of heat. Oil is generally the heating medium and the temperature varies between
55° and 58°C, the times of exposure varying between 10 and
15 min depending on temperature. In addition to oil, water
has also been used as the heating medium. The general time-
temperature relationship recommended is $1\frac{1}{2}$ min at 65.5°C,
or 15 min at 54.5°C. In either procedure, thermostabilization
produces a thin layer of coagulated albumen next to the inner
shell membrane, which closes the pores and thus prevents
escape of carbon dioxide. This procedure also retards microbial spoilage.

The old classic methods of dry packaging in materials such
as sawdust, wood ashes, bran, etc., and immersion in liquids
like borax, brine, lime water, and others are quite out of date;
however, water glass (sodium silicate) is still used in several
parts of the world.

Liquid Eggs

Preservation.—The methods of preservation discussed so
far apply to the preservation of shell eggs. However, in recent years a considerable percentage of eggs have been used
in liquid form. Liquid eggs are generally sold in the frozen
form; the new food laws dictate that all liquid eggs shall be
pasteurized before freezing.

Pasteurization.—There is still some confusion concerning
the exact time-temperature relationship for pasteurization of
liquid egg. However, 60°C for $3\frac{1}{2}$ min is considered a safe
limit. Pasteurization of yolk, albumen, whole egg, sugared
and salted eggs requires different heating temperatures and
time combinations.

Freezing.—There are no definite recommendations on the
freezing temperatures for the preservation of the functional
properties of egg on thawing. As far as can be ascertained
from the literature, freezing does not affect the functional
properties. However, an important physical change in terms
of increases in viscosity takes place in the egg yolk on freezing. This is often referred to as gelation, a complex phenomenon involving physicochemical changes in the proteins, lipids,

and water in the egg yolk. Addition of salt or sugar prevents the increase in viscosity. Other agents such as glucose, fructose, glycerol, and proteolytic enzymes have also been used for preventing gelation.

Drying.—Dehydration technology has made considerable advances from the earlier pan-drying and roller-drying procedures. At the present time, most egg solids are dried by spray-drying. In addition, the foam mat-drying and freeze-drying procedures are under study by some commercial concerns. Most of the liquid egg white is first desugared to remove glucose before drying. This prevents browning of the final product.

FUNCTIONAL PROPERTIES OF EGGS

Although the use of eggs in foods is based on their excellent nutritional properties, their functional properties cannot be overlooked. The functional properties are: (1) coagulation, (2) foaming, (3) emulsification, (4) browning, (5) binding.

Coagulation.—The coagulating properties of eggs on heating are primarily due to the ovalbumin and conalbumin of egg white and the yolk proteins. Some coagulation of albumen can be seen at 57°C, but only after long periods of heating. Visible coagulation begins at 60°C and egg albumen begins to thicken to a gel as the temperature approaches 62°C. At 70°C, the mass, although firm, is still tender, but at higher temperatures it becomes very firm. The yolk coagulates at a somewhat higher temperature than the albumen. The coagulation gives firmness to breakfast eggs, thickness to custards and pie fillings, and plays an important role in cream puffs and cakes. In addition to heat coagulation, eggs can be coagulated by acid, alkali, and salts. The incorporation of air, as in foaming, also causes surface coagulation. Chemically, the coagulation is due to the interchange of chemical bonds, particularly the sulfhydryl groups. Over-coagulation (higher temperatures, longer heating times) can cause exudation, or tough white, and textural problems in processed foods. Some important examples of coagulation in cooking eggs are poaching, frying, baking, scrambling; also in soufflés and custards.

Foaming.—The effectiveness of eggs as leavening agents depends on the amount of air incorporated and retained by them. Since egg yolk generally produces low foams, egg white is used more commonly than either egg yolk or whole egg. Such foams are used in puffy omelets, souffles, meringues, short cakes, angel food cakes, and sponge cakes. The factors which influence the foaming ability of eggs include age of the egg, quantity of egg white, speed and extent of whipping, and finally the type of additive. It has been commonly accepted that cream of tartar increases the stability of foam. The presence of egg yolk or any other oil (fat) decreases the foam volume considerably. Salts also appear to decrease the volume. The extent of heating as well as determining its use for a particular type of product is very important. On heating, the incorporated air extends slightly and then the albumen on the surface of the air coagulates, thus entrapping the air and giving the product a characteristic texture.

Emulsification.—This property is attributed to the lecithins of the egg yolk. The chief use of yolk as an emulsifying agent is in the manufacture of mayonnaise, which is an emulsion of oil, vinegar (acetic acid solution), and seasoning. Besides stabilizing the emulsion the yolk increases the nutritional properties of mayonnaise.

Browning.—The use of eggs in batters and dips is very common. The eggs help brown the foods by means of the Maillard reaction.

Binding.—The use of eggs in meat loaves utilizes this property. This adhesiveness is also used in the pharmaceutical industry.

Clarification.—Clarification of broths and consommés with eggs has been practiced by chefs for many years.

Table 16.8 summarizes the industrial uses of eggs.

Microbiology of Eggs.—Shell eggs are well protected by barriers like the cuticle, the shell, and the two membranes. However, care should be exercised during storage and handling to prevent any contamination. This is extremely important from a public health standpoint, particularly in regard to *Salmonella*. In general, *Salmonella* are fairly heat-sensitive organisms and are killed by 3 to 4 min heat treatments at 60°C. As the growth of microorganisms in the egg is governed by temperature, the lower the storage temperature, the better are the chances of preventing spoilage caused by microorganisms. In general, intact raw eggs have longer shelf-life than cooked products because of the presence of antibacterial sub-

TABLE 16.8

ıUSAGE OF EGGS AND EGG

COMPONENTS IN UNITED STATES

Type	Principal User	% of Total
Whole egg		
Frozen	B, I	31.5
Dried	B, I, M	19.0
		50.5
Albumen		
Frozen	B, C	12.2
Dried	B, C, M	16.4
		28.6
Yolk		
Frozen salted	S	6.9
Frozen sugared	B, D	5.3
Frozen plain	B, N	4.6
Dried	M	4.4
		21.2

[1] Based on 1966 statistics: B = bakeries; I = institutions; M = dry mix manufacturers; C = confectioners; N = noodles; S = salad dressing and mayonnaise; D = dairy and baby food. The manufacturing uses (dyes, synthetics, etc.) and medical uses (pharmacology and bacteriology) are relatively small.

stances, including lysozyme, conalbumin, and avidin. However, if contaminated by gram-negative organisms, fresh eggs can spoil.

A FEW IMPORTANT INDUSTRIAL PROBLEMS

Peeling Hard-cooked Eggs.—The shell does not peel free from the cooked white, it is difficult to remove and often takes part of the cooked white. The exact cause of this problem is not known, but it is most commonly seen with fresh eggs. It is probably due to electrostatic bonds between the membrane and the albumen. The best prevention method is to let the eggs stand at room temperature for 18 to 24 hr before boiling. Other methods suggested, including addition of vinegar, cracking at the air cell, etc., have disadvantages.

Brownish Discoloration of Cooked Egg Whites.—This is the amino-sugar type of browning where the glucose of the egg white combines with the amino acids of the albumen. It occurs generally in older eggs where the breakdown of the albumen has started. The eggs invariably have been heated for longer periods of time than recommended or have been kept at the steam tables for long periods. Prevention includes cooling the eggs as fast as possible after heating.

Greenish-black Discoloration of Yolk.—This is a common occurrence in old eggs. In simple terms, there is a chemical reaction between the hydrogen sulfide produced from the albumen and the iron of the yolk producing iron sulfide, which has a greenish-black color. Prevention involves the use of fresh eggs and the quick thorough cooling of hard cooked eggs after cooking. In liquid eggs used for scrambling, this reaction can also take place, especially when eggs are left on the steam table. Addition of small amounts of vinegar will prevent this discoloration.

Gelation of Egg Yolk.—This is caused by freezing of yolk and can be easily prevented by the addition of salt or sugar depending on their later usage.

Mushy Albumen.—Not a very common complaint, but it is mostly found in fresh eggs.

Large Milky Whites.—This defect generally occurs in very fresh eggs due to entrapment of carbon dioxide.

There are a number of other problems, which are summarized in Table 16.9.

NEW EGG PRODUCTS

Cornell University has been actively engaged in the development of new egg and poultry products for over a decade. Over 39 products were developed, 24 of which have been market-tested. Below is a selected list based primarily on success of the product and the degree of innovation. Some of these products were modified from those generally made at home to introduce convenience, while others were entirely new concepts.

Instant French Toast.—This product contained $\frac{1}{2}$ egg per slice and was sold already cooked and frozen. The only preparation required by the consumer was to heat the product in a toaster for several minutes. High-protein bread was used to prevent buckling in the center when grilling before freezing.

TABLE 16.9

OFF-ODORS AND FLAVORS IN EGGS

Material Used	Effect on Eggs	Remarks
Insecticides		
BHC	Taste and smell like BHC	*Do not use*
Malathion (liquid)	Taste and smell like cat urine	If needed, use at night—chemical carrier used may influence
Ronnel (Korlon)	Bad chemical taste and smell	*Do not use*
Sevin (wettable)	Slight bitter taste, especially in albumen	Do not spray on eggs
Packing material		
Moldy, dirty, damp filler-flats	Musty, cardboard smell and taste	Definitely will cause trouble. Oil keeps filler-flats damp for mold growth
Petroleum products		
Oil not fully refined	Chemical smell and flavor	Make sure that egg oil is odorless, tasteless, and colorless (approved)
Kerosene	Taste and smell like kerosene	Avoid kerosene fumes
Gasoline	Taste and smell like gasoline	Avoid gasoline fumes
Sanitizer-detergents		
Chlorine products (concentrated)	Slight bitter taste and chemical smell of chlorine gas trapped in	Follow directions of manufacturers
Products used in rinse		
Chlorine products similar to Clorox (concentrated)	Bitter taste and chemical smell	Follow directions of manufacturer. Be sure the product is being dispensed properly

Destainers		
Citric acid	Slight off-flavor if held in destainer too long	Follow direction of manufacturer
Apples		
All varieties (some worse than others)	Bad bitter, cardboard flavor and odor	*Do not* allow eggs to be stored near apples
Vegetables and citrus fruits		
Most vegetables and citrus fruits	Most vegetables and citrus fruits will import flavor and odor to eggs	Do not store eggs with citrus fruit or vegetables
Hen house odors		
Fumes of chicken manure	Possible to pick up odors and flavor if fumes strong and eggs are not gathered frequently	If odors bad, should gather eggs three times a day
Odors in egg room	Musty odors, etc., will be picked up by eggs	Keep egg rooms clean and free of odors

Source: Baker, R. C. 1964. Cornell Poultry Extension.

Hard-cooked Egg Roll.—This item enjoyed great success at the institutional level. The roll was prepared by sealing one end of a polypropylene tube, filling with four large broken-out eggs, then clipping shut. The rolls were cooked in water at 92°C for 20 min. Two day-old eggs are best for this product, because they are old enough for the albumen to be firm after cooking, and fresh enough so that the yolk will center in the roll.

Tren.—This was a beverage from apple juice and eggs. One 8-oz glass of Tren contained one egg, with sugar and malic acid added to provide tanginess. This product appealed to children especially.

Other egg products developed included frozen chiffon pies, 500-Calorie pies, frozen western egg, high protein cookies, and several others.

NEW POULTRY PRODUCTS

Chicken Sticks.—This product was made from raw stewing chicken. The ground meat was mixed with a binder and seasonings, formed, and then frozen. The frozen product was dipped in an egg batter and then rolled in corn flake crumbs.

Chicken Emulsion Products.—Several products were developed using chicken meat emulsions, including chicken franks (Bird Dogs), chicken bologna, and chick-a-lona (an uncured bologna). These products had good acceptance and are now being sold in several regions.

Poulet Supreme, Chicken Chunk Roll, and Chunk-a-lona.—These products are made from an emulsion similar to chick-a-lona with added pieces of poultry meat. Poulet supreme contained 80% pieces of meat, Chunk roll, 50% and Chunk-a-lona, 20%. These products sold very well and are really the predecessors of such modern products as turkey roll, loaves, and similar types of cold cuts on the market.

Other.—Some of the other products developed included chicken chili, chick-a-links (a chicken breakfast sausage), chicken steaks, smoked chicken, chicken hash, and bake-and-serve chicken loaf.

CHAPTER 17

J. Rakosky, Jr.

E. F. Sipos

Food Uses of Soy Protein in Products

Institutional foods, to be generally accepted, must not only be nutritious—they must be appealing, tasty, easily served, and attractively priced. To be accepted by the consumer over a period of time, variety is also a factor.

Soybean products of different types, used in a variety of ways, are contributing to these factors in making institutional foods generally acceptable. Not only are soybean products highly nutritious, but they possess many functional properties that are used advantageously in food applications. Of importance is the low cost of soy products compared with other food ingredients. This is especially true of the soy proteins compared with other proteins.

In most food applications soy proteins perform their functions efficiently when used at low levels. If protein fortification is desired they can be used at higher concentrations.

The functional properties of both soy proteins and soy lecithins have been used by food processors at an ever-increasing rate for the past 30 years. Most soy products are employed as ingredients in conventional foods that are generally accepted and widely distributed.

Recently a number of animal product substitutes have been made from soybean oil and/or soy protein products. These were intended to simulate some animal products that are to be avoided for various reasons—religious, dietary, and/or cost. In most cases these analogs are used to either extend the animal product in question or to replace it entirely in the food preparation.

HISTORICAL

The soybean had its origin in eastern Asia where it was cultivated and highly valued for food centuries before written records were kept. It was regarded as a staple crop that could be stored like other grains to provide against famine. Not only did the Chinese use soybeans as food, but the seed and the plant were also used for medicinal purposes.

Soybeans were first introduced into the United States around the turn of the century, and were grown primarily as a forage and pasture crop. The crop gradually became an important source of oil when cottonseed oil was in short supply. Shortly thereafter, the protein content of the seed also became an important consideration—first for animal feeds, later for industrial use, and finally for edible applications.

In the 40 years from 1924 to 1964 the U.S. crop increased from 5 to 700 million bushels. It became the No. 2 cash crop in 1967 (exceeded by corn) and has remained in that position until the present time.

Because the U.S. produced 73% of the world's supply of soybeans, large quantities are exported, making it the No. 1 dollar earner in the export market.

Although most of the soybeans produced in this country are grown in the Corn Belt, the crop is becoming increasingly important in the south and southeastern sections of the United States.

Currently, the best average yield per acre for the United States is 27.3 bushels (60 lb = 1 bushel). While the best average yield for a state is 33.5 bushels per acre, it is generally believed that average yields for the United States can be 50 bushels per acre. With this yield as a base, an acre of soybeans would produce 540 lb of oil and 1,140 lb of protein, as opposed to the current average U.S. yields of 295 lb of oil and 622 lb of protein.

SOYBEAN PLANT AND VARIETIES

The soybean plant (*Glycine max*) belongs to the family of legumes, and as such is able to utilize the nitrogen of the air through the action of bacteria on the roots (see Figs. 4.1 and 4.2). These bacteria of the genus *Rhizobium* live symbiotically with the plant in root nodules, where they convert the nitrogen of the air into a nitrate, a form of nitrogen the plant can utilize. In turn, the bacteria utilize carbohydrates and other substances found in the juices of the plant.

Varieties now grown in the United States may be divided into three general groups, namely commercial (grain), vegetable, and forage. Varieties for commercial seed production are preferably yellow seeds and are used largely for processing oil, meal, and soy flour; but these varieties may also be used for forage purposes if heavier rates of seeding are used. Those used principally for forage and green manure are the black- and brown-seeded varieties, which for the most part are low in oil but yield a finer and heavier forage than the commercial and vegetable varieties.

"The term 'vegetable varieties' has been applied to varieties introduced from oriental countries where they are used solely as green vegetable or dry edible soybeans. In extensive tests of the quality of the green and dry beans made by the Bureau of Human Nutrition and Home Economics, Department of Agriculture, and by departments of home economics of various agricultural colleges, the vegetable varieties have proved much superior to the field or commercial varieties in flavor, texture, and ease of cooking. Many of these vegetable types have been found through experiments to be superior to commercial types for soybean milk, soybean flour, soybean curd, salted toasted soybeans, and other food products. The varieties used for processing and forage purposes usually do not cook easily and have a raw "beany" flavor. Nearly all vegetable varieties cook easily and have a sweet or bland nutty flavor."

SOYBEAN PROCESSING

Field soybeans must be cleaned and freed of the extraneous matter that often accompanies a crop during harvest. This cleaning process is performed by selective screening and air cleaning. Before the soybeans are stored in one of the processing plant elevators, it is often necessary to dry them down to 13% moisture or lower for good storage stability.

When the soybeans leave the grain storage bins and enter the edible processing plant, they are screened again to remove any broken or damaged beans as well as any other foreign materials that may have entered the product or escaped the original cleaning. (See Soybean Processing Diagram in Fig. 17.1). The middle cut of the screened stream flows into double cracking rolls, where the bean is cracked to allow the hull to break away.

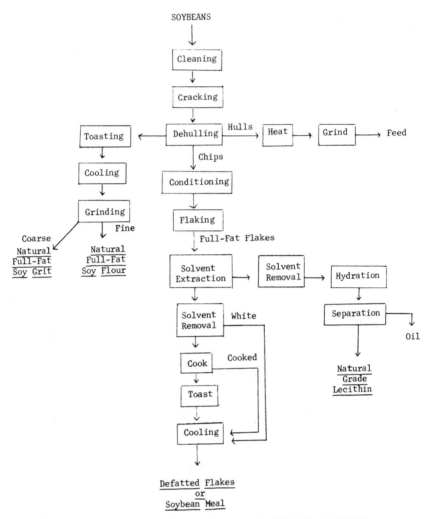

FIG. 17.1. SOYBEAN PROCESSING TO DEFATTED FLAKES

These rolls are corrugated and set so that the bean may be cracked into either quarters or eighths.

The hulls are removed from the cotyledons by air when the product stream passes through the double dehullers. The hulls are heat-processed, milled and sold for feed purposes.

In the production of a natural full-fat product, the dehulled cotyledons are toasted, cooled, and ground. A coarse grind results in a natural full-fat soy flour, which is of current interest in some of the specialty diets used in developing nations.

In the production of a fat-extracted flake, the cracked cóty-ledons (often referred to as chips or meats) are heat-treated in conditioners to make them plastic for the flaking process. Flaking is performed in huge rolls that are set to produce flakes of uniform thickness which is desirable for solvent extraction.

The oil is removed from the flake by commercial hexane in one of several types of countercurrent systems. The oil-rich hexane solution is heated to drive off the hexane from the residue, which is a crude soybean oil. The oil is degummed by steam hydration, centrifuged, and dried.

The gums obtained from this process are dried and sold as natural-grade lecithin, or are processed further into one of many types designed for specific applications.

After the defatted flakes leave the extractor the hexane is drained from the flakes and residual hexane is removed by heat and/or vacuum. In both of the hexane recovery steps, from the oil and the flakes, every attempt is made to recover all the hexane, for a number of reasons (economic, plant safety, and organoleptic).

After hexane removal, the defatted flake emerges with a protein content of 52 to 55%; depending on the amount of moist heat used, it can be a white, cooked, or toasted flake. It should be pointed out that flake color is also influenced by the degree of heat used. A heavy toast results in a golden brown color.

From a relative flavor standpoint the white product has a bitter, beany taste whereas the toasted product has a pleasant, nutty taste.

In some instances, hexane is removed from the flakes by a minimum of heat, as in a vacuum. This results in white flakes having a very high content of water-soluble protein, 80% or more. Such a product has a high enzyme activity, particularly lipoxidase.

The defatted flake may be coarse-ground (coarser than 100-mesh) to produce a soy grit (Fig. 17.2). It is possible to have a wide range of grit products based on particle size and degree of heat treatment.

If the soy flakes are ground to 100-mesh or finer, the product is a soy flour. Special lecithinated flours are made by the addition of lecithin and/or oil to the flour in a blending process.

Soy protein concentrate is produced from defatted soybean

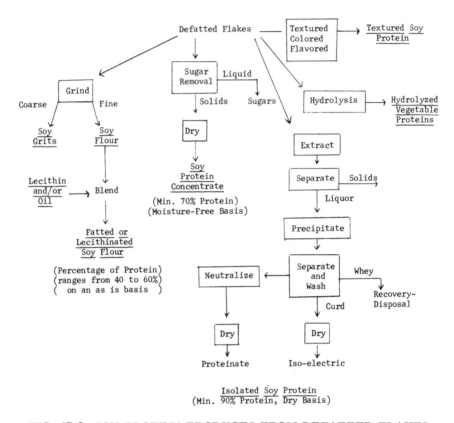

FIG. 17.2. SOY PROTEIN PRODUCTS FROM DEFATTED FLAKES

flakes by processes in which the protein is immobilized and the soluble sugars, mineral matter, etc., are removed, resulting in a protein content of 70% on a dry basis. Currently there are three methods by which soy protein concentrates are made. These methods differ as to the means used to immobilize the protein (heat, isoelectric, and organic solvent washes). All three methods are used commercially.

Edible isolated soy protein is produced by extracting a white flake with water or mild alkali. The protein-containing liquor is separated from flake residuum, and the protein in the liquor is precipitated with food-grade acid. The resulting curd is washed and spray-dried as the isoelectric product, or the curd is neutralized before spray drying to produce a water-dispersible product.

TEXTURED VEGETABLE PROTEIN

Soy proteins are playing an important role in the development of textured vegetable protein products. These products are quite versatile in that they can be used to simulate many food items such as various meat products, shredded coconut, and dried fruit and nuts. Currently texture is obtained commercially in two ways: (1) by a fiber spinning, or (2) by thermoplastic extrusion processes.

Spun Fibers

Fibers are prepared by extruding an alkaline dispersion of soy protein through spinnerettes into a coagulating bath. The resulting fibers are then stretched to impart toughness or chewiness to the product.

In the production of a simulated meat item, the fibers are combined with fat, coloring, flavoring, and heat-coagulable protein. They are then formed or shaped, and cooked. After fabrication, the product may be sliced, ground, or dried. These products may be consumed as-is or processed further into frozen, canned, or dried products.

Fabrication may also include several different processes that are recombined to simulate specific products. As an example, simulated bacon slices are made by laying down fibers randomly together with the edible binder. Some layers are colored to simulate lean meat; others are colorless to represent fat. The multi-layered slab is heat-set and transversely cut into slices.

Thermoplastic Extrusion

The thermoplastic extrusion process is also being used by a number of companies to produce various unique textures. The cost of these materials is less than that of the spun-fiber products because soy flours may be used instead of isolated soy protein.

The equipment used in making these products is similar to that for thermoplastic resin products, i.e., continuous extrusion cookers. The technology of making meat analogs by this route is similar to that of making snack foods. Depending on the equipment and other factors, the extruded particles may be compacted or expanded. In most cases it is the expanded form that is of greatest interest.

In this process a mixture of soy flour, water, flavoring, and coloring is subjected to heat and pressure for a predetermined time. This mass is extruded into the atmosphere or at a reduced pressure to allow expansion. Shape and size are determined by the conformation of the exit dies, as well as by the frequency that the extruded material is cut from the dies by a revolving knife. At this point the extruded material is still quite moist and further drying is necessary.

Meat Base Analog

Consideration of this subject would be incomplete if attention was not called to the patent disclosure of Coleman and Creswick (USP No. 3,253,931). This patent was assigned to the Thomas J. Lipton Company and is a description of the process used to prepare meats for dried soup mixes and dinners.

Since tenderness, color, and flavor in dried-meat preparations are hard to control by ordinary means, the problem was corrected by tearing down the meat structure and rebuilding it. In the process meat is mechanically reduced to fibers and then recombined with a premix consisting of isolated soy protein (sodium proteinate), egg white, fat, and salt. The combination is mixed with water to form a dough which is extruded through the shaped openings of a meat grinder. The particles are heat-coagulated and dried in a circulating oven until the moisture level reaches 2%.

The advantages obtained in using this method are: uniformity in size, shape, texture, and flavor. In addition, texture can be controlled by proper combination of egg white and isolated soy protein addition. Dehydration is achieved economically and rehydration is both rapid and uniform. The shelf-stability of the preparation is considered quite good.

It is interesting to speculate that here is a method whereby a simulated meat product can be formulated from inexpensive meat items such as poultry. Thus, using poultry meat fibers as a base, proper flavoring and structuring can lead to simulated pork, beef, ham, bacon, etc.

TABLE 17.1
CHEMICAL COMPOSITION OF SOYBEAN AND ITS COMPONENTS
ON DRY BASIS[12]

Components	Yield, %	Protein, %	Fat, %	Ash, %	Carbohydrate,[1] %
Whole soybean	100.0	40.3	21.0	4.9	33.9
Cotyledon	90.3	42.8	22.8	5.0	29.4
Hull	7.3	8.8	1.0	4.3	85.9
Hypocotyl	2.4	40.8	11.4	4.4	43.4

[1] Calculated by difference, 100-(protein + fat + ash); consists of crude fibre + N-free extract.

COMPOSITION AND NUTRITIONAL VALUE OF SOYBEAN PRODUCTS

Composition

Although the soybean at harvest can be said to contain 20% oil and 40% protein, it should be realized that the composition varies not only with the soybean variety but with other factors. These factors include all ecological influences such as climate, variations, soil condition, and year-to-year weather pattern variations.

The composition of the soybean and its component parts is shown on a dry basis in Table 17.1; Tables 17.2 and 17.3 show respective breakdowns of soybean oil and carbohydrate.

The polysaccharides present in soybeans are neutral arabinogalactan and acidic polysaccharide.

A breakdown of natural soybean lecithin is also shown in Table 17.2.

Most soy protein products are made from defatted flakes composed primarily of 52% protein and 31% carbohydrate. Since the production of soy grit and soy flour products is from defatted flakes ground to an appropriate size, the chemical composition of these products is similar to that of the defatted flakes. Usually the smaller the size of the particle the lower the moisture content. This can be attributed to the production of heat during the grinding process.

Soy protein concentrate which has a dry basis protein content of 70%, contains about 17% carbohydrate.

TABLE 17.2

APPROXIMATE COMPOSITION OF CRUDE SOYBEAN OIL

15% Saturated fatty acids
     9% Palmitic (C16)
     6% Stearic (C18)
80% Unsaturated fatty acids
     20% Oleic (C18−2H)
     52% Linoleic (C18−4H)
     7% Linolenic (C18−6H)
3% Natural lecithin (sp. gr. 1.04)
     20% Phosphatidyl choline[1]
     20% Phosphatidyl ethanolamine[1]
     21.5% Inositol phosphatides[1]
     34% Soybean oil[1]
     3% Sterols[1]
     1.5% Misc. (sugar, moist., etc.)

---

[1] Percent of natural lecithin fraction.

TABLE 17.3

CARBOHYDRATES IN SOYBEAN

Constituent	Average Amount, % Whole Bean
Cellulose	4.0
Hemicellulose	15.0
Stachyose	3.8
Raffinose	1.1
Sucrose	5.0
Other Sugars[1]	5.1

[1] Small quantities of arabinose, glucose, and verbascose are reported to be present.

Isolated soy protein is essentially pure protein. To qualify as an isolate it must have a minimum dry basis protein content of 90%. Many commercial preparations run as high as 97%.

Since textured vegetable protein products are essentially extruded soy flour products they will have composition similar to soy flours. The compositions of the three types of soy protein products are shown in Table 17.4.

Nutritional Value

Trypsin Inhibitor and Urease Activity.—It is widely recognized that the soybean as well as other legumes contains a
trypsin inhibitor that must be destroyed if one is to receive
full nutritional benefit from the protein. This was recognized
quite early in the animal-feeding studies. The soybean also
contains the enzyme urease, which breaks urea down into
ammonia and carbon dioxide.

Caloric Value of Soybean Components.—In giving consideration to the caloric content of soybeans only the fat, carbohydrate, and protein contents are considered.

For a general approach to the caloric content of the protein
preparation one may assign the values of 4 Calories per gram
for both protein and carbohydrate. For the oil, 9 Calories may
be used. As an example, the following can be considered for a
soy flour or soy grit:

Component	Percent	Calories/gm	Total Calories
Protein	52	4	218
Fat	1	9	9
Carbohydrate	30	4	120
Moisture	8.5	—	—
Ash	6.0	—	—
Fiber	2.5	—	—
			347

Thus it can be seen that there are 347 Calories in 100 gm of
the soy protein product. If lecithin is contained in the product
in question, the lecithin should be treated as fat for practical
purposes, i.e., 9 Calories per gm.

The soybean industry has been in the practice of listing all
analytical results except the carbohydrate or nitrogen-free
extract (NFE). NFE is not ordinarily obtained by analysis, but
by difference. This is done by adding together the moisture,
protein, fat, ash, and fiber and subtracting this sum from 100.
It is assumed that the remaining portion is NFE or carbohydrate.

The nutritional value of soy protein was an important consideration in the widespread usage of these products in animal
feeds. Although nutrition was an important consideration for
some in early edible utilization of these products, its impor-

TABLE 17.4

TYPICAL ANALYSIS OF SOY PROTEIN PRODUCTS

Analysis	Defatted Soy Flour	Soy Protein Concentrate	Isolated Soy Protein
Composition			
Moisture	6.5%	4.9	4.7
Protein (N × 6.25)	53.0%	67.6	91.8
Fat	1.0%	0.3	—
Carbohydrates (NFE)	31.0%	18.8	—
Fiber, crude	2.5%	2.6	0.1
Ash	6.0%	4.8	3.4
Caloric Content	1,665/lb	1,580/lb	1,666/lb
Essential amino acids for humans(gm per 16 gm nitrogen)			
Isoleucine	4.6	4.8	4.9
Leucine	7.6	7.8	7.7
Lysine	6.4	6.3	6.1
Methionine	1.4	1.4	1.1
Cystine (sparing action on methionine)	1.2	1.6	1.2
Phenylalanine	5.3	5.2	5.4
Threonine	4.2	4.2	3.7
Tryptophan	1.4	1.5	1.4
Valine	4.9	4.9	4.8

Vitamin Content			
Ascorbic acid (total)	12.60 mg/100 gm	5.70 mg/100 gm	10.90 mg/100 gm
Carotene	0.01 mg/100 gm	0.01 mg/100 gm	0.01 mg/100 gm
Thiamine	3.4 mcg/gm	4.5 mcg/gm	0.84 mcg/gm
Riboflavin	2.68 mcg/gm	1.81 mcg/gm	1.47 mcg/gm
Niacin	21.10 mcg/gm	11.60 mcg/gm	6.00 mcg/gm
Folic acid	2.62 mcg/gm	3.64 mcg/gm	0.09 mcg/gm
Mineral Content			
Calcium	0.17%	0.22%	0.30%
Phosphorus	0.732%	0.64%	0.77%
Potassium	2.70%	2.10%	0.20%
Sodium	0.011%	50 ppm	1.10
Iron	65 ppm	100 ppm	167 ppm

TABLE 17.5

NUTRITIONAL VALUE OF SOY PROTEIN PRODUCTS

Rat Feeding Studies: 10% Protein Diet—28 Days

Product	Protein Efficiency Ratio (ratio)
Soy flour (defatted)	2.16–2.48
+ 1.0% Methionine	2.97
Soy protein concentrate	2.02–2.48
+ 1.5% Methionine	3.09–3.24
Isolated soy protein	1.08–2.11
+ 1.5% Methionine	2.11–2.45

tance had not been considered by most people until after the White House Conference on Nutrition.

As shown in Table 17.4, soy protein products contain most of the nutrients considered important in nutrition. The protein products contain all the amino acids considered essential in human nutrition.

The value of soy proteins can be seen in the rat-feeding study resulting in PER values (protein efficiency ratio). This test is performed on young rats that have just been weaned. The animals are put on a diet that is complete for all nutrients, except that it is limiting in protein. The protein to be evaluated is added at a level of 10% of the diet and the rats are fed for 28 days. A built-in control diet usually includes caseinate. Consumption of the food is carefully recorded and the rats are weighed at the beginning and end of the test. The ratio of protein consumed and weight gain is recorded at the end of the test. This ratio is adjusted to a PER of 2.5 for casein. If the casein result is high, all values are adjusted downward; if it is low, all are adjusted upward proportionally.

Table 17.5 shows the PER values reported in the literature for the 3 classes of soy protein products.

All vegetable proteins when compared with animal proteins are inadequate or limiting in one or more essential amino acids: for wheat, e.g., it is lysine; for corn, it is both lysine and tryptophan; and for soy proteins, it is methionine. It can be seen in Table 17.5 that soy flours and soy protein concentrate are good nutritional protein sources *per se*. When supplemented with methionine they are further improved.

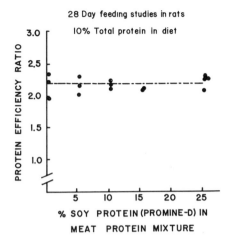

FIG. 17.3. NUTRITIONAL VALUE OF MEAT PROTEIN-SOY PROTEIN
MIXTURES

In most food applications soy protein products are not used
as the sole source of protein; on the other hand, in combination
with other proteins especially of cereal origin they effectively
improve the nutritional protein value of the food.

Of the soy protein products shown in Table 17.5 isolated soy
protein has the lowest PER. When this protein product was
used to replace meat protein in a sausage preparation in
amounts up to 25%, it was shown that there was little if any
change in the PER (see Fig. 17.3).

It is generally recognized that there is a relationship between the ingestion of legumes, such as navy beans, lima beans,
and soybeans, and the production of intestinal gas or flatulence.

Both Steggerda and Rackis and their co-workers have demonstrated that flatulence results when anaerobic bacteria act
on certain carbohydrate materials of bean products in the intestinal tract. It was shown that the low molecular-weight
sugars are responsible.

In comparative studies it was shown that soy flour products
produced approximately 1/3 less gas than navy bean meal.

In the production of soy protein concentrate and isolated soy
protein these sugars are removed or greatly reduced. Tests
performed on the portions removed show that the flatus factor
is present in quantity. Thus it would appear that if flatus is of
concern in the diet special consideration of soy protein products

should be given to soy protein concentrates and isolated soy protein.

UTILIZATION OF SOY PROTEIN PRODUCTS IN FOODS

Several past reviews have mentioned the various physical and chemical properties of soy proteins in the design of foods from a functional standpoint. These functional properties include gelling, emulsifying, emulsion-stabilizing, foaming, texture and fiber-forming, texture control, thickening, moisture and fat binding, and the like.

Utilizing one or more of these properties, Table 17.6 shows the food uses or areas of potential use for soy protein products.

Processed Meats and Meat-like Products

The largest area of current food utilization in the United States is in certain processed comminuted and coarsely ground meat products (see Table 17.6).

In finely chopped meats (e.g., frankfurter, bologna, etc.) isolated soy protein and fine mesh-size soy protein concentrate are used for moisture and fat-binding, fat-emulsifying, and meat emulsion-stabilizing properties. In tests on canned frankfurters and luncheon meats, processed under sterilizing conditions, Bocksch found that inclusion of isolated soy protein effected a considerable reduction in fat and jelly deposits.

In sausage products in the United States with a standard of identity, isolated soy protein and soy protein concentrate are permitted at 2% and 3-1/2%, respectively. In nonspecific items where there are no limitations on fat, moisture, or nonmeat ingredients of soy proteins or combinations with other additives (e.g., nonfat dry milk) are allowed.

To illustrate the utility of soy protein products in sausage and nonspecific emulsion-type meats, refer to some of the formulations shown in the appendix. Those formulations containing soy protein products have excellent eye appeal, good texture, no off-flavors, and result in substantial savings for the user while at the same time maintaining good nutritional quality.

Isolated soy protein is also used to advantage in canned-meat items, as it is not affected adversely by the high processing

temperatures. In this application there appears to be a protective action for the meat protein against the effects of heat.
Because of this property, it should play an important part in
items to be processed at higher temperatures and shorter
processing times.

It is also entirely possible to make a dispersion of isolated
soy protein in water in which an emulsion of fat will be locked
in upon heating. This is similar to the way the lean meat proteins of sausage or loaf items lock in the fat when the emulsion
is cooked. If one wishes to demonstrate this, make an emulsion
of 15% isolated soy protein (gelling type), 50% water, and 35%
lard. It will be found that the emulsion is extremely stable after
heating, and will withstand boiling, frying, or commercial canning temperatures without breakdown.

In coarsely chopped meats (e.g., meat patties, meat balls,
chili, Salisbury steaks, pizza toppings, and meat sauces) soy
protein concentrate is the product of choice. However, soy
grits and textured soy proteins (thermoplastically extruded)
are also used. The latter is used to good advantage in formulations exceeding 9% additive on a meat block basis. Products
made with soy proteins at the recommended levels have excellent eye appeal, good chewy texture, no off-flavors, and will
remain juicy after cooking. Due to the increased yield per
pound of meat, appreciable cost reduction can be realized.

Other Ground Meat Applications

Soy protein concentrate (20/60 mesh) or textured soy proteins
can also be used in the production of meat balls, chili, Salisbury
steaks, pizza topping, and meat sauces. These formulations
may contain 80 lb meat + 5.7 lb soy protein concentrate (20/60
mesh) or textured soy protein + 14.3 lb water.

As of this time, there is no restriction in additive-type patties
other than "sufficient for purpose."

In chili con carne, soy flour, soy grits, and soy protein concentrate are permitted up to a level of 8% in the preparation
in federally inspected plants.

As with meat patties, soy flour, soy grits, and soy protein
concentrate products are permitted in meat balls (in spaghetti)
and in Salisbury steak up to a level of 12%.

TABLE 17.6

MAJOR CURRENT AND POTENTIAL USES FOR VARIOUS SOY PROTEIN PRODUCTS

	Soy Protein Isolate	Soy Protein Concentrate	Soy Flour (grits)	Textured Soy Protein
Comminuted Meat Products				
Frankfurters	X	X		
Bologna	X	X		
Miscellaneous sausage	X	X		
Luncheon loaves	X	X		
Canned luncheon loaves	X	X		
Poultry products	X	X		
Coarsely Ground Meat Products				
Patties		X	X	X
Chili con carne		X	X	X
Sloppy joes		X	X	X
Meat balls		X	X	X
Pizza toppings		X	X	X
Bakery Products				
Cakes		X	X	
Cake mixes		X	X	
White bread			X	
Specialty breads		X	X	
Cookies, biscuits, crackers, etc.		X	X	
Pancakes			X	

Product				
Donuts			X	
Sweet goods			X	
Dairy-type Products				
Coffee whiteners	X			
Whipped toppings	X			
Frozen dessert	X			
Beverage powder	X			
Cheeses	X			
Dried Meat Bits	X			X
Infant Formulations	X		X	
Dried Soup Mixes	X			
Special Dietary Items		X	X	
Breakfast Cereal		X	X	

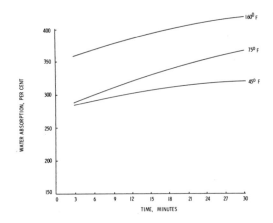

FIG. 17.4. RATE OF HYDRATION OF PROMOSOY 20/60

As with imitation sausage and nonspecific loaves, the government permits both soy flours and soy grits in soups, stews, scrapple, tamales, meat fries, pork and barbecue sauce, and beef with barbecue sauce "sufficient for purpose."

The following figures show the functionality of a commercially available soy protein concentrate (PROMOSOY 20/60, made by Central Soya Company, Incorporated).

(1) Hydration properties (Fig. 17.4).

(2) The rate at which the fat content of meat patties will drop with the addition of PROMOSOY 20/60, using different amounts of added water (Fig. 17.5).

(3) Shrink data (Figs. 17.6 and 17.7).

The Orientals not only recognized the flavoring properties of hydrolyzed vegetable proteins but used these products to an advantage in many of their food preparations to give their foods a meaty flavor.

Soy sauce or shoyu is obtained from a combination of soybeans and wheat by a fermentation process that takes as long as 1-1/2 years to complete. At the end of the fermentation the extract is heated and processed to produce a liquid sauce familiar to most of us.

In the United States, the major portion of protein hydrolyzates are prepared from soybean protein, wheat gluten, or milk protein by acid hydrolysis. However, a number of enzyme hy-

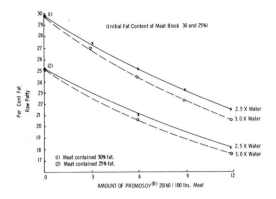

FIG. 17.5. PERCENT FAT IN RAW PATTY AT VARIOUS LEVELS OF
SOY PROTEIN CONCENTRATE AND VARIOUS LEVELS OF WATER
ADDITION

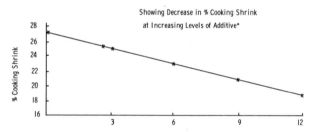

FIG. 17.6. % COOKING SHRINK

drolyzates are commercially available as flavoring agents
(using other combinations and other methods of hydrolysis).

The purpose of hydrolyzed vegetable protein (HVP) in processed meat products is to enhance their meaty flavor. Depending upon the preparation and type, HVP is used in concentrations usually ranging from 0.2 to 2% based on the final
weight of the products.

HVP is of particular value in those cases where bland products are used in conjunction with meats as extenders or binders.
They are also used extensively in simulated meat products
to contribute to the expected meat flavor.

Hydrolyzed vegetable protein is cleared for use in federally
inspected plants. The regulation simply states ''in amounts
sufficient for purpose.''

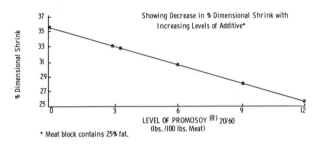

FIG. 17.7. % DIMENSIONAL SHRINK

SCHOOL LUNCH

One application of soy protein products that illustrates the benefits realized by its use is that concerning school lunch and the Type A Lunch.

In the April 17, 1970, issue of the *Federal Register*, revised regulations for the School Lunch Program were published. One section (G) of Part 225.9 states that, "The Child Nutrition Division (CND) may approve variations in the food components of the meals on an experimental or a continuing basis in any service institution where there is evidence that such variations are nutritionally sound and are necessary to meet ethnic, religious, economic, or physical needs."

In August 1970 the Department of Agriculture issued its "Position Statement on Engineered Foods," opening the door for innovation, and actually encouraging the use of engineered foods. Food and Nutrition Service (FNS) 219 Notice was published February 1971, allowing the use of textured vegetable proteins in school lunch. A late directive now permits the use of granular soy protein concentrate.

Accordingly, textured vegetable proteins and granular soy protein concentrate, when prepared and served in combination with meat, poultry, or fish, may be used as a meat alternate to fulfill part of the minimum requirement of 2 oz (edible portion as served) of cooked meat specified in Section 210.10 (a) (1) (ii) for the Type A School Lunch. It would also fulfill part of the meat and meat alternate requirement of item (b) in Section 225.0 (b) (4) (iii) of the Special Food Service Program for Children. The proportion of hydrated vegetable protein products (manufactured according to U.S.D.A. specifications) to uncooked meat in the combination shall not exceed 30 parts per 70 parts meat on the basis of weight.

The ratio of 30 parts hydrated vegetable protein product to 70 parts uncooked meat may be applied to the meat and meat alternate requirements of the lunch and supper food patterns for other age groups served under the Department's Child Feeding Programs.

DAIRY-TYPE PRODUCTS

Although isolated soy protein offers much potential in the manufacture of dairy-type products, these products are not produced in the United States in significant volume. A few, such as liquid coffee whitener, liquid whip topping, and an imitation milk, enjoy limited distribution in selected geographical areas. However, there is considerable development effort being devoted to a broad variety of dairy-type foods, which include coffee whiteners, whip toppings, imitation milks, convenience beverage powders, frozen desserts, sour cream, and cheese-like products.

Very little has been published on the use of soy protein isolate in dairy-like foods. Recently there has been much interest and grave concern in the United States over the introduction of filled and imitation milks. In part, the interest has centered on the utilization of soy protein isolate, together with vegetable fat, sugars, minerals, vitamins, and flavoring, to produce a beverage having milk-like qualities. There is much concern that such imitation milks will not fill the nutritional needs of the consumer. One must agree that because of the importance of fluid milk in milk-consuming areas of the world, and substitute should provide equivalent nutrition.

In the development of acceptable bland-flavored dairy-like products, the flavor contribution of soy protein isolate will be most critical. Properly processed and stored milk products have a complex flavor profile which is desired by consumers in milk-drinking areas of the world. At present, flavor is a deterrent to the wider utilization of soy protein isolate in certain simulated milk foods, but flavor improvements will be forthcoming because of the current emphasis on identifying the flavor components and flavor precursors in the source material.

Soybean curd or Tofu, often referred to as soybean cheese, has been a prominent source of food protein in certain Oriental diets. However, this is not truly a cheese since it is a bland product and is eaten either cooked or fried. Recent efforts in Israel have been devoted to exploring the utilization of isolated soy protein in fermented cheeses, such as soft cheeses, hard cheeses, and surface-ripened semi-hard cheeses. Some progress was made in all classes, but it is obvious that more work is necessary to develop commercial items having consumer acceptability.

For suggested formulations for Whipped Topping concentrate and frozen type Whipped Topping, see Appendix.

BAKING APPLICATIONS

In a general way when soy proteins are to be considered in baking applications, a number of factors must be taken into consideration: water-holding capacity, enzyme activity, water-soluble protein and fiber content, carbohydrate and lipid content, flavor, particle size, whether or not lecithin is necessary, food standards, and in some cases nutrition, compatibility, price, etc. Depending on the need at hand, these factors determine the type of protein to be selected among the many products available today.

Soy Flour.—Because of price and the compatibility of particulate fiber material with most bakery products, soy flour is the most widely used soy ingredient in this application area. The addition of soy flour in various baked goods formulation replaces up to 3% of the wheat flour, without any other formula adjustments other than that involving water. For every 1 lb of soy flour substituted in the formula an additional 1 lb or $1\frac{1}{2}$ lb of water usually must be added. Soy flours do not possess any of the gluten properties of wheat flour.

In the commercial white bread (buns and rolls) industry soy flour is accepted by many bakers as a regular ingredient. The protein additives most commonly used are nonfat dry milk with various blends of whey solids and gelatinized cornstarch with soy flour. Special process soy flour has been chemically treated and is distinguished from other types by its greater water absorption capacity and its higher protein content (60%). The breads produced have very good quality and the blends mentioned above are used by many bakers who want to retain some of higher priced nonfat milk products.

In cake formulations, nonfat dry milk was used extensively to enhance the crust color through the Maillard reaction. NFDM blends uniformly with other dry ingredients and does not interfere with the general flavor profile of commercial cakes. Since economically it has become necessary to reduce the amount of NFDM used, it can now be replaced by specially prepared soy flour up to 100% of the NFDM without impairing quality. At a 50% replacement level, it was found that aside from an increase in water absorption, no formula changes are necessary. With respect to additional absorption, it was demonstrated that a factor of 1.5 times the soy protein additive weight will yield optimum total absorption. With replacement levels at or above 75% dextrose must be included in the total sugar content (except devil's food). Leavening must also be increased but the added cost of leavening is more than offset by the increased yield of batter.

In cake doughnuts, egg solids are an important ingredient. These, too, can be reduced approximately in half and replaced by lecithinated soy flour in the formulation. One of the apparently good side effects is that when the donut hits the hot fat during frying it appears that a seal is formed at the surface in such a way that moisture is retained in the dough and fat absorption is lessened.

Phosphatides (lecithins) when present in flour are valuable for their emulsifying properties. When added to bread doughs produce more tender crusts, finer grain and texture, better general appearance, and longer lasting freshness. Maximum beneficial effects were associated with 0.25–0.5% lecithin based on the amount of wheat flour.

Other emulsifiers used in high protein breads are sodium stearoyl-2-lactylate and calcium stearoyl-2-lactylate. An excellent bread formula calls for 100% flour (14% moisture basis), 12% (variable) of soy flour or other protein-rich food stuffs, 3% yeast, 5% sugar, 2% salt, variable water, variable bromate, and 0.5% sodium stearoyl-2-lactylate.

Soy Protein Concentrate.—In specialty breads and high-protein toaster-type cookie, Williams *et al.* (1970) have used this 60% protein soy flour. These specialty breads contain 13 to 14% protein while ordinary white bread contains 8 to 9%.

The use of isolated soy protein needs further study, since it does not have the extensibility of wheat gluten and results in a decreased bread loaf volume; other factors also need further study before soy protein is used to improve the nutritional values of wheat products.

MISCELLANEOUS FOOD USES

Soy flour is used in many applications as a nutritional adjunct (e.g., baby formulations and foods, dietary wafers, breakfast cereals, pasta products, confections, etc.). It is used in many planned government-sponsored meals for school children and institutional feeding programs in areas where protein shortage exists.

Soy flour is part of standard of identity for margarine, and it can be used in all types of edible spreads.

Soy protein concentrate is a product of choice for certain dietary formulations. Because of its bland flavor, high PER, and its low flatulence activity, it is recommended for use in animal, baby, and geriatric foods. In the last two cases it is recommended because of the sensitivity of the intestinal tract of these individuals to gas formation. For these reasons it is an ideal protein source for a nutritional bar.

As mentioned before, soy protein concentrate is also permitted in school lunch in combination with meat as part of the protein requirement.

In the last several years, two hypoallergenic infant formulations containing isolated soy protein have appeared on the U.S. market.

A rather unusual and interesting use of isolated soy protein has been found in the spray-drying of banana purée. It was concluded that isolated soy protein at levels ranging from 4 to 20%, on a dry basis, may be used as an aid in drying the sticky banana mass, as an anticaking agent in the resulting powder, or as a nutritional supplement in banana powder for infant feeding.

CHAPTER 18

L. L. W. Smith

L. J. Minor

Carbohydrates

Plants in the presence of chlorophyll and light have the ability to produce the carbohydrate glucose: $6CO_2 + 6H_2O \rightarrow C_6H_{12}O_6 + 6O_2\uparrow$. This reaction in its entirety is called photosynthesis and takes place in the chloroplasts of the leaves. $C_6H_{12}O_6$ could be written $(CH_2O)_6$, representing a hydrated carbon. The general formula is $C_n(H_2O)_n$ such as $C_3H_6O_3$; $C_n(H_2O)_{2n}$; $C_6H_{12}O_6$; or $C_n(H_2O)_{2n-1}$, $C_{12}H_{22}O_{11}$ to a more complex form expressed as $(C_6H_{10}O_5)_n$.

Simple carbohydrates are called sugars or saccharides from the Latin word saccharon meaning sugar or glucose. Carbohydrates are polyhydroxy compounds with a keto or aldehyde group present or have the capability of reactions due to the formation of the keto or aldehyde groups. The hydroxy groups present represent the primary and secondary alcohol groupings; for example, glucose (a simple sugar) may be written as $CH_2OH(CHOH)_4CHO$, an aldehyde group, four secondary alcohol groups and a primary alcohol group.

Naming of carbohydrates is as follows:

(1) The general ending is-ose.

(2) The stem name indicates the number of carbons present such as triose, pentose, hexose.

(3) The name also indicates the major functional group present, aldose, ketose.

(4) Therefore the name of $CH_2OH(CHOH)_4CHO$ is an aldohexose, that of $CH_2OH(CHOH)_3CO(CH_2OH)$ is a ketohexose.

Classes of carbohydrates are generally of three types:

(1) Monosaccharides are carbohydrates that cannot be hydrolyzed to smaller units.

(2) Oligosaccharides are those which can be hydrolyzed to a few monosaccharides: of this group the disaccharides are the most important to the food group. The disaccharides are hydrolyzed to two smaller units, for example, $C_{12}H_{22}O_{11}$ (sucrose) upon the addition of a molecule of water yields two-$C_6H_{12}O_6$, one of which is glucose and the other fructose.

$$Sucrose + H_2O \longrightarrow glucose + fructose$$

Other disaccharides are maltose and lactose, which have the same molecular formula as sucrose.

(3) Polysaccharides are composed of multiple units such as starch, which upon hydrolysis may yield from 200 to 4000 units of glucose:

$$(C_6H_{10}O_5)_n + nH_2O \rightarrow nC_6H_{12}O_6$$

Other polysaccharides are glycogen and cellulose.

Many of these saccharides are linked together by a series of glycosidic linkages and may include other elements and materials.

The naturally occurring monosaccharides that are of particular interest are the aldohexoses and the ketohexoses. They have the same molecular formulas, $C_6H_{12}O_6$, but different spatial arrangements such as:

CHO	CH₂OH	CHO	CHO
H—C—OH	C=O	H—C—OH	HO—C—H
HO—C—H	HO—C—H	HO—C—H	HO—C—H
H—C—OH	H—C—OH	HO—C—H	H—C—OH
H—C—OH	H—C—OH	H—C—OH	H—C—OH
CH₂OH	CH₂OH	CH₂OH	CH₂OH
aldohexose glucose	ketohexose fructose	aldohexose galactose	aldohexose mannose

These compounds are capable of showing another form of isomerism called stereoisomerism. These isomers with the same molecular formula have a molecular configuration that has a definite effect on the passage of a plane of polarized light through each solution. These are called optical isomers.

Light which is passed through a Nicol prism separates one polarized ray from another, each ray vibrating in a single plane. One such ray passed through a sugar solution between two Nicol prisms will necessitate one prism being rotated to the left or right to achieve darkness again. This instrument is called a polarimeter and the rotation of the prism to the right is designated by a + (plus) sign and the number of degrees turned or to the left by a — (minus) sign and the number of degrees turned.

This phenomenon of stereoisomerism or optical isomerism is dependent upon (1) the plane of symmetry, (2) the center of symmetry or (3) a 4-fold alternating axis of symmetry; all of this depends upon a carbon atom that is attached to four different atoms or groups, called an asymmetric carbon.

Lactic acid is an example.

COOH | HO—C—H | CH₃   L   COOH | H—C—OH | CH₃   D   COOH HO⟨—⟩H CH₃   L   COOH H⟨—⟩OH CH₃   D

Drawn as a tetrahedron with the carbon in the center and maintaining the stable angle of 109°28', there can be 2 of these compounds that are mirror images, nonsuperimposable that have similar properties but rotate light to the right and to the left. These mirror images are called enantiomorphs. The center carbon is termed asymmetric and from the number of asymmetric carbon atoms the possible number of isomers can be predicted. In the case of lactic acid it is 2, the following formula is used in predicting $X = 2^n$ where $n = $ the number of asymmetric carbon atoms. Another example is glucose where $n = 4$. ˙ . $X = 2^4$ or 16 possible isomers. Isomers have the same basic *composition* but have different structural formulas or *constitution* and have different spatial arrangements or *configuration*, resulting in different molecular shapes or *conformation*. Another property of importance is the configuration of the "pentyl" carbon of the hexoses. To ascertain the proper or correct enantiomorph the symbols D and L were proposed which were based on the configuration of glyceryl aldehyde (aldotriose) as a reference configuration at the asymmetric carbon atom.

CHO
|
H—C—OH
|
CH₂OH

D + glyceraldehyde. This form rotates light to the right and the hydroxyl group is on the right side of the projection formula.

When it is on the left side it is designated as the L family. Therefore D (+) designates the configuration and the rotation, it could also read D (–) as well as L (–) and L (+). The D or L configuration of all other asymmetric compounds is defined according to whether the compound is similar to D- or L-glyc-eraldehyde. A *racemic* mixture contains equal quantities of D and L configurations, and is therefore optically inactive. A compound such as tartaric acid can be optically inactive within itself and is called a *meso* compound. Examples of the above are:

```
      COOH              HOOC                    COOH
       |                 |                       |
  H —— C —— OH      HO —— C —— H           H —— C —— OH
       |                 |                 -----+-----
 HO —— C —— H       H —— C —— OH           H —— C —— OH
       |                 |                       |
      COOH              HOOC                    COOH
```

    L-tartaric acid   D-tartaric acid   one-half a mirror image of the other or a *meso* compound and optically inactive.

equal quantities = racemic mixure, optically inactive

Optical isomers that are not mirror images or enantiomorphs are called diastereoisomers:

```
      COOH                          COOH
       |                             |
  H —— C —— OH                  H —— C —— OH
       |          and                |
  H —— C —— OH                 HO —— C —— H
       |                             |
      COOH                          COOH
```

The most important carbohydrate is glucose from the Greek "gleukos" meaning "must" or "sweet wine." It is also called dextrose, grape sugar, and blood sugar. The dextrorotatory form is the one occurring naturally. It is found along with fructose and sucrose in most plant juices. Honey is chiefly glucose and fructose. Glucose is present in the blood at an 0.1% level, and the free and combined form is one of the most abundant organic compounds in nature.

    Structures for monosaccharides have been shown as open- or straight-chain formulas; however, extensive studies of the properties of sugars has led to the conclusion that they also exist in the cyclic form. Glucose has an optical rotation of +113° when dissolved in water; after 5 hr this decreases to +52.5°. This phenomenon is termed mutarotation. All aldo-hexoses undergo mutarotation. This behavior is explained by the existence of two nonequivalent cyclic structures for each monosaccharide.

The carboxyl group and one of the hydroxyl groups in the chain can react to yield a cyclic hemiacetal. When this occurs the carboxyl carbon becomes asymmetric. Stable cyclic hemi-acetals are derived from 5- and 6-membered rings and are named from the names of the open-chained sugars. The result of the new asymmetric carbon atom produces two diastereo-isomers. These acetals are called glycosides and the two forms are designated as α (alpha) and β (beta).

Isomers of this type are known as *anomers* and the carbon atom responsible is known as the *anomeric* carbon atom. The *anomeric carbon* atom is generally the only one designated when showing these compounds in the cyclic form. The *ano-meric* carbon is the carbon linked to two oxygens in this cyclic formation.

These cyclic formulas, generally known as the Haworth formula, are used to show the perspective formula. As the carbon chain coils around and maintains its angle of 109°5' between carbons the following ring type results:

α-D-glucose β-D-glucose

The ring type resembles pyran.

Glucose is called glucopyranose in the ring formation.

In solution 36% is in the form of α-D-glucose and 64% is in the form of β-D-glucose. In solution their conformation may be that of the following:

(1) Chair form

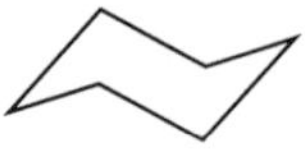

which is rather rigid and alternate atoms occupy two separate planes.

(2) Boat form

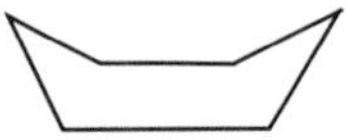

This form is flexible.

(3) Twist form

is about halfway between the chair and boat form.

One molecule exists in the flexible form for each 1000 molecules in the rigid chair form.

Fructose which forms a 5-membered ring resembles furan

and

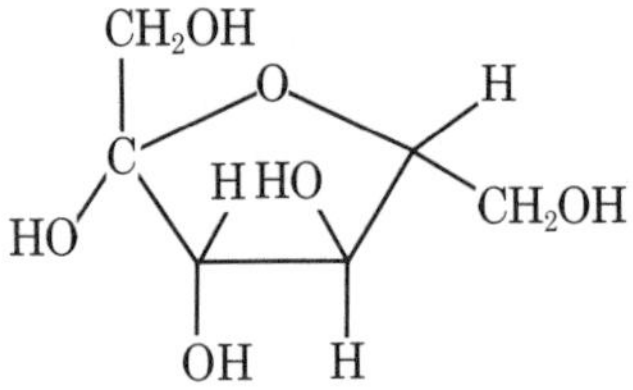

this formula represents β-D-fructofuranose. α-D-fructofuranose is

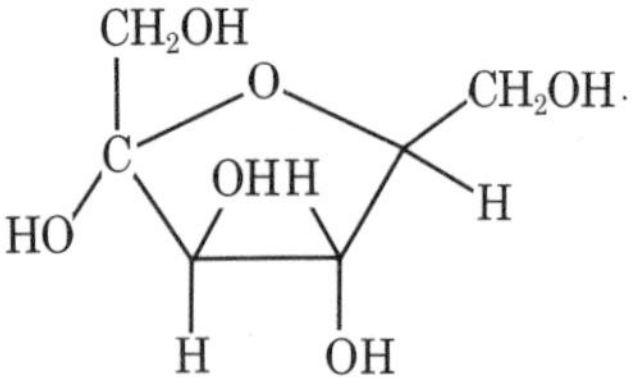

The disaccharides are formed by linking the monosaccharides together with the elimination of a molecule of water. The hydrolysis of maltose through the action of maltase (an enzyme) or the presence of H^+ will yield two molecules of glucose:

$$C_{12}H_{22}O_{11} + H_2O \longrightarrow 2C_6H_{12}O_6$$

Maltose represented by the Haworth formula shows linkages between the number 1 carbon atom of one molecule and the number 4 carbon atom of the other molecule.

α-maltose

Maltose is produced from the polysaccharide starch by the action of the enzyme diastase.

When two molecules of β-D-glucose are joined in a similar manner the product is called *cellobiose,* a hydrolysis product of cellulose, a polysaccharide:

This configuration is not acted upon by the enzymes present in the human digestive tract.

Lactose or milk sugar is the product of β-D-galactose and α-D-glucose.

β-lactose or α-D-gluco-β-D-galactopyrannoside

Cow's milk contains 5% of lactose which is present in the whey; human milk varies from 5 to 8%. Lactose, less sweet than sugar, has been used in the baking industry. Whey is one of the commercial sources of lactose.

Sucrose, cane sugar, beet sugar or maple sugar, is the product of α-D-glucose and β-D-fructose linked through the anomeric carbons:

Sucrose or α-D-glucopyranosyl-β-D-fructofuranoside.

When sucrose is hydrolyzed either through enzymatic action or H$^+$ it is said to be inverted to form invert sugar. This is related to the difference in rotation:

$$\text{Sucrose} + H_2O \longrightarrow \text{glucose} + \text{fructose}$$
$$[\alpha]_D^{20} + 66.50 \qquad\qquad [\alpha]_D^{20} + 52°7 \ [\alpha]_D^{20} - 92°4$$

A 50-50 mixture of glucose and fructose is called invert sugar.

Some Properties of Mono and Disaccharides

(a) Solubilities expressed as grams per 100 grams of H_2O at standard pressure.

	0°C	100°C
Glucose	56.5 gm	569.3 gm
Fructose	Very soluble	
Lactose	11.9	139.2
Sucrose	179.2	487.2

(b) Sweetness of the sugars on a comparative basis results in fructose judged the sweetest. When comparing equal concentrations with a 10% glucose solution, the relative sweetness is:

Lactose	0.55	The least sweet
Galactose	0.95	
Glucose	1.00	
Sucrose	1.45	
Fructose	1.65	The most sweet

Sweetness of sugars seems to bear a relationship to the angle and position of the hydroxyl group of the anomeric carbon

and the hydroxyl group of the number 2 carbon. The *cis* form
is sweeter, and it is suggested that the degree of hydrogen
bonding present may have more to do with taste perception
at the taste bud site.

There are other compounds that taste sweet that are not
of the carbohydrate configuration, such as saccharin, the
cyclamates or so-called synthetic sweeteners; even lead
acetate $[Pb(CH_3COO)_2]$, a deadly poison, tastes sweet.

The chemical properties of the sugars discussed to date are
of interest to the food field in two particular areas.

(a) As alcohols that can react with organic acids or inorganic
acids to form esters.

(b) The glycosidic linkage or ether linkage enables other
compounds to be formed.

(c) As aldehydes and ketones they react to oxidation reactions such as the alkaline solution of cupric salts.

The equation may be written as follows:

$$RCHO + 2Cu(OH)_2 \rightarrow RCOOH + CU_2O\downarrow + 2H_2O$$

Sugars that react with Fehling's solution [copper sulfate,
sodium hydroxide, and sodium potassium tartrate (Rochelle
salts)] or with Benedict's solution, which contains sodium
citrate instead of sodium potassium tartrate, are called *reducing sugars*. Glucose, fructose, lactose, and maltose will
react, but sucrose will not because it is not a reducing sugar.
Methods have been devised to determine content of reducing
sugar both qualitatively and quantitatively. The blue color of
the solutions may change to a bright green, yellow, orange
or brick red depending on the concentration of reducing sugars.
This test is used to detect the presence of glucose in the urine
or in the juices of fruits, vegetables or plants.

Another test used specifically for the presence of glucose
is made with paper impregnated with *o*-tolidine, an alkali,
and glucose oxidase giving a yellow color. This yellow tape
turns to shades of green that indicate the content of glucose.
Commercially the test is used to determine the approximate
concentration of glucose in potatoes to be used for French
fries or chips. An increase in glucose content indicates that
chips will be darker after frying. The browning or Maillard
reaction, which is chiefly responsible for the color, depends

partially upon the amount of glucose and/or reducing sugars present.

The potato is cut in half from the stem to the bud end; a piece of the tape is laid in between the halves and pressed to moisten. The two halves are separated and the ribbon of tape removed. After 1 min, the color of the tape is noted. If the tape remains yellow, it indicates that no glucose is present, and chips or French fries will fry a light color. If the tape turns green, it can be compared with a color chart supplied to determine the percent of glucose. If it becomes very dark, it is certain that chips or fries would be very dark. This test is generally performed on a sampling of five or more potatoes picked at random from a lot. Potatoes taken from cold storage 50°F or lower generally contain more glucose than those stored at a higher temperature. In cold storage the starch is converted to glucose during the respiration process; at higher temperatures, the reverse process takes place and the amount of reducing sugars is lowered. The frying operation produces a reaction basically between the reducing sugars and amino acids present (the Maillard reaction), which results in the golden brown color so desirable in fried foods. This color is also developed during the baking of bread, cakes, and pastry, and the roasting of meat. Besides color, the products of the Maillard reaction may also affect the flavor and odor of a food. Sometimes during the processing of foodstuffs, this reaction produces an off-color or flavor experienced in canned or evaporated milk, beer, or dried foods, etc.

The browning reaction, or nonenzymatic browning, is sometimes confused with the dehydration reaction of sucrose during pyrolysis, which gives caramel-like products and is called *caramelization*, or with the dehydration of starch by heating, which is termed *dextrinization* and also produces shades of brown coloration. Each of these nonenzymatic browning reactions produces a distinctive aroma, flavor or color, and in some foodstuffs it is possible that all three take place.

NATURAL STARCHES

The knowledge of starch and its chemistry is of great importance to the food technologist and processor because this product is used so widely in the manufacture of food products.

For example, when a food processor needs a neutral, edible filler, or when liquids such as water, milk, or juices are to be thickened, or where gels are required, there is usually a starch that will provide the desired characteristics.

The food industry comprises one of the largest consumers of starches and starch products, using more than 30% of total starch production. Table 18.1 lists a number of common foods in which starches provide their desirable properties and characteristics. The starches commonly used in these foods include: potato, corn, amioca, wheat, sago, rice and arrowroot, and tapioca flour. A short review of starch chemistry, with particular emphasis on the raw starches utilized in food products is attempted.

Characteristics of Starches

The colloidal properties of a particular starch in an aqueous dispersion are most important such as; dispersibility, clarity, organoleptic characteristics, viscosity, color, flow characteristics, gel and adhesive strength, and film properties. Table 18.2 lists the functions of starch dispersions and shows how they are used in particular foods. The first four of these functional uses of starch are dependent upon the colloidal nature of the starch hydrosols. These sols are strongly hydrophilic, structurally strong, and form quite permanent gels.

The inherent physical properties of any native raw starch, as distinguished from a modified starch, are principally dependent on its genetic origin, which determines its granule size, amylose-amylopectin ratio, and the molecular weight of the amylose and amylopectic polymers.

Starch Chemistry

Starch occurs in the form of white granules which are usually made up of an organized structure containing both a linear polymer (*amylose*) and a branched polymer (*amylopectin*) (see Figure 18.1). Each granule comprises a uniform mixture of these two types of polymers, which are oriented and associated in a crystal-like lattice. They are insoluble in cold water and relatively resistant to naturally occurring hydrolytic agents. In starches from some plants, such as potato, the

TABLE 18.1

STARCH UTILIZATION CHART

Food	Unmodified or Derivative	Enzyme-Converted	Dextrin	Pregelatinized	Thin-boiling	Oxidized
Bakery						
Cakes	x					
Cookies	x			x		
Dusting	x					
Flours	x					
Ice cream cones	x					
Macaroni	x					
Pie fillings						
Prepared mixes	x			x		x
Wafers	x					
Brewing	x	x		x		
Canned foods	x					
Soup	x					x
Thickeners	x					
Confectionery						
Caramels	x					
Chewing gum	x			x		
Dragee	x		x	x		
Dusting	x			x		
Gum work	x				x	x
Moldings	x			x		
Pan coatings			x			

Dairy food				
Condensed milk	x			
Stabilizers	x	x		
Desserts				
Pudding powders	x		x	x
Meat products				
Sausage	x			
Animal foods	x	x	x	
Baking powder	x		x	
Miscellaneous				
Condiments	x		x	
Rice polishes	x	x		
Salad dressings	x			x
Sugar, powdered	x			x
Yeast	x			
Films	x			

Source: Report of the Royal Commission of the New Brunswick Potato Industry, 1962.

TABLE 18.2

FUNCTIONS OF STARCH IN TYPICAL FOODS

Function	Foods
Thickening	Gravies, sauces, pie fillings, soups
Gelling	Gum drops, puddings (cooked)
Stabilizer	Beverages, syrups, salad dressings
Binder	Processed meat products
Moisture retention	Cake fillings, confectionery items
Coating agent (dusting)	Breads, confectionery items
Moulding	Gum drops, jellies, confectionery items
Diluent and flow-aid	Baking powder formulations

amylopectin may be esterified with a small amount of phosphate.

The two polymers differ in molecular weight and chemical structure: amylose consists of 200 to 1000 glucopyranose units joined through alpha-1,4-glucosidic linkages, whereas the branched or ramified polymer, amylopectin, is made up of chains of 1500 or more glucopyranose units. The linear polymer and the longer branches of the nonlinear polymer exhibit a pronounced tendency to orient and associate with other linear molecules.

Starch Gelatinization

The starch granules in a *sol* swell progressively as the temperature is raised to the range between 60° and 70°C. The temperature at which gelatinization begins is a characteristic of each particular type of starch. When heated above the temperature of gelatinization, the granules undergo an irreversible, sudden, rapid swelling, and the viscosity of the suspension increases greatly to form a paste or sol. On further increase of temperature, the final phase of the reaction is indicated by a rapid diffusion of starch from some granules and by the rupture of others, which leaves numerous formless sacs. Upon cooling, there is further stiffening and gelling of the sol, sometimes called "setback."

It is believed that the degree of retrogradation upon cooling is inversely related to the chain-length of the amylose molecule. Tuber starches (except in the case of sago) gel much less readily than corn or wheat, as is expected from the length of the chain of their amylose polymers.

There is also a difference in texture between gels formed from longer and shorter-chain amylose because orientation and association are more difficult in the longer chains. The degree of polymer association, which differs with each starch, may also explain, in part, the differences in gelatinization temperatures of different types of starch. This factor is illustrated in Table 18.2. Furthermore, it is indicated that small granules usually gelatinize at a slightly higher temperature than larger granules.

In general, root starches gelatinize more rapidly, and at lower temperatures; they yield clearer solutions, taste better, and hold water more tightly. When used with cereal starches, they may exert a stabilizing effect that reduces weeping or syneresis. On the other hand, root and stem starches, except in the case of sago, have relatively weak gel tendencies (primarily, because of the length of their amylose fraction). Therefore, the resulting textures of foods that include root starches are on the gummy or cohesive side (see Tables 18.3 and 18.4).

MODIFIED STARCHES

Recently starches have undergone physical and chemical modifications to obtain such properties as: (1) whiter color, (2) freedom from odor development, (3) improved gel strength and clarity, (4) higher enzyme susceptibility, (5) lower bacterial count, (6) improved flow characteristics (mobility), (7) greater paste stability, (8) paste viscosity in the desired range, (9) greater increased absorption in the cold.

Physically Modified Starches

Pregelatinized Starches.—These are precooked starches which are then dehydrated. Granule destruction is by grinding. The product or starch varies with the conditions of preparation. Pregelatinized starches are used in pie fillings, instant puddings, soup mixes, salad dressings, prepared breakfast cereals, bakery mixes, and other applications where thickening or stabilizing agents are needed and can be used without re-

TABLE 18.3

PHYSICAL AND CHEMICAL PROPERTIES OF RAW STARCHES

Starch	Average Granule Size, microns	Temperature at which Gelatinization begins in a 5% Solution °C	°F	Amylose Content, %	Glucose Units per Molecule of Amylose
Potato	33	63.9	147	22	980
Corn	15	80.0	176	28	480
Tapioca	20	62.8	145	18	980
Amioca	15	73.9	165	0–4	
Arrowroot	30–45	75.0	167	20	
Wheat	21	76.7	170	25	540
Rice	5	81.1	178	17	
Sago	31	73.9	165	27	420

TABLE 18.4

CHARACTERISTICS OF 5% AQUEOUS RAW STARCH
DISPERSIONS GELATINIZED AND COOLED

Starch	Taste	Texture	Clarity
Potato	Sl. Charact.	Long cohesive	Clear
Corn	Cereal	Short stiff gel	Opague
Tapioca	Bland	Long cohesive	Clear to translucent
Amioca (sorghum)	Cereal	Long cohesive	Clear to translucent
Arrowroot	Bland	Short cohesive	Translucent
Wheat (flour)	Cereal	Short soft gel	Slightly opague
Rice	Cereal	Short stiff gel	Slightly opague
Sago	Bland	Long cohesive	Clear to translucent

Source: *Food Techn. 13*, No. 1 (1959).

sorting to heat. They are used in marshmallows to absorb and retain water; in meat products as binders; and in the form of grits in the brewing industry.

Pregelatinized starch is *more susceptible to enzyme action.* Pelleted pregelatinized products of the type used in pearl tapioca puddings are made from corn and waxy corn starches.

Pregelatinized starches are also modified by acids, oxidizing agents, etc.

Starch Sponge.—Starch sponge is a 5 to 10% starch paste slowly frozen and thawed, and squeezed and dried to a brittle porous mass. Dried starch sponge will absorb 16 times its own weight of water. It is used in icings or as crunchy in-gredients in candies.

Starch Films.—Films of starch are prepared from both amy-lose and amylopectin fractions. *Amylose film* has greater ease of solution and is acted upon by digestive enzymes. Edible wrappers for food materials are made from amylose film. *Amylopectin film* is more brittle and weaker than amylose film, but is instantaneously soluble in water. It is used for individual packets for instant tea, laundry starch, dyes, etc.

Chemically Modified Starches

Only slight modification of starch molecules is necessary to effect drastic changes in properties. The various types include: (1) acid-modified, which yields thin-boiling starch, (2) oxidized starch, and (3) chemically derivatized starch. Their charac-teristics are as follows:

(1) *Acid-modified* (0.1N HCl or H_2SO_4 at 122°F for 6 to 24 hr)
  (a) lower paste viscosity
  (b) granules more fragile and easily broken during pasting
  (c) pastes tend to gel and form firmer gels than unmodified starch (gum drops, jelly beans)

(2) *Oxidized starches* (by peroxides, $KMnO_4$, O_3, dichromate, O_2, persalts, chlorine, halite and hypo-halite salts)
  (a) decrease or increase viscosity
  (b) greater stability and clarity of pastes
  (c) reduce bacterial count
  (d) produce whiteness
  (e) produce no odor
  (f) improve mobility as a powder

They are used in:

(a) Preparation of soups and sauces where *high thickening power* is desired.

TABLE 18.5

COMPANIES AND SOME OF THE TYPES OF STARCH ON THE MARKET

1. *National Starch and Chemical Corp.*, 750 Third Ave., New York, N.Y. 10017
   - (a) Clear Jel   Refined waxy maize
   - (b) Clear Jel S   Pregelatinized waxy maize
   - (c) Col Flo 67   Modified waxy maize
   - (d) Purity 69   Modified tapioca
   - (e) Crystal Gum   Low-viscosity tapioca blend
   - (f) Dry Flow   Hydrophobic

2. *A. E. Staley Mfg. Co.*, P.O. Box 151, Decatur, Ill. 62525
   - (a) Magnapol   Amylopectin (87%) corn
   - (b) Nepol   Amylose (90%) corn
   - (c) Mira Clear   Modified corn starch

3. *Morning Star, Nicol Inc., Paisley Division.* 109 W. 38th St., New York, N.Y. 10019
   - (a) Star Freeze   Modified tapioca
   - (b) Arogum   Oxidized potato starch
   - (c) Aroostoocrat   Pregelatinized potato starch
   - (d) Fruitfil   Modified tapioca
   - (e) Tendergel   Modified tapioca
   - (f) Arrowstar   Pregelatinized arrowroot
   - (g) Redisol 4&D.C.   Pregelatinized tapioca

4. *Hercules Powder Co.*, Wilmington, Delaware. 19899
   - (a) Starbake   Wheat starch
   - (b) HMD 981
   - (c) HMD 982   Acid modified raw wheat starch
   - (d) HMD 973

(e) Starvis   Gelatinized starch
(f) HMD 1300
(g) HMD 983   Acid modified pregelatinized
(h) HMD 984   wheat starch
(i) HMD 1199
(j) HMD 1198   Oxidized gelatinized wheat starch
(k) HMD 1197

5. *The Hubinger Company*, 601 Main Street, Keokuk, Iowa 52632
   (a) O.K. Cerioca No. 50   Blend of modified and waxy maize starches
   (b) O.K. Kremegel Starch   Refined starch
   (c) O.K. Bakers' Dusting
       Starch No. 632   Corn starch
   (d) Cerioca No. 100   Waxy maize modified

6. *American Maize Products Co.*[1] 250 Park Ave., New York, N.Y. 10017
   Use trade name Amaizo before starch products
   (a) 12 regular corn products including Fluftex
   (b) 10 waxy maize products including W-13 (cross linked)
   (c) 8 pregelatinized products including Amaizo Instant W13 (cross linked)

7. *Stein, Hall & Co.*, 605 3rd Ave., New York, N.Y. 10016
   (a) Ramalin   Amylopectin, potato
   (b) Ramalose   Amylose, potato and other starches

[1]Most of these are high amylose starches.

(b) As anticaking agents in baking powder, and are unique in that they do not depend upon paste or gel-forming properties. Their function is to hold moisture.

(c) Oxidation with calcium peroxide produces a starch of low-ered hot-paste viscosity, but on cooling provides a clear strong gel for use in *gum confectionery*.

(3) *Derivatized starches* (e.g., Clearjel) (Cross-linked starches) Treatment of alcohol groups yield esters and ethers. Com-plete substitution is possible. These modified starches are used in canning and in long cooking procedures or where agitation may be involved, in salad dressings where acetic acid is used, or fruit pie fillings of acidic nature, where marked resistance to acid breakdown is desired. These properties are explained by the crosslinking of OH groups.

(4) *Other modified starches* are those enzymatically treated as in the fermentation process during breadmaking.

Table 18.1 indicates the uses of the many types of starches, and Table 18.5 lists some of the companies that produce starches, especially the modified types. New ones are always being made, especially of the freeze-thaw stability type. These, of course, must be evaluated and approved by the FDA and placed on the GRAS list.

CHAPTER 19

D. A. Bodnar | # Products from Corn
Wet Milling

As the result of continuous advances in food science, corn
starch, corn syrup, and corn sugar—better known as *dextrose*
—enjoy ever greater use. Today, the **products** of corn refining
enhance the taste, improve the consistency, and contribute
various other qualities to more than 8,000 separate food items.
Catsup, sweet pickles, tartar and steak sauces, horseradish,
jams, jellies, and salad dressings are just a few. Others
include margarines, coffee whiteners, ice cream, candy
and confections, bread and other baked goods, frozen fruits
and vegetables, soups, novelty items, baby foods, pet foods,
and spices. Products refined from corn also find their way
into a host of nonfood uses ranging from papermaking to drilling oil wells.

The corn most often used by refiners is not sweet corn,
but standard No. 2 yellow dent hybrid corn. Commonly called
"field corn," it is recognized by the yellow dent in the top
of its kernel. The abundance of America's harvest is manifest
in that the refiners, who process about 225 million bushels of
corn every year, use only about 5% of the annual crop: 80%
never leaves the farm, another 10% is ground for animal
feed, 2.5% is used by the dry millers or cereal makers, and
2.5% is used by distillers. Many by-products of refiners
and distillers are sold as animal feed ingredients, so that
92% of the annual harvest winds up as animal feed.

Anatomy of the Corn Kernel

To understand the process of corn refining, it is first necessary to examine the structure of the corn kernel, for refining
if basically a method of separating the kernel's components
(Fig. 19.1).

The kernel is surrounded by a thin cellulosic, fibrous covering called the *hull*. A shallow layer of *gluten*—a substance containing most of the protein and valued for animal feeds—lies

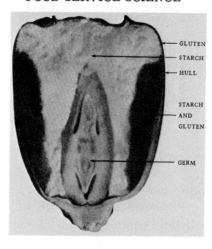

FIG. 19.1. THE CORN KERNEL

just under the hull. Adjacent to the gluten layer and bulging
toward the kernel's center is a mixture of starch and gluten
called *hard starch*. The germ, which contains almost all the
oil, lies under one side of the kernel on the depressed portion
of the front face. Surrounding the germ, above and on either
side, is starch. The kernel contains about 15% moisture,
60% starch, 9% protein, 5% oil, 5% hull, and 6% ash and other
solubles.

STARCH

Starch is the white substance that occurs often in higher
plants. Chemically speaking, it is a carbohydrate formed
by the combination or polymerization of dextrose. Its easy
identification is possible because it gives characteristic
blue or reddish colorations when stained with a dilute iodine
solution.

Starch has a granular structure, and each pound of starch
contains about three-quarters of a trillion granules. The
granule contains two types of starch molecules. Some molecules, called *amylose*, are linear, composed of several hundred successively attached dextrose units. Other molecules
are branched, and these are called *amylopectin* (Fig. 19.2).
About 73% amylopectin and 27% amylose characterize No. 2

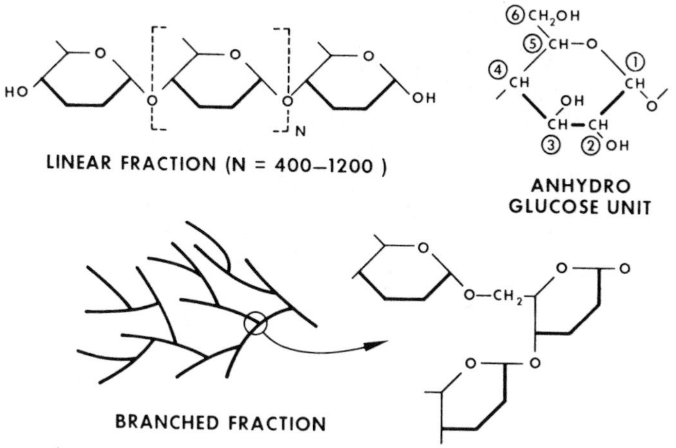

FIG. 19.2. ANHYDRO GLUCOSE UNIT, LINEAR FRACTION AND BRANCHED FRACTION OF STARCH

yellow dent hybrid corn starch. The "waxy" corn or Amioca that is sometimes used for special properties contains starch that is nearly all amylopectin. Two other types of corn starch are now finding use. These are referred to as high-amylose starches; one contains 55% amylose and the other 70% amylose. Hopefully, corn can soon be bred with even higher percentages of amylose.

Attractive forces between the amylose and amylopectin molecules account for the granule structure of starch. The theorized structure has the interlaced molecules of the starch fractions oriented in a radial direction in each concentric layer of the granule. Drawn together into bundles or "micelles," the molecules form a network that holds the granule together and prevents it from dissolving in cold water. A crystalline lattice is formed by the associated micelles, explaining the fact that a dark cross appears on the granule when examined under a microscope using polarized light. Sufficient energy will overcome the intermolecular forces in the granule, and this enables the refiner to make certain modifications in his starch (Fig. 19.3).

Properties of Starch

Although granular starches are insoluble in cold water, they lose their polarization crosses and start swelling when, suspended in water, they are heated beyond a certain temperature.

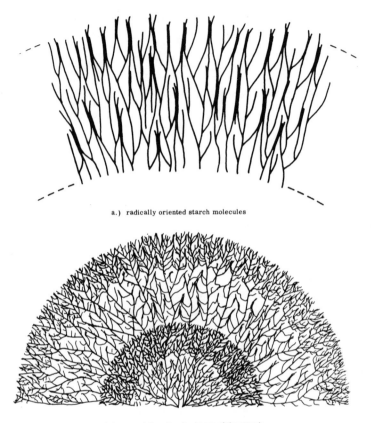

a.) radically oriented starch molecules

b.) concentric molecular layers of the granule

FIG. 19.3. SUBMICROSCOPIC STRUCTURE OF A STARCH GRANULE

This temperature is called the *gelatinization temperature* of the starch. Water enters the individual granules as they ·are heated to higher temperatures, and they continue to swell. As they expand and take up more volume, they start to "jostle" each other; the result is an increase in the viscosity of the slurry proceeding to the "pasty" form of cooked starch. Although the granules are exceptionally elastic, they become distorted and fragmented when vigorously stirred or when the heating is prolonged. This causes a viscosity decrease, although enough granules survive to impart "body" or consistency to the suspension.

One of the special properties of high-amylose starches is that they gelatinize only with great difficulty and do not dissolve

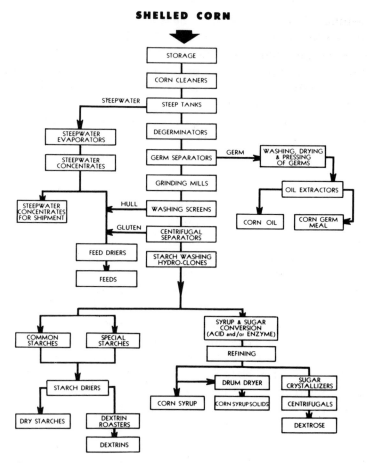

FIG. 19.4. SCHEMATIC OUTLINE OF THE CORN WET MILLING PROCESS

easily. On the other hand, the absence of amylose in "waxy" starch causes it to swell rapidly and fall apart under continuous cooking.

Processing

The corn arrives at the refinery either by rail or truck, and before processing, it is thoroughly cleaned by passage through a series of screens and air separators that remove both over- and undersized material, mostly broken pieces of corn cob, cracked kernels, and other grains (Fig. 19.4).

Steeping—The kernels must be softened before they can be separated into their components. This is done by steeping, or soaking the corn in stainless steel tanks for about 40 hr. Germination and most kinds of fermentation are prevented by adding a small amount of sulfur dioxide. Certain solubles that are leached out during steeping are recovered from the steepwater after the corn is removed and are used in livestock feeds. Portions of the steepwater are also used in several industrial fermentations, such as the manufacture of various antibiotics.

Milling.—The softened corn passes over a series of curved screens to separate it from water. A set of machines then tear the kernels apart and free the germ without crushing it. These are called *degerminating mills.*

The resulting mass is passed through two series of germ hydrocyclones that separate the lighter germ from the heavier starch, gluten and hulls by centrifugal action. The heavier fraction goes to another series of mills for finer grinding and then, after washing, passes over a sequence of curved screens where the hulls and grits are eliminated. The mixture of starch and gluten, or "mill starch," goes to the starch-separation department for further refining.

Starch Separation.—Huge centrifuges and small cyclones separate the starch from the lighter gluten using the same principle found in a cream separator. The starch fraction receives several washes and filterings, and then passes to the finishing departments for processing into various starch products of conversion into corn syrup or dextrose.

Types of Corn Starch

Common Starch.—Dried starch as it comes direct from the refining process with no further modification is known commercially as *common, regular, untreated,* or *unmodified* corn starch. Cooked in water, its solution is cloudy and non-cohesive; on cooling it has a tendency to set, or gel, depending on its concentration. It is thus referred to as "thick cooking" starch. Large quantities are used as paper and textile sizes and adhesives. Regular corn starch finds its way into such food items as salad dressings, puddings, canned foods, and confections. Other uses for regular corn starch are brewing, tabletting, and sugar grinding.

"Waxy" corn starch differs somewhat from regular corn starch in that it produces clear, fluid, and cohesive pastes. It is non-gelling and when used with other corn starches, it reduces their tendency to gel.

Numerous cold water-swelling or pregelatinized starches are now being marketed. Such starches are gelatinized, then dried on heated rolls or drums. The dried starch becomes viscous again when brought in contact with water. Pregelatinized thick-boiling starches are used as beater additives in papermaking, for making instant foods, and for drilling oil wells.

Thin-Boiling Starches.—Acid-modified or thin-boiling starches are usually converted in "milk form." A small amount of hydrochloric acid is added to a suspension of starch in water, and the solution is then heated to a temperature below the gelatinization point. The acid is neutralized after the desired conversion, and the starch is filtered and dried.

The acid apparently penetrates the looser molecular areas between the micellar bundles, hydrolytically breaking a few of the molecular chains. With the connecting network between the micelles weakened, the granules fall apart when gelatinized in hot water. This accounts for sizable reduction in viscosity.

Acid-modified starches are made over a wide viscosity range. They are designated by their relative fluidities (the reciprocal of viscosity), as 20, 40, 60, 75, and 90, etc. The higher the number designation, the lower the viscosity.

Textiles warp sizes and laundry starches are based on acid-modified starch. It is also the standard starch used for making candies such as orange slices and jelly beans, etc.

Oxidized Starches.—Oxidized starches are made in much the same way as acid-modified starches, except that sodium hypochlorite replaces the acid. By its oxidizing action, the hypochlorite introduces zig-zag discontinuities into the amylose. The net result is a limitation of the degree to which the molecules associate upon cooling. This increases stability against gelling. The applications of oxidized starches tend to be industrial because the products generally have a medicinal flavor and odor due to the hypochlorite treatment.

Specialty Starches.—In addition to the broad general types of starches, starches of a more specialized character have been developed. Some of these have been designed to meet the individual requirements of a single application. Others are useful for a variety of purposes. These starches may be modified to make them either thin-boiling, or even thicker-boiling than regular starch. They may incorporate certain fats or oils to provide products for molding confections such as gum drops or jelly beans. They may also incorporate chemical additives to provide "free flow" characteristics. These products can be used to dust bread doughs in much the same manner as flour, but at reduced cost and without the possibility of insect infestation.

Starch Derivatives.—Starch may be chemically combined with other substances to yield products of widely different characteristics. In the preparation of such products, it is common practive to attach to the starch molecules such sub-stituent groups as carboxyl, phosphate, alkylamine, car-boxymethyl, hydroxyethyl, hydroxypropyl, and others. The property possibilities of derivatized starches are almost limitless, and striking new starch derivatives of increased usefulness offer a great possibility for the future.

Dextrins.—When dry starch is subjected to acidic conditions and high temperatures, and roasted in the absence of water, the result is a modification of the starch terms "dextriniza-tion." This particular type of starch modification provides unique product properties which cannot be obtained in slurry type processes. Depending on the amount of acid used, the roasting temperature, and the duration of the roasting cycle, three general types of dextrins are produced. These are de-noted as white and yellow dextrins and British Gums. Ap-plications are generally restricted to adhesives, such as the familiar adhesive on envelopes and stamps. Some dextrins are used as binders or as cloud agents in select food applica-tions.

CORN SYRUP AND DEXTROSE

Manufacture

Corn syrup and dextrose are made by adding either acid or enzyme or both to a starch slurry to break the hydrolytic bonds that hold the starch molecule together, with the acid or enzyme acting as a catalyst. Chemically speaking, the degree to which the hydrolysis reaction has been carried out is measured by the chemical reducing power of the syrup. Starch *per se* has no significant reducing power, but each polymer unit, which is a dextrose molecule, does have reducing power. As each hydrolytic bond of the starch molecule is disrupted, a reducing end of a dextrose molecule is "freed." If the starch were completely hydrolyzed to dextrose, the hydrolysis product would exhibit the reducing power of dextrose. Thus, a comparison of the reducing power of a partially hydrolyzed starch product or syrup to the reducing power of dextrose would be its "dextrose equivalent." Technically defined, the Dextrose Equivalent or D. E., of a syrup is the total reducing sugar content calculated as percent anhydrous dextrose and expressed as a percentage of the total dry substance.

Acid-Converted Syrups.—Acid-converted corn syrups are generally made with hydrochloric acid. A starch slurry of about 35 to 40% dry substance is acidulated to about 0.12% acidity, based on the weight of starch to be converted. The reaction occurs in a large cooker, using a steam pressure of about 30 psig. As the reaction progresses, the gelatinized starch is converted first to polysaccharides of higher molecular weight and subsequently to sugars, mostly maltose and dextrose. The sugar content increases and the viscosity decreases as conversion proceeds (Fig. 19.5).

When conversion reaches the desired point, the entire contents of the reaction vessel is transferred to a tank where the acidity is reduced with sodium carbonate. In most cases, the pH is adjusted to between 4 and 5, slightly on the acid side, this aids in removing unwanted substances, prevents corrosion of equipment, and stops the conversion reaction. The salt resulting from the neutralizing reaction is ordinary table salt, sodium chloride.

The next step consists of skimming off the fatty substances that rise to the surface, using a device called a skimmer or with a fat-separating centrifuge. Suspended solid matter is removed by filtering. The filtrate is then evaporated to about 50% dry substance.

After the initial evaporation, the hydrolyzate is passed through carbon filters that effect further clarification and decolorization. Thus the resulting syrup is practically as clear and colorless as water. This process removes certain

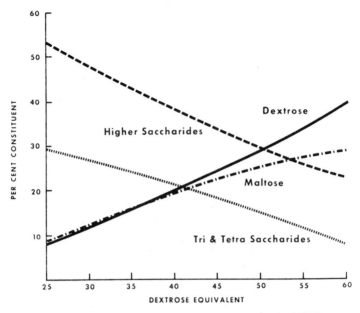

FIG. 19.5. ACID HYDROLYZED CORN SYRUP ANALYSIS

dissolved substances (protein and color bodies) and partially
removes soluble minerals. Further refinement of the syrup
can be obtained with ion-exchange resins. Trace impurities
are removed in a process analogous to that used in water
softening, except that the resins are quite specific in design
and purpose. Syrups refined with ion-exchange resins typically
have very good color and color stability.

After final filtration, part of the residual water is evaporated
to bring the syrup to the desired density or solids content.
This takes place in large vacuum pans, allowing the moisture
to be removed at temperatures below levels that would result
in thermal damage to the syrup. The syrup is then cooled
before loading into tank cars, tank trucks, or steel drums.

Acid-Enzyme Converted Syrups.—Acid-enzyme converted
syrups, or dual-conversion syrups, are made in essentially
the same way as acid-converted syrups, except that after
the syrup has been neutralized, clarified, and partially concentrated, an enzyme is added to advance the conversion
further. When enzyme hydrolysis has progressed to the desired level, the enzyme is inactivated. Adjustment of pH,
further refining, and final evaporation follow, as in the produc-

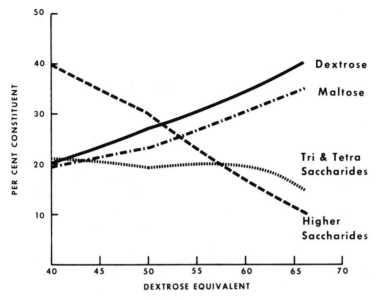

FIG. 19.6. ACID-ENZYME HYDROLYZED CORN SYRUP ANAL-
YSIS

tion of straight acid-conversion corn syrup (Fig. 19.6). The
final carbohydrate composition of corn syrups can be carefully
controlled by selecting enzymes which perform specific hydrolysis functions. One example is the hydrolysis of starch with
malt enzymes which consist largely of α-amylase enzyme (Fig.
19.7).

Dextrose

Dextrose, of course, is the product of complete conversion
of corn starch, and in anhydrous form is 100 D.E. Today,
all commercially available dextrose is produced by enzyme
hydrolysis utilizing the specific enzyme "amyloglucosidose."
The enzyme hydrolysis process produces dextrose of exceptionally high quality as compared to the dextrose previously manufactured by acid hydrolysis (Fig. 19.8). The
basic manufacture of dextrose is the same as that of corn
syrup, except that after purification and concentration, the
highly refined dextrose liquor is seeded with dextrose crystals.
Crystallization is then carried out under carefully controlled

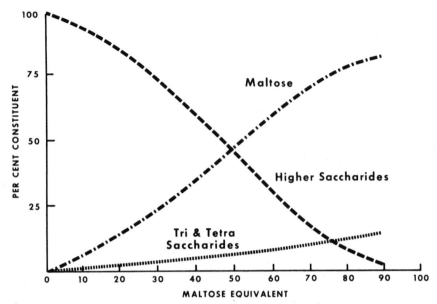

FIG. 19.7. MALT HYDROLYZED SYRUP ANALYSIS

rates of cooling in large crystallizers equipped with spiral
agitators.

After about 100 hr in the crystallizers, the crystalline
dextrose monohydrate is separated from the mother liquor
in centrifuges, washed, dried, and packed in 100-lb paper
bags. The mother liquor which has been separated from the
crystals by the centrifuges is clarified, concentrated, and
then passed through another crystallization cycle. Most dextrose prepared in this manner is actually dextrose monohydrate, with D.E. of 99+.

Anhydrous Dextrose.—Anhydrous dextrose requires still
further processing. Anhydrous dextrose has a different crystal
system, one not containing water. Crystalline dextrose monohydrate from the centrifuges is redissolved in water to form
a solution containing about 55% dry substance. Activated
carbon is added to this solution and the mixture is heated
to about 160°F for 30 min. The solution is then filtered until
perfectly clear, after which it is run into an evaporator for
crystallization. Seeding with crystals from a previous batch
is not required since graining conditions are effected by evaporation. Evaporation is continued until crystallization has
reached the desired stage. Centrifuging separates the crystals

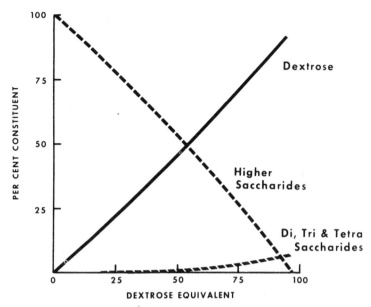

FIG. 19.8. GLUCOSIDASE HYDROLYZED SYRUP ANALYSIS

from the remaining liquid; then the crystals are washed with a hot water spray. Finally, the anhydrous dextrose is removed from the centrifuges, dried, pulverized and packed.

Physical Properties of Corn Syrups and Dextrose

Corn syrup and dextrose are essentially tasteless except for sweetness. The sweetening power of various corn sweeteners, compared with sucrose, is primarily dependent not only on the percentages of sweetener solids but also on the combination of sweeteners.

The effect of increasing concentration is evident when dextrose solutions are compared with sucrose solutions. A 2% solution of dextrose is about two-thirds as sweet as a sucrose solution of equivalent concentration. As the concentration is increased, the difference in sweetness is less apparent. In fact, at a level of 40% solids, sucrose and dextrose solutions appear to be equally sweet.

When corn syrup or dextrose is used in combination with sucrose, the resulting sweetness is usually greater than would be expected. For example, when tested at 45% solids, a mixture of 25% 42 D.E. corn syrup and 75% sucrose is considered to be as sweet as a sucrose solution of 45% solids.

Corn syrup, corn syrup solids, and dextrose are thoroughly compatible with other sweeteners and with food flavors. In canned fruit, for example, a liquid packing medium containing sucrose and a corn sweetener achieves optimum sweetness while providing superior body or density. Manufacturers of ice cream find that body and texture are improved by the use of corn sweeteners, and that a smoother product, with better melt-down results. In sherbets and ices, these sweeteners tend to eliminate crustation, promote smoothness, and inhibit separation of liquid from solids.

All corn sweeteners are readily soluble in water. Dextrose has a negative heat of solution, that is, it cools a mixture in which it is dissolved. This property is useful to bakers since it has a cooling effect on the dough.

Anhydrous dextrose melts at 295°F, while dextrose hydrate with a melting point of 180°F readily melts in a boiling water bath. Dried corn syrups or commercial corn syrup solids are noncrystalline, amorphous powders which do not have distinct melting points. Instead, they gradually soften or dissolve in their own trace moisture when heated.

Corn sweeteners are hygroscopic in varying degrees, and the degree of hygroscopicity increases as the D.E. increases. The higher conversion syrups, crude sugars and dextrose thus are employed as humectants, moisture conditioners, and stabilizers.

The higher saccharides give corn syrup its cohesive and adhesive properties. They have some of the desirable attributes of certain vegetable gums; therefore, corn syrups are used in a number of products requiring these characteristics. The higher saccharides also contribute the chewy texture desired in certain types of confections.

All the corn sweeteners, particularly the corn syrups, control the crystallization of sucrose and other sugars.

Dextrose, being a monosaccharide of molecular weight 180 compared with 342 for sucrose, has a relatively high osmotic pressure which enhances its effectiveness in inhibiting microbial spoilage in preserves.

Viscosity, one of the most important physical properties of corn syrups, is dependent on density, D.E., and tem-

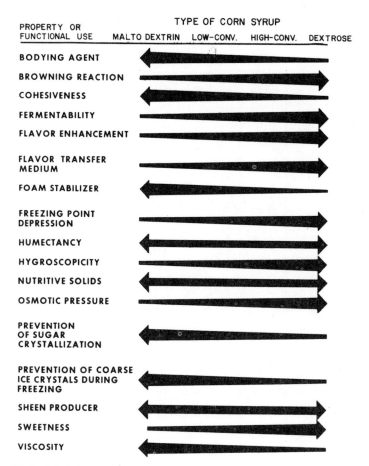

FIG. 19.9. PROPERTIES AND FUNCTIONAL USES OF CORN
SYRUP

perature. It decreases as D.E. and temperature are raised
but increases with higher density.

Chemical Properties of Corn Syrups and Dextrose

Fermentability is an important chemical property of corn
syrups and sugars in certain food applications. Dextrose
and maltose are readily fermentable by many organisms.
The fermentability of the corn syrups thus is roughly proportional to their content of dextrose and maltose—the higher
the D.E., the higher the fermentability. However, the property
of fermentability does not affect the storage life of corn syrups

TABLE 19.1

RELATIVE SWEETNESS OF CORN SWEETENERS COMPARED TO SUCROSE

Sweetener Type by Conversion Process	Dextrose Equivalent	Percent Solids	Relative Sweetness Values	
			Dry Basis %	As is Basis %
Enzyme	15	73.0	15	10
Enzyme	21	75.0	20	15
Enzyme	30	77.5	35	27
Acid	36	80.0	45	36
Acid	42	80.3	50	40
Acid/Enzyme (high maltose)	42	80.3	55	44
Acid	52	81.0	60	49
Acid/Enzyme	62	82.0	70	57
Acid/Enzyme	69	82.5	75	62
Enzyme/Enzyme/Enzyme (15% fructose)	75	82.0	80	65
Enzyme/Enzyme/Enzyme (42% fructose)	92	71.0	100	70
Enzyme/Enzyme	96	71.0	79	56
Enzyme—Dextrose	99+	91.5	80	73
Sucrose		100.0	100	100

In commercial formulations, these figures will not be absolute values, but should merely serve as a guide. Sweetener concentration, combination, and relationship to other ingredients present play an important role in the overall product sweetness. Temperature, texture, and other flavors in the food will also affect sweetness.

or sugars because they do not ferment unless diluted with water.

Dextrose has also the ability to combine with nitrogenous compounds at elevated temperatures to produce brown coloration. This property makes corn sweeteners useful in the manufacture of caramel color, promotes crust color in baking, and produces color and caramel flavor in other food products.

Dextrose, maltose, and certain polysaccharides of corn sweeteners are technically termed reducing sugars. This reducing property inhibits undesirable oxidative reaction in foods. It is useful in maintaining the bright red color in tomato catsup and strawberry preserves and in helping to retain desirable color in cured meats (Fig. 19.9).

RECENT PRODUCT DEVELOPMENTS AND INNOVATIONS

With the advances of food science, the uses for products from corn have increased continually. To meet these uses, the corn refiners have developed new and improved products. Some of the most current developments are found in the area of low conversion hydrolyzates. Either in liquid or dry form, the new products are designed as bulking agents, flavor carriers, bodying agents, etc. Their most prominent characteristics are very low hygroscopicity, high viscosity, and bland flavor.

Another new product is an edible packaging film. Although the present economics of film manufacture and some of its properties have not produced immediate and widespread use, it is filling a need in specific applications such as the dispersing of pre-measured enzymes, and flavors in packet form.

Finally, recent technology has produced fructose-containing corn syrups. Corn sweeteners have classically been combinations of dextrose and dextrose polymers. The applications of corn sweeteners have been limited in some areas by their sweetness, as dextrose is only about 80% as sweet as sucrose or table sugar. Now through enzyme and chemical technology, some of the dextrose present in corn syrups can be isomerized or changed to fructose, a very sweet sugar. This innovation provides for the manufacture of corn syrups with unprecedented sweetness levels, thereby increasing the application of corn syrups substantially (Table 19.1).

CHAPTER 20

L. L. W. Smith
L. J. Minor

Sweeteners, Candies, and Gums

SWEETNESS AND ARTIFICIAL SWEETENERS

Sweetness in food products is controlled by various factors, one of which is the acid content. The increase in acid decreases the sweetness, such as lemon in sweetened tea, and vinegar or acetic acid in the pickle industry. The reverse is true; increase in sugar decreases the effect of the acidity. These effects apply only to *small percentages*. The sugar-to-salt ratio seems to have a bearing on sweetness, at least at very low concentrations; however, no amount of sugar will wipe out the saltiness of over-salted potatoes. The presence of a hydrophilic colloid, such as starch, pectin, algin, etc., seems to decrease the sweetness of a product, permitting the use of more sugar, as in the making of jellies.

Sweetness varies with temperature. Warm or melted ice-cream is much sweeter than ice-cream served at −4 to −6°C. Sugars themselves tend to be sweeter at higher temperatures since the intramolecular bonds tend to break more at 60°C than at 20°C. Glucose is sweeter at higher temperatures, yet fructose seems sweeter at lower temperatures. Glucose sweetness increases with concentration; molecular complexes form more rapidly than with sucrose, adding to the complicated sweetness picture.

Sweetness in food products is therefore related to: (a) the sugar and acid ratio, (b) the sugar and salt ratio, (c) the hydrophilic colloid content, (d) the temperature, (e) concentration, (f) glucose and sucrose content, which has synergistic effects on sweeteners, and (g) the fact that sugar sweetness varies inversely with intermolecular bonding.

Artificial sweeteners have been on the market for many years, and as ill effects have been noted in animal testing, some have gradually been withdrawn and new ones added. Perhaps the one best known and used the longest to date is saccharin.

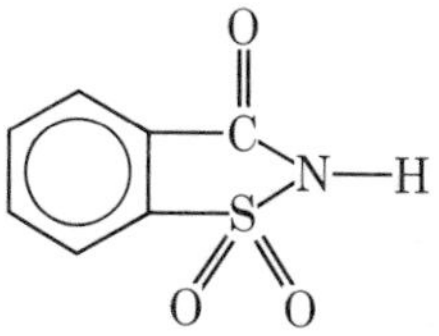

o-carboxylbenzenesulfimide or saccharin

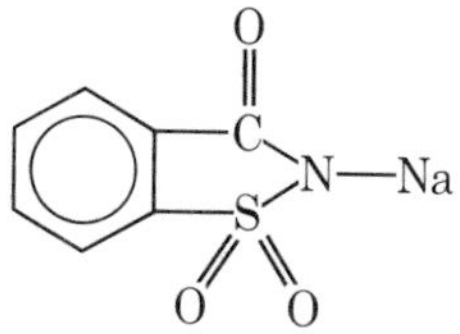

sodium o-carboxybenzine sulfimide or soluble saccharin

Saccharin has no food value and $\frac{1}{2}$ grain or one 0.03-gm tablet replaces 1 heaping teaspooon (10 gm) of sugar, indicating a sweetening power 300 times that of sucrose.

The cyclamates have been banned by the F.D.A. and removed from the GRAS list.

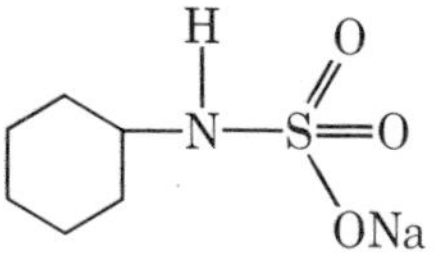

sodium cyclohexylsulfamate

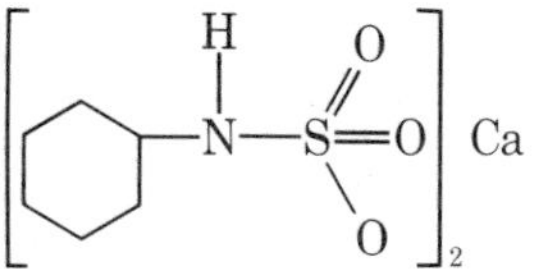

calcium cyclohexylsulfamate or Sucaryl

These compounds are 30 to 40 times as sweet as sucrose.

A combination of the two types, i.e., the saccharin and the cyclamate, in a ratio of 1 to 10 had been used to eliminate the bitter aftertaste left by saccharin. These are not used except in medical prescriptions for patients.

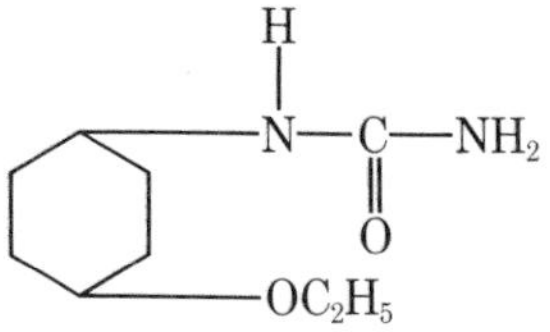

4-ethoxyphenylurea or dulcin

This compound was barred from use many years ago after deleterious effects were observed on dogs. It is 250 times as sweet as sugar.

Other sweeteners used in commercial productions are glucose combined with saccharin, the polyhydric alcohols, sorbitol and mannitol, and even glycerol, which has a sweet taste. Researchers are busy working on other products such as the dihydrochalcones obtained from citrus waste.

This particular compound would be rated at 2000 in sweetness. Sweetness seems to vary with the type of hydroxy and alkoxy groups substituted in the (x), (y), and (z) positions.

A naturally occurring sweetening agent from the fruit of "Dioscorecphyllum cuminsie" has been partially evaluated as being 1500 times as sweet as sucrose. This is a tropical fruit originally received from Nigeria and is indigenous to West Africa.

Another natural sweetener is derived from licorice root and is 50 times as sweet as sugar. It is *ammoniated glycyrrhizin*, $C_{42}H_{61}O_{16}NH_4 \cdot 5H_2O$

glycyrrluctinic acid glycoside or gly-cyrrluzinic acid

A patented product is sucrose-ammoniated glycyrrhizin sweetening agent. Other combinations of low caloric sweetening agents are fructose-rich corn syrup and sucrose or fructose combined with saccharin.

A new dipeptide sweetener formed from two amino acids is available for experimental use only, namely, aspartylphenyl-alanine methyl ester, a white crystalline powder with no discernible after-taste; it has from 100 to 200 times the sweetness of sucrose. Another type of sweetener on the market contains several amino acids, a polyglycerol, sorbitol and emulsified saccharin, and is only 6 to 7 times as sweet as sucrose. It will be of much interest to see the types of sweeteners which evolve and meet the F.D.A. standards.

CANDIES

Crystalline Candies

A standard crystalline candy, such as fondant, must have sugar crystals that are so small that the candy feels creamy and velvety on the tongue, and that remain small until the candy is consumed. Therefore, the problem in making fondant or any crystalline candy is to produce conditions under which only small crystals are formed. The process of making fondant involves: (1) complete solution of the sugar in water; (2) concentration of the sugar solution by cooking so that a high degree of supersaturation is obtained when the syrup is cooled to approximately 50°C; and (3) recrystallization of the sugar in a great number of very tiny crystals from this supersaturated solution.

Complete Solution of Sugar.—Solutions become most supersaturated when no nuclei are present to cause premature crystallization. Undissolved crystals of sugar may act as nuclei and "seed" the solution, thus starting crystallization before the solution is supersaturated enough to give tiny crystals. "Seeded" solutions give rise to large, coarse crystals. Therefore, *it is important to ensure the complete solution of all sugar crystals during the first part of the process of making fondant.* Using an *excess amount of water*, *stirring* the sugar solution, and *heating* the sugar solution will aid in dissolving all the sugar crystals. Contrary to the idea that stirring during cooking will cause a candy to be coarse-grained, stirring has no influence on the final texture of the candy *if stirring* *ceases* before the cooking period is over. Care must be taken *to prevent splashing* the syrup on the sides of the pan where it *may dry, recrystallize,* and thus *seed* the syrup as it is poured from the pan. Placing the lid on the pan during only the first few minutes of boiling will allow the steam vapor to condense and wash down any crystals that might have remained on the sides of the pan. Wiping the sides of the pan with a piece of wet cheesecloth tied around the tines of a fork is also a helpful procedure.

The premature formation of crystals may likewise be prevented by avoiding the formation of air bubbles when the hot syrup is poured onto the plate to cool and by not scraping the pan as the syrup is poured.

Proper Degree of Supersaturation. — For crystallization of sugar to occur, nuclei must be present in the solution. The formation of nuclei is possible only from a supersaturated solution. Supersaturation of a sugar solution is attained by boiling it to a certain temperature and then cooling it to a much lower temperature. Since the boiling point of a solution increases as the concentration increases, the final temperature to which a candy solution is cooked determines the concentration of the sugar solution. Because the solubility of sugar is directly related to the temperature of the solution, cooling the saturated sugar solution will result in a supersaturated solution. The higher the final temperature used in cooking the solution, the greater may be the degree of supersaturation.

A fondant which is usually boiled to 112°C at standard pressure would hold 80 gm sucrose in 100 gm solution. If the solution is cooled carefully, no crystallization will occur, and the sugar syrup will still contain 80 gm sugar. At 90°C, the solution will approach saturation since 100 gm of a saturated sucrose solution contain 80.6 gm sucrose at 90°C. Below 90°C, supersaturation develops until at 50°C the optimum degree of supersaturation is attained. Agitation of the solution at this temperature will give many fine crystals. A comparison of the values given for a sugar syrup cooked to 112°C and one cooked to 130°C shows that the degree of supersaturation in the latter syrup will be much greater than that in the former.

The final temperature of cooking is checked *most accurately* by a thermometer, but tests for the degree of concentration may be made by the following method. A small amount of the syrup is placed in cold water and gathered together and formed into a ball. The greater concentration of sugar, the harder will be the ball formed, as observed by holding it in the palm of the hand.

Crystallization of Sucrose.—The last step in making crystalline candies is the production of very many fine crystals. In order to obtain many fine crystals, a great number of nuclei must be present. Molecules of sugar attach themselves to these nuclei, and the crystals grow. The *size* to which they grow depends upon the *number of nuclei present* and upon the *rate at which crystallization occurs*. If a large number of nuclei are present, and crystallization is rapid, the crystals formed will be tiny and numerous, since the crystals come down too fast to concentrate upon a few nuclei, as long as there are other available nuclei. However, if there are only a few nuclei present and crystallization is slow, there will be only a few crystals, and these will grow large, since many sucrose molecules will have time to concentrate on each nucleus.

The nuclei may form spontaneously from a supersaturated solution as it cools. In this case, only a few nuclei develop, and the crystals become large. Dust particles may stimulate nuclei formation. Agitation, beating, or stirring the solution hastens the formation of nuclei. "Seeding" the solution will bring about the same results as spontaneous formation of nuclei in the solution.

Several factors influence the formation of nuclei. The four principal conditioning factors in the formation of small crystals are: (a) the absence of any previously undissolved crystals, (b) a high degree of supersaturation when crystallization is initiated, (c) extensive agitation when the desired concentration is attained, and (d) the presence of interfering substances. The first two conditions have been discussed.

Extensive Agitation at Desired Concentration.—If fondant is cooled without disturbance, spontaneous crystallization will occur, which has been shown to produce coarse, textured candy. Continuous agitation of the cooled supersaturated solution tends to prevent crystal growth by promoting the formation of many nuclei at one time. Beating must be continued until crystallization is complete. A cooled fondant syrup is clear and very stiff. As it is beaten, it becomes cloudy, opaque, and then whiter in appearance, losing its gloss and luster and becoming dull and dry. At this point, the candy becomes suddenly softer due to the heat of crystallization. When crystallization is complete, the heat disappears and the candy stiffens and should be kneaded or poured out at this stage.

If beating is stopped before crystallization is complete, the sugar molecules left in solution will grow on the crystals already formed, since there is no agitation to separate them. The result will be a grainy candy.

Presence of Interfering Substances. — Fondant can be made by heating only sugar and water, although it requires very careful handling to prevent the sugar molecules from clustering to form large crystals. This clumping of sugar molecules into large crystals may be prevented by the use of substances which interfere with crystal formation. These materials may be (a) substances that do not crystallize readily, such as dextrose, (b) substances that are adsorbed by the sugar crystals, and (c) substances that increase viscosity of the solution and thus decrease the molecular activity of the sucrose.

In fondant, corn syrup, invert sugar and/or some acid such as cream of tartar, lemon juice, or vinegar, which hydrolyzes the sucrose into invert sugar, are generally used to interfere with the crystallization of sucrose. In fudge, butter and the starch of chocolate and cocoa as well as the corn syrup act as interfering agents and aid in the formation of fine crystals. In divinity, egg protein is the interfering substance. In caramels, cream with corn syrup, or milk solids, may be used to prevent aggregation of sucrose crystals.

Substances that do not Readily Crystallize. — The principal substances that do not crystallize readily are other sugars, such as fructose, which crystallizes with the greatest difficulty. The ease of crystallization of sucrose from a mixture is much less than from a solution of sucrose alone. When crystallization does occur, it occurs all at once, and many fine crystals are formed at one time. Such a mixture can be obtained by adding invert sugar or by using an acid to change sucrose to invert sugar during the cooking period. The amount of invert sugar formed is influenced by several conditions: the length of the cooking time, the kind of acid, the concentration of the acid, the alkalinity of the water, and the temperature of heating.

Substances that are Adsorbed by Sugar Crystals. — If a foreign substance is strongly adsorbed by the sugar crystals, crystal growth is retarded because of the adsorbed layer of foreign material around the crystals. It may be retarded to such an extent that crystallization may never occur. *Fat, milk solids,* and *egg white* are adsorbed by sugar crystals, and because of this adsorption they aid in producing fine-grained or even amorphous candies. Other carbohydrates, such as starch and dextrins, may also be adsorbed, and may owe part of their capacity to interfere with crystallization to this property. Corn syrup is used rather commonly in the home, and it contains both glucose and dextrins.

Substances that Increase Viscosity of the Solution. — Substances that increase the viscosity of a solution of sucrose may prevent aggregation of the sucrose crystals by virtue of reducing molecular activity through the viscous syrup. Caramels do not crystallize, because the large quantities of milk solids and fat which are added, besides being adsorbed by sugar crystals, very definitely increase the viscosity of the candy mixture. Fine-textured fudge is produced by using corn syrup, butter, and cocoa or chocolate; all these increase viscosity, as does gelatin.

FONDANT

The factors controlling crystallization have been discussed. These factors are applicable to the preparation and the resulting structure of fondant.

Fondant made with cream of tartar becomes *snowy white* upon agitation due partly to small air particles whipped during beating and partly to the effect of the *action on the flavone* pigments in the sugar. If fondant is made with corn syrup, a *gray color* results, which may not be desirable. Fondant made with hard water has a *creamy color.* This may be the result of reaction of the alkaline salts in the water and the flavone pigments in the sugar, or it may be caused by caramelization.

When fondant stands for 24 hr it *"ripens"*: it becomes more moist, is more plastic, and can be kneaded more easily than before ripening. Perhaps it may even become sticky. Fondant is made up of crystals separated by a saturated sugar solution. When ripening occurs, the smallest crystals, which lie between the larger crystals and hold them more or less rigid, dissolve in the mother syrup, and the fondant becomes more plastic.

Candies that contain cream of tartar do not show any crystal growth during storage, while those containing corn syrup may become grainy.

Fondant centers of chocolate creams are firm to withstand handling; their liquefaction is brought about by the enzyme invertase after they are enrobed in the chocolate coating. The invertase is added to the fondant when it is softened for molding.

TEMPERATURES AND COLD WATER TESTS FOR SUCROSE SYRUPS

Temperature at Standard Pressure	Cold Water Test	Uses
112–115°C 234–240°F	Soft ball	Fondant, fudge, penuchi
118–120°C 244–248°F	Firmer ball	Caramels, or to be poured over beaten egg white
121–130°C 250–265°F	Harder ball	Pop corn balls, nougat divinities and some taffies
132–143°C 270–290°F	Soft-crack stage Separates into threads in cold water	Butterscotch and taffies
149–154°C 300–310°F	Hard crack stage	Brittles and glaces
160°C 320°F	Clear liquid	Barley sugar
170°C 338°F	Brown liquid	Caramel

When corn syrup (containing dextrins) and/or dextrins alone are used with sucrose in candies that do not require crystallization, the degree of hardness (cold water test) is at a lower temperature than when sucrose is used alone.

Amorphous Candies

Noncrystalline or amorphous candies solidify without the development of a definite crystalline pattern. Caramel, butterscotch, and taffy are examples of amorphous candy. Crystallization may be prevented by adding large quantities of glucose, fructose, corn syrup, fat, milk solids, and other foreign substances. Acids that produce invert sugar are used also.

In making amorphous candies as well as crystalline candies, *complete solution of sugar crystals is essential.* The final temperature of heating must be high enough to produce a highly viscous and concentrated solution. Upon cooling, formation of a crystal pattern is prevented by the high viscosity of the mixture and by rapid cooling of the syrup, so that the solution becomes very viscous before crystallization can occur.

GUMS

Gums are also food polymers that are finding more uses. Glickman's definition of a gum is any polymeric material that can be dissolved or dispersed in water to give viscous solutions or dispersions. This definition is based on the chief function of these hydrocolloids in food technology and leaves room for gelatin, casein, other protein materials as well as synthetic polymers both made and to be made. Glickman, likewise, classifies gums into three main categories: (1) natural gums; (2) modified natural or semisynthetic gums (those based on chemical modification of natural gums or gumlike materials); and (3) synthetic gums (those prepared by total chemical synthesis).

Gums are present in almost every natural food and are responsible for structure and texture. In prepared or convenience foods, they are used as additives to give the desired structural and textural consistencies to the product. These gums are necessary ingredients, and as such are not identified on the labels. They influence retention of water, reduction of evaporation rates, alteration of freezing rates, modify the crystal formation, and participate in some chemical reactions.

All gums are used in a wide range of specific food applications. Some typical functions are shown in Table 20.1.

Function of Gums in Food Products

There is an interplay between the viscosity and gelling characteristics of any specific gum and both are affected by temperature and concentration. Viscosity is defined as resistance to

TABLE 20.1

NATURAL POLYSACCHARIDES (HYDROCOLLOIDS)

	Polymer of	Charge	Use
A. Seaweed			
Agar-agar Insoluble in H_2O. Dispersed in hot H_2O. Forms strong gels. Will not melt up to 95°C	Polygalactose g.m.w. = 5000 to 160,000	Neutral Ⓝ	Icings, yogurt, baking Industry, culture medium For bacterial growth; removes tannins from wine
Carrageenan, "Irish moss," partially dispersed in cold H_2O; completely dispersed at 120–130°F	Sulfated D galactose alternate α1-3 β1-4 configuration. g.m.w. = 100,000–800,000	⊖ poly-anionic	Milk puddings, "Metracal"; creamed soups, kosher foods; "bloody Marys"; liquid coffee whiteners
Algins, readily dispersed in hot or cold H_2O. Freezing has no permanent effect. Requires more time to hydrate than starch or pectins	Mannuronic acid βD-1-4 linkage. No salt or propylene glycol ester. 3200 to 200,000 C_6 units	⊕ ⊖Ⓝ	Stabilizer; thickener; gelling agent; toppings; sausage casings; clarify beer; clarify wine; syn. potato chips; skin of artificial cherries; low-calorie foods; frozen spreads; instant puddings
Furcelleran, Danish agar; Dispersed in hot H_2O. Dispersed in hot milk. Successfully autoclaved	Polymer of galactose	Ⓝ	Excellent gelling ability; jelly icings; piping jelly; wine jelly, jams; confections; meat products; milk-based systems, puddings, milk drinks
B. Seed Gums			
Locust bean gums, "Carob." Seeds of locust	Polymer of galactose	Ⓝ	Does not gel; laxative, diuretic, relief of diarrhea; substitute for chocolate in health foods
Guar gum, India-seed	2:1 mannose to galactose; called a galactomannan	Ⓝ	Hydrates rapidly in cold H_2O; 0.3% in ice cream
C. Exudate Gums			
Gum arabic Exudate from sick acacia trees. Highly dispersed up to 50% conc	Galactose, glucauonic acid; Arabinose (5 C's) rhamnose = mannose with 6th C methylated; arabic acid	⊖	Viscous, jelly-like; similar to starch and used in confectionery products; emulsifiers of spices, mineral, vegetable & essential oils. Flavor fixative; vitamin glaze coatings; foam stabilizer 200 ppm for beer
Gum tragacanth, "goat horn shrub" oxidate. Highly	Galactose, glucuronic acid, Arabinose,	⊖	Thick and viscous; flavor emulsions; salad dressings; extruded confections;

	Polymer of	Charge	Use
dispersible; hydrates rapidly; resists acid hydrolysis	rhamocose, 6 dioxy L mannose CHO H—C—OH H—C—OH HO—C—H HO—C—H CH$_3$		bakery products; condiments; ice creams; sherbets; stabilizer in dry meringue mixes
Gum Karaya. Exudate—hydrates rapidly. g.m.w. = 9,500,000	Acetylated galactose, galacturonic acid, rhamnose	⊖	Resists acid hydrolysis; extruded sugar, confections, ice cream; sherbets, baking denture cream; bulk laxative; mucilage; stabilizer in French dressings; popsicles; prevents syneresis in cheese spreads

D. Starches

	Polymer of	Charge	Use
(a) Root (b) Seed Modified starches Types	Glucose; α linkage Glucose; α linkage	Ⓝ	Uses of starches Chapt. 18 Table 18

E. Cellulose Derivatives

	Polymer of	Charge	Use
CMC. Hydrates readily hot or cold	β linkage glucose	Ⓝ or anion- in character	Ice creams; icings, doughnut and cake mixes
—CH$_2$COOH attached to OH groups; R—O— CH$_2$COOH			Starch products; viscosity control agent; cheese spreads; dried dairy products
Methyl cellulose; hydrates readily in cold H$_2$O	Anhydroglucose units, methyl ether or methoxyl substituted or propylene glycol esters	Ⓝ	Bakery products; canned pie fillings; flavor emulsifiers; dietetic foods; high-strength water-sol. films or sheetings; stabilizer of foam

flow of a liquid system. The use of hydrocolloids depends upon the thickening of water media, the swelling of a particular hydrocolloid to perform its function in food stuffs. This could vary from forming and holding of emulsions of oil and water, stabilizing of liquid-solid-gas phases, and dispersion of liquid and solid phases to the stability of such phases.

Hydrophilic viscosities are affected by many factors, such as concentration, temperature, degree of dispersion, solvation, electrical charge, previous thermal treatment, previous mechanical treatment, presence or absence of other lyophilic colloids, age of lyophilic sol, and presence of electrolytes as well as nonelectrolytes. Lowe (1955) considers the above factors to be the "ten commandments of food preparation." The use of gums solely for thickening is common in such prod- ucts as pie fillings and puddings, beverage dry mixes, soup mixes, breading mixes, and dog foods where the addition of water forms a gravy-like sauce.

Hydrocolloid gels, on the other hand, are rigid systems that show resistance to flow under pressure and are capable of retaining a firm shape. They are generally composed of two phases: (1) a continuous network of solid materials and (2) a finely divided liquid phase which is enmeshed in the network. Gelatin can form both sol and liquid systems. Formation of a gel structure by long-chain polymers can be due to cross- linking of adjacent molecules to form a continuous network that will have the stability of a rigid state. The types of cross- linking or bonding are: (1) hydrogen bonding between nonionized carboxyl groups; (2) electrovalent linking such as between a negatively charged carboxyl group (COO^-) and a bivalent cation such as calcium; and (3) direct covalent linkage.

The texture of gels can vary from a smooth elastic gelatin- water gel to a short brittle carrageenan-water gel. Elastic gels generally exist when the cross-linking is low; a high degree of closely spaced cross-linking results in a more crys- talline-like structure and is more brittle. Then there are chewy gels used in the manufacture of synthetic meat products.

Factors which affect gels are sugar and acids. Sugar acts to separate polymer chains and sometimes is referred to as a plasticizer; however, it does compete with the polymer for water, thereby reducing the solubility or solvation of the poly- mer. Synergism is also shown by the action or combination of these hydrocolloids, such as carrageenan and locust bean gum. Carrageenan tends to give a brittle, crumbly gel, and the addition of a small amount of locust bean gum results in a gel that is more tender, elastic and stronger. Locust bean gum is sometimes used with pectins and agar gels. Guar gum, which has a chemical structure similar to locust bean gum, does not have this enhancing effect. Other gel structures are helped by nongelling hydrocolloids such as those of meringues, pie fillings and marshmallows. Carboxymethylcellulose and sodium algi- nate are reported to increase the sharpness of the gelation

point and to impart smoothness and workability. Incorporated
in a typical alginate dessert gel, the product will have freeze-
thaw stability.

In emulsions, mostly of the oil-in-water type, stability is
obtained by emulsifying, stabilizing and thickening or use of
the so-called surface-active agents. Gums are not typical long-
chained hydrophobic-hydrophilic compounds, but stabilize by
increasing the viscosity of the aqueous phase. The tendency of
the dispersed phase to coalesce is minimized and the emulsion
is stabilized by the protective effect based on the thickening
action of the gums. Examples of use of the above is gum tragacanth (and propylene glycol alginate) in preparing French
dressings. Starches are sometimes used in salad dressings
other than French for reasons of economy and ease of processing. Hydrocolloid stabilizers are also used in ice-creams,
sherbets and ices, and other frozen desserts. They improve
body, smoothness, and melt-down, and have excellent freeze-
thaw stability as in frozen puddings, etc. These hydrocolloids
are used in the preparation of liquid flavor emulsions, bottled
beverages, diet beverages, table syrups, and in some alcoholic
prepared mixed drinks. Here again the synergistic effect of
two gums is often better than either gum alone.

The importance of stabilizing suspensions is shown in preparing chocolate-flavored products, such as chocolate milk or
syrups, by the additional thickening action of hydrocolloids.
Carrageenans also have an affinity for small amounts of protein; this seems to be a chemical reaction. This is used to
advantage in suspending milk protein in buttermilk, yougurt and
other milk drinks. The gums cover the surface of the suspended
particles, acting as a protective colloid, and are attracted to
the aqueous or continuous phase.

Foams are closely related to emulsions and may be considered as agglomerations of gas bubbles separated by thin
films as well as dispersions of gas in a liquid or solid. These
are influenced more by temperature and air pressure, and
small changes in the surface tension of the film can result in
failure. These foams may be stabilized in a number of ways;
egg-white foams are set by heating, gelatin solutions after
whipping are cooled to set and stabilize the foam. Hydrocolloids
such as carrageenan, sodium alginate, and locust bean gum
are used to react with the protein to stabilize the above prod-

ucts. They also add to the viscosity of the systems. Icings of the meringue type use carboxymethylcellulose and in some instances where heat is not used, cold water-soluble carrageenans are employed as well as carboxymethylcellulose. Whipped toppings utilize locust bean gum, carrageenan and karaya to improve body and stability.

Hydrocolloids are used in crystallization procedures by (1) competing for the units that make up the crystal, (2) by having the ability to attach themselves to growing crystal surfaces and thus alter normal growth, and (3) by combining with impurities such as the Ca^{++} which would eliminate the effect of calcium on sugar crystallization. These effects are seen in ice creams, icings and in some confections.

These gums, especially gum arabic, are used as flavor fixation or encapsulating agents in spray-dried flavored powders. Microencapsulation or coacervation consists of depositing a complex protective colloidal film around microscopic oil droplets. Alginate sodium salts are also used and firmed by conversion to the calcium salts.

Many of these hydrocolloids have been used as edible protective films on food products. They have formed coatings for meats, vegetables, and other foods to prevent loss of moisture, oxidative rancidity, to retard bacterial growth and to improve the appearance and handling ease of the food stuffs.

The selection and application of hydrocolloids depends upon the usage, standards of identity, toxicity, permissive levels, cost and quality of the finished product. The latter factor can be divided into many categories, such as type, appearance, viscosity, odor, mouthfeel, hand feel, emulsification, synergistic effects, stability, preservation, etc. The mechanism of how the hydrocolloid works is not always clear.

PECTINS

Pectin substances are carbohydrate derivatives occurring in plant tissue, such as fruits. They may be classified in three categories:

Protopectin is a water-insoluble parent substance found in hard, immature fruit and citrus peel. It is converted to pectin during ripening.

Pectin is a general term for pectinates (salts and esters of pectinic acid) and pectinic acid. These are capable of forming gels when sugar and acid are present. These vary in degree of methylation from 1 to 14%.

Pectic acid is colloidal polygalacturonic acid mostly free of methoxyl ester groups. It is formed from pectin as the fruit becomes overripe.

Chemical Structure of Pectin

The pectin molecule is a polymer of galacturonic acid units linked together in a chain-like structure through carbons 1 and 4. The side chains are methoxyl groups or the corresponding acid.

Galactose

Galacturonic Acid   Methyl Galacturonate

Pectins from various sources differ in molecular size and degree of esterification. High-grade pectin may have a molecular weight of 200,000, and more than 1000 galacturonic units

Portion of a pectin chain (showing 1–4 linkage)

in one molecule. Low-grade pectins have shorter chains. Regular pectin (i.e., high-methoxylated pectin) contains from 7 to 14% methyl ester groups. Pectin containing less than 7% is called low-methoxy pectin (L.M. Pectin).

Mechanism of Pectin Gel Formation

Pectin molecules are elongated in shape; this property is responsible for their forming viscous sols when hydrated. This highly hydrophilic colloid carries a negative charge with its greatest stability in the neutral range. In gel formation, a dehydrating agent such as sugar or alcohol removes the protective water jacket from the hydrated pectin molecules. The addition of acid to a pH of below 3.5 results in electrical neutralization, so that the pectin aggregates form a gel.

Fruit Jellies

High-methoxyl pectins (7 to 14% methoxylated) are suitable for making fruit jellies. An aqueous solution of 0.3 to 0.4% pectin will gel when the pH is adjusted below 3.5 and 60 to 65% of the total weight is sugar. The *optimum pH* is between 3.0 and 3.3. Too little acid results in a soft gel or no gel, as the pectin may not be neutralized and precipitated. An increase in acid gives a tender gel which may show syneresis, and the time required for gelation may be decreased. The *optimum pectin content* varies between 0.5 to 1.0% and this depends upon the type of pectin, the pH, temperature and sugar concentration. The *optimum sugar* concentration is 60 to 65%; less than 60% gives a low yield and a tough stiff gel. Above 75% sugar gives a high yield, but the gel may be very soft in texture and may crystallize. A 60% sugar solution boils at 103°C at standard pressure.

Low-methoxyl pectins (1 to 7% methoxylated) form gels with little or no sugar provided the calcium ion (Ca^{++}) or other polyvalent ions are present to link the pectin molecules together. Calcium ion (10 to 30 mg/gm of pectin) unites with the carboxyl from one pectin chain and the carboxyl from an adjacent pectinate chain, thus forming the framework for the gel. Low-methoxyl pectins are not as sensitive to pH as regular pectin. They will form gels at a pH of 6.5 or as low as pH 2.5. A small amount of sugar (10 to 20%) imparts desirable physical characteristics to the gel. Pectin hydrates best when the calcium ion is absent; therefore, in making low-methoxyl products, the pectin is hydrated prior to the addition of the calcium salt. Low-methoxy pectin products are tomato aspic gels, canned fruit salads, vegetable gels, consomme and low-sugar diabetic gels, milk pudding gels and frozen strawberries to prevent excessive leakage from the thawed berries.

Pectins are commercially obtained from citrus albedo, a waste product of the citrus fruit industry, and from apple pomace. Both liquid (Certo) and dry forms (Sure Gel) are available. Acids such as citric and fumaric are generally mixed with commercial pectins. Sugar may be added to the dry pectin to prevent lumping. Fast- or slow-setting pectins are made for special purposes. A fast-setting pectin may be used in jams to prevent fruit pulp from floating to the top of the container. A slow-setting pectin is used in starch confectionery gels. Citrus pectin promotes friable jellies with little elasticity. Apple pectin is more elastic but tolerates less acid. Cranberry pectin produces firm jellies which do not spread.

Tests for Pectin Content of Fruit Juices

Alcohol Test.—Alcohol dehydrates and precipitates pectin. Add 15 ml (1 Tbsp) juice to 45 ml (3 Tbsp) 95% alcohol in a graduated cylinder. Invert slowly and return. Pour out in dish. If the extract is rich in pectin, a firm jelled mass will form. This is evidence that 3/4 to 1 cup of sugar may be

added to 1 cup of the extract. If the precipitate is in the form
of several lumps, the extract is medium in content of pectin
and requires more evaporation to secure a sufficient concentration. A few small stringy lumps indicate a very low
pectin concentration and the extract should be further concentrated or have pectin added before adding sugar.

Jelmeter Test.*—Viscosity of juice is an indication of pectin
content. Fill the calibrated glass tube or jelmeter to the top
with juice. Hold a finger against the lower opening when the
tube is partially filled. Then completely fill the tube, remove
the finger and allow the juice to flow for exactly 1 min, then
cover the bottom of the jelmeter again to stop the flow. Read
the nearest figure above or below the level of the juice. This
figure indicates the number of cups of sugar to add to each
cup of juice or the number of pounds of sugar to use with
each pound of juice.

Sugar Concentration

Sugar concentration is determined by the following tests.

Temperature.—Since sugar increases the boiling point of
the fruit juice solution, temperature can be used as a measure
of sugar concentration. When the temperature registers 3.5
to 4°C above the boiling point of water, the sugar concentration
will be approximately 65%.

Sheet test.—After the sugar is added to the juice, cook
until a sheeting test is obtained. When a spoon is lifted side-
wise from the hot mixture, the drops that cling to the edge
of the spoon just run together and "sheet" from the spoon
rather than falling as individual drops.

The *pH of fruit solutions* can be determined by the use of
Oxyphen papers and the Beckman pH meter.

----

*Formulations for cooked and uncooked gels are included in the
Appendix.

CHAPTER 21

H. W. Lawson | Fat and Oil Technology

This is an introduction into the subject of fats and oils, especially designed for students in Food Technology, Nutrition, and Hotel, Restaurant, and Institutional Management. This chapter covers the following topics involving fats and oils:

1. Nature, Structure, and Composition
2. Common Chemical Reactions
3. Physical Properties
4. Role of Fats in the Diet
5. Sources of Fats and Oils
6. Important Processing Steps
7. History of Usage of Fats and Oils
8. Packaging Techniques
9. Proper Handling, Transportation and Storage of Fat and Oil Products

For a more comprehensive study and for additional source material, the reader is referred to *Bailey's Industrial Oil and Fat Products*, Edited by Daniel Swern; and *Vegetable Fats and Oils* by E. W. Eckey. The sub-topics on "Essential" Fatty Acids, and Diet and Cardiovascular Disease are reprinted in part by permission of the Institute of Shortening and Edible Oils, Inc., from their publication *"Food Fats and Oils."*

The reader, prior to the study of this chapter, must realize that the subject of fats and oils comes under the more general term "lipid." This term is used to cover a variety of chemical substances such as food fats and oils, or tri-, mono - and di-glycerides, phosphatides, cerebrosides, sterols, terpenes, fatty alcohols, fatty acids, fat soluble vitamins, and other substances. Fats and oils are important sources of food energy and contribute greatly to the feeling of satiety to any meal. Fatty tissue of the body acts as a storage of energy as well as a cushion for the vital organs of the body. The thermal insulation of the body is provided by the fatty layers. In the food-service industry the cost of fats used in the kitchen is quite high. Fats are very much abused, because of ignorance with regard to their composition and proper care and use.

NATURE, STRUCTURE, AND COMPOSITION

Definition of Fats and Oils

This Chapter will be confined to the study of edible fats and oils, and exclude those used for inedible products. Edible fats and oils are of either plant or animal origin. Typical examples of plant derivatives include cottonseed and soybean oil, whereas those of animal origin include lard and butterfat. The term "fat" is generally used in reference to materials which are solid or semisolid at normal room temperature (70° to 75°F), and the term "oil" is used for those that are liquid under the same conditions. Example of fats are: vegetable shortenings, butter, and lard. An example of an oil would be a salad oil made from cottonseed, soybean, or corn oil. However, these distinctions between the terms "fats" and "oils" are not rigid, and it is rather common practice to use them interchangeably.

Basic Chemical Structure of Fats and Oils

Basically fats and oils may be considered as a mixture of triglycerides. The glycerol molecule has 3 carbon atoms, together with 5 hydrogen atoms and 3 OH or hydroxyl groups. It should be noted that there are 4 bonds or linkages to each of the 3 carbon atoms. When 3 fatty acids react with 1 glycerol molecule, a triglyceride is obtained. If only 2 fatty acids are attached to a specific glycerol molecule, a diglyceride is formed; and if only one fatty acid is attached, it becomes a monoglyceride.

$$
\begin{array}{c}
\text{H} \\
| \\
\text{H} - \text{C} - \text{OH} \\
| \\
\text{H} - \text{C} - \text{OH} \\
| \\
\text{H} - \text{C} - \text{OH} \\
| \\
\text{H}
\end{array}
$$

Glycerol

Each carbon atom continues to have four linkages. Any fatty acid which is not linked to a glycerol molecule in a fat or oil is referred to as a "free fatty acid." Natural fats contain

95 to 99% fat as triglycerides and mono- and diglycerides, plus 0 to 5% free fatty acids, and less than 0.1% other fatty substances.

Triglyceride Monoglyceride

Some of the more common fatty acids that will be found in naturally occurring fats and oils are butyric, lauric, palmitic, oleic, stearic, and linoleic. A 1-lb can of shortening, for example, will contain millions of fat molecules consisting of mixtures of the various fatty acids attached to glycerol molecules. The relative number of these various fatty acids and their particular placement on the glycerol molecules will determine the various characteristics of the fat product.

It was mentioned that some fatty materials are solid at room temperature, whereas others are liquid. Those that are liquid at room temperature are called oils, though sometimes they are referred to as "unsaturated" fats. This does not mean that all the fatty acids in that particular product are unsaturated, but merely that there is generally a preponderance of unsaturation which renders this specific product liquid. A further discussion of saturation and unsaturation, along with examples of structures of saturated and unsaturated fatty acids, will come later in this Chapter. For example, soybean oil has a preponderance of unsaturated fatty acids, making it a liquid, whereas lard has a greater proportion of saturated fatty acids, making lard a solid fat at room temperature. Coconut oil is a somewhat special case in that it is liquid at temperatures just above 78°F, in spite of the fact that it contains 85 to 95% saturated fatty acids. The reason for this is discussed in the next paragraph.

Chain length, or the number of carbon atoms in a fatty acid, also has a great influence on whether a fat is solid or liquid. Fatty acids have from 4 to 22 carbon atoms. Products containing high proportions of the longer-chain fatty acids (14 to 22) are more likely to be solid at room temperature, whereas those containing more of the shorter-chain fatty acids (4 to 12) are more likely to be liquid. Coconut oil is very high in lauric acid, which contains 12 carbon atoms; and about 60 to 65% of the fatty acids are of 14 carbon atoms or less. This is the reason for its liquidity at relatively low temperatures. Therefore, the two most important factors which render a fatty material solid or liquid are: (1) the average fatty acid chain length, and (2) the relative amount of saturated to unsaturated fatty acids.

Plastic fats or *shortenings* are generally represented as containing approximately 25% saturated and 71% unsaturated fatty acids. *Oils* or *liquid fats*, on the other hand, may contain approximately 22% saturated and 74% unsaturated fatty acids.

An illustration of a saturated fatty acid is:

$$R-\underset{\underset{H}{|}}{\overset{\overset{H}{|}}{C}}-\underset{\underset{H}{|}}{\overset{\overset{H}{|}}{C}}-\overset{\overset{O}{\|}}{C}-OH$$

saturated

Here, all the carbon atoms have four linkages to all the other atoms, including the other carbon atoms in the molecule. The R refers to the balance of the molecule. The R groups may represent saturated or unsaturated fatty acid chains and in this kind if there are at least two loose linkages between a pair of carbon atoms in a molecule, then it is an unsaturated fatty acid:

$$R-\overset{\overset{H}{|}}{C}=\overset{\overset{H}{|}}{C}-\underset{\underset{H}{|}}{\overset{\overset{H}{|}}{C}}-COOH$$

Two linkages, that is, a double bond, does not make this a stronger linkage between the two carbons in question; indeed it is actually a weaker linkage. An unsaturated fatty acid may react with hydrogen to break this double linkage, and form a saturated fatty acid. A polyunsaturated fatty acid has two or more points of unsaturation in a specific fatty acid molecule. Two sets of double bonds make this molecule more

TABLE 21.1
SATURATED FATTY ACIDS

I.U.P.A.C. Name	Common Name	No. of Carbon Atoms	Formula	Natural Source
Ethanoic	Acetic	2	CH_3COOH	
Butanoic	Butyric	4	C_3H_7COOH	Butterfat
Hexanoic	Caproic	6	$C_5H_{11}COOH$	Butterfat
Octanoic	Caprylic	8	$C_7H_{15}COOH$	Butterfat and coconut oil
Decanoic	Capric	10	$C_9H_{17}COOH$	Butterfat and coconut oil
Dodecanoic	Lauric	12	$C_{11}H_{23}COOH$	Coconut oil
Tetradecanoic	Myristic	14	$C_{13}H_{27}COOH$	Butterfat and coconut oil
Hexadecanoic	Palmitic	16	$C_{15}H_{31}COOH$	Palm, cotton-seed oil, butter, lard, tallow
Octadecanoic	Stearic	18	$C_{17}H_{35}COOH$	Most animal fats and cocoa butter
Eicosanoic	Arachidic	20	$C_{19}H_{37}COOH$	Peanut oil
Docosanoic	Behenic	22	$C_{21}H_{43}COOH$	Rapeseed oil, peanut oil

unstable, and it reacts more readily with hydrogen, oxygen, and other elements than a monounsaturated fatty acid.

$$R-\overset{\displaystyle \overset{H}{|}}{C}=\overset{\displaystyle \overset{H}{|}}{C}-\overset{\displaystyle \overset{H}{|}}{\underset{\displaystyle \underset{H}{|}}{C}}-\overset{\displaystyle \overset{H}{|}}{C}=\overset{\displaystyle \overset{H}{|}}{C}-\overset{\displaystyle \overset{H}{|}}{\underset{\displaystyle \underset{H}{|}}{C}}-COOH$$

polyunsaturated

Tables 22.1 and 22.2 show the names of the most important fatty acids occurring in nature together with their chain lengths

TABLE 21.2

UNSATURATED FATTY ACIDS

I.U.P.A.C. Name	Common Name	No. of Double Bonds	No. of Carbon Atoms	Formula	Natural Source
9-Decenoic	Caproleic	1	10	$C_9H_{17}COOH$	Butterfat
9-Dodecenoic	Lauroleic	1	12	$C_{11}H_{21}COOH$	Butterfat
9-tetradecenoic	Myristoleic	1	14	$C_{13}H_{25}COOH$	Butterfat
9-hexadecenoic	Palmitoleic	1	16	$C_{15}H_{29}COOH$	Animal fat, seed oils
9-octadecenoic	Oleic	1	18	$C_{17}H_{33}COOH$	Most fats and oils
6-octadecenoic	Petroselinic	1	18	$C_{17}H_{33}COOH$	Parsley seed oil
11-octadecenoic	Vaccenic	1	18	$C_{17}H_{33}COOH$	Butter fat, beef fat
9,12-Octadeca-dienoic	Linoleic	2	18	$C_{17}H_{31}COOH$	Most seed fats
9,12,15-Octadeca-trienoic	Linolenic	3	18	$C_{17}H_{29}COOH$	Soybean oil, linseed oil
9,11,13-Octadeca-trienoic	Elaeostearic	3	18	$C_{17}H_{29}COOH$	Tung oil
9-Eicosenoic	Gadoleic	1	20	$C_{19}H_{37}COOH$	Fish oils
5,8,11,14-Ei-cosatetraenoic	Arachidonic	4	20	$C_{19}H_{31}COOH$	Lard
13-Docosenoic	Erucic	1	22	$C_{21}H_{41}COOH$	Rapeseed oil

and numbers of double bonds. These R groups may contain
substituent groups such as (OH), or if unsaturated may present
cis-trans isomerism. The saturated fatty acids have the
general formula of $C_nH_{2n}O_2$ or $C_nH_{2n+1}COOH$; most are of the
straight-chain variety. The even number of carbon chains
C_4 to C_{24} are those that occur in fats. Those higher than C_{24}
occur in waxes. There are a few odd or uneven number of
carbon fatty acids that do occur naturally in very small amounts,
such as margaric (C_{17}); however, the C_{17} generally found
has proved to be a mixture of C_{16} and C_{18} acids.

CHEMICAL REACTIONS OF FATS AND OILS

The most important chemical reactions involving fats and
oils occur either at (a) the points of unsaturation on the fatty
acid chain, or (b) the point where the fatty acids are attached
to the glycerol molecule (the ester linkage).

Knowledge of some of the chemical changes which fats and
oils undergo is necessary to understand how the various fat
products are manufactured, as well as to cope with problems
encountered in storage, transportation, and usage of these
products.

Hydrolysis

As the name of the reaction implies, this is the reaction
of water with a fat. This results in the splitting of some of
the fatty acids from the fat or oil, yielding free fatty acids,
glycerol, and a mono and/or diglyceride.

$$
\begin{array}{c}
\text{H} \\
| \\
\text{H—C—O—C}\overset{\nearrow\text{O}}{}\text{—R} \\
| \\
\text{H—C—O—C}\overset{\nearrow\text{O}}{}\text{—R} + 3\text{HOH} \xrightarrow{\text{heat}} \\
| \\
\text{H—C—O—C}\overset{\nearrow\text{O}}{}\text{—R} \\
| \\
\text{H}
\end{array}
\qquad
\begin{array}{c}
\text{H} \\
| \\
\text{H—C—OH} \\
| \\
\text{H—C—OH} + 3\text{RCOOH} \\
| \\
\text{H—C—OH} \\
| \\
\text{H}
\end{array}
$$

Triglyceride   + Water ⟶   Glycerol + 3 Fatty Acids

Hydrolysis Reaction

This is an example of a reaction which takes place at the
junction of the fatty acids and the glycerol portion of the mole-

cule. As shown above, this reaction is carried to completion. Hydrolysis is accelerated by high temperatures and an excessive amount of water. This reaction is especially significant in the preparation of deep-fried foods, where the frying fat may be at a temperature of 350°F, and the food that is fried is high in moisture. A good example of this situation is the frying of French fried potatoes. Potatoes are high in water, which is over 80% of their weight before cooking, and during frying free fatty acids can develop at a fairly rapid rate. Moderate levels of free fatty acids, up to about 4%, do not necessarily have an adverse effect on frying fat performance, but excessively high levels may result in excessive smoking and even affect the flavor of the fried food.

The increase of free fatty acids decreases the smoke point of the fat.

% of FFA	Smoke Point, °F
0.05	440
0.10	400
0.50	350
0.60	300–325

This is certainly one of the most important chemical reactions. Another reaction which occurs at points of unsaturation or double bonds is hydrogenation.

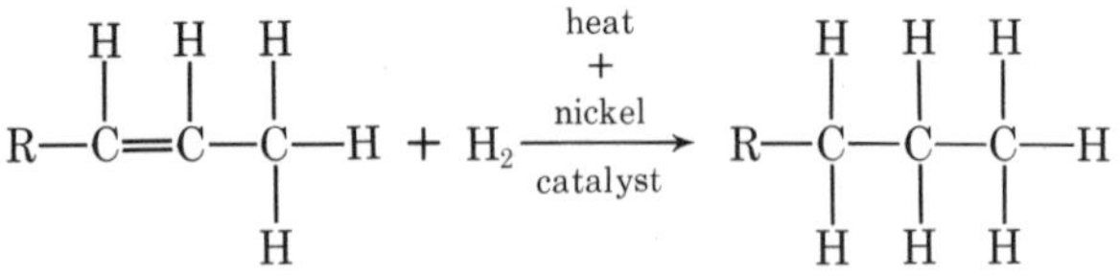

Hydrogenation Reaction

Gaseous hydrogen and elevated oil temperatures, often under pressure and in the presence of a suitable nickel catalyst, result in the hydrogen adding to the double bonds of unsaturated fatty acids to reduce their degree of unsaturation. This reaction is used to make fat products of greater flavor stability, minimizing the possibilities of oxidation, especially if fatty acids such as linolenic (three points of unsaturation on the same fatty acid) are originally present. Hydrogenation also permits the conversion of liquid vegetable oils into fluid shortenings and semi-solid plastic shortenings that are better adapted for use in deep frying, baking, etc. This is a reaction

system used by shortening manufacturers to optimize the
needed properties of fats and oils for specific uses.

Oxidation

Like hydrogenation, oxidation also occurs at the double
bonds or points of unsaturation.

$$R-\underset{\underset{H}{|}}{C}=\overset{\overset{H}{|}}{C}-\overset{\overset{H}{|}}{C}-H + O_2 \xrightarrow[\text{time}]{\substack{\text{light,}\\ \text{heat}}} R-\overset{\overset{H}{|}}{\underset{\underset{O-O}{|}}{C}}-\overset{\overset{H}{|}}{\underset{\underset{O}{|}}{C}}-\overset{\overset{H}{|}}{\underset{\underset{O-}{|}}{C}}-H$$

Oxidation Reaction

This is the reaction of a fat or oil with oxygen in the air;
with food this is to be avoided because it will adversely effect
the flavor of the fat and the food it is used in. In fact, considerable care is exercised during manufacturing, storage,
and usage either to keep this reaction from occurring or
to slow it down as much as possible.

In general, products containing high proportions of unsaturated fatty acids are more prone to oxidation than those containing lesser amounts of unsaturated acids. This is because
the double bonds are more unstable, and oxygen will more
readily react at these points of instability. However, proper
processing techniques can minimize this tendency.

The rate of oxidation increases with an increase in temperature, exposure to atmospheric oxygen, and contact with materials which are classified as pro-oxidants. An excellent
example of a pro-oxidant is the metal copper. Therefore,
care should be taken to keep copper, brass, and bronze out
of fat and oil processing systems, their packages, and in
food manufacturing plants which utilize fats or oils. In deep
frying, where the temperature of the fat is high, it is important to keep copper from coming into contact with fat,
especially at the surface where the fat is also in contact with
oxygen in the air. Examples of where copper contamination
can occur in deep-frying operations are copper thermocouples
and brass or bronze drain valves.

The reverse of a pro-oxidant is an antioxidant. Oils from
most vegetable sources contain antioxidants, called tocopherols.
Care should be taken to retain as much of these tocopherols

as possible during manufacturing, as they give a certain
amount of protection against oxidation to soybean and cottonseed salad oils and to vegetable shortenings during storage
and usage.

Lard, hydrogenated lards, and shortenings made from
meat fats are generally fortified or stabilized by adding
antioxidants, since they do not contain them naturally. They
are generally added at a very low level, such as a few parts
per million. Sometimes they are referred to as oxygen inter-
ceptors. Some of the most important ones commercially are
butylated hydroxyanisole and butylated hydroxytoluene, often
called BHA and BHT, respectively. Others used to a certain
extent are propyl gallate and citric acid.

Under normal circumstances, the oxidation of fats and oils
is a slow process. Slight degrees of oxidation will not be
noticed by most users, but after a time—usually measured
in months or years, depending upon storage conditions and
the stability of the product—oxidation can proceed to the point
where a rancid flavor and/or odor is noticed.

Antioxidants

Oxidative rancidity in fatty foods becomes evident by the
off odors and flavors produced, as well as by a change in
the texture of foodstuffs containing fatty material. The latter
appears as the gummy material that gathers at the opening
of a bottle of oil, mayonnaise, etc. It was found in the late
1940's that butylated hydroxyanisole (BHA) and (even earlier)
the *n*-propyl ester of gallic acid had antioxidant properties
in various fatty food materials. It was also discovered that
the combination of these two had added advantages, or were
synergistic and safe to use. At the same time it was necessary
to use something to remove traces of Cu and Fe, since these
metals act as catalysts for fat oxidation, and they also react
with antioxidant compounds to produce color problems. Citric
acid and other compounds were selected to act as the chelating
agents for these metals. The next problem was the variance
in solubility of these additives, and propylene glycol was
found to be the proper solvent of many possible combinations
of these three additives. Later BHT or butylated hydroxytoluene
and NDGA, nordihydroguaiaretic acid, were found to possess
antioxidant activity. The latter was obtained from the leaves

and twigs of a desert creosote bush, and recently it has been removed from the GRAS list of additives.

The antioxidants cleared for food use at present are:

(1) BHA (butylated hydroxyanisole or 2 and 3 isomers of *tert*-butyl-4-hydroxyanisole); (2) BHT (butylated hydroxytoluene or 2, 6-di-*tert*-butyl-4-methyl phenol); (3) Propyl gallate (*n*-propyl ester of gallic acid); (4) Dilauryl thiodipropionate; (5) Thiodipropionic Acid (3, 3^1-thiodipropionic acid); (6) Gum Guaiac; (7) Lecithin; (8) Tocopherols (tocopherols concentrate) mixed: Vitamin E); (9) THBP (2, 4, 5-trihydroxybutyrophenone); (10) Ethoxyquin (1, 2-dihydro-6-ethoxy-2, 2, 4-trimethylquino-line); (11) 4-Hydroxymethyl-2, 6-di-*tert*-butylphenol; (12) Glycine.

Of all these the first three are the most widely used.

Free radical oxidation of fatty substances is believed to take place in three stages, namely:

1. *Initiation*

$$\text{RH} \xrightarrow{\text{Initiator(s)}} \text{R} \cdot \qquad +\text{H}.$$
$$\text{fat molecule} \qquad\qquad \text{fatty free radical}$$

Initiators could be light (ultraviolet area) heat, heavy metals such as Cu and Fe.

2. *Propagation*

$$\text{R} \cdot + O_2 \longrightarrow \text{ROO} \cdot$$
$$\text{(peroxide free redicol)}$$
$$\text{ROO} \cdot + \text{RH} \longrightarrow \text{ROOH} + \text{R} \cdot$$
$$\text{hydroperoxide}$$
$$\text{ROOH} \longrightarrow \text{RO}. + .\text{OH}$$
$$.\text{OH} + \text{RH} \rightarrow \text{R}. + H_2O \text{ etc.}$$

During propagation, in the presence of catalytic agents, decomposition of hydroperoxides leads to formation of a wide variety of aldehydes, ketones, acids, etc. These compounds are responsible for the off odors and flavors characteristic of rancid fats.

3. *Termination* of the oxidation chain reaction occurs when the free radicals (autocatalysts) are deactivated or destroyed.

$$\text{R}. + \text{R}. \rightarrow \text{RR or R}. + \text{ROO}. \rightarrow \text{ROOR etc.}$$

Fat and oil antioxidants are substances that can react with the initiating and propagating radicals to give harmless products.

$$R^{\cdot} + AH \rightarrow RH + A$$

AH = antioxidant molecule

stable resonance hybrids

In other words antioxidants do not function by competing with the substrate for oxygen. They are not "oxygen absorbers." They act as free mechanism which is fundamental to oxidation.

Antioxidants are added to fats and oils as soon as possible to prevent any oxidized fat from accumulating. In addition to antioxidants other additives are used to prevent initiation of oxidative reactions and to counteract the catalytic effect of any heavy metals present, such as Cu and Fe. These additives are citric acid, monoisopropyl citrate, phosphoric acid, monoglyceride citrate and EDTA, and are called sequestering or chelating agents.

The low levels at which all of these compounds are added does not affect the odor or flavor of the fatty material. They are added directly or sprayed on, added to spices and seasonings or in antioxidant-treated packaging materials.

Polymerization

This is the reaction of a fat with itself in which relatively small molecules of fat or oil combine to form much larger molecules. It is unique in that polymerization may occur either at points of unsaturation on fatty acid chains, or at the juncture of the fatty acid and the glycerol molecule. Polymerization can occur in the deep frying of foods, where frying is done at temperatures ranging from 325° to 375°F. The reaction is accelerated by heat, oxygen, use of a poor quality frying fat, and poor frying practice, e.g., heating for long periods of time with little or no frying of food. This practice reduces the rate at which fat is removed from the kettle by absorption into the food, and in turn, the rate at which fresh fat is added to the system.

Polymerization is evidenced by deposits of a gum-like material around the sides of the frying kettle, frying baskets, commercial frying kettle conveyors, etc., especially where fat, metal, and air are in contact with each other. If polymerization is allowed to proceed to extremes, it can result in foaming of the fat. When the frying fat is still usable, the water in the foods being fried evolves as large bubbles and is quickly driven out of the fry kettle. However, when the frying fat polymerizes to a considerable extent and its viscosity increases, the moisture in the food evolves as very small bubbles during frying and rises slowly up the sides of the frying kettle. This is referred to as foaming. The extreme differences in the size of normal fat molecules and the polymerized molecules are an important factor in this phenomenon. Use of the proper type and amount of methyl silicone in a frying fat helps to retard the development of foam. When foaming occurs, the entire contents of the kettle or machine must be discarded and replaced with fresh fat.

In general, the rate of polymerization will increase with the degree of unsaturation in a fat or oil. However, by utilizing the latest processing techniques, including partial and very selective hydrogenation of vegetable oils along with the correct amount and type of antifoaming agents, shortenings high in polyunsaturation can be made to resist foaming as well as highly saturated fats.

Interesterification

This can be explained as a random migration of fatty acids from one fat molecule to another or from point to point within the same molecule in order to develop specific properties in the resulting new fat molecules. The site of this reaction is at the junction of the fatty acids and glycerol. One of the most important commercial reactions involves the production of monoglycerides and diglycerides from triglycerides. Monoglycerides are important as emulsifying agents in many food products. An emulsifier tends to hold fat and water together, whereas they would normally separate. An example of this is seen in mixing cake batters. In its simplest form, an example of interesterification is the reaction of triglycerides (containing 3 free fatty acids) with glycerol (no attached fatty acids) in the presence of a suitable alkaline catalyst to yield a mixture of mono and diglycerides.

$$
\begin{array}{c}
\underset{|}{CH_2OOCR} \\
\underset{|}{CHOOCR} \\
CH_2OOCR
\end{array}
+
\begin{array}{c}
\underset{|}{CH_2OH} \\
\underset{|}{CHOH} \\
CH_2OH
\end{array}
\xrightarrow[\text{Catalyst}]{\text{Alkaline}}
\begin{array}{c}
\underset{|}{CH_2OOCR} \\
\underset{|}{CHOOCR} \\
CH_2OH
\end{array}
+
\begin{array}{c}
\underset{|}{CH_2OOCR} \\
\underset{|}{CHOH} \\
CH_2OH
\end{array}
$$

Triglyceride   Glycerol   Diglyceride   Monoglyceride

Interesterification Reaction

Conjugated fats such as lecithin or similar products are produced either naturally or in the laboratory. A sugar molecule such as glucose may be substituted in the triglyceride molecule, thus adding to emulsification properties.

Flavor reversion is the development in some oils of a "fishy" type of flavor and may be the result of very slight oxidative activity. Hydrogenated or oils containing a high percentage of saturated fatty acids are very slow to oxidize as compared to those fats and oils of high degree of unsaturation.

Overheating of fats and oils results in the formation of acrolein, an acrid smelling product, that produces tears and permeates the atmosphere.

$$C_3H_5(OOCR)_3 + 3H_2O \xrightarrow{\Delta} C_3H_5(OH)_3 + 3RCOOH$$

$$C_3H_5(OH)_3 \xrightarrow{\Delta} CH_2{=}CHCHO + 2H_2O$$

acrolein or
propenal

PHYSICAL PROPERTIES

Many of the physical properties of fats and oils are of practical importance in understanding the nature of these materials.

Flavor

Almost all the animal and vegetable fats and oils consumed in the United States are preferred to have either as bland a flavor as possible, or a "butter-like" flavor. This preference depends upon the intended usage of the product. Butterfat, when fresh, has a distinctive and desirable flavor and aroma. However, if butterfat is permitted to become rancid, its flavor and aroma are no longer desirable, and in fact might be considered objectionable or distasteful by many consumers. The flavor of lard was at one time considered to be desirable in the United States, but today blandness or the absence of flavor in salad oils and shortenings is generally preferred.

The normal flavor of lard is still considered desirable in many parts of the world. Also, olive oil has a distinct flavor which is prized quite highly by people living in areas surrounding the Mediterranean Sea, and by a relatively small number of people in the United States, primarily those who were originally from this area, including Spain, Italy and Sicily.

Obviously, there is a place for some flavored fats for some specific purposes. Butter and margarines are good examples. In addition, some butter-like flavored fats are available for such uses as griddling, pan frying, sauce making, etc. Crude vegetable oils, such as cottonseed, soybean, corn, and peanut, have distinctive but undesirable flavors; but these oils can be processed to achieve the desired bland, neutral flavor.

Melting Point

This is the temperature at which a solid fat becomes a liquid oil. Each individual fatty acid has its own melting point, and since fats and oils are essentially mixtures of various fatty acids (e.g., stearic, oleic, linoleic, etc.), they will not have sharp melting points. As the temperature of a shortening rises, some fatty glycerides will melt; and as the temperature drops, some portions of this product will resolidify. The amount of the fat that is solid at a given temperature can be determined analytically.

The complete melting point of a fat is the temperature at which that particular product is completely melted. For shortenings, the complete melting point may be as high as 120°F. The complete melting point for a specific product may be quite misleading in studying its physical properties without knowing more about the ratio of solids to liquids at temperatures from 50° to 120°F. This information can be invaluable in developing a good understanding of the physical properties of a specific fat or oil.

Plasticity

From the previous discussion of melting points, it can be seen that a shortening which appears solid to the eye at room temperature can actually be composed of both solid fats and liquid oils. Fig. 22.1 will help to understand plasticity. At 70°F a typical shortening which appears solid will have 15 to 20% solids and hence 80 to 85% liquid oil. By proper processing techniques and storage control, this small percentage of solids can be made to hold all the liquid in a matrix of very small, stable, needle-like crystals. As the temperature drops, more of the oils solidify and the shortening becomes progressively firmer. On the other hand, as the temperature rises, more solid fats or fatty acids melt and the shortening becomes progressively softer until it has practically no "body" or plasticity at all; eventually it becomes completely liquefied.

A shortening manufacturer can make a shortening of any desired consistency or plasticity which way be desired by the users. If a shortening is desired which is workable over a wide temperature range, it should be made up of a combination of fatty acids ranging widely in melting points. By the same reasoning, fats or shortenings requiring a shorter temperature range of workability would utilize a greater amount of fatty acids of similar melting points.

Color

Whiteness is generally preferred except for butter, margarine, and some liquid and plastic shortenings which are intentionally given an added yellow color, usually obtained by the use of minute quantities of betacarotene.

Oiliness

These materials feel oily and they have the ability to form oily or lubricant films. In some food products their lubrication action is important.

Viscosity

Viscosity is occasionally used in determining the condition of fats used in deep frying. During use in the frying kettle, the viscosity of a frying fat or oil will tend to increase. This can be related to polymer development and tendency to foam, which have been discussed previously.

Emulsification

Triglycerides with three fatty acids attached to the glycerol molecule have very poor emulsification properties. However, monoglycerides with only 1 fatty acid attached to the glycerol molecule and 2 free hydroxyl groups on the glycerol take on some of the properties of both fats and water. The fatty-acid portion of the molecule acts like any other fat and readily mixes with these fatty materials, but these same monoglycerides also contain two OH groups which mix or dissolve in water. Thus monoglycerides tend to hold fats and water together. This is especially important in mixing cake batters, where it is necessary to hold the shortening and water (including liquids in materials such as milk and eggs) together to form a stable batter which will not readily separate.

The comparative average weights of various fats is as follows:

Fat	Gm in One Cup
Crisco	188
lard	220
oils	210
butter	224
margarine	224

Crisco is lighter since some air is whipped in during the manufacturing process. It is used here as a representative of the many plastic fats on the market.

Frying

The other major use of fats and oils is in frying: pan, griddle and deep-fat frying. The uses to which a fat is put necessitates knowledge of the composition and nature of fats in order to buy and use wisely. A good quality fat is necessary, since fat replaces some of the water lost during the drying process and becomes a part of the finished food. Fats are absorbed by food products, and they also play a role in the browning reaction to produce the fine flavor of such foods.

All foodstuffs that are fried contain moisture. This moisture is heated during frying and aids in the cooking of the food, though some is released as steam. In pressure-controlled fryers the steam is condensed and removed; in open fryers it must be removed through a ventilating system. Excess moisture often results in foaming; this increases the amount of oxygen and moisture present, which hastens breakdown of the fats. It can be controlled by not adding overly moist products to the fryer and by the purchasing of fats that contain methyl silicones or defoaming agents.

Other substances that tend to accelerate the breakdown of fats are crumbs, protein materials, and copper and iron ions from fittings, baskets, or utensils. The collection of crumbs in the bottom of a fryer acts as a catalyst for fat breakdown and must be filtered off daily. In some commercial operations this can be a continuous process. The presence of copper and iron ions can be controlled by the purchase of fats containing chelating agents or by using stainless steel equipment.

Another source of fat breakdown is salt, and a good operator does not salt the food over the kettle.

All fats tend to darken in the frying kettle, but this is not always an indication that the fat is unusable. During continuous deep-fat frying, fat is removed from the kettle chiefly by absorption and adsorption by the food being cooked. The other mode of loss is via steam, which generally collects in the ventilating system. If this system is over the fryer, drips can also catalyze fat breakdown. The loss of fat increases the percentage of breakdown products; this can be reduced by maintaining a constant quantity of fat in the fryer. This rate of addition of fresh fat is termed "fat turnover." Rapid fat turnover keeps the fat in good, usable condition. In a well-balanced frying operation, ideally speaking, it is seldom necessary to discard the fat. Methods for testing for the presence of free fatty acids aids in determining when to discard the fat.

A fat is chosen for frying that has a minimum smoke point of 425°F. As the free fatty acid and other breakdown products accumulate, the smoke point is rapidly lowered. Since most frying is conducted at 360° to 370°F, the small percentage of 0.6% of free fatty acid (FFA) will lower the smoke point to 300 to 325°F.

The other problem experienced is the production of off-flavored fried foodstuffs with the build-up of these breakdown products.

Some companies which handle fats provide guidelines for the care and use of their products and for cleaning the equipment.

Fats are stored covered, generally where it is cool and in the dark to inhibit rancid deterioration. Fats of dairy origin are stored under these conditions as they are more susceptible to absorption of foreign flavors and odors.

In purchasing fats for any frying area the following specifications are available. The following is a brief summary of the relative meaning of each value.

SPECIFICATIONS USED IN THE PURCHASE OF FATS

Color—The specific color of uncolored fats and oils is usually unimportant. They all tend to darken with use. The normal range of color is 3.0 red/30.0 yellow as Lovibond color readings.

Free Fatty Acid—Fresh fats and oils usually contain about 0.05% or less.

Iodine Value—This is a measure to indicate the degree of unsaturation or the number of double bonds present. The higher the value the greater the degree of unsaturation.

Peroxide Value—This describes the extent to which a fat or oil has already reacted with oxygen. The average for fresh fats and oils should be below 0.05 milliequivalent per kilogram (meq).

AOM Values—A.O.M. stands for *A*ctive *O*xygen *M*ethod, which is a quick method used to ascertain the relative shelf-life of fats and oils or products containing a high concentration of fats and oils. This is obtained by bubbling air through a hot sample of fat and determining the number of hours required for the peroxide value to become 100. Most AOM values vary up to 15 hr for unhydrogenated fats and 50 to 100 hr for normal shortenings. *Antioxidants* can increase the AOM values.

Saponification Value—This is the number of grams of the substance saponified by 56.1 gm (i.e., 1 equivalent) of potassium hydroxide.

Smoke Point—Minimum of 425°F for frying uses. Smoke point and fire points are used to decide whether traces of solvent remain in extracted oils.

Monoglyceride—An emulsifier, generally indicated as "percent mono."
Refractive Index—The refractive index of an oil is used to identify an
  oil through the ratio of the sine of an angle of incidence to the sine of
  the angle of refraction, when a ray of light of wavelength 589.3 m
  passes from air into the oil or fat.
Flavor—Characteristic of the oil; however, most oils and fats should
  have a bland flavor.
Price—Varies with the type and use and, of course, the market.

The tests for free fatty acids are simple and can be done
by any careful operator. The solutions and equipment can
be purchased from a laboratory supply house or a pharmacy.
Based on these methods, several manufacturing companies
have placed on the market kits for free fatty acid tests. Some
may be purchased, others are given when their particular
fats are purchased. Many reactions take place in the fryer,
and since the determination of all of them is an impossible
task, use of the free fatty acid test is one method of indication
of breakdown. Another is the change in color of the fried
products. Color charts and FFA kits are offered by the various
manufacturers.

The extra time required to correctly take care of the fat,
the fryer, and the food is certainly worth its monetary value
to the operator.

See Appendix for FFA test.

ROLE OF FATS IN THE DIET

Most of the fats produced in the world are consumed as
food. In considering their role in the diet, it is well to consider (a) their caloric functions, (b) their noncaloric food
functions, (c) their contribution in "essential" fatty acids,
and (d) the relationship between dietary fat and cardiovascular
disease.

Caloric Functions

Fats and oils are an important source of energy in the diets
of many of the world's people. Fats are the most concentrated
of all food materials, furnishing about 9 Calories of energy
per gram as compared with about 4 Calories per gram for
proteins and carbohydrates. It is interesting to note that the

caloric content of these materials is about the same, whether
the materials are of animal or vegetable origin, solid or
liquid, predominantly saturated or unsaturated, and regardless of chain length. Even when comparing mono-, di-, and
triglycerides, the average caloric differences are relatively
small—8.5, 9.2, and 9.4 Calories per gram, respectively.

Fats supply about 35 to 45% of the total per capita caloric
intake in the United States; in some Oriental countries, they
may supply less than 5% of the calories.

Noncaloric Function

Fats and oils help regulate the digestive process, and can
be said to control the feeling of hunger between meals. Therefore, even in reducing diets, a modest amount of fats and
oils is generally included, to prevent a person trying to lose
weight from getting abnormally hungry between meals.

The contribution of these materials to the eating qualities and
palatability of foods is very important. For example, fat or
shortening contributes tenderness to cakes, pie crusts, cookies,
coffee cakes, and many other baked goods; flakiness to pie
crust and Danish pastry; and the desirable character and eating
qualities associated with deep-fried foods such as doughnuts,
potato chips, and chicken.

"Essential" Fatty Acids

For many years those dealing with nutrition were little
concerned over differences in the chemical and physical character of food fats. In the early thirties work was done demon-
strating the essentiality of certain long-chain polyunsaturated
fatty acids, such as linoleic, linolenic, and arachidonic acids,
for growth and good skin and hair quality in rats. These acids
are termed "essential" because they are not synthesized
by the body. However, there is some evidence that arachiodonic
acid can be synthesized from dietary linoleic acid.

In infants the requirement for these essential fatty acids
has been clearly demonstrated. While the minimum requirement has not been determined for adults, there is no doubt
that they are "essential" nutrients. The normal American
diet usually provides at least the minimum "essential" fatty-

TABLE 21.3.
FOOD COMPOSITION (%) COOKED EDIBLE PORTIONS

Component	Porterhouse Steak (Beef)	Lamb Chop	Baked Potato	Apple	Cod Fish	Cake Canned Salmon	Roast Chicken
Water	37.0	35.5	75.1	84.4	64.6	62.4	53.5
Protein	20.0	16.9	2.6	0.2	18.9	22.5	25.2
Ash	1.4	0.8	1.1	0.3	1.2	1.7	0.9
Total carbohydrate	0.0	0.0	21.1	14.5	0.0	0.0	0.0
Fat	42.0	46.5	0.1	0.6	5.3	13.4	20.2
(% fat dry basis)	67.0	72.1	0.4	2.3	11.6	36.0	43.4

LIPID COMPOSITION (% OF TOTAL FATTY ACIDS)

Fatty acids	Beef	Salmon	Potato	Safflower Oil	Soybean Oil
Myristic	3.1	5.4	0.3	0.2	0.1
Palmitic	29.1	26.2	19.3	3.4	10.5
Stearic	18.9	6.3	5.4	5.3	3.2
Oleic	44.0	2.7	0.6	15.0	22.3
Linoleic	0.3	52.1	53.0	75.0	54.5
Linolenic	trace	1.8	19.7	0.4	8.3
Arachidic	trace	6.5	1.2	1.5	0.2
% of total lipid	98	10.0	11.5	95	98

Source: *Critical Review*, 1971. Vol. 2, Issue 3, p. 357.

acid requirement. According to publication No. 1147 of the National Research Council, "Dietary Fat in Human Health," animal experiments have shown that linoleic acid equivalent to 1 or 2% of the Calories meets the "essential" fatty-acid requirements. See Table 21.3.

Diet and Cardiovascular Disease

From about 1955, considerable interest began to develop in the possible relationship of dietary fats and oils to the incidence of heart and vascular disease. The interest has continued until the present time. While an association has been shown between many elements of the diet and the incidence of heart disease, no cause and effect relationship has been established. However, some medical and nutritional authorities believe that it might be advisable to make some adjustments in the fatty-acid composition of the overall diet, particularly for those individuals that are known to have heart disease or those groups that seemingly are most susceptible to it. The following quotation from a statement prepared by the American Heart Association (June 5, 1965) illustrates this attitude:

"One approach to the retardation or prevention of coronary heart disease through dietary control is based on the concept that lowering the concentration of cholesterol and other blood fats may lower the risk of developing coronary heart disease and heart attacks. Studies of population groups in the United States and elsewhere have disclosed an association between the level of cholesterol and other fats in the blood and the incidence of coronary heart disease. Thus, populations with a low concentration of cholesterol and other blood fats have a lower incidence of coronary heart disease than populations with higher concentrations. These findings are of importance because a relationship has been demonstrated between the habitual diet and the concentration of cholesterol and other fats in the blood. It has also been shown that in most persons, but not all, the level of cholesterol and other fats in the blood can be decreased and maintained at a lower value by conscientious and long-term adherence to a suitable diet.

"In most individuals, this would entail: (1) A significantly decreased intake of saturated fat; (2) A significantly increased intake of polyunsaturated fat, with polyunsaturated fats being substituted for saturated fats in the diet wherever possible; (3) A decreased intake of cholesterol-containing foods; (4) A caloric intake adjusted to achieve and maintain desirable weight (statistical evidence strongly supports a relationship between coronary heart disease and both hypertension and diabetes mellitus. Since obesity aggravates both of these conditions, it is reasonable to strongly recommend control of weight as well as careful management of high blood pressure and diabetes.)"

While the role of fat has probably received the greatest amount of attention with respect to cardiovascular disease, some work has indicated that other dietary components may also play an important part. In addition, other nondietary factors such as stress, exercise, cigarette smoking, hypertension, heredity, and body weight have been implicated.

FATS

Some important fats and their sources are:

Almond oil	Bitter and sweet almonds
Babassu oil	Nut palm (Brazil)
Cocoa butter	Seeds of cocoa
Castor oil	Castor bean
Chinese vegetable tallow	Seeds of tallow tree
Coconut oil	Coconut palm
Cohune oil	Seeds of palm (Central America)
Corn oil	Germ of corn
Cottonseed oil	Seeds of cotton plant
Fish and fish-liver oils	Menhaden, sardine, herring, cod, pilchard, salmon
Lard	Rendered pork fat
Linseed oil	Seed of flax plant
Neatsfoot oil	By-product of slaughter horses
Olive oil	Fruit of olive tree
Palm-kernel oil	Kernels of palm tree
Palm oil	Kernels of palm tree
Peanut oil	Seeds of peanut plant
Perilla oil	Seeds from perilla plant
Safflower oil	Safflower plant
Soybean oil	Soybean plant
Tallow	Fat from cattle, sheep, goats
Tung oil	Tung trees
Whale oil	Whales, also oil from dolphin, seal and porpoise

Greases (inedible lard) are called white, yellow, brown, garbage, or fleshing greases.

SOURCES OF FATS AND OILS

There are numerous sources of raw materials used in making edible food products. The most important and most significant sources of fats and oils are as follows:

Fats

As a general rule, these raw materials are solid in appearance at room temperature.

Butterfat.—As derived from cows' milk butter is a mixture of milk fat, water, salt, and added color. It is one of the most important fats, with a world production of about 8 billion lb, the United States accounting for about 15% of the total. Butterfat production and consumption has been decreasing slightly in the United States over the past 20 years. Butterfat is composed of a very unique variety of fatty acids; every member of the saturated fatty acid series (as well as some unsaturated acids), from butyric with 4 carbon atoms to behenic with 22 carbon atoms, is present. The fatty-acid composition of butterfat varies with the season of the year and with differences in the cows' feed; its consistency is normally softer in summer than in winter. Both table grade and butters earmarked for bakery and industrial food use contain about 80% butterfat.

Butterfat is both a desirable and an expensive raw material. Butter's distinct flavor and yellow color are, of course, important factors in its popularity, and butterfat continues to maintain a high image rating. Besides butter, butterfat appears in many other dairy products, such as milk, cheese, ice cream, coffee cream, whipping cream; and to a certain extent in some bakery products.

Lard.—Lard has always been an important source of edible fat. The U.S. production and consumption have been decreasing slightly over the past several years, and it is now averaging about 2 to $2\frac{1}{4}$ billion lb per year. Lard is the fat rendered from the fatty tissues of hogs; lard production, therefore, depends on the number of hogs slaughtered each year, and the size and composition of the hogs. In recent years the demand for somewhat leaner meat cuts from the hog has tended to lessen the supply of lard.

The composition, characteristics, and consistency of lard vary greatly according to the feed of the hogs as well as the part of the animal from which it was taken.

Tallows.—Edible tallow is obtained primarily from beef cattle. At room temperature it is harder and firmer than lard, and its food uses are limited. The U.S. production of edible tallow is about $1/2$ billion lb, and the world production of the edible type is about 1 billion lb.

Coconut Oil.—Coconut oil is obtained from copra, which is dried coconut meat. It is classified as a fat because it is solid at room temperature but it does become a liquid oil above 78°F. This fat is characterized by containing a high percentage of lauric acid (a 12-carbon chain saturated fatty acid), and other fairly short-chain fatty acids. Also, unlike almost all other fats and oils, coconut oil has a rather sharp melting point of about 76 to 78°F, due to a high content of low molecular weight fatty acids. It does not exhibit the usual gradual softening with an increase in temperature. Because of its high level of saturated fatty acids, coconut oil is quite resistant to oxidative changes, and therefore is used for cracker spraying and nut frying. Because of its sharp melting point, coconut oil is used in confections and cookie fillings. About 400 million lb per year is consumed as edible coconut oil in the United States.

Cocoa Butter.—This is a pale-yellow solid with the characteristic pleasant odor and flavor of cocoa. Most of the world's supply comes from Africa. The main uses of cocoa butter are in the manufacture of solid chocolate confections and coatings for chocolate and candies. The world production is 700 to 750 million lb, and the United States consumption is 190 to 200 million lb. Due to its unique and specific triglyceride content and crystal structure, cocoa butter is brittle below 80°F; slightly above this temperature it softens quickly and melts.

Oils

Soybean Oil.—Obtained from the seeds of the soybean, this oil has grown from an unimportant oil in the 1920's to become the most important vegetable oil produced in the United States. The world production of soybean oil is in the neighborhood of

10 billion lb, and in this country the annual production is well over 4 billion lb. Its main uses are in the manufacture of vegetable shortenings for baking and frying, liquid vegetable shortenings, margarines, and salad and cooking oils.

Soybeans can be easily grown under wide varieties of soil and climatic conditions. In addition, bumper crops were accelerated by the U.S. Government support of the domestic price of soybeans shortly after World War II. This program resulted not only in rapid technological advances in the processing of soybean oil and increased domestic usage, but also in quantities being exported to countries such as Spain, Greece, Iran, Morocco, Pakistan, and Turkey.

Cottonseed Oil.—This oil is obtained from seeds of the cotton plant. It was the most important vegetable oil produced during the first part of this century, but with a decreasing output of cotton in the United States, cottonseed oil has become short in supply and a more costly raw material. Its world supply is about $4\frac{1}{2}$ to 5 billion lb, the United States producing about $1\frac{1}{3}$ to $1\frac{1}{2}$ billion lb yearly.

Crude cottonseed oil has a strong flavor and odor and a dark reddish-brown color. It can be processed to a bland flavor and a rather clear color. Cottonseed oil is used in the preparation of shortenings and margarines and as a cooking and salad oil.

Peanut Oil.—The world production of peanut oil is 5 to 6 billion lb, but the United States produces only about 2 to 3% of this total. The crude oil is pale yellow and has the characteristic odor and a slight flavor of peanuts.

Olive Oil.—Though a very important cooking and salad oil in countries bordering on the Mediterranean Sea, olive oil is used in relatively small quantities in the United States. In general, the preference is for a bland-flavored oil in this country. The world production of olive oil is 2 to $2\frac{1}{2}$ billion lb, but only about 50 to 60 million lb are consumed in the United States.

Sunflower Seed Oil.—Grown and produced in large quantities in Russia, Argentina, and Hungary, this oil can be produced in the United States, but at the present time it is relatively unimportant in this country. The total world production is about 6 billion lb.

Corn Oil.—Although corn is one of the principal crops in the United States, only a small portion of it is used for obtaining corn oil. It is chiefly a by-product of corn-starch production. Between $\frac{1}{2}$ to 1 billion lb is consumed in this country in products such as cooking and salad oils, mayonnaise, and margarine.

Safflower Oil.—Safflower oil has been known since ancient times, but only in the past 20 years has it assumed any degree of commercial importance. Since 1950 the U.S. acreage has been growing, notably in Nebraska, Colorado, and California. Its growth can be attributed to its high linoleic (polyunsaturated) acid content (about 75 to 80%), the highest in this regard of the commercially available oils. Its use has been very limited because of short supply and high cost.

Marine Oils.—The commercially important marine oils are obtained from whale, cod, halibut, shark, and menhaden. They are not used for edible purposes in the United States, but in Canada about 60 to 70 million lb are used in margarines and shortenings.

Palm Oil.—Obtained from the pulp of the coconut palm, which is grown extensively in Africa, Indonesia, and Central and South America, palm oil is characterized by a relatively high level of palmitic acid (40 to 42%). Relatively minor quantites (about 135 million lb per year) are imported into the United States for use in shortening manufacture.

PROCESSING OF FATS AND OILS

Crude vegetable oils are extracted from seeds or nuts. In the United States this is now done primarily by solvent extraction, whereas in the past it was done by physical means such as the application of heavy pressure to the seed or nut. Lard is the fat removed from hogs. These crude oils or crude fats are graded by the refiner through a series of chemical and physical tests which determine their quality and potential uses. These raw materials are kept segregated in the refiner's storage tanks prior to processing. The following are the most important processing steps.

Refining

The first step in the refining procedure is to react the crude oil with an alkaline material to remove the free fatty acids.

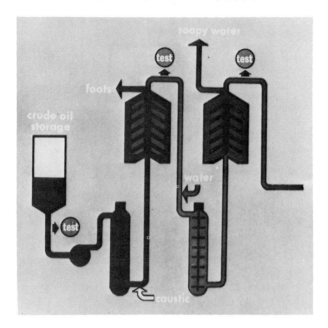

FIG. 21.1. CRUDE OIL REFINING

Free fatty acids are those which are not "tied" onto a glycerol
molecule, and an excessive quantity can contribute to an unsatisfactory flavor in a fat and detract from its frying life.
When the alkali reacts with the free fatty acids, soap is formed.
Obviously this must be removed; this is done by passing the
mixture of fat and soap through a continuous centrifuging
machine which separates the fat or oil from the soap, which
is sometimes referred to as "foots." The refined fat or oil is
water-washed to remove the final traces of soap, and is centrifuged again. Finally the refined material is dried to remove the residual water. Figure 21.1 outlines this procedure.

Bleaching

Bleaching of a fat or oil is the process of "decolorizing" it
so that the finished shortenings or salad oils will be light
in color. The prime purpose is to remove the coloring materials or pigments such as reds, yellows, and greens which
are present in the crude oil. An "active earth" or clay, such
as fuller's earth or diatomaceous earth, is intimately mixed

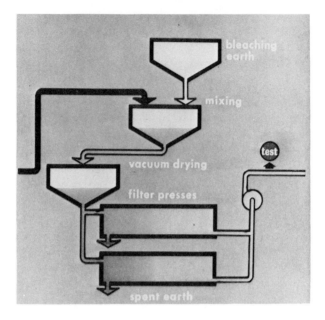

FIG. 21.2. BLEACHING

into the fat or oil. Fuller's earth, for example, is a natural bleaching earth consisting basically of hydrated aluminum silicate. Within recent years natural earths or clays have been replaced to a considerable extent by acid-activated clays which have considerably more bleaching power. The color pigments are adsorbed by the earth or clay, and then the oil is separated from earth or clay by filtration. This is shown in Fig. 21.2.

Hydrogenation

This is the manufacturing process which permits the production of both plastic solid shortenings and liquid shortenings from liquid oils. Hydrogen is added directly to points of unsaturation in the fatty acids. The hydrogenation process has developed as a result of the need to: (1) increase the oxidative stability of the fat or oil, and (2) convert liquid oils to the semi-solid form for greater utility in certain food uses.

Fatty acids with 2 double bonds, such as linoleic, can be hydrogenated to form fatty acids with 1 double bond, such as oleic, or with no double bonds, such as stearic. Likewise,

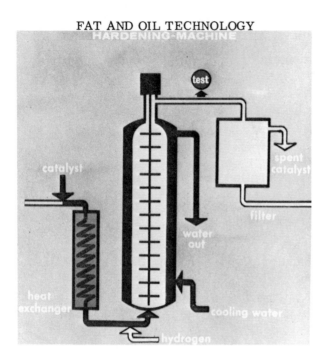

FIG. 21.3. HYDROGENATION

fatty acids with 3 double bonds (e.g., linolenic) can be hydrogenated to form fatty acids with 2 double bonds, 1 double
bond, or no remaining double bonds. As the degree of hydrogenation increases, the saturation of the fat and its firmness
at room temperature also increase. Obviously, its melting
point also increases. A diagram of the hydrogenation process
is shown in Fig. 21.3.

Hydrogenation is accomplished in a reactor where the oil
is completely melted and hydrogen gas is bubbled through it.
A nickel catalyst, which speeds up the reaction but does not
enter into the reaction itself, is also present. By careful
selection of temperature (250° to 450°F), pressure, and type
of catalyst, the oil may be selectively hydrogenated to obtain
the desired characteristics. The degree of hydrogenation is
pre-determined depending upon the type of intermediate or
final product desired. If an oil is completely hydrogenated,
it will be very hard, waxy, and brittle at room temperature.
Plastic shortenings are only partially hydrogenated to obtain
the proper balance between flavor stability and a workable
consistency over wide usage temperatures. It is customary
to blend materials which have received different degrees of

hydrogenation, in order to obtain the desired properties in the finished shortening. Liquid shortenings are also made from stocks of different degrees of hydrogenation to obtain the proper balance between flavor stability and pourability.

Winterizing

This process applies only to oils intended for making salad oils. Cottonseed oil, for example, contains some higher-melting fractions of triglycerides which refiners often refer to as stearine. To produce a salad oil from cottonseed oil, it is necessary to remove the stearine portions, which would crystallize out and form a haze in the oil when allowed to cool in a refrigerator. Also, if such an oil is used in making mayonnaise, these higher-melting fractions will solidify when the mayonnaise is refrigerated, which in turn will cause the mayonnaise to separate.

The process of removing the stearines is called winterizing. It is accomplished by lowering the temperature of the oil to a point where this material will crystallize or solidify out. Then the oil is filtered to remove the stearines. The remaining oil then has a much better resistance to crystallization or graining at the lower temperatures, and is referred to as a "salad oil" or "winter oil."

Although soybean oil is considered a natural winter oil because it does not have a tendency for its stearines to crystallize at a low temperature, historically it has not been used as a salad oil because the high level of unsaturated fatty acids in the unhydrogenated oil resulted in poor flavor stability. However, recent advances in selective and partial hydrogenation techniques of soybean oil (along with winterization) have resulted in some soybean oils of excellent flavor stability. Soybean oil, when properly processed, not only results in a salad oil with excellent flavor stability, but can also be lighter in color and can have even greater resistance to graining than winterized cottonseed oil.

Deodorizing

Deodorizing is a process which enables the production of a bland, neutral flavor in fats and oils so that the finished short-

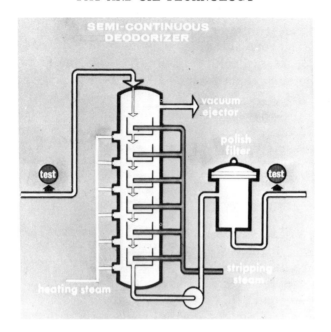

FIG. 21.4. DEODORIZING

ening or other fat food product will not impart any flavor of its own to the final food to be consumed. Deodorizing is accomplished in a "still" or a steam distillation chamber which literally boils or washes away objectionable odors and flavors present in the refined and bleached oil (see Fig. 21.4). Refined, bleached, and hydrogenated oils contain minor quantities (less than 0.1%) of materials which could impart undesirable flavors or odors to these oils. These materials are easily removed in the distillation process, which is carried out under low pressure and high temperature (about 400° to 450°F). Deodorizing is the final step in processing and is done just before plasticizing and packaging.

Plasticizing

In making shortenings it is important to develop the finest possible crystal structure in order to produce a shortening that is smooth in appearance and firm in consistency. This is accomplished through the final processing step of chilling the fat very rapidly in a scraped wall heat exchanger equipment resembling an ice cream freezer. During this rapid cooling along with vigorous agitation, it is customary to whip in about 10 to 15% of its own volume of air. The shortening is then packaged in such containers as 1- and 3-lb packages for house- hold use, and in 50-lb cartons and larger units for industrial food use. After packaging, the shortenings are "tempered" for 24 to 72 hr at about 85°F to further ensure proper crystal growth. These steps are shown in Fig. 21.5.

HISTORY OF FATS AND OILS USAGE

The types of fats and oils consumed by the American public have changed dramatically throughout the 20th century due to such factors as (a) changes in the availability of various raw materials, (b) technological advances in growing, extracting or rendering, and processing of raw materials, (c) availability of new crude fats or oils, and (d) changes in the demands for different types of products by the consumer. These factors are all interrelated, and in this section these changes will be described in approximate chronological order.

Early Shortening Usage (1900–1933)

Lard.—Around the turn of the century lard was the preferred fat for edible purposes. A plentiful supply was available as a by-product of pork production. Also at that time the distinctive flavor of lard was considered pleasing; at least it was pleasing in comparison with other available products such as beef tallow, mutton tallow, and the various marine oils. Lard was also superior in consistency, since it was softer at room tem- perature than the tallows and not as fluid as the marine oils.

Meat Fat Compounds.—This product consisted of a mixture of lard and cottonseed oil. It was a direct result of the rapid expansion in the acreage of cotton grown in the late 19th and early 20th century. These animal fat compounds utilized two by-products; lard from the slaughter of hogs and cottonseed oil from the production of cotton; therefore, this fat or shorten- ing was related to the economics of both industries. In making animal or meat fat compounds, large quantities of refined

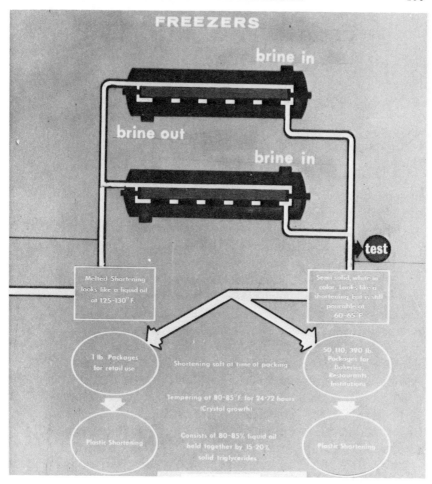

FIG. 21.5. FREEZING-PACKING

and deodorized cottonseed oil were mixed with a smaller quantity of a very hard animal fat or stearine, as it was sometimes called. This type of shortening had some advantages in consistency and workability over lard for some food uses, but it had poor stability to oxidative changes.

Standard Vegetable Shortening.—This product was the result of one of the most important technological advances in fats and oils, catalytic hydrogenation, which became a reality in the United States in 1911. Hydrogenation permitted the production of the first all-vegetable shortening. In making the first standard shortenings of this period, a large proportion of refined, bleached, and deodorized cottonseed oil was mixed with a small portion (15 to 20%) of cottonseed oil that had been previously hydrogenated to a considerable extent. This highly hydrogenated oil then replaced the meat fat stearine of the "compounds."

These early standard vegetable shortenings were, and still are, referred to as hardened shortenings. Even this product left something to be desired in consistency, stability, and flavor.

All-Hydrogenated, All-Vegetable Shortening.—After 1928, hydrogenation of all the oil eventually took place to improve the keeping qualities of the straight oil fraction, and thus the all-hydrogenated, all-vegetable shortenings were born.

During this 33-year period, other improvements were made to the processing of shortenings to make them blander in flavor and whiter in color. Constant improvements during this period and on up to the present time were made to the oil extracting, refining, bleaching, filtering, hydrogenation, deodorizing, and plasticizing steps. Solvent extraction permitted a higher yield of better-quality vegetable oils. Continous or semi-continuous methods of refining, bleaching, hydrogenation, and deodorizing were introduced, better earths were used for bleaching, and more efficient catalysts were employed in hydrogenation. Also, as fat crystallography became better understood, the stability, working, and creaming properties of shortening improved.

After 1930 when soybean crop yields became more and more significant, technology was called upon to utilize this oil, primarily to learn how to prevent off-flavor development. Improved refining and hydrogenation techniques not only overcame this problem, but have also resulted in soybean oil becoming a most desirable raw material. Today the major oil for both industrial and domestic edible use in the United States is soybean oil.

Development of Markets for Fats and Oils

Bland-flavored vegetable fats and oils found widening horizons of usage—in margarine, in mayonnaise and salad dressing, in whipped toppings, and eventually in frozen desserts. Cottonseed salad oil was superior to olive oil in blandness of flavor

TABLE 21.4.

BAKERS' AND HOUSEWIVES' FORMULAS (1925 TO 1933)

Ingredients	Baker's Formula	Housewife's Recipe
Flour	100%	100%
Sugar	90	118
Eggs	42	55
Liquid milk	58	66
Shortening	35	48
Baking powder	3	6
Salt	As desired	As desired
Flavor	As desired	As desired

and more attractive in price for mayonnaise and salad-dressing applications, especially with the development of the winterizing and "cold-proofing" process. Recent advances in hydrogenation, refining, winterizing, and packaging have resulted in excellent salad oils made from soybean oil.

With the higher stability and better consistency of fats, food processors (e.g., bakers and commercial fryers) found it possible to mechanize their processes, and were practically free of fat problems from high temperature exposure in ovens or fry kettles. Potato chips and doughnuts began to mount in acceptance. French-fried items, prepared commercially in restaurants and in the home, now awoke to their potential and soared in popularity. The homemaker, finding vegetable fats needed no refrigeration, were readily workable, and were bland in flavor, used greater and greater quantities in cooking.

Confidence in hydrogenated vegetable fats spread to the pharmaceutical field as creams, lotions, and ointments began to include these fats in their formulations.

Shortening Developments, 1933 to Present

"High-Ratio" Emulsifier Cake Shortening.—Before emulsifier-type shortenings were developed, a typical baker's cake formula was rather lean or low in sugar, shortening, milk, and eggs as compared with the average home cake recipe. When computed on the same basis, using flour as a base, the comparison was as shown in Table 21.4.

TABLE 21.5

EFFECT OF EMULSIFIER ON CAKE FORMULATION

Ingredients	Old Style Before 1933	High-Ratio After 1933
Flour	100%	100%
Sugar	90	140
Eggs	42	60
Liquid milk	58	95
Shortening	35	50
Baking powder	3	6
Salt	As desired	As desired
Flavor	As desired	As desired

It was not possible for the baker to move to a richer formula like the housewife because of the equipment and ingredients available to him at that time. However, in 1933 a new type of shortening containing substantial quantities of monoglycerides reached the market (most fats are predominantly triglycerides). As pointed out earlier, monoglycerides behave as emulsifiers. These emulsifiers were found extremely effective in promoting better dispersion of the shortening in cake batters. This type of shortening permitted the baker to make cake batters with higher proportions of sugar, shortening, milk, and eggs. This meant that richer cakes could be made with moister, softer, richer eating qualities, longer keeping qualities, better texture, and better flavor. Thus, the modern "High-Ratio" cake was born with the classic formula shown in Table 21.5.

This monoglyceride emulsifier principle was employed in both shortenings for the housewife and shortenings for cake bakers.

Sweet Dough Shortening.—It was a natural step to enrich sweet yeast dough and Danish pastry formulas through the use of emulsifier-type shortenings, to obtain softer, moister, longer-keeping products. The optimum emulsifier content of sweet dough shortenings was found to be considerably higher than the optimum level for cake shortenings. It is believed that high monoglyceride levels in yeast goods hold together certain water-soluble starch fractions during the baking operation which would otherwise be released to cause a toughening action.

Bread Shortening.—For years bread was made with lard as the only shortening, but the demand grew for softer bread which would remain soft for longer periods. It was natural to employ the same softening principles (monoglycerides) for bread as had been used for sweet dough and cake. Bread Standards which were promulgated in 1952 permit as much as 20% of the shortening by weight to be mono- and diglyceride mixtures. Later, liquid shortenings containing these emulsifiers came into prominence. Liquid bread shortenings have a significant advantage over solid shortenings in being pumpable at room temperature, whereas a solid shortening must be kept at about 150°F throughout the time that it is transported, stored, and used. Keeping fat at 150°F is not only a nuisance, but is undesirable from the standpoint of oxidative stability.

Prepared Cake Mixes.—It is in the area of prepared cake mixes that another renaissance took place in shortening. Monoglycerides were good for "wet" cake batters, but were less satisfactory in dry cake mixes. The problem stemmed in part from the inability to get sufficient creaming action or air incorporation under home-use conditions from a shortening so well dispersed in the mix. This need accelerated emulsifier research and gave birth to some new emulsifiers which are characterized by their quick aeration or foaming ability. Examples are lactic acid esters of mono-and diglycerides, polyoxyethylene sorbitan monostearate, and propylene glycol esters of fatty acids. Cakes resulting from shortenings containing these emulsifiers were moister and more tender than ever before. Consumer tests have time after time confirmed the demand for this type of cake. Some of these emulsifiers are now available in some commercial shortenings.

Fluid Shortening Developments, 1958 to Present

Fluid shortenings refer to those shortening products which have the opaque "creamy" white appearance of plastic shortenings, but are fluid at room temperature. They are generally free-flowing from about 50°F and melt completely at about

120°F. This area of shortening development has been so dramatic and represents such a significant technological advance that the resulting products should be considered separate from salad oil and plastic shortening developments.

Historically, plastic and solid shortenings were generally preferred to oils, except for salad oil purposes. In the field of deep frying, for example, solid shortenings enjoyed advantages in kettle stability; in cake and cookie baking they were preferred for creaming ability, cake size, grain and keeping qualities; and in bread and sweet dough baking solids were preferred for such reasons as higher water absorption, better grain, higher volume, and better keeping qualities.

From the seemingly impressive list of advantages for plastic shortening, it would seem as though there would be little incentive to develop fluid shortenings. However, some of the advantages for oils which existed were strong enough to cause the use of some vegetable oils in spite of other deficiencies. A few advantages of oils over plastic shortenings included: (a) convenience of storage in tanks, convenience in handling because of pourability, ease of measuring or metering, and pumpability; (b) products deep-fried in oils have livelier, less drab surface appearance, especially those sold in the frozen state; and (c) baked products have a softer texture, better eating qualities (e.g., less "waxy"), and better physical keeping qualities.

In addition to the above, interest continued to develop in the use of fats and oils higher in polyunsaturated fatty acids, or of higher polyunsaturate-to-saturate ratios than were found in the solid or plastic shortenings in use at the time.

Some of the developments and problems that had to be surmounted in making fluid shortenings included: (a) evolution of a non-settling or a non-separating system so that a sufficient quantity of fat solids could be introduced into the fluid portion; (b) the attainment of kettle stability in the deep-frying operation; and (c) the development of adequate creaming response for baking purposes. These problems were resolved in the mid to late 1950's, and this led to a number of important fluid shortening products.

Fluid Deep-Frying Shortening (1958).—Once the concept of a creamy white product which looked like a plastic shortening but poured like an oil was realized, frying stability character-

istics had to be built into the product. This was achieved by
proper processing of the oils and use of the proper type and
quantity of methyl silicone to prevent premature foaming.
Fluid shortening was also observed to provide excellent fried
food appearance, neither greasy nor dull, but a lively golden
brown. Fried foods have a good appearance, whether consumed immediately or refrigerated or frozen for later service.

Fluid Pan Frying and Griddling Shortening (1959).—These
products frequently contain an antisticking material such as
oxystearin or lecithin to alleviate sticking of foods on griddle
surfaces. Beta-carotene can be added to give a more golden
appearance to foods, and a butter-like flavor can also be
added for flavor impact when used in brushing on foods. The
products that utilize oxystearin instead of lecithin are also
satisfactory for deep frying and other uses where prolonged
heating is required. Lecithin-containing food products are
not normally used because they turn very dark in color under
these heating conditions.

Fluid Cake Shortening (1962).—The development of excellent
fluid cake shortenings had to await the discovery of the new
emulsifiers which were referred to in the prepared cake mix
section. Superior emulsification was needed to produce good
and stable baking foams without the creaming support normally
obtained from plastic fats. Excellent fluid cake shortenings
emerged which utilized either lactic acid or propylene glycol
esters to provide this emulsification. Propylene glycol esters
and lactic acid esters enable the liquid cake shortening to
aerate rapidly, and improve the dispersion of the shortening
throughout the other ingredients in the cake batter. Tiny cells
or bubbles of fat of microscopic size entrap extremely small
air bubbles. Small bubbles result in an even expansion of
the cake during the baking process.

Aside from mixing improvements and ease of scaling and
mixing, liquid cake shortening imparts greater softness, moist-
ness, and better keeping qualities to finished cakes. This
is due to two factors: (1) the fluidity of the shortening itself
(softer fat), and (2) the emulsifier systems employed in the
shortening.

Fluid Bread Shortening.—This need came about through the
development of continuous breadmaking operations in wholesale
bread plants. When switching from conventional or batch mak-

ing to continuous operations, a change in the type or quantity of fat types was found necessary. In the conventional method, lard and monoglycerides were used. However, when going to the new process, it was found that a third fat product was necessary (called "hard flakes," a completely hydrogenated hard fat) which contributed stability to the bread doughs and prevented collapsing sides in the baked bread. Addition of three types of fat products was somewhat burdensome, especially since they all had to be used in the completely melted state, about 150°F. Also, with three materials, there was the added danger of error in weighing or metering. Other difficulties noted were that at this high usage temperature, storage tanks had to be nitrogen-blanketed to slow down oxidation, and these tanks also required agitation devices to aid in melting and preventing resolidification.

Fluid bread shortenings were developed which had both the "hard flakes" and the emulsifier incorporated in one single product. These shortenings are stored and used at room temperature. The use of this type of shortening essentially eliminated the problems mentioned above.

PACKAGING

This is the era of the packaging revolution in all types of consumer products, as a trip through any modern supermarket will verify. Major food companies have spent millions of dollars just to find out what consumers find desirable about packages for specific products. Today's packages (a) afford greater product protection against breakage and loss in product quality, (b) are more sanitary, (c) are more eye-appealing, and (d) afford a greater degree of convenience.

Shortenings and oils have come in for their fair share of package innovations, both those sold direct to the consumer in supermarkets and in quantity to bakeries, restaurants, institutions, and food processors.

Consumer Products

Plastic packages for oils are beginning to appear. Easy opening and closing devices on shortening packages have also made their appearance in the trade, and are now commonly accepted as the norm. Packages are regularly improved to make them more eye-appealing.

Restaurant and Institutional Products

Five-quart cans for liquid frying shortening and all-purpose liquid fats have entered the picture, many times replacing the bulkier 50-lb shortening packages and 5-gal oil cans. The 5-quart can is (a) easier to store and inventory, (b) hermetically sealed for maximum product protection against oxidation, (c) more sanitary, and (d) lighter in weight, which is especially beneficial for female employees.

Retail and Wholesale Bakeries

Fifty-lb cube cartons with polyethylene liners are tending to replace larger packages like the traditional 110-lb tins and 400-lb steel drums. This again results in an easier handling, more convenient package. In addition, shortening packed in cubes uses less expensive packing materials than tins and drums. Some large bakeries use multiples of 50 lb of shortening in their formulas for various baked foods, which adds to convenience.

Food Processors

Bulk handling of fats and oils in food plants is eliminating the somewhat cumbersome system of shipping, receiving and storing drums of fats and oils. In a typical bulk handling system, the fat or oil product is shipped in tank trucks containing 30,000 to 45,000 lb, or in rail tank cars from 30,000 lb up to 150,000 lb in capacity. Tank-truck deliveries eliminate the need for a rail siding at the food processor's plant. Rail car deliveries will, of course, require a rail siding. The contents of the car or truck are removed by pumping into one or more holding tanks ranging in capacity from about 30,000 to 70,000 lb, depending upon the plant's needs. The plant tank capacity must obviously be larger than the amount of the deliveries. Tank storage requires considerably less space than trying to store an equivalent amount of fat or oil in drums. In addition, the cost to the food manufacturer is less than when he uses the same product in packaged form. This can result in sub-

stantial savings for a food manufacturer using from $\frac{1}{4}$ million
to several million lb of fat per year.

When fats or shortenings which are normally solid at room
temperature are handled in bulk, it is necessary that they be
heated to above their complete melting point during the entire
time they are stored and transported. Normally they are kept
at about 150°F. This means that heat must be applied constantly, that storage tanks must be agitated by some stirring
device, and often extra protection against oxidation is required. As the temperature of a fat or oil increases, the rate
of oxidation also increases. To minimize this reaction, storage
tanks are usually nitrogen-blanketed to help separate the fat
or oil from the oxygen in the air.

With the advent of fluid shortenings and, of course, the use
of liquid oils, both of which are fluid at room temperature,
many advantages in handling have accrued. As mentioned
before, they include no heating, no agitation, and less need
for oxidative protection.

PROPER HANDLING, TRANSPORTATION, AND STORAGE OF FAT AND OIL PRODUCTS

This refers to the treatment a fat or oil receives from the
time it is packed by a refiner until the time it is used up by a
consumer or by the various industrial fat users.

The normal routes of fats and oils to the retail baker and
the food service operator are as follows: (a) storage by the
manufacturer before shipping; (b) transportation to the jobber
or distributor; (c) storage by the jobber or distributor; (d)
transportation from the jobber to the customer; (e) storage
by the customer until it is used.

For the large wholesale baker and food manufacturer, two
of these steps are eliminated because the products go directly
from the manufacturer to the user.

If a shortening is handled properly under all five of the
above steps, it can be expected to retain its quality over a
considerable period of time. An industrial shortening im-
properly handled, however, can lose its good appearance,
good flavor, and good performance characteristics within a
few days.

A properly handled industrial shortening is one which is
stored at normal temperatures of 60 to 80°F, out of the reach

of sunlight, is properly rotated in storage and use, and is kept in storage space which is free from offending or undesirable odors. If a shortening becomes too cold and develops more fat solids and becomes hard, it can be brought back to room temperature without any impairment of quality or performance. The same is true of fluid shortenings; even if they become cold and firm enough to lose their fluidity, they can be brought back to room temperature without any loss in performance.

The consequences of storage at too high a temperature are lack of body and loss of creaming volume in plastic (solid) shortenings. These losses may be only temporary and can be restored by returning the product to room temperature, unless the exposure to abnormally high temperatures has been severe or long enough to cause partial melting. If this occurs, when the shortening resolidifies it will not return to its original smooth, creamy appearance; but the portion of the shortening that had been melted will be grainy and somewhat off color. Overheating may come about by sunlight hitting packages through a window in the storage area, or by packages sitting out on a warehouse dock; storage close to a radiator or steam pipe; or a direct draft from a heating blower. These are some of the ways in which shortening may be "heat-damaged." Shortening which has been heated to this extent, on cooling to room temperature, will lack its normal creamy white appearance and smooth texture. Also, shortening in this condition may not cream properly.

Fluid shortenings can also be heat-damaged to the extent that they will start to separate. However, it is much more difficult to heat-damage fluid shortenings than solid shortenings. Also, even when completely separated, fluid shortenings may perform normally for some uses.

Shortenings and oils in nonhermetically sealed packages stored in a room in which offensive odors are present, such as soap and cleaning compounds, will sometimes pick up these odors and pass them along to the finished foods, particularly uncooked cream icings. This handling abuse can be overcome by keeping the shortening away from all undesirable odors. While drums, cans, and cartons offer some degree of protection when unopened, bad odors can penetrate all but the airtight packs such as hermetically sealed 5-quart cans.

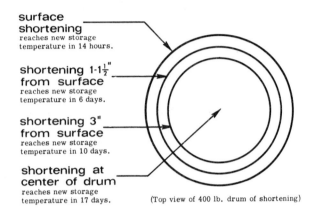

Diagram showing time required for all shortening in a steel
400 lb. drum to come to new storage temperature.

Temperature change due to change in storage conditions 27°F. *

surface
shortening
reaches new storage
temperature in 14 hours.

shortening 1-1½"
from surface
reaches new storage
temperature in 6 days.

shortening 3"
from surface
reaches new storage
temperature in 10 days.

shortening at
center of drum
reaches new storage
temperature in 17 days.   (Top view of 400 lb. drum of shortening)

* The time required for the shortening to come to the new storage
temperature would be the same regardless of whether the shortening
in the drum is cooled 27°F., or warmed 27°F.

FIG. 21.6. STORAGE TEMPERATURE CHANGE

Plastic shortening packed in 400-lb drums may require a long
time to alter the temperature of the entire contents of the drum.
An example of this is shown in Fig. 21.6.

THE FUTURE OF FATS AND OILS

The increased use of shortenings and oils of all kinds, both
industrial and retail, is a reflection of the growing appetite for
fat-bearing foods. Fat consumption itself is a measure of the
aggressiveness and the successfulness of countries. The world
fat consumption averages 23 lb per year per person as compared with 60 to 70 lb per capita for the United States, Canada,
and Western Europe. India is estimated at 15 lb per capita and
China at 5 lb per capita.

The ability of any country to purchase more fat-bearing foods
stems from the availability of more money for purchasing
food. As the standard of living in a country continues to flourish
not only here but abroad, and as the world's underdeveloped
countries are upgraded in living standards, there should be a
steadily increasing demand for fat-containing foods.

Some of the most important trends in the fat field include: (a) increased consumption of vegetable oils, along with a decrease in consumption of meat fats for shortening use; (b) decrease in the consumption of butter, along with an increase in the use of margarines; (c) new raw materials such as sunflower seed oil and rapeseed oil may become more prevalent; (d) Shortenings, fluid shortenings, and oils with higher levels of polyunsaturated fatty acids will be employed.

Undoubtedly in the years ahead further significant developments can be expected in the shortening, oil, and food emulsifier fields, and they will offer increasingly better properties to make fat-bearing foods even more delightful to the palate, more healthful, and even easier to use in food preparations.

CHAPTER 22

L. L. W. Smith | **Paints, Varnishes, and**
L. J. Minor | **Lacquers**

Paints, varnishes, and lacquers are liquid mixtures that provide air-dried or baked-on surface coatings that are protective
and decorative. Nearly $2\frac{1}{2}$ billion dollars were spent in the
United States on surface-coating materials in 1970. Of this
total, more than 95% was manufactured domestically, and 75%
was shipped from within a 500-mile radius from the point of
manufacture. Managers are responsible for the maintenance of
wood, metal, and masonry surfaces subjected to a variety of
atmospheric conditions. What coating system should be chosen
and how to apply it is knowledge that a manager needs.

PAINTS

Paint is composed of a liquid binder and solvent system called
the vehicle, in which one or more pigments are dispersed.
House paints are still hand-mixed by a few professional painters
from boiled linseed oil, turpentine, and white lead. The trend
in modern paints is in the direction of factory-made water-base
and oil-base coatings that employ water or organic solvents
as thinners to control viscosity and drying rate, and emulsified
synthetic resins as binders (film-forming agents).

Water-base paints are suitable for damp porous surfaces
exemplified by plaster and masonry, and have the advantage of
a cheap, odorless, nonflammable thinner. Latex and alkyd
emulsion types are used to protect wood, masonry, and metal
surfaces. Air pollution control and fire prevention favor the
use of water-base coatings whenever possible.

Gel paint is heavy-bodied and *thixotropic*, which means that
it is semi-solid at rest but fluid when stirred, shaken, or
brushed. When stress is removed it thickens, and has little
tendency to spill, drip, or run. This thixotropic quality is obtained by carefully incorporating small amounts of polyamide
resin into an alkyd resin vehicle.

Flat wall paints contain high pigment concentrations combined with viscous alkyd resin vehicles. *Alkyds* are prepared

512

by cooking soybean oil, phthalic anhydride, and soybean oil or other fatty acids together almost to the gel point. Alkyd flat wall paints are chosen by painters for use where hard wear is encountered or for areas that are difficult to paint. Today when application labor costs between 4 and 20 times as much as the paint, choice of a quality one-coat system may provide substantial savings.

Interior latex paints are based on emulsified polymers. Titanium dioxide, aluminum silicate, and clays are used as pigments, diatomaceous silicas being incorporated as "flatting" agents. Emulsion-type paints containing latex are susceptible to freezing and microbial attack during shipping and storage. Glycol additives protect against low temperatures, and phenylmercury salts act as preservatives and fungicides.

Heat-resistant paints contain aluminum pigments that yield oxide films that are nonconducting and heat-reflectant, and withstand temperatures up to 1000°F. Silicone/alkyd copolymer resin vehicles are used together with aluminum paste, metallic driers, and VM&P (varnish makers and painters) naphtha/xylene solvent systems.

Heat-resistant metal primer is a blend of zinc yellow and red iron oxide pigments in a silicone resin vehicle with plasticizer added to a 70:30 xylene/*n*-butanol solvent system. When baked on metal for 30 min at 440°F, a durable impact- and heat-resistant coating is obtained that has excellent adhesion to most metals.

Fire-retardant paints are formulated with highly chlorinated rubber binders and plasticizers that form puffed-up burned foams when subjected to fire. This foam insulation blisters, protecting the flammable wood or other surface beneath and preventing the flame from spreading. Antimony oxide pigment is combined with other fire-retardant materials in these high-cost formulations that are growing in popularity for specific architectural applications.

Exterior house paints of the organic solvent type include undercoaters or primers that are base coatings for new wood, flat house paints, gloss house paints, and shingle and shake paints. Besides turpentine, solvents or thinners for outside paint include mineral spirits, xylene, and toluene; binders consist of raw, heat-bodied, "boiled," and blown drying oils and alkyd resin polymers.

Undercoaters or primers for wooden surfaces are based on a 50-50 heat-bodied and raw oil system that controls penetration. Pigment volume concentrations are higher than in finish-coat paints and range from 35 to 40%; they consist of leaded zinc oxide and natural titanium dioxide. Fillers such as calcium carbonate (whiting), magnesium silicate (talc), diatomaceous silica and mica constitute 50% of the dry content. Diatomaceous silica gives "tooth," or ability to hold top coats to primer surfaces. Exterior wood should be primed immediately, and should not be allowed to weather prior to painting.

Flat house paints contain higher percentages of fillers than gloss types. An advantage of these coatings is that weathering does not affect surface appearance. However, dirt and mildew accumulation exceeds that for glossy coatings. Painters will often choose flat house paints to cover surface imperfections which are more noticeable when gloss house paints are applied.

Emulsion house paints have lower solids content and less covering power than oil house paints. Ease of application, brush or tool cleanup with water, fire hazard reduction, and second-coat application on the same day are some of their advantages. Before using emulsion paints over redwood and cedar, oil primers should be applied to prevent grain cracking and water staining. Emulsion paint films transmit considerably more water vapor than oil films, but blistering may occur.

Care must be taken to avoid freezing emulsion paints during shipping or storage. This causes the latex vehicle to coagulate and precipitate. Glycol compounds included in emulsion coatings provide some protection but are not one hundred percent safeguards.

Enamels are pigmented varnishes used to provide moisture, abrasion, and corrosion-resistant surfaces that are easily cleaned. Alkyd resin binders containing 30% phthalic anhydride and 60% soybean oil are pigmented with volume concentration ranges up to 25%. White gloss enamels utilize natural titanium dioxide as the principal white pigment due to its excellent hiding power. Naphtha and mineral spirits are compatible solvents with alkyd enamels.

Interior enamels are discolored by natural gas, ammonia cooking vapors, and cigarette smoke. There is no known remedy for the latter. Exterior enamels are formulated with titanium and zinc pigments rather than lead to eliminate the black sulfides that characterize leaded films. Marine varnishes and enamels made from tung oil alkyds are durable, attractive, and give excellent protection.

Semi-gloss coatings are combinations of enamel and flat wall paints, and accordingly combine the properties of each. Washability is better than that of flat wall coatings, and covering power on irregular surfaces is improved over that of enamels due to higher concentrations of alkyd varnish vehicle and pigment respectively. Lower cost and less sagging are additional advantages of semi-gloss paints over enamels. Reasons for choosing semi-gloss coatings over enamels include application to surfaces where less air pollution and corrosion are encountered or light reflectance must be reduced.

LACQUERS

Lacquers are solutions of resins such as acrylics in organic solvents which harden after the solvent evaporates from the film. They may be applied in clear or colored forms to paper, wood, cloth, or metal for the protection of art work. Sealant coatings for concrete block, anti-tarnishing sprays for copper, brass, silver, and gold; coatings for leather, glass, labels, upholstery fabrics, asphalt shingles, and rubber are other applications for clear acrylic lacquers. Ethanol, isopropanol, naphtha, and straight-chain hydrocarbon solvents are compatible with acrylics.

Cellulosic lacquers are used as clear or pigmented coatings made with resin plasticizers to increase adhesion, improve light and weather resistance, increase gloss, increase moisture and water resistance, and reduce costs. Nitrocellulose lacquers are tough and flexible, and may be combined with oil or modified-resin plasticizers and nonalkaline pigments in coatings for metal, woods, paper, leather, glass, masonry, plastics, rubber, and Masonite.

VARNISHES

Varnishes are oil vehicles modified with resins by cooking to high temperatures and then thinning with suitable hydrocarbon solvents, including mineral spirits, VM&P naphtha, toluene, and xylene. The incorporation of resins imparts de-

TABLE 22.1
RESIN COATINGS

Type	Source of Polymer	Classes	Uses
Alkyd (oil-modified) alcohol-acid polymers)	Fatty acids from oils, phthalic anhydride, and glycerin—other acids may be used e.g. maleic, adipic, fumaric, etc.	Short-oil, medium-oil, and long-oil, alkyds	Exterior paints for wood and metal, flat paints, enamels, varnishes note: alkyds may be combined with other resins to obtain specific properties
Aminoplast (urea-formaldehyde polymers)	Urea and melamine, formaldehyde react in mildly alkaline aqueous solutions	Urea aminoplasts, melamine aminoplasts	Metal primers and enamels (baked finishes), and catalyzed clear wood finishes
Phenolic	Phenol-formaldehyde polymers under acid or alkaline conditions	Nonoil-soluble, and oil-soluble resins	Coatings, molding plastics, adhesives for plywood, bonding metals, printing inks, marine varnishes, coil impregnating varnishes
Epoxy resins	Bisphenol A and epichlorohydrin under alkaline conditions	Epichlorohydrin/bisphenol A, amine adduct type, epoxy/polyamide, epoxy esters, epoxy phenolics	Coatings of excellent adhesion and chemical resistance, interior coatings for tanks, and pipelines, high glaze wall coatings, and heavy-duty floor coatings
Hydrocarbon resins	Coumarone and indene from coal-tar distillates	Coumarone-indenes, polydiene, polyethylene, polypropylene and rubbers	Aluminum paints, wall sealers, concrete paints, insulating varnishes, container coatings and floor coatings
Manilas	Philippines and Netherlands East Indies	Soft, half-hard, prime white soft, white soft, etc., obtained by tree-tapping	Spirit varnishes, paints, lacquers, sizing materials, japans, driers, waterproofing, printing inks, roofing, and paving compositions
Dammar	Singapore, Siam	Soft types obtained by tree tapping	Overprint varnishes, enamels, mill whites, lacquers, modifiers for alkyd resins in baking enamels
East India	East India	Batu, Black East India, and Pale East India semifossil exudates	Floor varnishes, priming coat for metal, enamels, sanding sealers, mill whites, abrasion-resistant floor varnishes, spar

		gathered from the ground	varnishes, aluminum paints
Accroides	Australia and Tasmania	Powdered red and yellow resins gathered from the ground	Binder in wallboard, resin substitute in paper coating, shellac substitute in spirit varnishes, lacquers and printing inks, finishes for wood, metal, and glass
Elemi	Philippines, Mexico, and Brazil	Yellow to brown resins	Plasticizer for lacquers applied to metal surfaces, in adhesives and cements, was compositions, printing inks, surface coatings applied to paper and textiles, and water-proofing compositions
Rosin	Southeastern U.S.	Gum rosin, and wood rosin graded according to color	Varnishes, paper sizing, linoleum, and printing inks; rosin esters are used in protective coatings
Shellac	Asia east of India from the lac bug that grows on tree twigs	Orange shellac, and white (bleached) shellac	Paints, stains, varnishes, wood sealer fast-drying for varnished floors, finish coat for floors, bowling alleys and bowling pins, and other wooden articles. Poor water and humidity resistance limit its uses
Asphalt and Pitches	Utah and Colorado (natural type), petroleum	Natural and petroleum types; Gilsonite, a hard, brittle natural resin	Gilsonite is cooked into oils to make black varnish in the same way as other hard resins are used for coatings as hardening agents for oil; automobile body under-coaters, acid and alkali resistant coatings, etc. Petroleum asphalts are used in roofing materials, underground wall coatings, waterproofing and paving compounds
Silicone resins	Silicon and organic halide reactions in the presence of powdered copper or silver catalysts	Hydrolyzed mono-, di-, and trisubstituted silanes, and their co-polymers with organic resins	High heat-resistant metal primers, heat resistant aluminum paint, weather and chemical resistant copolymers with alkyds, copolymers with epoxies and acrylics have greatly increased heat resistance for stove, heater, and duct coatings

Table 22.1 (continued)

Type	Source of Polymer	Classes	Uses
Natural resins (nonsynthetic)	Hardened exudations from trees	"Fossil types" dug from the ground "recent types" from living trees	Varnish resins for coatings unmodified by chemical processed where good weathering and chemical resistance are desired
Congo	Belgium Congo in Africa	Hard fossil from the ground	Production of varnishes and glycerin esters with good heat, moisture, dilute acid and alkali resistance and color retention, non-toxic and do not impart taste, and odor aqueous solutions
Kauri	New Zealand	Soft type from tapping living trees and fossilized resin from the ground	High-gloss coatings for furniture, oil varnishes, japans, lacquers, paint, cements, linoleum, and oil-cloth
Acrylic resins	Polymethyl and polyethyl methacrylates	Thermoplastic and thermosetting solids, liquids, and emulsions	Lacquer coatings, thermosetting finishes, and emulsion paints
Cellulosic films	Cellulose esters and ethers	Esters of inorganic and organic acids, and ethers	Lacquer coatings for metals, woods, paper, leather, plastics, glass, masonry, foil, fabrics, rubber, and "Masonite"
Vinyl resins	Polymers of vinyl chloride or vinyl acetate monomers	Vinyl chloride solution resins, and copolymer types	Phenolic, epoxy, and vinyl resin combination primers and coatings for furniture, exposed ducts and vents, lockers, outdoor furniture, nonskid clothes hangers, dishwasher interiors, and dish racks
Chlorinated rubber	Chlorination of rubber in solution	Chlorinated rubber, and chlorinated rubber blends with other resins	Chemical and corrosion-resistant wall coatings and metal coatings, marine hulls, masonry and swimming pool paints, fire-retardant paint, and rust preventive coatings for buried steel pipes
Urethane resins	Reactions between isocyanates and polyols, e.g., glycerin, ethylene glycol, alkyds, etc.	Drying oil modified, pre-polymers, blocked isocyanates, polyester/polyisocyanate	Baked coatings, solvent-free non-irritant liquid coatings for one-coat systems that are fast drying, and abrasion, water, and chemical resistant

sirable hardness to varnishes, enamels, and paints that improves abrasion, moisture, alkali, and acid resistance. A summary of resin coatings, types, sources, classes, and uses is given in Table 22.1

Wood furniture finishes may be clear lacquer or varnish or opaque paint types. Furniture woods are obtained from open-grain species, including oak, mahogany, walnut, elm and chestnut; or, nonporous maple, beech, gum, poplar, magnolia and cottonwoods, with birch and cherry as intermediate classes. Clear systems employ stains, fillers, sealers, and top coats.

Stains having clear, rich color that dry fast without raising the grain are obtained from aniline dyes dissolved in alcohol, aromatic hydrocarbons, and glycol ethers.

Sealers of low solids content are applied after staining and before filling the wood. A sanding-type sealer is applied after the filler, but before the finish coats. Sanding-sealers contain a higher percentage of solids due to incorporation of a sanding agent such as zinc stearate in the formula.

Fillers provide smoother surfaces and enhance the wood grain. They are formulated from 75% color pigments, and 25% unbodied linseed oil blended with short-oil varnish.

Finish lacquer coats may be clear or flat. The latter are clear coatings with a colloidal silica "flatting" agent. Finish coats consist of several film layers applied with a 1-hr drying period between coats. The final coat is rubbed after an overnight drying period.

FLOOR FINISHES

Floors are constructed of various materials other than wood, including: concrete, brick, skid-proof clay or ceramic clay tile; asphalt, vinyl, or vinyl-asbestos tile. New types of protective coatings are being developed and tested on a continuing basis to extend the life and improve the beauty of floorings.

Concrete is a conglomerate of gravel, pebbles, or broken stone embedded in Portland cement. Additives are responsible for 5 types of Portland cement for specific uses. Iron oxides are added to achieve greater surface hardness. Accordingly, the correct concrete should be specified for each application or use.

Coatings for concrete close the pores and prevent dusting due to abrasion, while providing a hard, continuous surface that is

easy to clean. A durable thin coating is obtained by applying
clear epoxy or polyurethane resin over new concrete previously
cleaned with a wash containing hydrochloric acid. Pigmented
epoxies or polyurethanes may be applied over primed older
concrete floors in greasy kitchen areas. Such coatings should
be applied by professionals. Concrete areas bordering swimming pools and similar walks or floors where wear is not
excessive may be improved by applying alkyd-resin enamels.
These coatings have excellent weather-resistance, and are
easily applied by brushing.

Asphalt, vinyl, or vinyl-asbestos tile floors laid over concrete, wood, or asphalt may be waxed, but yellowing and abrasion occur, and frequent stripping greatly raises maintenance
costs. Failure of tiles caused by breakage or loosening from
water seepage through joints demands frequent inspection and
repairs. A wet-dry vacuum is essential for cleaning these
floors, and mopping should precede vacuuming when necessary.

Terrazzo, brick, or tile floors are improved by applying
clear resin coatings. These prevent dirt penetration into pores
and mortar dusting. The coating should be thinly applied and
thoroughly dried before traffic is allowed, and renewed as wear
demands.

Wood floors in dance or exercise areas are preferably maple.
Sanding prior to protective coating should be done only by a
professional. After joints have been filled, stain is applied if
desired, and the wood is sealed with one or more coats of
shellac followed by 3 or 4 coats of clear varnish. A "gym
floor" coating may then be applied as a protection from hard
wear. This type can be applied after sanding.

RAW AND PROCESSED OILS

Raw and processed oils used in coatings are of vegetable or
marine origin. Chemically, they are esters of glycerol and
long-chain fatty acids called *glycerides*. Drying properties of
oils vary with the degree of unsaturation in the fatty-acid chain.
Oxygen taken up at the double bond sites accelerates drying by
polymerization. Linolenic acid with 3 nonconjugated double
bonds dries well whereas eleostearic acid with 2 conjugated
double bonds in the molecule dries faster.

Oils are vehicles that impart flexible films and drying properties to coatings. Linseed oil is the principal binder in house paints and in some alkyd resins. Tung oil (China wood oil) dries rapidly due to its high eleostearic acid content, and yields hard films with outstanding abrasion, water, and alkali resis-tance. Oiticica oil films are more brittle and have less water resistance than those from tung oil. Dehydrated castor oil dries rapidly, and has good color retention properties. Fish oils dry rapidly due to a high proportion of unsaturated fatty acids, and have a tendency to after-tack making them ideal rust-preventive coatings for the inside of automobile bodies. Coconut oil is nondrying but has excellent flexibility and color retention. Cottonseed oil is also nondrying, but its properties are inferior to those of coconut oil. Some important raw oil sources, properties, and uses is given in Table 22.2

Processed oils augment raw oils in coating formulations. These may be classified as "boiled," "heat-polymerized," and "blown" oils.

Boiled linseed oil is a misnomer. The oil is not brought to the boiling point, but is prepared by adding *metallic driers.* These may be oxides or naphthenates of manganese, lead, or cobalt combined with the hot oil. So-called "boiled" oil is thicker, darker, and faster drying than raw linseed oil.

Heat-polymerized linseed oil is prepared by prolonged heating at 500° to 600°F. Polymerization increases the oil's viscosity, and the bodied oil dries 6 times faster than raw oil.

Blown linseed oil is processed by heating the raw oil to 180° to 230°F as air is bubbled through. Oxidation followed by poly-merization increases viscosity. The "blown" product gives a harder film than heat-bodied oil, and is used in interior paints and enamels.

Modified oils are made by heat-treating soybean oil or other unsaturated oils with maleic anhydride. The reaction that occurs at the double bonds imparts faster drying and greater water resistance to the film. Water-soluble properties are imparted by reacting the modified oil with ammonia or amines.

Copolymer oils are heat-processed unsaturated oils with cyclopentadiene or other monomers added. Advantages of co-polymer oils are harder, faster-drying films.

Epoxidized oils are obtained by reacting unsaturated oils with peracetic acid. These are used as plasticizers to impart elasticity and flexibility to films.

TABLE 22.2
RAW OILS

Oil	Source	Properties	Uses
Linseed	Flaxseed	Yellow-amber-brown, contains linoleic and linolenic acids, a typical drying oil, soluble in turpentine, and petroleum ether	Varnishes, paints, synthetic resins, linoleum, etc.
Soybean	Solvent extraction or pressing of soybeans	Yellow liquid, semidrying, soluble in alcohol, ether, chloroform	Paints, varnishes, synthetic resins, margarine, shortening, etc.
Sunflower	Pressing of sunflower seeds	Pale yellow liquid, soluble in alcohol, ether, and chloroform	Varnishes, edible oil in Russia
Tung	Roasting, grinding and pressing tung nuts	Pale yellow-brown-liquid drying oil, soluble in chloroform, ether and oils	Varnishes, varnish driers, waterproofing compositions
Castor (dehydrated)	Hot-pressed castor beans with 5% of bound water	Pale yellow drying oil, imparts elasticity to and improves drying rate of linseed oil, soluble in alcohol, benzene, ether, and chloroform	Paints, lacquers, alkyd resins
Safflower	Pressed or solvent extracted from safflower seed	Light yellow drying oil, rich in linoleic acid, non-yellowing	Paints, varnishes, linoleum, foods
Coconut	Pressed from fresh nut meat and solvent extracted	White, semi-solid fat, soluble in alcohol, ether, and chloroform, nondrying, excellent color retention and elasticity	Alkyd resins, candles, foods; etc.

Drying oil tests include: iodine number, saponification number, specific gravity, index of refraction, color, melting point,
and solidifying point.

RESIN COATINGS

Resins are either *natural* solid or semisolid viscous materials
derived mostly from secretions of certain plants and trees;
or *synthetic* organic types produced by polymerization or condensation of a large number of molecules of 1, 2, or occasionally
3 relatively simple compounds.

Typical resins derived from natural polymers are: rubber,
chlorinated hydrocarbon polymers (neoprene); cellulose nitrate,
cellulose acetate, and methylcellulose; casein and zein proteins;
and miscellaneous ester gums, rosin, and lignin. Synthetic
classes include: acetal, acrylate, allyl, coumarone-indene,
fluorocarbon, furan, polyethylene, polypropylene, polystyrene,
vinyl and vinylidene resins derived by addition polymerization;
and alkyd, epoxy, melamine, phenolic, polyamide, polycarbonate,
polyester, polyurethane, polyether, silicone and urea-formalde-
hyde resins derived by condensation polymerization of small
molecules, with formation of water of some other simple molecule as a byproduct.

Resin coatings of various types, sources of the polymers,
classes, and uses are summarized in Table 22.1.

SOLVENTS

Solvents in surface coatings are used to solubilize drying oils
and resins, thus reducing the viscosity and improving brushing,
rolling, and spraying properties of the coating, and to control
the evaporation rate. Some types of solvents (hydrocarbon oils)
are also called thinners. Solvents range from water used in
latex emulsion paints to low boilers such as acetone, ethyl- or
butylacetate used in lacquers, and high boilers typified by VM&P
(varnish makers and painters) naphtha, mineral spirits, xylene,
and toluene used in varnish, house paint, and enamel.

Hydrocarbon solvents include straight- and branched-chain and
cyclic aliphatics (hexanes, heptanes and turpentine) and aromatics (benzene, toluene, xylene, naphtha, and petroleum ether).

Oxygenated solvents include alcohols, glycol ethers, ketones, and esters. These are typical lacquer solvents. Water is a special oxygenated solvent used in water emulsions.

Solvent tests include boiling range, flash point (closed cup), specific gravity, color, and refractive index.

Evaporation rates of solvents vary directly with film thickness, and the weight of solvent per unit area of evaporating surface. Lacquer films are thin, averaging less than 1 mil in thickness and are built up with multiple coats. Paint films vary between 1 and 3 mils thick, and are applied in one or more coats. Thixotropic paints with high solids give single-coat films measuring 10 to 20 mils.

PIGMENTS

Pigments are metallic substances that impart opacity and color to coatings. They are dispersed in the vehicle by milling, grinding, or merely mixing. White pigments include: titanium dioxide, zinc oxide, zinc sulfide, basic white lead carbonate, basic white lead sulfate, basic white lead silicate, and antimony oxide. Colored pigments are classed as inorganic and organic. Some inorganic pigments are: chrome yellows, oranges, and greens, zinc yellow, iron oxides, cadmium iron blue, ultramarine blue, red lead, siennas, nickel titanate, and molybdate orange. Organic pigments include: lithols, para reds, toluidine red and maroon toners, benzidine yellow, nickel azo yellow, thioindigo maroons and reds, rubine reds, phthalocyanine blue, carbon, lamp, and boneblacks.

Tints are defined by the American Society for Testing and Materials as: "a color produced by the mixture of white pigment or paint in predominating amount (50 percent or more) with a color pigment or paint."

PLASTICIZERS AND OTHER COATING ADDITIVES

Plasticizers are substances combined with a polymer to increase its plasticity, elasticity, and toughness. They may be classified as chemical, polymeric, or natural oils and modifications. Odor, taste, and toxicity must be absent from plasticizers approved by the FDA for use in containers and container linings. The approved list includes: butyl stearate, dibutyl sebacate, diethyl phthalate, epoxidized soybean oil, glycerol monooleate, triacetine, and triethyl citrate.

Metallic soaps are additives that modify flow properties or impart thixotropy, and aid in the suspension of pigments. They are the reaction products obtained by fusing or precipitating a metallic oxide or hydroxide with a weak organic acid. Settling and hard packing of pigments during storage of oleoresinous coatings is retarded or prevented by the incorporation of metallic soaps.

Metallic driers are liquid solutions of naphthenate, octoate, and tallate salts of cobalt, manganese, lead, calcium, zinc, or iron. They are used to control surface "skinning" and promote drying of coatings.

Flatting agents are additives that reduce light reflection by the dried coating film. Metallic carboxylates are dispersed in oleoresinous or lacquer vehicles as colloidal particles.

Sanding aids for lacquers are mainly zinc stearates mixed into a base coat that seals wood pores. This primer provides a "tooth" for the finish lacquer coats. Another application of zinc stearate is in lacquer top coats rubbed to a high gloss.

Preservatives and fungicides are added to latex, alkyd, epoxy, and other polymer type or oil emulsion coatings with water solvent to inhibit bacteria, molds, and fungi. Asphalt emulsions for roofs and driveways are susceptible to molds and require a mycostat. Typical preservatives are organo-mercurial salts, carbon disulfide derivatives, halogenated phenols, hexamethylenetetramine salts, and barium metaborate. Phenyl mercury salts are the most effective preservatives for aqueous coatings.

Fungal colonies impart black pigmentation to oil paint films on wood that are often mistaken for dirt. Molds may attack coatings under the humid conditions characteristic of breweries, food-packing plants, kitchens, shower rooms, and swimming pools.

Microbial inhibitors improve the appearance and extend the life of coatings besides eliminating an additional source of atmospheric contamination. Microbes quickly adapt to preservation additives, necessitating the constant development of new and more effective preservatives.

APPLICATION OF COATINGS

Coatings are applied by direct contact, for example, brushing, rolling, and dipping, and by spraying either with air or elec- trodeposition of the film. Air pollution is reduced when applica- tion is made by the electrodeposition spray method.

Brushes are available with either natural hog bristles or synthetic filaments set in vulcanized rubber or epoxy resin. Chinese hog bristle brushes with "flagged" tips (each bristle tip split in two or more parts) have heavier paint-loading capacity and leave finer brush marks than cheaper natural bristle types. Nylon brushes are ideal for latex paint, as hog bristles go limp as a result of excessive water absorption. Blending soft and stiff bristles improves performance and wearing quality of a brush.

Rollers require less practice and skill to manipulate than brushes. They cost less and larger areas can be covered in less time. Choosing them in accord with the application re- quires knowledge of different size cores, core materials, cover naps, and lengths.

Cabinets, fixtures, appliances, machines, and furniture that require refinishing should be sent out to reliable specialty shops, where uniform air-dried or baked-on coatings with the correct color, sheen, smoothness, hardness, and adhesion char- acteristics are applied economically by artisans who use specialized equipment.

FILM FAILURES

Faulty application causes many failures. Exterior painting conditions are best at temperatures of 75° to 80°F and a relative humidity of 50%. Film thickness is an important factor, and optimum thickness for outside wood surfaces is obtained by applying 1 coat of primer and 1 or 2 finish coats.

Moisture vapor accumulation inside buildings is often the cause of exterior-paint film failure. Vents should be provided to allow humid air to escape without being forced through out- side walls.

Kitchens require washable coatings that withstand moisture and chemical vapors from cooking and gas fuel. Ducts for hot vapors and heated pipes or other surfaces need heat-resistant paints. Adjacent areas should be painted with fire-retardant coatings. Coolers and meat-cutting rooms are cold and humid, indicating the need for latex emulsion paint or enamel.

Odorless paints are necessary in food handling or production areas, as foods absorb odors. Failures of painted surfaces in these areas may result in food contamination and must be carefully avoided. Tile walls and floors are best for food-manufacturing and storage areas; despite higher initial cost, these prove more economical over long periods due to low maintenance costs. Plaster or dry-wall ceilings with taped joints are generally used; these require suitable gloss or semi-gloss coatings for washability and light reflectance. Metal doors are generally chosen for use with tile walls, and these must be protected with suitable surface coatings.

The following general rules should prove helpful in avoiding coating film failures: (1) choose the correct coating system for the desired application; (2) carefully prepare the surface; (3) primers should be used over new surfaces; (4) favorable atmospheric conditions should prevail during the application of coatings; (5) new plaster and concrete should be cured to elimi-nate moisture and cleaned before applying coatings; and (6) drying time between coats should be adequate.

New materials are continually being developed and tested for use in coatings. An awareness of the advantages offered by these improved products is essential to progress.

CHAPTER 23

L. L. W. Smith
L. J. Minor

Nutrition

"You are what you eat," as foods affect your health and appearance from birth through adulthood to death. Nutrition may
be defined as the process by which plants and animals take in
and utilize foods. Only through adequate balanced nourishment
can the human machine function at its peak. Heredity plays an
important part in food habits, and so does the social climate.
For example, it is said that America is hamburger and "Coke"
crazy. This fad keeps growing as people stop at filling stations
for their stomachs as well as their gas tanks. Just as a high-
compression engine needs a high-octane gasoline to power it,
so does a well-trained athlete require a balanced diet. For unless a balance is maintained between energy input and output of
the body, either a depletion of protein, fat, carbohydrate, and
minerals will cause loss of weight and strength, or a surplus
will cause build-up of fatty tissue. Maintaining ideal weight
requires constant attention and personal discipline.

Food fads, diet-control preparations, and mechanical devices
for weight and body shape control are big money makers for
the entrepreneurs who promote them. Any benefits the customer
receives are negative or temporary. In other words, there is
no substitute for good food habits and regular exercise.

Absenteeism from work or school, fatigue and decreased
work output, and poor performance may be traced to common
colds, headaches, nose bleeds, and other common or chronic
ailments caused by omitting essential dietary factors. Food
habits may often be traced to a person's origin. Sea-coast
dwellers crave seafoods, midwesterners prefer beef, Americans
like hamburgers and hot dogs, people from the Eastern world
demand rice, and the English are fond of mutton. Religious
taboos and psychological blocks also may influence food habits.
For example, Middle Easterners avoid eating pork, Indians do
not eat beef, Hindus omit chicken and eggs, and dogflesh is
abhorred by Westerners other than American Indians or Es-
kimos.

Good food habits coupled with exercise make strong, well-formed bodies and add up to a vitalized personality. However, we do not simply eat and drink just to keep alive, but to be sociable and to obtain the psychological lift that a good meal provides.

Growth, maintenance, and repair of body tissues is dependent upon proper nutrition. Energy used in all activities must be provided by food intake. Hence, the study of foods and their balance for maintaining health is important.

Digestion of food precedes its absorption by the body. This begins with mastication in the mouth, and continues as the food passes through the stomach and intestines, where digestive chemicals liquefy it into simpler forms that can be absorbed by the body. Roughage, of course, passes through and aids in the elimination of body waste.

Nutrients may be divided into several classes, namely: oxygen, water, carbohydrates, fats, proteins, vitamins, and minerals. Miscellaneous food items such as salt, which provides sodium and chloride ions, and ethyl alcohol from alcoholic beverages that yield 7 Calories per gram oxidized, are especially important when dealing with heart patients or problem drinkers. Coffee, tea, and cola drinks may cause undesirable effects in persons who are sensitive to alkaloids without contributing significantly to nutrients unless cream, sugar, or milk are added.

Oxygen is a vital nutrient, which combines with carbohydrates, fats, and proteins to provide calories. Enzyme reactions involving biological oxidations also convert dietary materials into cellular constituents.

Water is second only to oxygen in importance as an inorganic nutrient. It provides the medium in which practically all metabolic reactions involving nutrients occur. In other words, it is concerned with all the chemical reactions in which protoplasm is built, destroyed, or converted, besides those that provide energy. The body needs about 1 ml of water per calorie of food intake under conditions of moderate temperature and movement. An adequate supply of water is especially necessary for infants and sick persons.

Carbohydrates furnish about 4 Cal/gm and include starches, simple sugars (glucose), and complex sugar (sucrose) which provide most of the energy requirements. Carbohydrates also

Any food that contains calories is "fattening" if the amount of calories consumed is greater than the amount used. The surplus is stored up in the form of fat. Potatoes provide a highly digestible bulk with relatively few calories (it would take about 10 pounds of potatoes to provide the daily caloric requirements of a young adult). Potatoes also contain generous quantities of important nutrients. As a source of vitamin C, potatoes are recognized as being a close second to citrus in providing each American's total supply.

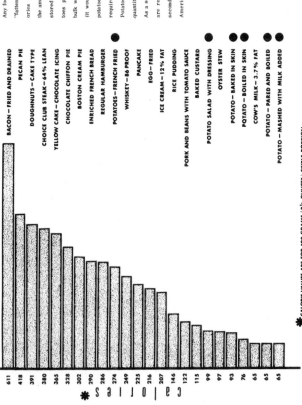

Food	Calories
BACON – FRIED AND DRAINED	611
PECAN PIE	418
DOUGHNUTS – CAKE TYPE	391
CHOICE CLUB STEAK – 64% LEAN	380
YELLOW CAKE – CHOCOLATE ICING	365
CHOCOLATE CHIFFON PIE	328
BOSTON CREAM PIE	302
ENRICHED FRENCH BREAD	290
REGULAR HAMBURGER	286
POTATOES – FRENCH FRIED	274
WHISKEY – 86 PROOF	249
PANCAKE	225
EGG – FRIED	216
ICE CREAM – 12% FAT	207
RICE PUDDING	146
PORK AND BEANS WITH TOMATO SAUCE	122
BAKED CUSTARD	115
POTATO SALAD WITH DRESSING	99
OYSTER STEW	97
POTATO – BAKED IN SKIN	93
POTATO – BOILED IN SKIN	76
COW'S MILK – 3.7% FAT	65
POTATO – PARED AND BOILED	65
POTATO – MASHED WITH MILK ADDED	65

* CALORIE VALUES ARE FOR 100 GRAMS (3½ OUNCES) EDIBLE PORTION

include pectins found in fruit skins; gums from trees and plants; algins, Irish moss and agar from seaweed, inulin from Jerusalem artichokes; and starches in flour, rice, corn, tapioca, arrowroot, sagopalm, and potatoes. Sugars include cane and beet table sugar, honey, invert sugar, and molasses, as well as glycogen or animal starch stored in liver. Cellulose, a carbohydrate polymer, provides roughage, and is found in lettuce, carrots, and other vegetables.

Fats furnish about 9 Cal/gm. These are either solid or liquid (in the form of oils), and include animal fats, or lard, suet, butter and chicken fat, and vegetable oils such as corn, cottonseed, soybean, safflower, sunflower, peanut, and coconut oils. They are either broken down into fatty acids and glycerol or absorbed directly as a store for body energy. Fatty acids essential to health that must be included in the diet are the polyunsaturated linoleic and linolenic acids; without an adequate amount of these, skin lesions may occur. Diets deficient in linoleic acid cause skin outbreaks in infants, have an adverse affect on reproduction and lactation, and lower resistance to radiation exposure.

Proteins are vital constituents of every living cell. Yet an adequate protein diet cannot be obtained by selecting food on the basis of protein content. Certain types of proteins support growth and maintenance of the animal body completely, while some fail to maintain a nitrogen balance, though the amount supplied should suffice. Proteins may be divided into two classes—animal proteins and vegetable proteins. Some important animal protein sources are meat, poultry, fish, milk and eggs; major vegetable proteins are found in cereals, nuts, and pulses such as peas, beans, and lentils.

Proteins (about 4 Cal/gm) consist of chains of amino acids, and from them the body tissues are built. There are 8 essential amino acids among the 20-odd types of amino acids, and these must be provided in the diet. To be effective, all the amino acids must be ingested at the same time in correct proportion, and a deficiency of any one of them will detract from their body-building value. Hence, the quality with respect to the amino-acid composition and concentration in proteins consumed is a determinant factor in well-being. Besides the 8 essential amino acids, arginine may be essential for adults and histidine for children. Animal protein is of greater nutritional value than vegetable protein. Gelatin is deficient in amino acids and when used as the sole source of protein, it cannot sustain life. Animal proteins contain the essential amino acids in proper proportions for body-building; vegetable proteins contain them, but not in the necessary proportions.

Recommended protein allowances by the Food and Nutrition Board of the National Research Council provide for 1 gm of protein per day per kilogram of body weight in adult men and women. The recommendation for pregnant women in the second half of pregnancy is 1.35 gm per kilogram of body weight and 1.7 gm per kilogram of body weight during lactation. Children and adolescents require 40 to 100 gm of protein daily, according to age (see Table 23.1).

*Metabolism.*is divided into *anabolism* or body buildups with nutrients, and *catabolism*, which involves the breakdown of nutrients to provide energy and waste products.

Metabolism of amino acids repairs and maintains existing cells and also supplies the necessary building blocks for the synthesis of specific cell proteins needed for the manufacture of new cells. This anabolic (building) activity includes structural proteins and components of cell protoplasm, intracellular and extracellular enzymes, hormones, and other nonproteinaceous amino-acid derivatives.

Any excess amino acids are catabolized (broken down) to simpler compounds liberating heat and energy or are converted to carbohydrate and fat; if energy requirements are met, the excess is stored as fat. During hunger or starvation amino acids are used to supply heat and energy to maintain essential body functions which take priority over anabolic activities.

Biologic value of food proteins is a function of amino acid composition, and is based on the percentage of absorbed nitrogen retained by the body for maintenance and growth. Proteins with a full spectrum of essential and nonessential amino acids have higher biological values than those that are lacking in essential amino acids upon digestion.

Digestion of a protein in the body by hydrolysis to its individual amino acids is necessary before these can be absorbed by the blood stream and transported to the metabolic pool. Cooking, baking, and toasting of proteins has a pronounced influence on their digestibility. Overheating may destroy lysine or interfere with enzymatic digestion by forming new chemical bonds. This is especially true in the absence of water when foods are broiled, fried, or roasted.

Absorption of food proteins by the intestinal mucosa is slight; the large molecules must be digested by hydrolytic enzymes in the gastrointestinal tract. Some polypeptides or proteins may pass the mucosal barrier entering the blood stream and cause allergic reactions in sensitive persons to specific food proteins. This may be a serious problem in the more permeable gastrointestinal tracts of very young infants.

Naturally occurring levorotatory amino acids are absorbed more easily than their D-isomers, and absorption of individual amino acids is a competitive selective process. Absorption rates for single amino acids do not apply to complex amino-acid mixtures.

Theoretically, there is an amino-acid pool that must be adequately filled with essential amino acids at the moment of absorption. Amino acids are mixed in the intestinal lumen, regulating the relative concentrations of amino acids available for absorption. This action in the intestine assures the simultaneous availability of an amino-acid mixture for optimal protein synthesis in body tissues.

Following absorption, the unused amino acids pass through the portal vein to the liver of lymphatic cells to the blood stream.

Egg protein is highest in biologic value, and close to it is milk protein (casein). All the essential amino acids can be supplied by egg or milk protein when provided in sufficient quantity to the diet. Gelatin is lacking in valine and tryptophan, two of the essential amino acids, and contains inadequate amounts of tyrosine; thus gelatin cannot serve as the sole source of protein. Addition of valine and tryptophan to gelatin in sufficient amounts makes normal growth and maintenance possible.

Fish, meat, and poultry proteins are high in biologic value. Cereal, bean, and nut proteins may contain the necessary amino acids but have low biologic value due to a shortage of one or more of the essential amino acids. Blends of these proteins or supplementation by other food proteins rich in the missing amino acids is essential to good nutrition. Soybeans provide an inexpensive source of nutritious protein that may shortly replace some animal protein in the diet.

TABLE 23.1

RECOMMENDED DAILY DIETARY ALLOWANCES[1]

Designed for the maintenance of good nutrition of practically all healthy people in the U.S.

	Age[2] years	Weight Kg	Weight Lb	Height Cm	Height In.	Kcal	Protein Gm	Fat-soluble Vitamins Vitamin A Activity IU	Fat-soluble Vitamins Vitamin D IU	Fat-soluble Vitamins Vitamin E Activity IU	Water-soluble Vitamins Ascorbic Acid Mg	Water-soluble Vitamins Folacin[3] Mg	Water-soluble Vitamins Niacin Mg equiv[4]	Water-soluble Vitamins Riboflavin Mg	Water-soluble Vitamins Thiamine Mg	Water-soluble Vitamins Vitamin B6 Mg	Water-soluble Vitamins Vitamin B12 μg	Minerals Calcium Gm	Minerals Phosphorus Gm	Minerals Iodine μg	Minerals Iron Mg	Minerals Magnesium Mg
Infants	0–1/6	4	9	55	22	kg × 120	kg × 2.2[5]	1,500	400	5	35	0.05	5	0.4	0.2	0.2	1.0	0.4	0.2	25	6	40
	1/6–1/2	7	15	63	25	kg × 110	kg × 2.0[5]	1,500	400	5	35	0.05	7	0.5	0.4	0.3	1.5	0.5	0.4	40	10	60
	1/2–1	9	20	72	28	kg × 100	kg × 1.8[5]	1,500	400	5	35	0.1	8	0.6	0.5	0.4	2.0	0.6	0.5	45	15	70
Children	1–2	12	26	81	32	1,100	25	2,000	400	10	40	0.1	8	0.6	0.6	0.5	2.0	0.7	0.7	55	15	100
	2–3	14	31	91	36	1,250	25	2,000	400	10	40	0.2	8	0.7	0.6	0.6	2.5	0.8	0.8	60	15	150
	3–4	16	35	100	39	1,400	30	2,500	400	10	40	0.2	9	0.8	0.7	0.7	3	0.8	0.8	70	10	200
	4–6	19	42	110	43	1,600	30	2,500	400	10	40	0.2	11	0.9	0.8	0.9	4	0.8	0.8	80	10	200
	6–8	23	51	121	48	2,000	35	3,500	400	15	40	0.2	13	1.1	1.0	1.0	4	0.9	0.9	100	10	250
	8–10	28	62	131	52	2,200	40	3,500	400	15	40	0.3	15	1.2	1.1	1.2	5	1.0	1.0	110	10	250
Males	10–12	35	77	140	55	2,500	45	4,500	400	20	40	0.4	17	1.3	1.3	1.4	5	1.2	1.2	125	10	300
	12–14	43	95	151	59	2,700	50	5,000	400	20	45	0.4	18	1.4	1.4	1.6	5	1.4	1.4	135	18	350
	14–18	59	130	170	67	3,000	60	5,000	400	25	55	0.4	20	1.5	1.5	1.8	5	1.4	1.4	150	18	400
	18–22	67	147	175	69	2,800	60	5,000	—	30	60	0.4	18	1.6	1.4	2.0	5	0.8	0.8	140	10	400
	22–35	70	154	175	69	2,800	65	5,000	—	30	60	0.4	18	1.7	1.4	2.0	5	0.8	0.8	140	10	350
	35–55	70	154	173	68	2,600	65	5,000	—	30	60	0.4	17	1.7	1.3	2.0	5	0.8	0.8	125	10	350
	55–75+	70	154	171	67	2,400	65	5,000	—	30	60	0.4	14	1.7	1.2	2.0	6	0.8	0.8	110	10	350
Females	10–12	35	77	142	56	2,250	50	4,500	400	20	40	0.4	15	1.3	1.1	1.4	5	1.2	1.2	110	18	300
	12–14	44	97	154	61	2,300	50	5,000	400	20	45	0.4	15	1.4	1.2	1.6	5	1.3	1.3	115	18	350
	14–16	52	114	157	62	2,400	55	5,000	400	25	50	0.4	16	1.4	1.2	1.8	5	1.3	1.3	120	18	350
	16–18	54	119	160	63	2,300	55	5,000	400	25	50	0.4	15	1.5	1.2	2.0	5	1.3	1.3	115	18	350

Age[2] years	Weight Kg	Weight Lb	Height Cm	Height In.	Kcal	Protein Gm	Fat-soluble Vitamins			Water-soluble Vitamins							Minerals				
							Vitamin A Activity IU	Vitamin D IU	Vitamin E Activity IU	Ascorbic Acid Mg	Folacin[3] Mg	Niacin Mg equiv[4]	Riboflavin Mg	Thiamine Mg	Vitamin B₆ Mg	Vitamin B₁₂ µg	Calcium Gm	Phosphorus Gm	Iodine µg	Iron Mg	Magnesium Mg
18–22	58	128	163	64	2,000	55	5,000	400	25	55	0.4	13	1.5	1.0	2.0	5	0.8	0.8	100	18	350
22–35	58	128	163	64	2,000	55	5,000	—	25	55	0.4	13	1.5	1.0	2.0	5	0.8	0.8	100	18	300
35–55	58	128	160	63	1,850	55	5,000	—	25	55	0.4	13	1.5	1.0	2.0	5	0.8	0.8	90	18	300
55–75+	58	128	157	62	1,700	55	5,000	400	30	55	0.4	13	1.5	1.0	2.0	6	0.8	0.8	80	10	300
Pregnancy					+200	65	6,000	400	30	60	0.8	15	1.8	+0.1	2.5	8	+0.4	+0.4	125	18	450
Lactation					+1,000	75	8,000	400	30	60	0.5	20	2.0	+0.5	2.5	6	+0.5	+0.5	150	18	450

Source: Natl. Acad. Sci.—Natl. Res. Council (1968).

[1] The allowance levels are intended to cover individual variations among most normal persons as they live in the United States under usual environmental stresses. The recommended allowances can be attained with a variety of common foods, providing other nutrients for which human requirements have been less well defined. See text for more-detailed discussion of allowances and of nutrients not tabulated.

[2] Entries on lines for age range 22–35 years represent the reference man and woman at age 22. All other entries represent allowances for the midpoint of the specified age range.

[3] The folacin allowances refer to dietary sources as determined by *Lactobacillus casei* assay. Pure forms of folacin may be effective in doses less than $\frac{1}{4}$ of the RDA.

[4] Niacin equivalents include dietary sources of the vitamin itself plus 1 mg equivalent for each 60 mg of dietary tryptophan.

[5] Assumes protein equivalent to human milk. For proteins not 100% utilized factors should be increased proportionately.

Deficiency of protein is encountered among two-thirds of the world's population. Small children after breast feeding is over suffer from malnutrition when they are fed cereal gruel. This disease is called *"Kwashiorkor,"* and is characterized by edema, potbelly, abnormal skin pigmentation, and liver damage. If at all possible at least one-third of dietary protein should come from meat, poultry, fish, eggs, and milk.

Special-purpose protein foods have been developed to feed undernourished children in underprivileged countries. Nonfat dry milk was distributed after World War II, followed by Incaparina, a blend of soy protein with vitamins and minerals. Now, the third generation is being fed Cerealina made from full-fat soy flour, cornstarch, and dry milk fortified with minerals and vitamins. This is mixed with water and sugar to make a "mingau" for the children costing four cents a serving.

Minerals in low percentages are required for regulating body processes. Iron, calcium, sodium, potassium, phosphorus, and iodine are the most essential minerals for health. See Table 23.7 on the inorganic elements present in the body, Table 23.9 on minerals in fresh fruit, and Table 23.8 on the function of metals in the body at the end of the chapter.

FUNCTIONS OF VITAMINS AND MINERALS AND DEFICIENCY EFFECTS

The main function of vitamins and minerals is the protection and regulation of health. *Vitamin D, calcium,* and *phosphorus* are necessary for the formation and maintenance of bones and teeth. Rickets, a softening and deformity of the bones, is caused by a vitamin deficiency. Without calcium, vitamin D is not effective, and a lack of vitamin D prevents utilization of dietary calcium by the body. Accordingly, both vitamin D and calcium must be present in the diet for either to be utilized by the body.

Iron is essential for oxygen transport in the body, and a deficiency causes anemia; *calcium* is essential to blood-clotting, together with vitamin K. Vitamin C increases the body resistance to infection, aids in healing wounds, and maintains healthy gums. Vitamin C is also called the antiscorbutic vitamin as it cures scurvy, a disease causing weakness, spongy gums, and anemia.

The B -group vitamins help convert food to energy, and maintain the tissues of the nervous system, and a deficiency of these
vitamins slows growth in children. *Nicotinic acid*, or niacin,
deficiency causes *pellagra*, a disease affecting skin and nerves.
Thiamine deficiency leads to beri-beri, a disease affecting both
the nervous and digestive systems.

Salt is important in the maintenance of body fluid concentration of sodium and chloride ions and the prevention of cramps.
Salt is lost in both sweat and urine. Maintenance of the correct
salt level requires a greater salt intake in hot climates due to
losses from perspiration.

Iodine regulates all the bodily processes, including energy
production through the thyroid gland. Goiter has been eliminated among residents in the Great Lakes fresh water region
of the United States by addition of iodine to diets via table salt
called iodized salt.

The general functions of each vitamin and mineral are summarized in Table 23.3. *Water* contains traces of minerals.
Hard water contains calcium, magnesium, and iron ions. Water
is softened by replacing calcium, magnesium, and iron with
sodium ions. This content of sodium may be prohibitive in the
drinking and cooking water used for people on low-salt diets.
An adequate supply of water is essential to nutritional processes. Man can live without food for a few weeks on stored
body fat, but if water is not provided, life ends after a few
days.

Energy requirements may be classified into three groups,
namely; basic metabolic activity including all the body processes essential to life (breathing, blood circulation, *food
digestion*, and *assimulation*). Basal metabolism refers to an
energy expenditure at a specific time, i.e., in the morning soor
after rising and 14 hr after the last meal. Sleeping and re-
clining activity is a condition of thermal neutrality requiring
530 cal/day. Sitting while reading, driving an automobile and
doing bench or desk work is sitting activity, and requires 630
cal/day. Standing activity, for example, playing billiards or
walking from room to room, burns 750 cal/day. Walking activity outdoors in commuting averages 360 cal/day. Other
activity such as sports or exercise uses 540 cal/day. Adding
these energy expenditures representing those of an average
22-year old male who weighs 70 kg gives a total daily ex-

penditure of 2,810 cal. An average 22-year old female weighing 58 kg expends 2,050 cal/day. (A kilocalorie is the heat required to raise 1 kg of water 1°C). The large Calorie (capitalized) or kilocalorie is equivalent to 1000 small calories. These values were determined by the National Research Council, Food and Nutrition Board, and published in 1968. Body energy is derived mainly from carbohydrates and fats although proteins in excess of the bodies daily needs also provide calories.

Metabolic needs include *sex, age*, and *size*. Women have more body fat than men and require fewer calories. Older people's activities are reduced, and so are their calorie requirements. Larger persons need greater numbers of calories than smaller ones to provide body heat and maintenance. *Activity* influences calorie requirements. Physically active persons adjust food intake to energy output, whereas inactive persons tend to ingest calories in excess of body needs. *Climate* affects energy requirements only when prolonged exposure to cold or heat is encountered. In mean temperatures below 14°C or above 38°C and accompanying increased physical activity, energy requirements are increased.

Pregnancy and lactation cause increased energy requirements of 200 cal/day and up to 1,000 cal/day, respectively.

In *infants, children*, and *adolescents*, calorie requirements decrease with age. During the first year of life allowances are gradually reduced from 120 cal/kg at birth to 100 cal/kg after 1 year. Growth rates of boys and girls after age nine show major differences necessitating caloric intake adjustments. Inactive children and adolescents suffer from obesity on calorie intakes below the norm, while extremely active children require larger amounts. Any surplus calories taken into the body are converted to fat. Thus decreased activity should be accompanied by diminished caloric intake. In normal satisfactory health just enough energy food should be eaten to fulfill the energy requirements and maintain body weight without gain or loss. Eating foods consisting mostly of carbohydrates or fat, or drinking alcohol could provide all the energy needs, but without amino acids, vitamins, and minerals the body functions deteriorate.

Carbohydrate metabolism consists of glycogen (animal starch) buildups in the liver as an energy reserve, and oxidation of carbohydrate in the cell to supply body energy. *Insulin*, a hormone secreted by the pancreas, functions in both the oxidation of glucose and the conversion of glucose to glycogen. Excess carbohydrate in the diet turns to fat, is stored in body tissues or synthesized into amino acids, or eliminated.

Fat metabolism involves the oxidation of fat to carbon dioxide, water, and energy or storage of fat as adipose tissue. Fat may be formed from amino acids or carbohydrates via enzyme reactions.

Faulty metabolism may be due to inborn or hereditary factors including diabetes mellitus, phenylketonuria, and galactosemia. *Diabetes mellitus* is caused by inability of the pancreas to provide sufficient insulin for the oxidation and storage of glucose. Excessive hunger, thirst, and urine output; accumulation of organic acids and acetone in the blood; weakness; and loss of body weight are symptoms borne by diabetics. Treatment with oral hypoglycemic agents, and adjustment of the patients diet are methods used to control diabetes. *Galactosemia* in infants is caused by a deficiency of the enzyme that converts galactose to glucose. Symptoms are failure to grow, galactose in the urine, liver enlargement, jaundice, mental retardation, and cataracts. Diets restricting lactose intake are used to treat galactosemia. *Phenylketonuria* in infants results from a shortage of a liver enzyme that converts one amino acid (phenylalanine) to another (tyrosine). Symptoms are eczema, motor disorders, musty-smelling urine, and mental retardation. Treatment consists of a synthetic diet low in the amino acid phenylalanine. Infants are tested for phenylketonuria at birth, for if not detected early, it may result in retardation.

DIGESTION AND ABSORPTION

Digestion is a mechanical and chemical process that begins when food is chewed and acted upon by the salivary enzyme *ptyalin*. Ptyalin hydrolyzes starch or dextrin to the disaccharide maltose.

From the mouth the comminuted food passes through the *esophagus* to the *stomach*. Here it is subjected to the chemical action of hydrochloric acid, the protein-splitting enzyme *pepsin*, and gastric *lipase* that acts on milk or egg fat. Pepsin hydrolyzes the protein chains to polypeptides of various chain lengths containing from 3 to several hundred amino acids.

TABLE 23.2
NATURAL SOURCES OF VITAMINS

Vitamin	Milk Group	Meat Group	Vegetable Group	Bread Group
I. Water-soluble				
Thiamine	Milk	Eggs, lean meat, liver	Fruits, legumes, yeast	Cereal grain, embryos
Riboflavin	Milk, cheese	Liver, eggs, meat	Leafy vegetables	Wheat germ
Niacin	—	Liver, kidney, lean meat, eggs, fish	Peanuts, yeast, green leafy vegetables	Bran
Pyridoxine	Milk	Liver	Yeast, legumes	Cereals
Pantothenic acid	Milk	Liver, kidney, eggs	Yeast	Wheat germ
Biotin	—	Kidney, liver, heart, egg yolk	Peanuts, cauliflower, mushrooms	
Folic acid	—	Liver, kidney	Dark green leafy vegetables, lima beans, nuts, lentils	Whole grain cereals
Vitamin B_{12}	Milk, cheese	Meats, scallops, sole, haddock, eggs	Peas, soybeans, beets, carrots	Wheat, oats, corn
Vitamin C	—	—	Citrus fruits, alfalfa, cabbage, green and red peppers, potatoes, raw turnip, tomato, pineapple	
II. Fat-soluble				
Vitamin A	Cream, butter	Fish, liver, oils, eggs	Carotenes, apricots, leaves of green plants	
Vitamin D	Evaporated milk, fortified fresh milk, fortified margarine	Fish liver oils, salmon, sardines, herring, liver, egg yolk		
Vitamin E	—	Egg yolk, meat	Lettuce, spinach, legumes	Cereal seed oils
Vitamin K	—	—	Alfalfa, spinach, cabbage, kale, carrot greens, tomatoes	

After 3 to $4\frac{1}{2}$ hr the partially digested food mixture, called *chyme*, moves into the *duodenum*, where it is chemically reduced to fatty acids and glycerol or di- and monoglycerides by pancreatic lipase, to simple sugars by pancreatic amylase, and to amino acids by pancreatic protease.

Undigested residues, unabsorbed end products of digestion, bile pigments, waste products, and water pass to the *colon*. No further digestion occurs, as there are no enzymes present in the colon. Water absorption is the principal function that occurs in the large intestine (colon).

Absorption of the soluble products obtained by digestive action occurs mainly in the small intestine, although water and small amounts of simple sugars pass through the mucosa of the stomach into the blood stream. Villi or lymph vessels that are fingerlike in shape and surrounded by capillaries line the small intestines. Nutrients taken in by the lymph vessel together with oxygen pass to the blood and tissues, whereas those absorbed by capillaries go from the portal vein to the liver.

Vitamins may be grossly classified as vitamin A, the vitamin B group, and vitamins C and D. Several other vitamins such as E and K are also required, and are present in any well-chosen diet. Incidentally, vitamins and minerals work with the enzymes to regulate energy and metabolic needs of the body. Often the vitamins are divided into water-soluble and fat-soluble classes. Vitamins A, D, E, and K are *fat-soluble*; the B group and vitamin C (ascorbic acid) are *water-soluble*. The three most important B-group vitamins are vitamin B, called thiamine, vitamin B_2, known as riboflavin, and nicotinic acid. Health is affected most by vitamins A, D, thiamine, riboflavin, and nicotinic acid (see Tables 23.2 and 23.3).

VITAMIN LOSSES IN COOKING AND FOOD PRESERVATION

Enzymes are protein substances that act as biologic catalysts, speeding up the processes of chemical breakdown in living tissue. Starch is converted to sugar by enzymes as fruit ripens. After harvest, enzyme activity leads to spoilage, for example, in fruits, vegetables, and meats.

Bacteria, yeasts, and molds also affect the condition of fresh food. These microorganisms act on the outer surfaces by feed-

TABLE 23.3
FUNCTIONS OF VITAMINS AND FIVE IMPORTANT MINERALS

	Bones and Teeth	Prevention of Anemia	Blood Clotting	Resistance to Infection	Healthy Gums	Healing of Wounds	Night Vision	Protection of Moist Tissues	Salt Level	Thyroid Function	Healthy Nervous System	Energy
Water-soluble vitamins												
Thiamine											X	X
Riboflavin											X	X
Niacin											X	X
Pyridoxine											X	X
Pantothenic Acid											X	X
Biotin											X	X
Folic Acid		X									X	X
Vitamin B$_{12}$		X									X	X
Vitamin C				X	X	X						
Fat-soluble vitamins												
Vitamin A							X	X				
Vitamin D	X							X				
Vitamin E											X	X
Vitamin K			X									
Minerals												
Calcium	X		X									
Phosphorus	X											
Iron		X										
Sodium									X			
Iodine										X		

TABLE 23.4

LOSS OF VITAMIN C IN CABBAGE COOKERY

Cabbage boiled in open sauce pan (etc.) showed large losses in vitamin C. Usually this loss is associated with the high concentration in the liquid drained from the cabbage. The higher retention of vitamin C was found in cooking with a small amount of water in a tightly covered pan

Method	Preparation of Cabbage	Loss of Vitamin C,%
Boiled	Shredded	78
Boiled	Coarsely shredded	74
Boiled	Cabbage wedges	65
Boiled	Cabbage 4 serving lots	62
Boiled	Cabbage 100 serving lots	72
Boiled	Cabbage army mess lots	88
Low pressure steamer	Cabbage 100 serving lots	70
Institutional steamer	Cabbage 100 serving lots	58
Pressure cooker	Cabbage 100 serving lots	47–77
Fried	Cabbage 100 serving lots	51.6
Electronic	Cabbage 100 serving lots	41

Adding cabbage to boiling water slowly resulted in less loss. Large pieces lose less than small pieces in the ratio of 58–24%

Loss after 30 min cooking	46%
Loss after 1 hr cooking	56%
Loss after 2 hr cooking	67%

The addition of salt as affecting loss is controversial
The addition of soda in small amounts seems to have no effect
Holding cooked cabbage

Refrigerator equals	25% loss
Steam table equals	64% loss
	72% loss at end of 1 hr
	92% loss at end of 2 hr

Source: Ohio Agriculture Experimental Station, 1954. Research Bulletin 742. The Effect of Cooking Method on Loss of Vitamin C.

ing on the nutrients, and tend to reduce palatability, decompose the structure, and produce toxic effects in the food.

A piece of meat that stands at room temperature for a day discolors and develops a strong odor. Yeast and mold contamination can make the meat unpalatable and bacterial action can produce toxic effects. Food that is to be held for future

TABLE 23.5

STEAM VS. BOILING[1]

Vegetable	Cooking Method	Loss of Dry Matter, %	Loss of Protein, %	Loss of Calcium, %	Loss of Magnesium, %	Loss of Phosphorus, %	Loss of Iron, %
Asparagus	Boiled	14.0	20.0	16.5	8.8	25.8	34.4
	Steamed	7.9	13.3	15.3	1.4	10.4	20.0
Beans, string	Boiled	24.6	29.1	29.3	31.4	27.6	38.1
	Steamed	14.2	16.6	16.3	21.4	18.8	24.5
Beetgreens	Boiled	29.7	22.2	15.9	41.6	44.9	43.1
	Steamed	15.7	6.9	3.8	14.1	14.0	24.5
Cabbage	Boiled	60.7	61.5	72.3	76.1	59.9	66.6
	Steamed	26.4	31.5	40.2	43.4	22.0	34.6
Cauliflower	Boiled	37.6	44.4	24.6	25.0	49.8	36.2
	Steamed	2.1	7.6	3.1	1.7	19.2	8.3
Celery	Boiled	45.4	52.6	36.1	57.1	48.7	—
	Steamed	22.3	22.3	11.6	32.4	15.7	—
Celery	Boiled	63.2	67.1	49.7	61.6	66.1	67.6
Cabbage	Steamed	38.3	33.5	16.3	32.6	30.2	44.1
Spinach	Boiled	33.9	29.0	5.5	59.1	48.8	57.1
	Steamed	8.4	5.6	0.0	17.8	10.2	25.7
Beets	Boiled	30.9	22.0	18.7	30.9	33.6	—
	Steamed	21.5	5.4	1.5	29.4	20.1	—
Carrots	Boiled	20.1	26.4	8.9	22.8	19.0	34.1
	Steamed	5.1	14.5	5.1	5.6	1.1	20.7
Kohlrabi	Boiled	33.6	23.2	27.8	40.4	27.7	51.7
	Steamed	7.6	1.0	1.0	14.3	7.7	21.3

Onions	Boiled	21.3	50.2	15.6	27.8	40.2	36.1
	Steamed	11.0	30.7	7.1	15.7	31.5	15.9
Parsnips	Boiled	21.9	13.3	11.4	46.8	23.7	27.6
	Steamed	4.6	20.0	4.2	8.2	5.7	8.1
Potatoes	Boiled	9.4	—	16.8	18.8	18.3	—
	Steamed	4.0	—	9.6	14.0	11.7	—
Sweet potatoes	Boiled	29.0	71.5	38.3	45.3	44.4	31.5
	Steamed	21.1	15.0	22.1	31.5	24.5	25.1
Rutabagas	Boiled	45.8	48.6	37.1	42.7	57.2	50.0
	Steamed	13.2	15.7	13.4	3.4	24.6	14.3
Average for all	Boiled	39.4	43.0	31.9	44.7	46.4	48.0
vegetables	Steamed	14.0	16.0	10.7	18.6	16.7	21.3

[1]This chart shows the dramatic savings of nutrients when steam is used in preference to a stock pot. There is a close relationship between nutrients, color, flavor, and texture.

Source: *Cooking for Profit*, August, 1965, page 15.

TABLE 23.6

COMPOSITION OF FOODS, 100-GRAMS (3 1/2-OZ) EDIBLE PORTION

Food and Description	Water, %	Food Energy, Cal	Protein, Gm	Fat, Gm	Carbohydrate Total, Gm	Fiber, Gm	Ash, Gm	Calcium, Mg	Phosphorus, Mg	Iron, Mg	Vitamin A Value, I.U.	Thiamine, Mg	Riboflavin, Mg	Niacin, Mg	Ascorbic Acid, Mg
Potatoes															
Raw	79.8	76	2.1	0.1	17.1	0.5	0.9	7	53	0.6	20	0.10	0.04	1.2	20[1]
Cooked															
Baked in skin	75.1	93	2.6	0.1	21.1	0.6	1.1	9	65	0.7	20	0.10	0.05	1.7	20
Boiled in skin	79.8	76	2.1	0.1	17.1	0.5	0.9	7	53	0.6	20	0.10	0.04	1.5	16
Boiled, pared before cooking	82.8	65	1.9	0.1	14.5	0.5	0.7	6	56	0.7	20	0.09	0.03	1.2	16
French fried	44.7	274	4.3	13.2	36.0	1.0	1.8	15	111	1.3	50	0.13	0.11	3.1	21
Fried from raw	46.9	268	4.0	14.2	32.6	1.0	2.3	15	101	1.1	40	0.12	0.07	2.8	19
Hash-browned after holding overnight	54.2	229	3.1	11.7	29.1	0.8	1.9	12	79	0.9	30	0.08	0.05	2.1	19
Mashed, milk added	82.8	65	2.1	0.7	13.0	0.4	1.4	24	49	0.4	40	0.08	0.05	1.0	10
Mashed, milk and table fat added	79.8	94	2.1	4.3	12.3	0.4	1.5	24	48	0.4	260	0.08	0.05	1.0	9
Canned															
Solids and liquids	88.5	44	1.1	0.2	9.8	0.2	0.4	(4)[2]	(30)	(0.3)	10	0.04	0.02	0.6	13
Dehydrated mashed															
Flakes without milk															
Dry form	5.2	364	7.2	0.6	84.0	(1.6)	3.0	35	(173)	1.7	Trace	0.23	0.06	5.4	32
Prepared, water, milk, table fat added	79.3	93	1.9	3.2	14.5	0.3	1.1	31	47	0.3	130	0.04	0.04	0.9	5

Granules without milk															
Dry form	7.1	352	8.3	0.6	80.4	1.4	3.6	44	203	2.4	Trace	0.16	0.11	4.9	19
Prepared, water, milk, table fat added	78.6	96	2.0	3.6	14.4	0.2	1.4	32	52	0.5	110	0.04	0.05	0.7	3
Granules with milk															
Dry form	6.3	358	10.9	1.1	77.7	1.5	4.0	42	237	3.5	60	0.19	0.30	4.2	16
Prepared, water, table fat added	81.4	79	2.0	2.2	13.1	0.3	1.3	31	44	0.6	90	0.03	0.05	0.8	3
Frozen															
Diced, to hash-brown															
Not thawed	81.0	73	1.2	Tr.	17.4	0.4	0.4	10	30	0.7	Trace	0.07	0.01	0.6	9
Cooked, hash-browned	56.1	224	2.0	11.5	29.0	0.7	1.4	18	50	1.2	Trace	0.07	0.02	1.0	8
French-fried															
Not thawed	63.5	170	2.8	6.5	26.1	0.6	1.1	7	67	1.4	Trace	0.14	0.02	2.1	20
Heated	52.9	220	3.6	8.4	33.7	0.7	1.4	9	86	1.8	Trace	0.14	0.02	2.6	21
Mashed															
Not thawed	80.4	75	1.7	0.1	17.1	0.4	0.7	16	39	0.7	30	0.07	0.03	0.8	6
Heated	78.3	93	1.8	2.8	15.7	0.4	1.4	25	42	0.6	140	0.06	0.04	0.7	4
Potato chips	1.8	568	5.3	39.8	50.0	(1.6)	3.1	40	139	1.8	Trace	0.21	0.07	4.8	16
Potato flour	7.6	351	8.0	0.8	79.9	1.6	3.7	33	178	17.2	Trace	0.42	0.14	3.4	(19)

Source: Composition of Foods, U.S. Dept. of Agriculture, 1963.
[1] Year round average. Recently dug potatoes contain about 24 mg. of ascorbic acid per 100 gm. The value is only half as high after 3 months of storage and about *one-third* as high when potatoes have been stored as long as six months.
[2] Parentheses indicate imputed value.

TABLE 23.7

INORGANIC ELEMENTS PRESENT IN MEASURABLE AMOUNTS
IN THE HUMAN BODY

	Metals	Nonmetals[1]
Essential	Calcium	Phosphorus
	Magnesium	Chlorine
	Sodium	Sulfur
	Potassium	Iodine
	Manganese	Fluorine[2,3]
	Iron	Selenium[2,3]
	Copper[2]	
	Zinc	
	Cobalt[3]	
	Molybdenum[2,3]	
Probably essential	Molybdenum[2,3]	Barium
		Bromine
	Strontium	Fluorine[2,3]
	Chromium	Selenium[2,3]
Nonessential	Aluminum	Arsenic[4]
	Lead[4]	Boron
	Nickel	Silicon
	Rubidium 20–40 ppm	

[1] The major components of the soft tissue of the human body are carbon, oxygen, hydrogen and nitrogen. These are not included in the listing because they exist in organic compounds.

[2] Can be toxic if present in greater than optimum amounts.

[3] Classification differs according to source.

[4] Highly toxic.

General Functions of Inorganic Elements:
1. Part of skeletal structure (Ca, P, F, etc.).
2. Maintenance of the colloidal state of body matter and regulation of some of the physical properties of colloidal systems—viscosity, diffusion, osmotic pressure (Na^+, Cl^-, Ca^{++}, K^+).
3. Regulating acid-base equilibrium—buffers (eg. $H_2PO_4^-/HPO_4^=$; H_2CO_3/HCO_3^-).
4. As a component or activator of enzyme and/or other biological units or systems.

Source: Crampton, E. W. & L. E. Lloyd. 1959. *Fundamentals of Nutrition*. San Francisco: W. H. Freeman & Co., 1964, pp. 205–260; National Research Council. 1964. Publ. 1146. Recommended Dietary Allowances, 6th ed. Washington.

TABLE 23.8
ESSENTIAL METALS IN BODY FUNCTIONS

Metal	Amount Present	Distribution	Effect of Deficiency
Ca	1,050 gm in 70-kg man 1.5% total body weight	99% in bones and teeth 10 mg/100 ml blood serum Weight ratio of Ca/P in bones is 2/1	Drop in blood Ca produces hyperirritability Tetany, Death

Functions

Formation of bones and teeth (approximately 1% of bone Ca exchanged daily)
Blood clotting
Regulation of cell fluids in osmosis
Reduces irritability of nerve and muscle cells
Enzyme activator important in fat catabolism, glycogen formation (carbohydrate storage), release of chemical energy for cell work

Recommended Daily Amounts

0.8 gm for adults and children under 9
1.4 gm for teenage boys, 15–18 yr
1.3 gm for teenage girls, 15–18 yr
Need increases during pregnancy
Need Vitamin D to aid in absorption
Best sources: milk, cheese

Metal	Amount Present	Distribution	Effect of Deficiency
Mg	35 gm in 70-kg man 0.05% total body weight	Similar to phosphorus 70% in skeleton 2.5 mg/100 ml blood serum	Drop in blood Mg produces vasodilation producing a decrease in blood pressure Hyperirritability Tetany, Death

Functions

Depresses nervous irritability
Activator of many enzymes, particularly important in carbohydrate metabolism

Recommended Daily Amounts

Not established
Requirements probably 2–300 mg/day for adult male; may be more
All milk diet for extended period or alcoholism can produce deficiency

Metal	Amount Present	Distribution	Effect of Deficiency
Na	105 gm in 70-kg man 0.15% total body weight	93% in extracellular fluid (i.e., plasma, interstitial fluids) Present entirely in ion form	Nausea, vomiting, vertigo, mental apathy, exhaustion, cramps, respiratory failure

Table 23.8 (*continued*)

Metal	Amount Present	Distribution	Effect of Deficiency

Functions

Maintains osmotic equilibrium between extracellular and intracellular
  fluid
Maintains normal pH in blood
Muscle contractility
Conduction of nerve impulses

Recommended Daily Amounts

Not established since deficiencies rarely encountered
Sodium may be restricted in certain disease conditions—diarrhea, vomit-
  ing or excessive perspiration may deplete sodium

Metal	Amount Present	Distribution	Effect of Deficiency
K	245 gm in 70-kg man 0.35% total body weight	Almost entirely within cells Present entirely in ion form	Muscle weakness Poor intestinal tome with distention Cardiac abnormalities Eventual failure of re-spiratory muscles

Functions

Maintains osmotic pressure regulation and acid-base balance within cell
Stimulating effect on muscle irritability
Enzyme activator important to energy release and storage

Recommended Daily Amounts

Minimum need probably about 0.8–1.3 gm/day about the amount in the
  usual U.S. diet

Metal	Amount Present	Distribution	Effect of Deficiency
Mn[1]	0.2 gm in 70-kg man 0.0003% total body weight	Primarily in liver also in skin, muscle, bone	Inhibits normal repro-duction and sexual de-velopment in animals

Functions

Activator of enzymes concerned with carbohydrate, protein and fat metabolism

Metal	Amount Present	Distribution	Effect of Deficiency
Fe	4.5 gm in 70-kg man 0.004% total body weight	75% in hemoglobin Remaining 25% pri-marily in liver, some in bone and spleen	Anemia

Functions

Essential for formation of normal red blood cells
Energy production in cells
Acts in enzyme systems both as a component of the enzyme or an activator

Table 23.8 (*continued*)

Metal	Amount Present	Distribution	Effect of Deficiency

Recommended Daily Amounts

Men 18 yr and older; 10 mg/day
Women 18–55; 15 mg/day
Boys and girls 9–15, 15 mg/day
Best sources: lean meat, liver, eggs, dried beans, molasses

Cu	0.1 gm in 70-kg man 0.0002% total body weight	Blood, liver, kidneys, heart, brain	Anemia Other specific disorders in farm animals

Functions

Helps in absorption of iron from gastrointestinal tract
Enzyme system in hemoglobin formation
Enzyme activator in other systems

Recommended Daily Amounts

Minimum intake about 2 mg/day
Ordinary diets provide 2–5 mg

Zn^1	Small	Liver, bones, epidermal tissue and blood	Unknown

Functions

Part of enzyme important in reaction causing CO_2 transportation and release by blood
Activator of other enzymes
Seems to increase action of two female reproductive hormones

Co	—	Vitamin B_{12}	—

Functions

Essential for formation of Vitamin B_{12} since humans cannot form this
molecule but must use it pre-formed. The need for cobalt is closely
associated with the need for B_{12}
Enzyme activator (?) may be B_{12} function

Recommended Daily Amounts

Cannot use free cobalt but only need it in form of vitamin B_{12}

Mo	—	—	—

Functions

Component of enzymes

Table 23.8 (*continued*)

Metal	Amount Present	Distribution	Effect of Deficiency
Si	—	—	Affects bones and teeth of rats and guinea pigs
Cr	—	—	Growth factor in experimental animals
Ba	—	—	Affects bones and teeth of rats and guinea pigs
P	700 gm in 70-kg man 1.0% total body weight	80% in bones and teeth 35–45 mg/100 ml blood; mostly in red blood cells Present in all tissue particularly nervous tissue	Unknown

Functions

Formation of bones and teeth; about 1% of bone phosphorus is exchanged daily
Form compounds that store chemical energy
Buffer systems in blood and urine: $(H_2PO_4^-/HPO_4^=)$
Important in carbohydrate and fat metabolism—participates in absorption of sugars from intestines and reabsorption of glucose from kidney tubules

Recommended Daily Amounts

Not established
If calcium and protein intake are adequate, phosphorus intake will be also

Cl	105 gm in 70-kg man 0.15% total body weight	Primarily extra cellular tissue Some in red blood cells and other tissue cells	Unknown

Functions

Osmotic pressure regulation
Chief anion of gastric juice
Exchanges with HCO_3^- in red blood cell during time CO_2 being carried by blood
May have some bearing on activity of salivary enzyme

Recommended Daily Amounts

Not established. Normally ingested in adequate amounts as NaCl

Table 23.8 (*continued*)

Metal	Amount Present	Distribution	Effect of Deficiency
S[1]	175 gm in 70-kg man 0.25% total body weight	Widespread	Unknown

Functions

Occurs almost entirely as component of organic compounds; especially protein
$SO_4^=$ in blood
Not an enzyme activator

I	0.03 gm in 70- kg man 0.00004% total weight	60% in thyroid gland, remainder in blood	Thyroid enlargement (goiter) Lower basal metabolic rate Poor cold toleration Mental symptoms

Functions

Essential for formation of thyroid hormone and thus essential for maintenance of normal basic metabolic rate

Recommended Daily Amounts

Not established. Good sources: seafood, water iodized salt

F	—	Bones and teeth	Increased number of dental caries

Functions

Part of structural molecule of bones and teeth

Recommended Daily Amounts

1 ppm in drinking water
Br

Function

Some growth increase found in experimental animals when diet supplimented
Se

Function

Biological catalyst

---

[1] Recommended daily amounts not established.

TABLE

Sample	Macro Elements				
	Nitrogen	Calcium	Magnesium	Phosphorus	Potassium
			mg/100 gm		*Citrus*
Grapefruit, sectioned without membrane					
Marsh, white seedless					
Calif.	138 ± 17	7.6 ± 3.8[2]	8.1 ± 2.8[2]	11.1 ± 3.2[2]	144 ± 18[2]
Fla.	101 ± 11	4.2 ± 1.7	8.7 ± 1.6	7.4 ± 1.6	150 ± 7
Marsh, pink seedless—					
Fla.	88 ± 7	4.4 ± 2.4[2]	7.9 ± 2.5	8.6 ± 2.9	127 ± 12[2]
Lemons, juiced, Eureka—					
Calif.	61 ± 8	3.7 ± 1.4	4.9 ± 1.1	4.5 ± 1.2[2]	127 ± 10
Limes, juiced, Persian—					
Fla.	70 ± 1	7.1 ± 2.5[2]	5.4 ± 2.0	7.4 ± 2.5	111 ± 4
Oranges, sectioned with membrane					
Navel					
Calif.	162 ± 8	23.7 ± 6.4	10.2 ± 3.2	15.8 ± 2.8	175 ± 17[2]
Fla.	103 ± 5	16.0 ± 6.8[2]	10.2 ± 2.9	12.6 ± 4.0	157 ± 12[2]
Valencia					
Calif.	167 ± 23	19.3 ± 5.2	10.0 ± 3.4	12.7 ± 2.6	164 ± 10
Fla.	122 ± 11	13.1 ± 7.2	9.9 ± 2.9	10.8 ± 2.1	180 ± 4
Temple—Fla.	94 ± 11	23.4 ± 5.4[2]	11.3 ± 2.5	10.5 ± 2.1	172 ± 12[2]
Tangelos, sectioned with membrane—Fla.	107 ± 5	15.6 ± 4.9[2]	11.2 ± 2.8	11.6 ± 1.8	174 ± 10[2]
Tangerines, sectioned with membrane, Dancy—Fla.	98 ± 8	16.6 ± 3.3	12.3 ± 3.6	10.0 ± 2.1	162 ± 7
					Deciduous Fruits
Apples					
Peeled					
McIntosh—N. H., 1 lot; Mass., 1 lot; Vt., 1 lot; New England, 1 lot	25 ± 3	1.8 ± 0.6[2]	2.6 ± 0.5	4.9 ± 1.0	92 ± 8[2]
Delicious					
N. Y.	26 ± 4	2.2 ± 0.7	3.2 ± 0.8	5.8 ± 1.2	122 ± 38[2]
Va.	18 ± 3	2.1 ± 1.0[2]	2.7 ± 0.3	6.1 ± 1.2	108 ± 5
Wash.	22 ± 2	1.3 ± 0.3	2.8 ± 0.8	6.1 ± 1.3	120 ± 4
W. Va.	23 ± 4	1.7 ± 0.5[2]	2.9 ± 0.4[2]	7.1 ± 1.2	128 ± 7[2]
Jonathan					
Va.	21 ± 1	1.8 ± 0.5	3.5 ± 0.8	5.1 ± 1.2	119 ± 8[2]
W. Va.	24 ± 3	2.3 ± 1.0	3.1 ± 0.9	5.3 ± 1.6	111 ± 20[2]
Stayman					
Va.[3]	17 ± 5	2.1 ± 1.0	2.6 ± 0.4	6.4 ± 0.9	120 ± 20[2]
W. Va.	22 ± 5	2.6 ± 1.0[2]	3.0 ± 1.0[2]	7.5 ± 1.6[2]	124 ± 8[2]
With peel					
McIntosh—N. H., 1 lot; Mass., 1 lot; Vt., 1 lot; New England, 1 lot	30 ± 5	2.4 ± 0.7	3.6 ± 0.4	5.4 ± 0.6	96 ± 10
Delicious—N. Y.[4]	30 ± 1	2.9 ± 0.6	4.7 ± 0.4	6.0 ± 1.1	139 ± 34
Jonathan					
Va.	28 ± 3	2.6 ± 0.2	4.8 ± 0.3	5.6 ± 0.8	124 ± 9
W. Va.	31 ± 3	3.1 ± 1.2	4.6 ± 0.6	5.7 ± 1.1	117 ± 24
Stayman—W. Va.[4]	26 ± 5	3.4 ± 1.6	4.8 ± 1.2	7.7 ± 1.5	131 ± 6
Apricots, with peel, unidentified—Wash.	148 ± 17	8.0 ± 3.9	9.3 ± 2.8[2]	14.8 ± 5.0	319 ± 49[2]
Berries, including seeds					
Blackberries (dewberries)—N. Car.	205 ± 61[2]	13.6 ± 4.1	19.8 ± 5.1	18.0 ± 6.0	212 ± 15[2]
Blueberries					
N. J.	103 ± 21[2]	4.1 ± 1.3	3.6 ± 0.8	11.1 ± 2.7	74 ± 3[2]
N. Car.	111 ± 14	5.2 ± 2.7[2]	4.7 ± 1.2[2]	10.7 ± 3.0	84 ± 4[2]
Cranberries—early, 3 lots; late black, 1 lot —Mass.	61 ± 11[2]	7.4 ± 2.3	4.5 ± 1.2	6.0 ± 2.2[2]	67 ± 4[2]
Raspberries—Md.	140 ± 4	13.4 ± 0.8	17.7 ± 2.8	12.0 ± 3.1	152 ± 10[2]
Strawberries					
Unidentified—Calif.	140 ± 12	15.2 ± 3.3	11.0 ± 2.4	21.1 ± 5.3	186 ± 11
Pocohantas, 2 lots; Armore, 1 lot; unidentified, 1 lot—local	77 ± 9	9.4 ± 3.3	7.3 ± 2.2	12.2 ± 4.5[2]	139 ± 17[2]
Massey, 1 lot; unidentified, 3 lots—N. J.	94 ± 6	12.4 ± 5.1	8.2 ± 1.8[2]	14.0 ± 4.1	159 ± 18[2]
Albritton, 2 lots; Klonmore, 1 lot; unidentified, 1 lot—N. Car.	107 ± 5	10.7 ± 3.9	10.9 ± 2.3	16.8 ± 5.0	174 ± 9

23.9[1]

	Micro Elements				
Aluminum	Boron	Copper	Iron	Manganese	Sodium

Fruits

mcg/100 gm

<10	64 ± 15	32 ± 13[2]	75 ± 39[2]	20 ± 12[2]	330 ± 168[2]
<10	30 ± 8[2]	56 ± 14	53 ± 18	11 ± 3[2]	407 ± 110[2]
<10	25 ± 5[2]	44 ± 12	44 ± 22	10 ± 3	380 ± 148[2]
<10	24 ± 3	29 ± 16[2]	32 ± 6[2]	8 ± 2[2]	547 ± 117[2]
<10	31 ± 11	30 ± 9	31 ± 13	8 ± 2	497 ± 93[2]
<10	124 ± 34	56 ± 30[2]	120 ± 33	27 ± 9	493 ± 129[2]
<10	147 ± 46	34 ± 9	102 ± 32[2]	27 ± 8	428 ± 109[2]
<10	149 ± 83[2]	37 ± 20[2]	91 ± 21[2]	23 ± 6[2]	340 ± 107[2]
<10	75 ± 21[2]	43 ± 13[2]	74 ± 20	20 ± 4	471 ± 250[2]
<10	67 ± 20[2]	38 ± 6[2]	76 ± 19	25 ± 8	1,832 ± 417[2]
<10	58 ± 13[2]	33 ± 5	88 ± 25	30 ± 8	1,268 ± 425[2]
24 ± 2	86 ± 18	28 ± 8	104 ± 34	32 ± 8	1,146 ± 227[2]
<20	134 ± 35	16 ± 4	50 ± 20	18 ± 5	142 ± 24
<20	80 ± 35	34 ± 19[2]	86 ± 76	20 ± 7[2]	425 ± 200[2]
<20	80 ± 30	25 ± 10[2]	55 ± 19	13 ± 3	201 ± 54[2]
<20	187 ± 95[2]	32 ± 14[2]	40 ± 8	10 ± 1	160 ± 28
<20	111 ± 74[2]	40 ± 9	53 ± 19[2]	16 ± 4[2]	372 ± 110[2]
20 ± 5	72 ± 38	38 ± 14	76 ± 27[2]	38 ± 16	237 ± 30
<20	103 ± 39	31 ± 12[2]	81 ± 33	28 ± 13[2]	248 ± 101[2]
<20	147 ± 77[2]	22 ± 6[2]	46 ± 13	15 ± 4[2]	324 ± 224[2]
<20	109 ± 32	30 ± 8	93 ± 78[2]	16 ± 8[2]	195 ± 55[2]
20 ± 10	154 ± 17	20 ± 2	74 ± 15	27 ± 7	168 ± 35
87 ± 16	88 ± 48	38 ± 20	132 ± 35	29 ± 9	516 ± 186
74 ± 25	94 ± 29	40 ± 4	124 ± 26	49 ± 10	243 ± 27
61 ± 25	126 ± 17	37 ± 9	122 ± 14	39 ± 14	263 ± 111
46 ± 25	141 ± 20	30 ± 5	151 ± 130	26 ± 11	217 ± 42
221 ± 142[2]	354 ± 94[2]	75 ± 45[2]	238 ± 83[2]	48 ± 27[2]	384 ± 173[2]
392 ± 237[2]	87 ± 36[2]	114 ± 45[2]	441 ± 168[2]	1,750 ± 879[2]	237 ± 138[2]
268 ± 70	46 ± 14[2]	40 ± 21	140 ± 36	92 ± 57[2]	208 ± 127[2]
240 ± 101[2]	53 ± 14[2]	21 ± 10[2]	142 ± 55[2]	404 ± 122[2]	316 ± 183[2]
<40	34 ± 8	58 ± 24	198 ± 60	157 ± 54[2]	768 ± 207[2]
391 ± 156[2]	98 ± 27[2]	60 ± 20	548 ± 87[2]	1,139 ± 163[2]	158 ± 57[2]
232 ± 136[2]	88 ± 25	24 ± 11[2]	335 ± 88	328 ± 133[2]	2,606 ± 1,290[2]
96 ± 53[2]	38 ± 6	38 ± 17[2]	198 ± 88[2]	260 ± 121[2]	1,063 ± 1,330[2]
242 ± 256[2]	46 ± 10	43 ± 12	224 ± 75[2]	224 ± 84[2]	543 ± 521[2]
56 ± 35[2]	42 ± 10	29 ± 21[2]	196 ± 70	193 ± 80[2]	410 ± 84[2]

TABLE 23.9[1] *(continued)*

Sample	Nitrogen	Calcium	Magnesium	Phosphorus	Potassium
					Deciduous
			mg/100 gm		
Cherries, pitted					
Bing					
Calif.	194 ± 48[2]	9.6 ± 3.3	16.2 ± 3.7	13.3 ± 4.4	250 ± 22[2]
Wash.	211 ± 29	10.7 ± 6.0[2]	14.5 ± 4.1[2]	14.6 ± 4.2[2]	266 ± 18[2]
Sour, unidentified—Pa.	146 ± 11	5.9 ± 2.2[2]	11.5 ± 2.2	10.6 ± 2.4	197 ± 11
Grapes, seeded					
Thompson seedless—					
Calif.[3]	121 ± 17	6.2 ± 2.0	5.8 ± 1.5	12.8 ± 2.5	200 ± 27[2]
Tokay—Calif.	82 ± 19[2]	5.2 ± 1.9[2]	6.2 ± 1.9[2]	11.6 ± 2.5	180 ± 47[2]
Nectarines, with peel					
Early LeGrand, 2 lots;					
red, 1 lot; Sun Grand,					
1 lot—Calif.	175 ± 38[2]	4.3 ± 2.3[2]	7.8 ± 2.8	17.2 ± 4.5	224 ± 34[2]
Sun Grand, 3 lots;					
LeGrand, 1 lot—Pa.	116 ± 63[2]	3.0 ± 1.4	4.7 ± 1.0	13.7 ± 2.3	210 ± 11[2]
Peaches, peeled					
Keystone—Ga.	128 ± 9	2.0 ± 0.9	8.0 ± 1.9	12.8 ± 2.9	200 ± 15[2]
Elberta—Pa.	95 ± 24[2]	1.6 ± 0.5	5.6 ± 1.0	13.9 ± 3.5	194 ± 22[2]
Dixired, 2 lots; Elberta,					
1 lot; Sunhigh, 1 lot;					
Triogem, 1 lot—					
S. Car.[3]	92 ± 14	1.4 ± 0.5	5.8 ± 1.8	12.0 ± 2.8	202 ± 12[2]
Early Red Free—Va.[3]	124 ± 3	1.6 ± 0.3	7.6 ± 1.9	10.6 ± 2.2	197 ± 52[2]
J. H. Hale—Wash.[3]	114 ± 15	2.3 ± 0.9	6.2 ± 1.7	12.0 ± 4.1	216 ± 33[2]
Pears					
Peeled					
Bartlett—Calif.	58 ± 11[2]	2.5 ± 0.9	5.0 ± 1.3	8.4 ± 1.6	117 ± 4
Anjou—Ore.	46 ± 9	3.9 ± 1.3	4.8 ± 1.6	8.0 ± 2.3	130 ± 11
With peel					
Bartlett—Calif.	63 ± 7	4.8 ± 1.7	6.5 ± 1.6	9.3 ± 1.7	129 ± 13[2]
Anjou—Ore.	52 ± 7	7.7 ± 2.9	5.2 ± 1.3	7.7 ± 1.7	140 ± 12
Plums, with peel					
Santa Rosa—Calif.	152 ± 13	1.8 ± 0.7	5.2 ± 1.4	11.9 ± 2.5	170 ± 14[2]
Yellow sweet—Kelsey,					
3 lots; unidentified,					
1 lot—Calif.	109 ± 12	1.9 ± 0.4	6.2 ± 1.5	10.4 ± 2.2[2]	192 ± 15[2]
					Sub-Tropical Fruits
Avocados					
Spring grown—Buenco,					
2 lots; Fuertes, 1 lot;					
unidentified, 3 lots—					
Calif.[5]	318 ± 78[2]	7.8 ± 2.3	35.9 ± 5.8	54.4 ± 19.5[2]	732 ± 63[2]
Winter grown, unidenti-					
fied—Calif.[5]	279 ± 35[2]	10.2 ± 3.9[2]	22.9 ± 7.8[2]	42.6 ± 10.9	526 ± 91[2]
Blackskin, 1 lot; green					
skin, 3 lots; unidenti-					
fied, 4 lots—Fla.	254 ± 36[2]	12.8 ± 7.6[2]	34.1 ± 7.5	39.1 ± 17.5[2]	488 ± 122[2]
Bananas (varieties uniden-					
tified)					
Ecuador	168 ± 37[2]	2.7 ± 0.7[2]	25.4 ± 4.7	16.4 ± 4.2[2]	373 ± 20[2]
Guatemala	214 ± 20	2.0 ± 0.4	22.0 ± 4.4	13.5 ± 4.2	394 ± 36[2]
Haiti	188 ± 14	3.2 ± 0.8	29.4 ± 8.7	14.5 ± 2.9	399 ± 21
Honduras	184 ± 47[2]	2.6 ± 0.7	23.8 ± 8.1	14.1 ± 4.7	375 ± 15
Jamaica	184 ± 26	3.3 ± 0.7	32.9 ± 8.0[2]	17.6 ± 3.2	378 ± 18
Panama	178 ± 26	2.5 ± 0.4	21.8 ± 5.1	18.0 ± 6.6[2]	398 ± 22
Figs, Kadota—Calif.	120 ± 18	32.1 ± 9.3	16.7 ± 4.7	13.7 ± 4.5	232 ± 31[2]
Mangoes, Haden—Fla.	70 ± 9	12.9 ± 4.4[2]	8.8 ± 2.3	7.1 ± 1.9[2]	164 ± 17[2]
Papayas, unidentified—					
Hawaii	114 ± 7	7.2 ± 1.6	7.6 ± 2.4	4.2 ± 0.8	334 ± 19[2]
Pineapples, unidentified—					
Puerto Rico	71 ± 6	2.2 ± 1.5	3.9 ± 1.6	3.0 ± 0.6	142 ± 15[2]
					Melons and Miscellaneous
Cantaloupes, unidentified					
Ariz.	149 ± 35	5.0 ± 1.4[2]	8.0 ± 1.6	12.9 ± 3.3	371 ± 22[2]
Calif.	136 ± 35[2]	4.6 ± 0.8	6.3 ± 1.3	9.0 ± 1.4	351 ± 36[2]
Md.	152 ± 43	7.7 ± 4.3[2]	11.7 ± 2.0	11.4 ± 5.3[2]	304 ± 67[2]
N. Car.	121 ± 26	4.6 ± 2.3[2]	6.8 ± 3.3[2]	7.2 ± 2.4	278 ± 50[2]
Honeydews, unidentified—					
Calif.	71 ± 40[2]	3.2 ± 0.7	6.7 ± 2.9	9.9 ± 5.1[2]	264 ± 50[2]
Watermelons, Charleston					
Gray					
Fla.	97 ± 15	2.9 ± 1.2	9.2 ± 2.1	6.8 ± 3.5[2]	121 ± 24[2]
S. Car.	102 ± 21	2.8 ± 0.7	13.1 ± 2.8	7.4 ± 2.2[2]	117 ± 13[2]

		Micro Elements			
Aluminum	Boron	Copper	Iron	Manganese	Sodium

Fruits

$mcg/100\ gm$

Aluminum	Boron	Copper	Iron	Manganese	Sodium
<30	222 ± 122²	84 ± 29²	225 ± 73	64 ± 18	411 ± 175²
<30	218 ± 70²	77 ± 31²	258 ± 100²	95 ± 88²	232 ± 39²
<30	32 ± 9	90 ± 14	263 ± 73	100 ± 30	136 ± 40²
63 ± 28²	262 ± 108²	128 ± 33	152 ± 52²	45 ± 30	3,405 ± 3,189²
<30	242 ± 60²	61 ± 22²	209 ± 71²	42 ± 10	976 ± 417²
136 ± 79²	276 ± 87	76 ± 19	164 ± 62	34 ± 6	139 ± 29
95 ± 34	161 ± 53	111 ± 32²	122 ± 81	38 ± 7	139 ± 25
<20	204 ± 40	63 ± 24	107 ± 38	43 ± 19	238 ± 106²
<20	212 ± 69²	66 ± 25²	90 ± 49²	48 ± 33²	85 ± 17
<20	145 ± 33	67 ± 24	82 ± 27	35 ± 17²	239 ± 77²
<20	128 ± 44²	65 ± 21²	100 ± 46²	53 ± 24	186 ± 64²
<20	227 ± 89²	67 ± 18²	79 ± 32²	32 ± 10²	128 ± 36²
<15	163 ± 79²	113 ± 21	48 ± 14	18 ± 5	250 ± 115²
<15	240 ± 164²	122 ± 21	67 ± 47	42 ± 44²	305 ± 82²
<30	212 ± 101²	118 ± 19	71 ± 30	32 ± 15	220 ± 69²
<30	168 ± 48	116 ± 19	104 ± 41	44 ± 32	336 ± 76
49 ± 20	304 ± 68	60 ± 27²	72 ± 31	21 ± 7²	287 ± 168²
<30	293 ± 114²	29 ± 14²	90 ± 43²	72 ± 52²	116 ± 67²
<20	971 ± 228²	316 ± 91	842 ± 306²	134 ± 32	14,342 ± 2,936²
<20	938 ± 401²	256 ± 69²	525 ± 171²	150 ± 97²	10,433 ± 12,120²
<20	688 ± 234²	251 ± 66²	526 ± 117	170 ± 115²	4,687 ± 3,460²
<40	98 ± 13	80 ± 39	172 ± 58	340 ± 460²	306 ± 204²
<40	64 ± 15²	80 ± 28²	146 ± 67²	61 ± 25²	184 ± 84²
<40	78 ± 32	84 ± 37	216 ± 51	84 ± 39²	168 ± 70²
<40	68 ± 22²	88 ± 41	138 ± 63²	92 ± 88²	180 ± 56
<40	76 ± 16	73 ± 14	192 ± 78	302 ± 356²	183 ± 25
<40	76 ± 21²	84 ± 29	133 ± 35	57 ± 22²	204 ± 63²
152 ± 88²	130 ± 54²	70 ± 18	366 ± 82	128 ± 37	1,074 ± 116²
<30	48 ± 16²	117 ± 24	90 ± 27	26 ± 6	246 ± 100²
<30	47 ± 6	14 ± 2	66 ± 12	9 ± 2	1,984 ± 423²
<30	26 ± 7	20 ± 8²	44 ± 17	2,128 ± 490²	142 ± 19

Fruits

Aluminum	Boron	Copper	Iron	Manganese	Sodium
14 ± 3	76 ± 19	50 ± 12	88 ± 29	23 ± 5²	13,630 ± 3,285²
14 ± 4	164 ± 78²	44 ± 14²	82 ± 19	22 ± 3	12,687 ± 4,244²
<10	48 ± 15²	21 ± 6	153 ± 29	52 ± 26²	7,189 ± 7,529²
<10	30 ± 6	22 ± 6²	97 ± 41²	46 ± 28²	3,094 ± 2,032²
17 ± 7²	59 ± 22²	41 ± 22²	63 ± 19	18 ± 5	9,073 ± 4,974²
<20	67 ± 39²	28 ± 27²	160 ± 62	28 ± 18	1,946 ± 573²
<20	33 ± 8	39 ± 15²	170 ± 48	48 ± 19²	1,924 ± 1,788²

TABLE 23.9[1] *(continued)*

Sample	Macro Elements				
	Nitrogen	Calcium	Magnesium	Phosphorus	Potassium
				Melons and Miscellaneous	
			mg/100 gm		
Rhubarb					
Hot-house grown, un-identified—Mich.	173 ± 14	5.4 ± 1.6	10.5 ± 1.7	21.0 ± 4.2	198 ± 9
Field-grown, unidenti-fied—N. J.	115 ± 12	79.2 ± 16.7	11.6 ± 2.2	7.2 ± 2.1	368 ± 22[2]

[1] Values are the mean of means of individual lots and standard deviations of all analyses (number of for flame photometric and colorimetric data).
[2] One of more lots significantly different (1% level) from the mean of the producing area.
[3] Five lots.
[4] Three lots.
[5] Six lots.
Source: *Journal American Dietetic Association*, 1968, Vol. 52, No. 3, March.

use should be preserved immediately by a suitable means, for example canning, freezing, dehydrating, or chemical treatment. *Chemical preservation* may utilize vinegar, sulfur dioxide, salt, wood smoke, or a combination of these, and radically alters the appearance and taste of food. Sulfur dioxide is used in some wines, fruit juices, and dried fruits.

Freezing stops the activity of organisms, and quick freezing has the least effect on food nutrients. Enzymes are inactivated by blanching or parboiling the food prior to freezing.

Cooking includes baking, grilling, steaming, boiling, roasting, and frying and halts microbial and enzyme action. The purpose of cooking is to make food more digestible, while improving its taste and appearance. Vitamin losses can be largely avoided by careful cooking and conservation of juices of liquid. The vitamin B group and vitamin C are lost mainly in boiling by *water leaching*; therefore a minimum amount of water is used and the resulting liquids are used in soups or gravies.

Cooking has relatively little effect on mineral retention in cooked foods. Three points should be noted concerning minerals, as follows: (a) cooking vegetables in hard water may increase calcium content slightly due to absorption and toughening texture; (b) iron absorption from foods by the body is increased by cooking; (c) sodium lost during boiling peeled potatoes or other foods is amply replaced by the addition of salt for taste.

Cooking time should be as short as possible to preserve the vitamins, since exposure to heat increases the rate of oxidative and hydrolytic vitamin destruction.

Cooking may cause losses up to 70% of the vitamin B group

Micro Elements					
Aluminum	Boron	Copper	Iron	Manganese	Sodium
Fruits					
		mcg/100 gm			
82 ± 34²	68 ± 16	30 ± 11	211 ± 29	91 ± 39²	182 ± 18
482 ± 174²	70 ± 30²	11 ± 2	207 ± 92²	300 ± 193²	7,142 ± 7,111²

determinations in standard deviation = 16 or more for nitrogen and spectrographic data; 8 or more

and vitamin C; but as the bulk of the food is reduced by cooking, this may more than compensate for the lesser vitamin content. Table 23.4 illustrates the results of the cooking losses of vitamin C in cabbage prepared and cooked under several conditions. Table 23.5 shows a comparison of boiling versus steaming of some vegetables in the losses of protein and the minerals, calcium, magnesium, phosphorus, and iron. The loss of dry matter could include some starch (glucose) as well as protein material and salts. Potatoes, raw, baked, boiled, fried, canned, frozen, and dehydrated, are chosen to show the variation in composition under many conditions of preparation (Table 23.6). The results here are based on a $3\frac{1}{2}$-oz or 100-gm serving portion. Similar studies of other food products can be made. This type of study is necessary for labeling under the new FDA rulings.

The study of the role of essential minerals is most important in nutrition and is therefore important to the producer of food products. Tables 23.7 and 23.8 briefly discuss these elements and their role in the metabolism of the body. Some of these, of course, are lost as salts in the cooking liquids. Specific amounts are difficult to determine since the method of preparation and cooking has much to do with this loss. Steaming, the use of small amounts of water, and the use of the cooking liquor in sauces, soups, etc., helps to utilize these minerals. Table 23.9 is a publication from the *Journal of the American Dietetic Association* of the minerals present in fruits. These are served raw, canned, frozen, or prepared in a solution of their own juices. In the latter case, the total food value of fruits is preserved for human consumption.

CHAPTER 24

M. A. Wolf | Food Additives, Essential
Tools of the Food Scientist

THE FOOD REVOLUTION

Scientists tell us that the number of each living species is controlled by the natural forces of food, disease, and enemies. These for man become the familiar famine, plague, and war. Each is a worthy subject for thought, but as our general subject is closely related to food we will set aside the others and concentrate on food and its influence on man's history.

Early in man's development he obtained his food primarily by hunting. Of course, when hunting was poor, he was forced to supplement his meat diet with other sources of food. By trial and error, many times no doubt with tragic results, he learned to use other foods such as fruits, roots, and seeds. Gradually he developed the habit of gathering an excess of these, which led to the practice of preserving and storing them against a time of want. Thus, man became a hunter-gatherer.

Later, probably quite by accident, he noticed that some of his seed or fruits sprouted and grew when he accidentally spilled them or purposely threw them out because they were spoiling. Gradually, he observed that the growth of such seeds or fruits could provide, in due time, a source of food close at hand. Slowly he realized this meant that he need not search for and gather these important food supplies from widely scattered areas. Thus man entered the agricultural stage of his development. In time he added to his growing skills animal husbandry, so that he need not spend so much time in providing himself with fresh meats.

With ever-increasing numbers to feed, man soon found that he must improve on his ability to provide himself with more food. Two great problems continually plagued him: inability to store foods for long periods of time, and the competition from insect and animal pests that also ate the food he wished for himself. These are the twin problems of prevention of spoilage and the protection of food against pests. Soon man initiated a

560

trial-and-error search for possible solutions to these increasingly serious problems. Even today the search is still being actively pursued albeit with greater skill and with better tools at his disposal.

Undoubtedly man learned early, probably by accident, possibly by keen observation, that if he dried his foods he could store them longer than if they remained fresh. This method of preserving food is still used. Salt was also found to have preservative effectiveness. That man discovered early the value of salt as a preservative is shown by the numerous references in history to his search for and defense of this precious commodity. So deeply imbedded is the value of salt in man's history that it has figured in his religion and even today there are wise sayings involving salt.

The use of fire has also played a great part in man's development. He used it to warm himself to protect himself from his animal enemies, and to cook his food. Probably quite by accident he discovered that if he hung his food in the smoke of his fires, the smoked food could be stored for longer periods of time. Thus, he discovered another method of preservation. Today we know that the smoke contains a complex array of chemicals which inhibit microbial growth and at the same time add to flavor and aroma.

With the passage of time man has discovered better methods of preserving his foods. But with each discovery other problems have arisen. For example some of these methods of preservation have been found to change food so that it does not taste or look the same, or that the texture or color is not as desirable. The food technologist is still wrestling with these problems.

Man soon encountered additional problems of crop and food production. For instance, he found he had to control unwanted plants that got into his crops and choked them out, so he developed methods of cultivation against these plant pests. In addition, insects found his crops and ate them, so he tried to control or combat these insects. Then, when man stored his food, he discovered that it frequently was devoured or made unfit to eat by insects as well as animals such as rats, so he had to develop methods to control these pests.

In his solution of the food dilemma, man has developed newer and better methods of protecting and preserving his

foods. Some of these utilize physical treatment such as canning, freezing, and freeze-drying. However, he has also developed many suitable chemicals which are highly useful to
supplement the physical techniques. As his understanding
of the foods has grown, he has found, in addition, that these
versatile chemicals can be used to enhance the desirability of
foods in many ways. All these chemicals which man adds to his
food are the food additives so necessary in the production of
the wholesome, nutritious, and appealing food we all enjoy
today.

FOOD ADDITIVES

Definition

The Food Protection Committee of the National Academy of
Sciences—National Research Council defines a food additive
as "a substance or mixture of substances, other than a basic
foodstuff, which is present in food as a result of any aspect of
production, processing, storage, or packaging. This term
does not include chance contaminants." Note that this definition covers any material that is added or gets into food at any
stage in its growth or preparation. The legal definition in the
Federal Food, Drug and Cosmetic Act is somewhat different.
It states that a food additive is "any substance the intended use
of which results or may reasonably be expected to result directly or indirectly in its becoming a component or otherwise
affecting the characteristic of any food ..." This definition
not only includes the substances covered in the first definition
but is broadened to include those materials that may reasonably be expected to affect a food's characteristics.

Types of Food Additives

A careful reading of these definitions leads to the conclusion
that there could be two major types of food additives. First,
are those that are added intentionally to improve or protect
the food or its characteristics in some desirable manner; and
secondly, are those that are not intentionally added—the incidental additives—such as substances that inadvertantly become a component of food during its production, processing,
storage, or packaging. These, for example, may result from

migration into foods of chemicals from the package, from washing the produce, or as minute residues of pesticides which are applied to the crop and carried over into the finished product.

Source of Food Additives

Some food additives are derived directly from foods themselves. Lecithin, a very useful additive, is made from soybeans and corn. However, many food additives are created in laboratories. Many of these chemical food additives duplicate those found in natural foods. Others, while not occurring in foods, are synthesized and used because they have been found to improve and enhance foods. Regardless of their source, whether isolated from foods or created in the laboratory, *all food additives are chemicals*. Failure to appreciate this fact can lead to considerable misunderstanding and fear. To many people the word "chemical" means something dangerous or foreign or at least "not natural." For example, most people would not be worried if told they are eating fats, but because they do not understand, they might become concerned—even frightened—when told they are eating triglyceride esters of palmitic, oleic, linoleic, and stearic acids, the chemists' name for these same fats.

Why Intentional Food Additives are Used

(1) *To improve the nutritive value of food.* It has been said that we are the result of the food we eat. In a real sense this is true. All the foods we eat are chemicals. Some food products contain all the chemicals needed for life, others may have an insufficient amount or none at all of the essential materials. Certain grains, such as corn and rice, are known to be lacking in adequate amounts of certain amino acids necessary to provide man with a complete diet. Because these grains are basic foods of a large number of people throughout the world, food scientists have improved these foods by enriching them with the necessary amounts of these amino acids, thus making these grains more adequate as a protein source.

Vitamins and other chemicals are also added to some foods to improve their nutritional value. The addition of Vitamin C has been shown to prevent the debilitating disease, scurvy. Essentially all milk today is fortified in some manner with Vitamin D because it helps prevent rickets. Iodine has been added to table salt because scientists discovered that in certain areas there was not a sufficient amount of naturally occurring iodine in food and water to provide the essential amounts of iodine needed to prevent goiter.

(2) *To enhance the flavor of certain foods.* The importance of flavor is beyond question. It has been said that flavor is to food what color is to sight. Poorly flavored foods may be excellent from a nutritional standpoint, but certainly not appetizing or tasty. It is difficult to imagine how our foods would taste without spices, essential oils, aromatic chemical flavorings, and flavor enhancers.

Because many natural flavors are not readily available, flavor chemists have learned to duplicate them in their laboratories. These flavors play an important part in our foods today, both to supplement naturally occurring flavors and to replace those which are inadequate at certain times of the year or which are lost during processing.

(3) *To maintain appearance, palatability, and wholesomeness of foods.* Today's food scientist is continually developing new processing techniques to maintain the color, flavor and texture, and wholesomeness of the food he produces. Nevertheless, these techniques do not always prevent some loss of desired properties; hence food additives are used to control these problems.

One of the common problems of food processing is that of the change of flavor and/or color caused by oxidation. Antioxidants are added to prevent or retard such changes. A notable example is the tendency of fats and oils to become rancid upon storage. The use of antioxidants makes possible the development of many highly successful "convenience foods," such as cake mixes, frozen bakery goods, and frozen "heat-n-serve" and deep-fried foods.

Microbial inhibitors may be added to foods to prolong wholesomeness and shelf-life. Such inhibitors are used to supplement the special precautions and good sanitary practices taken to prevent the presence of these organisms in or on foods.

(4) *To maintain or impart desirable properties to food products. Emulsifiers* are used to disperse tiny particles or glob-

ules of one liquid in another. Emulsifiers appear in a wide variety of food products such as salad dressings, bakery goods, candy and confections, beverages, and dairy products such as ice cream and frozen desserts, as well as in aerosols of dairy products.

Stabilizers and thickeners help maintain uniform texture and flavor in many food products such as chocolate milk, commercial ice creams and frozen desserts, jams and jellies, and in cake mixes, gelatins, and pudding mixes. They may also be used to protect and prevent evaporation of flavors.

Acidity-alkalinity control agents such as acids, alkalies, buffers, and neutralizing agents are used in foods to enhance flavor such as the tart taste in soft drinks, to intensify the fruit flavor in sherbets, and to add flavor and ''zip'' to cheese spreads.

Leavening agents such as yeast, baking powder, and baking soda are used in making certain foods light in texture.

Food colors both naturally occurring and those synthetically produced are added to enhance the eye-appeal of foods. They may be used to replace the natural color which may be lost in processing, to give color to manufactured products such as gelatine dessert, or to provide uniform color throughout the year in products such as butter.

Bleaching and maturing agents are used in wheat flour to make an elastic, stable dough. They are of special importance in flour milling and bread baking. Bleaching agents are also used to produce relatively white cheeses and to destroy undesirable colors in natural oils and fats.

Sequestering agents are used to remove trace amounts of substances which interfere in the processing of foods. Two examples are: the ''sequestering'' of trace amounts of copper and iron which catalyze oxidation of fats and oil, thereby enhancing the development of rancidity, and the sequestering of minerals which otherwise cause undesirable cloudiness in beverages.

Humectants are used to help maintain moisture in certain foods such as shredded coconut, marshmallows, and certain confections.

Anticaking agents. There is nothing so annoying as trying to pour certain powdered or granulated foods that have caked upon standing. Anticaking agents keep such products free-flowing.

Firming agents improve texture and characteristic shape of certain foods such as pickles, canned foods, and processed fruits.

Some others are: *clarifying agents, curing agents, foaming agents, expelling agents* for aerosols and *non-nutritive sweeteners,* to name a few. Food scientists will certainly develop newer and more useful food additives in the years to come as the demand for them arises. It is equally true that new food processing techniques may not be successful unless suitable food additives are discovered and available to solve some of the problems encountered.

SAFETY OF FOOD ADDITIVES

The job of developing a food additive is only half completed when the additive is shown to be useful. It must also be shown to be safe (defined as "the practical certainty that injury will not result from use of a substance in a proposed quantity and manner"). Hence, as soon as a chemical or a mixture of chemicals appears to be useful, toxicological studies are started on laboratory animals. Toxicity is defined as the capacity of a substance to produce adverse effects by other than mechanical means. These toxicity studies are frequently conducted at the same time the food scientist is completing his studies evaluating usefulness.

Single-dose oral studies on suitable laboratory animals, such as the rat, rabbit, guinea pig, and the mouse, are carried out to provide a basis for further, more extensive work. The studies give the first indication of the toxicological properties of the additive. Careful observation of the treated animals should disclose the probable adverse effects and the levels to be considered in further studies.

Next the toxicologist usually will undertake short-term feeding studies on rats and dogs. These investigations usually last for 90 days and are designed to establish the maximum daily intake of the additive that is without detectable adverse effects, as well as the nature of any adverse effects that may occur if too much of the additive is eaten. Both male and female animals are used. Suitable observations of the animals are made, including appearance and behavior, changes in the physical or chemical characteristics of both blood and urine, and changes in the various tissues. In addition observations may be made to establish the metabolic fate of the food additive.

Should the food scientist in his studies find that a prospective additive continues to show promise, the toxicologist will initiate long-term feeding studies which will provide the necessary basis for evaluation of its safety to humans. This study should show that the food additive can be fed in the diet of laboratory animals without causing any detectable adverse effects at a daily dosage level at least 100 times the amount that persons would be expected to ingest daily. In these studies, two points of reference need to be established: the first is the highest level than can be given to the animals without adverse effects, and the second is the lowest level that causes minimal adverse effects.

Because humans eat many foods containing additives during their lifetime, these tests normally run for the life span of the rat, and 2 years in the dog or some other nonrodent mammal. Again both sexes are fed. Normally the additive is mixed into the diet, but occasionally it is added to the drinking water. Sometimes with dogs, the additive is fed daily in a capsule. Life-time studies are highly desirable because of the need to evaluate the capacity of the additive to cause tumors. Unfortunately, man's knowledge of tumor development, at the present time, is not sufficient to permit a faster method of detection.

Keeping in mind that the toxicologist is looking for minimal adverse effects, he must select his animals carefully and design his experiment so that suitable definitive answers can be expected. To start with, the toxicologist will select healthy animals which are born at about the same time, and are uniform as to weight, appearance, and behavior. In the rat studies, very young animals equivalent to people of two or four years of age, are used.

During the course of feeding, the animals are weighed frequently and observed regularly to detect any changes in behavior and appearance or any indications of illness. Blood and urine samples are collected periodically and subjected to numerous tests designed to show possible adverse effects. When the rats have reached an age equivalent to the age of a

person of about 85 or 90, feeding of the additive is stopped
and the surviving rats are killed and examined.

At the time of necropsy, samples of blood and urine are
collected again. Each necropsied animal is observed visually
for any adverse tissue effects. Next the major organs such as
the liver, lungs, kidneys, heart, spleen, and in the males the
testes are removed from both the "control" and the treated
animals, trimmed of all adhering tissue, then weighed carefully
to see if there has been an increase or decrease in weight of
the organs, the "control" animals being those maintained
during the study on the same diet, but without the additive.

Finally, a goodly number of samples of tissue are saved
for later microscopic examination for adverse cellular changes.
In most studies, as many as 20 to 30 separate tissue samples
from each rat and 30 to 35 from each dog are taken.

As soon as the results from these studies are available, they
are evaluated to establish the "no-effect" level and the lowest
level that gave rise to the "barely detectable" or minimal
effects.

Based upon the results seen, it may be necessary to do
further experimental work on the material. Such work may
include studies designed to determine the effects on reproduction and to determine in more detail the absorption, metabolism,
distribution, and excretion of the additive. Then, and only
then, can the experienced toxicologist postulate the level at
which there is practically no risk to a person who might eat
the additive over his lifetime. In arriving at this safe level, a
number of factors must be considered, including the intended
use of the additive, the level of the additive encountered in the
foods of man, the types and number of foods which may contain
the additive, and the health of the people who may be eating it.
Prudence dictates that regardless of its toxicological properties, no more additive should be used than is absolutely
necessary to accomplish the desired effect.

Both intentional and unintentional (incidental) food additives
are studied in the above manner. However, before such studies
are initiated on an incidental additive, the additive must first
be shown to be present, and the amount likely to be encountered
in foods must be established. Obviously, if chemicals do not
get into foods they need not be evaluated.

When all the toxicological tests are completed and evaluated, the toxicologist and the food scientist join forces and put their information into a petition which is submitted to the appropriate governmental regulatory agency. None of the food additive may be used in food until approval is granted. This official approval is given only after careful study of the information given to establish both the safety and the effectiveness of the proposed food additive.

FOOD LAWS

The need to establish the safety of additives to foods is both a moral and a legal obligation. Governmental protection of the consumer has a long history going back to at least 300 B. C. Most of these laws have dealt with the problem of adulteration. In the United States the first consumer protection laws were those dealing with imported foods which might be adulterated.

Pure Food Law of 1906

The first major legislation regulating food in this country was the 1906 Federal Food and Drug Act, often called the Pure Food Law. It prohibited the adulteration of food; "adulteration" being defined as including: (1) the addition of any poisonous or deleterious substances to foods, (2) extraction of valuable constituents from foods, (3) concealment of inferiority, (4) substitution of other articles or mixtures of substances that would adversely effect the quality or strength of foods. The act also restricted certain labeling practices. The Department of Agriculture was made responsible for its administration.

It was considered a good law for its time. However, as the newer and more sophisticated developments in food technology appeared, it became evident that the Pure Food Law of 1906 needed modernizing. A new bill was introduced in Congress in 1933.

Federal Food, Drug and Cosmetic Act of 1938

After several years of hearings and many revisions, a new Act known as the Federal Food, Drug and Cosmetic Act of 1938 became law. It applied to exports and imports as well as foods in commerce between the states, within the District of Columbia and in U.S. Territories. It defined foods as "articles used as food and drink for man and other animals, chewing gum, and articles used for components of any such article." Adulteration of food was broadened to include food containing an added poisonous or deleterious substance unless the added substance was required and could not be avoided by good manufacturing practices and was safe at the level of use. The law also prohibited all kinds of cheating in foods such as: addition of a substance to increase bulk or weight, reduction of strength or quality, making an article appear to have a greater value, removal of a substance normally expected to be present, substitution of one product for another, or concealing of an inferior or damaged product.

This act also made labeling mandatory. The label was required to tell what was in the package and the weight or volume of the contents. At the same time the labeling must not be misleading. The label must also give the name and address of the manufacturer, packer, or distributor. All this information must be prominently displayed and easily read.

Among other things, this Act authorized the Secretary of Health, Education, and Welfare, the agency presently designated to administer the Act, to issue definitions and standards of identity, standards of quality and standards of fill of containers for foods where in his judgment such action would "promote honesty and fair dealing in the interest of consumers." Some foods so defined and standardized are chocolate and cocoa products, many bakery and dairy products, canned fruits and vegetables, tuna fish, egg products, and dressings for foods.

Major Amendments to the Federal Food, Drug and Cosmetic Act

The Miller Pesticide Amendment of 1954.—This amendment was designed to establish the procedure for the setting of safe amounts (commonly referred to as tolerances) for incidental additives caused by residues of pesticides. These residues may occur on or in fresh fruits, vegetables, and other raw agricultural commodities. Before a pesticide may be sold, the Department of Agriculture must certify that the pesticide proposed by the manufacturer is useful for the purposes claimed and the Food and Drug Administration must set the tolerances for the quantities that remain in or on the food based upon the scientific evidence submitted by the manufacturer.

The Food Additives Amendment of 1958.—The Federal Food, Drug and Cosmetic Law of 1938, while useful, was felt by many to have some deficiencies. First, the 1938 law placed the burden of proof of safety of food additives on the Food and Drug Administration. It was felt that this responsibility should be shouldered by the manufacturer of food additives. Hence, this responsibility, already taken by reputable manufacturers, was placed on them by this amendment. It also became incumbent on the manufacturer to show the effectiveness of additives. The Secretary was authorized to issue regulations permitting the safe use of additives. It also forbade the use of any substance as a food additive that was "found to induce cancer in man or animals, in any amount and under any conditions." This clause has caused a great deal of controversy.

The Color Additive Amendments of 1960.—These amendments brought the control of all color additives under one law and jurisdiction. It permits the manufacturer to apply for tolerances for color additives. As with food additives, no color can be approved in any amount if it is found to induce cancer in man or animals. This amendment further established a procedure for evaluating questions or differences of opinions arising over the induction of cancer. Such problems may be submitted to a scientific advisory committee if the matter requires the exercise of scientific judgment. The committee is composed of experts selected by the National Academy of Sciences.

Other Federal Laws are the Federal Meat Inspection Act of 1906, the Imported Meat Act of 1930, and the Poultry Inspection Act of 1959. All these require inspection and approval of the products in question. The meat and poultry inspection acts also require inspection of the slaughtering house and processing facilities. Specific use of any additive must be approved.

State and Local Laws.—The Federal laws all pertain to foods passing in interstate commerce but do not apply to shipments intrastate. These are governed by state and local pure food laws which are generally patterned after the Federal acts.

SUMMARY

A trip to a typical supermarket in the United States reveals that the American people have a great variety of foods from which to choose. These stores may carry from 3,000 to 6,000 different food items at present, and more are on the way. Many of these foods are of the "convenience food" variety that are appetizing, nutritious, and quickly prepared.

Intentional food additives are the touchstone for the production of these foods. For example, a typical ready-mixed cake contains the following additives: bleaching and maturing agents to condition the flour, anticaking agents in the baking powder and salt, antioxidants in the shortening, emulsifiers to improve texture, flavoring agents and colors to improve appeal, and a preservative to prevent spoilage while the mix is stored. The use of all these is controlled by a law which requires that they be useful as well as safe. No wonder the people of the United States are considered the best fed people of the world!

Selected References and
Recommended Journals

AMERICAN SOCIETY FOR TESTING AND MATERIALS. 1964. Book of ASTM Standards.

ANON. March 1972. *Soybean Digest*, Blue Book Issue. American Soybean Association, Hudson, Iowa.

BESSELIEVRE, E. B. 1965. *The Four R's: A Solution for Water Problem*. Highlights of the First International Water Quality Symposium.

BIBLIOGRAPHY HOTEL AND RESTAURANT ADMINISTRATION AND RELATED SUBJECTS. Ithaca, New York, School of Hotel Administration, Cornell University.

BOWERS, C. G. 1971. *A Guide to Profitable Meat Management*, Avi Publishing Co., Inc., Westport, Conn.

BRAVERMAN, J. B. S. 1963. *Introduction to the Biochemistry of Foods*, Elsevier Publishing Company, New York.

COMPOSITION OF FOODS, RAW, PROCESSED, PREPARED. 1963. Agriculture Handbook No. 8, Washington Agriculture Research Service, United States Department of Agriculture.

COPSON, D. A. 1962. *Microwave Heating*. Avi Publishing Co., Inc., Westport, Conn.

DEMAN, J. M. and P. MELMYCHYN. 1970. *Symposium: Phosphates in Food Processing*. Avi Publishing Co., Inc., Westport, Conn.

DESIMONE, D. V. 1971. *A Metric America*. National Bureau of Standards, Special Publication 345, U.S. Government Printing Office, Washington, D.C.

EDUCATIONAL MATERIALS CENTER. National Restaurant Association, 1530 N. Lake Shore Drive, Chicago, Ill.

ERICSON, M. H. 1973. Recipe Standardization, mimeo material. School of Hotel Administration, Cornell University, Ithaca, New York.

FLAMMABILITY INSTITUTE. 4001 W. Nichols Road, Detroit, Mich.

FOOD AND NUTRITION BOARD. 1968. National Academy of Sciences, National Research Council. Recommended Daily Allowances.

FOOD CHEMICALS CODEX. 1972. National Academy of Sciences, National Research Council, Washington, D.C.

FOOD INDUSTRIES MANUAL. 1970. Edited by Anthony Woolen, Chemical Publishing Company, New York.

FOOD SERVICE SANITATION MANUAL. 1962. U.S. Department of Health, Education and Welfare, Public Health Publication No. 934, U.S. Government Printing Office, Washington, D.C.

GLICKSMAN, M. 1969. Gum Technology in the Food Industry, Academic Press, N.Y.

GRAHAM, H. D. 1968. *The Safty of Foods, Symposium.* Avi Publishing Co., Inc., Westport, Conn.

GRISWOLD, R. N. 1962. *The Experimental Study of Foods*, Houghton Mifflin Co., Boston, Mass.

HANDBOOK OF CHEMISTRY AND PHYSICS. Chemical Rubber Co., Cleveland, Ohio.

HANDBOOK OF FLAVOR INGREDIENTS. 1968. Chemical Rubber Co., Cleveland, Ohio.

HANDBOOK OF FOOD ADDITIVES. 1968. Chemical Rubber Co., Cleveland, Ohio.

HANDBOOK OF FOOD PREPARATION. 1966. American Home Economics Association, Washington, D.C.

HARREL, C. G. AND R. J. THIELEN. 1959. *Conversion and Technical Data for the Food Industry.* 6th ed. Burgess Publishing Co., Minneapolis, Minn.

HEICHEL, H. H. 1971. Plants, Oxygen and People. Frontiers of Plant Science, Conn. Agricultural Experiment Station, Storrs, Conn.

HEID, J. L. AND MAYNARD A. JOSLYN. 1967. *Fundamentals of Food Processing Operation.* Avi Publishing Co., Westport, Conn.

HETRICK, J. 1969. Imitation Dairy Products—Past, Present and Future. Journal American Oil Chemists Society, 46, 58A.

INSTITUTE OF SHORTENING AND EDIBLE OILS, INC. October 1968. Food Fats and Oils.

KOSIKOWSKI, F. 1966. *Cheese and Fermented Milk Foods.* Published by Author, Distributed by Edwards Brothers, Inc., Ann Arbor, Michigan.

KOTSCHEVAR, L. H. 1961. *Quantity Food Purchasing.* John Wiley & Sons, Inc., New York.

LEE, S. January 1968. Tea and Coffee Trade Journal.

LEOPOLD, LUNA B. 1964. Water in the World. The Unesco Courier.

LEOPOLD, LUNA B. AND K. S. DAVIS. 1966. Water. Life Science Library.

LEVI, A. 1963. The Meat Handbook, 3rd. ed. Avi Publishing Co., Inc., Westport, Conn.

LONGREE, K. 1968. Quantity Food Sanitation, Interscience Publishers, New York.

MATZ, SAMUEL A. 1959. *Chemistry and Technology of Cereals as Food and Feed.* Avi Publishing Co., Westport, Conn.

MATZ, SAMUEL A. 1962. *Food Texture.* Avi Publishing Co., Westport, Conn.

MEYER, E. W. May 1967. Soy Protein Concentrates and Isolates. Proceedings of International Conference on Soybean Protein Foods, U.S. Department of Agriculture, Peoria, Ill., ArS-71-35. p. 142.

NATIONAL ACADEMY OF SCIENCES. National Research Council. 1972. Food Chemicals Codex. National Academy of Sciences, Washington, D.C.

NOLLER, C. R. 1962. *Structure and Properties of Organic Compounds, a Brief Survey*. W. B. Saunders Co., Philadelphia, Pa.

PAUL, PAULINE C. AND H. H. PALMER. 1972. *Food Theory and Applications*. John Wiley & Sons, Inc., New York.

POTTER, N. N. 1968. *Food Science*. Avi Publishing Co., Inc., Westport, Conn.

PROTECTING OUR FOOD. 1966. The Yearbook of Agriculture, U.S. - D.A., Superintendent of Documents, Washington, D.C.

Recommended Dietary Allowances, Seventh Revised Edition. 1968. Report of Food and Nutrition Board, National Research Council, Washington, D. C.

ROBINOWIEZ, E. 1967. Polishing. Scientific American, June, 91–99.

ROGERS, JOHN L. 1969. *Production of Precooked Frozen Foods for Mass Catering*. Avi Publishing Co., Inc., Westport, Conn.

SCHULTZ, H. W., E. A. DAY, AND L. M. LIBBEY. 1967. *Chemistry and Physiology of Flavors*. Avi Publishing Co., Inc., Westport, Conn.

SCHULTZ, H. W. 1960. *Food Enzymes*. Avi Publishing Co., Inc., Westport, Conn.

SMITH, ORA. 1968. *Potatoes, Production, Storing, Processing*. Avi Publishing Co., Inc., Westport, Conn.

STADELMAN, W. J. AND O. J. COTTERILL. 1973. *Egg Science and Technology*. Avi Publishing Co., Inc., Westport, Conn.

TALBURT, W. F. AND O. SMITH. 1967. *Potato Processing*. 2nd ed. Avi Publishing Co., Inc., Westport, Conn.

THORNER, M. E. 1972. *Commercial and Fast Food Handbook*. Avi Publishing Co., Inc., Westport, Conn.

TRESSLER, D. K., W. B. VAN ARSDEL, AND M. J. COPLEY. 1969. *Freezing Precooked and Prepared Foods*, Vol. IV. Avi Publishing Co., Inc., Westport, Conn.

THE ALMANAC OF THE CANNING, FREEZING, PRESERVING INDUSTRIES (annually). Edward E. Judge and Sons, Inc., Westminster, Md.

THE MERCK INDEX OF CHEMICALS AND DRUGS. 1968. 8th ed. Merck and Co., Rahway, N.J.

UNITED FRESH FRUIT AND VEGETABLE ASSOCIATION. 177 14th. Street, N.W., Washington, D.C.

U.S. GOVERNMENT PUBLICATIONS. Washington, D.C. Superintendent of Documents, U.S. Government Printing Office.

WEISS, T. J. 1970. *Food Oils and Their Uses*. Avi Publishing Co., Inc., Westport, Conn.

WILLIAMS, L. D., SIPOS, E. F., AND ZIEMBA, J. V. 1970. Makes baked goods more nutritious. Food Engineering. Dec., 59–61.

WINTER, RUTH. 1972. *A Consumer's Dictionary of Food Additives*. Crown Publishers, N.Y.

WOLMAN, ABEL. February 1961. Impact of Desalinization on the Water Economy. Journal American Water Works Association.

WOLMAN, ABEL. 1965. The Metabolism of Cities. Scientific American, *213*, No. 3.

Technical Journals

Cereal Chemistry
Chemical Abstracts
Food Engineering
Food Technology
Journal of Agriculture and Food Chemistry
Journal of American Dietetic Association
Journal of American Oil Chemists Society
Journal of Food Science
Journal of Home Economics
Journal of Nutrition
Journal of Poultry Science
Quick Frozen Foods
The Cornell Hotel and Restaurant Administration Quarterly
  (yearly bibliography)

Trade Journals

Bakers Digest
Bakers Weekly
Brewers Digest
Cooking for Profit
Fast Foods
Food Service Magazine
Ice Cream Reviews
Institutions
Poultry Meat
Snack Foods
The Canner
The Glass Packer
The National Provisioner
Chemical Marketing Reporter (Oil, Paint, and Drug Reporter)

Miscellaneous Useful Tables

TABLE A.1

TEMPERATURE CONVERSIONS, FAHRENHEIT TO CENTIGRADE, CENTIGRADE TO FAHRENHEIT

The table below can be used to convert °F. to °C. and vice versa. Locate the temperature to be converted (either F. or C.) in the center column (bold face). The number to the left gives corresponding °C.; to the right corresponding °F.

°C.	Reading in °F. or °C. to be Converted	°F.	°C.	Reading in °F. or °C. to be Converted	F.	°C.	Reading in °F. or °C. to be Converted	°F.
−128.9	−200	−328.0	−0.6	31	87.8	21.7	71	159.8
−73.3	−100	−148.0	0.0	32	89.6	22.2	72	161.6
−62.2	−80	−112.0	0.6	33	91.4	22.8	73	163.4
−51.1	−60	−76.0	1.1	34	93.2	23.3	74	165.2
−45.6	−50	−58.0	1.7	35	95.0	23.9	75	167.0
−40.0	−40	−40.0	2.2	36	96.8	24.4	76	168.8
−34.4	−30	−22.0	2.8	37	98.6	25.0	77	170.6
−28.9	−20	−4.0	3.3	38	100.4	25.6	78	172.4
−23.3	−10	14.0	3.9	39	102.2	26.1	79	174.2
−17.8	0	32.0	4.4	40	104.0	26.7	80	176.0
−17.2	1	33.8	5.0	41	105.8	27.2	81	177.8
−16.7	2	35.6	5.6	42	107.6	27.8	82	179.6
−16.1	3	37.4	6.1	43	109.4	28.3	83	181.4
−15.6	4	39.2	6.7	44	111.2	28.9	84	183.2
−15.0	5	41.0	7.2	45	113.0	29.4	85	185.0
−14.4	6	42.8	7.8	46	114.8	30.0	86	186.8
−13.9	7	44.6	8.3	47	116.6	30.6	87	188.6
−13.3	8	46.4	8.9	48	118.4	31.1	88	190.4
−12.8	9	48.2	9.4	49	120.2	31.7	89	192.2
−12.2	10	50.0	10.0	50	122.0	32.2	90	194.0
−11.7	11	51.8	10.6	51	123.8	32.8	91	195.8
−11.1	12	53.6	11.1	52	125.6	33.3	92	197.6
−10.6	13	55.4	11.7	53	127.4	33.9	93	199.4
−10.0	14	57.2	12.2	54	129.2	34.4	94	201.2
−9.4	15	59.0	12.8	55	131.0	35.0	95	203.0
−8.9	16	60.8	13.3	56	132.8	35.6	96	204.8
−8.3	17	62.6	13.9	57	134.6	36.1	97	206.6
−7.8	18	64.4	14.4	58	136.4	36.7	98	208.4
−7.2	19	66.2	15.0	59	138.2	37.2	99	210.2
−6.7	20	68.0	15.6	60	140.0	37.8	100	212.0
−6.1	21	69.8	16.1	61	141.8	48.9	120	248.0
−5.6	22	71.6	16.7	62	143.6	60.0	140	284.0
−5.0	23	73.4	17.2	63	145.4	71.1	160	320.0
−4.4	24	75.2	17.8	64	147.2	93.3	200	392.0
−3.9	25	77.0	18.3	65	149.0	100.0	212	413.6
−3.3	26	78.8	18.9	66	150.8	115.6	240	464.0
−2.8	27	80.6	19.4	67	152.6	137.8	280	536.0
−2.2	28	82.4	20.0	68	154.4	160.0	320	608.0
−1.7	29	84.2	20.6	69	156.2	182.2	360	680.0
−1.1	30	86.0	21.1	70	158.0	204.4	400	752.0

TABLE A.2

GRAMS-POUNDS-OUNCES CONVERSION

Gm	Lb	Oz	Gm	Lb	Oz	Gm	Lb	Oz	Gm	Lb	Oz
14.18		0.5	609.53	1	05.5	1204.88	2	10.5	1800.23	3	15.5
28.35		1.0	623.70	1	06.0	1219.05	2	11.0	1814.40	4	00.0
42.53		1.5	637.88	1	06.5	1233.23	2	11.5	1828.58	4	00.5
56.70		2.0	652.05	1	07.0	1247.40	2	12.0	1842.75	4	01.0
70.88		2.5	666.23	1	07.5	1261.58	2	12.5	1856.93	4	01.5
85.05		3.0	680.40	1	08.0	1275.75	2	13.0	1871.10	4	02.0
99.23		3.5	694.58	1	08.5	1289.93	2	13.5	1885.28	4	02.5
113.40		4.0	708.75	1	09.0	1304.10	2	14.0	1899.45	4	03.0
127.58		4.5	722.93	1	09.5	1318.28	2	14.5	1913.63	4	03.5
141.75		5.0	737.10	1	10.0	1332.45	2	15.0	1927.80	4	04.0
155.93		5.5	751.28	1	10.5	1346.63	2	15.5	1941.98	4	04.5
170.10		6.0	765.45	1	11.0	1360.80	3	00.0	1956.15	4	05.0
184.28		6.5	779.63	1	11.5	1374.98	3	00.5	1970.33	4	05.5
198.45		7.0	793.80	1	12.0	1389.15	3	01.0	1984.50	4	06.0
212.63		7.5	807.98	1	12.5	1403.33	3	01.5	1998.68	4	06.5
226.80		8.0	822.15	1	13.0	1417.50	3	02.0	2012.85	4	07.0
240.98		8.5	836.33	1	13.5	1431.68	3	02.5	2027.03	4	07.5
255.15		9.0	850.50	1	14.0	1445.85	3	03.0	2041.20	4	08.0
269.33		9.5	864.68	1	14.5	1460.03	3	03.5	2055.38	4	08.5
283.50		10.0	878.85	1	15.0	1474.20	3	04.0	2069.55	4	09.0
297.68		10.5	893.03	1	15.5	1488.38	3	04.5	2083.73	4	09.5
311.85		11.0	907.20	2	00.0	1502.55	3	05.0	2097.90	4	10.0
326.03		11.5	921.38	2	00.5	1516.73	3	05.5	2112.08	4	10.5

340.20	1	12.0	935.55	2	01.0	1530.90	3	06.0	2126.25	4	11.0
354.38	1	12.5	949.73	2	01.5	1545.08	3	06.5	2140.43	4	11.5
368.55	1	13.0	963.90	2	02.0	1559.25	3	07.0	2154.60	4	12.0
382.73	1	13.5	978.08	2	02.5	1573.43	3	07.5	2168.78	4	12.5
396.90	1	14.0	992.25	2	03.0	1587.60	3	08.0	2182.95	4	13.0
411.08	1	14.5	1006.43	2	03.5	1601.78	3	08.5	2197.13	4	13.5
425.25	1	15.0	1020.60	2	04.0	1615.95	3	09.0	2211.30	4	14.0
439.43	1	15.5	1034.78	2	04.5	1630.13	3	09.5	2225.48	4	14.5
453.60	1	00.0	1048.95	2	05.0	1644.30	3	10.0	2239.65	4	15.0
467.78	1	00.5	1063.13	2	05.5	1658.48	3	10.5	2253.83	4	15.5
481.95	1	01.0	1077.30	2	06.0	1672.65	3	11.0	2268.00	5	00.0
496.13	1	01.5	1091.48	2	06.5	1686.83	3	11.5	2282.18	5	00.5
510.30	1	02.0	1105.65	2	07.0	1701.00	3	12.0	2296.35	5	01.0
524.48	1	02.5	1119.83	2	07.5	1715.18	3	12.5	2310.53	5	01.5
538.65	1	03.0	1134.00	2	08.0	1729.35	3	13.0	2324.70	5	02.0
552.**83**	1	03.5	1148.18	2	08.5	1743.53	3	13.5	2338.88	5	02.5
567.00	1	04.0	1162.35	2	09.0	1757.70	3	14.0	2353.05	5	03.0
581.18	1	04.5	1176.53	2	09.5	1771.88	3	14.5	2367.23	5	03.5
595.**35**	1	05.0	1190.70	2	10.0	1786.05	3	15.0	2381.40	5	04.0
2395.58	5	04.5	2934.23	6	07.5	3472.88	7	10.5	4011.53	8	13.5
2409.75	5	05.0	2948.40	6	08.0	3487.05	7	11.0	4025.70	8	14.0
2423.93	5	05.5	2962.58	6	08.5	3501.23	7	11.5	4039.88	8	14.5
2438.10	5	06.0	2976.75	6	09.0	3515.40	7	12.0	4054.05	8	15.0
2452.28	5	06.5	2990.93	6	09.5	3529.58	7	12.5	4068.23	8	15.5
2466.45	5	07.0	3005.10	6	10.0	3543.75	7	13.0	4082.40	9	00.0
2480.63	5	07.5	3019.28	6	10.5	3557.93	7	13.5	4096.58	9	00.5
2494.80	5	08.0	3033.45	6	11.0	3572.10	7	14.0	4110.75	9	01.0

Table A.2 (*continued*)

Gm	Lb	Oz	Gm	Lb	Oz	Gm	Lb	Oz	Gm	Lb	Oz
2508.98	5	08.5	3047.63	6	11.5	3586.28	7	14.5	4124.93	9	01.5
2523.15	5	09.0	3061.80	6	12.0	3600.45	7	15.0	4139.10	9	02.0
2537.33	5	09.5	3075.98	6	12.5	3614.63	7	15.5	4153.28	9	02.5
2551.50	5	10.0	3090.15	6	13.0	3628.80	8	00.0	4167.45	9	03.0
2565.68	5	10.5	3104.33	6	13.5	3642.98	8	00.5	4181.63	9	03.5
2579.85	5	11.0	3118.50	6	14.0	3657.15	8	01.0	4195.80	9	04.0
2594.03	5	11.5	3132.68	6	14.5	3671.33	8	01.5	4209.98	9	04.5
2608.20	5	12.0	3146.85	6	15.0	3685.50	8	02.0	4224.15	9	05.0
2622.38	5	12.5	3161.03	6	15.5	3699.68	8	02.5	4238.33	9	05.5
2636.55	5	13.0	3175.20	7	00.0	3713.85	8	03.0	4252.50	9	06.0
2650.73	5	13.5	3189.38	7	00.5	3728.03	8	03.5	4266.68	9	06.5
2664.90	5	14.0	3203.55	7	01.0	3742.20	8	04.0	4280.85	9	07.0
2679.08	5	14.5	3217.73	7	01.5	3756.38	8	04.5	4295.03	9	07.5
2693.25	5	15.0	3231.90	7	02.0	3770.55	8	05.0	4309.20	9	08.0
2707.43	5	15.5	3246.08	7	02.5	3784.73	8	05.5	4323.38	9	08.5
2721.60	6	00.0	3260.25	7	03.0	3798.90	8	06.0	4337.55	9	09.0
2735.78	6	00.5	3274.43	7	03.5	3813.08	8	06.5	4351.73	9	09.5
2749.95	6	01.0	3288.60	7	04.0	3827.25	8	07.0	4365.90	9	10.0
2764.13	6	01.5	3302.78	7	04.5	3841.43	8	07.5	4380.08	9	10.5
2778.30	6	02.0	3316.95	7	05.0	3855.60	8	08.0	4394.25	9	11.0
2792.48	6	02.5	3331.13	7	05.5	3869.78	8	08.5	4408.43	9	11.5
2806.65	6	03.0	3345.30	7	06.0	3883.95	8	09.0	4422.60	9	12.0
2820.83	6	03.5	3359.48	7	06.5	3898.13	8	09.5	4436.78	9	12.5
2835.00	6	04.0	3373.65	7	07.0	3912.30	8	10.0	4450.95	9	13.0

2849.18	6	04.5	3387.83	7	07.5	3926.48	8	10.5	4465.13	9	13.5
2863.35	6	05.0	3402.00	7	08.0	3940.65	8	11.0	4479.30	9	14.0
2877.53	6	05.5	3416.18	7	08.5	3954.83	8	11.5	4493.48	9	14.5
2891.70	6	06.0	3430.35	7	09.0	3969.00	8	12.0	4507.65	9	15.0
2905.88	6	06.5	3444.53	7	09.5	3983.18	8	12.5	4521.83	9	15.5
2920.05	6	07.0	3458.70	7	10.0	3997.35	8	13.0	4536.00	10	00.0

TABLE A.3

FLAME AND WIRE TEMPERATURES

Maximum Flame Temperatures (at 1.0 Atm Pressure) Temperature			Color of hot iron wire or heating element indicative of temperature	
Gas	°K	°C	Color of Wire	Temperature (°C)
natural gas-air	2200	1926.85		
carbon monoxide-air	2370	2096.85	dull red	500–650
hydrogen-oxygen-air	2930	2656.85	cherry red	650–750
acetylene-oxygen	3410	3136.85	orange	750–900
aluminum-oxygen	3800	3526.85	yellow	900–1100
hydrogen-fluorine	4300	4026.85	white	over 1100
cyanogen-oxygen	4800	4526.85		
carbon subnitride-oxygen	5300	5026.85		

TABLE

Direct-reading table for adjusting yield of recipes with ingredient amounts given in weights (a). (This
It may be used along with Table 2 which

Abbreviations in Table
oz. = ounce
# = pound

25	50	75	100	200	300	400
(b)	(b)	(b)	¼ oz.	½ oz.	¾ oz.	1 oz.
(b)	(b)	(b)	½ oz.	1 oz.	1½ oz.	2 oz.
(b)	(b)	(b)	¾ oz.	1½ oz.	2¼ oz.	3 oz.
¼ oz.	½ oz.	¾ oz.	1 oz.	2 oz.	3 oz.	4 oz.
(b)	(b)	(b)	1¼ oz.	2½ oz.	3¾ oz.	5 oz.
(b)	¾ oz.	(b)	1½ oz.	3 oz.	4½ oz.	6 oz.
(b)	(b)	(b)	1¾ oz.	3½ oz.	5¼ oz.	7 oz.
½ oz.	1 oz.	1½ oz.	2 oz.	4 oz.	6 oz.	8 oz.
(b)	(b)	1¾ oz.	2¼ oz.	4½ oz.	6¾ oz.	9 oz.
(b)	1¼ oz.	2 oz.	2½ oz.	5 oz.	7½ oz.	10 oz.
(b)	(b)	2 oz.	2¾ oz.	5½ oz.	8¼ oz.	11 oz.
¾ oz.	1½ oz.	2¼ oz.	3 oz.	6 oz.	9 oz.	12 oz.
(b)	(b)	2½ oz.	3¼ oz.	6½ oz.	9¾ oz.	13 oz.
(b)	1¾ oz.	2¾ oz.	3½ oz.	7 oz.	10½ oz.	14 oz.
1 oz.	2 oz.	2¾ oz.	3¾ oz.	7½ oz.	11¼ oz.	15 oz.
1 oz.	2 oz.	3 oz.	4 oz.	8 oz.	12 oz.	1#
1 oz.	2¼ oz.	3¼ oz.	4¼ oz.	8½ oz.	12¾ oz.	1# 1 oz.
(b)	3½ oz.	3½ oz.	4½ oz.	9 oz.	13½ oz.	1# 2 oz.
(b)	3½ oz.	3½ oz.	4¾ oz.	9½ oz.	14¼ oz.	1# 3 oz.
1¼ oz.	2½ oz.	3¾ oz.	5 oz.	10 oz.	15 oz.	1# 4 oz.
(b)	2¾ oz.	4¼ oz.	5½ oz.	11 oz.	1# ½ oz.	1# 6 oz.
1½ oz.	3 oz.	4½ oz.	6 oz.	12 oz.	1# 2 oz.	1# 8 oz.
(b)	3¼ oz.	4¾ oz.	6½ oz.	13 oz.	1# 3½ oz.	1# 10 oz.
1¾ oz.	3½ oz.	5¼ oz.	7 oz.	14 oz.	1# 5 oz.	1# 12 oz.
2 oz.	3¾ oz.	5¾ oz.	7½ oz.	15 oz.	1# 6½ oz.	1# 14 oz.
2 oz.	4 oz.	6 oz.	8 oz.	1#	1# 8 oz.	2#
2¼ oz.	4¼ oz.	6½ oz.	8½ oz.	1# 1 oz.	1# 9½ oz.	2# 2 oz.
2¼ oz.	4½ oz.	6¾ oz.	9 oz.	1# 2 oz.	1# 11 oz.	2# 4 oz.
2½ oz.	4¾ oz.	7¼ oz.	9½ oz.	1# 3 oz.	1# 12½ oz.	2# 6 oz.
2½ oz.	5 oz.	7½ oz.	10 oz.	1# 4 oz.	1# 14 oz.	2# 8 oz.
2¾ oz.	5½ oz.	8¼ oz.	11 oz.	1# 6 oz.	2# 1 oz.	2# 12 oz.
3 oz.	6 oz.	9 oz.	12 oz.	1# 8 oz.	2# 4 oz.	3#
3¼ oz.	6½ oz.	9¾ oz.	13 oz.	1# 10 oz.	2# 7 oz.	3# 4 oz.
3½ oz.	7 oz.	10½ oz.	14 oz.	1# 12 oz.	2# 10 oz.	3# 8 oz.
3¾ oz.	7½ oz.	11¼ oz.	15 oz.	1# 14 oz.	2# 13 oz.	3# 12 oz.
4 oz.	8 oz.	12 oz.	1#	2#	3#	4#
4½ oz.	9 oz.	13½ oz.	1# 2 oz.	2# 4 oz.	3# 6 oz.	4# 8 oz.
5 oz.	10 oz.	15 oz.	1# 4 oz.	2# 8 oz.	3# 12 oz.	5#
5½ oz.	11 oz.	1# ½ oz.	1# 6 oz.	2# 12 oz.	4# 2 oz.	5# 8 oz.
6 oz.	12 oz.	1# 2 oz.	1# 8 oz.	3#	4# 8 oz.	6#
6½ oz.	13 oz.	1# 3½ oz.	1# 10 oz.	3# 4 oz.	4# 14 oz.	6# 8 oz.
7 oz.	14 oz.	1# 5 oz.	1# 12 oz.	3# 8 oz.	5# 4 oz.	7#
7½ oz.	15 oz.	1# 6½ oz.	1# 14 oz.	3# 12 oz.	5# 10 oz.	7# 8 oz.
8 oz.	1#	1# 8 oz.	2#	4#	6#	8#
8½ oz.	1# 1 oz.	1# 9½ oz.	2# 2 oz.	4# 4 oz.	6# 6 oz.	8# 8 oz.
9 oz.	1# 2 oz.	1# 11 oz.	2# 4 oz.	4# 8 oz.	6# 12 oz.	9#
9½ oz.	1# 3 oz.	1# 12½ oz.	2# 6 oz.	4# 12 oz.	7# 2 oz.	9# 8 oz.
10 oz.	1# 4 oz.	1# 14 oz.	2# 8 oz.	5#	7# 8 oz.	10#
11 oz.	1# 6 oz.	2# 1 oz.	2# 12 oz.	5# 8 oz.	8# 4 oz.	11#
12 oz.	1# 8 oz.	2# 4 oz.	3#	6#	9#	12#
13 oz.	1# 10 oz.	2# 7 oz.	3# 4 oz.	6# 8 oz.	9# 12 oz.	13#
14 oz.	1# 12 oz.	2# 10 oz.	3# 8 oz.	7#	10# 8 oz.	14#
15 oz.	1# 14 oz.	2# 13 oz.	3# 12 oz.	7# 8 oz.	11# 4 oz.	15#
1#	2#	3#	4#	8#	12#	16#
1# 1 oz.	2# 2 oz.	3# 3 oz.	4# 4 oz.	8# 8 oz.	12# 12 oz.	17#
1# 2 oz.	2# 4 oz.	3# 6 oz.	4# 8 oz.	9#	13# 8 oz.	18#
1# 3 oz.	2# 6 oz.	3# 9 oz.	4# 12 oz.	9# 8 oz.	14# 4 oz.	19#
1# 4 oz.	2# 8 oz.	3# 12 oz.	5#	10#	15#	20#
1# 5 oz.	2# 10 oz.	3# 15 oz.	5# 4 oz.	10# 8 oz.	15# 12 oz.	21#
1# 6 oz.	2# 12 oz.	4# 2 oz.	5# 8 oz.	11#	16# 8 oz.	22#
1# 7 oz.	2# 14 oz.	4# 5 oz.	5# 12 oz.	11# 8 oz.	17# 4 oz.	23#
1# 8 oz.	3#	4# 8 oz.	6#	12#	18#	24#
1# 10 oz.	3# 4 oz.	4# 14 oz.	6# 8 oz.	13#	19# 8 oz.	26#
1# 12 oz.	3# 8 oz.	5# 4 oz.	7#	14#	21#	28#
1# 14 oz.	3# 12 oz.	5# 10 oz.	7# 8 oz.	15#	22# 8 oz.	30#
2#	4#	6#	8#	16#	24#	32#
2# 2 oz.	4# 4 oz.	6# 6 oz.	8# 8 oz.	17#	25# 8 oz.	34#
2# 4 oz.	4# 8 oz.	6# 12 oz.	9#	18#	27#	36#
2# 6 oz.	4# 12 oz.	7# 2 oz.	9# 8 oz.	19#	28# 8 oz.	38#
2# 8 oz.	5#	7# 8 oz.	10#	20#	30#	40#
2# 12 oz.	5# 8 oz.	8# 4 oz.	11#	22#	33#	44#
3#	6#	9#	12#	24#	36#	48#
3# 4 oz.	6# 8 oz.	9# 12 oz.	13#	26#	39#	52#
3# 8 oz.	7#	10# 8 oz.	14#	28#	42#	56#

A.4
table is primarily for adjusting recipes with original and desired portion yields which can be divided by 25.
is similarly constructed for measures)

Basic Information
1 pound = 16 ounces
1 pound = 454 gm.

500	600	700	800	900	1000
1¼ oz.	1½ oz.	1¾ oz.	2 oz.	2¼ oz.	2½ oz.
2½ oz.	3 oz.	3½ oz.	4 oz.	4½ oz.	5 oz.
3¾ oz.	4½ oz.	5¼ oz.	6 oz.	6¾ oz.	7½ oz.
5 oz.	6 oz.	7 oz.	8 oz.	9 oz.	10 oz.
6¼ oz.	7½ oz.	8¾ oz.	10 oz.	11¼ oz.	12½ oz.
7½ oz.	9 oz.	10½ oz.	12 oz.	13½ oz.	15 oz.
8¾ oz.	10½ oz.	12¼ oz.	14 oz.	15¾ oz.	1# 1½ oz.
10 oz.	12 oz.	14 oz.	1#	1# 2 oz.	1# 4 oz.
11¼ oz.	13½ oz.	15¾ oz.	1# 2 oz.	1# 4¼ oz.	1# 6½ oz.
12½ oz.	15 oz.	1# 1½ oz.	1# 4 oz.	1# 6½ oz.	1# 9 oz.
13¾ oz.	1# ½ oz.	1# 3¼ oz.	1# 6 oz.	1# 8¾ oz.	1# 11½ oz.
15 oz.	1# 2 oz.	1# 5 oz.	1# 8 oz.	1# 11 oz.	1# 14 oz.
1# ¼ oz.	1# 3½ oz.	1# 6¾ oz.	1# 10 oz.	1# 13¼ oz.	2# ½ oz.
1# 1½ oz.	1# 5 oz.	1# 8½ oz.	1# 12 oz.	1# 15½ oz.	2# 3 oz.
1# 2¾ oz.	1# 6½ oz.	1# 10¼ oz.	1# 14 oz.	2# 1¾ oz.	2# 5½ oz.
1# 4 oz.	1# 8 oz.	1# 12 oz.	2#	2# 4 oz.	2# 8 oz.
1# 5¼ oz.	1# 9½ oz.	1# 13¾ oz.	2# 2 oz.	2# 6¼ oz.	2# 10½ oz.
1# 6½ oz.	1# 11 oz.	1# 15½ oz.	2# 4 oz.	2# 8½ oz.	2# 13 oz.
1# 7¾ oz.	1# 12½ oz.	2# 1¼ oz.	2# 6 oz.	2# 10¾ oz.	2# 15½ oz.
1# 9 oz.	1# 14 oz.	2# 3 oz.	2# 8 oz.	2# 13 oz.	3# 2 oz.
1# 11½ oz.	2# 1 oz.	2# 6½ oz.	2# 12 oz.	3# 1½ oz.	3# 7 oz.
1# 14 oz.	2# 4 oz.	2# 10 oz.	3#	3# 6 oz.	3# 12 oz.
2# ½ oz.	2# 7 oz.	2# 13½ oz.	3# 4 oz.	3# 10½ oz.	4# 1 oz.
2# 3 oz.	2# 10 oz.	3# 1 oz.	3# 8 oz.	3# 15 oz.	4# 6 oz.
2# 5½ oz.	2# 13 oz.	3# 4½ oz.	3# 12 oz.	4# 3½ oz.	4# 11 oz.
2# 8 oz.	3#	3# 8 oz.	4#	4# 8 oz.	5#
2# 10½ oz.	3# 3 oz.	3# 11½ oz.	4# 4 oz.	4# 12½ oz.	5# 5 oz.
2# 13 oz.	3# 6 oz.	3# 15 oz.	4# 8 oz.	5# 1 oz.	5# 10 oz.
2# 15½ oz.	3# 9 oz.	4# 2½ oz.	4# 12 oz.	5# 5½ oz.	5# 15 oz.
3# 2 oz.	3# 12 oz.	4# 6 oz.	5#	5# 10 oz.	6# 4 oz.
3# 7 oz.	4# 2 oz.	4# 13 oz.	5# 8 oz.	6# 3 oz.	6# 14 oz.
3# 12 oz.	4# 8 oz.	5# 4 oz.	6#	6# 12 oz.	7# 8 oz.
4# 1 oz.	4# 14 oz.	5# 11 oz.	6# 8 oz.	7# 5 oz.	8# 2 oz.
4# 6 oz.	5# 4 oz.	6# 2 oz.	7#	7# 14 oz.	8# 12 oz.
4# 11 oz.	5# 10 oz.	6# 9 oz.	7# 8 oz.	8# 7 oz.	9# 6 oz.
5#	6#	7#	8#	9#	10#
5# 10 oz.	6# 12 oz.	7# 14 oz.	9#	10# 2 oz.	11# 4 oz.
6# 4 oz.	7# 8 oz.	8# 12 oz.	10#	11# 4 oz.	12# 8 oz.
6# 14 oz.	8# 4 oz.	9# 10 oz.	11#	12# 6 oz.	13# 12 oz.
7# 8 oz.	9#	10# 8 oz.	12#	13# 8 oz.	15#
8# 2 oz.	9# 12 oz.	11# 6 oz.	13#	14# 10 oz.	16# 4 oz.
8# 12 oz.	10# 8 oz.	12# 4 oz.	14#	15# 12 oz.	17# 8 oz.
9# 6 oz.	11# 4 oz.	13# 2 oz.	15#	16# 14 oz.	18# 12 oz.
10#	12#	14#	16#	18#	20#
10# 10 oz.	12# 12 oz.	14# 14 oz.	17#	19# 2 oz.	21# 4 oz.
11# 4 oz.	13# 8 oz.	15# 12 oz.	18#	20# 4 oz.	22# 8 oz.
11# 14 oz.	14# 4 oz.	16# 10 oz.	19#	21# 6 oz.	23# 12 oz.
12# 8 oz.	15#	17# 8 oz.	20#	22# 8 oz.	25#
13# 12 oz.	16# 8 oz.	19# 4 oz.	22#	24# 12 oz.	27# 8 oz.
15#	18#	21#	24#	27#	30#
16# 4 oz.	19# 8 oz.	22# 12 oz.	26#	29# 4 oz.	32# 8 oz.
17# 8 oz.	21#	24# 8 oz.	28#	31# 8 oz.	35#
18# 12 oz.	22# 8 oz.	26# 4 oz.	30#	33# 12 oz.	37# 8 oz.
20#	24#	28#	32#	36#	40#
21# 4 oz.	25# 8 oz.	29# 12 oz.	34#	38# 4 oz.	42# 8 oz.
22# 8 oz.	27#	31# 8 oz.	36#	40# 8 oz.	45#
23# 12 oz.	28# 8 oz.	33# 4 oz.	38#	42# 12 oz.	47# 8 oz.
25#	30#	35#	40#	45#	50#
26# 4 oz.	31# 8 oz.	36# 12 oz.	42#	47# 4 oz.	52# 8 oz.
27# 8 oz.	33#	38# 8 oz.	44#	49# 8 oz.	55#
28# 12 oz.	34# 8 oz.	40# 4 oz.	46#	51# 12 oz.	57# 8 oz.
30#	36#	42#	48#	54#	60#
32# 8 oz.	39#	45# 8 oz.	52#	58# 8 oz.	65#
35#	42#	49#	56#	63#	70#
37# 8 oz.	45#	52# 8 oz.	60#	67# 8 oz.	75#
40#	48#	56#	64#	72#	80#
42# 8 oz.	51#	59# 8 oz.	68#	76# 8 oz.	85#
45#	54#	63#	72#	81#	90#
47# 8 oz.	57#	66# 8 oz.	76#	85# 8 oz.	95#
50#	60#	70#	80#	90#	100#
55#	66#	77#	88#	99#	110#
60#	72#	84#	96#	108#	120#
65#	78#	91#	104#	117#	130#
70#	84#	98#	112#	126#	140#

Table A.4 (continued)

25		50		75	100	200	300	400
3#	12 oz.	7#	8 oz.	11#	4 oz.	15#	30#	45#	60#
4#		8#		12#		16#	32#	48#	64#
4#	4 oz.	8#	8 oz.	12#	12 oz.	17#	34#	51#	68#
4#	8 oz.	9#		13#	8 oz.	18#	36#	54#	72#
4#	12 oz.	9#	8 oz.	14#	2 oz.	19#	38#	57#	76#
5#		10#		15#		20#	40#	60#	80#
5#	4 oz.	10#	8 oz.	15#	12 oz.	21#	42#	63#	84#
5#	8 oz.	11#		16#	8 oz.	22#	44#	66#	88#
5#	12 oz.	11#	8 oz.	17#	4 oz.	23#	46#	69#	92#
6#		12#		18#		24#	48#	72#	96#
6#	4 oz.	12#	8 oz.	18#	12 oz.	25#	50#	75#	100#
7#	8 oz.	15#		22#	8 oz.	30#	60#	90#	120#
8#	12 oz.	17#	8 oz.	26#	4 oz.	35#	70#	105#	140#
10#		20#		30#		40#	80#	120#	160#
11#	4 oz.	22#	8 oz.	33#	12 oz.	45#	90#	135#	180#
12#	8 oz.	25#		37#	8 oz.	50#	100#	150#	200#

(a) This table was adapted from conversion charts developed by the Nutrition Services Division of
(b) The amounts cannot be weighed accurately without introducing errors.   Change to measure-

TABLE
Direct-reading table for adjusting yield of recipes with ingredient amounts given in measurement.   (This
It is intended for use along with Table I which

Abbreviations in Table
t. = teaspoon
T. = Tablespoon
c. = cup
qt. = quart
gal. = gallon
(r) = slightly rounded
(s) = scant

Measurement needed for number

25	50	75	100	200	300	400
¼ t.	½ t.	¾ t.	1 t.	2 t.	1 T.	1 T. + 1 t.
¼ t.(r)	½ t.(r)	1 t.(s)	1¼ t.	2½ t.	1 T. + ¾ t.	1 T. + 2 t.
¼ t. + ½ t.	¾ t.	1 t. + ½ t.	1½ t.	1 T.	1½ T.	2 T.
½ t.(s)	¾ t.(r)	1¼ t.(r)	1¾ t.	1 T. + ½ t.	1 T. + 2¼ t.	2 T. + 1 t.
½ t.	1 t.	1½ t.	2 t.	1 T. + 1 t.	2 T.	2 T. + 2 t.
½ t.(r)	1 t. + ½ t.	1¾ t.(s)	2¼ t.	1½ T.	2 T. + ¾ t.	3 T.
½ t. + ⅛ t.	1¼ t.	2 t.(s)	2½ t.	1 T. + 2 t.	2½ T.	3 T. + 1 t.
¾ t.(s)	1¼ t. + ⅛ t.	2 t.(r)	2¾ t.	1 T. + 2½ t.	2 T. + 2¼ t.	3 T. + 2 t.
¾ t.	1½ t.	2¼ t.	1 T.	2 T.	3 T.	¼ c.
1 t. + ½ t.	2¼ t.	1 T. + ¼ t. + ⅓ t.	1½ t.	3 T.	¼ c. + 1½ t.	⅓ c. + 2 t.
1½ t.	1 T.	1½ T.	2 T.	¼ c.	¼ c. + 2 T.	½ c.
1¾ t. + ⅛ t.	1 T. + ¾ t.	1 T. + 2½ t. + ⅛ t.	2½ T.	¼ c. + 1 T.	¼ c. + 3½ T.	½ c. + 2 T.
2¼ t.	1½ T.	2 T. + ¾ t.	3 T.	½ c. + 2 t.	½ c. + 1 T.	¾ c.
2¼ t. + ⅛ t.	1 T. + 2¼ t.	2 T. + 1½ t. + ⅛ t.	3½ T.	¼ c. + 3 T.	½ c. + 2½ T.	¾ c. + 2 T.
1 T.	2 T.	3 T.	¼ c.	½ c.	¾ c.	1 c.
1 T. + 1 t.	2 T. + 2 t.	¼ c.	⅓ c.	⅔ c.	1 c.	1⅓ c.
2 T.	¼ c.	¼ c. + 2 T.	½ c.	1 c.	1½ c.	2 c.
2 T. + 2 t.	⅓ c.	½ c.	⅔ c.	1⅓ c.	2 c.	2⅔ c.
3 T.	6 T.	½ c. + 1 T.	¾ c.	1½ c.	2¼ c.	3 c.
¼ c.	½ c.	¾ c.	1 c.	2 c.	3 c.	1 qt.
¼ c. + 1 T.	½ c. + 2 T.	¾ c. + 3 T.	1¼ c.	2½ c.	3¾ c.	1¼ qt.
½ c.	⅔ c.	1 c.	1⅓ c.	2⅔ c.	1 qt.	1¼ qt. + ⅓ c.
⅓ c. + 2 t.	¾ c.	1 c. + 2 T.	1½ c.	3 c.	1 qt. + ½ c.	1½ qt.
6 T. + 2 t.	¾ c. + 4 t.	1¼ c.	1⅔ c.	3⅓ c.	1¼ qt.	1½ qt. + ⅔ c.
¼ c. + 3 T.	¾ c. + 2 T.	1¼ c. + 1 T.	1¾ c.	3½ c.	1¼ qt. + ¼ c.	1¾ qt.
½ c.	1 c.	1½ c.	2 c.	1 qt.	1½ qt.	2 qt.
½ c. + 1 T.	1 c. + 2 T.	1½ c. + 3 T.	2¼ c.	1 qt. + ½ c.	1½ qt. + ¾ c.	2¼ qt.

500	600	700	800	900	1000
75#	90#	105#	120#	135#	150#
80#	96#	112#	128#	144#	160#
85#	102#	119#	136#	153#	170#
90#	108#	126#	144#	162#	180#
95#	114#	133#	152#	171#	190#
100#	120#	140#	160#	180#	200#
105#	126#	147#	168#	189#	210#
110#	132#	154#	176#	198#	220#
115#	138#	161#	184#	207#	230#
120#	144#	168#	192#	216#	240#
125#	150#	175#	200#	225#	250#
150#	180#	210#	240#	270#	300#
175#	210#	245#	280#	315#	350#
200#	240#	280#	320#	360#	400#
225#	270#	315#	360#	405#	450#
250#	300#	350#	400#	450#	500#

the New York State Department of Mental Hygiene, Albany, New York.
ment by using conversion table as suggested in bulletin.

A.5
table is primarily for adjusting recipes with original and desired portion yields which can be divided by 25.
is similarly constructed for adjusting weights)

Basic Information

Measuring spoons
1 T.
1 t.
½ t.
¼ t.
for ¾ t. combine ½ t. + ¼ t.
for ⅛ t. use half of the ¼ t.

Equivalents
3 t. = 1 T.
4 T. = ¼ c.
5 T. + 1 t. = ⅓ c.
8 T. = ½ c.
10 T. + 2 t. = ⅔ c.
12 T. = ¾ c.
16 T. = 1 c.
4 c. = 1 qt.
4 qt. = 1 gal.

of portions indicated below

500	600	700	800	900	1000
1 T. + 2 t.	2 T.	2 T. + 1 t.	2 T. + 2 t.	3 T.	3 T. + 1 t.
2 T. + ¼ t.	2½ T.	2 T. + 2¾ t.	3 T. + 1 t.	3 T. + 2¼ t.	4 T. + ½ t.
2½ T.	3 T.	3½ T.	4 T.	4 T. + 1½ t.	5 T.
2 T. + 2¾ t.	3½ T.	4 T. + ¼ t.	4 T. + 2 t.	5 T. + ¾ t.	5 T. + 2½ t.
3 T. + 1 t.	4 T.	4 T. + 2 t.	5 T. + 1 t.	6 T.	6 T. + 2 t.
3 T. + 2¼ t.	4½ T.	5 T. + ¾ t.	6 T.	6 T. + 2¼ t.	7½ T.
4 T. + ½ t.	5 T.	5½ T.	6 T. + 2 t.	7½ T.	8 T. + 1 t.
4 T. + 1¾ t.	5½ T.	6 T. + 1¼ t.	7 T. + 1 t.	8 T. + ¾ t.	9 T. + ½ t.
5 T.	6 T.	7 T.	½ c.	½ c. + 1 T.	½ c. + 2 T.
¼ c. + 3½ T.	½ c. + 1 T.	½ c. + 2½ T.	¾ c.	¾ c. + 1½ T.	¾ c. + 3 T.
½ c. + 2 T.	¾ c.	¾ c. + 2 T.	1 c.	1 c. + 2 T.	1¼ c.
¾ c. + ½ T.	¾ c. + 3 T.	1 c. + 1½ T.	1¼ c.	1¼ c. + 2½ T.	1½ c. + 1 T.
¾ c. + 3 T.	1 c. + 2 T.	1¼ c. + 1 T.	1½ c.	1½ c. + 3 T.	1¾ c. + 2 T.
1 c. + 1½ T.	1¼ c. + 1 T.	1½ c. + ½ T.	1¾ c.	1¾ c. + 3½ T.	2 c. + 3 T.
1¼ c.	1½ c.	1¾ c.	2 c.	2¼ c.	2½ c.
1⅔ c.	2 c.	2⅓ c.	2⅔ c.	3 c.	3⅓ c.
2½ c.	3 c.	3½ c.	1 qt.	1 qt. + ½ c.	1¼ qt.
3⅓ c.	1 qt.	1 qt. + ⅔ c.	1¼ qt. + ⅓ c.	1½ qt.	1½ qt. + ⅔ c.
3¾ c.	1 qt. + ½ c.	1¼ qt. + ¼ c.	1½ qt.	1½ qt. + ¾ c.	1¾ qt. + ½ c.
1¼ qt.	1½ qt.	1¾ qt.	2 qt.	2¼ qt.	2½ qt.
1½ qt. + ¼ c.	1¾ qt. + ½ c.	2 qt. + ¾ c.	2½ qt.	2¾ qt. + ¼ c.	3 qt. + ½ c.
1½ qt. + ⅓ c.	2 qt.	2¼ qt. + ⅓ c.	2½ qt. + ⅔ c.	3 qt.	3¼ qt. + ⅓ c.
1¾ qt. + ½ c.	2¼ qt.	2½ qt. + ½ c.	3 qt.	3¼ qt. + ½ c.	3¾ qt.
2 qt. + ⅓ c.	2½ qt.	2¾ qt. + ⅔ c.	3¼ qt. + ⅓ c.	3¾ qt.	1 gal. + ⅔ c.
2 qt. + ¾ c.	2½ qt. + ½ c.	3 qt. + ¼ c.	3½ qt.	3¾ qt. + ¾ c.	1 gal. + 1½ c.
2½ qt.	3 qt.	3½ qt.	1 gal.	1 gal. + 2 c.	1 gal. + 1 qt.
2¾ qt. + ¼ c.	3¼ qt. + ½ c.	3¾ qt. + ¾ c.	1 gal. + 2 c.	1¼ gal. + ¼ c.	1¼ gal. + 2½ c.

TABLE A.5 (*continued*)

25	50	75	100	200	300	400
½ c. + 4 t.	1 c. + 2 T. + 2 t.	1¾ c.	2⅓ c.	1 qt. + ⅔ c.	1¾ qt.	2¼ qt. + ¼ c.
½ c. + 2 T.	1¼ c.	1¾ c. + 2 T.	2½ c.	1¼ qt.	1¾ qt. + ½ c.	2½ qt.
⅔ c.	1⅓ c.	2 c.	2⅔ c.	1¼ qt. + ⅓ c.	2 qt.	2½ qt. + ⅔ c.
½ c. + 3 T.	1¼ c. + 2 T.	2 c. + 1 T.	2¾ c.	1¼ qt. + ½ c.	2 qt. + ¼ c.	2¾ qt.
¾ c.	1½ c.	2¼ c.	3 c.	1½ qt.	2¼ qt.	3 qt.
¾ c. + 1 T.	1½ c. + 2 T.	2¼ c. + 3 T.	3¼ c.	1½ qt. + ½ c.	2¼ qt. + ¾ c.	3¼ qt.
¾ c. + 4 t.	1⅔ c.	2½ c.	3⅓ c.	1½ qt. + ⅔ c.	2½ qt.	3¼ qt. + ⅓ c.
¾ c. + 2 T.	1¾ c.	2½ c. + 2 T.	3½ c.	1¾ qt.	2½ qt. + ½ c.	3½ qt.
¾ c. + 2 T. + 2½ t.	1¾ c. + 4 t.	2¾ c. + ½ t.	3⅔ c.	1¾ qt. + ⅓ c.	2¾ qt.	3½ qt. + ⅔ c.
¾ c. + 3 T.	1¾ c. + 2 T.	2¾ c. + 1 T.	3¾ c.	1¾ qt. + ½ c.	3 qt. + ¼ c.	1 gal.
1 c.	2 c.	3 c.	1 qt.	2 qt.	3 qt.	1 gal.
1¼ c.	2½ c.	3¾ c.	1¼ qt.	2½ qt.	3¾ qt.	1¼ gal.
1½ c.	3 c.	1 qt. + ½ c.	1½ qt.	3 qt.	1 gal. + 2 c.	1½ gal.
1¾ c.	3½ c.	1¼ qt. + ¼ c.	1¾ qt.	3½ qt.	1¼ gal. + 1 c.	1¾ gal.
2 c.	1 qt.	1½ qt.	2 qt.	1 gal.	1½ gal.	2 gal
2¼ c.	1 qt. + ½ c.	1½ qt. + ¾ c.	2¼ qt.	1 gal. + 2 c.	1½ gal. + 3 c.	2¼ gal.
2½ c.	1¼ qt.	1¾ qt. + ½ c.	2½ qt.	1¼ gal.	1¾ gal. + 2 c.	2½ gal.
2¾ c.	1¼ qt. + ½ c.	2 qt. + ¼ c.	2¾ qt.	1¼ gal. + 2 c.	2 gal. + 1 c.	2¾ gal.
3 c.	1½ qt.	2¼ qt.	3 qt.	1½ gal.	2¼ gal.	3 gal.
3¼ c.	1½ qt. + ½ c.	2¼ qt. + ¾ c.	3½ qt.	1½ gal. + 2 c.	2¼ gal. + 3 c.	3¼ gal.
3½ c.	1¾ qt.	2½ qt. + ½ c.	3½ qt.	1¾ gal.	2½ gal. + 2 c.	3½ gal.
3¾ c.	1¾ qt. + ½ c.	2¾ qt. + ¼ c.	3¾ qt.	1¾ gal. + 2 c.	2¾ gal. + 1 c.	3¾ gal.
1 qt.	2 qt.	3 qt.	1 gal.	2 gal.	3 gal.	4 gal.
1¼ qt.	2½ qt.	3¾ qt.	1¼ gal.	2½ gal.	3¾ gal.	5 gal.
1½ qt.	3 qt.	1 gal. + 2 c.	1½ gal.	3 gal.	4½ gal.	6 gal.
1¾ qt.	3½ qt.	1¼ gal. + 1 c.	1¾ gal.	3½ gal.	5¼ gal.	7 gal.
2 qt.	1 gal.	1½ gal.	2 gal.	4 gal.	6 gal.	8 gal.
2¼ qt.	1 gal. + 2 c.	1½ gal. + 3 c.	2¼ gal.	4½ gal.	6¾ gal.	9 gal.
2½ qt.	1¼ gal.	1¾ gal. + 2 c.	2½ gal.	5 gal.	7½ gal.	10 gal.
2¼ qt.	1¼ gal. + 2 c.	2 gal. + 1 c.	2¾ gal.	5½ gal.	8¼ gal.	11 gal.
3 qt.	1½ gal.	2¼ gal.	3 gal.	6 gal.	9 gal.	12 gal.
3 qt. + 1 c.	1½ gal. + 2 c.	2¼ gal. + 3 c.	3¼ gal.	6½ gal.	9¾ gal.	13 gal.
3½ qt.	1¾ gal.	2½ gal. +2 c.	3½ gal.	7 gal.	10½ gal.	14 gal.
3½ qt. + 1 c.	1¾ gal. + 2 c.	2¾ gal. + 1 c.	3¾ gal.	7½ gal.	11¼ gal.	15 gal.
1 gal.	2 gal.	3 gal.	4 gal.	8 gal.	12 gal.	16 gal.
1 gal. + 1 c.	2 gal. + 2 c.	3 gal. + 3 c.	4¼ gal.	8½ gal.	12¾ gal.	17 gal.
1 gal. + 2 c.	2¼ gal.	3¼ gal. + 2 c.	4½ gal.	9 gal.	13½ gal.	18 gal.
1 gal. + 3 c.	2¼ gal. + 2 c.	3½ gal. + 1 c.	4¾ gal.	9½ gal.	14¼ gal.	19 gal.
1¼ gal.	2½ gal.	3¾ gal.	5 gal.	10 gal.	15 gal.	20 gal.
1¼ gal. + 1 c.	2½ gal. + 2 c.	3¾ gal. + 3 c.	5¼ gal.	10½ gal.	15¾ gal.	21 gal.
1¼ gal. + 2 c.	2¾ gal.	4 gal. + 2 c.	5½ gal.	11 gal.	16½ gal.	22 gal.
1¼ gal. + 3 c.	2¾ gal. + 2 c.	4¼ gal. + 1 c.	5¾ gal.	11½ gal.	17¼ gal.	23 gal.
1½ gal.	3 gal.	4½ gal.	6 gal.	12 gal.	18 gal.	24 gal.
1½ gal. + 1 c.	3 gal. + 2 c.	4½ gal. + 3 c.	6¼ gal.	12½ gal.	18¾ gal.	25 gal.
1½ gal. + 2 c.	3¼ gal.	4¾ gal. + 2 c.	6½ gal.	13 gal.	19½ gal.	26 gal.
1½ gal. + 3 c.	3¼ gal. + 2 c.	5 gal. + 1 c.	6¾ gal.	13½ gal.	20¼ gal.	27 gal.
1¾ gal.	3½ gal.	5¼ gal.	7 gal.	14 gal.	21 gal.	28 gal.

500	600	700	800	900	1000
2¾ qt. + ⅔ c.	3½ qt.	1 gal. + ⅓ c.	1 gal. + 2⅔ c.	1¼ gal. + 1 c.	1¼ gal. + 3⅓ c.
3 qt. + ½ c.	3¾ qt.	1 gal. + 1½ c.	1¼ gal.	1¼ gal. + 2½ c.	1½ gal. + 1 c.
3 qt. +1⅓ c.	1 gal.	1 gal. +2⅔ c.	1¼ gal. +1⅓ c.	1½ gal.	1½ gal. +2⅔ c.
3¼ qt. + ¾ c.	1 gal. + ½ c.	1 gal. + 3¼ c.	1¼ gal. + 2 c.	1½ gal. + ¾ c.	1½ gal. + 3½ c.
3¾ qt.	1 gal. + 2 c.	1¼ gal. + 1 c.	1½ gal.	1½ gal. + 3 c.	1¾ gal. + 2 c.
1 gal. + ¼ c.	1 gal. + 3½ c.	1¼ gal. + 2¾ c.	1½ gal. + 2 c.	1¾ gal. + 1¼ c.	2 gal. + ½ c.
1 gal. + ⅔ c.	1¼ gal.	1¼ gal. + 3⅓ c.	1½ gal. + 2⅔ c.	1¾ gal. + 2 c.	2 gal. + 1⅓ c.
1 gal. + 1½ c.	1¼ gal. + 1 c.	1½ gal. + ½ c.	1¾ gal.	1¾ gal. + 3½ c.	2 gal. + 2½ c.
1 gal. + 1⅔ c.	1¼ gal. + 1⅓ c.	1½ gal. + 2 c.	1¾ gal. + 1⅔ c.	2 gal. + 1⅓ c.	2¼ gal. + 1 c.
1 gal. + 3¾ c.	1¼ gal. + 3½ c.	1½ gal. + 3¼ c.	1¾ gal. + 3 c.	2 gal. + 2¾ c.	2¼ gal. + 2½ c.
1¼ gal.	1½ gal.	1¾ gal.	2 gal.	2¼ gal.	2½ gal.
1½ gal. + 1 c.	1¾ gal. + 2 c.	2 gal. + 3 c.	2½ gal.	2¾ gal. + 1 c.	3 gal. + 2 c.
1¾ gal. + 2 c.	2¼ gal.	2½ gal. + 2 c.	3 gal.	3¼ gal. + 2 c.	3¾ gal.
2 gal. + 3 c.	2½ gal. + 2 c.	3 gal. + 1 c.	3½ gal.	3¾ gal. + 3 c.	4¼ gal. + 2 c.
2½ gal.	3 gal.	3½ gal.	4 gal.	4½ gal.	5 gal.
2¾ gal. + 1 c.	3¼ gal. + 2 c.	3¾ gal. + 3 c.	4½ gal.	5 gal. + 1 c.	5½ gal. + 2 c.
3 gal. + 2 c.	3¾ gal.	4¼ gal. + 2 c.	5 gal.	5½ gal. + 2 c.	6¼ gal.
3¼ gal. + 3 c.	4 gal. + 2 c.	4¾ gal. + 1 c.	5½ gal.	6 gal. + 3 c.	6¾ gal. + 2 c.
3¾ gal.	4½ gal.	5¼ gal.	6 gal.	6¾ gal.	7½ gal.
4 gal. + 1 c.	4¾ gal. + 2 c.	5½ gal. + 3 c.	6½ gal.	7¼ gal. + 1 c.	8 gal. + 2 c.
4¼ gal. + 2 c.	5¼ gal.	6 gal. + 2 c.	7 gal.	7¾ gal. + 2 c.	8¾ gal.
4½ gal. + 3 c.	5½ gal. + 2 c.	6½ gal. + 1 c.	7½ gal.	8¼ gal. + 3 c.	9¼ gal. + 2 c.
5 gal.	6 gal.	7 gal.	8 gal.	9 gal.	10 gal.
6¼ gal.	7½ gal.	8¾ gal.	10 gal.	11¼ gal.	12½ gal.
7½ gal.	9 gal.	10½ gal.	12 gal.	13½ gal.	15 gal.
8¾ gal.	10½ gal.	12¼ gal.	14 gal.	15¾ gal.	17½ gal.
10 gal.	12 gal.	14 gal.	16 gal.	18 gal.	20 gal.
11¼ gal.	13½ gal.	15¾ gal.	18 gal.	20¼ gal.	22½ gal.
12½ gal.	15 gal.	17½ gal.	20 gal.	22½ gal.	25 gal.
13¾ gal.	16½ gal.	19¼ gal.	22 gal.	24¾ gal.	27½ gal.
15 gal.	18 gal.	21 gal.	24 gal.	27 gal.	30 gal.
16¼ gal.	19½ gal.	22¾ gal.	26 gal.	29¼ gal.	32½ gal.
17½ gal.	21 gal.	24½ gal.	28 gal.	31½ gal.	35 gal.
18¾ gal.	22½ gal.	26¼ gal.	30 gal.	33¾ gal.	37½ gal.
20 gal.	24 gal.	28 gal.	32 gal.	36 gal.	40 gal.
21¼ gal.	25½ gal.	29¾ gal.	34 gal.	38¼ gal.	42½ gal.
22½ gal.	27 gal.	31½ gal.	36 gal.	40½ gal.	45 gal.
23¾ gal.	28½ gal.	33¼ gal.	38 gal.	42¾ gal.	47½ gal.
25 gal.	30 gal.	35 gal.	40 gal.	45 gal.	50 gal.
26¼ gal.	31½ gal.	36¾ gal.	42 gal.	47¼ gal.	52½ gal.
27½ gal.	33 gal.	38½ gal.	44 gal.	49½ gal.	55 gal.
28¾ gal.	34½ gal.	40¼ gal.	46 gal.	51¾ gal.	57½ gal.
30 gal.	36 gal.	42 gal.	48 gal.	54 gal.	60 gal.
31¼ gal.	37½ gal.	43¾ gal.	50 gal.	56¼ gal.	62½ gal.
32½ gal.	39 gal.	45½ gal.	52 gal.	58½ gal.	65 gal.
33¾ gal.	40½ gal.	47¼ gal.	54 gal.	60¾ gal.	67½ gal.
35 gal.	42 gal.	49 gal.	56 gal.	63 gal.	70 gal.

TABLE

Direct-reading table for adjusting yield of recipes with ingredient amounts given in measurement. This
8, yields of 20 and 60

Abbreviations in Table

t. = teaspoon
T. = tablespoon
c. = cup
qt. = quart
gal. = gallon
(r) = slightly rounded
(s) = scant

(*a*) = too small for accurate measure; use caution

8	16	20	24	32	40	48
(*a*)	(*a*)	⅛ t.(s)	⅛ t.	⅛ t.(r)	¼ t.(s)	¼ t.
(*a*)	⅛ t.(r)	¼ t.(s)	¼ t.	¼ t.(r)	½ t.(s)	½ t.
¼ t.(s)	¼ t.(r)	½ t.(s)	½ t.	¾ t.(s)	¾ t.(r)	1 t.
¼ t.	½ t.	½ t.(r)	¾ t.	1 t.	1¼ t.	1½ t.
¼ t.(r)	¾ t.(s)	¾ t.(r)	1 t.	1¼ t.(r)	1¾ t.(s)	2 t.
½ t.(s)	¾ t.(r)	1 t.	1¼ t.	1¾ t.(s)	2 t.	2½ t.
½ t.	1 t.	1¼ t.	1½ t.	2 t.	2½ t.	1 T.
½ t.(r)	1¼ t.(s)	1½ t.	1¾ t.	2¼ t.(r)	1 T.(s)	1 T. + ½ t.
¾ t.(s)	1¼ t.(r)	1¾ t.(s)	2 t.	2¾ t.(r)	1 T. + ¼ t.	1 T. + 1 t.
¾ t.	1½ t.	1¼ t.(r)	2¼ t.	1 T.	1 T. + ¾ t.	1 T. + 1½ t.
¾ t.(r)	1¾ t.(s)	2 t.	2½ t.	1 T. + ¼ t.(r)	1 T. + 1¼ t.	1 T. + 2 t.
1 t.(s)	1¾ t.(r)	2¼ t.(r)	2¾ t.	1 T. + ¾ t.(s)	1 T. + 1½ t.	1 T. + 2½ t.
1 t.	2 t.	2½ t.	1 T.	1 T. + 1 t.	1 T. + 2 t.	2 T.
1½ t.	1 T.	1 T. + ¾ t.	1⅓ T.	2 T.	2½ T.	3 T.
2 t.	1 T. + 1 t.	1 T. + 2 t.	2 T.	2 T. + 2 t.	3 T. + 1 t.	¼ c.
2½ t.	1 T. + 2 t.	2 T. + ¼ t.	2½ T.	3 T. + 1 t.	¼ c. + ½ t.	¼ c. + 1 T.
1 T.	2 T.	2½ T.	3 T.	¼ c.	¼ c. + 1 T.	⅓ c. + 2 t.
1 T. + ½ t.	2 T. + 1 t.	2 T. + 2¾ t.	3½ T.	¼ c. + 2 t.	⅓ c. + ½ T.	¼ c. + 3 T.
1 T. + 1 t.	2 T. + 2 t.	3 T. + 1 t.	¼ c.	½ c.	⅓ c. + 4 t.	½ c.
1 T. + 2¼ t.	3 T. + 2¾ t.	¼ c. + 1¼ t.	⅓ c.	¼ c. + 3 T.	½ c. + 2½ t.	⅔ c.
2 T. + 2 t.	½ c.	⅓ c. + 2 T.	½ c.	⅔ c.	¾ c. + 4 t.	1 c.
3 T. + 1¾ t.	⅓ c. + 5 t.	½ c. + 2¾ t.	⅔ c.	¾ c. + 2 T.	1 c. + 5½ t.	1⅓ c.
¼ c.	½ c.	½ c. + 2 T.	¾ c.	1 c.	1¼ c.	1½ c.
⅓ c.	⅔ c.	¾ c. + 2 t.	1 c.	1⅓ c.	1⅔ c.	2 c.
⅓ c. + 4 t.	¾ c. + 4 t.	1 c. + 2 t.	1¼ c.	1⅔ c.	2 c. + 4 t.	2½ c.
⅓ c. + 5¼ t.	⅔ c. + 3½ T.	1 c. + 5¼ t.	1⅓ c.	1¾ c. + 1¼ t.	2 c. + 3½ T.	2⅔ c.
½ c.	1 c.	1¼ c.	1½ c.	2 c.	2½ c.	3 c.
½ c. + 2¼ t.	1 c. + 5¼ t.	1⅓ c.	1⅔ c.	2 c. + 3½ T.	2⅔ c.	3⅓ c.
½ c. + 4 t.	1 c. + 3 T.	1⅓ c. + 2 T.	1¾ c.	2⅓ c.	2¾ c. + 1½ T.	3½ c.
¾ c.	1⅓ c.	1⅔ c.	2 c.	2⅔ c.	3⅓ c.	1 qt.
¾ c.	1½ c.	1¾ c. + 2 T.	2¼ c.	3 c.	3¾ c.	1 qt. + ½ c.
¾ c. + 1¼ t.	1½ c. + 2¾ t.	1¼ c. + 3 T.	2⅓ c.	3 c. + 2 T.	3¾ c. + 2 T.	1 qt. + ⅔ c.
¾ c. + 4 t.	1⅔ c.	2 c. + 4 t.	2½ c.	3⅓ c.	1 qt. + 2½ T.	1¼ qt.
⅔ c. + 3½ T.	1¾ c. + 1¼ t.	2 c. + 3½ T.	2⅔ c.	3½ c. + 1 T.	4¼ c. + 3 T.	1¼ qt. + ⅓ c.
⅔ c. + ¼ c.	1¾ c. + 4 t.	2¼ c. + 2 t.	2¾ c.	3⅔ c.	4½ c. + 4 t.	1¼ qt. + ½ c.
1 c.	2 c.	2½ c.	3 c.	1 qt.	1¼ qt.	1½ qt.

A.6
table is primarily for use with recipes with original or desired portion yields which can be divided by portions are also included)

Basic Information

Measuring Spoons
1 T.
1 t.
½ t.
¼ t.
for ¾ t. combine ½ t. + ¼ t.
for ⅛ t. use half of the ¼ t.

Equivalents
3 t. = 1 T.
4 T. = ¼ c.
5 T. + 1 t. = ⅓ c.
8 T. = ½ c.
10 T. + 2 t. = ⅔ c.
12 T. = ¾ c.
16 T. = 1 c.
4 c. = 1 qt.
4 qt. = 1 gal.

56	60	64	72	80	88	96
¼ t.(r)	¼ t.(r)	¼ t.(r)	¼ t. + ⅛ t.	½ t.(s)	½ t.(s)	½ t.
½ t.(r)	½ t.(r)	¾ t.(s)	¾ t.	¾ t.(r)	1 t.(s)	1 t.
1¼ t.(s)	1¼ t.	1¼ t.(r)	1½ t.	1¾ t.(s)	1¾ t.(r)	2 t.
1¾ t.	1¾ t.(r)	2 t.	2¼ t.	2½ t.	2¾ t.	1 T.
2¼ t.(r)	2½ t.	2¾ t.(s)	1 T.	1 T. + ¼ t.	1 T. + ¾ t.	1 T. + 1 t.
1 T.(s)	1 T. + ⅛ t.	1 T. + ¼ t.	1 T. + ¾ t.	1 T. + 1¼ t.	1½ T.	1 T. + 2 t.
1 T. + ½ t.	1 T. + ¾ t.	1 T. + 1 t.	1½ T.	1 T. + 2 t.	1 T. + 2½ t.	2 T.
1 T. + 1 t.	1 T. + 1¼ t. + ⅛ t.	1 T. + 1¾ t.	1 T. + 2¼ t.	1 T. + 2¾ t.	2 T. + ½ t.	2 T. + 1 t.
1 T. + 1¾ t.	1 T. + 2 t.	1 T. + 2¼ t.	2 T.	2 T. + ¾ t.	2 T. + 1¼ t.	2 T. + 2 t.
1 T. + 2¼ t.	1 T. + 2½ t.	2 T.	2 T. + ¾ t.	2½ T.	2 T. + 2¼ t.	3 T.
1 T. + 2¾ t.(r)	2 T. + ¼ t.	2 T. + ¾ t.	2 T. + 1½ t.	2 T. + 2¼ t.	3 T.	3 T. + 1 t.
2 T. + ½ t.	2 T. + ¾ t.	2 T. + 1¼ t.	2 T. + 2¼ t.	3 T.	3 T. + 1 t.	3 T. + 2 t.
2 T. + 1 t.	2½ T.	2 T. + 2 t.	3 T.	3 T. +1 t.	3 T. + 2 t.	¼ c.
3½ T.	3 T. + 2¼ t.	¼ c.	¼ c. + 1½ t.	¼ c. + 1 T.	⅓ c. + ½ t.	⅓ c. + 2 t.
¼ c. + 2 t.	¼ c. + 1 T.	⅓ c.	⅓ c. + 2 t.	⅓ c. + 4 t.	⅓ c. + 2 T.	½ c.
⅓ c. + ½ T.	⅓ c. + 2¾ t.	⅓ c. + 4 t.	¼ c. + 3½ T.	½ c. + 1 t.	½ c. + 3½ t.	½ c. + 2 T.
¼ c. + 3 T.	¼ c. + 3½ T.	½ c.	½ c. + 1 T.	½ c. + 2 T.	½ c. + 3 T.	¾ c.
½ c. + ½ t.	½ c. + 2¼ t.	½ c. + 4 t.	½ c. + 2½ T.	⅔ c. + 1 T.	¾ c. + 2½ t.	¾ c. + 2 T.
½ c. + 4 t.	½ c. + 2 T.	⅔ c.	¾ c.	¾ c. + 4 t.	¾ c. + 2½ T.	1 c.
¾ c. + ½ T.	¾ c. + 4 t.	¾ c. + 2 T.	1 c.	1 c. + 5 t.	1 c. + 3½ T.	1⅓ c.
1 c. + 2½ T.	1¼ c.	1⅓ c.	1½ c.	1⅔ c.	1¾ c. + 4 t.	2 c.
1½ c. + 1 T.	1⅔ c.	1¾ c.	2 c.	2 c. + 3½ T.	2¼ c. + 3 T.	2⅔ c.
1¾ c.	1¾ c. + 2 T.	2 c.	2¼ c.	2½ c.	2¾ c.	3 c.
2⅓ c.	2½ c.	2⅔ c.	3 c.	3⅓ c.	3⅔ c.	1 qt.
2¾ c. + 2½ T.	3 c. + 2 T.	3⅓ c.	3¾ c.	1 qt. + 2½ T.	4½ c. + 4 t.	1¼ qt.
3 c. + 2 T.	3⅓ c.	3½ c. + 2½ t.	1 qt.	4¼ c. + 3 T.	4¾ c. + 2 T. + 1 t.	1¼ qt. + ⅓ c.
3½ c.	3¾ c.	1 qt.	1 qt. + ½ c.	1¼ qt.	1¼ qt. + ½ c.	1½ qt.
3¾ c. + 2 T.	1 qt. + 2½ T.	4¼ c. + 3 T.	1¼ qt.	1¼ qt. + ⅓ c.	1½ qt. + 5 t.	1½ qt. + ⅔ c.
1 qt. + 4 t.	1 qt. + ¼ c. + 2 T.	1 qt. + ⅔ c.	1¼ qt. + ¼ c.	5½ c. + 3 T.	1½ qt. + ¼ c. + 2½ T.	1¾ qt.
1 qt. + ⅔ c.	1¼ qt.	1¼ qt. + ⅓ c.	1½ qt.	1½ qt. + ⅔ c.	1¾ qt. + ⅓ c.	2 qt.
1¼ qt. + ¼ c.	1¼ qt. + ⅔ c.	1½ qt.	1½ qt. + ¾ c.	1¾ qt. + ½ c.	2 qt. + ¼ c.	2¼ qt.
5¼ c. + 3 T.	5¾ c. + 1½ T.	1½ qt. + ¼ c.	1¾ qt.	1¾ qt. + ¾ c.	2 qt. + ½ c. + 1 T.	2¼ qt. + ⅓ c.
5¾ c. + 1 T.	1½ qt. + ¼ c.	1½ qt. + ⅔ c.	1¾ qt. + ½ c.	2 qt. + 5 T.	2¼ qt. + 3 T.	2½ qt.
1½ qt. + ¼ c.	1½ qt. + ⅔ c.	1¾ qt. + 2 T.	2 qt.	2 qt. + ¾ c. + 2 T.	2¼ qt. + ¾ c. + ½ T.	2½ qt. + ⅔ c.
1½ qt. + ¼ c. + 3 T.	1½ qt. + ¾ c. + 2 T.	1¾ qt. + ⅓ c.	2 qt. + ¼ c.	2¼ qt. + 2½ T.	2½ qt. + 1½ T.	2¾ qt.
1¾ qt.	1¾ qt. + ½ c.	2 qt.	2¼ qt.	2½ qt.	2¾ qt.	3 qt.

Table A.6 (continued)

8	16	20	24	32	40	48
1 c. + 4 t.	2 c. + 2½ T.	2⅔ c. + 2 t.	3¼ c.	1 qt. + ⅓ c.	5⅓ c. + 4 t.	1½ qt. + ½ c.
1 c. + 5¼ t.	2 c. + 3½ T.	2¾ c. + ½ T.	3½ c.	4¼ c. + 3 T.	5½ c. + 1 T.	1½ qt. + ⅔ c.
1 c. + 2 T. + 2 t.	2¼ c. + 4 t.	2¾ c. + 2½ T.	3½ c.	1 qt. + ⅔ c.	5¾ c. + 1 T.	1¾ qt.
1 c. + 3½ T.	2¼ c. + 3 T.	3 c. + 1 T.	3⅔ c.	4¾ c. + 2 T.	1½ qt. + 2 T.	1¾ qt. + ⅓ c.
1¼ c.	2½ c.	3 c. + 2 T.	3¾ c.	1¼ qt.	1½ qt. + ¼ c.	1¾ qt. + ½ c.
1⅓ c.	2⅔ c.	3⅓ c.	1 qt.	1¼ qt. + ⅓ c.	1½ qt. + ⅔ c.	2 qt.
1⅔ c.	3⅓ c.	1 qt. + 2½ T.	1¼ qt.	1½ qt. + ⅔ c.	2 qt. + ¼ c. + 1 T.	2½ qt.
2 c.	1 qt.	1¼ qt.	1½ qt.	2 qt.	2½ qt.	3 qt.
2⅓ c.	1 qt. + ⅔ c.	5¾ c. + 1½ T.	1¾ qt.	2¼ qt. + ⅓ c.	2¾ qt. + ⅔ c.	3½ qt.
2⅔ c.	1¼ qt. + ⅓ c.	1½ qt. + ⅔ c.	2 qt.	2½ qt. + ⅔ c.	3¼ qt. + ⅓ c.	1 gal.
3 c.	1½ qt.	1¾ qt. + ½ c.	2¼ qt.	3 qt.	3¾ qt.	1 gal. + 2 c.
3⅓ c.	1½ qt. + ⅔ c.	2 qt. + ⅓ c.	2½ qt.	3¼ qt. + ⅓ c.	1 gal. + ⅔ c.	1¼ gal.
3⅔ c.	1¾ qt. + ⅓ c.	2¼ qt. + 2½ T.	2¾ qt.	3½ qt. + ⅔ c.	1 gal. + 2⅓ c.	1¼ gal. + 2 c.
1 qt.	2 qt.	2½ qt.	3 qt.	1 gal.	1¼ gal.	1½ gal.
1 qt. + ⅓ c.	2 qt. + ⅔ c.	2½ qt. + ¾ c. + 1½ T.	3¼ qt.	1 gal. + 1⅓ c.	1¼ gal. + 1⅔ c.	1½ gal. + 2 c.
1 qt. + ⅔ c.	2¼ qt. + ⅓ c.	2¾ qt. + ⅔ c.	3½ qt.	1 gal. + 2⅔ c.	1¼ gal. + 3⅓ c.	1¾ gal.
1¼ qt.	2½ qt.	3 qt. + ½ c.	3¾ qt.	1¼ gal.	1½ gal. + 1 c.	1¾ gal. + 2 c.
1¼ qt. + ⅓ c.	2½ qt. + ⅔ c.	3 qt. + 1⅓ c.	1 gal.	1¼ gal. + 1⅓ c.	1½ gal. + 2⅔ c.	2 gal.
1½ qt. + ⅔ c.	3¼ qt. + ⅓ c.	1 gal. + ⅔ c.	1¼ gal.	1½ gal. + 2⅔ c.	2 gal. + 1⅓ c.	2½ gal.
2 qt.	1 gal.	1¼ gal.	1½ gal.	2 gal.	2½ gal.	3 gal.

56	60	64	72	80	88	96
1¾ qt. + ⅓ c. + ¼ c.	2 qt. + 2 T.	2 qt. + ⅔ c.	2¼ qt. + ¾ c.	2½ qt. + ¾ c. + 1½ T.	2¾ qt. + ¾ c. + 3 T.	3¼ qt.
1¾ qt. + ¾ c.	2 qt. + ⅓ c.	2 qt. + ¾ c. + 2 T.	2½ qt.	2¾ qt. + 2 T.	3 qt. + ¼ c.	3¼ qt. + ⅓ c.
2 qt. + 3 T.	2 qt. + ¾ c.	2¼ qt. + ⅓ c.	2½ qt. + ½ c.	2¾ qt. + ½ c. + 2 T.	3 qt. + ¾ c. + 1½ T.	3½ qt.
2 qt. + ½ c. + 1 T.	2¼ qt. + 2½ T.	2¼ qt. + ¾ c.	2¾ qt.	3 qt. + ¼ c.	3¼ qt. + ¼ c. + 3 T.	3 qt. + 2⅔ c.
2 qt. + ¾ c.	2¼ qt. + ¼ c. + 2 T.	2½ qt.	2¾ qt. + ¼ c.	3 qt. + ½ c.	3 qt. + 1¾ c.	3 qt. + 3 c.
2 qt. + 1⅓ c.	2½ qt.	2¾ qt. + ⅓ c.	3 qt.	3 qt. + 1⅓ c.	3 qt. + 2⅔ c.	1 gal.
2¾ qt. + ⅔ c.	3 qt. + ½ c.	3¼ qt. + ⅓ c.	3¾ qt.	1 gal. + ⅔ c.	1 gal. + 2⅓ c.	1¼ gal.
3½ qt.	3¾ qt.	1 gal.	1 gal. + 2 c.	1¼ gal.	1¼ gal. + 2 c.	1½ gal.
1 gal. + ⅓ c.	1 gal. + 1½ c.	1 gal. + 2⅔ c.	1¼ gal. + 1 c.	1¼ gal. + 3⅓ c.	1½ gal. + 1⅔ c.	1¾ gal.
1 gal. + 2⅔ c.	1¼ gal.	1¼ gal. + 1⅓ c.	1½ gal.	1½ gal. + 2⅔ c.	1¾ gal. + 1⅓ c.	2 gal.
1¼ gal. + 1 c.	1¼ gal. + 2½ c.	1½ gal.	1½ gal. + 3 c.	1¾ gal. + 2 c.	2 gal. + 1 c.	2¼ gal.
1¼ gal. + 3⅓ c.	1½ gal. + 1 c.	1½ gal. + 2⅔ c.	1¾ gal. + 2 c.	2 gal. + 1⅓ c.	2¼ gal. + ⅔ c.	2½ gal.
1½ gal. + 1⅔ c.	1½ gal. + 3½ c.	1¾ gal. + 1⅓ c.	2 gal. + 1 c.	2¼ gal. + ⅔ c.	2½ gal. + ⅓ c.	2¾ gal.
1¾ gal.	1¾ gal. + 2 c.	2 gal.	2¼ gal.	2½ gal.	2¾ gal.	3 gal.
1¾ gal. + 2⅓ c.	2 gal. + ½ c.	2 gal. + 2⅔ c.	2¼ gal. + 3 c.	2½ gal. + 3⅓ c.	2¾ gal. + 3⅔ c.	3¼ gal.
2 gal. + ⅔ c.	2 gal. + 3 c.	2¼ gal. + 1⅓ c.	2½ gal. + 2 c.	2¾ gal. + 2⅔ c.	3 gal. + 3⅓ c.	3½ gal.
2 gal. + 3 c.	2¼ gal. + 1½ c.	2½ gal.	2¾ gal. + 1 c.	3 gal. + 2 c.	3¼ gal. + 3 c.	3¾ gal.
2¼ gal. + 1⅓ c.	2½ gal.	2½ gal. + 2⅔ c.	3 gal.	3¼ gal. + 1⅓ c.	3½ gal. + 2⅔ c.	4 gal.
2¾ gal. + 2⅔ c.	3 gal. + 2 c.	3¼ gal. + 1⅓ c.	3¾ gal.	4 gal. + 2⅔ c.	4½ gal. + 1⅓ c.	5 gal.
3½ gal.	3¾ gal.	4 gal.	4½ gal.	5 gal.	5½ gal.	6 gal.

FOOD SERVICE SCIENCE

FOOD PRODUCT	Size of Can	Approximate Net Weight or Volume*
Apple Butter	No. 10	7 lbs. 8 oz.
Apple Juice	46-oz.	1 qt. 14 fl. oz.
Apples	No. 10	6 lbs.
Apple Sauce	No. 303	1 lb.
Apple Sauce	No. 10	6 lbs. 12 oz.
Apricot Halves (med.)	No. 2½	1 lb. 13 oz.
Apricot Halves (med.)	No. 10	6 lbs. 10 oz.
Asparagus Cuts	No. 303	1 lb.
Asparagus Cuts	No. 10	6 lbs. 5 oz.
Asparagus Spears (med.)	No. 2	1 lb. 3 oz.
Asparagus Spears (med.)	No. 10	6 lbs. 7 oz.
Beans, Baked	No. 300	15½ oz.
Beans, Baked	No. 10	6 lbs. 14 oz.
Beans, Green	No. 303	1 lb.
Beans, Green	No. 10	6 lbs. 5 oz.
Beans, Kidney	No. 303	1 lb.
Beans, Kidney	No. 10	6 lbs. 12 oz.
Beans, Lima	No. 303	1 lb.
Beans, Lima	No. 10	6 lbs. 9 oz.
Beans, Wax	No. 303	1 lb.
Beans, Wax	No. 10	6 lbs. 5 oz.
Beets	No. 303	1 lb.
Beets	No. 10	6 lbs. 8 oz.
Blackberries	No. 303	1 lb.
Blackberries	No. 10	6 lbs. 7 oz.
Blueberries	No. 300	15½ oz.
Blueberries	No. 10	6 lbs. 6 oz.
Carrots	No. 303	1 lb.
Carrots	No. 10	6 lbs. 9 oz.
Catsup, Tomato	No. 10	7 lbs. 3 oz.
Cherries, Red Tart Pitted	No. 303	1 lb.
Cherries, Red Tart Pitted	No. 10	6 lbs. 7 oz.
Cherries, Sweet	No. 303	1 lb.
Cherries, Sweet	No. 10	6 lbs. 12 oz.

*Weights will vary slightly depending on density of sirup or specific gravity of products.

A. 7
SERVINGS PER CAN

1 oz. servings	2 oz. servings	3 oz. servings	4 oz. servings	5 oz. servings	Servings governed by number of pieces or average portion
					120 (1 oz. average portion)
46	23	15	11	9	
96	48	32	24	19	36 (six 9-inch pies)
16	8	5	4	3	
108	54	36	27	21	
					7 (3 to 4 halves)
					25 (3 to 4 halves)
16	8	5	4	3	
101	50	33	25	20	
					5 (6 spears)
					25 (6 spears)
15	7	5	4	3	
110	55	36	27	22	
16	8	5	4	3	
101	50	33	25	20	
16	8	5	4	3	
108	54	36	27	21	
16	8	5	4	3	
105	52	35	26	21	
16	8	5	4	3	
101	50	33	25	20	
16	8	5	4	3	
104	52	34	26	20	
16	8	5	4	3	
103	51	34	25	20	36 (six 9-inch pies)
15	8	5	4	3	
102	51	34	25	20	36 (six 9-inch pies)
16	8	5	4	3	
105	52	35	26	21	
					115 (1 oz. average portion)
16	8	5	4	3	
103	51	34	25	20	36 (six 9-inch pies)
16	8	5	4	3	
108	54	36	27	21	

Table A. 7 (*continued*)

FOOD PRODUCT	Size of Can	Approximate Net Weight or Volume*
Chili Con Carne	No. 300	15½-16 oz.
Chili Con Carne	No. 10	6 lbs. 12 oz.
Corn, Cream-Style, Whole Kernel	No. 303	1 lb.
Corn, Cream-Style, Whole Kernel	No. 10	6 lbs. 10 oz.
Corned Beef Hash	1 lb.	1 lb.
Corned Beef Hash	No. 10	5 lbs. 8-14 oz.
Crab Meat		6½ oz.
Cranberry Sauce	No. 300	1 lb.
Cranberry Sauce	No. 10	7 lbs. 5 oz.
Figs	No. 2½	1 lb. 14 oz.
Figs	No. 10	7 lbs.
Fruit Cocktail	No. 2½	1 lb. 13 oz.
Fruit Cocktail	No. 10	6 lbs. 12 oz.
Fruits for Salad	No. 2½	1 lb. 13 oz.
Fruits for Salad	No. 10	6 lbs. 12 oz.
Grapefruit Sections	No. 303	1 lb.
Grapefruit Sections	46-oz.	3 lbs. 2 oz.
Grapefruit Juice	46-oz.	1 qt. 14 fl. oz.
Grapefruit Juice	No. 10	3 qts.
Ham, Spiced (Pork Prod.)	12Z Oblong	12 oz.
Ham, Spiced (Pork Prod.)	6 lb. Luncheon Meat	6 lbs.
Hams, Whole		9-11 lbs.
Hams, Whole		11-13 lbs.
Hominy	No. 2½	1 lb. 13 oz.
Hominy	No. 10	6 lbs. 9 oz.
Jams	No. 10	8 lbs. 8 oz.
Jellies	No. 10	8 lbs. 6 oz.
Mixed Vegetables	No. 303	1 lb.
Mixed Vegetables	No. 10	6 lbs. 8 oz.
Mushrooms	No. 4Z	6¾ oz.
Mushrooms	Jumbo	1 lb. 8 oz.
Okra	No. 10	6 lbs. 3 oz.
Olives, Ripe	No. 2½	1 lb. 2 oz.
Olives, Ripe	No. 10	4 lbs. 2 oz.

*Weights will vary slightly depending on density of sirup or specific gravity of products.

1 oz. servings	2 oz. servings	3 oz. servings	4 oz. servings	5 oz. servings	Servings governed by number of pieces or average portion
15	7	5	4	3	
108	54	36	27	21	
16	8	5	4	3	
106	53	35	26	21	
					3-4 ($\frac{1}{2}$ to $\frac{2}{3}$ cup)
					18-24 ($\frac{1}{2}$ to $\frac{2}{3}$ cup)
					4 ($1\frac{1}{2}$ oz. average portion)
					16 (1 oz. average portion)
					117 (1 oz. average portion)
					7 (3 figs)
					25 (3 figs)
29	14	9	7	5	
108	54	36	27	21	
29	14	9	7	5	
108	54	36	27	21	
16	8	5	4	3	
50	25	16	12	10	
46	23	15	11	9	
96	48	32	24	19	
					4 (2 slices — $3\frac{1}{2}$" x $1\frac{3}{4}$" x $\frac{3}{8}$")
					32 (2 slices — $3\frac{1}{2}$" x $1\frac{3}{4}$" x $\frac{3}{8}$")
					20-35 (2 slices — 4" x 3" x $\frac{1}{8}$")
					35-45 (2 slices — 4" x 3" x $\frac{1}{8}$")
29	14	9	7	5	
105	52	35	26	21	
					136 (1 oz. average portion)
					134 (1 oz. average portion)
16	8	5	4	3	
104	52	34	26	20	
6	3	2	—	—	
24	12	8	6	4	
99	49	33	24	20	
					(3 olives — average portion; number of servings per can varies with size of olives)

Table A. 7 (continued)

FOOD PRODUCT	Size of Can	Approximate Net Weight or Volume*
Onions	No. 10	6 lbs. 5 oz.
Orange and Grapefruit Sections	No. 303	1 lb.
Orange and Grapefruit Sections	46-oz.	3 lbs. 2 oz.
Orange Juice	No. 2	1 pt. 2 fl. oz.
Orange Juice	46-oz.	1 qt. 14 fl. oz.
Orange Juice	No. 10	3 qts.
Peach Halves (med.)	No. 2½	1 lb. 13 oz.
Peach Halves (med.)	No. 10	6 lbs. 10 oz.
Pear Halves (med.)	No. 2½	1 lb. 13 oz.
Pear Halves (med.)	No. 10	6 lbs. 10 oz.
Peas; Black Eye Peas	No. 303	1 lb.
Peas; Black Eye Peas	No. 10	6 lbs. 9 oz.
Pickles, Whole — Dill, Sour, Sweet	No. 10	3 qts. 9 fl. oz.
Pickles, Sliced	No. 10	3 qts. 9 fl. oz.
Pickles, Mixed	No. 10	3 qts. 9 fl. oz.
Pickles, Chow Chow	No. 10	3 qts. 9 fl. oz.
Pickles, Relish	No. 10	3 qts. 9 fl. oz.
Pimientos	4Z	4 oz.
Pimientos	7Z	7 oz.
Pimientos	No. 2½	1 lb. 12 oz.
Pineapple—Chunks, Crushed and Tidbits	No. 2	1 lb. 4 oz.
Pineapple—Chunks, Crushed and Tidbits	No. 10	6 lbs. 12 oz.
Pineapple — Sliced	No. 2	1 lb. 4 oz.
Pineapple — Sliced	No. 10	6 lbs. 12 oz.
Pineapple Juice	46-oz.	1 qt. 14 fl. oz.
Pineapple Juice	No. 10	3 qts. 2 fl. oz.
Plums	No. 2½	1 lb. 14 oz.
Plums	No. 10	6 lbs. 12 oz.
Potatoes, White Dehydrated	No. 10	6 lbs.
Potatoes, White Whole	No. 10	6 lbs. 6 oz.
Potatoes, Sweet	No. 3 Vac.	1 lb. 2 oz.
Potatoes, Sweet	No. 2½	1 lb. 13 oz.
Potatoes, Sweet	No. 10	6 lbs. 6 oz.
Preserves	No. 10	8 lbs. 8 oz.

*Weights will vary slightly depending on density of sirup or specific gravity of products.

1 oz. servings	2 oz. servings	3 oz. servings	4 oz. servings	5 oz. servings	Servings governed by number of pieces or average portion
					25 (3 to 4 onions)
16	8	5	4	3	
50	25	16	12	10	
18	9	6	4	3	
46	23	15	11	9	
96	48	32	24	19	
					7 (2 halves)
					25 (2 halves)
					7 (2 halves)
					25 (2 halves)
16	8	5	4	3	
105	52	35	26	21	
					($\frac{1}{2}$ to 2 pickles — average portion; number of servings per can varies with size of pickles)
					100 (1 oz. average portion)
					100 (1 oz. average portion)
					100 (1 oz. average portion)
					100 (1 oz. average portion)
20	10	6	5	4	
108	54	36	27	21	
					5 (2 slices)
					25 (1 large or 2 small slices)
46	23	15	11	9	
98	49	32	24	19	
					7 (2 to 3 plums)
					25 (2 to 3 plums)
					150 (1 cup)
					25
					4
					5
					25
					136 (1 oz. average portion)

Table A. 7 *(continued)*

FOOD PRODUCT	Size of Can	Approximate Net Weight or Volume*
Prunes	No. 2½	1 lb. 14 oz.
Prunes	No. 10	6 lbs. 14 oz.
Pumpkin	No. 10	6 lbs. 10 oz.
Raspberries, Black	No. 303	1 lb.
Raspberries, Black	No. 10	6 lbs. 6 oz.
Raspberries, Red	No. 303	1 lb.
Raspberries, Red	No. 10	6 lbs. 7 oz.
Rhubarb	No. 10	6 lbs. 9 oz.
Salmon	½ lb. Flat	7¾ oz.
Salmon	1 lb. Tall	1 lb.
Sardines and Pilchards	¼ Oblong	3¼ oz.
Sardines and Pilchards	½ Oblong	8 oz.
Sardines and Pilchards	¾ Oblong	11 oz.
Sardines and Pilchards	No. 1 Oval	15 oz.
Sauerkraut	No. 2½	1 lb. 11 oz.
Sauerkraut	No. 10	6 lbs. 3 oz.
Soup, Condensed	No. 1 Picnic	10½-12 oz.
Soup, Condensed	46-oz.	3 lbs. 2 oz.
Soup, Condensed	No. 10	6 lbs. 8 oz.
Soup, Ready-to-Serve	No. 211 Cyl.	12 fl. oz.
Soup, Ready-to-Serve	No. 2½	1 pt. 12 fl. oz.
Soup, Ready-to-Serve	No. 10	3 qts.
Spinach	No. 10	6 lbs. 2 oz.
Sirup: Blended, Cane, Maple	No. 10	3 qts.
Tomatoes	No. 303	1 lb.
Tomatoes	No. 2½	1 lb. 12 oz.
Tomatoes	No. 10	6 lbs. 6 oz.
Tomato Juice	46-oz.	1 qt. 14 fl. oz.
Tomato Juice	No. 10	3 qts.
Tomato Paste	No. 10	7 lbs. 2 oz.
Tomato Puree	No. 10	6 lbs. 9 oz.
Tuna	No. ½	7 oz.
Tuna	No. 1	13 oz.
Turnip Greens	No. 10	6 lbs. 2 oz.

Weights will vary slightly depending on density of sirup or specific gravity of products.

1 oz. servings	2 oz. servings	3 oz. servings	4 oz. servings	5 oz. servings	Servings governed by number of pieces or average portion
					7 (2 to 3 prunes)
					25 (2 to 3 prunes)
106	53	35	26	21	48 (eight 9-inch pies)
16	8	5	4	3	
102	51	34	25	20	36 (six 9-inch pies)
16	8	5	4	3	
103	51	34	25	20	36 (six 9-inch pies)
105	52	35	26	21	
7	3	2	2	1	
16	8	5	4	3	
					1½ servings
					2 servings
					3 servings
					4 servings
27	13	9	6	5	
99	49	33	24	19	
					4 (¾ cup)
					16-18 (¾ cup)
					32 (¾ cup)
					2 (¾ cup)
					4 (¾ cup)
					16 (¾ cup)
98	49	32	24	19	
					48 (2 fl. oz. average portion)
16	8	5	4	3	
28	14	9	6	5	
102	51	34	25	20	
46	23	15	11	9	
96	48	32	24	19	
114	57	38	28	22	
105	52	35	26	21	
7	3	2	2	—	
13	6	4	3	—	
98	49	32	24	19	

TABLE A. 8

FRUITS AND VEGETABLES, CONTAINERS

Cans commonly used in canning fruits, vegetables, juices:
Container dimensions, capacities, and conversion factors

Industry Designation	Dimensions	Total Capacity Avoir. oz. Water at 68°F	No. 303 Equiv- alent	No. 2 Equiv- alent	No. 2½ Equiv- alent
6Z	202x308	6.08	0.360	0.295	0.204
8Z Short	211x300	7.93	.470	.386	.266
8Z Tall	211x304	8.68	.514	.422	.291
No. 1 Flat	307x203	8.89	.527	.433	.298
No. 1 Picnic	211x400	10.94	.648	.532	.367
No. 211 Cylinder	211x414	13.56	.803	.660	.455
No. 2 Vac. (12Z Vac)	307x306	14.71	.871	.716	.494
No. 300	300x407	15.22	.902	.741	.511
No. 1 Tall	301x411	16.70	0.989	.813	.561
No. 303	303x406	16.88	1.000	.821	.567
No. 300 Cylinder	300x509	19.40	1.149	0.945	.651
No. 2	307x409	20.55	1.217	1.000	.689
No. 303 Cylinder	303x509	21.86	1.295	1.060	.734
No. 3 Vacuum	404x307	23.9	1.416	1.162	.802
Jumbo	307x510	25.8	1.528	1.254	.866
No. 2 Cylinder	307x512	26.4	1.564	1.284	0.886
No. 2½	401x411	29.79	1.765	1.450	1.000
29Z	307x700	32.5	1.925	1.580	1.091
32Z (Quart)	307x710	35.5	2.103	1.729	1.192
3 Cylinder (46 oz.)	404x700	51.7	3.063	2.515	1.735
No. 5 Squat	603x408	68.1	4.034	3.314	2.286
No. 10	603x700	109.43	6.483	5.325	3.673

[1]The first figures in this column represent the diameter of the container and the second figure the height. The first digit in each number represents inches and the second two digits sixteenths of an inch, i.e., 307 is $3\frac{7}{16}$ in.

Source: National Canners Association.

TABLE A.9

FRUITS AND VEGETABLES, CONTAINERS

Case conversion factors for canned fruits and vegetables

Container Designation	No. Containers per Case	Factors to Multiply by to convert to:		
		24/303's	24/2's	24/2$\frac{1}{2}$'s
6Z	48	0.72	0.59	0.41
8Z Short	72	1.41	1.16	.80
8Z Tall	48	1.03	0.84	.58
No. 1 Flat	48	1.05	0.87	.60
No. 1 Picnic	48	1.30	1.06	.73
No. 211 Cylinder	24	0.80	0.66	.46
No. 2 Vac. (12Z Vac.)	24	.87	.72	.49
No. 300	24	.90	.74	.51
No. 1 Tall	24	0.99	.81	.56
No. 303	24	1.00	.82	.57
No. 300 Cylinder	24	1.15	0.94	.65
No. 2	24	1.22	1.00	.69
No. 3 Vacuum	24	1.42	1.16	0.80
No. 2$\frac{1}{2}$	24	1.77	1.45	1.00
29Z	12	0.96	0.79	0.55
32Z (Quart)	12	1.05	0.86	.60
No. 3 Cylinder	12	1.53	1.26	.87
No. 5 Squat	6	1.01	0.83	.57
No. 10	6	1.62	1.33	0.92

Source: National Canners Association.

TABLE A.10

FRUITS AND VEGETABLES, CONTAINERS

Shipping containers most commonly used for fresh fruits and vegetables

Commodity	Shipping Container	Approximate Net Weight[1] lb
Fresh fruits		
Apples	Bu. basket	40–50
	Fiberboard box, tray pack	37–48
	Fiberboard box, cell pack	37–44
	Fiberboard box, bulk pack	38–50
	Film bag 3, 4, 5, 10 lb (packed 4 to 15 bags to the master container)	36–48
Apricots	Lug, Brentwood	24–25
	Lug, L.A.	27–30
	Lug	12
	Lug	14
	4-basket crate	26
Avocados		
California	Lug	12–15
Florida	1-layer flat or $\frac{1}{4}$ bu. wood or fiberboard box	13–14
Florida	4/5 bu fiberboard box or carton	36–40
Bananas	Fiberboard folding box	25–50, mostly 40
All berries		
California	12 1-pt tray or carton	11–12
other	24 qt crate	36
	24 pt crate	18
	12 pt crate	9
	16 qt crate	24
Cherries	Lug, Calex	18–20
	Lug, Campbell	15–16
	Lug, wood	12–14
	Lug or carton	20
Cranberries	Box or fiberboard carton, $\frac{1}{4}$ barrel	25
	1-lb film bag or carton (packed 24 to the master container)	24
Figs	Flat, 2 layer	12–15
California	9-basket crate	12–15
Grapefruit, Florida	$1\frac{3}{5}$ bu wirebound box	85
	4/5 bu wirebound or fiberboard box	$42\frac{1}{2}$
	Film or mesh bags	4–5–8
	Mesh bags	20
Grapefruit, Texas	$1\frac{2}{5}$ bu wirebound box	80
	7/10 wirebound or fiberboard box	40
	Bags	5–8
	Mesh bags	20
Grapefruit, California Desert Valleys, and Arizona	7/10 bu fiberboard box, carton	32

Table A.10 (*continued*)

Commodity	Shipping Container	Approximate Net Weight[1] lb
Grapefruit (California, "other" areas)	7/10 bu fiberboard box, carton	33½
Grapes, Table		
California	Lug	27–28
	Lug	24
	Flat	17–20
	Chest, sawdust pack	20–22
	Chest, sawdust pack	32–34
Eastern	8 2-qt crates	24–25
	12-qt basket	18–20
Grapes, juice (Cal.)	Lug	26–28
	Lug	36–42
Lemons		
California and Arizona	7/10 bu fiberboard carton	38
Limes		
California and Florida	Fiberboard box, carton—4/5 bu	40
	Fiberboard box, carton—2/5 bu	20
	Fiberboard box, carton—1/5 bu	10
	Fiberboard master container	
	12 1-lb pks.	12
	36 1-lb pks. or 24 1½-lb	36
Mangoes, Florida	1 layer flat	13
	Box or carton	40
Nectarines, California	Flat	10
	Standard peach box	20–24
	Lug, Sanger	22–24
	Lug, L.A.	30
	4-basket crate	30–32
Oranges	1⅗ bu wirebound box	90
Florida	4/5 bu wirebound or fiberboard box	45
	Film or mesh bags	4–5–8
	Mesh bags	20
Texas	1⅖ bu wirebound box	85
	7/10 bu wirebound or fiberboard box	42½
	Bags	5–8
	Mesh bags	20
(California and Arizona)	7/10 bu fiberboard carton	37½
	Bags	2–8
Peaches		
(West)	Lug, L.A., wooden	22–28
	Western peach box	16–20
	Lug, Sanger	20
	Flat—1 layer	10
	Wood or fiberboard crate or carton	18–22
	4-basket crate	27

Table A. 10 (*continued*)

Commodity	Shipping Container	Approximate Net Weight[1] lb
(All other states)	Bu. basket	46–52
	1$\frac{1}{9}$ bu crate	50–55
	3/4 bu basket, carton or crate	35–42
	1/2 bu basket	23–28
Pears		
(West)	Standard wood box or carton	40–54
	Lug, L.A. or 2-layer carton	22–28
	1/2 standard box	30
	3/4 bu. basket	38–41
prickly, California	Lug	20
Persimmons,		
California	Lug	20
Plums California		
and Idaho	Fiberboard box carton	25–30
California	Standard peach box	20–24
	Lug, Sanger	24–28
	Lug, L.A.	32
	4-basket crate	28–34
Prunes (Northwest)	1/2 bu basket, carton or lug	28–30
	4-basket crate	28–30
	Fiberboard carton	20
	Wooden box	15
	Wooden box	12
Pomegranates	Lug, L.A.	28
Tangerines		
Florida	4/5 bu. wirebound or fiberboard box	47$\frac{1}{2}$
California	Carton	25
Fresh Vegetables		
Anise		
California	W.G.A. crate	75
Texas	Wirebound crate	35–40
Artichokes, California	1/2 box	20–26
	Fiberboard box, carton	22
Asparagus,		
All	Pyramid crate	26–32
	Pony crate	12
California	Fiberboard box, carton containing	
	1$\frac{1}{2}$ lb consumer pkgs.	31
	3-qt basket—loose	10
Beans		
Lima, all	Bu. hamper or basket	28–32
Snap, all	Bu. hamper or basket	28–32
Beets		
Bunched	Wirebound crate	45
	1/2 W.G.A. crate	40–45
	Carton containing 18 bunches	15
Topped, all	Open mesh sack	50

TABLE A.10 (*continued*)

Commodity	Shipping Container	Approximate Net Weight[1] lb
Broccoli	Wirebound crate	25
	Pony crate	40–42
	1/2 crate, wirebound	20–22
	Crate, 14 film-wrapped bunches	20–23
Brussels sprouts	Tray, 12-pt cups	12–14
	Wirebound crate, 24 1-pt cups	22–26
	Fiberboard box, carton	25
	Drums	25
Cabbage, all	Wirebound crate	50
	W.G.A. crate	70–100
	Mesh bag	50
	Paper bag	50–60
	Carton, fiberboard	44–70
Carrots,		
Topped, all	Open mesh bags	50
	Wirebound crate	50
	Wirebound crate	80
	Burlap sack	70–85
	4 doz. 1-lb film bags packed in mesh bag or carton	50
	2 doz. 2-lb film bags packed in mesh bag or carton	50
	Bushel baskets	50
Bunched	2/3 crate	45–52
	S & W crate, 6 doz.	87
Cauliflower, all	Fiberboard box, 1 layer, wrapper leaves removed, film wrapped	16–23
	Fiberboard box, 2 layers wrapper leaves removed, film wrapped	23–35
	Crate, lettuce	55–62
	L.A. crate	50–53
	W.G.A. crate	50–60
Celery, all	16 in. nailed or wirebound crate	55–70
	1/2 size carton	30–33
	2/3 carrot crate	72–75
	Pony crate	40
	Crate, lettuce	72–90
	Fiberboard box, 16 in. packed with 2 doz. film bags	50
	Fiberboard box, 16 in. packed with 1 doz. film bags	25
Chinese cabbage	1.45 bu wirebound box	50–55
	1-1/8 or 1-1/9 bu crate or carton	40
Corn,		
All	Wirebound crate.	40–60
	Mesh or multi-wall bag	45–50
(Texas)	Mesh bag—$\frac{1}{2}$ bu	22–30

TABLE A.10 (*continued*)

Commodity	Shipping Container	Approximate Net Weight[1] lb
Cucumbers, all	Bu. basket, carton, hamper or crate	47–55
	Fiberboard carton	20–22
	1-1/9 bu crate	55
	.57 bu wirebound crate	27
	1/3 bu fiberboard carton	19
	1/4 bu fiberboard carton	14
	Lug, L.A.	28–32
Eggplant, all	Bu. basket or hamper	30–34
	1-1/9 bu crate	35
Escarole, endive, and chicory	16 in. wirebound or nailed crate	36
	Bu. basket	25
	1-1/9 bu wirebound crate	25–28
Garlic	Open mesh sack	25
	Open mesh sack	50
	Fiberboard box, carton	30
	Fiberboard box	25
	Nailed crate	50
	L.A. Lug	28–30
Greens: Collards, mustard, turnip, and spinach	Bu. basket, hamper, or crate	18–25
Lettuce and romaine		
All	Fiberboard box, carton	38–55
	Wirebound crate	40
	1-1/9 bu crate	26
Hothouse	Basket	5
	Basket	10
Melons		
Cantaloups	Jumbo crate	80–89
	Standard crate	70–85
	Fiberboard carton, Eastern flat	15–18
	1/2 size carton	$31\frac{1}{2}$
Honeydew	Honeydew flat or crate	35–47
	Jumbo honeydew crate	52
	Standard honeydew crate	48
	Carton	$31\frac{1}{2}$
Onions		
Dry, all	Open mesh sack	50
	Open mesh sack	25
	Open mesh sack	10
	Open mesh sack	5
	Fiberboard carton	48–50
	Film bags, packed in master containers	$1\frac{1}{2}$, 2, 3, 5, 10
Green	Wirebound crate	15–20
	Wirebound crate	38
	16-in. fiberboard carton	25–30
	Carton, 4 doz. bunches	15–18
	Open lug	10–16
	Crate	60–65

TABLE A.10 (*continued*)

Commodity	Shipping Container	Approximate Net Weight[1] lb
Okra	Basket, $\frac{1}{2}$ bu	15
	Bushel basket or hamper	30
Parsley	16-in. crate	19
	Wirebound crate	26
	Nailed crate	18–20
	1/2 L.A. crate	24
Peas, green, unshelled	Bu. hamper or tub	28–30
Peppers, green, all	Bu. basket, hamper or crate	28–30
	1-1/9 bu crate	28–33
	Fiberboard carton	30–34
Potatoes, all	Burlap sack	50–100
	Fiberboard carton	50–55
	Paper bag, with or without mesh window	5, 10, 15, 20, 25, 50
	2 and 3-lb. film-wrapped cardboard boats packed in master containers	50–55
	Mesh or film bag	3, 5, 8, 10, 15, 20, 25
Radishes		
topped	12-qt basket, 30 6-oz film bags	$11\frac{1}{4}$
	Cartons, 30 6-oz film bags	$11\frac{1}{4}$
	25-lb. film bags	
bunched	Crate, 5 doz. bunches	30–40
	Carton, wax-treated, 4–5 doz. bunches	30–40
	W.G.A. crate, 8–10 doz. bunches	80–90
	W.G.A. crate, packed loose, unlidded, 6 doz. bunches	45–55
Rhubarb		
Field	Box	20
Hothouse	Box	15
	Case, 10 5-lb carton	50
Squash		
Summer	Bu. basket, hamper or crate	40–45
	1/2 bu wirebound crate	21
	Lug, L.A.	24–27
Winter	Bu. basket, hamper or crate	50
Sweetpotatoes[2]	Bu. basket, crate or hamper	50
	Fiberboard box carton	36–46
	Fiberboard box carton, uncured	40–50
	1/2 bu carton, hamper, or basket	22–25
Tomatoes	Lug, L.A.	30–34
	8-qt climax basket	9–11
	12-qt climax basket	18–20
	16-qt climax basket	27
	Wirebound crate	58–62
	1/2 bu basket or hamper	30
	5/8 bu hamper	33–35
	Wirebound crate	40

TABLE A.10 (*continued*)

Commodity	Shipping Container	Approximate Net Weight[1] lb
	Wooden flat or nailed box	15–25
	Fiberboard carton	8, 18, 20, 30, 40, 60
Turnips		
Bunched	Wirebound crate	42
	1/2 W.G.A. crate	35–40
	W.G.A. crate	70–80
Topped	Open mesh sack	50
	Film sack	25

[1] Actual weights larger and smaller than the range shown may be found. It is suggested that the mid-point of the range be used where a single value is desired.

[2] The usual weight of sweet potatoes when harvested averages 55 lb. Weight is lost in curing or drying.

TABLE A. 11

SEASONING WITH SPICES AND HERBS[1]

Spice	Uses
Allspice	Pot roast, fish, eggs, pickles, sweetpotatoes, squash, fruit
Anise seed	Cookies, cakes, breads, candy, cheese, beverages, pickles, beef stew, stewed fruits, fish
Basil	Tomatoes, noodles, rice, beef stew, pork, meat loaf, duck, fish, veal, green or vegetable salad, eggplant, potatoes, peas, carrots, spinach, eggs, cheese, jelly
Bay leaf	Soups, chowders, pickles, fish, pot roast, variety meats, stews, marinades
Caraway seed	Green beans, beets, cabbage, carrots, cauliflower, potatoes, sauerkraut, turnips, zucchini, goose, lamb, pork, spareribs, beef or lamb stew, marinades for meats, cake, cookies, rice, rye bread
Cardamon	Baked goods, pickles, grape jelly, puddings, sweetpotatoes, squash, fruit soups
Cayenne pepper	Meat dishes, spaghetti, pizza, chicken, fish, eggs, cheese, vegetables, pickles

Table A.11 (*continued*)

Spice	Uses
Celery seed	Potato salad, fruit salad, tomatoes, vegetable stuffings, pickles, breads, rolls, egg dishes, meat loaf, stews, soups. Celery salt may be used in any of the above, but the amount of salt used in the recipe must be reduced.
Chili powder	Tomato barbeque sauces, dips, egg dishes, stews, meat loaf, chicken, marinades for meats, cheese, bean casseroles, corn, eggplant
Cinnamon	Beverages, bakery products, fruits, pickles, pork, ham, lamb or beef stew, roast lamb, chicken
Cloves	Fruits, pickles, baked goods, fish, stuffings, meat sauces, pot roast, marinades for meats, green beans, Harvard beets, carrots, sweetpotatoes, tomatoes. Use **whole** to stud ham, **fruit, glaz**ed pork or beef
Curry powder	Curried beef, chicken, fish, lamb, meat balls, pork, veal, eggs, dried beans, fruit, dips, breads, marinades for meats
Dill seed	Pickles, pickled beets, salads, sauerkraut, green beans, egg dishes, stews, fish, chicken, breads
Fennel seed	Egg dishes, fish, stews, marinades for meats, vegetables, cheese, baked or stewed apples, pickles, sauerkraut, breads, cakes, cookies
Garlic	Tomato dishes, soups, dips, sauces, salads, salad dressings, dill pickles, meat, poultry, fish, stews, marinades, bread
Ginger	Pickles, conserves, baked or stewed fruits, vegetables, baked products, beef, lamb, pork, veal, poultry, fish, beverages, soups, Oriental dishes
Mace	Baked products, fruits, meat loaf, fish, poultry, chowder, vegetables, jellies, pickles, breads
Marjoram	Lamb, pork, beef, veal, chicken, fish, tomato dishes, carrots, cauliflower, peas, spinach, squash, mushrooms, broccoli, pizza, spaghetti, egg dishes, breads, soups
Mint	Punches, tea, sauces for desserts, sauces for lamb, mint jelly, sherbet, vegetables, lamb stew, lamb roast
Dry mustard	Egg and cheese dishes, salad dressings, meat, poultry, vegetables
Mustard seed	Cucumber pickles, corned beef, coleslaw, potato salad, boiled cabbage, sauerkraut

Table A.11 (*continued*)

Spice	Uses
Nutmeg	Hot beverages, puddings, baked products, fruits, chicken, seafood, eggs, vegetables, pickles, conserves
Onion powder	Dips, soups, stews, all meats, fish, poultry, salads, vegetables, stuffing, cheese dishes, egg dishes, breads, rice dishes. If onion salt is used, reduce the amount of salt in the recipe
Oregano	Tomatoes, pasta sauces, pizza, chili con carne, barbeque sauce, vegetable soup, egg and cheese dishes, onions, stuffings, pork, lamb, chicken, fish
Paprika	Beef, pork, veal, lamb, sausage, game, fish, poultry, egg dishes, cheese dishes, vegetables lacking in color, pickles
Parsley	Soups, coleslaw, breads, tomato and meat sauces, stuffings, broiled or fried fish, meats, poultry
Pepper	
Black	Meats, poultry, fish, eggs, vegetables, pickles
Red	Meats, soups, cheese dishes, sauces, pickles, poultry, vegetables, spaghetti sauce, curried dishes, dips, tamale pie, barbequed beef and pork
White	White or light meats, vegetables
Poppy seed	Pie crust, scrambled eggs, fruit compotes, cheese sticks, fruit salad dressings, cookies, cakes, breads, noodles. Sprinkle over top of fruit salads, vegetables, breads, cookies and cakes
Poultry seasoning	Stuffings, poultry, veal meat loaf, chicken soup
Rosemary	Lamb, poultry, veal, beef, pork, fish, soups, stews, marinades, potatoes, cauliflower, spinach, mushrooms, turnips, fruits, breads
Saffron	Baked goods, chicken, seafood, rice, curries
Sage	Stuffings for poultry, fish, and other meats, sauces, soups, chowders, poultry, fish, beef, pork, veal, marinades, lima beans, onions, eggplant, tomatoes, cheese, potatoes
Sesame seed	Sprinkle canapes, breads, cookies, casseroles, salads, noodles, soups, and vegetables, Add to pie crust, pie fillings, cakes, cookies, dips, and stuffings
Tarragon	Sour cream sauces, casseroles, marinades, pot roasts, veal, lamb, fish, poultry, egg dishes

Table A.11 (*continued*)

Spice	Uses
Thyme	Meat, poultry, fish, vegetables
Tumeric	Cakes, breads, curried meats, fish, poultry, egg dishes, rice dishes, pickles
Vanilla	Baked goods, beverages, puddings

[1]There is no general rule for the correct amount to use of a spice or herb—the pungency of each differs and its effect on different foods varies.

Source: U.S. Dept. of Agriculture

Miscellaneous Formulations

SOYA PROTEIN FORMULATIONS
FOR WHEAT PRODUCTS

Frankfurter	Weight
Lean beef (90% lean)	55.0
Pork jowls	45.0
Soy protein additive (soy protein isolate)	2.5
or (soy protein concentrate)	4.0
Corn syrup	2.0
Dextrose	2.0
Salt	2.5
Water	35.0
Spice, cure, seasonings to suit	

Frankfurter	
Beef plates	35.0
Pork stomachs	28.0
Pork or beef hearts	27.0
Pork back fat	10.0
Soy protein additive (soy protein isolate)	2.5
or (soy protein concentrate)	4.0
Corn syrup	2.0
Dextrose	2.0
Salt	2.5
Water	3.0
Spice, cure, seasonings to suit	

Imitation Frankfurter	
Lean beef (90% lean)	100.0
Beef plates	80.0
Pork jowls	50.0
Beef hearts	20.0
Beef tongue trimmings	100.0
Soy protein additive (soy protein isolate)	15.0
or (soy protein concentrate)	17.0
Corn syrup	10.0
Dextrose	10.0
Salt	12.0
Water (soy protein isolate)	140.0
or (soy protein concentrate)	135.0
Spice, cure, seasonings to suit	

612

Soya protein formulations (*continued*)
Meat Patties

Ingredients	Pounds	%
A. Meat[1]	100	79.8
Soy protein concentrate (20/60 mesh)	6	4.8
Water[2]	18	14.4
Salt[3]	1.25	1.0
Total	125.25	100.0
B. Meat[1]	100	72.9
Soy Protein Concentrate (20/60 mesh)	9	6.6
Water[2]	27	19.6
Salt[3]	1.25	.9
Total	137.25	100.0

[1]Two or more meats can be blended to make desired fat level, (recommended 30% fat).

[2]Water can be adjusted to either 2.5 or 3.0 times the amount of concentrate added. The final amount will depend on the machinability of the mix.

[3]It is recommended that at usage levels above 6% of dry soy protein concentrate (20/60 mesh), a small amount of seasoning mix should be incorporated into the basic meat blend. This could include: pepper 1.5 oz and onion powder 4.5 oz per 100 lb meat.

Manufacturing Procedure

1. Grind meats through 1 in. plate.
2. Place required amount of meats in mixer to give desired batch size.
3. Add soy protein concentrate (20/60 mesh), which has been hydrated for approximately 10 min in required amount of water. Mix 5 min.
4. Remove mixture from mixer and grind through 1/8" plate.
5. Shape into patties and freeze.

Alternate formulations can be made to meet specific requirements in aiding the processor in selecting optimum formulations based on economics and quality.

SOYA PROTEIN FORMULATIONS FOR WHIPPED TOPPINGS

Dry Concentrate Whipped Topping
Vegetable fat	40.0%
Sucrose	15.5

Soya Protein Formulations (*continued*)

Corn syrup solids 42 DE	4.0
Salt	0.025
Dextrose and cellulose gum	0.30
Soy protein isolate	0.25
Dextrose and vegetable gum	0.50
Polysorbate 60	0.30
Sorbitan monostearate	0.15
Water	38.9
Flavor and color	Q.S.
	———
	100.0%

Processing

1. Heat water to 160°F.
2. Add fat, Polysorbate 60, Sorbitan Monostearate, melt in with agitation.
3. Premix all dry ingredients and add to above, continue agitation.
4. Mix until uniform.
5. Pasteurize at 160°F for 30 min.
6. Homogenize 1000 + 500 psi.
7. Cool to 40°F.
8. Refrigerate or freeze.

For whipping: Dilute 2 parts of concentrate with 1 part of water.

2. Frozen Type Whipped Topping

Vegetable fat	25.0%
Sucrose	20.0
Dextrose or corn syrup Solids	3.0
Soy protein isolate	1.0
Stabilizer	1.0
Polysorbate 60	0.6
Polyglycerol stearate	0.2
Water	49.2
	———
	100.0%

Flavor and color to suit

Processing

1. Place water in vat and heat to 160°F.
2. Add the Polysorbate 60 and the Polyglycerol Stearate.
3. Add vegetable fat and mix to melt.
4. Dry-blend soy protein isolate,[1] stabilizer, corn syrup solids, portion of sucrose, and add to liquid mix.
5. Add balance of sucrose and stir.
6. Pasteurize at 160–165°F, for 30 min.
7. Homogenize mixture using 2000 + 500 psi.

8. Cool to 40°F, using surface or plate cooler.
9. Store overnight at 40°F.
10. Whip in suitable device such as Votator CR-6 using nitrogen gas. Bring to desired specific gravity.
11. Place in plastic containers and freeze at −30 to 40°F..

[1]PROMINE-F made by Central Soya Company, Incorporated.

SOYA PROTEIN FORMULATIONS FOR HIGH PROTEIN BREAD

Sponge

Ingredients	Lb
Patent flour	552
Yeast	23
Monocalcium phosphate	2
Yeast food	3
Water	314

Dough

Ingredients	Lb
Patent flour	278
Vital wheat gluten	20
Soy protein concentrate	90
or soy flour 60% protein	100
Sucrose	51
Salt	21
Vegetable shortening (plastic)	25
Emulsifier	4
Yeast	7
Water	384

BAKERY FORMULA HIGH PROTEIN BREAD[1] SPONGE METHOD

Sponge Lb	Sponge Oz	Ingredients	Dough Lb	Dough Oz
75	---	Flour (Northwest)	25	---
46	---	Water (approximately)	24	---
2	4	Yeast	---	---
---	4	Yeast food	---	---
---	---	Salt	2	4
---	---	Sugar	4	8
---	---	Nonfat dry milk solids	8	---

[1]This is the original Cornell Formula Bread developed by Dr. Clive McCay to contain the essential nutrients, vitamins, minerals, and amino acids.

---	---	Soy flour (full fat)	6	---
---	---	Shortening	3	---
---	---	Wheat germ	2	---

Mixing Time

4–5 min	8–10 min
65 rpm	65 rpm

Temperature Set

76°F	79–80°F

Time

4 hr 30 min	30 min floor time

Note: During pan proof too much steam or moisture should not be applied to doughs containing high percentages of nonfat dry milk solids and soy flour. If too much moisture is present in the proof box the resulting crust will be somewhat tough in character and will have a foxy red color. It is also well to give the bread a little less proof before going to the oven. When this dough is properly mixed and fermented it will have a very good oven spring. Temperature of proof box should be about 92° to 95°F with enough humidity so the loaves will not form a top crust.

Baking

This type of bread, because of the high percentage of nonfat dry milk solids as well as soy flour, will color more quickly in the oven as compared with milk-free bread. Temperature of oven should be such that the loaves will start to color in about 10 to 12 min after being placed in the oven, approximately 400° to 420°F. Flash heat, or temporary excessive oven temperature at the start of the baking process, should be avoided inasmuch as it will cause a rapid crust formation which will color too deeply and sometimes burn before the inside of the loaf is properly baked. The bread should be baked for a little longer period of time. Under-baked bread will invariably have an aroma suggestive of greenness and will have a bitter flavor. Its texture will be over-moist and clammy. It will not slice and wrap well. A pound loaf should be baked for at least 32 min.

FORMULATION OF GELS

A. *Uncooked Grape Jelly*   Yield: 3 cups
   $\frac{1}{3}$ cup *powdered* pectin (Sure-Jell)
   1 3/8 cups grape juice
   1 7/8 cups sugar

1. *Add slowly* the powdered pectin to 1 cup of the grape juice, mixing constantly with an electric mixer at lowest speed.

2. Allow the *pectin-juice mixture to stand 45 min,* stirring occasionally.

3. Mix together the remaining 3/8 cup of grape juice and 7/8 cup of the sugar. All the sugar will not dissolve.

4. To the pectin-juice mixture, add slowly the remaining 1 cup of sugar, mixing until all the sugar is dissolved. Combine this with the juice-sugar mixture and continue mixing *at low speed* until all the sugar is dissolved. Do not over-mix.

5. Put the mixture into containers; cover and let stand at room temperature until gelled, about 24 hr.

6. Store in the refrigerator.

B. *Uncooked Raspberry Jam*   Yield: 2 cups

  1 cup pureed raspberries
  $1\frac{1}{3}$ cups sugar
  2 Tbsp. *liquid* pectin (Certo)

1. To the pureed frozen sweetened raspberries, *mix in slowly* all the sugar. Let stand for 20 min, stirring occasionally.

2. To the fruit-sugar mixture, add the liquid pectin. Mix for 3 min at lowest speed with electric mixer.

3. Pour the mixture into containers; cover and let stand at room temperature until gelled, about 24 hr.

4. Store in refrigerator.

C. *Tomato Aspic or Grape Jelly* with *Low Methoxy Pectin* Yield: 1 cup

  $1\frac{1}{2}$ Tbsp. lemon juice
  1 cup Tomato juice or 1 cup grape juice (sweetener added)
  1 Tbsp sugar
  3.5 gm L.M. Pectin
  $\frac{1}{4}$ tsp salt
  $\frac{1}{4}$ tsp calcium chloride ($CaCl_2$ $2H_2O$) Food Grade

1. Dissolve the calcium chloride in $\frac{1}{4}$ cup tomato juice.

2. Mix remaining ingredients and any dry spices and add slowly with stirring to the remaining tomato juice.

3. Heat this to boiling temperature *stirring constantly.*

4. Add slowly to the hot mixture the tomato juice containing the dissolved calcium chloride.

5. Boil for a minute or two, stirring constantly then pour into molds.

6. Refrigeration is not necessary for gel formation but will hasten gelation.

Free Fatty Acid Tests

Method I—(developed by Armour & Co.)

APPARATUS:
1. 25 ml graduated automatic buret
2. 250 ml Erlenmeyer flasks, wide-mouth
3. 50 ml graduated cylinder, with additional mark at 32.5 ml
4. Dropping bottle for indicator

REAGENTS:
1. Sodium hydroxide solution, $0.1N$
2. Isopropyl alcohol
3. Alkali blue 6B solution. (Saturated solution of alkali 6B powder in alcohol.)[1,2]

PROCEDURE:
1. Measure 50 ml isopropyl alcohol into Erlenmeyer flask.
*2. Add 20 drops or more of alkali blue indicator until a dark blue color appears.
3. While swirling or shaking flask, add $0.1N$ sodium hydroxide solution drop by drop from buret until color just changes from *blue* to *red*. *Caution*: only a few drops will be required.
4. Add 32.5 ml of oil[3] to the *red-colored* alcohol in Erlenmeyer flask. Shake flask vigorously to mix. Color will change to *blue*.
5. Fill buret to top mark with $0.1N$ sodium hydroxide solution. Make certain this is done before each test is made.
6. Titrate sample with sodium hydroxide until the odor changes *from blue to red which persists*.
7. Read buret to nearest 0.1 ml. Each 1 ml is equal to 0.1% FFA; each 0.1 ml is 0.01% FFA. For example, 5.2 ml equals 0.52% FFA.
8. Repeat titrations until results check within 0.5 ml. Fat should be discarded if percentage is greater than 1%.

Note: [1]If desired, the alkali blue indicator can be mixed with alcohol to avoid the necessity of adding it separately for each determination.

[2]Preparation of alkali blue 6B indicator solution: To each 100 ml of alcohol add 1 ml of $1N$ HCl solution and 10 gr of alkali blue 6B powder. Shake solution vigorously dissolve powder. A small amount of powder will remain undissolved. If desired, the solution may be filtered to remove the excess powder. Alkali 6B blue powder is obtained from: Krackeler & Campbell, Inc., Port of Albany, Albany, New York 12202. It can be obtained direct from the above or through most laboratory supply houses.

[3]Solid fat must be *warmed and measured as oil*.

Method II. Use of A-1 Reagent (Potato Chip Institute International)

APPARATUS:
1. 25 ml graduated buret
2. 10 ml graduated cylinder
3. 50 ml Erlenmeyer flasks or small capped vials (3-oz)

REAGENTS:
A-1 reagent (100 ml $0.1N$ NaOH and 10 ml 1% phenolphthalein solution made up to one liter with neutral 95% alcohol).

PROCEDURE:
1. Measure 10 ml of fat into an Erlenmeyer flask. If the fat is solidified, warm to liquefy.
2. Fill buret with A-1 reagent. Record initial reading.
3. From the buret, titrate slowly the A-1 reagent into the Erlenmeyer flask containing the oil sample. Rotate or shake flask continuously while adding small portions of A-1 reagent. Watch for pink color. Continue to add A-1 reagent until a definite pink color persists for 1 min.
4. Record final reading. Calculate percent of free fatty acids by multiplying the number of milliliters of A-1 reagent used by 0.03. If this percentage is greater than 0.6%, the fat is no longer usable.
5. Repeat titrations until results check within 0.5 ml.

Method III. Use of indicator test paper (Smith, Smith and Davis)

APPARATUS:
1. 30-50 ml vial
2. Small wire screen, as drying rack
3. Treated indicator paper
4. 20% NaOH or KOH

PROCEDURE:
1. Place spot of oil on treated indicator paper.
2. Place spot of fresh oil on opposite side as control.
3. Dip paper in sodium hydroxide solution for 10 sec. Remove.
4. Place on wire screen for 3 min.
5. Oil containing 1% FFA[1] or more will remain cherry red. Oil with less than 1% FFA will tend to lose the cherry red color.

[1]Free Fatty Acid Kits

(1). Keating of Chicago, Inc., 715 S. 25th Avenue, Bellwood, Illinois 60104; Shortening test kit (cost $10.50) contains enough material for 30 tests; (2) Armour and Company, Kankakee, Illinois 60901; (3) C. P. C.; (4) Color charts, etc. from Procter & Gamble.

Calculations Used in Food Analysis Index

ONE OF THE problems in training new chemists in a food testing laboratory is that of acquainting them with the calculations commonly used. If they are provided with equations into which they can feed data, and examples making use of actual test data, almost immediate use can be made of their work.

The calculations shown here are some of the more common ones used in many food laboratories. For the most part, they are based on methods of analysis found in the three major references cited below.

The equations are set up for the express purpose of feeding data into them with the expectation of performing calculations correctly.

The specific examples are the result of actual analyses. The values shown as answers are in line with current government specification requirements. They represent desirable levels in good-quality foods, and may be used as indications of the reasonableness of analytical data. The number of significant figures shown in an answer is indicative of the precision expected of the answer for the particular analysis. Likewise, the number of significant figures shown for sample weights, volumes, and normalities is indicative of the number of significant figures that should be achieved in practice.

The usefulness of the calculations is extended by the use of factors. For example, the calculation for "PROTEIN, PERCENT," gives factors for converting percent nitrogen into percent protein in a wide variety of foods. The factors were obtained from the references.

REFERENCES:

CEREAL LABORATORY METHODS, American Association of Cereal Chemists, Inc., 1955 University Avenue, St. Paul, Minnesota 55104.

OFFICIAL AND TENTATIVE METHODS OF THE AMERICAN OIL CHEMISTS' SOCIETY, American Oil Chemists' Society, 35 East Wacker Drive, Chicago, Illinois 60601.

OFFICIAL METHODS OF ANALYSIS OF THE ASSOCIATION OF OFFICIAL AGRICULTURAL CHEMISTS, Association of Official Analytical Chemists, P.O. Box 540, Benjamin Franklin Station, Washington, D.C. 20044.

[1]This Section was prepared by Charles H. Coleman and is reprinted from the *1970 IFT World Directory and Guide*, pages 326–331 with permission of the Institute of Food Technologists.

CALCULATIONS USED IN FOOD ANALYSIS

ACIDITY, PERCENT:

$$\frac{(ml\ base)\ (N\ base)}{(meq.^*\ wt.\ acid)\ (100)} = percent\ acid.$$
$$(g\ sample)$$

*NOTE: meq. = milliequivalent.
   Meq. wt. acetic acid = 0.06005,
   citric acid = 0.06404.

EXAMPLE:

$$\frac{(25.20\ ml\ NaOH)}{(0.1000\ N)\ (0.06005}{meq.\ wt.\ acetic\ acid)}}{(100)}{(3.000\ g\ vinegar)} = 5.0\%\ acetic\ acid.$$

ACIDS FREE FATTY, PERCENT:

$$\frac{(ml\ base)\ (N\ base)}{(meq.\ wt.\ free\ fatty\ acid^*)\ (100)} = percent\ free\ fatty\ acids.$$
$$(g\ sample)$$

*NOTE: meq. wt. oleic acid = 0.282, lauric acid = 0.200, palmitic acid = 0.256.

EXAMPLE:

$$\frac{(10.00\ ml\ NaOH)}{(0.0100\ N)\ (0.282\ meq.}{wt.\ oleic\ acid)\ (100)}}{(28.2\ g\ sample)} = 0.10\%\ oleic\ acid\ (free\ fatty\ acid).$$

ADDED MOISTURE IN SAUSAGE:

$$\frac{(W)-(4P)}{[1-(0.01W)]+(0.04P)} = percent\ added\ moisture.$$

W = percent moisture, P = percent protein = (6.25) (%N) Correct if necessary for protein in added material.

EXAMPLE:

$$\frac{(60\%\ moisture)-}{[(4)\ (14\%\ protein)]}}{\{1-[(0.01)\ (60\%\ moisture)]\}+[(0.04)}{(14\%\ protein)]} = 4.2\%\ added\ moisture.$$

ALIQUOTS, USING IN CALCULATIONS:
See, "DILUTIONS, USING IN CALCULATIONS."

ASH, PERCENT:

$$\frac{(grams\ ash)\ (100)}{(grams\ sample)} = percent\ ash.$$

EXAMPLE:

$$\frac{(0.0700\ g\ ash)\ (100)}{(5.000\ g\ pepper)} = 1.4\%\ ash.$$

CAFFEINE, BAILEY-ANDREW METHOD:

$$\frac{(ml\ acid)\ (N\ acid)}{(0.014\ meq.\ wt.\ N)}{(^*3.464)\ (dilution)\ (100)}}{(g\ sample)\ (aliquot)} = percent\ anhydrous\ caffeine.$$

*NOTE: 3.464 converts nitrogen to caffeine.

EXAMPLE:

$$\frac{(15.26\ ml)\ (0.1000\ N\ HCl)}{(0.014)\ (3.464)}{(500\ ml)\ (100)}}{(5.000\ g\ instant\ coffee)}{(200\ ml)} = 3.7\%\ anhydrous\ caffeine.$$

CALORIES:

Calories = [(9) (g fat) + (4) (g protein) + (4) (g carbohydrate)]

EXAMPLE:

Using a sample of 100 g of enriched white bread made with 5-6% nonfat dry milk, and analyzing 35.0% moisture, 3.8% fat, 9.0% protein, 2.0% ash, and 50.2% carbohydrate by difference:
Calories = [(9)(3.8)+(4)(9.0)+(4)(50.2)] = 271 calories.

NOTE: The factors of 9, 4, 4 are general; more exact factors are available in *COMPOSITION OF FOODS*, Agriculture Handbook No. 8, Agriculture Research Service, United States Department of Agriculture, Washington, D.C. 20402, Revised December 1963, page 160, TABLE 6. This reference gives a value of 275 calories for the food used in the above calculation.

CARBOHYDRATE BY DIFFERENCE:

% Carbohydrate = (100%)-[(% moisture)+(% fat)+ (% protein)+(% ash)]

EXAMPLE:

% Carbohydrate, enriched white bread (5-6% nonfat dry milk) = (100%)-[(35.0% moisture)+(3.8% fat)+ (9.0% protein)+(2.0% ash)] = 50.2%.

COLORIMETRY:

$$\frac{(Cs)\ (Ax)}{(As)} = Cx$$

C = concentration; A = Absorbance = log_{10} 100 - log_{10} percent transmission; s = standard; x = unknown.

CAUTION: As should be adjusted to approximately equal Ax; otherwise close adherence to Beer's law is necessary.

EXAMPLE:

Cs = 0.94 g ethyl vanillin/100 ml.
Ts = 37.5% = transmission of standard. (Log_{10}100-log_{10} 37.5 = 0.426 = As).
Tx = 36.0% = transmission of sample. (Log_{10}100-log_{10} 36.0 = 0.444 = Ax).
$$\frac{(0.94\ g/100\ ml)\ (0.444)}{(0.426)} = 0.98\ g\ ethyl\ vanillin/100\ ml\ sample.$$

DEXTROSE EQUIVALENT:

$$\frac{(g\ reducing\ sugar^*)\ (100)}{(g\ Total\ Solids)} = D.\ E. = Dextrose\ Equivalent.$$

*NOTE: Reducing sugar is calculated as dextrose.

EXAMPLE:

$$\frac{(0.4000\ g\ reducing\ sugar)}{(100)}}{1.000\ g\ total\ solids} = 40 = D.\ E.$$

DILUTIONS, USING IN CALCULATIONS:

$$\frac{(g\ found^*)\ (100^{**})}{(volume)}}{(g\ sample)\ (aliquot)} = percent^*$$

* Of characteristic being determined.
**Factor for percent, Factor for parts per million = 1x10⁶.

NOTE: Volumes and aliquots may be continued indefinitely when used as factors.

EXAMPLE:

If 10 ml aliquot of 250 ml original volume is made up to 200 ml, 5 ml aliquot of the 200 used in the determination, the calculation would be:

$$\frac{(0.001 \text{ g found}^\circ)\ (100)}{\underset{\begin{subarray}{c}(10 \text{ g sample})\\ (10 \text{ ml})\ (5 \text{ ml})\end{subarray}}{(250 \text{ ml})\ (200 \text{ ml})}} = 10\%^\circ$$

DRY BASIS (db):

$$\frac{(\text{percent found}^\circ)\ (100)}{(100\% - \text{percent moisture})} = \text{percent}^\circ \text{ (db)}.$$

$^\circ$ Ash, protein, etc.

EXAMPLE:

$$\frac{(0.0294 \text{ g ash})\ (100)\ (100)}{\underset{(100\% - 13.5\% \text{ moisture})}{(5.000 \text{ g flour})}} = 0.68\% \text{ ash (db)}.$$

EGG IN DRESSING:

Percent yolk (on a 43% solids basis) = (94.26P) - (2.192N).

P = percent of P_2O_5 (See "PHOSPHORUS PENTOXIDE" for calculation of P_2O_5.); N = percent total nitrogen.

EXAMPLE:

[(94.26) (0.0562% P_2O_5)] - [(2.192) (0.137% nitrogen)] = 5.0% egg yolk.

EGG, WHOLE, IN ALIMENTARY PASTES:

75.5 {[(percent P_2O_5) (1.1)] - (0.055)} = percent whole egg.

See "PHOSPHORUS PENTOXIDE" for calculation of P_2O_5 in unknown. The factor 1.1 makes up for manufacturing loss. The factor 0.055 subtracts lipoid P_2O_5 due to flour.

EXAMPLE:

75.5 {[(0.171% P_2O_5) (1.1)] - (0.055)} = 10.0% whole egg in noodles.

EGG YOLK IN ALIMENTARY PASTES:

58 {[(percent P_2O_5) (1.1)] - (0.055)} = percent egg yolk.

See "PHOSPHORUS PENTOXIDE" for calculation of P_2O_5 in unknown. The factor 1.1 makes up for manufacturing loss. The factor 0.055 subtracts lipoid P_2O_5 due to flour.

EXAMPLE:

58 {[(0.136 P_2O_5) (1.1)] - (0.055)} = 5.5% egg yolk in noodles.

FAT OR OIL, PERCENT:

$$\frac{(\text{g found})\ (100)}{(\text{g sample})} = \text{percent}.$$

EXAMPLE:

$$\frac{(0.8000 \text{ g fat})\ (100)}{(4.000 \text{ g ground beef})} = 20.0\% \text{ fat}.$$

FIBER, CRUDE, PERCENT:

$$\frac{(\text{Loss in weight}^\circ)\ (100)}{(\text{g sample})} = \text{percent crude fiber}.$$

$^\circ$ Loss in grams due to ashing undigested organic matter.

EXAMPLE:

$$\frac{(0.2500 \text{ g loss})\ (100)}{(2.500 \text{ g nutmeg})} = 10.0\% \text{ crude fiber}.$$

IODINE NUMBER:

ml 0.1 N $Na_2S_2O_3$ used by blank.
-ml 0.1 N $Na_2S_2O_3$ used by sample.
—
$^\circ$ml $Na_2S_2O_3$ equivalent to I_2 added by sample.

$$\frac{(^\circ\text{ml})\ (\text{N } Na_2S_2O_3)}{\underset{(\text{g oil})}{(0.12691 \text{ meq. wt. iodine})}} = \text{iodine number}.$$

EXAMPLE:

$$\frac{(20.49 \text{ ml } Na_2S_2O_3)}{\underset{(0.2000 \text{ g paprika oil})}{(0.1000 \text{ N})\ (0.12691)}} = 130 \text{ iodine number}.$$

LANE-EYNON SUGAR METHOD:

$$\frac{(\text{Factor}^\circ)\ (\text{dilution})}{(\text{g sample})\ (\text{titer})\ (10^{\circ\circ})} = \text{percent sugar}.$$

$^\circ$ From table, Official Methods of Analysis of the AOAC.
$^{\circ\circ}$ Percent multiplier/mg to g factor = 100/1000 = 1/10.

EXAMPLE:

A 1.5 g sample of sirup is made up to 200 ml and gives a titer of 26.8 ml using 25 ml Lane-Eynon reagent (Soxhlet soln) for a factor of 120.6 for dextrose. The percent dextrose would be calculated as follows:

$$\frac{(120.6)\ (200 \text{ ml})}{\underset{(10)}{(1.5000 \text{ g sirup})\ (26.8 \text{ ml})}} = 60.0\% \text{ dextrose}.$$

MEAT CONTENT:

$$\frac{\%\ \text{meat nitrogen}^\circ\ \text{x } 100}{\text{Factor}^{\circ\circ}} = \%\ \text{lean meat}.$$

$^\circ$ NOTE: Nitrogen from added cereals, milk, etc., must be subtracted from total nitrogen to obtain meat nitrogen.

EXAMPLE:

Using sample of carcass beef analyzing 60% lean, 40% fat, 49.4% moisture, 14.9% protein = [(2.384% N) (6.25)]

$$\%\ \text{lean meat} = \frac{2.384\%\ N\ \text{x } 100}{4.0} = 60\%$$

$^{\circ\circ}$ Factor for various meats = % lean meat/ % protein.
    4.0 for choice beef = 60/15
    4.7 for choice lamb = 77/16.5
    4.6 for medium fat pork = 47/10.2
    4.4 for medium fat veal = 84/19.1

MOISTURE, PERCENT BY DRYING:

$$\frac{(\text{g lost}^\circ)\ (100)}{(\text{g sample})} = \text{percent moisture}.$$

$^\circ$ Empirical method calculates all volatile matter lost during drying as moisture.

EXAMPLE:

$$\frac{(0.2700 \text{ g lost})\ (100)}{(2.000 \text{ g flour})} = 13.5\% \text{ moisture}.$$

MOISTURE, PERCENT BY TOLUENE DISTILLATION:

$$\frac{(\text{ml water found})\ (\text{sp. gr.})\ (100)}{(\text{g sample})} = \text{percent moisture}.$$

EXAMPLE:

$$\frac{(1.00 \text{ ml water found}) (100)}{(50.00 \text{ g dehydrated fish})} = 2.0\% \text{ moisture.}$$

NOTE: The references interpret (vol./wt.) (100) as percent.

MOISTURE, ADDED, IN SAUSAGE:
See "ADDED MOISTURE IN SAUSAGE."

MOISTURE BASIS (mb) 14%:

$$\frac{(\text{percent found}^*) (86)}{(100\% - \text{percent moisture})} = \text{percent}^* \text{ on a } 14\% \text{ moisture basis.}$$
*Ash, protein, etc.

EXAMPLE:

$$\frac{(0.0294 \text{ g ash } (100) (86)}{(5.000 \text{ g flour}) (100\% - 13.5\%)} = 0.58\% \text{ ash } (14\% \text{ moisture basis}).$$

MOISTURE-FREE BASIS (Mfb):
See "DRY BASIS (db)."

MOISTURE IN BREAD:
(100% - percent solids*)=percent moisture.
*See, "SOLIDS IN BREAD, PERCENT."

EXAMPLE:
(100% - 65% solids)=35% moisture.

OIL OR FAT PERCENT:
See "FAT OR OIL, PERCENT."

OIL, VEGETABLE IN SALAD DRESSING:
(Percent total oil)-[(percent egg yolk) (0.256)] =percent vegetable oil.

EXAMPLE:
(41.3% total oil)-[(5.0% egg yolk) (0.256)]=40.0% vegetable oil.

PARTS PER MILLION (ppm):

$$\frac{(\text{g found}^*) (10^6)}{(\text{g sample})} = \text{parts per million (ppm).}^*$$
*Of characteristic being determined.
NOTE: Parts per million also=mg/kg=g/1000kg.

EXAMPLE:

$$\frac{(25.00 \text{ ml NaOH}) (0.0100 \text{ N}) (0.032 \text{ meq. wt. SO}_2) (10^6)}{(32.00 \text{ g dehydrated potatoes})} = 250 \text{ ppm SO}_2.$$

PERCENTAGE OF WEIGHT:

$$\frac{(\text{g found}^*) (100)}{(\text{g sample})} = \text{percent.}^*$$
*Of characteristic being determined.

EXAMPLE:

$$\frac{(95 \text{ g through U.S.\#40 sieve}) (100)}{(100 \text{ g pepper})} = 95\% \text{ through U.S. \#40 sieve.}$$

PERCENTAGE OF WEIGHT USING COMBINED DILUTIONS* AND MILLIEQUIVALENT WEIGHT:

$$\frac{(\text{ml}) (\text{N}) (\text{meq. wt.}) (100) (\text{volume}^*)}{(\text{g sample}) (\text{aliquot}^*)} = \text{percent.}$$
*May be expanded, see "DILUTIONS IN CALCULATIONS."

EXAMPLE:

$$\frac{(15.60 \text{ ml NaOH}) (0.1000 \text{ N}) (0.06404 \text{ meq. wt. citric acid}) (200 \text{ ml vol.}) (100)}{(10.00 \text{ g synthetic beverage powder}) (10.00 \text{ ml aliquot})} = 20.0\% \text{ citric acid.}$$

PERCENTAGE USING MILLIEQUIVALENT WEIGHT IN TITRATIONS:

$$\frac{(\text{ml}) (\text{N}) (\text{meq. wt.}) (100)}{(\text{g sample})} = \text{percent.}$$

EXAMPLE:

$$\frac{(25.20 \text{ ml NaOH}) (0.1000 \text{ N}) (0.06005 \text{ meq. wt. acetic acid}) (100)}{(3.000 \text{ g vinegar})} = 5.0\% \text{ acetic acid.}$$

PEROXIDE VALUE OF FATS:

$$\frac{(\text{ml}) (\text{N}) (1000)}{(\text{g sample})} = \text{milliequivalents of peroxide per kilogram.}$$

EXAMPLE:

$$\frac{(5.00 \text{ ml Na}_2\text{S}_2\text{O}_3) (0.100 \text{ N}) (1000)}{(5.000 \text{ g shortening, AOM})} = 100 \text{ meqs. peroxide per kg.}$$

PHOSPHORUS PENTOXIDE, PERCENT:

$$\frac{(\text{ml NaOH}) (\text{N}) (0.003086^*) (100)}{(\text{g sample})} = \text{percent P}_2\text{O}_5.$$
*Milliequivalent weight of P_2O_5 using volumetric ammonium molybdate method.

EXAMPLE:

$$\frac{(22.03 \text{ ml NaOH}) (0.1000 \text{ N}) (0.003086 \text{ meq. wt. P}_2\text{O}_5) (100)}{(5.000 \text{ g noodles})} = 0.136\% \text{ P}_2\text{O}_5.$$

POTASSIUM IODIDE IN SALT:

$$\frac{(\text{ml Na}_2\text{S}_2\text{O}_3) (\text{N}) (0.02776^*) (100)}{(\text{g sample})} = \text{percent KI.}$$
*Milliequivalent weight of KI by the bromine-oxidation method.

EXAMPLE:

$$\frac{(14.00 \text{ ml Na}_2\text{S}_2\text{O}_3) (0.005 \text{ N}) (0.02776 \text{ meq. wt. KI}) (100)}{(10.00 \text{ g sample of salt})} = 0.02\% \text{ KI.}$$

POUNDS PER GALLON FROM GRAMS:

$$\frac{(3.785^*) (\text{g/ml}) (1000)}{(28.35) (16)} = \text{pounds (avoirdupois) per U.S. gallon.}$$
*NOTE: There are 3.785 liters per U.S. gallon, 28.35 grams per ounce, and 16 ounces per pound avoirdupois.

EXAMPLE:

$$\frac{(3.785) (10.00 \text{ g/10.00 ml}^*) (1000)}{(28.35) (16)} = 8.34 \text{ pounds avoirdupois per U.S. gallon.}$$
*Water in air at 3.98°C.

PROPORTION:

a/b=c/d   c =ad/b
a =bc/d   d=bc/a
b=ad/c

EXAMPLE:
Problem: If there are 2 g of fat in 10 g of beef, how many g of fat would be in 140 g of beef?

$$\frac{2 \text{ g fat}}{10 \text{ g beef}} = \frac{c \text{ g fat}}{140 \text{ g beef}}, \quad c = \frac{(2)(140)}{(10)} = 28 \text{ g fat.}$$

PROTEIN, PERCENT:

$$\frac{(\text{ml acid})(\text{N acid})(0.014 \text{ meq. wt. nitrogen})(\text{factor}^\circ)(100)}{(\text{g sample})} = \text{percent protein.}$$

°Factors for converting nitrogen to protein:
3.464 for caffeine.
5.55 for gelatin dessert powder, and gelatin.
5.7 for wheat and wheat products; alimentary pastes, baked products of wheat.
6.25 for plants, cereals other than wheat, fruits, nuts, meat and meat products, dog food, wines, yeast.
6.38 for milk and milk products, cheese, ice cream, etc.
20.36 for piperine.
Report nitrogen in water as nitrates, and nitrogen as % N for fish, mayonnaise, and products not specified.

EXAMPLE:

$$\frac{(32.00 \text{ ml HCl})(0.1000 \text{ N})(0.014)(6.25)(100)}{(2.000 \text{ g sausage})} = 14.0\% \text{ protein in sausage.}$$

PROXIMATE ANALYSIS: (Rational interpretation of quantitative analysis so as to approach 100% analysis.)
See, "CARBOHYDRATE, BY DIFFERENCE."

SALT (NaCl) PERCENT:

$$\frac{(\text{Ml AgNO}_3)(\text{N AgNO}_3)(0.05845 \text{ meq. wt. NaCl})(100)}{(\text{g sample})} = \text{percent NaCl.}$$

EXAMPLE:

$$\frac{(12.83 \text{ ml AgNO}_3)(0.1000 \text{ N})(0.05845 \text{ meq. wt. NaCl})(100)}{3.000 \text{ g meat product}} = 2.5\% \text{ salt (NaCl).}$$

SIZE, PERCENT FOR SIEVE TESTS:

$$\frac{(\text{g passing through, or retained})(100)}{(\text{g sample})} = \text{percent through (or retained).}$$

EXAMPLE:

$$\frac{(95 \text{ g through U.S. } \#40 \text{ sieve})(100)}{(100 \text{ g pepper})} = 95\% \text{ through U.S. } \#40 \text{ sieve.}$$

SOLIDS IN BREAD, PERCENT:

$$\frac{(B)(C)}{(A)} = \text{percent solids.}$$

A=loaf weight; B=weight after air drying; C=percent solids after oven drying.

EXAMPLE:
A bread roll weighed 100 g at time of receipt. The weight after air drying was 76.47 g. Percent solids after oven drying was 85%.

$$\frac{(76.47)(85)}{(100)} = 65\% \text{ solids.}$$

SOLIDS, PERCENT (Direct Method):

$$\frac{(\text{g solids})(100)}{(\text{g sample})} = \text{percent solids.}$$

EXAMPLE:

$$\frac{(0.825 \text{ g solids})(100)}{(5.000 \text{ g mustard})} = 16.5\% \text{ solids.}$$

SOLIDS, PERCENT (Indirect Method):

$(100\%) - (\% \text{ moisture}) = \text{percent solids.}$

EXAMPLE:
$(100\%) - (6.0\% \text{ moisture}) = 94.0\%$ solids; potatoes, white, dehydrated.

SUGAR IN WATER RATIO (Condensed Milk):

$$\frac{(\% \text{ sugar})(100)}{(100 - \text{TMS})} = \text{Ratio of sugar in water.}$$

TMS=Total Milk Solids=(fat + solids-nonfat.) Solids-nonfat may be abbreviated SNF.

EXAMPLE:
Analytical data: Moisture = 28.1%°
              Fat   = 8.9%
              SNF   =18.0%
              Sucrose =45.0%
°(100% - % Total Solids.)

$$\text{Ratio} = \frac{(45.0\%)(100)}{(100 - 26.9)} = 61.6\%$$

$(\text{TMS}) = (8.9\% + 18.0\%) = (26.9)$

SULFUR DIOXIDE, PARTS PER MILLION (ppm):

$$\frac{(\text{ml NaOH})(\text{N NaOH})(0.032 \text{ meq. wt. SO}_2)(10^6)}{(\text{g sample})} = \text{ppm SO}_2.$$

EXAMPLE:

$$\frac{(25.00 \text{ ml NaOH})(0.0100 \text{ N})(0.032 \text{ meq. wt. SO}_2)(10^6)}{32.00 \text{ g dehydrated potatoes}} = 250 \text{ ppm SO}_2.$$

TIN PLATE (BENDIX METHOD):

$(\text{Ml Na}_2\text{S}_2\text{O}_3 \text{ of Blank - ml Na}_2\text{S}_2\text{O}_3 \text{ for back titration})(\text{N Na}_2\text{S}_2\text{O}_3)(0.05935 \text{ meq. wt. stannous Sn})(17.28^\circ) = $ pounds Sn per base box.
°Factor is based on use of sample area of 8 square inches compared to area of 67,720 square inches in a base box. Analysis by Bendix Method, Ind. Eng. Chem. Anal. Ed., 15, 501 (1943).

EXAMPLE:
Both sides of a disc having a total of 8 square inches of tin plated surface were tested. $(20.00 \text{ ml Na}_2\text{S}_2\text{O}_3 - 7.80 \text{ ml Na}_2\text{S}_2\text{O}_3)(0.1000 \text{ N})(0.05935)(17.28) = 1.25$ pounds tin per base box.

VOLATILE OIL, ml/100 g (BY STEAM DISTILLATION):

$$\frac{(\text{ml oil})(100)}{(\text{g sample})} = \text{ml}/100 \text{ grams.}$$

$$\frac{2.0 \text{ ml oil})(100)}{} = 2.0 \text{ ml}/100 \text{ g of black pepper.}$$

EXAMPLE:

$$\frac{(2.0 \text{ ml oil})(100)}{(100 \text{ g black pepper})} = 2.0 \text{ ml}/100 \text{ g of black pepper.}$$

VOLUMETRIC EQUATION, GENERAL:

$N_1 V_1 = N_2 V_2$
N=normality; V=volume. Any one symbol may be unknown value.

EXAMPLE:
10.00 ml of 0.1000 N HCl=V_2 of 0.0100 N HCl
$V_2 = (10)(0.1000)/(0.0100) = 100.0$ ml

Index